JANE GRIGSON'S
FISH BOOK

Illustrated by Yvonne Skargon

PENGUIN BOOKS

PENGUIN BOOKS

Published by the Penguin Group
Penguin Books Ltd, 27 Wrights Lane, London W8 5TZ, England
Penguin Books USA Inc., 375 Hudson Street, New York, New York 10014, USA
Penguin Books Australia Ltd, Ringwood, Victoria, Australia
Penguin Books Canada Ltd, 10 Alcorn Avenue, Toronto, Ontario, Canada M4V 3B2
Penguin Books (NZ) Ltd, 182–190 Wairau Road, Auckland 10, New Zealand

Penguin Books Ltd, Registered Offices: Harmondsworth, Middlesex, England

This edition first published in Great Britain by Michael Joseph 1993
Published in Penguin Books 1994
1 3 5 7 9 10 8 6 4 2

Some of the material in this book first appeared in *Fish Cookery*,
published by the International Wine & Food Publishing Company in 1973,
and in a Penguin paperback edition in 1975

Printed in England by Clays Ltd, St Ives plc
Set in Monophoto Baskerville

Jane Grigson's
Fish Book

Jane Grigson was brought up in the north-east of England where there is a strong tradition of good eating, but it was not until many years later, when she began to spend three months of each year working in France, that she became really interested in food. *Charcuterie and French Pork Cookery* was the result, exploring the wonderful range of cooked meat products on sale in even the smallest market towns. This book has also been translated into French, a singular honour for an English cookery writer.

After taking an English degree at Cambridge in 1949, Jane Grigson worked in art galleries and publishers' offices and then as a translator. In 1966 she shared the John Florio prize (with Father Kenelm Foster) for her translation of Beccaria's *Of Crime and Punishment*. It was in 1968 that Jane Grigson began her long association with the *Observer* magazine, for which she wrote right up until her untimely death in 1990; *Good Things* and *Food with the Famous* are both based on these highly successful series of articles. In 1973 *Fish Cookery* was published by the Wine and Food Society, followed by *The Mushroom Feast* (1975), a collection of recipes for cultivated, woodland, field and dried mushrooms. She received both the Glenfiddich Writer of the Year Award and the André Simon Memorial Fund Book Award for her *Vegetable Book* (1978) and for her *Fruit Book* (1982) and was voted Cookery Writer of the Year in 1977 for *English Food*. A compilation of her best recipes, *The Enjoyment of Food*, was published in 1992 with an introduction by her daughter, the cookery writer Sophie Grigson. Most of Jane Grigson's books are published in the Penguin Cookery Library.

Jane Grigson died in March 1990. In her obituary for the *Independent*, Alan Davidson wrote: 'Jane Grigson left to the English-speaking world a legacy of fine writing on food and cookery for which no exact parallel exists . . . She won to herself this wide audience because she was above all a friendly writer . . . the most companionable presence in the kitchen; often catching the imagination with a deftly chosen fragment of history or poetry, but never failing to explain the "why" as well as the "how" of cookery.'

Jane Grigson was married to the late poet and critic Geoffrey Grigson.

CONTENTS

There are two cookery writers that most cooks put in a class of their own: Elizabeth David, sadly whom I never knew, and Jane Grigson, who I wished I'd known better. Jane was the queen of her subject and yet was completely unintimidating. She was clever, interesting and kind. She had a terrific sense of fun, a real love of life and an amazing sense of humour. Her laugh, which was sometimes a rather wicked giggle, was infectious. She always cheered everyone up.

Jane invited my husband and me to lunch with her at Broad Town after I'd only met her once, very briefly. I was nervous: I thought it would be like going to see the Headmistress, but I couldn't have been more wrong. Both William and I loved her on sight and didn't want to leave.

I have always admired Jane, and am endlessly dipping into her books. Anything that I know that I find riveting about food has usually come from her. However, until I was most flatteringly asked to write the foreword to this book, I'd never sat down and read so much of her at one sweep. One thing I find interesting is that these days we all talk about the need for books to be user-friendly − but Jane invented all that years ago. The fascinating introductions to sections or recipes continually answer half-asked unspoken questions. None of the writing is contrived − so often in books you feel that the publisher has said to the author, can you write a 'bit of an intro'. Not so with Jane.

The introductions in the *Fish Book* are a combination of fun and intellect. They are so alive that you can hear Jane telling you about Romesco peppers or the Marquis of Goulaine's cook, Clémence. The recipes themselves assume a certain amount of basic knowledge but also give encouraging remarks like 'don't despair' should the sauce curdle; she suggests some simple and effective remedies.

This book is filled with fascinating information. It is not written by someone who has simply researched the subject; it is written by someone who for twenty years or so *lived* the subject and must have kept copious notes. It is a timeless book. I do not believe it could ever be out of date as I doubt it was ever 'in date'. It is a very generous book. Most of us forget from whose original recipe a new idea has been developed – but not Jane. She knows the history of the classic dishes and, although she has invented many new recipes herself, she constantly credits originators of recipes or stories. She is occasionally sharp with the reader. She remarks, for instance, that in 1826 a Mrs Johnston, writing on behalf of Meg Dods, noted that curried halibut is 'good as long as you make up your own blend of spices'. Jane says that it 'is rather daunting to think that, 160 years later, cookery writers are still saying the same thing. Are lazy practices eternal?'

Jane constantly flatters us – she assumes that we know so much more about poetry and history than probably many of us do. She is a great teacher because she gradually leads us in to new topics. And she writes so well that the book becomes almost unputdownable. The introduction to the section on eels makes one of the most charming stories I have read. If that sounds unlikely, read it. It begins with the discovery by the Danish biologist Johannes Schmidt who, after twenty-five years of research back-tracking eel larvae, eventually arrived right over their spawning ground. She recounts the epic journey of the eel to and from the Sargasso Sea. The trouble is that, by the end, you are so moved by the tenacity of the eels that Jane's clear instructions on their preparation and cooking has a quality of somewhat Roald Dahl-like ruthlessness.

I love the constant, almost throwaway, bits of information. How many cookery books tell you that 18 fathoms is 118 feet, that the Venetians invented double-entry bookkeeping, assume that the reader knows all about the great Brazilian balloonist Alberto Santos Dumont, tell you that akee is properly the name of a tree originally from West Africa, and was introduced to Jamaica from Guinea by Captain Bligh of the *Bounty*? (You must read on to find out more about its poisonous potential.) Who but Jane would know that Grimod de la Reynière discovered brandade? Do you know why red mullet is sometimes called sea woodcock? Because, like woodcock, the red mullet is cooked with its liver. You must read about the scavenging life of a shrimp and discover that tempura was originally brought to Japan by the Jesuit missionaries with Francis Xavier in the sixteenth century.

Jane destroys myths – John Dory cannot really be St Peter's fish as John Dory is a salt water fish that could not survive in the Sea of Galilee. St Peter's fish is more probably a kind of trout that flourishes in Galilee – 'a pleasant but not outstanding fish'. Unfortunately, it has no finger marks nor a coin in its mouth.

At Leith's School we divide into two camps – those of us who love coriander and those of us who hate it. Jane explains that to some people it can taste like soap and that this is a chemical effect and cannot be changed. I will now be much more sympathetic to those who loathe a herb I love.

Sole is one of her favourite fish. She writes sadly that its behaviour and lifestyle is not that interesting. 'The most dramatic episode of its life is when the left eye of the perfectly normal, fish-shaped larva moves up and over the head to the right side, as the sole flattens into its characteristic shape.' That is how to write about cooking, or anything else: clear, funny, interesting and learned. Don't let me keep you from reading Jane Grigson's work for another moment.

Caroline Waldegrave is closely involved with the Jane Grigson Trust, and is Managing Director of Leith's School of Food and Wine, which she opened with Prue Leith in 1975. In May 1991 the proceeds of a Leith's School fund-raising dinner were used to set up the Jane Grigson Library at Guildhall Library. Caroline Waldegrave was a member of the Health Education Authority from 1985 to 1988 and, as Chairman of the Guild of Food Writers for two years, until March 1993, she was actively involved in the Guild's campaign to improve institutional food, specifically in hospitals. She is the author, or co-author with Prue Leith, of numerous cookery books. She is married to William Waldegrave MP; they have four children.

NOTE

The sections of this book that Jane Grigson revised before her death in 1990 are indicated by a dagger next to the chapter title. Although the chapters without a dagger were not revised by her, they have been updated to include material from her books and articles which were published after *Fish Cookery* first came out in 1973.

Asterisks that appear in the text refer to recipes in the chapter Court Bouillons, Batters, Butters & Sauces at the beginning of the book.

INTRODUCTION

The problem with a book on fish is how to stop writing it. To start with, there are fifty-two species of edible fish (including many different varieties) listed by the White Fish Authority. This does not include either shellfish or freshwater fish. It leaves out the extensive choice of cured fish, as well as fish imported from abroad to be sold to foreigners living and working here.

Think of this when you next visit your fishmonger. Count the choice of fish for sale. And count how many different kinds you have eaten in the last few months. You may then agree with me that fish is one of the great untapped areas of exploration, for curiosity, and for the delight of the cook and her family and friends.

Compare this abundance with the choice of meat. How often do you come across an animal you have never heard of before? At least, heard of in culinary terms. For me, the answer is, 'once', and that was when I visited the strange shop of Monsieur Paul Corcellet in Paris – he had ready-prepared elephant's trunk, python, crocodile and monkey for sale. Yet with fish one never seems to come to the end of perfectly reasonable possibilities.

To begin with, we eat too little of the best fish. We know about them, we may order them in restaurants on occasion, but we buy and cook them rarely. I am talking about sole, lobster, eel, scallops, oysters, clams, trout and salmon trout, monkfish or squid. We think they are too expensive, and go off and buy steak instead, or a large joint. Partly, this is convention. I read a statement one day which struck me as particularly foolish. The writer remarked that fish could not be served as a main course when men were present, as they needed steak or some other good red meat.

Why? The protein content of fish is as high as the protein content of meat. It is more easily digested, too – a point which concerns more men, I suspect, than women. And in the cooking of sole with its sauces, or of lobster, there is far more implied compliment to the guests than in grilling even the finest Scottish steak.

I suppose, too, that most of us grow up with the firm impression that fish means cod and plaice, overcooked and coated with greasy batter or coloured substances of unpleasant flavour. Certainly I was startled, when I first crossed the Channel, to find out that there were far more fish to eat than anyone had allowed me to believe. Later on, as we spent longish periods working in Europe, I discovered that many of the 'exotic' fish we had been enjoying swam in quantity and quality around the coasts of Great Britain, as well as in the Mediterranean and the Bay of Biscay, and off the Breton coast. Squid, for instance, and monkfish – two of the great delicacies of Italian and French cookery.

At the weekly stall in our local market at Montoire, forty-four miles north-west of Blois and 150 miles from the sea at Nantes, we can usually count between thirty and thirty-five different kinds of fish to buy. They are stiff-alive, as fishmongers say, with freshness. The owner's wife, Madame Soarès, took our education in hand, persuaded us into trying new fish, and told us how to cook them. With gestures and vivid phrases, she described the sauces, the flavours, the pleasure we would have at supper that night.

I wish I could take our fishmongers in England to that stall in Montoire, and keep them there for a few months! Some of them have increased their range of fish to sell to our new communities of Chinese and Italians and so on, but few of them can tell a doubtful English customer how to cook these new creatures, or what they taste like. One has the idea that they have never tried them themselves at home. They lack the warm enthusiasm of Madame Soarès – 'Here's some parsley for you. Have a lemon, too. And why not buy a handful of shrimps – they'll make a finish to the sauce! *Extrà!*'

The main fish authorities could be more help. They are anxious that we should eat more fish, it is true, but only more of the same few kinds. Their interest is in shifting the gluts of plaice and cod. They do not think of pointing out the special virtues of huss, let alone of the rarer John Dory. In the end it is up to the customers who enjoy good food to insist, and complain, and learn about fish, and complain again but more knowledgeably, so that things can be changed a little more rapidly.

Jane Grigson (1973)

CHOOSING, CLEANING & COOKING FISH

CHOOSING FISH

General advice – if you see a fish at the fishmonger's that is strange to you, buy it, but do not expect much advice on how to cook it. Ask the name and look it up in the index at the back of this book when you get home.

More specifically – choose fresh fish, fish with a bright eye, red gills and no more than a seaweedy smell. Stale fish will look miserable; the eyes will be sunken or opaque, the skin gritty or dry or blobbed with yellow slime, it will smell, and you will be able to push the flesh in easily with your finger. As you may have concluded already, the buyer of fish needs character for all this sniffing and prodding. Getting good fish is easier once you find a fishmonger you can trust, but if he sells you poor fish, *go back and tell him so.*

The naming of fish is a tricky business. One name may be used for quite different species. Local names abound. There are misleading inducements: certain fish which bear labels saying 'rock salmon' and 'rock turbot' have nothing in common with 'salmon' and 'turbot'. When you go on holiday, foreign names add to the confusion. Because of this intricately knotted muddle, the United Nations has produced the *Multilingual Dictionary of Fish and Fish Products*, an international compilation with names from fifteen languages, which attempts to straighten matters out with an elegant system of indexing. Local names are there, as well as the Latin ones. A book to be recommended to anyone who enjoys eating fish. (I can also recommend the *Atlas of the Living Resources of the Seas*, published by the Food and Agricultural Organization of the United Nations in 1972, again with an index but this time in three languages – English, French and Spanish; from her Majesty's Stationery Office.)

CLEANING FISH

Although the fishmonger should do this for you, it is as well to know what to do. Cut off spiky fins and other extrusions first. Remove scales by pushing them up the wrong way with the blunt edge of a knife – spread newspaper round to catch the scales which fly about. Rinse quickly. Remove innards through the gills, or by slitting up the belly. Retain the livers and roes; they are often good to eat. Rub any stubborn traces of blood with a little salt. Cut off heads or not, as you please.

SKINNING AND BONING FLATFISH   If you have to skin the fish yourself, make a cut across, just above the tail. Raise a corner of it and with salted fingers – salt gives a better grip – pull the skin slowly at first and then with a quick tug. Do the same thing with the other side.

I have a preference, with flatfish, for cooking them whole, on the bone, complete with head, but there are times when they must be filleted. This is easy with flatfish. Run a small, sharp knife along the central division of one side. Then scrape gently from the head end of the centre towards the side, keeping the knife close to the bone, until the whole fillet is raised. Repeat on the other side of the central division. Turn the fish over, and remove the last two fillets the same way. Therefore, four fillets come off one flatfish.

BONING WHOLE FISH, HERRING, ETC   Cut off the head, slit the belly, and clean. Lay the fish on a board, cut side down, and press along the backbone steadily. Turn it over and pick out the backbone and the other small bones, which will be sticking up.

COOKING FISH

BOILING   A method only suitable for soups, when every scrap of flavour is to be extracted from the fish for the benefit of the liquid.

BRAISING, BAKING AND ROASTING   This includes all methods of cooking fish in the oven; sometimes on a bed of herbs and vegetables; sometimes with fish stock or wine, as well as butter and oil. Instructions are given with each recipe, as they can vary a great deal.

COOKING IN FOIL *For large fish* – Few of us have the space to store an enormous fish kettle that may be used only once or twice a year. Foil solves the problem and we can wrap the fish up without the least worry that it will lose flavour to the water or bouillon. And it cannot become too dry either. *See* the method for cooking salmon in foil on p. 306.

For medium fish – Place the foil on a baking sheet, and the fish on the foil. Pour over 4–6 tablespoons of good dry white wine, or put a lump of butter forked up with herbs into the cavity. Fold the foil round the fish, making a baggy parcel; finally, twist the edges into a firm seal.

For the method of cooking fish in paper, en papillote, *see* p. 60.

FRYING For finer fish, shallow-fry in clarified butter* or olive oil. Unclarified butter mixed with oil is a second best expedient, but the flavour will not be so good. Unclarified butter on its own burns easily.

Keep deep-frying for fish in batter and for whitebait. The temperature should be gas 5, 185–190 °C (365–375 °F).

GRILLING Slash small plump fish, such as herring, mackerel, and mullet diagonally two or three times, brush with clarified butter or olive oil, and grill for 4–8 minutes a side.

Flatfish – Brush with clarified butter and seasoning. Allow 4–6 minutes a side, but timing depends on the thickness of the fish; chicken turbot will take longer than sole, for instance.

Fish steaks – These need not be turned while grilling. Set them in a well-buttered grill pan, brush the tops with clarified butter, season, and cook for up to 15 minutes. They are done when the flesh turns opaque and the central bones can be moved easily.

Boned fish and fillets – Always grill the fleshy, cut side first, brushing with butter and sprinkling with salt and pepper. When it is almost done, the fish can be turned over to give the skin a chance to be become brown and crisp.

POACHING This is the correct way of cooking fish in water or other liquids, which should be kept just below boiling point. For timing and court bouillon recipes, *see* p. 7.

Even shellfish such as crabs and lobsters should not be boiled hard. *See* relevant sections.

STEAMING The fish is laid on a buttered plate, or piece of foil, and set over a pan of simmering water until cooked. For success, the fish must be fresh, really fresh, and well seasoned. It is a method much better exploited by Chinese than by European cooks: they add aromatics such as spring onion, ginger and soy sauce. In the West, steamed fish has the dull sound of sick-room cookery, which is unfair as it can be delicious.

TO KNOW WHEN FISH IS COOKED   Pierce the thickest part with a larding needle or skewer (*not a fork*). The flesh should be opaque, and part easily from the bone. Never overcook fish. It is surprising how little time it takes compared with meat. Take into account the fact that it will continue to cook slightly while keeping warm in the oven, and while being dished up and brought to the table.

COURT BOUILLONS, BATTERS, BUTTERS & SAUCES

COURT BOUILLONS

Until the introduction of kitchen foil, whole fish, or large pieces, were always cooked in a flavoured liquid or court bouillon. When the liquid was no more than salted water, the result was frequently a disaster, particularly if the fish had been allowed to boil rapidly. Few dishes are more disgusting than cod cooked in this way (the French call fish boiled in water *poisson à l'anglaise*). In religious households it cast additional gloom over Good Friday, and many other Fridays as well. I think that it has been the main reason for the general unpopularity of fish.

Now that foil has superseded the fish kettle things are better. Appropriate seasonings and aromatics are parcelled up with the fish, which cooks in its own juices plus a little butter or white wine. The flavour stays where it should, in the fish itself, and in the small amount of essence left in the foil as sauce. (*See* sauce Bercy*.)

Sometimes though, a court bouillon is essential for fish soup, for a sauce requiring a fair amount of the liquid in which the fish was cooked, for poaching turbot or skate, or for boiling live shellfish. Generally, vegetables and spices are simmered in the liquid for half an hour to extract their maximum flavour. When cool or just tepid the liquid is strained over the fish, which it should just cover. The pan, set over a moderate heat, comes slowly to the boil and is then allowed to do no more than simmer or shake slightly for the appropriate length of time, which is as follows:

¾–1 kg (1½–2 lb) fish 7–10 minutes
2 kg (4 lb)   15 minutes
3 kg (6 lb)   20 minutes
4–5 kg (8–10 lb)   30 minutes

If the fish is to be eaten cold, ignore these times. Instead, bring the pan slowly to the boil, give it time for a couple of strong bubblings, then remove it from the heat and allow it to cool. Because larger quantities of bouillon take longer to come to the boil and longer to cool down, this method is successful with large as well as small fish.

When cooking salmon, I combine the foil and bouillon methods. The fish is wrapped up in greased foil (use butter for hot salmon, oil for cold, to avoid congealed fat ruining the flavour and appearance), with a seasoning of salt and pepper. The parcel goes into enough cold water to cover it well. If you want it hot, follow the times given above: I use the second method for cold salmon. This is quicker than baking the salmon in the oven, yet it has the advantages of keeping all the flavour and moistness in the fish itself.

1. GENERAL PURPOSE COURT BOUILLON   This makes an excellent start to fish soups.

> 2 carrots, sliced
> 2 leeks, sliced ⎫
> 2 shallots, sliced ⎬ or 2 mild onions
> 16 lightly crushed black peppercorns
> 1 heaped teaspoon pickling spices
> bouquet garni of appropriate herbs
> 600 ml (1 pt) water
> 600 ml (1 pt) dry white wine or dry cider
> 1 tablespoon white wine vinegar

Simmer vegetables and spices in the liquid for half an hour. Allow it to cool and cook the fish according to instructions above. If you want to make a fish soup with the bouillon afterwards, tomatoes can be added, with a little sugar; cream and a couple of egg yolks make a final thickening. Fish cooked in the bouillon can be cut up or liquidized to give the soup body – or it can be left whole and served as the next course with bread and butter, or potatoes and butter, in the Breton style. Shellfish such as prawns or mussels can provide a final garnish. In other words a court bouillon can be the start of many good meals, from the homely to the luxurious.

2. SIMPLE COURT BOUILLON   For salmon, skate, salt cod.

> 1 carrot sliced
> 1 onion, sliced

12 lightly crushed black peppercorns
salt to taste
1¼ litres (2 pt) water
2 tablespoons white wine vinegar

3. SALTY COURT BOUILLON For crab and lobster, prawns, shrimps, etc.

seawater, plus salt or plain salted water (an egg should be able to float in it)

4. WHITE COURT BOUILLON For turbot, brill, smoked haddock.

600 ml (1 pt) milk ⎫
600 ml (1 pt) water ⎬ or *1¼ litres (2 pt) milk*
1 thick slice lemon
salt, pepper (for smoked haddock, omit salt)

5. WHITE WINE COURT BOUILLON For marinaded herring, mackerel, jellied trout, Écrevisses à la nage (p. 464).

1 bottle dry white wine
3 medium carrots, sliced
4 onions, sliced or 6 shallots
bouquet garni
1 rounded teaspoon black peppercorns
salt
extra flavourings: *chilli, aniseed, celery, tarragon*

For whole fish, reduce by rapid boiling to half quantity and leave until tepid. Put in fish, bring to the boil, allow two bubblings, then remove pan from heat and leave to cool. For écrevisses and other small shellfish put into boiling reduced bouillon, cook for 10 to 12 minutes and leave them to drain in a colander: for à la nage dishes, serve a little bouillon with the shellfish.

FISH STOCK (Fumet de poisson)

The delightful name of *fumet de poisson* means scent or bouquet of fish. In reality, it is no more than fish stock, and the good thing about it is that it is simple and cheap to make. There are now fish stock cubes available and some fish stock ready made up by certain manufacturers, but there is nothing quite like one's own fumet de poisson.

Most fishmongers will give you the necessary trimmings. Ask especially for turbot and sole bones because they have a high proportion of gelatine which improves the texture of the stock; monkfish, whiting, cod and haddock are all suitable. Avoid oily fish debris – such as mackerel, herring, etc.

Makes 2 litres (3½ pt)

1–1½ kg (2–3 lb) fish bones and heads
l onion, sliced
l carrot, sliced
white part of 1 small leek, sliced
1 stalk celery, sliced
bouquet garni
10 black peppercorns
450 ml (15 fl oz) dry white wine or good dry cider
2 teaspoons white wine vinegar
2 litres (3½ pt) water

Put all the ingredients in a large pan, adding the water last. Bring slowly to the boil, skimming until the liquid is clear. Cover the pan and simmer it – fish stock should never boil – for about 30 minutes. Do not be tempted to cook it longer or the stock will taste gluey. Strain the stock through a double-muslin-lined sieve. Salt is not added, since the stock may well need to be reduced if you are making a sauce.

NOTE Any left over can be stored in two ways: either in conveniently sized pots in the freezer or else in the form of a fish glaze that can be kept for weeks in the refrigerator.

To make fish glaze – Strain the stock into a wide, shallow pan and boil it down to a tenth or even a twentieth of its original volume, depending on how concentrated it was in the first place. When the liquid is thick and syrupy, pour it in a little container and cover it when cold. A teaspoonful will add flavour to many fish sauces without you having to make stock.

Aspic Jelly

Leave the strained fish fumet of the main recipe to cool. You will then be able to see how much extra gelatine it requires to achieve a firm set: this will depend on the bones used, the quantity of skin, etc. Clarify with the shell and white of an egg (*see* ingredients which follow).

To get the jelly to brushing consistency, stand the bowl of fumet in a bowl of warm water until it begins to melt. Brush it over the fish, which should be placed on a wire tray. When the first coat is dry, put decorations in place with a dab of jelly, then brush over again until the desired thickness is obtained. Left-over jelly can be chopped and placed round the fish.

If you don't wish to make a fish fumet, an ordinary aspic jelly will do instead. Put into a saucepan:

> *450 ml (15 fl oz) water*
> *90 ml (3 fl oz) white wine vinegar*
> *½ onion, chopped*
> *½ carrot, chopped*
> *½ stalk celery, chopped*
> *rind and juice of ½ lemon*
> *30 g (1 oz) gelatine*
> *crushed shell and white of 1 egg*

Bring all the ingredients slowly to the boil, whisking to dissolve the gelatine. A thick white foam will develop on top. Remove from heat when boiling, leave 10 minutes, then strain through a cloth. When the stock is tepid, add either 120 ml (4 fl oz) dry white wine, or 90 ml (3 fl oz) Madeira, Marsala or sweet sherry – these two amounts may be adjusted to taste: the flavour should be strong, not overpowering.

NOTE For coating cold fish, many people prefer the flavour of jellied mayonnaise*.

SHELLFISH STOCK

This robust stock I find handy to have in the freezer, along with more classic fish stocks, as a spicy base for soups and stews. Adjust the quantity of tomato to what you are likely to need – 1 or 2 ripe tomatoes will just help the sweetness without being too identifiable, whereas a medium can or 4 huge ripe tomatoes will give a more definite accent. You can use wine as part of the stock, or 2 or 3 tablespoons of sherry vinegar: on the whole I stick to water – then add reduced red or white wine or a little sherry vinegar when the stock comes into use.

It is prudent to ask the fishmonger in advance to save you lobster, crab and other shellfish debris, as well as the heads and bones of the best white fish, otherwise he will fling them into the dustbin as he prepares his display and may have nothing to give you when you turn up at the shop.

Makes about 3¾ litres (6 pt)

2½ kg (5 lb) mixed shellfish and fish debris
5 cloves garlic, in their skins
2 large onions in their skins, each stuck with 1 clove then quartered
2 medium leeks, sliced
2–4 tomatoes or a medium can (see *above*)
1 medium to large carrot, coarsely grated
2 outer stalks celery, sliced
30 g (1 oz) parsley
2–3 bay leaves
2–3 sprigs of basil or fennel branches
4 sprigs of fresh thyme or 1 teaspoon dried thyme
1 or more hot red chillies
1 good pinch of saffron strands or 1 piece of dried orange peel
salt, freshly ground black pepper

Put the large shellfish and fish debris into a large pot. Crush the garlic with the blade of a knife and add it, with the skin still attached, to the pot. Put in all the other ingredients, plus 4 litres (7 pt) of water. Bring to the boil, then continue to boil steadily but not too vigorously for 30 minutes. Strain through a double layer of muslin. Add seasoning according to your proposed use for the stock.

TWO BATTERS

EGG WHITE BATTER

125 g (4 oz) plain flour
pinch of salt
1 tablespoon olive oil
generous 150 ml (5 fl oz) lukewarm water or beer
white of 1 large egg

Mix the flour and salt with the oil and the water or beer, beating well together. Cover and leave in the kitchen, *not the refrigerator or cold larder*, until required. This gives the flour a chance to ferment slightly, which improves the texture of the batter. Just before the batter is required, beat the egg white stiff and fold it in carefully.

WHOLE EGG BATTER

This is a tempura batter from Japan, which is quick and simple to make, and very light; it is particularly good for large prawns.

Break an egg into a measuring jug. Add four times its volume of water, then five times its volume of flour. Whisk well until smooth.

SAVOURY AND OTHER BUTTERS

The underlying principle of northern fish cookery is butter. So long as you have butter and the usual seasonings, you can do without many other things. Butter comes before wine, cream or eggs.

A fresh trout fried in clarified butter is food for the most demanding. So is Dover sole, brushed with melted butter, then grilled and served with maître d'hôtel butter as sauce and seasoning. A cod, salmon or halibut steak baked in well-buttered foil is a delicious thing to eat. And what about the sauces – how many of them begin and end with butter? Can you imagine eating whitebait or smoked salmon without brown bread and butter? What about shrimps potted in mace-flavoured butter? And all the traditional English pastes made from smoked haddock and smoked salmon, bloaters and kippers, pounded up with butter? Think, too, of the things we serve with fish – well-buttered spinach, new potatoes in parsley butter, sorrel or gooseberries melted to a purée in butter, and slices of mushroom stewed in butter. Have you ever tried mussels or oysters baked in garlic butter?

Butter is the flavour one misses most if margarine or some kind of innominate dripping has been used instead, or one of the tasteless oils of modern cookery. The only alternative for frying and grilling is olive oil and occasionally lard or bacon fat. But for all sauces except mayonnaise, vinaigrette and tomato sauce, which do need olive oil, butter is essential.

The best butter to choose is unsalted, preferably from Normandy. Lightly salted butters such as the Danish Lurpak do almost as well, but Normandy butter is best. And the finest comes from Isigny, a small port on the Cherbourg peninsula. This is easy to buy in Britain nowadays; use plenty, and avoid meanness. It is better to buy a cheaper fish than to economize on butter. Our own butters are made from sweet cream (most European butter is prepared from ripened cream), and have a fair amount of salt added to them: for these two reasons they are not as good for savoury butters.

CLARIFIED BUTTER

Small quantities of butter can be clarified and strained into the frying pan for immediate use, but if you cook a lot of vegetable dishes and fish, it is worth making it in quantity. Store it in a covered jar in the refrigerator: it will keep for weeks. The great advantage of clarified butter is that it burns at a higher temperature than unclarified. Any cook will see the advantage of this. It also contributes to a particularly pure butter flavour that enhances the quality of simple dishes.

Cut up two or three packets of butter and bring them to the boil in a heavy pan. Boil for 1 minute, then set aside to cool for 10 minutes. Strain through a damp muslin so that the white salty crust is held back, leaving a clear yellow oil. This will solidify when completely cold.

Concentrated butter is sometimes available. It is a little better for frying than butter, but as it has some milk solids put back in it, it does not fry at such a hot temperature as clarified butter. It is, however, easy to clarify.

BEURRE MANIÉ

This is a kneaded butter – a useful substance for thickening sauces, soups and stews at the end of the cooking time. A tablespoon of butter is mashed together with a tablespoon of flour to form a paste. This is divided into knobs, which are stirred one by one into the *almost boiling* liquid until it reaches the desired thickness. Allow 5 minutes over a moderate or slow heat. If the sauce begins to boil it will taste floury.

This sounds odd – one simmers a béchamel or velouté sauce for at least 20 minutes to lose the flavour of flour in the roux. But with beurre manié one keeps the sauce below simmering point and cooks it for no longer than 5 minutes with exactly the same purpose.

BEURRE NOISETTE

Butter cooked to a golden-brown, in other words to a nut or *noisette* colour. Capers, lemon juice and parsley are often added. A last minute sauce, an essential part of Raie au beurre noir, p. 487.

SAVOURY BUTTERS

ANISE BUTTER   Mix 1 tablespoon Pernod or pastis with 125 g (4 oz) butter.

BEURRE COLBERT   Add 2 teaspoons of finely chopped tarragon to the beurre maître d'hôtel below, plus 2 or 3 tablespoons of meat glaze or rich meat jelly from underneath beef dripping.

BEURRE MAÎTRE D'HÔTEL   As far as fish is concerned, this is the most useful of the savoury butters, particularly with grilled sole, salmon, turbot, cod – in fact, with almost any other fish.

> *250 g (8 oz) lightly salted butter*
> *60–75 g (2–2½ oz) chopped parsley*
> *lemon juice to taste*

Soften the butter to a thick cream, then mix in the parsley and lemon juice. Mint, savory, tarragon or chive butter can be made by substituting the herb for all or part of the parsley.

You can form the butter into a roll, wrap it in foil and store it in the refrigerator; then neat round slices can be cut off as required.

GARLIC BUTTER   Cream 250 g (8 oz) unsalted butter. Add 3 large cloves of garlic, finely chopped, 30 g (1 oz) chopped shallot, onion or spring onion, 50 g (1½ oz) chopped parsley, 1–2 teaspoons of fine sea salt, and freshly ground black pepper. This butter is especially useful for mussels and shellfish baked in scallop shells or small pots.

LIME BUTTER   Lime butter is even nicer with fish than maître d'hôtel. Here is a recipe for it given by Skeffington Ardron in *The Guardian*.

To 60 g (2 oz) lightly salted butter, add 2 teaspoons fresh lime juice, 2 teaspoons grated peel, 1 teaspoon chopped chives, a pinch of powdered thyme, and a very small pinch of grated ginger.

MONTPELLIER BUTTER (Elizabeth David's version) Weigh out 125 g (4 oz) of the following, in approximately equal amounts – watercress, spinach and tarragon leaves, parsley, chervil. If you grow salad burnet, the French *pimprenelle*, add some of that, too. If you have no chervil, double the quantity of parsley.

Pour boiling water over the herbs, leave for 1 minute, then drain and dry as completely as possible. Pound in a mortar, with 6 anchovy fillets, 2 tablespoons capers, 4 miniature gherkins, the yolks of 1 raw and 3 hard-boiled eggs. When all is smooth, mash into 125 g (4 oz) soft butter. Sieve and mix in 5 or 6 tablespoons of olive oil gradually. Finally sharpen with a little lemon juice. Store, covered, in the refrigerator where it will keep for several days, but remove in good time or it will be too hard to spread over the cold salmon, or whatever other fish you are eating it with. It can also be served with hot grilled, fried or poached fish.

I find that this process is much speeded by using a blender. Put the herbs and pickles in together, using the olive oil to keep them moving. When smooth add the eggs and mash into the softened butter by hand, or use an electric beater.

MUSHROOM BUTTER Cream 250 g (8 oz) unsalted butter. Add 3 large cloves of garlic, finely chopped; 75 g (2½ oz) mushrooms, finely chopped; a slice of cooked ham, finely chopped; and 60 g (2 oz) chopped parsley; finally, add salt and freshly ground black pepper.

MUSTARD BUTTER Cream 125 g (4 oz) unsalted butter. Add 1 tablespoon French mustard (or to taste), then season with salt and freshly ground black pepper. Use with herring and mackerel.

ORANGE BUTTER Although this butter can be made with sweet oranges quite successfully, it is best made with Seville oranges. To 125 g (4 oz) unsalted butter, add 4 teaspoons orange juice, 4 teaspoons grated peel, 2 teaspoons of tomato concentrate (or to taste), and season with salt and freshly ground black pepper.

See individual sections for butters based on the following: Anchovy, Lobster, Prawn & Shrimp, Smoked Salmon.

HOT SAUCES

ELIZA ACTON'S RICH MELTED BUTTER

This is a useful basic sauce for fish and comes from Eliza Acton's *Modern Cookery*. Many flavourings can be added to it – hard-boiled egg, lobster, oyster, crab, anchovy essence, some pounded anchovy fillets with mace and cayenne, or shrimps.

> *1 dessertspoon plain flour*
> *½ saltspoonful salt*
> *300 ml (½ pt) cold water*
> *125–175 g (4–6 oz) butter*

'Mix to a very smooth batter a dessertspoonful of flour, a half-saltspoonful of salt, and half a pint of cold water: put these into a delicately clean saucepan, with from four to six ounces of well-flavoured butter, cut into small bits, and shake the sauce strongly round, almost without cessation, until the ingredients are perfectly blended, and it is on the point of boiling; let it simmer for two or three minutes, and it will be ready for use. The best French cooks recommend its not being allowed to *boil*, as they say it tastes less of flour if served when it is just at the point of simmering.'

BÉCHAMEL SAUCE

This is the most useful sauce of home cookery. If you have a freezer, make it in quantity from time to time and store it in containers of every size from 3 tablespoons up to 600 ml (1 pt). The recipe following gives 600 ml (1 pt) more or less, depending on how far you reduce it.

> *600 ml (1 pt) milk*
> *1 large shallot* or *medium onion, stuck with 2 cloves*
> *1 carrot, quartered*
> *5-cm (2-inch) piece celery stalk*
> *bouquet garni*
> *salt, pepper*
> *60 g (2 oz) butter*
> *60 g (2 oz) plain flour*

Bring the milk slowly to the boil with the vegetables, bouquet and seasoning. Leave it over a very low heat to infuse for half an hour; it should not boil, just keep it very hot.

Melt the butter in a heavy pan, stir in the flour and cook to a roux for two minutes, without browning it. Gradually stir in the flavoured milk, through a strainer. Do this off the heat and use a balloon whisk. Return it to the heat, stir and bring to simmering point, then leave it to cook down steadily to the consistency of double cream. Stir occasionally. Making this sauce well can take an hour or even longer. Of course you do not need to stand over it all the time, but you should give it a chance to mature.

QUICK METHOD   Make a butter and flour roux as above. Meanwhile bring the milk to the boil, then add it to the roux gradually. Put in the vegetables, bouquet and seasoning and simmer steadily, with the occasional stir, for at least 15 minutes, preferably 25. Strain before serving or storing.

ANISE SAUCE   Into the béchamel, stir in Pernod, anisette or pastis Ricard, all aniseed-flavoured, until the taste is delicate but noticeable. This sauce should be served immediately.

SAUCE AURORE   It is easy to see how this most beautiful of the béchamel variations was given its name. The flush of colour, from the mixture of ivory béchamel and coral tomato purée, has a Homeric tone of early morning rose. Some recipes are content to achieve this effect with a couple of squirts from a tube of tomato concentrate, but this does not give the right texture at all, or the right delicacy of flavour.

In classic French cookery, sauce aurore partners fine white fish – turbot, sole, monkfish – as well as chicken, and eggs and some vegetables of the more watery character.

Instead of béchamel sauce, a mornay or velouté sauce can be used.

> *300 ml (10 fl oz) béchamel sauce*
> *up to 300 ml (10 fl oz) tomato sauce**
> *60 g (2 oz) butter*

Heat the béchamel sauce to boiling point, then stir in the tomato sauce gradually, stopping when you get to the flavour and colour you prefer. So much depends on the original quality of the tomatoes that one cannot be precise. Bring to the boil again, remove from the heat and whisk in the butter in little bits. Check the seasoning.

Serve with turbot baked in milk, sole, a tailpiece of fresh cod or monkfish – any firm white fish of quality.

SAUCE CHIVRY   I like herb sauces. They mean summer when so many fish are at their best – and look their best, served with a pale green sauce. I like walking down the garden – the genius of man having placed the herb patch as far away from the kitchen as possible, on the principle, I suppose, that exercise is good for cooks – past catalpa and hibiscus, to find chives, tarragon, and parsley, which flourish at the foot of a most entangling rose.

Recipes for herb sauces and butters usually glide over the main pitfall. They state 1 tablespoon, or 3 sprigs, with authority. What this apparently firm direction means is 'a handful, more or less, as opposed to a sackful'. Reflect on this: last year we split a bushy tarragon plant in two, half for Wiltshire, half for our tiny garden in the Bas-Vendômois. In France eight or nine leaves will permeate a chicken: here I use three times as many and still don't quite achieve the same result. There is a veil between us and the sun in England, a lack of clarity of light. To be fair, I should remark that a Vendômois friend grows basil in a successful quantity, but it hasn't the flavour of Ligurian or Provençal basil – again the sun. So be guided by the season, and by your own taste and climate. Be prepared to use far more than I – or anyone else – suggest.

> *tarragon, chives, chervil, parsley, watercress*
> *1 glass dry white wine*
> *450 ml (15 fl oz) béchamel sauce*
> *150 ml (5 fl oz) cream*
> *90 g (3 oz) spinach (1 handful)*
> *60 g (2 oz) butter*

Chop equal quantities of the first four herbs, with half the amount of watercress (which has a strong flavour, so must not be allowed to be too dominant). Put half into a small pan with the wine, and boil down until there is about a tablespoon or two of liquid left. Add to the béchamel sauce with the cream, and leave to simmer. Cook the spinach with the remaining herbs. Press out all liquid, and combine this greenery with the butter. When you are ready to serve the sauce, stir in the spinach butter gradually until the flavour seems right to you: don't let the sauce boil while you do this, or the flavour of the butter will be spoilt.

A good sauce with poached salmon or bass, or with any really fresh fish of a non-oily kind.

NOTE   Keep this sauce for summer. Don't be tempted to try it with dried herbs.

CREAM SAUCE　This expression is sometimes used as a polite way of saying béchamel, but it should be béchamel sauce with a generous amount of cream added. If this makes the sauce too thin, boil it down. Add a final knob of butter before serving and a squeeze of lemon juice if you like.

CURRY SAUCE　When making the béchamel, cook a medium-sized chopped onion slowly in the butter, and add 2 teaspoons of curry powder with the flour. Finish in the usual way. It is much improved by the addition of 150 ml (5 fl oz) cream, beaten with an egg yolk, particularly if it is being served with scallops. Remember not to let the sauce boil once the cream and egg yolk have been added. This is a true French sauce, with the curry powder being used as a spicing ingredient; it has no real relationship to Indian cooking.

MORNAY AND MUSTARD SAUCES　*See* the velouté variations on p. 22 and apply the same seasoning to a béchamel base.

MUSHROOM SAUCE　Either cook 175 g (6 oz) mushrooms in 60 g (2 oz) butter and add them to a béchamel sauce; or cook the mushrooms in the butter for the sauce with a tiny chopped clove of garlic. Add flour, then the hot milk in the usual way. Flavour with plenty of black pepper and a little lemon juice; cream does not come amiss. However, *see* Anchovy and mushroom sauce, p. 50.

PARSLEY SAUCE　To the béchamel, add up to 150 ml (5 fl oz) double cream and reduce slightly. Finish with about 60 g (2 oz) chopped fresh parsley, a few drops of lemon juice and a knob of butter. This is a good sauce, if rich and made with plenty of parsley.

SAUCE SOUBISE　The Hôtel Soubise in the Marais district of Paris, that once belonged to the great Soubise family, now houses the French archives. It is a building of elegance, beautiful statues and colonnade but not an onion dome in sight.

The sauce was invented by Marin, chef to Charles de Rohan, Marquis de Soubise, at the beginning of the eighteenth century. It has a particularly delicate flavour. Chop a large onion. Put it into a pan and cover it with boiling water. Cook for 3 minutes, then drain and return it to the pan with a tablespoon of butter. Cover the pan and stew the onion, without colouring it, until soft. Pour in 300 ml (10 fl oz) béchamel sauce and simmer for 15 minutes. Sieve or blend to make a smooth sauce. Stir in 4 or 5 tablespoons of double cream – the better the cream, the better the flavour – and heat through. Add salt.

See individual sections for other sauces, i.e. Anchovy sauce, Anchovy and mushroom sauce, Crayfish sauce (Sauce Nantua), Lobster sauce, Mussel sauce, Prawn sauce, Shrimp sauce.

VELOUTÉ DE POISSON

The success of a velouté sauce depends on a good stock – the same recipe can be used with meat and poultry stocks instead of fish fumet – and on the gentle reduction that matures the flavour and makes the texture as velvety as possible. The sauce can be served on its own, or used as the base for further complexities. It is fine, for instance, to add mussel or oyster liquor and then reduce again, perhaps with some cream (*see* sauce Normande below).

Makes about 600 ml (1 pt)

60 g (2 oz) butter
4 tablespoons plain flour
1 litre (1¾ pt) fumet de poisson*
about 100 g (3½ oz) chopped mushroom stalks (optional)
crème fraîche or double cream, to taste
salt, pepper

Melt the butter, stir in the flour and cook it for 1 minute, stirring most of the time. Meanwhile heat the fumet to boiling point. Pour it on to the roux gradually, off the heat, using a whisk to make the sauce as smooth as possible.

Now add the mushroom stalks, if you have them. Bring the sauce back to boiling point, stirring. Lower the heat, or put the pan over another pan of simmering water and leave the sauce to reduce by almost half. Allow at least 45 minutes: it will take longer to reduce over water than if it is directly on the stove (in which case I would recommend that you use a heat-diffuser to make sure it cannot catch). If a skin forms, whisk it in.

Finally add as much crème fraîche or cream as consistency, flavour and your taste demand. Strain out the mushroom stalks if used and season it according to the end you have in mind for the sauce. Serve it very hot.

SAUCE ALLEMANDE   Make the velouté sauce. Beat up 2 egg yolks with 60 ml (2 fl oz) of single and 60 ml (2 fl oz) of double cream. Pour in a little of the sauce, return to the pan and stir steadily over a low heat (*don't boil*) until the sauce is very rich. Use with the finest white fish, poached or baked in white wine or fish stock; the stock is used in making the basic velouté sauce.

SAUCE ANDALOUSE   Make the velouté. Peel and chop 2 very large tomatoes. Cook them in a little olive oil, with a clove of garlic, crushed. When they are reduced to a purée, add to the sauce, plus 2 canned peppers, chopped small. (Fresh peppers can be used but they must first be seeded, then boiled, peeled and chopped.) Last of all stir in some chopped parsley. A good sauce for mullet of all kinds, and any firm fish such as tuna.

MORNAY SAUCE   Add 2 heaped tablespoons grated Parmesan, 2 tablespoons grated Gruyère and some grated nutmeg. Dry Cheddar can be substituted for Gruyère but you will need more of it for a good flavour. Do not allow the sauce to boil once the cheese is added.

NOTE   This sauce can also be made with béchamel.

MUSTARD SAUCE   To the velouté sauce, made with half milk and half fumet de poisson, add a teaspoonful of French mustard – or more, according to taste – just before serving. More successful than mustard added to béchamel.

SAUCE NORMANDE   Today's version of a very grand sauce is subtly different every time you make it because the juices from cooking the varying garnishes are added to it. Should you be using prawns or shrimps, boil up their shells with some water or fish stock, whizz the whole thing in the processor and strain off the liquid through a cloth: it can go into the sauce as well.

Makes 600 ml (1 pt)

600 ml (1 pt) velouté de poisson
up to 500 ml (18 fl oz) fish fumet*
oyster, mussel and prawn or shrimp cooking liquor
liquor from cooking a mushroom garnish (optional)
4 egg yolks
125 ml (4 fl oz) crème fraîche or double cream
60 g (2 oz) unsalted Normandy butter, cut up
salt, pepper, chilli powder (cayenne pepper), lemon juice

Heat the velouté in a wide pan with the fumet and shellfish liquors and the mushroom liquor if you have it, and reduce it to 600 ml (1 pt).
Beat the egg yolks with half the crème fraîche or cream, stir in a

little sauce and then stir this back into the pan, keeping the heat low. Keep stirring, without boiling, until the sauce is thick.

Off the heat, stir in the butter and the rest of the cream. Season to taste. A few drops of lemon juice will improve the flavour if double cream is used.

SAUCE NORMANDE (a simpler version)   Use when a creamy sauce is needed for a gratin, or to go with a fish pie, or with some poached fish of a firm texture.

> *60 g (2 oz) butter*
> *3 tablespoons plain flour*
> *150 ml (5 fl oz) fish stock or liquor from shellfish or light meat stock*
> *300 ml (10 fl oz) double cream or single and double mixed*
> *salt, pepper*
> *dash of wine vinegar*

Make the sauce in the usual way, adding the vinegar just before serving, when the pan is off the heat. Sherry or Madeira can be used instead; or dry white wine or vermouth, in which the fish has been cooked. Reduce it to a few tablespoons after removing the fish.

POULETTE SAUCE   Make the velouté sauce with a few more mushrooms than usual – about 125 g (4 oz) in all. Beat up 2 egg yolks with 2 tablespoons double cream, and incorporate this with the hot sauce, which should not be allowed to boil. Season with lemon juice and chopped parsley. An excellent sauce for mussels or eel, and the liquid from cooking that fish is used to make the velouté sauce.

SAUCE AU CIDRE

This is a Normandy sauce, like the white wine sauce which follows.

> *1 onion or 2 shallots, chopped*
> *trimmings of the fish, plus its bones*
> *150 g (5 oz) butter*
> *about 600 ml (1 pt) cider*
> *bouquet garni*
> *salt, pepper*
> *3 tablespoons plain flour*
> *2 egg yolks*
> *60 ml (2 fl oz) double cream*
> *lemon juice*

Fry the onion or shallot, and the trimmings of the fish, very gently, in 30 g (1 oz) of butter. When the onion begins to soften, pour in the cider, plus 150 ml (5 fl oz) water. Add the fish bones, bouquet and a seasoning of salt and pepper. Simmer steadily for half an hour, with the lid off the pan; there should then be between 450 and 600 ml (¾–1 pt) of stock.

Make a roux with 60 g (2 oz) of butter and the flour, add the strained stock, and complete the sauce as if it were a velouté, thickening it with the egg yolks beaten into the cream. Just before serving, whisk in the last 60 g (2 oz) of butter and season with salt, pepper and lemon juice.

SAUCE AU VIN BLANC

This is one of many similar recipes (*see* sauce Bercy*) which makes a good general sauce for many fish.

> *300 ml (10 fl oz) white wine*
> *1 litre (1½ pt) water*
> *1 kg (2 lb) fish bones*
> *bouquet garni*
> *1 carrot, sliced*
> *1 onion, sliced*
> *60 g (2 oz) butter*
> *3 tablespoons plain flour*
> *125 ml (4 fl oz) double cream* ⎫
> *125 ml (4 fl oz) single cream* ⎭ *or 250 ml (8 fl oz) double cream*
> *salt, pepper*

Put the first six ingredients into a large pan and boil steadily for half an hour. Strain off and measure the liquid. If necessary boil down again to 450 ml (15 fl oz). Use this stock, and the cream, to make a velouté sauce in the usual way. Let it mature and thicken by slow simmering.

CREAM SAUCES MADE WITH CREAM AND BUTTER

Twenty or so years ago, one used to come across people who would throw up their hands in horror at the thought of cream and butter sauces. Nowadays, crème fraîche has changed all that – although one would wish it were a little more readily available. Otherwise, you can use half soured, half double cream.

SAUCE À LA CRÈME NORMANDE

This wonderful sauce is the simplest I know. Once it was made on both sides of the Channel (there are recipes for it in eighteenth-century English cookery books); now you find it nowhere but in Normandy or under Norman influence. Serve it with salmon and salmon trout, or with wild river trout if you can get it. Use it as a binding sauce for mushroom fricassee – or to reheat a little left-over cooked turbot or salmon.

A chopping of *fines herbes* is the usual flavouring, but nutmeg could be used instead. If you confine yourself to tarragon, with a little chervil, it makes an admirable sauce for braised or poached chicken.

For about 300 ml (10 fl oz) cut up 175 g (6 oz) unsalted butter and melt it gently in a 21-cm (8½-inch), heavy frying pan, preferably a non-stick one. Pour in 200 ml (7 fl oz) crème fraîche or half soured and half double cream. Stir all the time with a wooden spoon as the sauce bubbles down to a rich thickness. Do not let it gallop but bubble it steadily to the consistency you need, which will be thicker for a binding sauce than for pouring.

Should the sauce show a tendency to oiliness, which can happen if you work too fast or, I suspect, if the cream is not the freshest and best, rapidly stir in a tablespoon of very cold water, off the heat. Season to taste.

SAUCE VERTE DE CHAUSEY

The Îles Chausey, several miles out from Granville in Normandy, once provided granite for the quays and cathedrals and monasteries of that coast, including Mont St Michel. Whether this sauce was made there, I have not been able to discover. Perhaps it was named for its dark, speckled-green colour, rather the effect of granite. The mustard makes it a good sauce for gurnard, garfish, herring, mackerel, saithe or huss. If you cut down the mustard, or increase the cream and butter, it goes well with salmon. It is a great improver of the cod family.

Makes about 250 ml (8 fl oz)

30 g (1 oz) finely chopped shallots
2 cloves garlic, finely chopped
2 tablespoons chopped parsley, plus extra, to taste
125 g (4 oz) unsalted butter
1 scant tablespoon Dijon mustard
dash of white wine vinegar
125 ml (4 fl oz) crème fraîche or half soured, half double cream
1 tablespoon chopped tarragon
salt, pepper

Cook the shallots and garlic with the parsley very slowly in half the butter in a smallish non-stick frying pan or sauté pan. When they are tender add the rest of the butter and then the mustard and vinegar. Stir until the mixture bubbles again, and pour in the crème fraîche or cream. Keep stirring and let the sauce thicken a little. Off the heat, add the chopped tarragon, extra parsley, salt and pepper.

You can serve the sauce as it is, but I prefer to smooth it further in the blender. A few short bursts is enough, leaving plenty of speckled interest. Reheat the sauce gently. This sauce is served warm rather than boiling-hot.

EGG AND BUTTER SAUCES

SAUCE HOLLANDAISE AND DERIVATIVES

I can never decide which gives me greater pleasure – making a hollandaise sauce, which is in effect a hot mayonnaise, or eating it. Its origins are elusive but one thing is certain: it is not Dutch at all, but French. Sometimes it is called sauce Isigny, a genuflection to the hometown of France's best butter.

3 tablespoons white wine vinegar
3 tablespoons water
12 white peppercorns
3 large egg yolks
250 g (8 oz) unsalted or lightly salted butter
salt, lemon juice

Boil the first three ingredients down to a tablespoon of liquid. Strain into either a pudding basin or the top pan of a double boiler. When cool, beat in the yolks. Stand the basin, or top pan, over a pan of barely simmering water. Keep the heat steady, being careful not to overheat. Now add the butter in chips, beating them in with a wooden spoon gradually. Or, and this works well, melt the butter and beat it in as if you were making mayonnaise; you can do this off the heat if you like, so long as both egg yolks and butter are warm.

When the sauce is very thick, add a final seasoning of salt and lemon juice. If you have to keep it waiting, turn it into a *tepid* bowl or jug or sauceboat and stand it in a pan of *tepid* water. Overheating at this point can curdle the best hollandaise. If at any moment you think the hollandaise is overheating, plunge the base of the bowl or pan into cold water.

Should the sauce curdle, try whisking in a tablespoon of ice cold water. If this doesn't work, break a fresh egg, put the yolk into a clean basin and beat in the curdled sauce gradually. It doesn't take long, so don't give way to despair.

CAVIARE SAUCE   Fold 3–4 tablespoons of pressed caviare into the finished mousseline sauce, *see* below. Adjust the seasoning. For the finest fish – sole, turbot, trout, really fresh bass, John Dory.

CUCUMBER HOLLANDAISE   *See* Grilled pompano with cucumber hollandaise, p. 62.

MALTESE SAUCE   Stir in the grated rind of a blood orange, and use the orange juice instead of lemon for the final seasoning. A Seville orange makes an even better flavour. Delicious with firm white fish.

MOUSSELINE SAUCE   Whip up 125 ml (4 fl oz) double cream. Fold into the sauce just before serving, and readjust the seasoning. Good with a solid fish like salmon.

SAUCE TRIANON   Use lemon juice (1 tablespoon) and sherry medium-dry (2 tablespoons) instead of vinegar.

SAUCE BÉARNAISE

This is a nineteenth-century sauce, invented by a chef at the Pavillon Henri IV at St Germain-en-Laye, and named for that great French king, who came from Béarn, close to the Basque country, on the Spanish border. This chef had the idea of spicing the egg and butter innocence of hollandaise with a reduction of wine, tarragon, shallot and wine vinegar, seasoned with plenty of coarsely ground black pepper, a simple addition, perhaps, but it quite changes the character of the sauce. Serve with grilled fish of fine flavour and substance – salmon, sunfish, tuna, pompano, large mackerel.

> *1 heaped tablespoon chopped shallot*
> *2 tablespoons chopped tarragon and chervil*
> *4 tablespoons tarragon vinegar*
> *4 tablespoons white wine*
> *good grating of black pepper*
> *egg yolks and butter, as for hollandaise**
> *1 tablespoon chopped tarragon and chervil for finishing*
> *pinch of salt*
> *pinch of cayenne pepper*

Put the shallot, tarragon and chervil, vinegar, wine and black pepper into a small pan. Boil down until about 2 tablespoons of liquid is left. Put into a large pudding basin, and when cool add the egg yolks. Continue as for hollandaise sauce. Strain, and whisk in about a tablespoon of chopped tarragon and chervil. Add salt and cayenne. Serve in a warmed sauceboat.

SAUCE CHORON   This is the most famous variation of the béarnaise sauce, and is called after a Normandy chef, Choron, who came from Caen. It is usually served with grilled meat or poultry, but goes very well with fish; *see* Bar en croûte, p. 353.

Make a béarnaise, above. Then flavour the sauce to taste with seasoning and about 3 tablespoons of tomato purée (preferably home-made), adding it gradually. If you feel at this point that the consistency could be improved, add 2 good tablespoons of whipped cream which will make the sauce bulkier and lighter.

OTHER HOT SAUCES

SAUCE À L'AMÉRICAINE

This sauce comes, in spite of its name, from southern France. So it is important to use olive oil and garlic, and to liven the tomatoes up with sugar and black pepper, should you happen to be cooking in a less sunny climate. There is no substitute for cognac, apart from the other grape brandies.

In its classic version, this sauce is cooked with the dish in the style of a stew (*see* Lobster à l'américaine, p. 213.) But if you can only buy ready-boiled lobster, or if you serve the sauce with a fish that can't stand the fierce reduction, for instance huss or hake or quenelles of whiting, here is a recipe allowing for this:

750 g (1½ lb) tomatoes, peeled and roughly chopped
150 ml (5 fl oz) olive oil
500 g (1 lb) cheap white fish
seasoned flour
125 g (4 oz) chopped shallot or mild onion
125 g (4 oz) chopped carrot
1 large clove garlic, crushed
75 ml (2½ fl oz) cognac
shell of lobster, crab or prawn
300 ml (10 fl oz) dry white wine
150 ml (5 fl oz) strong beef stock
salt, pepper, cayenne pepper, sugar
tarragon and chervil or parsley
1 good tablespoon butter

Cook the tomatoes to a thick purée in half the olive oil. Cut the white fish into large cubes, turn them in seasoned flour and fry in the rest of the olive oil with the shallot, carrot and garlic. When the fish is lightly browned, add the warmest cognac and set it alight. Turn the mixture, so that the flames last as long as possible. Add lobster, crab or prawn shell, the wine, stock and tomatoes. Season with plenty of black pepper and ½ teaspoon of salt. Cook vigorously for half an hour, or until the sauce looks thick rather than watery. Remove as much shell as possible, then briefly liquidize. Correct the seasoning, add herbs, and reheat. Stir in the tablespoon of butter, pour over the cooked fish and serve.

If you are using ready-boiled lobster, reheat it in the sauce before adding the butter.

NOTE As with sauce aurore*, the important thing is to use real tomatoes. By all means help the flavour with a little tomato concentrate, if it seems necessary, but never make tomato concentrate a substitute for tomatoes.

SAUCE BERCY

This intense concentration of onions, wine and meat essence usually accompanies plainly-cooked food such as grilled steak or liver. But if the juices from a foil-baked fish are substituted for meat essence, it goes equally well with bass, bream or salmon.

1 heaped tablespoon chopped shallot or *onion*
1 level tablespoon butter
150 ml (5 fl oz) white wine
salt, pepper, lemon juice
chopped parsley

About 25 minutes before the fish is cooked, put the shallot or onion and the butter into a small heavy pan. Cook gently until golden and transparent. Add the wine and boil hard until there is about a couple of tablespoons of liquid left. Remove from the heat. Transfer the cooked fish to a warm serving plate. Pour the juices from the foil, about 300 ml (10 fl oz) of fish fumet, into the onion and wine mixture. Reheat, and correct the seasoning with salt, pepper and lemon juice to taste. The amount required is bound to vary according to the type and quantity of seasoning put into the foil package with the fish. Add some chopped parsley and serve very hot in a separate sauceboat.

Remember that this is intended to be a concentrated sauce, to be eaten in small quantities. If the juices in the foil were too abundant and watery – though this is unlikely – the sauce must be reduced a second time before the final seasoning.

NOTE   A more copious amount of sauce can be provided by adding up to 150 ml (5 fl oz) of double cream or thicken with beurre manié*.

BEURRE BLANC

The château of La Goulaine, south of Nantes, has a reputation for Muscadet, the wine of the district. It also has a reputation for being the birthplace of beurre blanc, one of the best of fish sauces. The first reputation is well-bestowed; I am not quite so sure about the second. A love of good food is often garnished with undeclared fairy tales. But this one has plausibility.

One day towards the turn of the century, so the story goes, the Marquis of Goulaine's cook, Clémence, was preparing a dinner party. She asked a helper to get on with the béarnaise, while she attended to other things. When everything was dished up, Clémence glanced at the béarnaise and realized that the egg yolks had been forgotten. No time to make a fresh sauce; the mistake – which tasted surprisingly good – was sent up. After dinner Clémence was summoned to the dining-room. She arrived red-faced and ashamed, expecting trouble. Instead, the 'new sauce' was praised. She was asked to repeat the mistake many times, and when she left the château to open a restaurant at la Chébuette, a mile or two away on the banks of the Loire, her beurre blanc soon became a speciality of the region, from Nantes to Angers and Tours.

As you would expect, beurre blanc is served with shad, brochet and salmon from the Loire. Try it, too, with saltwater fish such as turbot, sole, John Dory, brill and whiting. The fish should be poached in a half-wine, half-water court bouillon*, baked in foil, or braised. *Not* a sauce for fried fish.

The trick consists in not overheating the sauce, which is very much a last-minute sauce. The first time you make it, have a bowl of ice cubes handy for quickly cooling the base of the pan. Make a reduction of wine vinegar and shallots as for the béarnaise sauce*. Cut up 250 g (8 oz) butter, chilled until firm, into cubes. Whisk in the butter, bit by bit, keeping the heat very low; it should melt to a cream – raise the pan from the stove to make sure it does not get too hot. Season to taste.

If you have a total collapse, don't despair. Beat a couple of egg yolks in a basin over a pan of simmering water, and add the butter/ shallot mixture gradually until you have the thicker and yellower sauce more usually known as hollandaise*.

SAUCE À LA CRÉOLE

A tomato sauce made sweeter, and a little hotter, by the addition of peppers and a discreet seasoning of chillis.

> *250 g (½ lb) chopped onion*
> *2 large stalks celery, chopped*
> *3 fresh red peppers, seeded, chopped or 4 canned peppers*
> *1 small green chilli or ½ teaspoon crushed hot chilli flakes*
> *60 g (2 oz) butter*
> *1 kg (2 lb 3 oz) can of tomatoes*
> *thyme*
> *salt, pepper*
> *basil*

Fry the onion, celery, peppers and chilli in the butter, gently at first until they begin to soften, then a little more strongly until they brown lightly. Pour in the contents of the can of tomatoes, add a sprig or two of thyme, plenty of freshly ground black pepper and only a little salt (because the sauce is to be reduced). Leave the lid off the pan so that the liquid has a chance to evaporate, and cook until the sauce becomes a stew.

Remove the sprigs of thyme, check the seasoning and add more salt or chilli flakes if required. Add a final chopping of fresh basil.

Like the marinara sauce*, sauce à la créole makes an excellent basis for fish stews. When the flavour is to your liking, add some lightly-browned fish such as turbot, brill, hake, shark, monkfish, or squid, and cook for another 5 or 10 minutes. (*See* Sunfish à la créole p. 474.) If using mussels or clams, open them in a large saucepan and remove the shells, before adding them to the sauce – stir in the strained shellfish liquor too.

THREE GOOSEBERRY SAUCES

These gooseberry sauces and the sorrel ones below have a remarkably similar taste, as Elizabeth David remarks in *French Provincial Cooking*. The two acidites are interchangeable. I must confess, though, to never having eaten gooseberry sauce with salmon, because when the fruit is at its small, acid-green best, salmon is unpleasantly expensive. Mackerel, at their finest, arrive with the first gooseberries; nobody can complain at the price of either, though Parson Woodforde, the greediest of Norfolk parsons in the eighteenth century, did complain, in his diary, when the spring was late and he had to eat the first mackerel of the season without gooseberry sauce.

In spite of this, it is the French and not the English who christened this hardy fruit *groseille à maquereau* – which is odd, at first sight, because the gooseberry grows super-abundantly in the British Isles (and indeed as far north as the Arctic Circle), and gooseberry sauces are more common in our old cookery books than in French ones. Perhaps the reason is that we use gooseberries in so many ways, for pies or tarts, for boiled puddings and for jam, whereas in France it is largely a question of gooseberries with mackerel.

1. The first sauce is made by substituting 250 g (8 oz) gooseberries for the sorrel leaves in the recipe for sorrel sauce (*see* p. 35). Strain the purée through a sieve and add the boiled cream and the fish stock or juice.

2. The second sauce requires:

> *500 g (1 lb) gooseberries*
> *30 g (1 oz) butter*
> *1 egg or 3 tablespoons béchamel sauce**
> *1 teaspoon sugar*
> *ground ginger or freshly grated nutmeg*

Top and tail the gooseberries (it is easiest to use scissors for this). Cook over a low heat with the butter, until soft enough to put through a sieve or *mouli-légumes*. Beat in either the egg or the sauce. Reheat without boiling, and season with the sugar, and the ginger or nutmeg, to taste.

3.   The third sauce includes fennel:

> *500 g (1 lb) gooseberries*
> *30 g (1 oz) butter*
> *3 tablespoons béchamel sauce**
> *1 heaped dessertspoon of fennel leaves, chopped*
> *nutmeg, salt, pepper, lemon juice, sugar*

Prepare and cook gooseberries as described above until one taken from the pan will give between the fingers without collapsing completely. Drain, and set aside while you make a béchamel sauce in the usual way. Let the sauce reduce, simmering, up to the consistency of thick cream. Mix in the gooseberries and the chopped fennel, and add the seasonings to taste: the sugar should not be added unless the gooseberries are very young and tart. Reheat gently.

The gooseberries may be sieved into the sauce, instead of being left whole.

MARINARA OR ITALIAN TOMATO SAUCE

This is the basis for fish stews and soups, and for pasta sauces. One of the girls in our family once worked in Rome. The first time she came home on holiday, she pushed me affably from the stove. 'I'm going to show you how to make a proper tomato sauce,' she announced. 'First, you must put in some chopped carrot – and second, you mustn't keep stirring it once it comes to the boil.'

> *1 medium onion, chopped*
> *1 medium carrot, chopped*
> *1 generous tablespoon olive oil*
> *1 clove garlic, crushed*
> *1 kg (2 lb) tomatoes, peeled and chopped or 1 kg (2 lb 3 oz) can of Italian*
>   *tomatoes*
> *salt, pepper*

Brown the onion and carrot lightly in the oil. Add the remaining ingredients and bring to the boil, stirring. Leave to simmer, uncovered, until the sauce reduces to a fairly thick stew – at least 30 minutes. Sieve or not, as you please.

A glass of red wine may be added to the ingredients above. And the sauce may be finished by the addition of a nice lump of butter and some cayenne or chilli flakes, but be careful not to overdo them.

This is one of the most useful of all fish sauces. Small fish, squid, shrimps or prawns, clams and mussels can all be added to it, or cooked in it, to make the most satisfactory fish stews. Dilute with fish stock, add some shellfish, and you have a delicious soup.

ROMESCO SAUCE

One of the most famous sauces of Spanish cookery, from the province of Tarragona where the small hot Romesco peppers are grown. In this country I would recommend you buy fresh red chillis and hang them up to dry in your kitchen. The other essential ingredient – except of course for tomatoes – is hazelnuts, which add texture and their oil to the sauce.

> *2 huge tomatoes, Marmande or Eshkol type*
> *3 fine fat cloves garlic*
> *24 hazelnuts, blanched* or *12 each almonds and hazelnuts*
> *2 large red home-dried chillis, seeded*
> *salt, pepper*
> *250 ml (8 fl oz) olive oil*
> *2 tablespoons sherry vinegar* or *1 each wine vinegar and dry sherry*
> *chopped parsley*

Bake the whole tomatoes and whole, peeled garlic in a moderate oven for about 15 minutes. After 10 minutes add the nuts and chillis. Transfer to the blender, scraping the tomato pulp free of its skin, and blend to a purée, adding the seasoning and the olive oil – gradually – to make a smooth sauce. Finally stir in the vinegar or vinegar and sherry, and correct the seasoning.

SAMPHIRE SAUCE

This recipe comes from Alan Davidson's *North Atlantic Seafood*;

For 500 g (1 lb) fish, take 375 g (12 oz) prepared samphire, well washed and with the hard bits of stalk near the roots cut off, and cook it for 10 minutes in a covered pot of 4 tablespoons water. Drain it and use an electric blender to turn it into a purée, incorporating 90 g (3 oz) butter in it. The purée is then heated and poured over the fish as a sauce. It has a marvellously bright green colour – any other so-called green sauce would go even greener with envy – and a delicious flavour. But it is quite salty, so on no account add salt.

TWO SORREL SAUCES

There was a time, twenty or so years ago, that the French were leaving their countryside in large numbers, leaving behind them houses they could not sell. Many a time I remember walking along a lane, and seeing a cluster of farm buildings over a hedge. There would be no barks to greet one's arrival, no flutter and squawk of fowls on the dung heap. One would see nothing hanging from the nails by the kitchen door. Passing by the house, one would come to the kitchen garden, overgrown perhaps but undeniably there. Pushing the gate open, freeing it from the overhanging rose, one would stumble over a lusty patch of sorrel, placed where it was easy to grab a handful to flavour the evening's soup, or to make a sauce for the fish brought home from the market. How grateful that clear flavour is in the spring, sharp as lemon juice to one's tired winter taste.

This recipe comes from Elizabeth David's *French Provincial Cooking*.

> *1 large handful sorrel leaves (approx. 125 g/4 oz)*
> *30 g (1 oz) butter*
> *125 ml (4 fl oz) each single and double cream (250 ml/8 fl oz in all)*
> *stock or juice from cooking the fish*
> *salt, pepper*

Remove the toughest stems from the sorrel. Wash and melt it to a purée in the butter. This takes no more than three or four minutes. In a saucepan, bring the cream to the boil, stir in the sorrel and 3 or 4 tablespoons of stock from cooking the fish. If the fish has been fried or grilled, add some water to the pan juices, boil up well and use them instead of stock. Season to taste. Serve with mackerel, salmon, white fish, shad, pike.

The next recipe came from Mrs Stevenson when she was at the Horn of Plenty near Tavistock in Devon. She served it with the delicious Tamar salmon.

about 30 leaves of sorrel, 1 large handful
30 g (1 oz) butter
500 g (1 lb) unsalted butter
4 egg yolks
2 tablespoons water
salt, lemon juice

Make a sorrel purée as above. Put the unsalted butter into a saucepan, cut in chunks, and bring to the boil over a gentle heat. Meanwhile, beat the egg yolks and water in a large pudding basin. Set the basin over a pan of barely simmering water. Keep stirring the yolks, and as the butter comes to a frothing boil, pour a little of it on to the yolks. Go on beating – a wooden spoon is best for this – and add the butter slowly: the mayonnaise process. As the sauce thickens the butter may be added more rapidly. Watch the water underneath – it should not boil.

When the sauce coats the spoon, take the basin from the pan and stir in the sorrel purée to taste. Add salt and lemon juice if required.

NOTE   Of course there is no reason why the sorrel purée shouldn't be added to the conventionally made hollandaise sauce*. This method, though, is quicker.

FRESH TOMATO SAUCE

Skin, seed and chop 2 large tomatoes or 500 g (1 lb) of well-flavoured smaller tomatoes. Cook a small chopped onion and 2 chopped cloves of garlic in a little olive oil. Stir in the tomato, raise the heat. If you want a Latin-American accent, add a chopped, seeded chilli and a final seasoning of coriander. If you prefer the Italian style, omit the chilli and use basil as the final herb. Salt, pepper, sugar as necessary. Cook as briefly as possible so that you concentrate the flavour without losing freshness and texture.

COLD SAUCES

MAYONNAISE

I believe that the best mayonnaise, in particular if it is to go with cold fish, should be made with olive oil. A light-flavoured oil – mayonnaise emphasizes the fruity flavour – but an oil tasting of olives.

When strong flavourings such as curry powder are to be added, corn or groundnut oils may be substituted. Never spoil mayonnaise with malt vinegar. Red and white wine vinegar, tarragon vinegar or, most usually, lemon juice are the sharpeners to use.

Mayonnaise is a sauce that rarely fails if you take reasonable precautions beforehand – the ingredients should be at least at room temperature.

> *1 large* or *2 standard egg yolks*
> *wine vinegar* or *lemon juice*
> *1 teaspoon Dijon mustard* (*optional*)
> *150 ml* (*5 fl oz*) *light olive oil*
> *salt, pepper, herbs, etc.*

HAND OR ELECTRIC BEATER METHOD   Warm the bowl and spoon or beater with hot water, then dry. Quickly put in the egg yolk with a teaspoon of vinegar or lemon juice, and mustard if appropriate to the dish. Beat thoroughly together, then add the oil, drop by drop at first, then more steadily as the mixture thickens. When the oil is absorbed, add vinegar or lemon juice to taste, seasonings and herbs.

BLENDER METHOD   Use two yolks or one whole large egg. Put the egg into a warmed blender with the vinegar or lemon juice and mustard. Turn to top speed, having covered the blender. After 10 seconds, remove the central cover of the lid and gradually pour in the oil and seasonings. On account of the very high speed, you can put in the oil more rapidly from the start, though it is prudent to go gently at first.

REMEDIES FOR CURDLED MAYONNAISE
(1)   The moment you suspect curdling, whisk in a tablespoon of boiling water. This is often enough to bring the sauce back.
(2)   Put another egg yolk into a clean bowl and add the curdled mixture drop by drop at first, then the remainder of the oil, plus extra to bring the quantity up to 250 ml (8 fl oz).
(3)   Put a tablespoon of Dijon mustard into a clean, warmed bowl, instead of another egg yolk, then continue with method 2. This is handy to know if you are out of eggs, and the dish will stand the extra mustard flavour.

AILLOLI AND AILLADE   *Ailloli*, the garlic mayonnaise from Provence, gives its name to the great spread of cold food for which that part of France is so famous. Salt cod and other fish provide the centrepiece (*see* p. 100). The sauce can quite well accompany the salt fish in simpler combinations or even alone; though I think a modifying salad of some kind is a good idea.

> up to 8 cloves garlic
> salt
> 2 egg yolks
> 300 ml (10 fl oz) Provençal olive oil
> pepper
> lemon juice

Crush the garlic with a little salt in a mortar, or blender. (The first time you make the recipe start with 4 cloves of garlic; when everyone has got used to the idea, work up gradually to 8.) Add the egg yolks and finish the mayonnaise with the rest of the ingredients.

The unexpected ingredients of *aillade*, another garlic mayonnaise, are hazelnuts and walnuts. To me, this is the ideal sauce for a simpler arrangement of cold fish:

> 8 large shelled hazelnuts
> 8 shelled walnuts
> 3–6 cloves garlic
> salt
> 2 egg yolks
> 300 ml (10 fl oz) Provençal olive oil
> pepper
> lemon juice

Grill the hazelnuts lightly, until the skins can easily be rubbed off; pour boiling water over the walnuts, and remove their skins. Crush the nuts with the garlic and a little salt in a mortar or blender, and continue with the mayonnaise in the usual way.

AVOCADO SAUCE Avocado makes a good sauce for salmon and salmon trout in particular, though it also goes well with crab and lobster.

> 2 ripe avocados
> juice of 1 small lemon
> 1 large garlic clove, crushed
> 300 ml (10 fl oz) soured cream
> salt, pepper
> 2 spring onions, chopped (see recipe)

Peel, stone and mash the avocados with the lemon juice and garlic. Mix in the cream gradually. Taste and season with salt and pepper. Finally mix in the onion, if the sauce is to be served with cold fish. If the sauce is for hot fish, omit the onion and warm the basin over a pan of simmering water until the sauce is reasonably hot, but nowhere near boiling point.

CURRY MAYONNAISE   This sauce, which is simple to make, goes well with the strong flavours of fish like pickled herrings. Add 1 teaspoon of finely grated onion and 1 teaspoon of curry powder or paste to the 2 egg yolks of the basic mayonnaise ingredients (which, in this case, may be made with corn or groundnut oil) and finish in the usual way.

In Scandinavia, a curry mayonnaise made with curry powder and an equal amount of chopped chutney is served with prawn dishes.

GASTRONOME MAYONNAISE   Mix 150 ml (5 fl oz) mayonnaise with 100 ml (3½ fl oz) soured cream, 1 level tablespoon each of tomato paste and chopped tarragon, plus 1 teaspoonful tarragon vinegar. Serve this with cold fish, especially turbot and sole. This recipe comes from Bengt Petersen's *Delicious Fish Dishes*.

GREEN MAYONNAISE   Every cookery book gives sauce rémoulade, sauce tartare, sauce ravigote – all versions of mayonnaise. These sauces use herbs and sharp pickles, such as gherkins, anchovies or capers, with the occasional spice of some raw, chopped onion or shallot; the kind of sauce that each cook can alter to her own taste.

Here is a less commonly encountered herb mayonnaise, a green sauce of distinction. As a rule it is served with salmon, salmon trout and shellfish, but it goes with cold white fish too, turbot or John Dory, for instance.

According to the resources of your garden or neighbourhood, assemble one or other of these herb mixtures:

either
15 g (½ oz) each parsley, chervil, tarragon, chives, sorrel, salad burnet
30 g (1 oz) spinach and watercress leaves
or
30 g (1 oz) each parsley, tarragon, chervil, chives
45 g (1½ oz) each spinach and watercress leaves

Make your basic mayonnaise. Blanch the herbs for 2 minutes in boiling water. Pour out into a sieve and run under the cold tap. Leave to drain. Press the last moisture out, and pound to a paste either with pestle and mortar, or in a liquidizer with a little of the mayonnaise. Mix into the mayonnaise just before serving.

JELLIED MAYONNAISE FOR CHAUDFROID   Instead of coating a cold, poached fish with aspic jelly*, jellied mayonnaise may be used instead.

The mayonnaise is made in the usual way, using 300 ml (10 fl oz) of oil and 2–3 egg yolks. Fold in gently 150 ml (5 fl oz) of firm aspic jelly, or 150 ml (5 fl oz) water in which 8 g (¼ oz) gelatine has been dissolved, while the gelatine is on the point of setting but still liquid. *Use at once.*

LIGHT MAYONNAISE   Add 60–90 ml (2–3 fl oz) soured cream to mayonnaise at the end of making it. Chopped green herbs, especially chives, are a good addition.

MALTESE MAYONNAISE   Grate the rind of an orange, preferably a blood orange, into the bowl, before putting in the egg yolks with 1 tablespoon of lemon juice. Flavour at the end with the juice from the orange, and a little more lemon juice instead of vinegar, if extra sharpness is required. Good with cold white fish.

MUSTARD AND DILL MAYONNAISE   The proportions for this superb Scandinavian sauce can be varied to suit your taste. The egg yolk may be omitted, in which case the sauce is a variant of vinaigrette. Serve with pickled salmon, trout or herring, boiled crab or lobster.

> 2 tablespoons French or German mustard
> 1 tablespoon white sugar
> 1 large egg yolk
> 150 ml (5 fl oz) corn or groundnut oil
> 2 tablespoons wine vinegar
> 1 generous teaspoon dill weed
> salt, white pepper

Beat the first three ingredients together, and finish the mayonnaise in the usual way.

PAPRIKA MAYONNAISE   Flavour a basic mayonnaise with 1 level tablespoon of tomato concentrate, 1 tablespoon chilli sauce and a finely shredded red pepper.

PERNOD REMOULADE   A piquant sauce good with many of the round fish – grilled grey mullet, sea bass, John Dory, sea bream – and with mackerel.

> basic mayonnaise
> 1 dessertspoon chopped sweet-sour pickled cucumber
> 1 dessertspoon each chopped parsley and tarragon
> about 1 tablespoon Pernod

Fold the other ingredients into the basic mayonnaise, using the above measurements as a guide only.

SAUCE RAVIGOTE   Chop a handful of parsley, tarragon, watercress, chives, chervil and a thick slice of onion. Mix with a heaped teaspoon of Dijon mustard, a dessertspoon of drained capers and a chopped hard-boiled egg. Gradually mix in 3 or 4 tablespoons of olive oil, then wine vinegar to taste. Chopped anchovies and gherkins are often added as well as capers.

SAUCE TARTARE   This is either a mayonnaise or a vinaigrette seasoned with shallots or spring onions, and *fines herbes*, plus capers and gherkins to taste. The sauce should be thick and speckled with these ingredients.

See individual sections for other kinds of mayonnaise, i.e. Anchoiade (Anchovy mayonnaise), Crab mayonnaise, Lobster mayonnaise.

HORSERADISH SAUCE WITH FRESH WALNUTS

One November at the turn of the century, the great chef Escoffier was invited to a shooting weekend in the Haute-Savoie. Saturday lunch began with a dish of *ombles-chevalier* (a speciality of the lac du Bourget, in nearby Savoie) which had been cooked, and left to cool, in white wine from his host's own vineyard. The surprising thing was the sauce which accompanied the fish; it was made from horseradish, and the juicy fresh walnuts which are so delicious an item of French meals at that time of year.

Now *omble-chevalier*, or arctic char, isn't likely to come our way very often, but there is no reason why the exquisite sauce shouldn't be served with trout of various kinds (including salmon trout), other char, and grayling, which have been poached in a white wine court bouillon.

> 150 g (5 oz) shelled walnuts
> 1 dessertspoon caster sugar
> 2 tablespoons white breadcrumbs
> 300 ml (10 fl oz) double cream
> pinch of salt
> 1 dessertspoon lemon juice or wine vinegar
> 150 g (5 oz) grated horseradish

If you have been able to buy fresh walnuts, you will find that the pale skin is easily removed; older walnuts need to have boiling water poured over them before the darkened skins can be rubbed off. This sounds a fiddly business, but it is worth doing because the sauce will taste much more delicate without the slight bitterness one can get from walnuts. Chop them finely, and mix with the sugar, breadcrumbs, cream, salt and part of the lemon juice or wine vinegar. Now add the horseradish slowly, to taste (if you have no fresh horseradish, use one of the prepared brands – again to taste), and the rest of the lemon juice or vinegar, as necessary. The sauce can be made in the blender. For ways of using horseradish with hot fish, *see* Poached turbot with horseradish, p. 435, and Carpe au bleu with horseradish sauce, p. 70.

ROUILLE

A fiery sauce of Mediterranean origin, which is served with Bouillabaisse fish soups and stews, or with fish in a large mixture such as ailloli garni. Here are two recipes:

1.   Pound in a mortar 2 cloves of garlic and the flesh of 2 small red chilli peppers. Add the liver of bream or red mullet, if they are appearing in the final dish.

Squeeze out a thick, crustless slice of white bread in a little fish stock. Add to the garlic and pepper. Stir in gradually, as if you were making a mayonnaise, 3 tablespoons of olive oil and a little fish stock, or the juices from cooking the fish in foil.

2.   If a richer sauce is required, pound 3 cloves of garlic with the 2 red peppers. Beat in 2 egg yolks, then gradually add 250 ml (8 fl oz) olive oil, and season with French mustard, salt and pepper. This is excellent with salt cod or cod fritters.

SAFFRON SAUCE

This beautiful sauce for fish was given to me by Tom Hearne when he was at the Hole in the Wall restaurant in Bath. It is for steaks of pike, hake, turbot, halibut or bass, baked in the oven with a little fish stock.

Serves 4

generous pinch of saffron
600 ml (1 pt) fish stock*, heated
125 g (4 oz) butter
60 g (2 oz) plain flour
1 small red and 1 small green pepper, seeded and cut into strips
1 clove garlic, crushed and chopped
150 ml (5 fl oz) cream
2 tablespoons Madeira
lemon juice

Dissolve the saffron in the stock (this should be made with some dry white wine and a splash of vinegar). Make a roux with half the butter and the flour: moisten it with stock. Cook down to the consistency of double cream.

Meanwhile, soften the peppers with the garlic in the remaining butter over a low heat. When they are soft, add this mixture to the sauce and simmer for 10 minutes. Pour in the cream, Madeira and lemon juice to taste. Add the juices, much reduced, from the fish.

Arrange the fish on a serving plate or individual plates. Carefully pour the sauce round it, and arrange the pepper strips on top.

SKORDALIA

This is the Greek equivalent to the Provençal ailloli, made without egg yolks as it is a sauce eaten by tradition in Lent, with slices of aubergine and courgette, dusted with flour and fried, and with boiled beetroot and potatoes. On Clean Monday in Greece, the Monday after the last day of the Carnival, when everyone ate themselves to a stupor, it was served with salt cod soaked and deep fried in batter. Nowadays, skordalia often appears on Greek menus with all kinds of fish fried in batter. It is an improver of white fish in general, served hot or cold.

See p. 232 for recipes.

TAHINA CREAM SALADS

In cooking, as in much else, one homes continually on the Middle East as the central knot of our world. So in Claudia Roden's *A Book of Middle Eastern Food*, one finds the ancestors of Escoffier's walnut and horseradish sauce in the tarator sauce below, or in these sesame meal salads. I give her proportions.

> *1–3 cloves garlic*
> *salt, about ½ teaspoon*
> *150 ml (5 fl oz) lemon juice or juice of at least 2½ lemons*
> *150 ml (5 fl oz) tahina (sesame seed) paste*
> *½ teaspoon ground cumin (optional)*
> *6 tablespoons chopped parsley or 2 only, to garnish*
> *sliced hard-boiled eggs, to garnish*

Mix first five ingredients in an electric blender or with a beater. Parsley in quantity can be mixed into the salad, or else the smaller amount can be used as a garnish with the egg.

Serve with baked fish or cold fish. Or serve on its own as an hors d'oeuvre, mixed with a tin of chopped, well-drained anchovies.

> *1 clove garlic*
> *salt, about ½ teaspoon*
> *150 ml (5 fl oz) lemon juice or juice of at least 2½ lemons*
> *150 ml (5 fl oz) tahina paste*
> *5 tablespoons ground almonds*
> *5 blanched almonds to garnish*

Mix first five ingredients in a blender or with a beater, using a little water to soften the mixture if necessary for creaminess. Turn into a bowl, and decorate with a daisy of whole almonds.

Serve with cold fish: John Dory, turbot, sole, cod.

> *125 g (4 oz) walnuts*
> *2 cloves garlic*
> *salt, about ½ teaspoon*
> *3–4 tablespoons tahina paste*
> *juice of 2 lemons*
> *a little water if necessary*
> *4 tablespoons chopped parsley*

Mix as above, folding parsley in at the end.

Serve with fried mussels, baked fish or cold fish.

TARATOR SAUCE FROM THE MIDDLE EAST

I usually make this recipe – from Claudia Roden's book – with walnuts, in the Turkish style. This is because we bring them home by the kilo, every autumn, from our neighbour's tree in France. After the hard work of the vintage is over, he finds walnut picking a pleasant job. The tree grows at the foot of a steep slope, and one suddenly sees his head, and the heads of nephews, cousins, and friends, popping out of the leaves like Jacks in the Green. Down below wife and children bash at the branches with sticks, and the nuts come raining to the ground. We munch steadily for days, walnuts with the new wine, walnuts with new bread, walnuts fried with apples to go with *boudins noirs*. And when I get back to England and electricity, we drink walnut soup and enjoy this sauce with fish; with the bass, bream or John Dory, mussels, or cod steaks to liven them up.

If your abundance happens to be hazelnuts, almonds or pine kernels, they can be used instead of walnuts.

> *2 slices white bread, crusts removed*
> *125 g (4 oz) nuts*
> *150 ml (5 fl oz) olive oil*
> *3–4 tablespoons wine vinegar*
> *1–2 cloves garlic, crushed*
> *salt, pepper*

Dip the bread in water and squeeze it dry. Crumble roughly and add to the nuts, which should have been finely ground. Mix in the olive oil gradually, beating all the time, then the vinegar and garlic. Season with salt and pepper.

The simplest way is to put all the ingredients, except salt and pepper, into the liquidizer, and whirl at top speed until you have a smooth sauce. Finally season to taste.

VINAIGRETTE OR FRENCH DRESSING

Basic cookery books give the ingredients for this sauce as three tablespoons of oil to one tablespoon of wine vinegar, but I find this far too strong. Five to one is a better proportion, at least to start with, although the final quantities will depend on the oil and vinegar used and the opinion of the person who is making it.

The usual seasonings, beyond salt and pepper, are garlic, a hint of sugar, perhaps mustard, and plenty of chopped green herbs such as parsley and chives, with tarragon and basil to add a different note from time to time.

For a plain green salad, or a salad of one vegetable (cooked or raw), olive oil is the best choice. Olive oils vary as much in flavour as wines, but as there is only a limited variety on sale in this country choice is not too bewildering. My own preferences are for the green oils of Tuscany, Umbria and Greece (Minerva brand usually), and for the golden oils of Beaumes-de-Venise in Provence. Walnut oil I use for certain salads, on special occasions. A tasteless oil is good for mixed salads.

Take care with wine vinegar. The best is made in Orléans still. I go for Martin-Pouret brands as I have seen the way they are matured in casks in the old-fashioned manner which give their virtues a chance to develop.

Malt vinegar is not suitable for a sauce deriving from wine-growing countries.

For a green salad, mix the dressing in the bowl; cross the salad servers over it to make a platform for the rinsed and dried salad green. Chill if you like, but do not turn the salad until you are ready to eat it or the softer greenery will collapse unpleasantly.

ABALONE *see* A FEW WORDS ABOUT . . . ABALONE

ALLIS SHAD *see* A FEW WORDS ABOUT . . . SHAD

AMERICAN SHAD *see* A FEW WORDS ABOUT . . . SHAD

† ANCHOVY

Engraulis encrasicholus

The other day, the fishmonger gave me a handful of fresh anchovies, a rare occurrence in England (and in the States, too; although there are plenty of them, no one bothers to catch them. The Mediterranean is the place where the art of the anchovy is practised). They had come, muddled into a load of sprats, from Brixham – which quite often happens in winter months – and were the same length. The heads have a more pointed appearance: the bodies are slimmer, and rounded. We grilled them and ate them with rye bread and butter, and a seasoning of lemon juice. They were not so fat as sprats, nor so finely flavoured as herrings or the fresh sardines we buy in France.

I suspect that they should be eaten straight from the sea as they are in Italy. On Ischia, they are boned and baked in olive oil, flavoured with oregano; lemon juice is squeezed over them just before serving. Sometimes they are laid on a bed of breadcrumbs, covered with a 'piecrust' of crumbs and cheese bound together with olive oil, and seasoned with garlic, capers and olives. Rather like some of the baked sardine recipes (p. 330).

It seems, too, that absolute freshness is necessary for good anchovy preserving, because they disappear quickly from the docks after a catch is landed, presumably carried straight off to be processed. There are small businesses in the various ports, each with its own 'secret' variation of the recipe. If you are on holiday in the Mediterranean, in Spain, Italy and France particularly, it is worth seeking out the local anchovies. One of the best presents I have ever had was a large tin of whole, salted anchovies which my sister brought back from

Collioure near Perpignan. The small picturesque port – don't trip over the easels – is mainly devoted to anchovy, sardine and tuna fishing. Similar anchovies in salt sometimes may be bought from Italian delicatessen stores (the best ones come from Gorgona, an island off the Tuscan coast at Leghorn) and some Greek-Cypriot grocers. Before use, they have to be filleted and soaked for several hours, but the flavour is delicious. The oblong tins of anchovies on sale here are more convenient, but tiny; it is pleasing to have a bottomless pit of anchovies in the larder for a change. (Incidentally, 'Norwegian anchovies' are really sprats, put down in salt and bay leaves.)

The antiquity of the trade pleases me. It goes back to the ancient Greeks and Romans who relied heavily on a sauce called *garum* or *liquamen* (*garon* is Greek for shrimp, but many other fish were used, including the anchovy). The intestines, liver and blood were pickled in salt, the superb Mediterranean sea salt which still makes a moon landscape of shining white on many parts of the coast. After weeks in the hot sun, a dark rich essence was produced and sold in trade-marked bottles. I read recently that a similar product was used in Turkey, for marinading fish, until the last century.

Anyone who has looked at Rosemary Brissenden's or Sri Owen's or Jennifer Brennan's books of South-East Asian cookery will notice the ubiquity of fish sauce in Thai cooking. It seems the precise equivalent of *garum*. So does the Nuoc Mam of Vietnam and the *blachan* and *trasi* used all over South-East Asia, made from prawns or shrimps, salted, dried, pounded and rotten, then formed into cakes. Right back to fifth century Athens. All these fishy sauces were and are used to enhance meat dishes, rather as the Chinese use soy sauce.

I trust this will encourage you to believe me when I suggest that anchovies and anchovy essence can enrich our own meat cookery. If you have ever eaten pork pies from the Melton Mowbray area, you were not I expect aware that they were probably seasoned with anchovy essence. Try it to flavour a steak and kidney stew or pie. (Substitute it for oysters, which are now too expensive to be used recklessly as a seasoning, as they once were.) If you have no wine, anchovy essence wonderfully improves a shin of beef stew. Anchovy mayonnaise (p. 54) goes well with cold beef and baked potatoes. In the past legs of lamb were stuck with slivers of anchovy as well as garlic.

With vegetables, less persuasion is needed. Most people know and like cauliflower boiled in the usual way, then dressed with anchovies, melted butter and breadcrumbs (or chicory, or Florentine fennel, or celery). The finest of such dishes comes from Piedmont.

ANCHOVY BUTTER

Add 6–8 anchovy fillets, well mashed, to 125 g (4 oz) unsalted butter.

ANCHOVY, GARLIC AND CAPER SAUCE

An eighteenth-century sauce that goes beautifully with hard-boiled eggs – halve them across, spread the sauce on a dish and put the eggs, cut side down in neat rows on top. Allow 6–9 eggs. Serve it with cooked haricot beans, salt cod and grilled white fish, or tuna.

Serves 6

10–12 large cloves garlic, in their skins
8–10 anchovy fillets
2 tablespoons small capers
dash of wine vinegar
salt, pepper
about 12 tablespoons olive oil

Simmer the garlic in water to cover for 7 minutes. Cool under the tap, remove their skins and put them into a blender (better than a processor for this kind of sauce) with the anchovies, capers, vinegar and a little seasoning. Whizz to a purée, then slowly add the oil to make a sauce of mayonnaise consistency. Taste and adjust seasonings.

This is a strong sauce – you could use half sunflower or safflower oil and half olive oil to make it blander.

ANCHOVY SAUCE

Liquidize 6 anchovy fillets with 3 tablespoons of unsalted butter. Reheat this mixture and stir into the béchamel sauce* just before serving.

NOTE I much prefer a simpler anchovy sauce for fish, particularly for white fish of the cod type which can do with a little assistance. Melt 125 g (4 oz) unsalted butter and add a finely chopped clove of garlic; simmer slowly for 5 minutes. Meanwhile, crush 6 to 8 fillets of anchovy. Stir them into the melted butter, keeping on a low heat until the anchovies have disintegrated into the sauce. Check the seasoning, and add some freshly ground black pepper. This is excellent with Crostini alla provatura, p. 53.

ANCHOVY AND MUSHROOM SAUCE

Sliced mushrooms, both cultivated and wild, fried in butter, go well with many fish. I'm not so sure about mushroom sauce. The béchamel seems to dull the savour. One day, though, I found a Swedish recipe in which anchovies were used to season mushrooms, and I took the hint. A surprising combination, but it works well. The flavour of each ingredient, clear and piquant, raises béchamel sauce to the most interesting deliciousness.

> *450 ml (15 fl oz) béchamel sauce**
> *175 g (6 oz) mushrooms, chopped*
> *½ clove garlic, crushed*
> *3 tablespoons butter*
> *½ tin (4–5 fillets) anchovies*
> *150 ml (5 fl oz) double cream*
> *salt, black pepper*
> *chopped dill weed* or *parsley*

As the béchamel sauce simmers, fry mushrooms and garlic gently in the butter. After about 10 minutes, add the roughly chopped anchovy fillets. Stir well, and add the cream, which should bubble down to make a thickish sauce. Tip the mushroom mixture into the béchamel, season and leave to simmer together for 10 minutes or so until you are ready to serve the fish. Add the chopped herbs at the last minute.

Excellent with all the firm white fish, and with mullet, huss, snapper, and so on.

BAGNA CAUDA

One late November, we were invited to join a truffle hunt in Piedmont. White truffles, in those parts. The hotel smelled of them since the owner was also a truffle dealer. We ate them for dinner, went to bed in a haze of truffled air, woke up to them, ate breakfast in their pervading presence. As the splendid meals arrived, truffles were shaved fast and furious on to our plates, priceless morsels showering off in all directions in a fine spray to the floor from the edge of the special graters while the large flakes fell generously over the pasta or game before us. In the snowy morning, we were taken off to watch the dogs of Alba working in the woods. They leapt on the leash, thin and ravenous, like medieval hounds on a tapestry, finding truffles with such ease that we felt they had been planted there in advance for our benefit.

At midday we were taken off to a vast barn, out of the way of truffles, to a great spread of vegetables encircling a pot of gently bubbling anchovy sauce, a bagna cauda. We dug in with stalks of celery and cardoon, slices of Florentine fennel, chicory, peppers, carrots and Calabrese, stirring up the garlicky salt brew.

Next night we had bagna cauda again, this time in special little pots with nightlights underneath. It was served at the Belvedere restaurant at La Morra, and to honour the occasion truffles were sliced into the sauce. This is the recipe they gave us, and I have used it ever since – though minus truffles, I am afraid.

Serves 6

18 plump cloves garlic, skinned, sliced
milk
18 large salted anchovies, soaked, filleted, chopped or 3 × 50 g (1¾ oz) tins
  anchovy fillets in oil
60 g (2 oz) unsalted butter
250 ml (8 fl oz) olive oil
6 eggs (optional)
1–2 white truffles (optional)
a variety of raw vegetables, cut in handy pieces
grissini or *bread sticks* or *long bread 'soldiers'*

In a small pan, simmer the garlic in enough milk just to cover it. The milk should gradually reduce in the 7–10 minutes it takes for the garlic to become tender – watch it, or the pan will catch. Put in the anchovies, cut in pieces, with their oil if they are tinned. Crush them down over a very low heat, using a pestle or potato masher. Work in the butter, then the oil gradually. The sauce will become thick and brown, with the oil separating out. This can be done in advance.

Put the eggs and truffles, if used, into a basket. Prepare the vegetables and arrange them in another shallow basket, or put pieces on individual plates which will eventually hold small pots of sauce. Put the bread into a jar.

Just before the meal, bring the anchovy sauce back to simmering point. Pour it into six warm pots, preferably the special kind for bagna cauda with little lights beneath them. Put a pot on each plate to serve. At table, grate a little truffle into the sauce and then each person dips pieces of vegetable into their pot, stirring up the piquant sediment into the oil. When the sauce is almost gone, break an egg into the remains and stir it round fast so that it scrambles in the warmth. Eat the egg with the sticks of bread.

If you don't have the appropriate pots, you might do better to have one central fondue pot over a nightlight, with everyone dipping into it. It is more difficult, then, to manage the eggs, but they are hardly necessary if the bagna cauda is providing the first course of a meal, rather than the meal itself.

PAUL BAILEY'S ANCHOVY SALAD

This anchovy salad of Paul Bailey's has a dark rich appearance, and a clean savoury taste, that make it an ideal start to a meal. Guests look furtively round the table, serving spoon in hand, as they count heads, trying to work out just how much they can decently help themselves to. Mainly Paul uses dried tomatoes put up in olive oil by the Italian firm of Carapelli: they are particularly soft and luscious. Dried tomatoes, sold by weight, can also be used: if they are very dry, soak them in a little very hot water before putting them into the salad.

Serves 6–8

4 large red peppers, roasted or grilled and skinned
5 small tins anchovy fillets in olive oil, 50 g (1¾ oz) size
about ⅓ jar dried tomatoes
pepper, basil leaves, olive oil

Make this salad several hours before the meal, if possible. This gives everything a chance to settle down well together.

Cut the peppers into strips, discarding the seeds. Split the anchovy fillets longways. Arrange both in a shallow bowl with the tomatoes, add pepper to each layer and display the various pieces to make an appetizing streaky effect of colour. Scatter in some torn up basil leaves. Pour in the oil out of the anchovy tins, plus enough extra olive oil to come almost to the top. Just before serving, scatter the top with torn basil leaves and extra coarsely-ground pepper.

Serve with a coarse country bread without too positive a flavour.

CANAPÉS À LA CRÈME

Serves 1

1 round of bread
butter
3–4 anchovy fillets
1 tablespoon clotted cream

Take the round of bread from a slice 1¼ cm (½ inch) thick, with a large scone cutter. Fry it pale brown in butter (clarified is best). Quickly arrange anchovies on top and place on a very very hot dish. Cover with clotted cream and serve immediately. The contrast between hot crisp bread, sharp anchovy, and cold grainy cream is excellent – whipped cream does not give the same result at all.

CROSTINI ALLA PROVATURA

An Italian rarebit, improved by anchovies – spectacularly improved.

Provatura was a cheese made from buffalo's milk which has, according to Elizabeth David's *Italian Food*, almost disappeared from the market. Even in Rome, this dish is now usually made with mozzarella cheese. Other substitutes are bel paese, Gruyère, and provolone – originally another buffalo milk cheese, though in fact it is now usually made from cow's milk, like mozzarella, and is much less tasty in consequence.

The general point of the recipe is to improve cheese-on-toast with a sauce of anchovies melted in butter. Mrs David's recipe suggests putting slices of cheese – nice thick slices – on rounds of French bread. These are then arranged, slightly overlapping each other, in an ovenproof dish, and put into a fairly hot oven until the bread is crisp and the cheese melted but not runny. For the sauce for 6 to 8 crostini, soak 4 or 5 fillets of anchovies in warm water for 10 minutes. Heat them in 60 g (2 oz) of butter, having chopped them up first. Pour over the crostini and serve immediately.

Ada Boni, this century's Mrs Beeton of Italian cookery, has alternating chunks of cheese and bread on skewers, cooked over a wood fire or in a fairly hot oven (gas 6, 200°C/400°F). The sauce is similar, but the proportion of butter to anchovies is higher.

Incidentally, this sauce is excellent with veal or pork tenderloin escalopes, or on vegetables, or slightly dull white fish. Remember that leg of veal to be boiled for *vitello tonnato* is often larded with anchovy fillets. This was common practice in the past, in England, with beef, too.

HARICOTS À L'ANCHOIADE

This is an example of the agreeable southern French habit of eating garlicky mayonnaise sauces with hot food, such as soup, vegetables and fish. Anchoiade is often served with boiled salt cod and boiled potatoes. It can also be stirred into fish and tomato soup or fish and saffron soup, instead of a peppery rouille*. Try it with hard-boiled eggs, instead of the usual mayonnaise. Delicious. Or with baked potatoes and cold beef.

Serves 6

500 g (1 lb) haricot beans
salt
9–10 anchovy fillets
2–3 cloves garlic
1 large egg yolk
150 ml (5 fl oz) olive oil
chopped parsley

Soak and boil the beans in unsalted water in the usual way. Add salt when the beans are just cooked, and give them another 5 minutes.

In the meantime pound anchovies, garlic, and the egg yolk to a paste. Add the oil (which must be olive oil) gradually, as if you were making a mayonnaise*. If you use a blender, include some of the egg white when the anchovies, garlic and yolk are being whirled to a paste.

When everyone is ready for the meal, drain the beans and fold in the anchoiade. Sprinkle with parsley. Serve immediately. The dish can be eaten cold, but the flavours are clearer and lighter when hot.

ANCHOIADE DE CROZE A splendid elaboration of the simple anchoiade of Provence, which was given – in *Les Plats régionaux de France* – by Count Austin de Croze. In the twenties, he was one of the leaders, with Curnonsky, of the new interest in the food of France outside Paris, and the grand restaurants of the haute cuisine.

Serves 12

60 g (2 oz) finely chopped parsley, chives, tarragon
2 good sprigs green fennel leaves, finely chopped
2 cloves garlic, finely chopped
1 small onion, finely chopped
3 dried figs, finely chopped
1 small dried red pepper
12 blanched almonds
12 anchovies in oil or 12 anchovies in brine, washed
4 or more tablespoons olive oil
lemon juice

1 tablespoon orange-flower water
12 brioches, bridge rolls or finger rolls
black olives

Mix the ingredients up to and including the figs. Pound the next four together to a paste. Combine the two mixtures. Add lemon juice to taste, and then the orange-flower water – go slowly because it has a surprisingly dominating flavour. (If you want to do the chopping and pounding in a blender, you will need more olive oil.) Open the brioches, or rolls. Spread the top side with the anchoiade, and brush the bottom side of the cut with olive oil. Close the rolls, and heat for 5–10 minutes at gas 6–7, 200–220 °C (400–425 °F). Serve surrounded by black olives.

JANSSON'S TEMPTATION

The name of this dish is an incitement to culinary myth-making. For instance: 'Eric Janson, the Swedish religious reformer who founded Bishop Hill, Illinois, in 1846, preached rigorous asceticism to his followers, no liquor and a diet that barely sustained life. One day, according to legend a zealous Jansonist discovered the prophet feasting . . .' But as Jansson is a Swedish equivalent of Smith or Jones, why look any further for a meaning than 'Everyone's Temptation'? A gloss which is perfectly convincing when one has tasted this piquant gratin of potatoes, onions, anchovy and cream. Don't use milk instead of cream, as many Swedes do these days, or the beauty of the title will escape you.

Norwegian 'anchovies' should be used but they are tricky to find.

Serves 6

3 large onions
1 kg (2 lb) potatoes
3 tins anchovies
freshly ground black pepper
300 ml (10 fl oz) double or whipping cream
60 g (2 oz) butter

Peel and thinly slice the onions. Peel the potatoes and cut them into matchstick strips (a mandolin cutter saves time). Grease a shallow oval gratin dish with a butter paper. Arrange about half the potato strips in an even layer, then make a lattice of the anchovies on top. Cover with the onions and the rest of the potatoes. Season well with pepper only. Pour over the oil from the anchovy tins and half the cream. Dot with the butter and bake in a hot oven (gas 7, 220 °C/ 425 °F) for half an hour. When the potatoes begin to look appetizingly brown, lower the heat and pour over the rest of the cream. Taste the cooking juices and add salt if necessary. Return to the oven until the potatoes are cooked.

A lunchtime dish, to be followed, prudently, by no more than a salad and some fruit.

NOTE   The amount of cream can be varied in quantity (upwards) and type (mix in some single cream).

PISSALADIÈRE

If you are a cook living in the Mediterranean, the sun does half the work for you. Tomatoes and onions have acquired a concentration of sweet richness: olive oil, olives and anchovies flavour them to perfection. This combination is known to us all in the form of the pizza which has sadly become a cliché – I have even seen it described as an American national dish and, to be fair, people like Alice Waters have turned it into an elegant creation of the most skilful cooking. Mostly, though, it is plain awful, unless you find yourself in Naples where it all began and where in some *pizzerie* you will find the real original rustic sort of dish, baked in the right sort of oven.

At home you will do better with the Pissaladière – no connection, in spite of the similar sounds. Pizza means pie. Pissaladière takes its name from *pissala*, the modern descendant of those vigorous Roman confections known as *garum* and *liquamen* (*see* Anchovy Introduction). It can have a little tomato flavouring – Italian influence – but really it is an onion tart. You can make it on a bread base, like a pizza, but the contrast of a crisp sort of pastry, *pâte brisée* or shortcrust is really more agreeable. (It may be heresy to admit this.)

Serves 6

2 kg (4 lb) onions, sliced
3 cloves garlic, finely chopped
olive oil
1 large bay leaf
½ teaspoon thyme
salt, pepper
2 tablespoons tomato concentrate or well-reduced purée (optional)
25–28-cm (10–11-inch) pastry case, baked blind
2–3 teaspoons pissala or about 9 anchovy fillets, soaked
60 g (2 oz) black olives, preferably the tiny niçois kind

Cook the onions and garlic slowly in a little olive oil, with the bay leaf and thyme. Cover the pan to begin with, then remove it so that the mixture does not become watery. Season, having regard to the anchovies and olives, and mix in the tomato if used. Spread the pastry with pissala, if that is what you are using. Put the onions on top evenly. Dispose the anchovy fillets and olives on top of them.

Pour over a little olive oil and bake in a fairly hot oven, gas 6, 200°C (400°F) for 20 minutes or so, until the pastry is properly cooked and the olives are beginning to wrinkle.

Eat hot or warm with a glass of red wine – splendid picnic food.

SALADE NIÇOISE

When Mediterranean dishes are taken up by northerners, they become a kind of dustbin. Pizza is a sad example. We lose all sense of the basic austerity of the south. Salade niçoise was once the simple food of a none too wealthy community. Tuna fish has, for instance, been far too much of a luxury to be included until recently. To us, on the other hand, tiny broad beans and young violet-leaved artichokes and basil are luxuries. They are what give the salad its special character, along with tiny black niçois olives. Don't spoil it with cooked French beans and potatoes. If you can't get broad beans or artichokes young and tender enough to eat raw, steam or boil them lightly before adding them to the salad.

Serves 4–6

500 g (1 lb) tomatoes, quartered, skinned
salt
½ clove garlic
3 hard-boiled eggs, quartered
1 cucumber, peeled, thinly sliced
2 small green peppers, seeded, thinly sliced
6 spring onions, sliced
175 g (6 oz) shelled small broad beans or 8 small, trimmed violet-leaved
*   artichokes, thinly sliced*
12 salted anchovy fillets, soaked, cut in 4 or about 300 g (10 oz) cooked or
*   canned tuna, flaked*
100 g (3½ oz) small black olives
olive oil, large basil leaves, black pepper

Sprinkle the cut sides of the tomatoes with a little salt and drain them in a colander.

Rub the salad bowl with the cut clove of garlic, then discard it. Salt the pieces of egg lightly. Arrange the vegetables in the bowl, and put the tomatoes with them. On top, scatter the eggs, anchovy or tuna and olives. Pour over about 4 tablespoons of olive oil and tear the basil leaves over everything. Pepper well and chill for about half an hour.

Salade niçoise is served as a first course very often, or as lunch with plenty of bread. If you are going on a picnic, slice a shallow round loaf of bread across, remove most of the crumb and brush it with olive oil vinaigrette. Pack it with the salad ingredients, wrap it in cling film and chill under a light weight. This wonderful snack is known as *pan bagna*.

SCOTCH WOODCOCK

I am not keen on names which give an affected impression of the reality – rock turbot and rock salmon are two flagrant examples, however hallowed they may be by antique regional use. Scotch woodcock is another. In extenuation, I suppose that woodcock has become as legendary as the phoenix, except to millionaires and game-keepers: one can hardly be angry at a comparison one is never likely to be able to make.

This recipe comes from that wonderful book *The Scots Kitchen* by F. Marian McNeill: 'Take six small rounds of buttered toast, spread them with anchovy paste, arrange on a dish and keep hot. Melt two tablespoons of butter in a saucepan, put in three tablespoons of cream and the raw yolks of three eggs, and stir over the fire until the mixture is a creamy mass.' (Don't boil, or you will have scrambled or curdled eggs.) 'Add a little finely-chopped parsley and a dash of cayenne. Heap on the rounds of toast and serve very hot.' I suggest you use anchovy butter instead of anchovy paste on buttered toast – see p. 49.

Mrs Beeton suggests using 150 ml (5 fl oz) cream instead of butter and cream. In either case, double cream gives the best flavour and consistency.

ANGLER-FISH *see* MONKFISH

ARGENTINE *see* A FEW WORDS ABOUT . . . SMELT

BLUEFISH & POMPANO

Pomatomus saltatrix & Trachinotus carolinus

In his *North Atlantic Seafood*, Alan Davidson joins these two fish to-gether in one section although they are in fact of different species. The gracefully shaped bluefish, long, with a blue-green shine on its grey body, comes in to the Atlantic coast of America by the million every summer. It is a most ferocious animal – 'an animated chopping machine' – of carnivorous and wasteful habits. Its progress through the sea is marked by the bloody remains of other fish which had the misfortune to cross its path.

It is quite a good eating fish, not very firm but fairly oily. This means it grills well, and needs rather positive flavours to go with it. The recipes for Herring baked with cucumber on p. 183 and Red snapper créole on p. 479 can both be adapted to bluefish.

The pompano is one of America's most famous delicacies. It is also caught in the Mediterranean (this is the *Trachinotus ovatus*, or the round pompano), but the place to eat it is undeniably at Antoine's restaurant in New Orleans. As with bluefish, it is good baked or grilled with cucumber.

BLUEFISH BUSTANOBY

Many herring and mackerel recipes are suitable for bluefish. It is rich enough to take the sharpness of gooseberries, or the contrasting smoked flavour of bacon. In this recipe from the *Long Island Sea Food Cook Book*, by J. George Frederick, smoked ox tongue is used.

Serves 6

1 ½ kg (3 lb) bluefish
3 tablespoons mushroom juice
½ glass Chablis or *other dry white wine*
pinch of salt, pepper
3 tablespoons tomato sauce
1 tablespoon cooked smoked beef tongue, finely minced

Clean and store the bluefish. Dry it and place in a buttered ovenproof dish. Add mushroom juice (obtained by stewing mushrooms *gently* in butter so that they exude their moisture), the wine and seasoning. Cover with buttered paper and put into a fairly hot oven (gas 5, 190°C/375°F) for half an hour. Pour off the juices into a pan, add the remaining ingredients to them, and boil for 2 minutes. Pour over the fish and serve.

GRILLED BLUEFISH

Clean the fish, and bone it from the back, so that it opens out like a kipper. Brush with melted butter and put under the grill cut side up. When it is nearly done, turn it over and grill the other side.

Serve with melted butter sharpened with capers or lemon juice, or with pats of maître d'hôtel butter*. Mussel or oyster sauce can go with it, or a béarnaise*.

ANTOINE'S POMPANO EN PAPILLOTE

One of the best known recipes for pompano was devised in New Orleans at the beginning of this century by the son of the Marseillais founder, Antoine Alciatore. The occasion was, I believe, the visit to that city by the great Brazilian balloonist, Alberto Santos-Dumont. Like the Alciatores, he was French by origin, and no doubt appreciated the fine contents of the papillotes which had puffed up in the oven to the shape of one of his own dirigibles.

The early 1900s were the era of paper-bag cookery. The en papillote method had long been known, but was generally unsatisfactory because the taste of paper clung to the food inside. This problem was overcome by the development of special paper which did not have this disadvantage. In England, Spicers created the famous Soyer bag, at the instigation of Nicholas Soyer, grandson of the great chef, whose *Paper-bag Cookery* was published in 1911. Nowadays we use foil, which is completely neutral, and has the extra advantage over paper of being more efficiently twisted into a seal. Soyer demonstrated that almost anything could be cooked by this method, from cakes to huge joints of beef, but I think it is most successful of all with fish. If you cannot buy pompano, do not despair. Use fillets of any good firm fish instead – John Dory, turbot or brill, salmon trout, rainbow trout or bass. The rich crab sauce is excellent with this type of fish.

Serves 6

6 fillets pompano
salt, pepper
skin, bones and head for stock
1 chopped shallot or 1 heaped tablespoon chopped onion
90 g (3 oz) butter
600 ml (1 pt) dry white wine
250 g (8 oz) crab meat
250 g (8 oz) shelled prawns
½ clove garlic, chopped
250 g (8 oz) onion, chopped
1 sprig thyme
1 bay leaf
1 heaped tablespoon plain flour
2 egg yolks

Season the fish. Simmer skin, bones, etc. in 1 litre (1¾ pt) water for 30 minutes, strain into a measuring jug (there should be about 450 ml/ 15 fl oz of stock). Cook the shallot in 30 g (1 oz) butter until it begins to soften; add fillets. When they are lightly coloured on both sides, pour in the wine and simmer until the fish is just cooked and no more. Strain off the wine and set it aside. Leave the fish to cool.

Meanwhile, lightly fry crab, prawns and half the crushed garlic in another 30 g (1 oz) of butter. Add the onions and the remaining garlic. Cook gently for 10 minutes, covered. Add herbs and 300 ml (10 fl oz) of the fish stock. Make a thick sauce in the usual way with the remaining butter, the flour and the stock. Incorporate the white wine in which the fish was cooked, and the crab and onion mixture. Thicken further with the egg yolks. Correct seasoning. Remove the thyme stalks and bay leaf.

If you want to present the pompano properly, cut six paper or foil hearts large enough to contain the fillets. (Otherwise cut six oblongs, about 23 × 30 cm/9 × 12 inches.) Brush them lightly with oil. Put a layer of sauce on one half of each heart, then the fish and more sauce. Fold over the other side and twist the edges tightly together to make a close seal. Put these parcels on a baking sheet; place them in a very hot oven (gas 8, 230 °C/450 °F) for about 10 minutes.

NOTE This is said, by Marion Brown in *The Southern Cook Book*, to be the genuine recipe from Antoine's. I have seen variations elsewhere in which crab meat alone was used, no prawns, and 125 g (4 oz) of sliced mushrooms added to the onions.

There is no reason why such a delicious sauce should not be served with pompano, and other fish, which have been poached in white wine, without the en papillote finish.

BAKED POMPANO WITH PRAWN OR SHRIMP STUFFING

Serves 6

1 pompano
salt, black pepper
1 small onion, chopped
1 tablespoon butter
60 g (2 oz) breadcrumbs
milk
1 heaped tablespoon parsley
175–250 g (6–8 oz) shelled prawns or shrimps
white wine or cream

Clean and season the fish. Make the stuffing; melt the onion in the butter until soft. Squeeze out the breadcrumbs in a little milk. Add to the onions and stir in the parsley off the heat. Chop the prawns or shrimps roughly and mix them in. Season to taste, and stuff the fish.

Butter an ovenproof baking dish and lay the pompano in it. Pour a little white wine over it – about a glassful – or some cream. Bake in a moderate to fairly hot oven (gas 4–5, 180–190 °C/350–375 °F) for three-quarters of an hour.

GRILLED POMPANO WITH CUCUMBER HOLLANDAISE

Split and bone the whole pompano, or buy 6 fillets. Brush with melted butter, season, and grill with the cut side up. When the fish is almost cooked, turn it over and grill the other side if you like, but this is not necessary – the fish can be cooked completely without being turned over.

Serve with this sauce:

1 large cucumber
salt
*hollandaise sauce**
Tabasco sauce

Slice the cucumber thinly. Put it into a colander, sprinkle with salt, and leave to drain for at least an hour. Rinse if the slices are too salty, gently squeeze them dry in a clean tea towel, and then chop roughly. Make the hollandaise sauce, incorporating a dash of Tabasco with the seasonings at the beginning. Fold in the cucumber just before serving, and adjust the seasoning.

BONITO *see* TUNA

† BRILL

Scophthalmus rhombus

There is one particular category, a category not much dwelt upon in food matters though I am sure it occupies a fair amount of the psychologist's time, that corrals a sad group in many spheres of existence. It makes life hell in some families. It dents the morale of towns, suburbs and villages, schools and shops. I refer to the *almost as good as* category – for instance, Edward is almost as brave/tough/handsome as his brother Andrew. In food matters, this category can be exploited in unfortunate ways by devious businessmen – for instance, sponge-cake-with-additives-to-give-a-200-year-shelf-life is *almost as good as* the one you make at home with eggs, sugar and flour. Carob and that extraordinary stuff they coat biscuits with these days is *almost as good as* chocolate. Sometimes the *almost as good as* category is expanded so vigorously that it knocks out the tip-top category it was once compared with. People stop asking for the real thing because they have forgotten what it tastes like, even that it ever existed. Ice cream, sausages and properly reared, properly hung meat.

Whenever brill comes up, it is firmly placed in that category, too. Brill is *almost as good as* turbot. Actually, the gap is quite a large one. And perhaps I am being over-sensitive and even paranoid in suspecting that the fish trade keeps turbot from us, keeps sole from us, keeps wild salmon from us, so as to make us forget such things. Then we will stop demanding them, and they will have an easier time selling us brill, lemon sole and farmed salmon. Less worry about conserving stocks, which means less trouble with quotas. Eventually we shall end up with a choice between fish fingers and crab sticks. All fishermen will have to do is to run their vacuum cleaners over the sea bed, and transfer the haul to processing plants.

We have not, thank goodness, come quite to that point though in some fishing communities it seems uncomfortably near. Let us enjoy brill while we may, because it is a good fish of the second rank and worthy of our attention. I should perhaps add that the name is occasionally used for a most distinguished flatfish of the Pacific coast of America, the petrale sole. Although biologically the fish are not the same, they can be cooked in the same ways; recipes, too, for turbot, sole and other flatfish are all suitable as well. That goes without saying.

With all these flatfish or flounders, it is a question of sorting out the appropriate treatment. The first division comes with firmness – in this, sole and turbot have a supreme advantage since firmness combined with sweetness in fish is the most desirable of qualities. You underline this excellence with the finest sauces. Alternatively, you underline it by doing the least you possibly can so that nothing gets in the way, and serving it with the finest wine, the best bread. I remember the surprise of eating the very best oysters at Wheeler's in London, oysters in lavish quantities, and being served 'brown' bread of such poor quality that one suspected it had come from a plastic packet of sliced bread.

Brill may not be of this high standing, but it is worth fresh and lively treatment. You could also try it with cheese: either bake it and pour a Welsh rabbit over it, or give it the more measured treatment of sole cooked with Parmesan (p. 384). The fillets are good for frying – Alan Davidson gives a delightful Swedish recipe for cooking the fillets this way in butter with a panful of chanterelle (girolle) mushrooms. But then, almost all white fish of second and lower quality is extraordinarily improved when cooked with mushrooms of any kind, even cultivated mushrooms. Try it, too, with samphire sauce*.

HOW TO CHOOSE AND PREPARE BRILL

Brill do not have the slightly diamond outline of the turbot, and they are in general smaller. The dark skin is smooth. Both sides need scaling, which is not the case with turbot.

When you are baking the fish whole, you can also cut through the dark skinned side. With flatfish, this is the equivalent to slashing the plumpest part of a round fish when grilling or baking it. Cut along the lateral line to the bone.

You may like to take the opportunity of easing the flesh a little away from the bone and introducing seasoning and butter. Place the brill down on its slashed side.

BAKED BRILL IN PORTUGUESE STYLE

A pleasant summery dish that depends for success on the quality of the tomatoes.

Serves 4

1 large brill, scaled and cleaned
salt, pepper
70 g (2½ oz) butter
1 large onion, thinly sliced
leaves of 2 sprigs thyme
1 tablespoon chopped parsley
1 bay leaf
125 ml (4 fl oz) dry white wine, preferably Portuguese
3 tomatoes (about 340 g/12 oz), skinned, seeded, coarsely chopped
½ clove garlic, finely chopped
pinch of sugar

Preheat the oven to gas 7, 220 °C (425 °F). Choose a heat- and oven-proof gratin or earthenware dish that accommodates the brill.

Slash down the dark side of the brill, along the central bone and scrape the flesh from the bones on either side to make a pocket. Season it inside and smear in a good tablespoon of butter.

Using a heat-diffuser mat if necessary, put the dish over a low heat and melt just enough butter to cover the base with a thin layer. Add the onion, thyme, parsley and bay leaf, and cook until the onion begins to look transparent and tender, without browning. Lay the brill in the dish, dark side down. Pour over the wine and lay a butter paper (or a buttered greaseproof paper) on top of the fish. When everything is bubbling away, transfer the dish to the oven and leave it there for 10–15 minutes, or until the fish is ready.

Meanwhile, cook the tomato in a generous tablespoon of butter with the garlic, salt, pepper, and a pinch of sugar if the tomatoes need its help. Aim to end with a fresh-tasting, choppy purée of a sauce.

When the fish is ready, stir the remaining butter into the tomato and pour it round the brill, stirring it slightly and as best you can into the juices. Serve with plenty of bread, and the wine that you used for the cooking.

BRILL WITH VERMOUTH

Dry white vermouth is an excellent wine for cooking fish. When the amount of liquid being used is small, its pronounced flavour and concentration gives a better result than dry white wine. Use extra dry Martini, Noilly Prat, or Chambéry.

Serves 6

6 × 125–175 g (4–6 oz) portions brill fillet
salt, pepper
4 tablespoons melted butter
breadcrumbs made from day-old bread
4 tablespoons finely chopped shallot
3 tablespoons chopped parsley
10 tablespoons vermouth
60–90 g (2–3 oz) unsalted butter

Season the fish with salt and pepper, a little in advance, if possible.

Switch on the oven to gas 8, 230 °C (450 °F).

Brush the top side of each piece of brill with melted butter and press it down into a tray of breadcrumbs to coat it. With a butter paper, grease an ovenproof dish that will take the fillets in a single layer, fairly closely. Scatter the shallot and most of the parsley over the base, and put the fillets on top, crumb side up. Sprinkle the rest of the melted butter over the crumbs. Pour the vermouth round the sides of the fish.

Bake for about 10 minutes, or until the brill is cooked. Remove the fish to six warm plates. Strain the cooking juices into a small pan and whisk in the unsalted butter. Season to taste. Pour the sauce beside the pieces of fish and scatter it with a little of the remaining parsley.

CAPELIN *see* A FEW WORDS ABOUT . . . SMELT

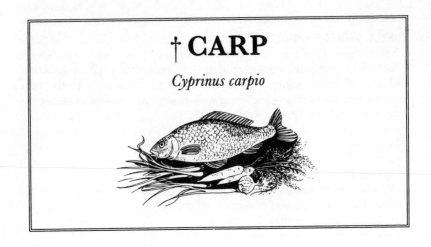

† CARP

Cyprinus carpio

For centuries, carp have been the pet fish of domestic waters. Frank Buckland described them as 'water-sheep – herbivorous – gregarious – of a contented mind'. Still at great houses, like the château of Chantilly in France, they rise in crowds to the surface of moat or lake to be fed (not, I believe, on account of the bell which is rung, but because they see people collecting together and have learnt that this means food). Another of the French châteaux, Chambord, has given its name to a much-truffled preparation of carp in the princely style.

The first carp I encountered came from no such elegant waters, but from the river Loir, in May. The clammy creature was handed to me by a friend who observed that he had brought his lunch with him. I recognized the handsome large-scaled fish from Chinese plates and paintings, but I had not the least idea of how to cook it. Neither did I know that it should have been soaked in vinegar and water in case it had a muddy flavour.

As it turned out, I was lucky. That carp had been kind enough to avoid the murkier depths of the Loir. And the only means I had of cooking it – foil, a double row of bricks with a grill, and charcoal – were just right for its fresh liveliness of flavour. Butter, shallots, parsley and white wine all went into the package, and we remember its taste many years later.

Our second carp did not turn out so well. It was not *Cyprinus carpio* from the Loir, but a Mirror carp, a variety which has been bred for fish-farming. It looked strange, even amongst the exotic fish of Soho. The skin had a soft, wash-leather appearance, an opulent nudity, as the huge scales were few and dotted in single rows. That fish must have been a long way from home, because the flavour had faded. In fact, carp are good travellers. I should have been more careful to choose a livelier looking specimen. Although one could not expect the wild freshness of river-caught carp, these domestic varieties please the Chinese, and the Germans, and the French, all in their very different ways serious eaters of good things. Obviously carp are not selling in large quantities all over the world just because they are tough survivors and easily fed. (Some of the ponds extend to thousands of acres.)

I have learnt since that the carp is a surprisingly interesting fish for the cook, as I hope you will agree after reading the following recipes. It should be added that, for the eater, the flesh is firm and sweet, the arrangement of bones satisfyingly comprehensible. The soft roe is a great delicacy. If it is not required specifically in the recipe, turn to p. 430 and make the Curé's omelette with it.

TO CHOOSE AND PREPARE CARP

The male carp with a soft roe is generally preferred to the female: its flavour is thought to be better.

A problem with carp is the likelihood that it will taste muddy. There are two ways to counteract this. First you can salt the fish, either sprinkling salt over the slices, or soaking the whole carp in a brine. As well, you can soak it for 5 minutes in water acidulated with vinegar – say 6 tablespoons to 1 litre (1¾ pt) of water. Take advice from the fishmonger.

However, before you get to this stage, you should scrape off the scales – unless it is Christmas Eve and you want to keep them on as good luck charms for the coming year. Then cut out the gills, wash and dry the fish. Now put it on a flat surface, remove the fins and cut the tail shorter and slit the belly so that you can remove the innards. Do this carefully, as inside there is a gall sack that should be removed intact or else the fish will remain bitter; you should also remove the thickest part of the intestine. The rest of the innards should be left inside, and neither they nor the cavity should be washed with water or the special characteristic flavour of the carp will be spoiled.

Now you can salt the fish, and give it a vinegar bath, before tackling one of the following recipes.

CARPE AU BLEU WITH HORSERADISH SAUCE

Serves 6

1³⁄₄–2 kg (3¹⁄₂–4 lb) carp
150 ml (5 fl oz) wine or tarragon vinegar
court bouillon no. 2*
300 ml (10 fl oz) double cream
60 g (2 oz) ground almonds
1 teaspoon sugar
grated horseradish to taste or prepared horseradish
salt

After cleaning it, tie the carp in a circle, nose to tail. (Do not wash or scale.) Put it into a pan. Bring the vinegar to the boil and pour it over the fish. Add the court bouillon, bring to the boil, and simmer until the carp is cooked. Drain and serve with the following sauce.

Bring cream, almonds and sugar to the boil. Stir in grated or prepared horseradish to taste and season with salt. A little lemon juice can also be added.

CARP STUFFED WITH CHESTNUTS

This is a more conventional recipe, from *The Alice B. Toklas Cookbook*, though again there is the sweet note, in this case of chestnuts.

Serves 4

1¹⁄₂ kg (3 lb) carp
450 ml (15 fl oz) dry white wine
salt
cracker crumbs
2 generous tablespoons melted butter

STUFFING
1 medium onion, chopped
2 shallots, chopped
1 clove garlic, crushed
2 generous tablespoons butter
5-cm (2-inch) thick slice of bread
dry white wine
1 tablespoon chopped parsley

1 teaspoon salt
¼ teaspoon each pepper, mace, powdered bay leaf, thyme
12 chestnuts, boiled, peeled and roughly chopped
1 egg

First make the stuffing. Cook the onion, shallots and garlic until soft and golden in the butter. Cut the crusts off the bread, dice it and soak in a little dry white wine. Squeeze out the surplus. Mix the rest of the stuffing ingredients together and put into the cleaned carp. Sew or skewer together and leave for 2 hours.

Bake for 20 minutes in a fairly hot oven, preheated to gas 5, 190 °C (375 °F), with the white wine and salt. Sprinkle with cracker crumbs, pour over the melted butter and put back into the oven for another 20 minutes. Serve with noodles.

CATIGOT

Catigot or *catigau* is a freshwater fish stew from southern France. Two or more varieties are cooked in white wine, the sauce thickened with egg yolks. Bacon fat or lard is used instead of olive oil or butter. This recipe is based on one from *La Cuisine Rustique – Languedoc* by André Bonnaure.

Serves 4–6

500 g (1 lb) eel
750 g (1½ lb) carp
1 large onion, sliced
1 medium carrot, sliced
2–3 cloves garlic, crushed
lard or bacon fat
175 ml (6 fl oz) dry white wine
salt, pepper
3 egg yolks
½ tablespoon wine vinegar
croûtons of bread fried in lard or cooking oil and rubbed with garlic

Skin and clean the eel. Scale and clean the carp. Cut them into chunks about 4 cm (1½ inches) wide. Cook the onion, carrot and garlic, until lightly coloured, in just enough lard to cover the base of a saucepan. Put the pieces of fish into the pan. Pour in the wine and add water to cover. Season, and cook over a good heat for 10 minutes or until the fish is tender.

Meanwhile, beat the egg yolks with the vinegar. When the fish is cooked, strain a little of its liquid into the egg yolk mixture, stirring all the time. Return to the pan and keep over a low heat, *without boiling*, until the sauce is thickened. Turn into a serving dish and serve with the croûtons tucked around the edge.

CHINESE CARP WITH CHICKEN FAT SAUCE

The Chinese consider that the flavour of chicken fat enhances the soft delicacy of carp. The fish will be fried in the fat with spring onion and ginger: soy sauce, sherry and some water are then added so that the carp can finish cooking more comfortably. Kenneth Lo gives a slightly more elaborate version of the sauce, which is well worth trying.

Serves 4–6 with other dishes

1¼ kg (2½–3 lb) carp
salt
1½ tablespoons plain flour
5 tablespoons chicken fat
2 slices fresh ginger, peeled, cut into shreds
2 cloves garlic, chopped
4 spring onions cut into 2½-cm (1-inch) lengths
3 tablespoons soy sauce
1 tablespoon hoisin sauce
1 teaspoon chilli sauce
2 teaspoons sugar
2 tablespoons sherry
1 packet tofu, 300 g (10 oz)
175 ml (6 fl oz) chicken stock

Clean the carp completely and rub with salt outside and in the cavity. Leave for an hour, then dry and rub the flour into the fish.

In an oval flameproof casserole, heat the chicken fat. In it stir-fry the ginger, garlic and half the spring onion for 1 minute. Then add the sauces, sugar and sherry. Lay the carp on top, cook for 2 minutes, then turn it over and give it 2 minutes more. Meanwhile, cut the tofu into 12 pieces and put them against the inside of the pot. Add the stock and remaining spring onions. Cover and simmer 10 minutes. Serve straightaway in the cooking pot.

HALASZLÉ KALOCSAI

Kalocsa fish soup is made with carp from the Danube, in a great iron pot, set on the banks of the river for preference. The right peppers to use are the hot cherry peppers that are much grown in Hungary, but fresh hot red chillis can be substituted. Other river fish can be used.

Serves 4–6

1 kg (2 lb) carp, cleaned
15 hot cherry peppers or 2 long fresh red hot chillis, 1 broken
  to expose the seeds
125 g (4 oz) chopped onion
3 teaspoons tomato paste
2 tablespoons paprika
salt

Chop the head and tail from the carp and put them into a large pot with the peppers or chillis, the onion, tomato paste, paprika and 1 litre (generous 1¾ pt) water. Bring to the boil and simmer for 1 hour. Remove the head and tail. Then cut the fish into steaks, put them into the soup and simmer for up to 30 minutes. Do not be tempted to stir the soup or the fish will break up; just shake the pot from time to time. Add salt to taste, give it another 2 minutes and serve with bread.

NOTE If you persuade the fishmonger to skin the carp for you, put that in with the head and tail to flavour the broth.

KARP NA SZARO (Karpfen in Polnische sauce)

In Poland and East Germany it is usual to have carp in grey sauce (*szary sos*) on Christmas Eve. The fish is cooked with its scales on and everyone treasures a scale or two in their purse to bring them good luck in the coming year. Sometimes the sauce is made with a mixture of beer and red wine, or with red wine alone – carp in red wine is a New Year's Eve dish in some parts of Germany.

Serves 6

1 ½ kg (3 lb) carp, prepared and cut into steaks, the head split
salt
3 tablespoons butter
2 tablespoons plain flour
1 litre (1¾ pt) liquid, half brown beer (not bitter) and half beef stock
 or one-quarter beer, one-quarter red wine, half beef stock
 or half red wine, half beef stock
125 g (4 oz) chopped onion
3 tablespoons chopped green herbs
¼ teaspoon allspice or 2 cloves
3 prunes, stoned, chopped
60 g (2 oz) chopped Pfefferkuchen, pain d'épices *or gingerbread*
lemon juice, pepper, sugar
60 g (2 oz) blanched almonds
60 g (2 oz) raisins

Put the carp pieces in a dish with the head and sprinkle with salt (unless it has already been salted). Set aside for an hour.

Cook the butter to the fragrant brown stage, stir in the flour off the heat. Cook gently to a coffee-coloured roux. Gradually stir in the liquid, and add the onion, herbs, spices, prunes and spice or ginger cake. Simmer for 30 minutes, then sieve into a pan that will take the pieces of carp. Taste the sauce, and add lemon juice, pepper and sugar to taste. When it tastes right, put in the almonds and raisins, and the pieces of carp which have been drained and dried. It is sensible to put the head in the bottom of the pan. Simmer until cooked.

Check the seasoning and serve in a warm shallow serving dish.

Carpe à la juive

This simpler version of the previous recipe makes a good cold dish. A strange thing about the carp is the unanimity with which it is treated across the world – as if everyone agreed to emphasize what Kenneth Lo described as its 'uncomplicated sweet-freshness'. I cannot think there is any connection between central European and Chinese methods, because the carp recipes of mainland Europe seem to be living fossils of the sweet-sour style of medieval cookery. Interesting, though, that such recipes should have survived for carp, when so many other medieval recipes for other fish have not. This Jewish style comes from Lorraine.

Follow the recipe above, leaving the carp whole if you have a fish kettle. Prepare and scale it. Then cook as above,

substituting	fish stock or water for the liquid
	wine vinegar for lemon juice
	bouquet garni for chopped herbs
omitting	prunes and spice/ginger cake
	spices
doubling	quantities of almonds and raisins.

Remove the cooked fish to an oval serving plate, re-forming the steaks into something of the carp's original shape if you have had to cut it up. Reduce the cooking liquor, if need be, to make a stronger flavour, then remove the bouquet. Check seasoning and pour over the fish. The sauce sets to a jelly. Serve chilled.

MEURETTE DE CARPE

Serves 4

125 g (4 oz) mushrooms, sliced
1 medium onion, chopped
90 g (3 oz) currants
3 large cloves garlic
bouquet garni
1 bottle red Burgundy
salt, pepper
1–1¾ kg (2–3½ lb) carp
4 tablespoons butter
1 tablespoon plain flour

Simmer the mushrooms, onion, currants, garlic, bouquet garni and wine together for half an hour, uncovered, until the wine has reduced by a good third. Season. Clean the carp and cut into pieces. Add to the pan, cover, and simmer for another 20 minutes, or until the fish is cooked.

Mash butter and flour together, and use it to thicken the sauce (beurre manié*). Reheat and serve with croûtons of bread fried in butter. Remove the bouquet garni before serving, and the head of the carp.

VERSENYI BATYUS PONTY

Carp in a bundle, Verseny style, is a recipe of George Lang's from his masterpiece of a book, *The Cuisine of Hungary*. It is served with a horseradish soured-cream sauce – a velouté made with beef stock and

milk, flavoured with a little sugar, vinegar or lemon juice and 125 g
(4 oz) grated horseradish which has soaked in a little boiling water
for 2 minutes. Last of all 125 ml (4 fl oz) soured cream.

Serves 4–6

1 kg (2 lb) carp fillet, cut in 1 piece
salt
3 tablespoons plain flour
1 tablespoon paprika
4 tablespoons clarified butter
1 egg white, slightly beaten to break it up

DOUGH
175 g (6 oz) plain flour
125 g (4 oz) butter
1 egg yolk
1 tablespoon soured cream
1½ teaspoon salt

Make the dough first. Rub together the flour and butter until you
have a crumbly mixture. Mix in the egg yolk, soured cream and salt.
Knead on a lightly floured board to make a dough. Chill in the
refrigerator for at least an hour.

Switch on the oven set at gas 5, 190 °C (375 °F). Salt the fish and
roll it in the flour and paprika mixed. Shake off any excess. Fry
slowly in the butter on both sides.

Choose an ovenproof dish measuring 23 × 15 cm (9 × 6 inches). Roll
out the dough into a rectangle. Line the dish with one end of the
dough. Put the fish on top. Fold the rest of the dough over and round
the fish. Brush over with egg white. Bake 40–45 minutes.

NOTE If you can only buy smaller pieces of carp fillet, make
individual pasties.

CARPET-SHELLS *see* A FEW WORDS ABOUT . . .
CARPET-SHELLS

CATFISH *see* A FEW WORDS ABOUT . . . CATFISH

CERO *see* MACKEREL

CHAR *see* TROUT

CLAMS

Venus mercenaria, Mercenaria mercenaria

Everybody knows that clams are American. It is true that in Scotland scallops are often known as clams, and that we use the phrase 'as tight as a clam' about secretive people, but clams really belong to our rosier knowledge of American life. There is clam chowder for a start (not in fact a Red Indian dish, but an adaptation of the name and recipe of a French fish stew, *see* below). We have probably heard rather enviously of New England clambakes, those summer feasts on the beach when the shellfish are steamed on a bed of seaweed over red hot stones, along with lobster, chicken, sausages and a variety of vegetables. If we remember pioneering tales, we can probably recollect that wampum, the Red Indian money, consisted of strings and belts of clam shells (hence the second word of the specific name, *Venus mercenaria*).

It is not generally known that the bubbling dishes of *praires farcies grillées*, served in Norman and Breton restaurants (*see* Huitres farcies grillées, p. 256), are clams, real American clams, of the kind known as quahaug, quahog or hard clams. Efforts were first made to introduce them into France in the second half of the nineteenth century. Now they are acclimatized all down the Atlantic coast of France. As one sops up the last garlicky juices, one does not spend much time regretting the American clams that are *not* acclimatized in Europe – the cherry stone, little neck and butter clams which are eaten raw like oysters; the long razor clams which come to the table fried as well as in chowders; the soft clams which rejoice in the local names of gaper, maninose, nannynose, old maid and strand-gaper. I am sure that none of them can equal the *praires farcies* – or at least surpass them.

Clams are among the easiest shellfish to grow commercially. It is true that they take four years, almost as long as an oyster; but they are more good-tempered, less of a risk. As demand increases, so will production. It does seem ridiculous to go to France to eat them, let alone America, when we could be enjoying them at Southend or Torquay or in our own kitchens. Like many other shellfish, clams are best in the summer months. We tend to be superstitious about eating them when the month lacks an R (as we once were about eating pork). It seems that this is a groundless form of masochistic self-denial. Apparently only the native oyster, not the Portuguese but *Ostrea edulis*, should be avoided in July and August, because, as one authority put it, the shells are 'full of gritty little babies'.

HOW TO PREPARE CLAMS

Having found your clams, how are you going to open them? If they are fresh and alive, use the oyster method, *see* p. 254. A few moments in warm water makes it much easier to push a knife through the hinges.

Some cookery books suggest using the mussel method (a large pan, covered, over a moderate heat) or, for the large ones, the scallop method (a few moments in a fairly hot oven, gas 6, 200 °C/400 °F, until they begin to open). Clams which have been deep-frozen are the easiest of all. Put them in warm water to thaw, until the shells just begin to gape. Finish the job off with a knife, oyster fashion. Keep deep-frozen clams for cooking.

Once the black-tipped siphon has been removed, all of the clam meat can be eaten. The coral foot and pinkish-white muscles are firmer than the central body part: for some recipes, it is a good idea to chop these parts, while leaving the soft part whole. Most oyster, mussel and scallop recipes can be adapted to clams – especially the one for Huîtres farcies grillées. Oysters Rockefeller (p. 261) is also particularly suitable.

CLAMS AU NATUREL

Fresh clams can be eaten raw on the half-shell, like oysters. Lemon juice and cayenne pepper can be served with them, plus the usual wholemeal or rye bread and butter, and a white wine such as Muscadet.

In *The Boston School Cookbook*, Fanny Farmer recommends that clams should be served with individual dishes of melted butter, sharpened with a little vinegar or lemon juice; the clam liquor should be strained, and served in glasses, for drinking at the same time.

Certainly clam liquor should be cherished, like oyster and mussel liquor.

CLAM CHOWDER

Being English, and of a tranquil disposition, I hesitate to offer comments on one of America's sacred institutions. Even to suggest a recipe verges on impiety. But now that we have our own clam-producing beds, I can't duck the issue, or any missiles that may come my way in consequence. It is strange how the monotheistic spirit has entered the kitchen. Each clam-chowder missionary expects everyone to bow down before his one true recipe (it is the same with Bouillabaisse in France). Tomatoes or no tomatoes? Milk or water? Onions – how many? Fanny Farmer instructs readers to take a pint of hard clams or a dozen large clams and one thinly sliced onion . . . In response Louis P. de Gouy thunders, 'A dozen clams forsooth! . . . Men and women of Rhode Island and Massachusetts Bay never sat down to less than a peck of clams apiece.' A peck, if I may remind the new metricians, is quarter of a bushel – think of a bushel basket for picking apples – in other words two gallons. They were gods in their appetite, the men and women of those days, cast in a gigantic mould. Here is one of them, Ishmael in *Moby Dick*, describing his first encounter with chowder at the Try Pots Inn run by Mrs Hosea Hussey in Nantucket: 'Oh! sweet friends, hearken to me. It was made of small juicy clams, scarcely bigger than hazel nuts, mixed with pounded ship biscuits, and salted pork cut up into little flakes; the whole enriched with butter . . .'

Walt Whitman, too, would have found Fanny Farmer and her Boston School a little on the meagre, ladylike side:

> The boatman and clam-diggers arose early and stopt for me,
> I tuck'd my trowser-ends in my boots and went and had a good time;
> You should have been with us that day round the chowder-kettle.[1]

---

[1] *Song of Myself.*

Here, therefore, is Louis P. de Gouy's recipe from *The Gold Cook Book* (1948):

'Take 4 or 5 dozen good soft clams, if your family is a small one . . . Then take 6 large onions and ½ pound [250 g] of the finest salt pork. Cut the pork in half-inch [1¼-cm] dice and brown them slowly in an iron skillet,[2] then add the onion slices to the pork fat and let them turn to golden-brown rings. Meanwhile wash the live clams, using a brush to get rid of all sand, and heat them slowly in a pan till the shells open. Save the juice, cut off the long necks and remove the coarse membrane, then chop half of the clams, not too finely, and keep the rest whole. Put pork, onions, clam juice, and 1 quart of boiling water in a kettle,[2] add 3 large peeled tomatoes, 1 bunch of leeks cut finely, 2 stalks of celery, finely minced, 2 young carrots, diced, 1 tablespoon of parsley, chopped, ½ teaspoon of thyme leaves, 2 large bay leaves, 1 teaspoon of salt, ½ generous teaspoon of freshly ground black pepper, a slight grating of nutmeg, and let the mixture boil up smartly. Then reduce to the simmering point, and put in 3 large potatoes, peeled and cut in neat small dice. Prepare a roux by browning 2 rounded tablespoons of flour in 2 rounded tablespoons of butter, and make it smooth and creamy by stirring in broth from the kettle. Put all the clams into the kettle before the potatoes begin to soften, and simmer slowly until the potatoes are just tender, then stir in the roux and 2 large pilot biscuits[2] coarsely crumbled, and add 1 teaspoon of Worcestershire sauce and a dash of Tabasco sauce. Serve sizzling hot.

'If preferred, omit the tomatoes and add instead 1 cup [125 ml/ 4 fl oz] of scalded cream.'

CLAMS FARCIES

As well as the recipes for grilled and stuffed oyster or mussels, try this delicious mixture. Bacon and mushrooms are good with most of the small shellfish.

Serves 6

48 clams
125 g (4 oz) mushrooms
4 slices bacon, crisply cooked

[2] Skillet and kettle mean frying pan and saucepan. An American quart equals 32 liquid ounces, as opposed to the Imperial quart of 40 ounces. Pilot biscuits are ship's biscuits – cream crackers will have to do instead.

1 tablespoon chopped parsley
breadcrumbs (see *recipe*)
salt, pepper
butter

Like oyster shells, clam shells need to be settled firmly on a supporting base if they are not to wobble about during cooking. Tin pans with a thick layer of sea salt are one solution: the clams can be pressed down into the salt. I prefer large 'platters' of bread, in which holes have been made with a small scone cutter; the shells rest in the holes, and any juice which bubbles over is sopped up – to your ultimate benefit – by the bread. Having settled this point, open the clams, and pour off their liquor into a jug.

To make the stuffing, chop the mushrooms finely and crumble the bacon. Mix them together with the parsley and strained clam liquor. Stir in enough breadcrumbs to make a normal stuffing consistency – spreadable, but not sloppy. Season to taste. Divide this mixture between the shells, to cover the clams. Dot with butter and bake in a moderate oven (gas 4, 180 °C/350 °F) for about 12 minutes, until they are nicely browned and bubbling.

CLAM FRITTERS

Although soft shell clams are recommended for this recipe from *The American Heritage Cookbook* hard clams can be used instead. So can mussels.

By my estimate, 3–3½ kg (6–7 lb) of clams in the shell should produce the required amount, or 4 kg (8 lb) of mussels.

Serves 6

375 g (12 oz) clams, drained
2 eggs, separated
80 g (2¾ oz) white breadcrumbs, toasted
1 teaspoon salt
½ teaspoon pepper
½ dessertspoon chopped parsley
½ dessertspoon chopped chives
generous 60 ml (2 fl oz) milk
butter or vegetable oil

Chop the drained clams finely. Beat the egg yolks, then mix in the clams, breadcrumbs, seasoning and herbs. Add enough milk to make a heavy batter. Beat the egg whites stiffly. Fold them into the mixture just before you intend to cook it. Heat the butter or oil in a frying pan. Drop spoonfuls of the mixture into it and cook in the usual way.

Although the recipe doesn't say so, lemon quarters are a good garnish: their juice cuts the richness of the fritters.

CLAMS MORNAY

You will need a prepared base for the clam shells, see p. 81. Alternatively, you can discard the shells, and divide the sauce and clams, on the same principle, between six little pots.

Serves 6

48 clams
butter
175 ml (6 fl oz) dry white wine
Mornay sauce*
125–175 g (4–6 oz) grated Gruyère cheese
3 tablespoons breadcrumbs

Open, remove and drain the clams, retaining the liquor. Fry the clams for 2 minutes only in just enough butter to cover the base of the pan. Pour in wine and simmer for 4 or 5 minutes – don't overcook. Drain the clams carefully and set aside; add the reserved clam liquor to the cooking liquor, and reduce until you have a strongly concentrated essence. Add this gradually to the Mornay sauce, stopping before it becomes too salty.

Put some of the sauce into the shells, lay the clams on top and then cover with some more sauce. Mix the grated Gruyère and breadcrumbs, and sprinkle over the top. Brown lightly in the oven, or under the grill – the latter is simpler, and more easily controlled. Serve immediately.

This is a good recipe, too, for scallops – 18 should be enough for 6 people.

COLCHESTER CLAMS WITH SAMPHIRE

The biggest indictment of our catering trade is fish – or rather the lack of it. You can spend a thousand days at the seaside without being able to sit down in a café to a platter of seafood – lobster, crab, mussels, oysters, shrimps, prawns, whelks, winkles – served on ice with a bowl of proper mayonnaise. In seaside hotels, the one item of fish on the menu will be frozen or dull or overcooked, most likely all three. We need the influence of the new cooking from France, with its insistence on fish. Thank heavens that it begins to show – though this is often indignantly denied – in our best restaurants, the brave hundred (according to one food guider) that care about ingredients.

In fact, I think that the best turbot I have ever eaten was in Norfolk when Melanie de Blank had her hotel in Shipdham. Many of her ingredients came from her husband's London shops, but the fish was splendidly local. She took advantage, too, of the samphire that covers the salt marshes of the flat Norfolk coast. In summer, you can pick it yourself (wellingtons are a prudent measure), or buy it from village stalls outside farmhouses and from fishmongers. Take home plenty because it freezes well. Steam or blanch it in unsalted water, after picking it over and cutting away brown stem lengths, and serve it with butter like asparagus. You pick it up, nibble off the tender tops and then chew the green lower sections from their central strings.

In this recipe, samphire is teamed with Colchester clams (mussels or oysters could be used instead), and the sauce is flavoured with saffron – not in these days from Saffron Walden but from Spain. Only use the stringless green tips of samphire, serving the rest at another meal: 1 kg (2 lb) should provide enough.

Serves 6

6 handfuls of samphire tips
36 clams
150 ml (5 fl oz) dry white wine
2 small shallots, chopped
1 medium carrot, chopped
pinch of saffron, steeped in a little hot water
300 ml (10 fl oz) crème fraîche or half each soured and double cream
julienne shreds of carrot and leek, blanched, to garnish

Wash and steam or blanch the samphire. Drain well. Scrub the clams. Bring the wine, chopped shallots and carrot to the boil, put in the clams, cover and leave for 2 minutes. Remove the clams, if open; otherwise leave a little longer until they open. Set aside six clams in their shells. Remove the remaining clams and discard the shells. Strain the liquor into a wide shallow pan, add the saffron and its liquor, and boil down to concentrate the flavour. Stir in the cream(s), and boil slightly to thicken. Off the heat, stir in the clams and cool. Add seasoning, if necessary.

Put the samphire on six plates, spoon over the clams with their sauce, and decorate with the julienne and the reserved clams in their shells.

SPAGHETTI ALLE VONGOLE

Small clams in a tomato sauce are often served with spaghetti in central and southern Italy. In the north, in Venice, they would be added to a risotto with a lump of butter rather than tomato sauce.

Serves 6

500 g (1 lb) spaghetti
3 kg (6 lb) clams, washed
1 large onion, chopped
3 cloves garlic, chopped
3 tablespoons olive oil
400 g (14 oz) can tomatoes
60 g (2 oz) chopped parsley (large bunch)

Cook the spaghetti in plenty of boiling salted water in the usual way, until it is cooked but not slimily soft. Drain and keep warm until the sauce is finished.

Start the sauce as soon as the spaghetti goes into the pan. Open the clams in a large pan over a moderate heat, discard the shells and strain off the liquid from the fish. Brown the onion and garlic lightly in the oil. Add the tomatoes and some of the clam liquor. Boil down to a rich sauce. Add clams, which will be adequately cooked, just to re-heat them. Remove sauce from the stove, stir in the parsley and pour over the spaghetti, mixing it well.

† COD, LING, COLEY, POLLOCK, POLLACK, etc.

Gadidea spp.

Cod, oh dear not *cod. Again.* I used to dislike it, or perhaps I used rather to feel bored by it when it was the bottom fish on the marble slab. When I was first writing *Fish Cookery* in 1971, I noted that there were a number of things you could do with it, but were they worth your while? Although Escoffier had remarked that if cod were only rarer, 'It would be held in as high esteem as salmon; for when it is really fresh and of good quality, the delicacy and delicious flavour of its flesh admit of its ranking among the finest of fish,' when it came to the count, he had only been moved to give six recipes to it in his *Guide Culinaire*, by comparison with sole which had 182.

Fifteen years later, the laugh is on me: in those days, cod was forty-five per cent of the total wet fish landings in Britain; by 1985, it had dropped to just over thirteen per cent. A figure that would, I think, have surprised Escoffier. As I write now, in December 1986, there are reports of reduced breeding stocks with national quotas in the EEC adjusted accordingly. Prices are at £900 per tonne, whereas two years ago they were £700 and in 1982, £300. The conclusion of the article in *The Independent*, from which these figures come, is that prices cannot continue to rise. With more and more farmed salmon and the lowering of salmon prices accordingly, will there be parity of esteem? Perhaps not over the whole consumer range, since the magic of the

word salmon may take a year or two to dispel, but many friends I
have talked to agree that they would rather eat top quality cod than
some of the farmed salmon one sees around.

This rarity of the real thing has drawn attention to the lesser
relations. I exclude from this category haddock (p. 148), hake and
whiting (pp. 161 and 446), which have strong identities of their own.
They are all fish of fine quality. Somewhat less glorious, though
adequate for stocks, soups, fish pies, fish cakes possibly, fish fried in
batter, and for salting, is a bevy of fish with a confused
nomenclature. From the cook's point of view, all one actually needs
to know is that they are all cooked like cod, haddock and hake.
Nevertheless, here is a modest attempt to disentangle some of them,
with French names to help if you are catering for the family abroad and
are bewildered by the much greater choice of fish in the markets:

ling (*Molva molva*; *lingue* or *julienne*)

coley, coalfish,
black pollack, rock (*Pollachius virens*; *Lieu noir*, *colin noir*)
salmon, etc.

pollack, Dover hake,
lythe, Margate hake, (*Pollachius pollachius*; *Lieu jaune*, *colin jaune*)
pollock, etc.

Alaska pollack or
pollock (*Theragra chalcogrammus*)

You will see that pollack or pollock covers at least three realities.

Having acknowledged the lesser fry, let us return to the king of the
cod fishery, *Gadus morhua*, once the most important food fish in
northern Europe. It has all the freshness and crispness of form that
cold seas can give it. The English name, cod, goes back to the year
dot pretty well. No etymologist can work out where it has come from.
One thing is sure, it has no connection with the Greek *gados* from
which the first element in the Latin name derives. Obeisance should
be made to its majestic importance, but it should also be pointed out
that – from the eater's point of view – there is cod and cod. Go for
the small inshore fish that haven't been bruised around in ice in a
ship's hold for weeks. Official sizing this side of the Atlantic goes by
length:

small codling: less than 54 cm (21 ½ inches)
codling: 54–63 cm (21 ½–25 ¼ inches)
sprag: 63–76 cm (25 ¼–30 inches)
cod: over 76 cm (30 inches)

This gives you some idea of what to ask for, if your fish kettle measures 60 cm (24 inches). Assuming, that is, that you want to cook it whole as they do in Norway for Christmas dinner. There you choose your fish on the quay as it swims around in the tanks. The fishmonger dispatches and cleans it, and you take it home to poach and serve with a traditional mustard or egg sauce, or with melted butter and fine grated horseradish.

Another place where small codling are given their due is Boston (Boston, Mass., not Boston, Lincs.). It appears there, and so does haddock, under the name of scrod. They measure the fish there by weight:

scrod: ¾–1¼ kg (1½–2½ lb), less than 50 cm (20 inches)
market: 1¼–5 kg (2½–10 lb), 50–75 cm (20–30 inches)
large: 5–12½ kg (10–25 lb), 75–100 cm (30–40 inches)
whole: over 12½ kg (25 lb), over 100 cm (40 inches).

People fly across the States for it, I gather. One keen traveller ran out of the airport and jumped into a cab: 'Take me some place good where I can get scrod!'

The cab drive sat back and paused, admiringly: 'That's a question I've been asked many times. But never in the pluperfect.'

Nowadays in Boston, sadly, and in Gloucester, cod fishing is not the vast trade it once was. Down at the pierhead auction with George Berkowitz who runs five of the best fish restaurants in Boston (each with a fishmonger's counter beside the till, so that inevitably you walk out with supper after enjoying your lunch), I heard complaints of the great Russian ships which have invaded the traditional fishing grounds and hoover up the seabed like a carpet. In Europe, memories of the cod war with Iceland a few years ago are still sharp in many people's minds. Its virtues, now we are unable to take it for granted, are more apparent.

Really fresh cod, not overcooked, falls apart in large firm creamy flakes, and the bones are easy to avoid. Its clean aplomb can be toned down to delicacy with a fine sauce, or underlined with shellfish or bacon, tomatoes, peppers, spices, wine. In batter, quick from the pan with a squeeze of lemon, it is perfect food for hungry people. Smashed down in the blender or processor, cod makes an excellent fish pudding. I use it as a substitute for unobtainable species of fish when trying out a stew. The cod chowders of America's eastern seaboard are infinitely variable, warming food for a cold night.

Cod may not yet be regarded as an epicure's delight, but as the fish of human martyrdom, of the tragedy of lost lives, it does have a splendid novel to itself. In *Pêcheurs d'Islande*, Pierre Loti turned the sufferings of this dangerous trade into a work of art, a sustained elegy for the tough, inarticulate Bretons who spent the summer in a frail 'house of planks', rocking on the North Sea in the pale void of the nights, 'under the gaze of this sort of spectral eye which was the sun'. Beneath them, the 'innumerable fish, myriads and myriads, all alike, gliding noiselessly in the same direction, as if they had a goal in their perpetual journeying. They were the cod which were executing their evolutions together . . . Sometimes, with a sudden stroke of the tail, they all turned together, showing the gleam of their silvered bellies and then the same stroke of tail, the same turn were propagated through the entire shoal in slow undulations, as if thousands of metal blades had given, under water, each a little flash.' Again and again, one of the men – who worked in pairs – hauled in the lines heavy with fish, the live cod allowed themselves to be caught, 'it was rapid and incessant, this silent fishing. The other gutted with his large knife, flattened, salted and counted, and all the time the soused fish which was to make their fortune on their return was piling up behind them, streaming and fresh.'

Nowadays, the cod fishermen spend winters there as well, in vast modern trawlers with wireless, and refrigerated chambers for the catch. They have a better chance against the ice and tumult of those bitter seasons off Iceland and the North Cape. It is still hard going, though, for the smaller inshore boats out from the Massachusetts ports, whose living is so precarious that they turn for home at the last possible moment, fearing to lose any possible chance of the fish that may just turn their sorties from loss to profit.

Some years ago, I was ticked off by a reader on account of my liking for salt cod. 'Poverty food,' she said, 'and in this country, we are beyond the need for that kind of thing.' Certainly the need for salt fish inland for the many fast days of Christianity long ago is no longer with us. The Reformation saw to that and, if it hadn't, modern refrigerated transport would have done so in our time. Now we can eat it for pure pleasure, an extra item in our diet, just as buckling or kippers, ham or bacon, make extra variations on the basic themes of herring and pork.

Salt cod was originally the product of Holland and Scandinavia in the Middle Ages. I have read that Portuguese fishermen who were also after the cod in Greenland waters were setting up their drying tenters on the shores of America and Canada decades before Columbus set sail in 1492. Portugal is reputed to have a salt cod recipe for each day of the year: certainly my own favourite salt cod recipe is Portuguese (p. 103), followed by the creamy savoury pounded salt cod made in Languedoc and northern Italy. It is interesting that the best recipes all come from the destinations of the trade, rather than from its original homes in Holland, Iceland and Norway. In those countries, until quite recent times, you could see green and stony fields white over with fish, laid to dry in an unending patchwork. Nowadays the fish is hung up on racks in huge sheds where the drying is properly regulated and no longer affected by the uncertain weather. The main market was and still is the Mediterranean, with stops on the Atlantic coasts of Spain and Portugal. The ships brought back wheat and dried fruit.

Along with the salt cod went stockfish, which is made from the same members of the *Gadidae* family, cod, hake, coley and so on, but without the salting process. The fish is simply split and dried. This is the board-like fish that hangs in high rows, fringing shops in Ghana and other parts of Africa, still its main market. You will not find it easy to obtain in Britain or America. In some languages, the word stockfish is used interchangeably with the word for salt cod. And one can make use of them interchangeably in the same recipes, with adjustments of soaking time and seasoning. They are a sombre reminder – like black and red herrings (p. 191) – of the days of slavery: boats full of salt cod would set out from Boston for Spain and Africa, keeping back a little of their cargo to feed the people that were then crammed into the empty holds for the journey to the West Indies. Their place was taken by the sugar and molasses of the plantations that the slaves were imported to produce, and so back to Boston. This means, of course, that another source of good salt fish recipes is the Caribbean and Brazil.

HOW TO CHOOSE AND PREPARE COD

Whether you are buying whole fish, fillets or steaks, the top quality comes from inshore codling. It should look particularly bright and fresh; the steaks should have a milky whiteness that draws your eye.

Do not let this put you off coley (also called saithe and coalfish), which is a most unalluring dark greyish-pink colour. Often it is a good second best; it whitens in the cooking and tastes pleasant enough. For Bergen fish soup, below, one of the finest and most delicate of all fish soups, it is essential. You will find it works well in cod chowders (p. 515), too, and for fish stocks when you cannot get hold of fish bones and trimmings. I admit it is not the best of the cod-like fish – hake, haddock, whiting would be most people's preference – but I feel protective towards it ever since I heard an old lady say to a fishmonger, 'Oh, and give me a bit of coley for the cat!'

Cod's head and shoulders used to be a favourite of the Victorian family table. There are good pickings, but today we are more squeamish. If you have a modern young fishmonger with a genteel trade, you may be able to get the cod's head from him for very little (an older man may well have a better idea of its worth). Use the head for fish stock, removing the cheeks, jaw muscle, and so on, when they are just cooked. Or make soup – see the Salmon head soup on p. 318 – using the cooked fish as a final garnish. The reason people ate the cod's head and shoulder in the past was because they were quite sufficient for a dish, and also because it is difficult to cook a whole cod evenly – 'when the thick part is done, the tail is insipid and overdone'. Codling is all right cooked whole, however.

Another comment from Mrs Beeton is that fresh cod can be a little watery in the cooking. If you rub salt into it a couple of hours beforehand, it will stiffen and flavour it. In fact, I find most fish are improved by seasoning in advance, giving the salt time to penetrate. Obviously this works better with steaks and fillets than with whole, unskinned fish: even so, rubbing salt into the cleaned cavity and over the skin does help.

BERGEN FISH SOUP

This soup was the great delight of a trip we made several years ago now. We were part of a group of journalists from all over the world who were being taken to visit the salmon farms that are staked out in the narrows of the low rocky coast. In between lectures, there was some lovely food, especially one evening at the Royal Hotel, where we were staying: the chef gave us his recipe for the great local speciality, which is made – by choice – from coley.

Serves 8

1 kg (2 lb) coley fillet, cubed
1 kg (2 lb) fish bones, heads, etc.
1 large onion, finely chopped
1 large leek, trimmed, sliced
2 medium-sized bay leaves
salt, pepper
1 teaspoon sugar

white wine vinegar
2 medium carrots, cut in julienne strips
white part of 2 leeks, cut in julienne strips
1 tablespoon plain flour
2 tablespoons butter
3 egg yolks
150 ml (5 fl oz) each double and soured cream
chopped chives

FISH BALLS
250 g (8 oz) haddock fillet, skinned
½ teaspoon salt
2 teaspoons plain flour
2 teaspoons cornflour or cornstarch
2 tablespoons soft butter
pepper, nutmeg
225 ml (7½ fl oz) cold boiled milk
4 tablespoons cold boiled cream

Make a stock by simmering the first five ingredients together in plenty of water to cover. Give them 45 minutes, then strain off the stock into a clean pan. Season with salt, pepper and sugar. Liven the flavour with a teaspoon of vinegar, taste and then add a splash or two more but do not overdo it. Pour off enough of the stock into a shallow pan to make a 2-cm (¾-inch) depth for poaching the fish balls, which can be made while the stock simmers.

Reduce the haddock, from the fish ball ingredients, and the salt to a fluffy purée in a blender or processor, and add the rest of the ingredients in turn, one by one. Chill the mixture, if this is convenient, while you get on with the soup.

To the large pan of stock, which should be at simmering point, add the carrot shreds. Give them a minute's cooking, then put in the leek. Mash the flour into the butter and add it to the pan in little bits, keeping the soup below simmering point from now on. Beat the egg yolk and creams, whisk in a ladleful of soup and pour back into the pan. Stir for 5 minutes and taste again for seasoning. Put in the chives. Keep warm without further cooking.

To poach the fish balls, heat the shallow pan of stock to simmering point. Form little balls, quite tiny ones, with two teaspoons, slipping them into the stock. After 2 minutes, taste one. If it feels light and soft, without any hint of flour, the fish balls are done. You may well not need all the mixture, which can be kept for another occasion (it is tricky making a smaller quantity).

Place the fish balls in the soup, and add their stock to the pan as well. The final result is a creamy white soup, with streaks of colour from the carrot and leek, beautiful and delicate, not insipid.

COD WITH MUSHROOMS

The important thing is to cook the mushrooms and cod together so that the flavours intermingle. A surprisingly good dish. Aim to keep the mushrooms in a light juice, rather than a lot of liquid.

Serves 6

6 × 175–250 g (6–8 oz) cod steaks
salt, pepper, nutmeg
6 slices of crustless bread cut to the size and shape of the cod
125 g (4 oz) clarified butter
seasoned flour
375 g (12 oz) mushrooms, caps sliced, stalks chopped
1 clove garlic, crushed, skinned, chopped
1–2 tablespoons chopped parsley

Put the steaks on a dish and season them, then set aside while you fry the bread until brown and crisp on one side only, in half the butter. Place the bread, cooked side down, on a hot dish and keep warm.

Dry the fish, turn it in the flour and fry it in the remaining butter. Add the mushrooms and garlic when you turn the cod. Remove the cod when done, putting it on top of the bread. Give the mushrooms a little longer if necessary, and season them. Put them round the cod, sprinkle a little parsley on top of the fish and serve.

NOTE Instead of slices of bread, you could fry small bread dice or coarse breadcrumbs and scatter them over the dish before serving. A crisp contrast makes a dish of this kind much livelier.

FISKEPUDDING (Fish pudding)

If you visit a Stockholm market, you may well see on the fish stalls a regimentation of what looks like collapsed kugelhupf cakes. A sad and weak-kneed array, to an outsider at least. They are likely to be interspersed with plastic tubs. Customers come along quite briskly all the same. The fishmonger wraps the chosen collapsible in foil, presumably for reheating, and hands over a plastic tub as well. Everyone seems happy. Try this recipe and you will see why. Having a processor is the secret.

Serves 4–6

375 g (12 oz) cod fillet
130 g (generous 4 oz) butter, softened
2 large egg yolks
2 level tablespoons plain flour
150 ml (5 fl oz) double cream
150 ml (5 fl oz) milk
1½ teaspoons salt
1 teaspoon sugar
pepper
2 large egg whites
extra butter, for greasing the mould
2–3 tablespoons fine breadcrumbs
1 tablespoon finely chopped parsley

Scrape the fish from the skin, removing any bones. Process with the butter, yolks, flour, cream and milk and the seasoning, gradually and in batches if necessary. Whisk the whites in a bowl and fold in the fish mixture. Taste for seasoning.

Grease a 1¼ litre (2 pt) kugelhupf pottery or metal ring mould with butter. Mix crumbs and parsley and shake them about in the mould to coat it. Tip out any surplus.

Put in the fish mixture, cover with buttered paper and steam or cook in a bain-marie in a moderate oven, preheated to gas 4, 180° (350°F) for an hour or until firm to the touch. Ease with a knife, turn out on to a hot dish and serve with shrimp or prawn sauce, p. 281 – that is what the plastic pots contained in the Stockholm market.

POACHED CODLING WITH OYSTER SAUCE AND MELTED BUTTER

Here's English cooking for you and, if well done, it is very well worth eating. Do not jib at the quantity of salt: if the fish is whole, you will find it agreeably seasoned and no more, just as you do when baking a whole fish or whole chicken in a mound of sea salt (p. 367). Oyster sauce is a special treat with chicken and turkey, as well as with white fish of firm quality.

Serves 6

1 ½ kg (3 lb) codling, cleaned
coarse sea or rock salt
sprigs of parsley
small new potatoes, boiled

SAUCE
24 large or 36 medium oysters, opened
60 g (2 oz) butter, softened
2 teaspoons plain flour
cream
cayenne pepper

BUTTER
250 g (8 oz) unsalted or lightly salted butter, cut in dice

Start with the sauce. Tip the oysters with their juice into a bowl. Swish each oyster about in the liquor to get rid of bits of shell and put it into a small pan. Strain the liquor over them, through a cloth. Bring to simmering point and hold them there until they look plump. Remove immediately and strain off the liquor into a measuring jug. Mash the butter and flour together and put into the top pan of a double-boiler. Add enough cream to the oyster liquor to bring it up to 300 ml (10 fl oz), and add a pinch of cayenne. Leave near the stove for last-minute cooking.

For the melted butter, bring the diced butter to boiling point in a small pan. Let it bubble briefly, then leave for the sediment to settle. Pour off into a small jug, for later reheating.

To poach the cod, lay it on the strainer tray of the fish kettle. Pour over enough water to cover it properly, measuring as you go. Stir in enough sea salt to make a brine, allowing 90 g to every 2½ litres of water (or 3 oz to 2½ pt). Bring up to a rolling boil, standing the kettle over two burners, then immediately lower the heat so that the water barely trembles. Poach the fish for 10–15 minutes, keeping it submerged by laying a dish on top. Test after 10 minutes by giving the first dorsal fin a little tug: if it comes out easily, the fish is done. Remove it to a hot serving dish and keep warm while you complete the oyster sauce.

Have the lower part of the double-boiler half full of boiled water. Pour the oyster and cream mixture into the top part and set it in place. Stir steadily until the sauce thickens: it should become very hot, but not boil. Stir in the oysters and give them a few moments to heat through, without further cooking. Remove and pour into a hot jug.

Stand the little jug of melted butter in the double-boiler to heat up.

Surround the cod with sprigs of parsley and boiled potatoes. Serve with the two jugs of sauce and melted butter.

VERY FRESH COD NORWEGIAN STYLE

A fish straight from the tank should be cleaned – preserve liver and roe – and cut in 'finger-thick slices'. Keep the head. Put all the fish into a bowl under a running tap until about 30 minutes before the meal, then drain.

Boil water with salt, as above, in a fish kettle. Lower the fish on the strainer tray, then remove the kettle from the heat when water returns to the boil. The slices will be almost cooked. Give them a minute or two more if necessary; the head will not need much longer.

Meanwhile, simmer any roe in salted water separately, tied in muslin, until just firm, about 10 minutes, then serve in slices with the cod. The liver should be chopped and cooked in the minimum of barely salted water with a splash of vinegar: this makes one sauce. Provide another such as hollandaise * or, in nineteenth-century style, an oyster sauce (p. 263). And boiled potatoes. Tuck bunches of parsley around the cod's head, slices and roe.

CRAB STICKS ALIAS POLLOCK (OR CROAKER)

The crab stick or, in some circles, krab stik – is a phenomenon of 'high tech'. A fairly recent phenomenon. A fishmonger in Cirencester market gave us a couple free in, I would say, 1983 when they were new on the British scene. Looking first at their rouged cheeks, and then pushing the thready synthetic sweetness round our mouths, we never thought they would come to anything. If someone had told us that a vast industry in Japan is devoted to such things, we would not have believed them. Yet now crab sticks lurk in the corner of every fishmonger's slab.

I would say that they are spurned by the knowing customer here. Certainly it never occurred to me that crab sticks would appear in the revision of *Fish Cookery* until a trip to Paris in 1986. Three of us were taken by SPOEXA to the great food fair that is held there every other year. One evening we went to an elegant restaurant, the Quai des Ormes: among the dishes ordered was pasta with crab sauce. When it came, we were startled to see that the final flourish was an artistically squashed crab stick. Three days later, when I was with friends in Aix en Provence, the cook of the family came home from market with a new treasure. Just the thing, the fishmonger had assured her, for a nice crab salad, little batons of claw meat.

When I said, 'Ah, crab sticks!', she was mortified. Next day, we paid the fishmonger a visit. He swore they were the real thing – look at the fibres, Mesdames, and the colour that you always find on crab close to the shell. Obviously he believed himself. His sincerity was touching. It made us very nervous. Nothing is more impermeable than a gastronomically sincere French fishmonger – except perhaps a gastronomically sincere French chef. The implications are daunting. Watch out when you next go to France. Be wary of crab on the menu.

If crab sticks are not crab, what are they? That, as I discovered from a seafood quarterly, *Ocean Leader*, published in Seattle, is more interesting than you might suppose, and far more ancient.

The idea goes back a thousand years, to ingenious Japanese fishermen who for one or another reason were too far from home to get back and sell their catch in time. To save what they could, they boned and chopped the fish to a jellied hash that they called *surimi*. This was mixed with something starchy and salt, and cooked. The resulting paste was then moulded round bamboo sticks (*chiku*) in rings (*wa*), for later sale. This faceless edible surimi is a kind of marine tofu. It can be made from many fish, though nowadays it comes mainly from the vast catches of Alaskan pollock (and croaker) in the Bering Sea.

The Japanese used knives, pestles and mortar – until machines came along to take over. The processing of surimi is similar to the production of comminuted meat (i.e. meat, bones, gristle, etc. which are pulverized to a paste), the glue and 'meat content' of hot dogs, sausages, the more ineffectual pâtés. Surimi has the advantage of being springy in texture when it has been warmed and moisturized to the correct state. Then it is 'extruded in a thin layer on to a stainless steel belt followed by a flame and steam heat set to yield a strong and cohesive sheet of product. This sheet passes through knives which cut the fibers lengthwise, but not completely through. The fibers thus produced are collated by rolling or bunching the sheet together and coating with an outer layer of the surimi mixture. The product is then printed with a food grade coloring agent, wrapped and heat processed before final packaging. Similar products' – e.g. shrimp, scallops, lobster – 'may be prepared by an extrusion process similar to spaghetti production.'

There it is. Now you know.

What irritates me is that this kind of thing can be pleasant enough to eat. From surimi, the Japanese have developed a kind of fish cake, flavoured with mirin, salt and sugar, called *kamaboko*; it comes in various cylindrical and semi-cylindrical forms, sometimes coloured red on the outside, or cut to show a red spiral design. In a Vietnamese restaurant, you may get prawn paste pressed round a short piece of sugar cane, rather in the style of that ancient *chikuwa*, that is really good. It seems that once big food business lays its high-tech hands on processing, all virtue, all art goes. Theoretically, artificial flavouring and textures could surely be as fine and lively in their own way as natural ones. Why should an artificial flavouring not be up to the standard, say, of the best perfumes from France?

With the size of the potential market, the expense of employing good tasters and sniffers would be nothing by comparison with the other costs. But then big food business is bent on selling the most tawdry product it can get away with at the highest price the public (i.e. the fools) will pay: 'With the right dye, flavoring and processing technology, surimi can be made into just about anything. The best profit margins, though, come from imitating shellfish – generally regarded by consumers as luxuries ... high tech will never replace the real thing' – ah, but will it drive it out? Think of the effect frozen chicken has had on the availability of decent poultry – 'but more importantly it represents a whole new market for the consumer who can't tell, or afford, the difference. In the United States, where processed food is king, that's just about everybody.'

That is why the respectable if humdrum pollock and croaker are being turned into crabless crab. It is so easy. Easy for the manu-facturer. Easy for his accountants to rake in the cash. Easy for the fool of a consumer to unwrap a packet and serve up with loveless love, and a glass of milkless milk.

STOCKFISH, SALT COD OR KLIPFISH, AND LUTEFISK

HOW TO PREPARE IT

STOCKFISH   This is the oldest form of preserved cod and its relations, being air-dried, without salt. The fish are beheaded, slit and gutted, then hung up in pairs, in the dry cold air of Norwegian winters, on wooden tenters like the framework of some ancient Viking homestead. The fish lose about four-fifths of their weight by evaporation, but none of their nutritional advantages. Only water has gone. The main European market is Italy where *stoccafisso* is even more popular than *baccalà* (salt cod). Nigeria and Cameroon are big buyers, too, of this useful storage item that requires no refrigeration. Humidity rather than heat is what spoils it.

All you need do is soak it for about thirty-six hours. It can then be used interchangeably with salt cod, though obviously you will need to add salt to the recipe.

SALT COD OR KLIPFISH   This came up as a rival to stockfish in the seventeenth century as far as Norwegian exports are concerned. As a product, it had been around much earlier. One English writer recorded in 1555 that Cabot himself had named Newfoundland and the country Baccallaos, 'because that in the seas thereabouts he found so great multitudes of certain big fishes . . . which the inhabitants call Baccallaos'. How this ties in with the Spaniards, I do not know, since it seems to be from their use of the term *bacalao* that the word spread through various European languages. The French use *morue* for preserved cod, *morue sèche* for stockfish, *morue verte* for salted cod that has not been dried out: the word for fresh cod is *cabillaud*, from the Netherlands' *kabeljauw* and adopted in the thirteenth century. Be wary of this when you use French recipes.

The true klipfish (*klippfisk* in Norway) is the split kite of creamy-coloured flatness, backed with the silky grey of the skin. Plump, moister salt cod, the French green cod, which has been more lightly salted, is often to be found in sealed packages these days. The weight loss is obviously much less: something you need to take into account when buying it.

As with stockfish, you need to soak salt cod however light the cure. In earlier times, people left the boards of fish to regain tone in the central fountain, or in a country stream. If you have a spare sink – and no water meter – you can imitate the system by cutting the cod up into pieces, placing them in a colander and standing the colander under a gently running tap.

I confess I have found this idea picturesque rather than necessary. Forty-eight hours, with one change of water, has always been adequate in my experience for even the most obdurate board of dried-out salt cod. More lightly salted cod requires twenty-four to thirty-six hours. The sensible thing is to chew a bit after soaking and judge accordingly. This is not unpleasant. Norwegians sometimes tease out the dry cod into a loose shreddy mass, and chew it to induce a thirst. After the initial surprise, I found this quite good, like biltong or jerky but with a clean fishy taste.

If salt cod is not available in your shops, you could follow some of today's chefs – and Mrs Beeton – by salting your own fresh cod (or hake or coley or pollock or ling). Sprinkle a tablespoon of fine sea salt over 1 kg (2 lb) cod fillets and leave for upwards of 2 hours. Turn the fish occasionally. Unless your hand slipped with the salt, or you left it a particularly long time, this domestic salt cod will need no more than a quick rinse. Again, taste it before submitting it to water.

TO COOK STOCKFISH, SALT COD AND KLIPFISH Put the piece or pieces into a pan and cover generously with cold water. Slowly bring to the boil, lower the heat and simmer for 5–8 minutes. Alternatively, bring to the boil, clap on the lid, remove to the side of the stove and leave for 15 minutes.

Drain and pick out the bones. Some recipes suggest discarding the skin, but this always seems to me a mistake, since it adds an extra succulence to the final dish.

In some dishes, you do not need to give salt cod this pre-cooking. Most recipes will make this clear, but with a little experience you will be able to judge for yourself.

NOTE Small lumps and humps of salt cod, the so-called tongues or cheeks (following), which are a great delicacy, are treated in the same way. Since they are special, and more expensive, you are justified in serving them in smaller quantity than the less rich salt cod from the body of the fish. Bearing this in mind, you can use them for any stockfish or salt cod recipe.

COD'S TONGUES, CHEEKS A particular delicacy of this salted and dried fish trade is the small nobbly bits from the head. I once bought some in Tours market. As far as I can remember, they were labelled *joues de morue*, cheeks of salt cod, though perhaps *bajoues* was the word since they really come from underneath the jaw where there is a tender muscle roughly the shape of an arrow-head. In some books they are called *langues* or tongues, a reference to their shape. I recognized what they were from meals we had eaten in Basque towns in Spain where these little nuggets – taken more often, in those parts, from hake than cod – are known as *kokotzas* and eaten fresh. They are cooked in olive oil with garlic and hot chilli, a little parsley and some stock; the milky liquor that emerges from them binds the sauce, making it particularly succulent.

Salted pieces can be cooked in the same way, once soaked. Or you could fry them gently in a little olive oil and simmer with some tomatoes, stirring in a spoonful or two of pesto as a finishing touch. I once used them for Bacalhau à Bras (p. 103), and it was even better than usual. The price is higher, naturally, for these diminutive luxuries, but they are richer and can be served in smaller quantities than the normal salt cod.

LUTEFISK OR LYE FISH   A most particular speciality of Scandinavia, this has not made many converts in the outside world. You begin with stockfish which is soaked for a week, then submerged in a lye of birchwood ashes and slaked lime. After this, the fish is soaked for a further week, with daily changes of water. For cooking, the lutefisk is tied into a cheesecloth bag and poached in boiling water. Salt is added after the water boils so that the cooked fish will 'shiver', this being the test of first class lutefisk. The jellied texture and special flavour are not to everyone's taste. Even Alan Davidson, whose inclination is towards every kind of fish in whatever form human ingenuity can devise, was cautious on the subject in his *North Atlantic Seafood*.

Despite the Christmas importance of lutefisk in Norway, Sweden and Finland, and in their settlements overseas, Mr Davidson was not convinced. He concluded that it survives as a fossil, its origin having been in past exigencies of climate and rough transport. A pamphlet I have from one of the producing firms, in Norway, instructs the cook to poach or steam the lutefisk, then provide 'bacon fat, mustard sauce, grated brown cheese' – this I take to mean *gjetöst* – 'syrup, pease pottage or white sauce, to choice, accompanied by boiled potatoes and thin wafer crispbread'. The melted bacon fat, hot with little bits of bacon in it, seems intended, Mr Davidson says, to obscure an unpleasing taste that need not have been there in the first place.

AIOLI GARNI WITH SALT COD

The most spectacular dish of summer holidays in Provence is *aioli*, or *ailloli garni*, or *le grand aioli*. At its most flamboyant, it is a Matisse-coloured salad of salt cod and other fish; vegetables fresh and dried, raw and cooked; hard-boiled eggs, snails, and lemon quarters. With it comes a huge bowl of a special garlic mayonnaise. The flavour has nothing to do with rubbing a clove of garlic discreetly round a salad bowl. It comes from clove after clove after clove. So important is this sauce that the dish carries its name of aioli – *ail* being French for garlic – with all the rest reduced to the status of a garnish, lordly abundance being just an excuse as it were for eating the sauce. Although the classic mayonnaise has a way of dominating nomen-clature – *mayonnaise de saumon, mayonnaise de homard* – I think no other name touches the grandeur of aioli garni which often appears as *le grand aioli*.

The start of a dish of this kind is a visit to the market, to see what vegetables are at their best. The salt cod you will have in stock: it should already be soaking, and have been soaking for about thirty-six hours.

Bear in mind the balance of your dish, what you can assemble by way of eggs, snails, semi-dried or dried beans. The obvious lack so far is crispness – celery, radishes, chicory, cardoon, Florentine fennel, sweet peppers; you serve them raw. Then there are vegetables that need only light cooking – sugar peas, string beans, cauliflower, sprouting broccoli of various kinds.

Deal with all your items, poaching the salt cod, cooking the dried beans and so on, cutting the raw vegetables, and arrange everything on a huge dish, interspersed with lemon quarters, the egg, snails, etc.

Now make the aioli* itself, and put it into a large bowl or bowls depending on the number of people involved. Serve with cloth napkins, as large as possible. Like anchoiade (p. 54) this kind of communal buffet dish can be excessively uncomfortable unless attention is paid to detail.

BACALAO AL PIL-PIL

Salt cod can be cooked in olive oil made piquant and spicy with dried chillis and garlic, in the same way as elvers or prawns (pp. 127 and 284). The thing about this particular method is that the juices of the cod do not emerge to make the sauce creamy as in the next recipe. Use a flat-bottomed earthenware glazed pot of a sturdy kind which can go straight to table: on electric rings or gas, it is prudent to use a heat-diffuser mat.

This recipe gives you a good way of using up the thin tail end of salt cod. The sharp cooking means that the plump kind is unsuitable, since the fish should be permeated with the flavours.

For four people, soak 500 g (1 lb) salt cod. Then cook, bone and drain it well. Leave on the skin and cut it into handy pieces for eating. Dry them on kitchen paper.

Heat up the pot you intend to use with enough oil to cover the base comfortably. In it, cook 4 quartered cloves of garlic until they are golden brown, together with 2 small hot dried chillis (if you are not accustomed to this kind of dish, taste the oil occasionally and remove the chillis when it is piquant enough).

Put in the cod, skin side down. Cook for a minute or two, moving

the bits about to avoid sticking. Then turn and cook briefly again.
Serve immediately (put back the chillis for the sake of appearance and
the name of the dish) with plenty of bread to mop up the delicious oil.

BACALAO IN ITS OWN SAUCE (Bacalao ligado)

A favourite book of mine is *Gastronomia Vasconum*, a collection of
Basque recipes by Juan D° de Echevarria, in five languages, published
by Eduardo Izquierdo in Bilbao. I do recommend it. A number of
recipes in this book are adapted from it, including this one. The
magic, to me at any rate, of much Spanish and Portuguese cookery
comes from the effects one can get by using heavy rustic earthenware
pots directly on the heat. They are very cheap to buy on the spot,
and I find they last for many years if treated reasonably carefully.

You will sometimes find that this dish is what comes to table, in
restaurants, under the name of Bacalao al pil-pil (*See* preceding recipe).

Soak and lightly cook 500 g (1 lb) salt cod. Remove the bones and
drain it well. Dry carefully before frying it.

In an earthenware pot, heat up 250 ml (8 fl oz) olive oil. In it fry
4 cloves of garlic, sliced across. Remove when they are golden brown,
and keep for garnishing.

In a second pot, heat up a further 250 ml (8 fl oz) olive oil with
2 sliced cloves of garlic. When they are brown, put them aside with
the other garlic. Keep the oil warm.

Into the first pan, put the cod, skin side up and add 125 ml (4 fl oz)
water or light beef or veal stock. Shake the pot to and fro, adding the
warm oil bit by bit. The sauce should turn creamy. Take care that
the cod does not stick. Scatter the browned garlic slices on top and
serve immediately.

NOTE It is wise to practise this technique with small quantities.
Should you come to disaster – i.e. should the sauce not turn to a
consistency somewhere between thick cream and mayonnaise – reduce
the whole thing to a thready purée in the processor, or with an
electric beater, to a version of Brandade, p. 104.

MEXICAN BACALAO

This recipe came from friends in Stockport who had it from a Mexican
girl who worked for them a few years ago. When she left, they missed
her beautiful presence but consoled themselves with this legacy that
she had bequeathed them. It is a marvellous dish for a party, or for a

holiday time, since it keeps well in the refrigerator for at least a week and can be eaten hot or cold.

I give the ingredients exactly as they came to me. The salt cod to use is the plump kind in plastic packages, which will not swell a great deal in the soaking. Should you be the lucky grower of good tomatoes, use them instead of canned purée, either wholly or in part. The essential thing, though, is to stick to preserved red peppers, the kind that come from Eastern Europe in jars.

Serves 8–10

1 kg (2 lb) salt cod, soaked for 24–36 hours
600 ml (1 pt) olive oil
10 cloves garlic, whole but peeled
6 large onions, sliced
2 handfuls of small parsley sprigs
5 × 150 g (5 oz) cans Italian tomato purée or 2 × 400 g (14 oz) cans
*   passata or canned tomatoes, chopped*
375 g (12 oz) preserved red peppers, drained, sliced
16–20 green olives
2 teaspoons sugar
salt, pepper

Remove any bones from the fish and flake it. Heat the oil in a large sauté pan or earthenware dish and fry the garlic until it is deep brown. Scoop out and discard the garlic. Put in the onion. Lower the heat and cook gently until it is transparent. Add the fish and stir together for a minute or so. Next, put in the parsley sprigs, then the tomato – if the sauce looks sinister at this point, don't worry as it comes out all right in the end. Simmer for 15 minutes. Add the peppers and olives. Simmer again until the fish is tender and the sauce blended – about 30 minutes. Sprinkle on the sugar and taste for seasoning.

Serve hot with a risotto (saffron risotto makes a fine contrast) or cold with a rice salad.

BACALHAU À BRAS

This much-loved dish of the vast salt cod repertoire of Portugal is a winner. It is savoury and unusual – to the Anglo-Saxon experience at least – and completely delicious with its balance of cod and potatoes, egg and olives. If you are feeling hard up, increase the potatoes and decrease the cod. The name puzzled me, but apparently it is the inventor. Blessings on Mr Bras!

Serves 8–9

1 kg (2 lb) salt cod, well soaked or 750 g (1½ lb) salt cod cheeks
1 kg (2 lb) potatoes, peeled
groundnut or sunflower oil for deep-frying
500 g (1 lb) onions, sliced
4 tablespoons olive oil
175 g (6 oz) butter
1 large clove garlic, sliced
salt, pepper
12 large eggs, beaten
1 small bunch parsley, chopped
24–30 black olives

Flake and cut the cod into rough strips, discarding any bone. Shred the potatoes into matchsticks and deep-fry them until they are soft and lightly coloured but not brown and crisp like chips. Drain well.

Soften the onion in the olive oil and a third of the butter over a low heat. Add the garlic and cook a little faster so that the onion is nicely caught with brown in an appetizing manner: do not overheat the fat or it will burn. Add the fish and continue cooking for another 5 or 6 minutes, stirring often. Add seasoning, then put the whole thing into a bowl and mix in the potatoes. All this can be done an hour or two in advance.

For the final stages, you need two large sauté pans – another solution, better from the point of view of flavour, is to cook a generous half of the mixture, then the rest for second helpings.

Melt the remaining butter and stir in the fish and potato to heat through. Pour in the beaten egg and go on stirring until the whole thing is bound lightly – *do not overcook*. Turn on to a warm dish, sprinkle with parsley, decorate with the olives and serve.

BRANDADE DE MORUE

Brandade has had its devotees ever since Grimod de la Reynière 'discovered' it in Languedoc and wrote down the recipe at the end of the eighteenth century. He concealed the name of the place where he first ate this cream of salt cod, which has led to much pleasurable but fruitless speculation. (Like Lobster à l'américaine – or armoricaine.) Was the place Béziers, the ancient cathedral town between Sète and Narbonne? Or was it Nîmes, where one cooked food shop at least sends brandade to customers all over France? To add to the mystery, an almost identical dish, *baccalà mantecato*, is a great speciality of Venice and the Veneto.

Brandade is a fascinating dish to make. Poor-looking greyish-white boards of dried cod are transformed into richness by the gentle attentions of olive oil and cream. Less gentle are the attentions of the cook, who must keep up a steady crushing of the ingredients, combined with a shaking of the pot (the name is said – by Grimod de la Reynière – to come from *brandir*, an old verb meaning to stir, shake and crush with energy, for a long time: one may wonder on what other occasion it might have been employed). Such a slow transformation of substances may sound tiresome in a busy life, but it has its own relaxed pleasure, and a delicious result. A consolation – fruit is the only possible follow-up. The modern recipe has changed little. I use cream, you may prefer to use rich milk and some butter instead.

Serves 6

¾–1 kg (1½–2 lb) dried salt cod
500–600 ml (1 pt) olive oil
1 large clove garlic, crushed, finely chopped (optional)
300 ml (10 fl oz) single cream or milk and cream
salt, pepper, nutmeg, lemon juice
18 small triangles of bread fried in olive oil
2 tablespoons finely chopped parsley

Soak the cod and cook it in the usual way. Remove and discard all bony parts, but keep the skin. This is often discarded, but as Ali-Bab remarks in his *Gastronomie Pratique*, it helps the flavour and the consistency of the brandade, being gelatinous.

Put the pieces of cod, and skin if used, into a stoneware or enamelled iron casserole, over a low, steady heat (with a heat-diffuser mat underneath, if gas is used). Have the oil, and garlic if used, together in a small pan, keeping warm. The same goes for the cream or milk and cream. Pour a little oil on to the cod, and crush the two together with a wooden spoon, moving the pan about. Then add some cream, or milk and cream. Continue in this way until oil and cream are finished. You should now have a coherent creamy mass, very white if you have omitted the skin, white flecked with grey if you haven't. Season with salt, pepper, nutmeg and lemon juice.

The thing to avoid is overheating, which could cause the brandade to separate. Should this happen, take the unorthodox step of putting the mixture into a bowl and beating it vigorously and, if possible, electrically. Or use the processor.

Serve either in the cooking dish (though this will probably be too large), or on a plainly coloured earthenware dish. Dip one corner of each triangle of fried bread first in the brandade, and then into the parsley, before tucking the croûton into the edge of the brandade as a garnish.

Any left over can be reheated another day, and served in tiny pastry cases. Or it can be made into little cakes – bind it with one or two eggs – dipped in egg and breadcrumbs, and fried.

NEW ENGLAND SALT COD DINNER

This kind of food is only good if it is properly done. You need to feel that it is something to relax over when you are really hungry and the weather is cold. The temptation is to cook the vegetables in a muddle, all together (except the beetroot of course) which usually means that nothing is quite right. The trickiest part for a cook in Britain will be finding salt belly of pork: fat green streaky bacon can be substituted, though these days you are most likely to get a watery fluid from it than proper fat.

Alan Davidson gives a very similar recipe to this one in *North Atlantic Seafood*. His version adds carrots, and substitutes egg sauce for parsley sauce.

Serves 6

750 g (1½ lb) salt cod, soaked, simmered until just tender
6 potatoes, boiled in their skins
6 boiled onions
12 small beetroot, baked in foil in the oven or boiled
parsley sauce made with cream*
175 g (6 oz) skinned salt pork, diced small

When the cod and vegetables are all ready, arrange them on a hot serving plate – skin the beetroot first, and the potatoes if you like. Keep them warm. Reheat the sauce and pour it into a jug.

Last of all, fry the salt pork in a heavy pan so that the fat runs from it and the little bits turn brown and crisp. Pour into a small hot jug, for people to help themselves, or else pour over the fish.

NEWFOUNDLANDERS' PIE (Tourte des Terre-Neuvas)

As one reads in Pierre Loti's novel (*see* Cod Introduction), the men who went fishing to Icelandic waters were known as *les islandais*, the icelanders. Others who went to Newfoundland were *les Terre-Neuvas*, and this is their recipe. I would say a dish for rejoicing when – if – they returned home in September.

Serves 6

500 g (1 lb) salt cod, soaked, simmered
375 g (12 oz) boiled potatoes, peeled, sliced
1 large onion, chopped
3 shallots, chopped
125 g (4 oz) butter
3–4 tablespoons chopped parsley
salt, pepper
750-g (1½-lb) piece of puff pastry
250 ml (8 fl oz) crème fraîche

While the cod and potatoes cool, stew the onion and shallots in half the butter until yellow and tender. Stir in the parsley and seasoning.

Roll out half the pastry to fit a 25-cm (10-inch) tart tin. Pile on the cod and potato in layers, interspersed with the onion and shallot mixture. Brush the pastry rim with water.

Roll out the remaining pastry large enough to make a lid. Cut a 4-cm (1½-inch) hole from the centre. Put the lid in place, pressing down the edges closely together. Decorate or score as you please. Brush over the top with a little of the cream. Chill half an hour, together with the circle cut from the lid.

Preheat the oven to gas 7, 220°C (425°F). When the temperature is set, slip in a baking sheet. Give it 3 or 4 minutes to heat up, then put the tart on the baking sheet. Place the circle of pastry beside it. Bake for 15 minutes, check the browning of the pastry and remove the circle if it is done. Give the tart another 15 minutes, lowering the heat if necessary.

Remove to a hot serving dish. Pour the rest of the cream into the pie through the central hole. Put on the circle of pastry and serve.

SALT COD FRITTERS

The kite-shaped boards of salt cod hanging from the fishmonger's hooks look far too unyielding and dry for fritters. In fact, they work quite well (especially if you use only the thickest part) but results will be even better if you use the undried salt cod that you buy in packages. Be sure to soak the fish well. You do not *need* to cook it, but I think that the result is a little better if you give it 5 minutes' gentle simmering. Then drain and cool it.

Cod's cheeks or tongues are good for tiny fritters: soak well and cook briefly as above.

Serves 6

750 g (1½ lb) salt cod, soaked
batter with beaten egg white*

SERVE WITH:
lemon quarters
or *skordalia and beetroot salad, p. 232*
or *tomato sauce* plus a chopping of walnuts, black olives and capers*
or *tomato and red pepper salad*
or *mayonnaise**
or *mayonnaise derivatives – tartare, aioli, anchovy, etc.*

Simmer the fish for up to 5 minutes in water (or use half water, half milk). It should be just tender enough to eat with pleasure. After removing bones and, if you like, any skin, drain and dry it extremely carefully. Cut it into roughly 5-cm (2-inch) pieces.

Make the batter and the sauce or salad before you start deep-frying the cod. Have everyone sitting ready, as fritters are best from the pan.

Heat the oil to 180°C (350°F). Dip each piece in the batter and deep-fry. Be careful not to overload the pan. When the batter coating is crisp and a deep golden colour, the fritters are done.

SALTFISH AND AKEE

One of the great dishes of salt cod cookery from Jamaica is worth making in quantity since the left-overs taste so good served in the halves of a very ripe breadfruit baked in buttered foil in the oven. Or it can be used as a stuffing for some of the livelier squashes, crooknecks or patty pans. Or as a filling for pasties and little tarts.

Akee, which we have to buy in tins, in Britain at any rate, looks like heaped billows of scrambled egg. The texture is soft and succulent. Ask anybody what it is and they would be pushed to give you an answer. And when you tell them the answer, they might well be keen to avoid it. Akee is properly the name of a tree, originally from West Africa, that was introduced to Jamaica from Guinea by Captain Bligh of the *Bounty* at the end of the eighteenth century. Hence its botanic name, *Blighia sapida*. The fruits are red and warty. When fully ripe, they burst open to show round black seeds, like berries, each one reposing in a creamy yellow cushion, a surreal padded egg cup – the aril – which is the part you eat. But, and this is quite a 'but', unless the fruit has 'ripened to the point of voluntary opening, it is a deadly poison. No overly ripe, fallen, discoloured or unripe fruit dare be eaten,' (I quote from *The Joy of Cooking* by Rombauer and Beck) 'and the greatest care must be used to remove all seeds before cooking as these are always poisonous.' So too is the pinkish pulp inside.

What heroine of the hearth I wonder first discovered the joy of eating akee, the right part in precisely the right condition to be eaten? Did she conduct controlled experiments with the tribe? Did she thoughtfully consider a succession of gastronomic deaths and reach – at last – the right conclusion? It is perhaps a relief to open a tin, rather than trust the judgement of a market seller.

The dish can of course be made without akee, but it neither looks nor tastes quite so good. It has occurred to me to use girolles instead, for their colour and consistency, but I have never had both girolles and salt cod in the house together. Scrambled egg is not a bad substitute at all visually, and it tastes fine if not exactly right.

Serves 6–8

500 g (1 lb) salt cod, soaked and simmered
500 g (1 lb) akee (contents of a large tin)
125 g (4 oz) salt pork, diced
lard or bacon fat (see recipe)
175 g (6 oz) chopped onion
1 green sweet pepper, seeded, cut in strips
1 teaspoon green chilli, seeded, chopped
4 spring onions or Welsh onions or very young leeks, chopped
good pinch of thyme
375 g (12 oz) tomatoes, skinned, seeded, chopped
6–8 streaky bacon rashers, fried crisp
1 tomato cut in 8 wedges
parsley or watercress to garnish

Drain, cool and flake the cod, discarding any bones and skin. If you are using fresh akee, put it into boiling water and simmer until tender: salt it cautiously (in view of the saltiness of the fish). Otherwise drain the tinned akee. Mix with the fish.

In a large sauté pan, fry the pork in its own fat, adding a little lard or bacon fat if necessary. When the dice are brown, scoop them with a slotted spoon into the bowl of akee and cod. In the fat remaining, fry the onion, pepper, chilli, spring onions or leeks, thyme and tomatoes, adding each item as the one before it wilts and softens. Cook to an unwatery sauce. Put in the akee, cod and pork to heat through. Check the seasoning.

Turn it on to a hot dish, scatter with crumbled or chopped crisp bacon, the tomato wedges and parsley or watercress, and serve.

ZURRUKUTUNA

A soup that can be turned into a meal by the addition of poached eggs. If you are lucky enough to have a supply of those dried Spanish peppers called ñoras, this is an occasion to use them. The first substitute would be other dried mild peppers (e.g. anchos), then grilled, seeded and skinned red peppers. The last resort would be canned peppers, or bottled peppers. This is a particularly useful store cupboard dish for winter meals.

Serves 4

250 g (8 oz) salt cod, soaked, cooked or 175 g (6 oz) dried salt cod, soaked, cooked
2 ñoras, soaked or 2 fresh red peppers, quartered, seeded, grilled
olive oil
4 large cloves garlic, halved
4 slices stale bread, crusts removed
4 tablespoons finely chopped onion
black pepper
4 poached eggs (optional)
cayenne pepper

Bone and flake the cod. Remove the skin if you like. Scrape the fleshy part from the ñoras, discarding the skin; or skin and purée the fresh peppers.

Heat enough oil in an earthenware pot on top of the stove (use a heat-diffuser if necessary) to cover the base comfortably and fry the garlic to a light brown. Remove, crush and add to the peppers. In the oil, fry the bread until it, too, is nicely browned on both sides.

Pour off any surplus oil, add the onion with the peppers and garlic to the pot, season with black pepper and pour on 1 litre (1¾ pt) water. Simmer for 15 minutes, crushing the bread down so that it disintegrates into the water. Add the cod and simmer for a further 15 minutes. Add extra water at this stage, if the soup is too thick, and adjust the seasoning.

Have ready four very hot bowls, pour in the soup and slip a poached egg into each one, if you like. Dust the soup lightly with cayenne pepper. Serve immediately.

COLEY see COD

CONGER EEL see A FEW WORDS ABOUT . . . CONGER EEL

CRABS

Before the war, I remember that one of the few attractive things about our depressed town was the regular arrival of fisherwomen from Cullercoats, further up the coast, in Northumberland. They came with baskets of crabs and other fish balanced on their heads. They swung down the hill by our house in long striped skirts. Their weatherbeaten faces were shaded – incongruously it seemed to me – by the prettiest of lilac-sprigged sunbonnets. They were tough, unsmiling, magnificent if you like, and their fish was fresh, their crabs the best in the world. On rare days when we went to Seahouses or St Mary's lighthouse, we would stop by the row of little houses at Cullercoats and choose a crab to take home, weighing them thoughtfully in our hands to see if they felt heavy for their size. No crabs were ever so good.

Of course you will not agree with me – particularly if you live in Maryland, where crabs have restaurants to themselves. I am not sure if I agree with myself either, having tasted now the sweet spider crabs from the Atlantic coast of France; but those Cullercoat crabs set up a standard of deliciousness in my memory, however embroidered by time, which I cannot escape from. The point is that in this country at least, crab is a luxury that many people can afford, without feeling guilty. The price of lobsters have soared, scallops have joined them, oysters are not yet the poor man's food, as they once were and as they may be again. Prawns and scampi, toughened by freezing, are a disappointment. But fresh crabs, like fresh mussels, are an unalloyed pleasure.

Unless your fishmonger is beyond reproach, the crab you boil yourself is far superior to the ready-to-eat kind. Be wary about ready-to-eat crab meat too. Sometimes it is mixed with foreign substances to pad it out. This may be approved by health inspectors, but does absolutely nothing for the true crab. Crab is a rich filling substance – it should not be weighed down by stodgy and concealed matter.

There is no way out of it. Boiling and excavating your own crab is best. It is also a pleasure. Particularly if you can find someone to read to you, as you jab away.

HOW TO PREPARE CRABS

The point of success lies in salting the water adequately. Even seawater needs extra strength. An egg should float in the brine – use about 175 g (6 oz) salt to 2–2¼ litres (3½–4 pt) of water. Put in the crab, fasten on the lid, and bring it to the boil, or rather to the simmer. Give it 15 minutes for the first 500 g (1 lb); 10 minutes for the second, third and so on. Remove from the pan to cool.

When the crab is cold, lay it on its back. Twist off the legs and claws. Push back and remove the pointed flap, and take out the central body part – a large mass of thin bone, crab meat and 'dead men's fingers'. Remove the small mouth part, too, by pressing down on it: it will snap away.

Have two basins ready. Scoop out all the soft yellowish-brown meat from the shell – the best part – and put it in one basin. Add any yellowish meat still adhering to the central body. Crack the large claws and remove the sweet pinkish-white meat and put it into the second basin. The quick part of the work is now over. Settle down with a larding needle or crochet hook, a small mallet and a teaspoon, and poke out all the residue of delicious white fibres from the central body, and the meat from the legs. Be careful not to add tiny pieces of thin shell to the basin. A good ¾–1 kg (1½–2 lb) crab can yield 375 g (12 oz) of edible deliciousness if you are prepared to be a little patient. This is enough for three people, or more if you are going to add sauces, salad ingredients and so on.

The large shell can be turned into a container for the crab. You will notice a beautifully curved line on the undershell. Give a few hard taps on the inner side of it, by the gaping hole, and the rough pieces will fall away along the line. Scrub out the shell, and brush it lightly with oil if you want to give it a gloss.

CRAB MAYONNAISE AND CRAB LOUIS

A good way of serving crab is to make it the focal point of a large salad. There is nothing original in the idea. To the usual ingredients, add slices of avocado pear (brushed with lemon juice to stop them blackening); this goes well with crab and mayonnaise. Hard-boil some eggs, cream the yolks with crab meat and a little mayonnaise, and fill the whites with this mixture. Try differently flavoured mayonnaise sauces.

Here is one version of an American mayonnaise, the main point of which is the chilli sauce. Sometimes finely chopped green pepper is included.

Crab Louis

Mix together the following ingredients:

> Serves 6
>
> *mayonnaise, made with 2 egg yolks, 150 ml (5 fl oz) oil and the usual*
> *   flavourings**
> *125 ml (4 fl oz) double cream, whipped*
> *60 ml (2 fl oz) chilli sauce*
> *2 tablespoons grated onion*
> *2 tablespoons chopped parsley*
> *dash of cayenne* or *Tabasco*
> *1 teaspoon green pepper (optional)*
> *extra lime or lemon juice*

Arrange the crab meat on lettuce cover with the dressing and add the usual hard-boiled eggs, tomatoes and so on.

ACHILTIBUIE CRAB SOUFFLÉ

Mark Irvine's Summer Isles Hotel, north-west of Ullapool in Scotland, is so far from the main road, along a single track, that he reckons it is a test of character for any guest arriving the first time. We certainly wondered where we were going to end up, the country would have seemed deserted if it had not been for the astonishing number of cars, even lorries, that we made way for. After 25 km (16 miles), we found ourselves on a narrowing tongue of land between beautiful pale sandy bays and turned left to Achiltibuie village and an hotel of reassuring comfort and warmth.

Sarah Irvine presides in the kitchen and has a much wider range of ingredients than you would think possible in such a place. She flavours her soufflés with crab bought from the fishermen in the village, or with her husband's artichokes. He seems able to grow anything, either in his hydroponicum behind the hotel, or in plastic tunnels on the land which slopes down to the sea.

Serves 8–10

butter and dry crumbs for 2 soufflé dishes, or 8–10 individual dishes
90 g (3 oz) butter
60 g (2 oz) plain flour
450 ml (15 fl oz) milk
½ small bay leaf
100 g (3½ oz) grated onion
salt, pepper
1 tablespoon anchovy essence
2 teaspoons made English mustard
375 g (12 oz) crab meat
8 eggs, separated

Brush the dishes with soft butter and scatter with crumbs. Shake out the surplus.

Make up the soufflé base by melting the butter, stirring in the flour and cooking it gently for 2 minutes. Heat the milk and stir it in to make a smooth sauce. Add the bay leaf, onion and seasoning. Cook for about 20 minutes, tasting from time to time and removing the bay leaf before it becomes too dominant. Remove the pan from the heat and add the anchovy essence, mustard and crab meat. Beat in the egg yolks. Whisk the whites until stiff and fold them in, a little at first to slacken the mixture.

Divide the mixture between the dishes. Bake the larger soufflés at gas 6, 200°C (400°F) for 12–15 minutes, the smaller ones for 7–9 minutes. Serve immediately.

VARIATION   Instead of crab, use the cooked and sieved bases of 8 artichokes, and use crumbled dry Stilton to flavour the sauce rather than anchovy and mustard. Allow about 175 g (6 oz), but add it to taste.

BRETON CRAB SOUP

One evening in 1884, Edmond de Goncourt and Emile Zola were invited to dinner by their publisher, Charpentier. It was so delicious that de Goncourt wondered if Charpentier was about to abscond with the cash, and became slightly nervous about the money owing on his novel *Chérie*. The star turn was crab soup, a Breton dish little known in Paris at that time. It was like a shellfish bisque, but 'with something finer to it, something tastier, something more of the ocean'.

> 2 medium-sized cooked crabs
> 1 carrot, sliced
> 1 onion stuck with 3 cloves
> bouquet garni
> 250 ml (8 fl oz) dry white wine, preferably Muscadet
> fish, veal or chicken stock
> 150 g (5 oz) rice
> up to 150 ml (5 fl oz) single cream
> salt, pepper, cayenne

Remove the meat from the cooked crabs and set it aside. Put all the debris into a pan with the carrot, onion, bouquet, wine and enough stock to cover everything generously. Simmer for 30 minutes. Extract the toughest pieces of claw shell, then whizz the rest in a liquidizer to extract every hint of flavour into the liquid. Pour through a sieve into the rinsed out pan – do not press too hard, just enough to extract the softer part.

In a separate pan, meanwhile, cook the rice in some more stock, or water. When very tender, put it into the liquidizer with most of the crab meat (keep enough for the garnish). Blend to a purée and add to the crab shell stock. Taste and dilute further if necessary with more stock or water. Add cream to taste and reheat to just under boiling point. Put in extra seasoning, with a good pinch of cayenne, and the crab pieces you kept for the garnish. Leave for another 5 minutes, still without boiling, then serve with croûtons or bread fried in butter.

CHILLED GUMBO BISQUE

The gumbo stews of the southern states of America are often given their defining character by okra. Here is a delicious soup in which they may seem subdued: nonetheless they are essential to the satin smoothness and unusual flavour of the soup. This recipe is an anglicized version of a bisque devised by a New York friend to use up a can of crab claws. I never find canned shellfish satisfactory – it is almost as tasteless as the frozen kind – and prefer to use fresh crab claws which are sometimes sold separately, or fresh prawns in their shells. The important thing is to have some hard debris to flavour the stock, as well as soft meat for finishing the soup.

> 300–375 g (10–12 oz) fresh boiled crab claws or prawns in their shells
> 1 litre (1¾ pt) fish or chicken stock, plus 450 ml (15 fl oz) water
>   or 1 kg (2 lb) fish trimmings plus 1½ litres (2½ pt) water
>   and 250 ml (8 fl oz) dry white wine or cider
> 100 g (3½ oz) chopped celery
> 100 g (3½ oz) chopped onion
> ½ green pepper, chopped
> 2–3 tablespoons butter
> 250 g (8 oz) okra
> 1 medium can tomatoes (approx. 400 g/14 oz)
> 100 g (3½ oz) rice
> salt, pepper, cayenne

Shell crab claws or prawns. Put the debris into a large pan. Set aside the meat. To the pan, add stock and water, or fish trimmings, water and wine or cider. Simmer for 45 minutes to extract the flavours, then strain into a measuring jug and add water to make 1½ litres (2½ pt). Meanwhile, soften the celery, onion and pepper in butter. Prepare and cut the okra in slices 1 cm (½ inch) thick. Add them with stock, tomatoes and rice to the vegetables. Season. Cover and simmer for an hour. Purée in the blender, dilute further if you like, then chill overnight or for at least 4 hours. Serve with some or all of the crab meat or prawns.

CRAB OR SHRIMP SOUP

Crabs, shrimps, prawns and freshwater crayfish can all be used to make a bisque, even the tiny crabs you pick up on holiday.

Use the Bisque de homard recipe (p. 211) as a guide. You will need 1–1½ kg (2–3 lb) of crab or shrimps. Substitute water for fish stock and add 500 g (1 lb) or more of good tomatoes. With tiny shellfish there is obviously no point in attempting to separate the meat from the shell, but it is important to break them up in a rough and ready fashion, about halfway through the main cooking time, so that none of their flavour is wasted.

For a more southern flavour, substitute olive oil for butter, include garlic and saffron in the herbs, and cook some fine pasta (forget the rice) in the soup after it has been sieved.

This recipe shows that no fish, however tiny, are useless to the cook, so long as the quantity is there.

CRAB TART (Tarte soufflée au crabe)

Use crab meat that is fresh for this tart, preferably from crabs you have cooked yourself. The recipe is easily adapted to other shellfish, with appropriate changes or additions to the seasoning.

In Britain, we like our pie pastry to be short and crumbly; if we need something stronger, for instance for raised pies, we use a hot water crust. The French *pâte brisée* lies somewhere between the two; it has to hold the filling for an open flan or tart, and yet be crisp and thin. One thing that our shortcrust and *pâte brisée* have in common is the need for coolness and quick working; marble is the ideal surface. Water should be iced; one's hands cool. Rests for the dough in the refrigerator are essential, both before and after rolling. The one utensil you really need is a dough scraper.

Serves 6–8

FOR THE PÂTE BRISÉE
200 g (7 oz) plain flour, plus extra if necessary
pinch of salt
1½ egg yolks
about 3 tablespoons iced water
100 g (3½ oz) cold but malleable butter, cut in four

FOR THE FILLING
about 500 g (1 lb) meat from two large crabs
salt, pepper, cayenne, mace to taste
3 eggs, separated
200–250 ml (7–8 fl oz) crème fraîche or half soured, half double cream
about 1 tablespoon each grated Parmesan and Gruyère cheese

For the pastry, sift the floor and salt on to a marble slab or cold Formica surface. Make a well in the centre and put in the egg yolks, 2 tablespoons iced water and the butter. With your fingers, work the yolk mixture together, crushing the butter. Then gradually pull in the flour until you have a soft dough. Add the extra iced water if needed. Use the dough scraper to help you form the ball of dough which should not be tacky. Press the dough away from you with the heel of your hand, two or three times, using a light sprinkling of flour if necessary. Wrap in foil, parchment or cling film and chill for at least 30 minutes or up to 2 days – after that, you can store in the freezer.

When you are ready to make the tart, roll out the dough to line a 23–25-cm (9–10-inch) shortcrust pastry case and chill again. Preheat the oven to gas 7, 220°C (425°F) and bake the pastry case blind until firm but not coloured.

For the filling, check over the crab meat to make sure that there are no bits of shell in it. Season it to taste. Beat in the egg yolks, and the crème fraîche or creams, and add the grated cheese gradually to taste. Whisk the whites until they are stiff and then fold them in. Pile the filling into the tart and put in the oven at the same temperature as the pastry case was baked. Lower the oven to gas 5, 190°C (375°F) after 2 or 3 minutes and leave the tart for a further 30 minutes, or until the filling is puffed and slightly browned. If you like a creamy centre, remove the tart from the oven while it is wobbly under the crust in the middle.

Serve with a salad and rye or wholemeal bread.

GRAPEFRUIT AND CRAB SALAD

In hollowed-out grapefruit shells, put a salad made of crab meat mixed with some of the fruit's skinned, diced segments, after first lining the shell with a lettuce leaf, so that it frills slightly over the edge. The rest of the grapefruit flesh can be used for another dish. If you like, also add some diced cucumber or tomato, with wedges of hard-boiled egg.

Put a spoonful of mayonnaise on top of each filling, to which you can add a little brandy if you like. Put a neat piece of grapefruit on top. Serve chilled, with extra mayonnaise and brown bread and butter.

You may substitute shelled prawns for the crab.

POTTED CRAB

In the past, potted meats and fish and shellfish were a practical way of storing food since the top layer of clarified butter kept out the air and preserved the contents underneath in a reasonable manner. They were our equivalent to pâtés and terrines in French cookery. What they often depended on for success was hard pounding by some poor young creature learning his or her trade in the kitchen. As this kind of labour disappeared, so did potted meat and fish, although odd examples survived – often very nastily – in some parts of the country where they had always been made by butchers: some Midlands potted beef I tasted on one of my tours of Britain was as disgusting as any we had been served in our northern boarding school during the war.

Now there is a revival of such dishes, thanks to the introduction of electric mixers, blenders and processors. Indeed, potted kipper and mackerel pastes have become too much of a cliché for comfort.

Potted shellfish can be very successful. The first recipe I give below is Elizabeth David's traditional formula, which is followed by a more elaborate version from Michael Quinn.

Elizabeth David's Potted Crab

This is one of the best ways of eating crab, very rich and delicious. It is taken from her pamphlet *English Potted Meats and Fish Pastes*. This method of serving crab is particularly successful as a lunch dish, to be followed by a green salad, or a salad of purple-sprouting broccoli. It works well for lobster, too.

Serves 4–6

1 kg (2 lb) crab, boiled
black pepper, mace, nutmeg, cayenne pepper
lemon juice
salt (see *recipe*)
about 250 g (8 oz) slightly-salted or unsalted butter
clarified butter to seal

Pick all the meat from the crab, being careful to keep the firm and creamy parts separate. Season both with spices and lemon juice – salt may be necessary if you bought the crab ready boiled. There will be about 375 g (12 oz) meat.

Choose an attractive round stoneware pot, or an oval one. Pack the crab meat into it, in layers. (If you prefer it, use four to six individual pots or soufflé dishes.) Melt the butter and pour it over the crab meat. There should be enough just to cover it – the quantity required will depend on the amount of crab meat you had the patience to pick out of the shell, and on whether you used one or half-a-dozen pots. It is only fair to point out that Danish – especially Lurpak – or French butter gives the best result with potted meat and fish: it is made in a different way from English butter, and has a milder flavour and better consistency for this kind of dish.

Leave to cool, then cover with clarified butter: a thin layer if the crab is going to be eaten within twenty-four hours; a 1-cm (½-inch) layer if it is being kept for a few days – in this latter case, add a foil covering so that the butter does not dry out and contract from the edge of the pot, so spoiling the seal.

Michael Quinn's Potted Crab

Serves 6

75 g (2½ oz) chopped shallot
2 tablespoons dry white wine
2 tablespoons Noilly Prat
pinch of mixed spice
pinch of cinnamon
pinch of ginger
pinch of crushed coriander seeds
pinch of cayenne pepper
pinch of nutmeg
400 g (14 oz) unsalted butter, cubed
300 g (10 oz) white crab meat
300 g (10 oz) brown crab meat
salt

Put shallots, wine, Noilly Prat and spices into a pan and boil down to a juicy purée, with the shallot tender and the liquor reduced to just over a couple of tablespoons. Stir in the bits of butter, and when they are melted, simmer for 20 minutes. Remove, cool 30 minutes and sieve into a bowl.

Set the bowl over ice and whisk until thick and creamy but not hard. Mix in the crab meat. Taste and add salt and other extra seasoning as required. Spoon into six pots, cover with foil and chill in the refrigerator. Serve with brown bread and butter, and with some bitter-leaved salad.

SOFT-SHELL CRABS

Soft-shell crabs are a speciality of Venice, and of the southern coast of North America. They are not a separate species, but crabs which are 'moulting' – i.e. they have shed their shells, and the new one is still fragile. This sudden loss of weight means that they rise to the surface and can easily be caught. The Venetian molecchie, a May delicacy, are tiny, about 2½–5 cm (1–2 inches) across. They are washed, then soaked for a while in beaten egg (which they largely absorb). Just before the meal, they are drained, shaken in flour and deep-fried. One eats the whole thing, shell, claws, the lot, and it tastes like a crisp delicious biscuit.

In America the crabs are larger – two or three are a reasonable portion – but they are treated in much the same way. Sometimes they are grilled and brushed with melted butter. Tartare sauce or a similarly flavoured mayonnaise is served with them.

SEAFOOD PUDDING (Strata)

This is one of the best bread-and-butter puddings, but made with crab or prawns. For economy, a proportion of lightly cooked and flaked white fish can be used with the crab or prawns, but never more than half.

Serves 6

butter
12 slices from a small sandwich loaf
meat from a large crab or 250 g (8 oz) shelled crab or shelled prawns
salt, pepper, cayenne
1 tender celery stalk, chopped finely
1 tablespoon chopped onion
150 ml (5 fl oz) mayonnaise
3 tablespoons mixed herbs – chopped parsley, tarragon, chervil and chives
3 tablespoons grated Parmesan cheese
approx. 175 g (6 oz) Gruyère, fontina or Gouda cheese, grated
4 eggs
250 ml (8 fl oz) milk
250 ml (8 fl oz) single cream

Butter the bread and cut off the crusts. Season the crab or prawns. Mix the celery and onion with the mayonnaise, herbs and Parmesan and then fold into the shellfish. Make six sandwiches with the mixture.

Butter a dish that will take the sandwiches in a single layer. Cut them in half and place in the dish. Dot with the grated Gruyère, fontina or Gouda. Beat the eggs with the milk and cream and pour into the dish. Leave in the fridge for 2 hours or longer (overnight will not hurt).

Bake in the oven, preheated to gas 4, 180°C (350°F), for 30–40 minutes, lowering the heat as the top browns.

CRAWFISH *see* LOBSTERS

CROAKERS & DRUMS *see* A FEW WORDS ABOUT . . .
  CROAKERS & DRUMS

CUTTLEFISH *see* SQUID

DAB *see* SOLE

DOGFISH *see* A FEW WORDS ABOUT . . . DOGFISH

DOLPHINFISH *see* A FEW WORDS ABOUT . . .
  DOLPHINFISH

DORADO *see* A FEW WORDS ABOUT . . . DOLPHINFISH

DUBLIN BAY PRAWNS *see* LOBSTERS

†EELS & ELVERS

(*Anguilla anguilla* & *Anguilla rostrata*)

I love eel. Sometimes I think it is my favourite fish. It is delicate, but rich; it falls neatly from the bone; grilled to golden brown and flecked with dark crustiness from a charcoal fire, it makes the best of all picnic food; stewed in red wine, cushioned with onions and mushrooms, bordered with triangles of fried bread, it is the meal for cold nights in autumn; smoked and cut into elegant fillets, it starts a wedding feast or a Christmas Eve dinner with style and confidence. Its skin is so tough that it was used to join the two parts of a flail together (think of the strain on that join as the flails thumped down to winnow the corn at harvest), or to make a whip for a boy's top, or to bind the elastic to his catapult. The eel has picturesque habits, often lurking in old mill leats under willow roots, until it is seduced by a waisted eel-trap set by the sluice gate.

It has mystery, too. Aristotle wondered why no eel was ever found with roe or milt. This question had become a matter for poetry, or poetical prosing, by the time of Izaak Walton – 'others say, that as pearls are made of glutinous dew drops, which are condensed by the sun's heat in those countries, so Eels are bred of a particular dew'. The true poet, though, of this strange creature, was not Izaak Walton, or any other mystified ancient, but a biologist; the great Danish biologist Johannes Schmidt. In 1922, after twenty-five years of back-tracking eel larvae, he came right over the spawning ground, the correct 'particular dew'.

The first larva was found by chance near the Faroe Islands in 1904; a willow-leaf of transparency, 77 mm (3 inches) long and, as it turned out, three years old. Other smaller larvae were found in the following years, further away from the coasts of Europe. Schmidt realized that if he could follow this trail of diminishing larvae, he would come to their home. Which he did in 1922 (the First World War had held things up). Right over the spawning ground, at the seaweedy eastern side of the Sargasso Sea, he brought up in his net the tiniest larvae of all – 5 mm (¼ inch) long.

Millions of them radiate out in all directions. Elvers of the American eel, *Anguilla rostrata*, share the same spawning grounds as the European eel's, but veer to the west and have only a short journey to make by comparison. In a year, they reach the East Coast and wriggle in vast troops up rivers from the Gulf of the St Lawrence to Mexico. Of the elvers of *Anguilla anguilla*, only those caught in the Gulf Stream survive and make the journey to Europe. There, almost in sight of land, the willow-leaf becomes a wriggling, vigorous, worm-like object, the glass-eel or elver, ready to swarm up the rivers of Europe from the Atlantic, the Mediterranean and the Black Sea. (Apparently the slowness of larval growth increased over unimaginable time, as the continents drifted slowly apart: the eels clung tenaciously both to their spawning ground, and to their familiar rivers, however long the journey between them became.)

The elvers now come together in broods. They can be seen stringing along for miles in a yard-wide cordon or eel-fare (from which we have the word elver), pushing upstream at night with a strength incredible to anyone who has bought 500 g (1 lb) of elvers, feeble, thread-like things, from Gloucester market. Winds, tides, the hours of daylight, and of darkness which is their travelling time, all affect their speed, but they aren't stopped by obstacles in their way. One French biologist remarked that he had seen them pass waterfalls, weirs, locks. He had seen them climb vertical walls, lock walls, even coming out of the water so long as there was a little moisture. The bodies of the casualties stick to the walls to make a sort of ladder for the push of elvers behind. They can wriggle themselves through the narrowest cracks ... 'and so they manage to populate the smallest stretches of water, even those which might seem to have no connection at all with a river'.

It is at night, between ebb and falling tide, that the Severn elver-fisherman sets out. He carries a scoop net, and a bucket for the catch; he has a lamp too, and sticks to support it. The elvers are mainly dispatched to the eel farms of northern Europe, but some are kept for the housewives of the Severn area as a spring delicacy for suppertime.

If you live anywhere near Gloucester, it is worth making a visit in March (or April according to the season) to find elvers, to see the elver-fisherman's equipment in the Folk Museum in Westgate Street, and buy an excellent illustrated guide to the Severn Fishery collection, by John Neufville Taylor. At Frampton-on-Severn, there is an annual elver-eating competition: the record – 500 g (1 lb) in a minute – is held by the village garage mechanic.

The elvers which survive the journey, and the attentions of fishermen, grow slowly to maturity in the hidden crannies of streams. Young eels are yellowish at first (yellow eels are not worth eating), then after eight years or more their flanks turn to silver and they are ready for the long swim home. In autumn, the ones who can return downstream, avoiding nets stretched across many rivers, and barriers of basketwork and reeds, with more or less success. These silver eels, mature eels, are the best. They are caught in tons at the mouths of some rivers: at Comacchio on the Po, it has been known for 1,000 tons to be caught in a single night. A favourite dish there is a simple soup of eel layered with slices of onion, carrot, and celery and seasoned with parsley and lemon rind. The eel is covered with water, and halfway through the cooking a spoonful or two of tomato concentrate and wine vinegar are added.

Once in salt water, the silver eel streaks out for the Sargasso Sea, thousands of miles away, fathoms down, along dark cold currents, with no light or fishing nets to impede its path. Eel from the Black Sea may take a year, but eel from Western Europe will do it in about six months, ready to spawn in the spring.

Only the European eel, *Anguilla anguilla*, makes so arduous and – to our mind – so moving a journey (other species, *Anguilla rostrata*, or *japonica*, or *australis*, have their spawning grounds comparatively close to the streams of North America, or Japan or Australia). As the salmon knows its way back to the river where it was born, so the eel knows its way back to the Sargasso Sea – but how much longer a journey that is. Mature eels are never found returning to Europe, so it seems that once they have spawned they die exhausted by the double effort: 'The Sargasso Sea is at once their grave, and the cradle of their descendants.'[1]

As to the elvers which are sent to eel-farms, they are destined to lead a pampered life, with the result that they will reach maturity in only two or three years. At Le Croisic in Brittany, old salt-marsh workings have been turned into great basins to accommodate the elvers or *civelles* of the Loire. Their seawater is regularly changed to

[1] L Bertin

avoid pollution, they are anxiously scrutinized for the first hints of disease, and their favourite food is flung to them in abundant quantity. Fish-farming seems to be more satisfactory than intensive meat-farming, because the end-product has a much better flavour. Nobody, I think, could tell the difference between eel-farm eels and the ones we are often given from the Loire. Both are absolutely delicious, the occasion for rejoicing.

WHAT TO DO WITH ELVERS

Elvers are extremely filling; I think you will find that 750 g (1 ½ lb) is enough for four people with good appetites. When you set out to buy them, take an old, clean pillowcase into which the fishmonger can tip them. At home, add a large handful of kitchen salt to the elvers, and swish the pillowcase about in a big bowl of water. Squeeze firmly to remove as much water as possible. Then add another handful of salt, and repeat the process with more cold water. This may be enough to get rid of the slight sliminess of the elvers, but be prepared to wash them a third time, and to pick them over continuously to get rid of bits of twig and grass, the general murk of the full river.

Exhausted after an evening's work at the swirling mass, I can never face cooking and eating them at once. Some go into water in a covered bowl in the refrigerator for the next day: the rest, divided into convenient quantities, are tied into plastic bags set in refrigerator boxes and put into the freezer for later use, without further preparation. The cold kills them. They store well. This I learned in Spain, surprised to be served elvers at several restaurants at the end of September, right out of season: my informant, a knowing waiter in a Salamanca restaurant just by the covered market, added that quantities of elvers came in from Britain as Spanish rivers could not provide enough of such a favourite delicacy. This reminded me bitterly that it is impossible to buy eels in most parts of Britain – and America – because they are flown off to Holland. There are few treats more appreciated by North Europeans than smoked eel and schnaps.

GLOUCESTER STYLE   Fry 8 rashers of very fat bacon until crisp. Take the rashers from the pan, and fry 500 g (1 lb) elvers in the bacon fat. When they turn white – after a few seconds – stir in a couple of beaten, seasoned eggs, to make a kind of omelette. Eat with the bacon. Don't overcook the elvers; the omelette should just be set, not at all leathery.

KEYNSHAM STYLE   Keynsham is a small town between Bath and Bristol which, according to the 1748 edition of Defoe's *Tour through Great Britain*, used to supply both cities with elver cakes. The elvers were well seasoned and baked in shortcrust pastry for about 20 minutes. Modern oven setting would be fairly hot (gas 5, 190°C/375°F).

LOIRE STYLE   Put 500 g (1 lb) elvers into a saucepan and cover them with cold water. Add some salt and a bay leaf. Bring the water to boiling point and simmer until they are white. Line a colander with muslin and pour the eels into it – leave them to cool.

When you want to eat the elvers, melt 100 g (3½ oz) butter in a large frying pan with a crushed clove of garlic. Allow the garlic to cook slowly in the melted butter for a few seconds, then add the elvers. Turn them about over a gentle heat until they are coated with the butter and very hot. Sprinkle them generously with chopped parsley; serve straightaway with bread and butter and dry white wine.

SPANISH STYLE   *Angulas en cazuelita*, elvers in little pots, come bubbling hot to table in Spanish restaurants, with little flat wooden forks to spear them with. For 3 or 4 people, you need about 500 g (1 lb) elvers. Heat 8 tablespoons of olive oil with 2 red hot chillies, slit into two and seeded. Crush them down into the oil so that they colour it slightly, and put in 4 large, skinned, halved cloves of garlic: keep the heat moderate so that the oil is well-flavoured by both items before the garlic turns a deep golden brown. At this point, remove the garlic and chillies, and tip in the elvers, swirling them round in the pan until they are opaque. This takes a minute or two, not long. Salt them, then divide between three or four well-heated earthenware pots and rush them to table. Provide plenty of bread and dry white wine.

WHITEBAIT STYLE   Turn the drained and dry elvers into a plastic or paper bag with some seasoned flour and shake them about so that they are coated with flour. Tip into a chip basket, allowing surplus flour to fall off (into the sink or on to a piece of paper). Fry them in hot deep fat for a few moments until they are crisp; give them a second frying time at a higher temperature, like chips, if they aren't crisp in a few moments the first time. Serve with lemon quarters, and brown bread and butter.

To my way of thinking, the Loire and Spanish styles are the best way of eating elvers. Some cookery books allow 250 g (8 oz) per person: I find that 125 g (4 oz) is plenty. With any slightly unusual food, you should never give people the chance to feel surfeited, because this will increase any lurking quivers of revulsion. Small quantities, well cooked, leave a desire for more on another occasion.

HOW TO CHOOSE AND PREPARE EELS

Eels should be bought alive. Insist on this (unless your fishmonger can be trusted when he says the eels on sale have just been killed that morning). Then ask the fishmonger to kill it for you.

Many recipes demand skinned eel, but for grilling and baking I find that the skin acts as a valuable barding layer. And when it is crinkly brown and charred from a fire of charcoal or vine prunings, it is good to eat as well: those who don't like it can easily cut it away at this stage. Certain dishes would be less appealing with the dark skin of the eel, matelote or a pie for instance, but consider the matter before you rush in to have it skinned.

Although the fishmonger will skin the eel for you – and he should have no hesitation, considering the price you are about to pay – it is prudent to know exactly what to do in case an angling husband or neighbour presents you with an eel in a bucket of water. If you are really squeamish, ask someone to hold it down while you kill it with one blow at the back of the head with a cleaver, and chop the rest rapidly into chunks without skinning them. I don't like doing this; it makes me understand why people about to be beheaded were often anxious about the axeman's aim.

A better system is to kill the eel by piercing through the back of the head, through the spinal marrow, with a strong skewer; it is fair to ask the angler to do this. Now suspend the eel from a strong hook, using a slip loop of rope. Make a circular cut with a Stanley knife just below the rope, right through the skin. Sprinkle the cut with salt and, with the assistance of pliers, ease the skin away from the body for about ½–1¼ cm (¼–½ inch), enough to provide a grip. Now pull the skin down the body as if you were removing a tight glove, pliers in one hand and a piece of skin in the other. This can be tricky. I must admit that I've sometimes swung round an eel as if it were a rope-swing on a streetlamp. But once you get going, it is easy. Untie the eel, cut off and discard the head, chop the rest into appropriately sized pieces, and wash and clean them. A warning – pieces of eel may continue to jerk about in a disconcerting way. Leave them for a while in a covered pot.

CHICKEN WITH EEL IN THE DIGOIN STYLE (Poulet de ferme étuvé à la digoinaise)

This old Burgundian recipe, like the pochouse on p. 505 from the last part of the nineteenth century, I would say, comes from Alexandre Dumaine, now alas dead, once one of the finest chefs in France, contemporary and friend of the great Fernand Point, the inspiration and founder of today's nouvelle cuisine. Dumaine's restaurant, the Côte d'Or at Saulieu 72 km (45 miles) west of Dijon, was a high place of French gastronomy when I started writing about food in the sixties (we could never afford to go there, something I still regret). Then he retired to another part of Burgundy, his native town of Digoin, where the canal goes over the Loire in a beautiful stone bridge with barges bringing china clay for the porcelain factories. Among other things, he encouraged and trained Jean-Paul Billioux who, of all odd, square, ugly places, had made the Hôtel de la Gare famous for its food.

I give the recipe as reported by Alexander Watt, in *The Art of Simple French Cookery*, a book he dedicated to Dumaine who was at that time, after Point's death in 1954, France's greatest chef. It was a dish of his father's time, which he was still eating frequently, 'avec émotion'. For today's tastes, you can omit the flour and concentrate the sauce by boiling it down. The country bread Dumaine speaks of was – is – not wholemeal but a huge loaf of coarser, more chewy texture than the usual French bread, though still light and holey: there really is no substitute – I use thick slices of bread made from unbleached white flour, though it is heavier than I would like.

Serves 4

> *1 generous kg (2¼ lb) chicken, cut into 8 pieces*
> *250 g (8 oz) eel, cut into 4 lengths*
> *60 g (2 oz) butter*
> *1½ tablespoons plain flour*
> *175 ml (6 fl oz) dry white wine*
> *250 ml (8 fl oz) water*
> *bouquet garni*
> *2 cloves garlic, crushed, skinned*
> *salt, pepper*
> *6 slices country bread, fried in butter*

No need to skin either chicken or eel pieces – you need the richness for the sauce. Melt the butter in a large heavy sauté pan. Put in the chicken and eel. Cover and leave to cook gently for 10 minutes – this is stewing rather than frying. Turn, cover again and leave for a further 10 minutes: the pieces should not brown or catch the heat.

Remove the chicken and eel to a plate. Spoon off any clear fat. Stir in the flour, cook very gently for a couple of minutes, then stir in the wine and water to make a sauce. Add the bouquet and garlic, and season. When everything is simmering harmoniously, put back the chicken and eel. Cover again and stew until everything is tender. Dumaine suggests 50 minutes for this, which indicates a very low heat indeed. I find 30 minutes is about right if you are using an electric hob rather than gas: it is sensible to remove chicken breast pieces and the thinnest length of eel before they overcook.

Put the six newly-fried pieces of bread on to a serving dish. Arrange boned pieces of chicken and boned eel (remove the skin if it looks raggy) on the bread. Keep it all warm. Taste the sauce for seasoning; adjust it by boiling down or by adding extra liquid so that it has consistency without heaviness. Strain and pour a little over the chicken and eel, the rest round the bread. Serve very hot, with extra bread.

EEL IN THE GREEN (Anguille au vert)

The idea of eel undulating through the greenery of a stream is one that has much appealed to cooks. Sedgmoor eel stew (p. 138) gives the simplest style of all; then there is Guy Mouilleron's jellied eel mousse with watercress sauce (p. 137), and this great classic of Belgian and French cookery, Anguille au vert. The recipe below gives the simplest combination of greens, and sorrel is essential: watercress could be used instead of spinach (one English restaurateur's recipe includes onion, chives, parsley and young nettle leaves, as well as wild sorrel for its extra sharpness).

If you don't grow sorrel in your garden – or on your 17th-floor kitchen windowsill – put sorrel seed at the top of your shopping list. A cook without sorrel to hand is a deprived creature, a subject for lamentation.

Serves 6

1½ kg (3 lb) eel, skinned
salt, pepper
125 g (4 oz) clarified butter

3 handfuls (about 175 g/6 oz) sorrel, shredded
3 handfuls (about 175 g/6 oz) spinach, shredded
1 handful parsley (about 60 g/2 oz), chopped
6 sage leaves, chopped
8 tarragon leaves, chopped
375 ml (12 fl oz) dry white wine
3 large egg yolks
125 ml (4 fl oz) whipping or double cream (optional)
lemon juice
6 slices fried bread, if dish it to be eaten hot

Cut up the eel into pieces that will fit nicely on to the bread, for eating hot. For cold eating, cut them into fewer, longer pieces. Season and fry them in the butter until they begin to brown, then put in the sorrel and spinach. As they cook down, add the herbs and wine. Simmer until the eel is tender, about 15 minutes depending on thickness. Take the pan from the heat. Bone the eel pieces and arrange them on the hot bread on a serving dish or on six plates, and keep them warm: for cold eating, arrange the boned fillets on a serving dish and put it near the stove while you finish the sauce.

In the pan, beat the egg yolk with the cream if used, and some of the hot herby liquor. Put the pan back on the heat, stir in the egg yolk mixture and continue stirring until the sauce thickens gently, without coming near boiling point. Check the seasoning, sharpen agreeably with lemon juice and pour over the eel. Serve either very hot with very hot plates, or chilled.

AN EEL PIE WORTHY OF EEL-PIE ISLAND

From the seventeenth century until recently, people went to enjoy themselves at Twickenham Eyot in the Thames – in other words Eel-Pie Island. Boating parties, anglers, picnickers, gathered on its leafy acres, and bought eel pies from the inn. How sad that the famous inn should have ended up as a hippy battleground. Here is a recipe from *The Cook's Oracle* by Dr William Kitchiner. It was published in 1843, when Eel-Pie Island was at the height of its prosperity, and soon after the inn had been enlarged to include a splendid assembly room.

The interesting thing is that this recipe, which I thought had vanished from our cookery many years before, turned up again recently when I was preparing *British Cookery* in the winter of 1983–84. It is on the menu of the Old Fire Engine House restaurant in Ely, close to the Fens where eels still flourish. The proprietor, Ann Jarman, told me that she found the recipe in a local Women's Institute publication. Another example – there must be hundreds – of a dish once in the national repertoire surviving as a regional oddity. American cookery is full of such fossils – transparent tarts and oyster loaves being two conspicuous examples of once popular dishes that in this country we no longer make.

'Skin clean and bone two Thames eels. Cut them in pieces and chop two small shallots. Pass the shallots in butter for five minutes, and then add to them a small faggot of parsley chopped, with nutmeg, pepper, salt and two glasses of sherry. In the midst of this deposit the eels, add enough water to cover them and set them on the fire to boil. When boiling-point is reached, take out the pieces of eel and arrange them in a pie-dish. In the meantime, add to the sauce two ounces [60 g] of butter kneaded with two ounces [60 g] of flour, and let them incorporate by stirring over the fire. Finish the sauce with the juice of a whole lemon, and pour it over the pieces of eel in the pie-dish. Some slices of hard-boiled egg may be cunningly arranged on the top, and in it *amung* the lower strata. Roof the whole with puff pastry; bake it for an hour. And lo! A pie worthy of Eel-Pie Island. It is a great question debated for ages on Richmond Hill whether this pie is best hot or cold. It is perfect either way.'

NOTE   Use dry or medium-dry sherry – or white wine if you prefer it. Put into a hot oven (gas 8, 230°C/450°F), and after about 20 minutes – by which time the pastry should be well risen – lower the heat to moderate (gas 4, 180°C/350°F). No need to bone the eel: there should be about 1 kg (2 lb). Light fish stock can be used instead of water, and you may not need all the beurre manié to thicken it.

ITALIAN GRILLED AND BAKED EEL

Grilled eel is very popular in Italy: bay leaves are used, sometimes a little rosemary. In the north, a dish of Mostarda di Cremona will go with it; this is a mixture of many fruits pickled in a mustard and garlic-flavoured syrup, and exquisite chutney of some antiquity. Montaigne sampled it twice in 1581, near Cremona, on his way back to France. Very good, he said, but omitted to mention what he ate it with. It is usually a relish for meat, poultry and game, but if you can get a jar from an Italian grocery, do try it with eel. A mustard sauce could be substituted, but would not have the same enchantment and deliciousness.

Recipes for grilling eel can easily be adapted to the oven. Some friends of ours, who spend the summer at Lake Bracciano to the north of Rome, are able to buy the most enormous fat eels. They cut them into chunks about 5 cm (2 inches) long, and arrange them on a grid in a roasting pan. They are brushed with olive oil, seasoned and topped with a bay leaf for each chunk. The pan goes into a hot oven (gas 5, 190 °C/375 °F) until the eel is cooked, i.e. when the flesh can be prised easily from the bone. It is essential to place the eel on a grid or rack of some kind, so that the fat can drain away. Serve with lemon quarters, or with the Mostarda di frutta from Cremona.

The apotheosis of eel in Italy is the magnificent Capitone arrostito, one of the ritual dishes of the Christmas Eve dinner, the *cenone*, the start of the festival. In all Roman Catholic countries, this meal is always *margo*, lean, a fasting meal without meat. Fasting is one of those ideas which puzzle Protestants, they take it to mean going without food (or else eating badly cooked boiled fish on Friday): I remember fellow pupils at school fainting away in the cold church at early communion because they had had nothing but sips of water. To learn that oysters followed by monkfish or lobster is just as virtuous, whereas steak and chips or sausage and mash would be sinful – I know which I would rather have any day – make Protestants suspicious of the honesty of the Roman Catholics. Or rather it did in the part of the world where I grew up.

Capitone arrostito makes a good excuse for Romans to visit the huge and glittering Piazza Vittorio market to choose a fine fat eel, most probably from the lagoon at Comacchio. For 6 people, you need at least 1½ kg (3 lb) or a bit more since it is a feast you are preparing. It needs to be skinned, for elegance.

At home, cut the eel into 5- or 8-cm (2- or 3-inch) pieces. In a large bowl, beat together a vinaigrette of 250 ml (8 fl oz) olive oil, 4 tablespoons lemon juice or wine vinegar, salt and pepper. Add 2 or 3 bay leaves. Put in the well-washed pieces of eel, mixing them up thoroughly. You can also add a good handful of breadcrumbs. Leave for 2 hours or longer.

Drain the pieces, then thread them on to long skewers if you have an electric spit, or on to six individual skewers if you intend to grill, barbecue or oven-roast them. Between each piece put a bay leaf, and on long skewers use chunks of bread at each end to help keep the eel in place as the spit turns. If you are baking the eel, stand the skewers on a rack in a pan so that the fat can drip away freely.

However you decide to cook the eel, it should come into contact at first with high heat. With an oven, preheat it to gas 8, 230 °C (450 °F). You can lower the temperature later if there is a risk of scorching. With indoor grills and electric spits, preheat them for 15 or

20 minutes. With charcoal, make sure that it has reached that ashy grey-looking stage that conceals the fierce red heat of the coals beneath.

As the eel begins to drip, baste it with left-over marinade and keep basting it with fresh fine breadcrumbs that will catch the heat and turn into a golden-brown coating by the time the eel parts from the bone and is cooked.

Have ready a very hot serving dish and plates. Intersperse the skewers of eel with lemon wedges and little bunches of parsley.

MATELOTE OF EEL (Matelote d'anguille)

Unlike many of the smaller French rivers, the Loir has never been canalized into straight, poplar-lined elegance. It runs into a medieval diversity of side streams and leats, which once turned the wheels of a hundred and more mills from Proust's Illiers-Combray down to Angers. A paradise for eels. And for eel fishermen – after a successful inspection of their nets they return to house or *cave* for wine. Most of the catch goes into a tank for the time being, but one or two are strung up and skinned. Meanwhile, a bundle of vine prunings is reduced to embers between two rows of bricks to make a rough barbecue. The pieces of eel are rubbed with coarse grey sea salt, placed on an iron rack over the heat and grilled gently to golden brown. I don't think it is imagination to declare that eel grilled over vine prunings is the best way of all to cook it.

However, most of the Loir eels that are sold at market or to hoteliers will go into the richer, more elaborate dish of matelote. At least once every visit to Trôo, we go to the Hôtel de France at La Chartre-sur-le-Loir to eat Monsieur Pasteau's matelote, a dish that in the twenty-five years we have been eating it never varies in quality. According to books of local cookery, Monsieur Pasteau also grills eel and serves it with grilled mushrooms, smoked bacon and tomatoes, plus straw potatoes and sauce tartare: there is also a recipe for pieces of eel, well seasoned and lavishly buttered, that are made into a pasty of puff pastry, in the style of an apple turnover.

These two dishes I have never seen on the menu, but I can vouch for the matelote which is stewed in red wine of the district, often with mushrooms from the old quarry caves that warren the low cliffs of the Loir. At Vouvray, on the great Loire, white wine is the natural choice. So it is at Saumur, and in Anjou where the dish is often called *bouilleture de Loire*. There, too, prunes are used to set off the delicate flavour of eel. They were once produced in Touraine, at Huistnes in particular, but now come from Agen far to the south –

even (in small type, at the bottom corner of the packet) from
California. It is surprising how well prunes go with river fish such as
perch and lampreys – they are browned in butter, sprinkled with
flour and left to stew or bake for half an hour in wine, with soaked
prunes. Eel, though, seems to demand a little extra grandeur.

Serves 8

1 kg (2 lb) eel, skinned and cut up
3–4 tablespoons marc or brandy
4 tablespoons oil
salt, freshly ground black pepper
1 bottle white wine plus 1 large egg yolk and 90 ml (3 fl oz) double cream
     or 1 bottle red wine plus 1½ tablespoons plain flour and 2 tablespoons butter
2 cloves garlic, crushed (optional)
175 g (6 oz) chopped shallot or onion
white of 1 leek, chopped (optional)
bouquet garni

Also choose an appropriate garnish:

LOIR   20–30 small glazed onions
          20–30 small button mushrooms, cooked in butter
          triangles of bread fried in butter
          chopped parsley

ANJOU   as above, plus 25 large prunes
          quarters of hard-boiled egg (optional)

VOUVRAY   20–30 small glazed onions
          strips of streaky green bacon, browned in butter
          20–30 small button mushrooms, cooked in butter
          25 large prunes (optional)

Turn the pieces of eel in the brandy and oil, season well and leave for
several hours or overnight. At the same time, put the prunes, if used,
to soak in half the bottle of wine.

A good hour before the meal, simmer the rest of the wine with
garlic, if used, onion, leek and bouquet garni for half an hour. Arrange
the eel and prunes, with any liquor from them, in a large pan, and
strain the seasoned wine over them. The eel and prunes should be
just covered. Stew gently for 20–30 minutes until the eel is cooked.
Meanwhile prepare the garnish.

To thicken the sauce: either mash butter and flour together, dividing the mixture into small lumps, then add them to the red wine stew gradually, stirring all the time so that the sauce thickens smoothly; or beat the egg yolk and cream, whisk in a little of the simmering white wine stew, and return to the cooking pot, which should be kept below the boil so that the sauce thickens without curdling.

Correct the seasoning, pour into a serving dish and arrange the garnish on top. With triangles of bread, dip one corner into the sauce, then into chopped parsley, and tuck the opposite corner into the stew.

MATELOTE D'ANGUILLE DE TANTE MARIE

A recipe from the Vendômois that is really a good and homely dish. Things from the garden, onions and flageolet beans and Jerusalem artichokes, mushrooms from the quarry caves where they are grown in the cool darkness, and eel from the sluices on the many mill leats and streams that flow into the Loir, all speak of that genuine local cooking which varies from house to house according to what is to hand. The eel is almost always skinned, on account of its fattiness, but if you find this too difficult, give the pieces a quick browning over a high heat in a heavy greased pan before you put them into the sauce.

Serves 4

1 eel weighing about 600 g (1¼ lb), skinned, cut up
salt, pepper
60 g (2 oz) unsalted butter
1 level tablespoon plain flour
300 ml (10 fl oz) water from cooking dried beans or peas or vegetable stock
bouquet garni
12 medium-sized mushrooms
about 500 g (1 lb) Jerusalem artichokes, peeled, diced
300 ml (10 fl oz) Gamay or other red wine
12 small pickling onions
extra butter
sprinkling of sugar

Sprinkle the eel with salt and pepper and set aside. Melt the butter in a heavy pan, stir in the flour and cook for 1 minute. Moisten with vegetable water, add the bouquet, mushrooms and artichokes. When the artichokes are almost tender, pour in the wine.

In the meantime, brown the onions in the extra butter with a sprinkling of sugar to help them caramelize. Add them to the pan with the wine. Boil for 3 minutes, steadily, check the seasoning and put in the eel pieces. Lower the heat to a simmer and give the eel 20 minutes. If some of the pieces are thin, it is prudent to check after 15 minutes and remove them if the flesh is parting easily from the bones. Put them back just before serving.

Provide bread and more of the Gamay or other wine used in the cooking.

GUY MOUILLERON'S JELLIED EEL MOUSSE WITH WATERCRESS SAUCE

When Guy Mouilleron left the Relais at the Café Royal to open his own restaurant, Ma Cuisine, in Walton Street in London, this was one of the most popular dishes on the menu. He gave me the recipe, which is a pattern for fish terrines of all kinds, and a base for elaborations of your own.

Serves 8

2 eels, weighing about 1¼ kg (2½ lb) in all, skinned, filleted
salt, pepper, nutmeg
3 egg whites
500 ml (17 fl oz) double cream, well chilled

SAUCE
1 bunch or handful of watercress
150 ml (5 fl oz) double cream, whipped
salt, pepper

For the fish mousse, cut off 375 g (12 oz) of the messiest looking eel fillet. Season the rest and set it aside for the moment.

Chill the blender goblet or bowl of the processor in which you will be making the mousse. When it is thoroughly cold, set it in motion and drop on to the whirling blades the 375 g (12 oz) of eel fillet, lubricating the mixture with the egg whites. Chill the whole thing again, then put it back in place, switch on and pour in the cream. Season it well. You should have a rich white coherent billowy-looking mixture.

Take a stoneware or earthenware terrine respectable enough to appear on the table. Put in a layer of the mousse, then a layer of eel fillets that had been set aside. Repeat and then finish with a layer of the mousse. Cut butter papers to fit into the terrine, on top of the last layer of mousse, then cover the whole thing right over with foil.

Either steam the mousse for an hour or put it into a pan of boiling water to come halfway up the side and bake in a moderate oven, preheated to gas 4, 180°C (350°F) for the same time. Remove the terrine to a cool place, and when cold, chill overnight.

To make the sauce, remove enough leaves from the bunch of watercress to make a tablespoon when chopped. Blend or process the rest of the leaves with the minimum of water to make a murky slush. Sieve and add to the whipped cream. Season and fold in the leaves.

Serve the mousse in slices, cut from the terrine at the table, with a spoonful of the sauce. Provide brown bread to eat with it.

SEDGMOOR EEL STEW

The landscape of Sedgmoor in Somerset is a medieval creation. Monks from such abbeys as Athelney and Glastonbury drained the marshes by digging long canals known as rhines (pronounced reens). A paradise for eels. Here is one local recipe, very simple and direct.

Allow 250 g (8 oz) of eel per person. Skin and cut it into appropriate pieces, discarding the heads as usual. Put the pieces into a shallow pan that will take them in a single layer – a non-stick sauté pan is ideal, or an enamelled pan. Cover with rough or dry cider. Simmer until tender – at least 15 minutes. Remove the pieces to a serving dish, seasoning them and seasoning the liquor. Mash together 2 tablespoons each of butter and flour. Add this mixture bit by bit to the simmering liquid, until it thickens lightly (you may not need it all). Put in a great deal of chopped parsley. Check the seasoning and pour the sauce over the eel.

You can make this dish grander in various ways. Serve the eel on croûtons of bread, as in Anguille au vert, p. 130. Reduce the cooking liquor slightly and enrich it with clotted cream before adding the parsley – this means you can do without the flour-and-butter mixture (beurre manié). But really this is a country dish: if you want something grander, I would go for the Anguille au vert and leave this recipe alone.

ELVERS see EELS.

FLAKE see A FEW WORDS ABOUT . . . DOGFISH

FLYING FISH see A FEW WORDS ABOUT . . . FLYING FISH

FOGAS *see* PERCH

FRESHWATER CRAYFISH *see* A FEW WORDS ABOUT . . .
FRESHWATER CRAYFISH

GARFISH *see* A FEW WORDS ABOUT . . . GARFISH

GRAYLING *see* TROUT

† GREY MULLET

Mugil cephalus and spp.

There are about 100 species of mullet spread about the warm and temperate seas of the world, a fact which may surprise you in view of their comparative scarcity at the fishmongers'. In the eastern Mediterranean, though, and in the Black and Caspian Seas, they are abundant enough to provide roes for Taramasalata (p. 530), and that piquant substance known as Botargo (p. 529), once prized by Rabelais and Pepys as a stimulus to thirst, but now difficult to find in northern Europe.

Our grey mullet is likely to come from the sea off Cornwall and the west of England during the summer and autumn months. The fish move in shoals, sometimes coming right into estuaries and ports where the brackish polluted water may give them a muddy taste. I have never experienced this with grey mullet, but if you have reason to think they have been caught in such places, wash them in several changes of salted, vinegared water.

Grey mullet, also known as striped mullet in North America and black mullet in Florida, looks a little like sea bass, silvery in colour, but clouded and pointed with dark grey. A svelte creature. The flesh is reasonably firm and delicate, the price reasonable. Its success depends on its freshness. Elsewhere in the world, the different species do not have the same muddy inclination and the fish is better thought of.

In Senegal, the cooks of Saint-Louis prepare a complexity of stuffed mullet. The fish is slit down the back, the flesh and innards carefully prised from the skin. The edible parts are chopped and mixed with breadcrumbs, tomato, garlic, parsley and chilli, then packed back into the skin, which is sewn together. The resurrected fish lies on a bed of tomato, fried potato, cooked carrot and turnip for baking. A tricky operation of a kind I am never tempted to perform.

The ways of Hawaii seem to me more sympathetic. There, mullet – *amaama* – may simply be steamed until half done, then gently finished in coconut milk. Or it may be made into little parcels and baked, *see* below. I have a weakness, too, for the Green Fisherman's recipe from *Pinocchio*. He floured mullet and flung it into a huge frying pan of olive oil which smelt like newly-snuffed candles. It was part of a Fritto misto, which also included red mullet, hake, sole, anchovies and spider crabs – and nearly included Pinocchio, too – all freshly caught, straight from the sea. How good it must have tasted, absolutely delicious. It improves most fish to be fried in olive oil, I would say.

Another way is to grill mullet. Larger ones can be boned and cut into pieces and strung on skewers with bits of fat bacon and bay leaves, for cooking en brochette. Small ones can be grilled whole after being scaled, cleaned and slashed three times on each side. Brush them with oil or clarified butter*, and serve them with a tomato sauce*, or hollandaise and its derivatives*. Or with sauce andalouse*, which may sound a little old-fashioned with its velouté base, but which goes well with mullet of all kinds.

My own feeling is that grey mullet is best cold, since it has a chance to lose any hint of pappiness and firm up. Plainly baked or steamed or poached, it goes well with mayonnaise. And the cold Provençal olive treatment – p. 143 – is a winner.

HOW TO PREPARE MULLET

Scale the mullet carefully. Both roe and liver are worth saving, and many people treasure the extraordinary length of gut compressed into the cavity – over 2 m (6½ ft) for a fish weighing 500 g (1 lb).

BAKED MULLET PARCELS (Lawalu amaama)

To make this Hawaiian dish as it should be, you need leaves from that Scrabbler's godsend, the ti tree, otherwise known as the tree of kings or the good luck tree. For each little parcel you need one leaf, split into two longways. The first piece is wrapped round the bits of fish in one direction, the second at right angles to it. The whole thing can then be tied up neatly with a bit of raffia.

In our less exotic situation, the long green husks that enclosed a head of sweetcorn may be used, or a homely square of foil. I am sure that something is lost, perhaps the ti leaf has as much to contribute by way of flavour as a vine leaf, but the result is genial all the same.

Serves 4

2 mullet, each weighing at least 500 g (1 lb)
4 rashers of unsmoked streaky bacon
4 bay leaves, split in 2
8 very thin slices of onion
1 small green pepper, seeded
salt, pepper

Slice each fish across into 4 pieces about 5 cm (2 inches) long. Keep the wrapping in mind – if you are using leaves or husks you may need to adjust the size of the slices. Discard the heads and thin tail end, putting them into the freezer stock bag.

Cut a piece of bacon to go on top of each slice, then arrange the bay leaves, onion and a neat strip of green pepper on top (you will not need all the pepper). Season as you go, remembering the saltiness of the bacon. Tie up the parcels.

You can put the parcels into a baking dish with a thin layer of water in the base, and give them about 20 minutes in a hot oven preheated to gas 7–8, 220–230 °C (425–450 °F). Or you can steam them for 30 minutes until the contents of the parcels feel firm. It is wise to have an extra trial parcel as a tester, if you are not used to steaming.

BAKED GREY MULLET WITH JERUSALEM ARTICHOKES AND BLACK OLIVES

One of the discoveries of modern cooking – presumably in the wake of the new interest in Mediterranean eating – has been how well fish goes with certain vegetables. I was brought up to think that only a few potatoes were permissible with fish. But then with a northern diet the alternative vegetables, in wintertime at least, would have been cabbage or turnip or swede which were far too strong, watery and unbuttered to do anything but overwhelm the excellent fresh cod and haddock. This particular combination was a happy accident: I have repeated it since with red mullet and various breams. It works with cod, but would be overwhelming with the more delicate white fish.

Serves 4–6

2 large grey mullet, weighing at least 500 g (1 lb) each
salt, pepper
1 kg (2 lb) Jerusalem artichokes
2 tablespoons butter
2 tablespoons olive oil
1 large tomato, skinned, seeded, chopped
1 bunch spring onions, about 10, sliced
250 ml (8 fl oz) medium-dry white wine, e.g. Vouvray
about 18 small black olives

Clean the mullet and season the cavities. Set aside. Peel and dice the artichokes – this should give you about 750 g (1 ½ lb), in other words you will lose about a quarter of their weight, though some varieties are smoother and less knobbly these days.

Switch on the oven to gas 7, 220 °C (425 °F).

In a sauté pan, heat the butter and oil and stew the tomato briefly. Setting aside a little of their green part for a final garnish, put the rest of the spring onions into the pan with the artichokes and the wine. Stir everything well, cover and stew gently until the artichokes are tender. If the mixture begins to look watery, remove the lid and raise the heat: you need to have the whole thing as dry as possible without allowing it to catch. Sieve or put through the coarse plate of a vegetable mill. Check for seasoning and spread into a baking dish. Put the mullet on top and bake for 15 minutes.

Meanwhile cook the olives briefly in boiling water. Dot them around the fish, check on its state and give it another 5 minutes in the oven or longer, until cooked. Scatter with the onion green that you set aside, and serve with bread.

GREY MULLET WITH OLIVES (Mulet aux olives)

In Provence in the past, and in some families still, Christmas begins on 24 December, the eve of the festival, with the *Gros Souper* or Big Supper. It is full of symbolism and mystery. First there is the business of the yule log, which has to be cut from a fruit-bearing tree. It must also be large enough to burn for three nights and days. The oldest and youngest members of the party carry it at either end, and with the family make a procession three times round the room before laying it on the hearth. The grandfather sprinkles the log with *vin cuit*, blessing it in the name of the Trinity. Then he lights it, and with the youngest grandchild says 'Cacho-fio, bouto-fio, Dieu nous allègre', a blend of Provençal and French meaning 'Let the log burn, God brings us happiness'. And everyone sits down to supper.

No meat, game or poultry is served as everyone will be going off to Midnight Mass and it is still Advent. The table is covered with three cloths and three candles burn, for the Trinity. At one end of the table is a bowl of green sprouting wheat, at the other sprouting lentils: the seeds were sown on 4 December, St Barbara's Day. Twelve rolls for the twelve Apostles and a large loaf for Christ are marked with the cross before anyone eats them. And seven dishes are served for the seven wounds of Christ on the cross. They are made from vegetables, eggs and fish – one of them will be mullet with olives, another with salt cod with raita. There will be anchoiade (p. 54) with celery and cardoons with an anchovy sauce (p. 49). As far as the mullet is concerned, there are a number of variations you can make to the basic recipe, and I recommend that you eat it cold.

Once the seven dishes have been dispatched, and a salad of curly endive to remind us of the curly head of the Infant Jesus, the thirteen desserts are put on the table so that people can chat and nibble away until it is time to leave for the church. But that is another story.

Serves 4

1 kg (2 lb) grey mullet
salt, pepper
1 small handful of parsley leaves
2 large cloves garlic
3 tablespoons olive oil
seasoned flour
juice of 1 large lemon or 4 tablespoons dry white wine
2 bay leaves
125 g (4 oz) mixed black and green olives, blanched for 3–4 minutes
*   in boiling water*
slices of lemon or orange to decorate

Preheat the oven to gas 7, 220 °C (425 °F).

Season the cavity of the mullet. Chop parsley and garlic together. Heat the oil in a shallow, flameproof baking dish that will hold the mullet comfortably, and cook the parsley mixture for about 3 minutes over a low heat.

Turn the fish in the flour, shaking off any excess, and put it into the oil. After a few seconds, turn it over. Add the lemon juice or white wine, bay leaves, olives and 200 ml (7 fl oz) of water. Season and simmer 5 minutes, then put into the oven.

Allow 10 minutes for 2 mullet, 15 minutes for 1 large one. Baste once.

When the fish is just cooked – it is particularly important to avoid overcooking if the mullet is to be eaten cold, since it will cook a little more in its own heat – remove it from the oven and pour off the juice into a shallow pan through a strainer. Boil it down steadily to a good flavour: it should be quite sharp, but pleasantly so. Pour over the fish, adding any debris of parsley and olives from the strainer. If the bay leaves look fagged out, discard them, and add a couple of fresh ones.

TO EAT HOT   Serve immediately with plenty of bread and dry white wine, and slices of lemon or orange ranged neatly down the mullet.

TO EAT COLD   Leave to cool, turning the fish from time to time. Serve chilled, so that the juices have a chance to turn to a light parsley-flecked jelly. Decorate finally with a few slices of lemon or orange.

MULLET BAKED WITH FENNEL AND PASTIS

I used to cook mullet en papillote, but now feel that this treatment is only suitable for very firm fish. Baking in a hot oven works better.

Serves 6

6 mullet
salt, pepper
3 heads of fennel, cut into strips, the leaves saved and chopped
3 tablespoons pastis
1½ teaspoons thyme
1½ teaspoons fennel seed
olive oil
lemon wedges

STUFFING
roes and liver from the fish, if any or *3 pairs herring roes, soft or hard*
6 tablespoons fine breadcrumbs
1 teaspoon thyme
1½ teaspoons fennel seed
3 tablespoons chopped shallot or *onion*
3–4 tablespoons butter
salt, cayenne pepper

Preheat the oven to gas 7, 220 °C (425 °F).

Season the mullet cavities with salt and pepper. Blanch the fennel strips in boiling salted water until they are almost tender. Mix the pastis with thyme and fennel seed, then add it to the drained fennel strips and put them into an oiled ovenproof baking dish.

For the stuffing, crush the roes and mix them with the breadcrumbs and most of the leaves saved from the fennel. Crush thyme and fennel seed in a mortar and add to the crumbs. Soften the shallot or onion slowly in the butter: when it is soft and yellowish, add to the crumbs. Stuff the mullet with this mixture – season the mixture with salt and cayenne pepper first – and put the fish on top of the fennel strips in the dish, head to tail. Brush them over with oil, season and bake in a hot oven, gas 7, 220 °C (425 °F). Test after 15 minutes. Be prepared to give them a little longer. Scatter with the last of the chopped fennel leaves and serve with lemon wedges.

MULLET IN CHARENTE STYLE (Meuille à la charentaise)

The butter of the Charente is famous and it combines well with the vegetables that come from the neighbouring market gardens of the Marais, just to the north. I once read that Rabelais had introduced the tomato to France, sending seeds from Rome to his friend and master, the abbot of Maillezais, but I have never seen any real evidence that this was true – although it is agreeable to sit by the abbey ruins on one of the Marais canals and think about such things. Certainly tomatoes, garlic and onions now flourish in those parts – all the good things of that favoured region come together in this recipe.

Serves 6

6 mullet, about 250 g (8 oz) each
salt, pepper
175 g (6 oz) butter
6 cloves garlic, halved
leaves of 1 handful of parsley
500 g (1 lb) tomatoes, skinned, seeded, chopped
4 tablespoons dry white wine
cayenne pepper, sugar (see *recipe*)
3 tablespoons finely grated Parmesan

Season the mullet cavities with salt and pepper. Preheat the oven to gas 6, 200 °C (400 °F).

Reduce two-thirds of the butter, the garlic and parsley to a crumbly chopped mass in the processor. Cook the tomatoes down to a purée in a shallow pan buttered with a little of the remaining butter. Add the wine. Do not overcook – you want to keep the freshness of the tomato flavour. Season with cayenne, and a pinch or two of sugar if the tomatoes are on the tasteless side.

Meanwhile, bake the mullet in a buttered shallow dish for about 10 minutes. Pour over the very hot sauce, scatter with the Parmesan and put back into the oven until the mullet are cooked. About another 10 minutes.

GROUPERS *see* SEA BASS

GURNARD *see* A FEW WORDS ABOUT . . . GURNARD

† HADDOCK

Melanogrammus aeglefinus

After cod comes the haddock – at least in the way of popular consumption. And in some regions it is preferred to cod, for instance in the West Riding of Yorkshire where fish and chips means haddock and chips. Alan Davidson points out that discriminating Icelanders also prefer haddock to cod. This makes me feel that they are offered a superior strain, or perhaps just a fresher fish. The haddock one gets here under the normal humdrum circumstances of life is, in my experience, an uninspiring if estimable acquaintance. Chances are that you buy it because sole or turbot or halibut are too dear, because it is *there* on a thin day for choice and you cannot think of anything else. Faced with a fillet of haddock, the heart does not sing.

The tragic realities of fishing cod that lie behind the history of New England and the western countries of Europe, that have stimulated great novels such as *Pêcheurs d'Islande* and *Captains Courageous* and a host of songs, are not so apparent in the matter of fishing haddock. Perhaps it is something to do with the name. It has a jaunty, diminutive air – like bullock or hillock – that does not seem to have appealed to the poet's or novelist's ear. The haddock's main cultural achievement is to have become identified with St Peter, like the John Dory. After the Transfiguration, Jesus and St Peter arrived in Capernaum on the shores of Galilee, where the ruins of the synagogue of that time may still be seen. Immediately the local customs people were after them. Christ knew that being locals and not strangers they were not liable, but said precisely to St Peter, 'Notwithstanding, lest we should offend them, go thou to the sea, and cast an hook, and take up the fish that first cometh up; and when thou hast opened his mouth, thou shalt find a piece of money: that take, and give it unto them for me and thee.'

The dark round marks behind the head, above the pectoral fins, are by legend the fingerprints of St Peter. The silly thing is that neither the haddock nor the John Dory could possibly have been the fish since they live in the sea, and the Sea of Galilee is a freshwater lake.

An interesting point about haddock is that being softer and smaller-flaked than cod, it is not as suitable for long-term drying and salting. Small haddocks, rizzered haddock, may be lightly salted and hung up to dry when the air is clear, to make a breakfast dish next day, but their particular virtues are best shown off by smoking. The fisherfolk of eastern Scotland developed a couple of famous cures for haddock. I do not know how long ago, but presumably in the eighteenth century, if not earlier: they became more widely known in the rest of the country and abroad in the nineteenth century as Finnan haddie or haddock and Arbroath smokies. These are two of the great delicacies, when properly done.

HOW TO BUY AND PREPARE HADDOCK

As with cod, the finest part of the haddock is behind the head (which also has its pickings). As a change, instead of cooking a whole bass or salmon, why not buy a whole haddock of 1–1½ kg (2–3 lb)? You can then stuff and bake it in a hot oven, say at gas 7, 220 °C (425 °F), using a light mixture of breadcrumbs, herbs with a little green onion, perhaps some chopped mushrooms or hard-boiled egg and some lemon juice. Or you might poach it in very salty water, as if it were cod, see p. 94, and serve it with clear melted butter and fine shreds of grated horseradish, or with an hollandaise sauce*. Freshness is the key to success.

As with so many others of the cod family, pre-salting is a surprising improvement. You might go further by salting it liberally and leaving it for twenty-four hours; it will then need rinsing before you cook it. We had home-salted fish once at Joigny, at the Lorains' À La Côte St Jacques, with very young, neat root vegetables – simple and good.

ESCOFFIER'S GRATIN OF HADDOCK WITH COURGETTES

I was idling through Escoffier's *Guide Culinaire* one day, enjoying the nomenclature of kings and princesses, archdukes, admirals and opera stars, *les grandes horizontales* and the smart resorts they adorned, the characters and places of history which give such a picture of that age and its more frivolous preoccupations, when the words 'earthenware dish' caught my eye. The Empress Eugénie or the American soprano Mary Garden may be honoured in porcelain and crystal dishes, what has earthenware to do with Escoffier? It appeared in a trim little recipe, very direct, after a dish dedicated to the Great Condé in which sole fillets covered with a white wine sauce were picked out with lines of buttered tomato purée and decorated like shields with crosses piped in the same purée (perhaps this was the device of that famous soldier?). The earthenware dish recipe was also for sole, but I find it most useful for the many more times I have haddock to cook, and other less glorious fish of the cod family. It must entirely have reminded Escoffier of the implicities of his childhood in Provence.

Choose an earthenware dish that will just accommodate in a single layer the number of haddock fillets you are intending to cook. Butter it, put in the fish, skin side down, and season. Set aside for 30 minutes.

Preheat the oven to gas 5–6, 190–200 °C (375–400 °F).

Peel and slice enough young courgettes to make a single layer on top of the fish. Butter a sauté pan and put in the slices with 2–3 fine ripe tomatoes that have been skinned, seeded and roughly chopped. You need enough to make a light moistness. Add a few drops of lemon and some seasoning. Cook gently until almost done. When you turn the slices, add 2–3 sprigs of basil.

Spread the courgettes over the fish evenly. Sprinkle with a layer of crumbs from day-old bread. Bake for upwards of 15 minutes – time will depend on the thickness of the fish – 'so as to cook the fillets and brown the crumbs at the same time. Serve in the dish just as it is.'

GREEN FISH SOUP

A most attractive and unusual soup that demands no particular local genius of a fishmonger or greengrocer. Anyone could make it, I would say, anywhere above – or below – the tropics. Something of a relief to the writer of a fish cookery book. One spends so much time trying to come by a few squid or an ambulant crab or prawns that are not weighed down with icy jackets. For this original soup made from such unoriginal ingredients, we have to thank Marion Jones of the Croque-en-bouche restaurant in Malvern. She is a cook of verve and ingenuity.

Serves 8

1 medium onion, thinly sliced
1 small leek, thinly sliced
2 tablespoons butter
3 tablespoons plain flour
1 litre (1¾ pt) fish stock, flavoured with fennel
salt, pepper, nutmeg
500 g (1 lb) skinned fillet of haddock, whiting, hake or ling, cut up
375 g (12 oz) sprouting broccoli or Calabrese, prepared weight
about 6 tablespoons single cream (optional)

Sweat onion and leek in the butter until soft, without colouring them. Stir in the flour, cook gently for a few minutes, then stir in half the stock. Simmer for 10 minutes. Season the liquid and add the fish. Cook for 1 minute and leave to cool down. Blend at top speed, or process and sieve until very smooth.

Meanwhile, chop all the broccoli or Calabrese except for a few flowering heads to use as garnish. Cook in enough salted water to cover, resting the heads on top so that they steam; do not put the lid on the pan. Remove the heads carefully and set aside. Sieve the rest of the contents of the pan into the soup, liquor included. Or use the blender. Dilute further to taste with the remaining fish stock and, if necessary, a little extra water.

Reheat carefully, check the seasoning and stir in the cream, if used. Float the broccoli or Calabrese heads on top.

GRILLED HADDOCK WITH LIME AND GINGER BUTTER

When you experiment with fish and unaccustomed spices and flavourings, you can minimize possible disaster by grilling it plainly and then blending the new items into a flavoured butter. Not that I anticipate anyone would dislike haddock with lime and ginger butter, which is a delicate combination, lovely to look at since lime zest gives a general pale green tone, speckled with flecks of green onion. The ginger is the mystery.

Serves 2

2 fillets of haddock, each weighing 250 g (8 oz)
salt, pepper
2 limes
125 g (4 oz) unsalted or Lurpak butter
peeled slice of ginger, 1 ½ cm (½ inch) deep
2–3 teaspoons chopped onion green or chives
sunflower or groundnut oil
a little melted butter, extra onion green or chives

Put the haddock on a dish, skin side down. Sprinkle it with salt and pepper. Remove the zest of the limes with a zester or fine grater and put it into the processor or blender. Squeeze the juice of one lime over the fish and set it to one side. Squeeze the juice of the second lime into the processor or blender. Add the butter, cut up, and grate or chop in the ginger. Whizz to a cream, then add the onion green or chives to taste and salt. Scrape out the butter into a pot. You could chill it and cut it into neat slices, if you prefer.

Just before the meal, preheat the grill. Slip a metal serving dish underneath prior to cooking.

Drain and dry the haddock. Brush the skin side with oil. Take out the heated dish from under the grill. Put the fish on it skin side down and brush the top of the fillets with melted butter. Put back under the grill. Keep an eye on it, and brush over with more butter after 2 minutes. After another 2 minutes, check to see if it is ready. When it is cooked, serve scattered discreetly with chopped onion green or chives and serve with the butter.

FINNAN HADDOCK

Fine Finnan, or Findon, haddock is a most excellent fish. The cure was first developed in the village of Findon, about 9½ km (6 miles) south of Aberdeen. I hope there is a statue there to the inventor (though I doubt it), since these days the name of the village is on the lips even of Americans 1,600 km (1,000 miles) away where, in New England at least, they may find haddock cured in the proper manner. The distinguished author of *The Encylopaedia of Fish Cookery*, A. J. McClane, attributes its first popularization to John Ross more than a century ago in Findon. (The firm of John Ross is still curing Finnan haddie in Aberdeen.) In fact, Finnan haddock was widely appreciated much earlier than that. Sir Walter Scott described a comparative tasting organized by some of 'our Edinburgh philosophers' who 'tried to produce their equal in vain. I was one of a party at a dinner where the philosophical haddocks were placed in competition with the genuine Finnan fish. These were served round without distinguishing whence they came; but only one gentleman of twelve present espoused the cause of philosophy.' He claimed, and I am sure he may well be right, that 'a Finnan haddock has a relish of a very peculiar and delicate flavour, inimitable on any other coast than that of Aberdeenshire.'

Most of us have to put up with second best, which can still be very good. Incidentally you can tell a Scottish Finnan haddock from one cured in England by looking at the backbone. It should lie to the right of the split fish. In the London cut cure, developed for the London market and the south, it lies to the left.

Because of the small completeness of the proper Finnan haddie, opened out into a kite shape, it is easily distinguished from smoked cuts of cod. Take a look at the skin side too: there you will see the two dark fingerprint marks where St Peter grabbed the fish – an honour which the haddock shares with the John Dory (p. 203). The beautiful golden silvery tones of Finnan haddock come from the cold-smoking alone, no dye is used. Or rather no dye should be used. If you suspect the colour of something labelled Finnan haddock, or its shape, make firm enquiries before you buy. The Finnan cure can produce one of the finest of all smoked fish, a great treat costing little, and it should not be traduced.

In France, on menus or in shops – and in French cookery books – the word *haddock* indicates the smoked fish (*aiglefin* is the word for fresh haddock). Go carefully before you order it in a restaurant. In my experience, it usually comes grilled with maître d'hôtel butter*. If the fish was plump and the cure mild, this works well. If not, your *haddock* will be dry in the mouth and very salty.

In Scotland, there are local variations of the split haddock Finnan cure. Eyemouth haddock and Glasgow Pales, for instance, are even more lightly brined and smoked.

CAISSES À LA FLORENCE

Don't be put off by the strange-sounding combination of ingredients in this recipe from *The Gentle Art of Cookery* by Mrs C. F. Leyel and Miss Olga Hartley. It is particularly delicious if you take the trouble to use Finnan haddock – or Arbroath smokies – and I would suggest you set aside a little of the cooked fish when you are making other, more large-scale dishes in this section. About half a fish, for a trial run.

You will also need some very large prunes, three or four per person. Soak and stone them if necessary.

Mash – or process – the boned and skinned fish with enough double cream to make a smooth, thick paste. Flavour it with cayenne. I doubt you will need more salt.

Stuff the prunes with this mixture.

Cut broad fingers of bread that will accommodate two or three prunes each, and fry them in butter. Any left-over haddock paste can be spread on top. Then divide the prunes between them. Put into a moderately hot oven to warm through. They do not need to be cooked, just warmed enough for pleasant eating.

CULLEN SKINK

The origin of this soup is mysterious. In recent years, with the revival of interest in local dishes, it has become popular in a number of the better Scottish restaurants. The name gives it an air of ancient mystery. Yet all paths lead back only half a century to Marian McNeill's *The Scots Kitchen*, which first came out in 1929.

Skink means shin of beef. It has also been used to indicate soup for at least 150 years. For even longer, the shores of Scotland east of Inverness – where Cullen lies – and down round to Aberdeen and Arbroath have been famous for cured haddock. Yet there is no mention of the soup in that earlier quarry of Scots recipes, *The Cook and Housewife's Manual* by Meg Dods, of 1826. Or in the splendid compilation from recipes left by Lady Clark of Tillypronie that came out in 1909.

Perhaps we shall never know. Perhaps when Marian McNeill describes it as 'a cottage recipe from the shores of the Moray Firth', she is concealing some very special visit to a friend with a more than usual skill who, on her own – or on his own – arrived at this most successful soup, without any promptings from the past.

Serves 4

1 Finnan haddock, skinned
1 onion, chopped
600 ml (1 pt) milk, boiled
about 150 g (5 oz) mashed potato
2 tablespoons butter
salt, pepper

Put the haddock into a pan and pour on enough boiling water to cover it. Bring back to the boil, add the onion and simmer until cooked. Remove the fish, extract the bones and put them back into the pan. Simmer for a further hour, strain into a clean pan and heat up. When boiling, pour in the hot milk, and add the haddock which you have flaked meanwhile. Simmer a few minutes, then stir in mashed potato until you arrive at the consistency you like best. Add the butter, with seasoning to taste.

VARIATION Betty Allen of Airds Hotel, Port Appin, and one of Scotland's best cooks, makes Cullen skink by sweating the onion in butter until golden, then adding 1 kg (2 lb) of Finnan haddock cut in 4 pieces and 600 ml (1 pt) water. This is simmered for 30 minutes. The fish is drained, the bones and skin discarded, and the soup finished with milk and potatoes as above. Cream and chives are the final additions.

FINNAN HADDOCK WITH EGG SAUCE

It may seem odd to use a French recipe for one of our best-known national dishes. I think, though, that this one is worth giving for its careful instructions. It comes from Ali-Bab's *Gastronomie Pratique*, first published in 1912 with a grand, augmented edition in 1928. Nowadays we expect recipe writing to be informative as to quantity and method, but with writers of the past, cookery books were more a collection of reminders and new ideas. Minutely detailed recipes given in a French periodical of the nineties, *Pot-au-feu* by Madame Saint-Ange (her great work was published in 1927), and then Henri Babinski's *Gastronomie Pratique* (Ali-Bab was his pen name) must have been an unimaginable relief to the Dora Copperfields of those days – just as Julia Child and Simone Beck are now to those whose taste in food is far beyond their skill as cooks.

Another point about very precise recipe writing is that it gives a far more accurate idea about the tastes of the past. If only those fifteenth-century cookery manuscripts gave precise quantities of the many spices that were used, we should be much better placed to discover whether our ancestors were practising a style of cookery that was refined and oriental in style, or closer to the dark blends of Christmas puddings and mincemeat.

Serves 6

3 Finnan haddock, about 1 kg (2 lb)
milk and water for poaching
1 kg (2 lb) firm potatoes, boiled, peeled and sliced
100 g (3½ oz) clarified butter

SAUCE
100 g (3½ oz) butter
1 small carrot, sliced
1 small onion, sliced
1 small turnip, sliced
4 tablespoons plain flour
450 ml (15 fl oz) boiled milk
bouquet garni
salt, pepper, nutmeg
100 ml (3½ fl oz) single cream
2 hard-boiled eggs, chopped
a little chopped parsley
a little lemon juice

Start with the sauce (it can be made in advance, up to the final additions). Melt half the butter and cook the sliced vegetables in it until they are lightly coloured but not brown. Stir in the flour, cook for 2 minutes, then moisten with the hot milk. Put in the bouquet with a little salt, pepper and nutmeg. Let it brew for an hour, reducing gently to a nicely pourable consistency. Strain it into a clean pan, without pressing the vegetables through (they are for flavouring rather than consistency).

About half an hour before the meal, poach the haddock in milk and water to cover. Drain and remove the bones. Some people may also like to discard the skin. Halve the haddock longways into six fillets and put them on to a hot dish. Keep them warm.

Fry the sliced potatoes in the clarified butter until they are golden crisp. Just before serving, put them round the haddock.

To finish the sauce, bring it to simmering point and beat in the remaining butter and the cream. Stir in the egg and parsley. Taste to see if the seasoning needs adjustment. Heighten the flavour with a little lemon juice, if you like. Pour the sauce into a hot sauceboat and serve it with the haddock and potatoes.

NOTE Don't waste the haddock poaching milk, haddock bones and the vegetable debris from the sauce. Simmer them all together and then sieve into a clean pan (the carrot adds an appetizing orange tone). This makes a lovely soup basis, which you can enrich with a couple of egg yolks beaten up in a little cream.

KEDGEREE

This favourite Victorian breakfast dish was a convenient assemblage of yesterday's cold fish and yesterday's cold boiled rice. Unless the cook had a generous hand with the butter, I feel it was not always an inspiriting start to the day. The dish is based on Indian cookery, but the name is closer to the Hindi name, *khichri*, than to the recipe for it. *Khichri* was – and is – a mixture of rice and lentils with various seasonings; it might be eaten with fish or meat, or it might be eaten on its own. By whose genius the final dish was evolved, I do not know; but one thing is sure, *kedgeree* made with freshly cooked smoked haddock and freshly cooked rice is an excellent dish – not for breakfast perhaps, but for lunch or supper.

My own favourite recipe has always been Elizabeth David's from *Spices, Salt and Aromatics in the English Kitchen*. My husband preferred a neighbour's version that she had from somebody who had spent years in India before retiring to Cheltenham. Other people like additions of salmon and prawns. With the two basic recipes following, you have a good start for ingenuity. I would suggest that it is worth noting the way that the rice in recipe 1 is flavoured thoroughly with mace, very successful.

(1) Serves 4–6

175 g (6 oz) long grain rice, preferably Basmati
2 blades of mace
90 g (3 oz) butter
1 large Finnan haddock, poached, skinned and boned
2 hard-boiled eggs, mashed or chopped
salt, pepper
1 raw egg, beaten
at least 6 tablespoons single cream
2–3 tablespoons chopped parsley

Rinse and boil the rice until tender with the 2 blades of mace; drain well. Heat two-thirds of the butter in a sauté pan and flake the haddock into it. Stir for a few minutes. Mix in the rice and, when it is piping hot, the eggs. Check for seasoning. Off the heat, add the raw egg and cream, the rest of the butter and enough parsley to give a good speckled effect. Taste and add extra cream, it you like. Turn out on to a hot dish and serve on hot plates, as quickly as possible.

(2) Serves 3

1½ Finnan haddock
1 medium onion, sliced
2 tablespoons olive oil
1 scant teaspoon curry powder
2 tablespoons sultanas
125 g (4 oz) long grain rice, preferably Basmati
salt, pepper
2 hard-boiled eggs
chopped parsley
butter
lemon wedges and mango chutney

Pour boiling water over the haddock. Leave 2 or 3 minutes, then drain, skin and flake into pieces.

Cook the onion gently until pale yellow in the oil in a sauté pan. Stir in the curry powder and cook for a minute, stirring. Add the sultanas and rice, plus 600 ml (1 pt) water. Bring to boiling point and cook steadily for 10 minutes. Put in the haddock and seasoning and complete the cooking of the rice, which should be tender. The water will have been absorbed: towards the end of cooking time, keep an eye on things and prevent sticking by pouring in a little more water, or freeing the bottom layer of rice with a fork.

Turn on to a hot serving dish. Arrange the hard-boiled eggs and parsley on top with little knobs of butter here and there. Serve with lemon wedges and chutney.

OMELETTE ARNOLD BENNETT

The Savoy Hotel in the Strand was the scene of Arnold Bennett's novel, *Imperial Palace*. He describes its inner life and workings so well that you begin to feel part of its enveloping claustrophobic world. Outside nothing mattered, nothing held the two main characters except what related to the hotel's existence and triumph. The novel was published in 1930, the year before he died, and by then he had known the Savoy for many years, often stopping there for a late supper after the theatre. One of his favourite dishes was this omelette, which still appears regularly on the restaurant menu.

Serves 3

250 g (8 oz) cooked, flaked Finnan haddock
3 tablespoons Parmesan cheese
salt, pepper
6 eggs, beaten
a little butter
3–4 tablespoons double cream

Switch on the grill at top heat, allowing time for it to warm up.

Mix the fish with the cheese and season it. Cook the eggs in butter in an omelette pan. When the underneath part is firm but the top quite liquid, spread the fish over it and pour on the cream. Place under the grill until lightly browned and bubbling. Slide on to a serving dish without attempting to fold the omelette over.

ARBROATH SMOKIES, ABERDEEN SMOKIES, PINWIDDIES

Small haddock, quite little ones, are used for this particular cure. The fish are beheaded, gutted and washed. Then they are tied by the tail, two by two together, and brined. The last stage, after they have been hooked over rods to drip dry, is the smoking at a temperature sometimes as high as 85°C (180°F). This gives the skins a deep coppery-brown look and cooks the inside to a flaky opaque creaminess that is quite different from the close, semi-transparent firmness of cold-smoked fish.

The cure originated in Auchmithie on the eastern coast of Scotland among the fishing families that inhabit the rocky cliff. Then it spread to Arbroath, 5½ km (3½ miles) away, a busy and prosperous port. The fame of the local smokies spread gradually at the end of the nineteenth century, but they have never quite managed to become as popular as Finnan haddock. At good fishmongers in the south of Britain you may see smokies from time to time, and they are easily recognized since they are strung together in pairs. And I would say that their most distinguished appearance is at Aston Clinton in Buckinghamshire, where Michael Harris has served Bell Inn smokies for many years. They are one of his specialities and much appreciated.

Using small white soufflé dishes, one for each person, he puts in a layer of chopped, skinned and seeded tomato with seasoning, then a thick layer of flaked smokie fillets. The whole thing is covered with good thick Jersey cream and baked in a hot oven until lightly browned. Most delicious. You could add a fine grating of Parmesan or nicely dried out Cheddar.

Traditional Scottish ways are to steam or heat the smokies in an oven or under a grill, then to open them up, remove the backbone and pepper the inside well. Spread with butter, close the fish again and continue to heat gently. Be careful not to overdo the heat, since the fish are already cooked.

If you would like to buy smokies by post, ring or write to R. R. Spink & Sons, 13 High Street, Arbroath, Tayside, Scotland (0241–73246).

† HAKE & SILVER HAKE

Merluccius merluccius & *Merluccius bilinearis*

In the years since *Fish Cookery* first came out, I have once or twice been in trouble for not paying enough attention to hake. Protests came from Northern Ireland and from English readers living in Spain. My lack of judgement – or rather experience, to be fair – upset me even more when Alan Davidson declared that the first page of his *North Atlantic Seafood*, the magistral companion to *Mediterranean Seafood*, written in Vientiane where he was then ambassador, was a recipe for hake. A friend there gave him this splendid dish for hake set in its own jelly and served with a cucumber cream sauce, which came not surprisingly from Portugal. I give a resumé on p. 163.

On further investigation, it seems that while the Irish may fish hake in abundance and eat it, for all I know, every Friday and fast day of their lives, they do not treat it well. There is a lack of culinary enthusiasm about Irish cooking that drove even an optimist like the writer Maura Laverty to despair. She had learned about fish in Spain, wonders at the scarcity and price of fish in Ireland – 'In this country, each Friday brings such a realization of the financial disadvantages of being a Catholic that one has to think quickly of its spiritual advantages in order to remain in a state of grace.' Seems to me as if they suffer the disadvantages of Puritanism along with Catholicism. Even in the wry cheeriness of her *Kind Cooking*, with its charming decorations by Louis le Brocquy and dreadful photographs that look as if they had been supplied by the PR departments of sundry food manufacturers, Maura Laverty reduces the huge possibility of the North Atlantic ocean to the single word Fish – as in Fish curry, Fish baked in milk – for most of the recipes of the small section concerned.

That was in 1950, so perhaps I am being unfair, and Maura Laverty's gifts were not Elizabeth David's (her *Book of Mediterranean Food* came out in the same year, and began a quiet revolution in our kitchens). All the same, as far as hake is concerned, I turn firmly south, and in particular to Spain and Portugal. North Americans have a minor appreciation of two or three hake species. In Gloucester, they salt fresh hake for a few hours, then treat it in a similar manner to the New England salt cod dinner, i.e. it is poached and served with a number of vegetables including beetroot, p. 106. A. J. McClane in his capacious *Encyclopaedia of Fish Cookery*, has this to say: 'During our winter months after a sudden temperature drop, it's not unusual for a coldkill of hake to occur along the beaches of New York and New Jersey. Thousands of "frostfish" are washed ashore and collected by savants who dwell by the waterside. This bounty is usually harvested at night by walking the surf edge with a flashlight. Sea gulls quickly consume the frozen hake at dawn's first glow.'

Where I differ from Mr McClane is in his estimate of hake as having a 'coarser, less bland-tasting flesh' than cod. Perhaps this applies to American species. I would say quite the contrary about hake in Europe. The reason for its popularity in the Iberian peninsula may well have something to do with its availability, but there are a number of people who would still choose hake over haddock and cod who live much further north.

TO CHOOSE AND PREPARE HAKE

If you want to cook a whole fish, there is something to be said for choosing a hake rather than a more expensive sea bass or a farm salmon. Ask the fishmonger to scrape and clean the fish for you. Follow the Norway method with cod (p. 95), or – if you are making a cold dish – follow Alan Davidson's recipe, opposite.

Slices of hake are best from the head end of the fish. And they benefit greatly from a preliminary salting, as do cod, haddock and whiting steaks and fillets. This might be said of most fish, but the difference is particularly outstanding with the *Gadidae* family, since the salt improves the texture of the fish, not just its flavour. I have done test cookings of hake to see the difference salting makes – half the slices salted, half untouched until cooking time. The difference was spectacular. All you need do is range the slices in a dish, sprinkle a pinch of salt over each one and leave them for an hour at least. Longer will not do any harm at all: turn the slices, if you can, after an hour, for even distribution. As a general guide to quantity, allow a tablespoon to each 1 kg (2 lb) of fish.

Heads of hake, like cod and haddock head, are excellent for fish soup (p. 498).

HAKE IN ASPIC (Pescada en geleia)

A fine dish of summer eating that Alan Davidson gave in his *North Atlantic Seafood*, in memoriam Peter Ratcliffe, C.B.E., the friend who supplied the recipe. If ever there was a man who belonged to Petrarch's enviable band of civilized people – *Nos autem cui mundus est patria velut piscibus aequor*, people to whom the wide world is home as the sea is to fish – it must be Alan Davidson. Perhaps I am wrong in detecting a faint note of homesickness for Europe in the picture he gives of the two of them in Vientiane, far from any sea, talking of the book Alan was planning, and the friend offering this recipe from his other home on the Minho river in Portugal. A recipe which gave the stimulus to start writing.

Serves 6–8

fish stock*
1 kg (2 lb) piece of hake, cut in thick 2-cm (¾-inch) slices
3 tablespoons chicken broth
gelatine (see *recipe*)
2 tablespoons capers
3 tablespoons lemon juice

SAUCE
1 large cucumber, peeled, cut in thin strips
300 ml (10 fl oz) double cream
3 tablespoons lemon juice
2 tablespoons finely chopped onion
2 tablespoons finely chopped chives
plus: *chopped parsley and thin cucumber slices to decorate*

Bring the stock to boiling point, put in the hake and adjust heat to maintain a simmer. After 5 minutes, check the fish and remove the moment it is tender. Discard skin and bone, divide the pieces into a convenient size and put into an attractive dish that they will almost fill.

Strain the stock through a muslin: there should be nearly 1 litre (1¾ pt). Add the chicken stock and enough gelatine – *see* instructions on packet – to set the quantity of liquid. Add the capers and lemon juice. Pour this over the fish, which should be covered, and the dish full almost to the top. Put it in the refrigerator to set, at least 4 hours, but leave 6 to be sure, or 8. When almost set, decorate with parsley and halved cucumber slices.

For the sauce, dry the cucumber. Whip the cream and mix it with lemon juice to taste, then cucumber, onion and chives. Serve chilled with the aspic.

HAKE IN A GREEN SAUCE (Merluza en salsa verde)

This is a charming and simple dish for spring and early summer especially. Serve it with asparagus or very young peas. Some Spanish hake recipes of this kind include slices of potato fried first in the oil, but I prefer small new potatoes, halved after cooking and turned in parsley, for their freshness.

Serves 6

6–12 slices of hake, according to size
salt, lemon juice, plain flour
olive oil
4 large garlic cloves, halved
125 ml (4 fl oz) light stock or water
6 tablespoons dry white wine
½ dried ñora or other sweet pepper
plenty of chopped parsley (see *recipe*)

Season the hake with salt and lemon juice and leave for at least an hour. Before cooking, drain, dry and turn in flour.

In a large earthenware pot, heat enough olive oil to cover the base comfortably and cook the garlic until it is golden brown. Remove it and put in the hake, adding the stock or water, the wine, pepper and about 3 tablespoons of chopped parsley. If you like, you can crush the garlic to a paste and add it to the pot, otherwise discard it.

As the fish cooks – turn it once – shake the pot so that a sauce forms, pushing it to and fro so that it never loses contact with the heat but the liquid keeps moving.

Just before serving, add extra parsley to refresh the colour and put asparagus or peas round the dish, with potatoes.

HAKE ON THE PLATE (Merluza al plato)

This is a Spanish way of cooking hake that is simple, quick and most delicious to eat. Indeed, it is a recipe that I came back to again and again, especially with fish of the cod family though it also works well with flounders and steaks of turbot and brill. The balance of crispness, smoothness, richness and the savoury hints of garlic and lemon seem to me exactly right.

Serves 6

6–12 slices of hake, according to size
salt, lemon juice
olive oil
3 slices of bread, wholemeal, wheatmeal or white
leaves of 1 small bunch of parsley
3 large cloves garlic, quartered
mayonnaise made with light olive oil and lemon juice*

Salt the hake, allowing a ¼ teaspoon for the large steaks, less for the smaller ones. Sprinkle with a little lemon juice. Leave for an hour or longer.

Preheat the oven to gas 7, 220 °C (425 °F).

Choose a baking dish that will accommodate the fish in a single layer, fairly closely but not jammed together. Brush it out generously with oil. Cut the hardest crusts from the bread. Reduce parsley and garlic to a crumble in the processor, adding the bread gradually.

To cook, turn the steaks in the olive oil in the dish and range them tidily. Put the crumble mixture on top and drip a little oil over each one. Bake for about 15 minutes. Test the thickest slice and be prepared to allow a little longer if it is still pink. Quite often it is enough to shut the oven door, turn off the heat and leave for 5 minutes.

Serve with the mayonnaise or with two sauces as in the next recipe, and, if it is the season, small new potatoes.

HAKE WITH TWO SAUCES (Merluza con mahonesa y salsa de pimientos)

A variation of the *salsa verde* dish, but here the hake is cooked in one piece. I have adapted the recipe from one given in *Spanish Cooking* by Maite Manjón and Catherine O'Brien. It is a dish for high summer, when the asparagus accompaniment to hake is no longer possible.

Serves 6

1½ kg (3 lb) piece of hake on the bone, cleaned
salt
olive oil
125 g (4 oz) chopped onion
175 ml (6 fl oz) dry white wine
leaves of 1 medium-sized bunch of parsley
1 clove garlic, crushed, finely chopped
2 tablespoons chopped shallot
3 large red peppers, quartered, seeded, grilled, skinned
375 ml (12 fl oz) mayonnaise made with light olive oil and lemon juice*
cayenne pepper

Rub the hake over with a little salt and leave for an hour. Choose a dish that will accommodate it nicely. Switch on the oven to gas 7, 220°C (425°F).

Put a thin layer of oil into the dish. Scatter the onion over it, pour on white wine and sprinkle with a light chopping of parsley leaves and the garlic. Put the fish on top and brush it over with oil. Bake until cooked, about 25 minutes, but start testing after 20.

Meanwhile, make the pepper sauce by simmering the shallot in a little oil under tender. Do not colour it. Strain in the juices from the fish when it is cooked (discard the onion etc. in the sieve) and boil down to concentrate the flavours. Purée the peppers in a liquidizer or processor or through a sieve, and flavour to taste with the shallot reduction.

Fillet the fish and put the two pieces side by side on a hot serving dish, skin side up. Spoon the mayonnaise over it, then streak with the pepper sauce, sprinkle on some cayenne and put back in the oven for 10 minutes to heat the sauces.

KOKOTZAS

As I explained on p. 99, these are the gullet muscles cut from beneath the lower jaw of a fish. They can be taken from any of the cod family, but in the Basque country, where they are a great treat, they come invariably from hake. From their form, they are often misleadingly called 'tongues' in French and English, which can be offputting. You may find it more helpful to think of them as blunted arrowheads. Small quantities for this recipe, as you will need a patient fishmonger, or a fishmonger in the Iberian peninsula, who will collect them for you. Salted and soaked kokotzas can be cooked in the same way.

For 2 or 3 people, season 250–300 g (8–10 oz) kokotzas and set them aside. Choose a glazed flat earthenware dish that will accommodate them nicely in a single layer. Heat up 5 tablespoons of olive oil in it and fry a large quartered clove of garlic in it until golden brown, then scoop it out, and put in the kokotzas with a tablespoon of chopped parsley, a small hot dried chilli (or a fresh one) and 90 ml (3 fl oz) water or light stock. Raise the heat.

Have ready 5 more tablespoons of olive oil, heated up in a small pan and cooked for a few minutes on its own. As the kokotzas cook, add this oil gradually and keep the pot moving to and fro; the juices should merge into a creamy sauce. Taste from time to time and remove the chilli when the mixture is piquant enough for your taste.

MAIA HAKE (Pescada à Maiata)

A Portuguese recipe for hake from Carol Wright's *Portuguese Food* and one of the best ways I know of baking white fish fillets; whiting or John Dory or brill are every bit as suitable as hake. The idea of cooking mayonnaise in this way sounds bizarre, but try it. Remember that the Portuguese are the world's masters in the use of eggs and have confidence.

Serves 6

4 large egg yolks
up to 400 ml (14 fl oz) oil, part olive, part sunflower according to taste
lemon juice or wine vinegar
salt, pepper
750 g (1½ lb) hake fillets
juice of ½ lemon
750 g (1½ lb) potatoes, scrubbed
extra olive and sunflower oil
1 small onion, finely chopped (optional)

Make a mayonnaise in the usual way with the yolks, oil, lemon or vinegar and seasoning to taste.

Put the fillets skin side down in one layer in a baking dish, of a size to leave enough space to take the potatoes eventually. Sprinkle them with seasoning and the juice of half a lemon. Set aside.

Preheat the oven to gas 4, 180 °C (350 °F). Then boil the potatoes until they are almost tender. Run them under the cold tap, peel them and cut them into dice. Fry them in the extra oils until they are a nice golden-brown: they should not be a deep colour and crisp, but melting and even-toned. Arrange them round and between the pieces of fish. Spoon the mayonnaise mainly over the fish but a little over the potatoes; the exposed potatoes can be sprinkled with onion.

Bake for 20–30 minutes until the fish is just cooked and the mayonnaise lightly browned.

† HALIBUT

ATLANTIC, PACIFIC & CALIFORNIA

Hippoglossus hippoglossus, H. stenolepis &

Paralichthys californicus

The halibut is, or at least can be, the most monstrous of the flounders. In the Atlantic, specimens have been caught measuring over 2 m (6½ ft), nearly 3 m (9¾ ft) occasionally, in length and over 1 m (3¼ ft) wide – potentially a most flattening experience for halibut fishermen. I have occasionally seen fish measuring about half this magnificent length: they seemed quite big enough at the time, though nothing by comparison.

The name 'halibut' seemed odd at first. What kind of name could it be? As usual, the big *Oxford English Dictionary* provided the answer. It signifies 'holy flounder', 'holy flatfish', a northern name, nothing Mediterranean about halibut; in other words, a fish much eaten on fast days, Fridays, Wednesdays, the eve of holy days. It first appeared on record in English, an item on a banquet menu, in the 1420s. A grand occasion, obviously held on a fast day, in honour of Richard Flemming, Bishop of Winchester. Other fish were salmon, eel, 'good pike and fat', lampreys, trout, sturgeon, porpoise, perch, whelks, sea bream, crab, gudgeon, haddock, gurnard, plaice, tails of cod and ling. Quite a shopping list for the local fishmonger.

The strange things is that after that glamorous occasion, it makes no appearance in cookery books, as far as I can discover, until the nineteenth century. No recipes, no comment. Perhaps it was all too commonly served up dry and overcooked. Everyone knew what to do with it, and did it without enthusiasm.

Halibut's one moment of glory, gastronomic glory, occurs on 25 April 1784, at Olney, when the poet William Cowper turned his skill *To the Immortal Memory of the Halibut on which I dined this day*. Mind you, Cowper was using the halibut to send up the dull stupidity – he was 'as dry as the remainder biscuit after a voyage' – of the notable Dr Blair, an Edinburgh academic who fancied himself on poetry. Blair was all for Ossian and his wild Scottish fake romanticism. He ticked Virgil off for not sticking to things that 'fill the nation with astonishment' – e.g. thunderbolts splitting mountains, when writing about a storm in the *Georgics*, but descending to the obvious such as wind and rain. Cowper could not, he confessed, conceive 'that wind and rain can be improper in the description of a tempest'. And in returning thanks to the friend who had sent both Blair's lectures and the halibut, he took off into the Sublime, laughter barely restrained, à la Dr Blair, all preposterous grandeur:

> Where hast thou floated, in what seas pursued
> Thy pastime? When wast thou an egg new-spawn'd,
> Lost in th' immensity of ocean's waste?
> Roar as they might, the overbearing winds
> That rock'd the deep, thy cradle, thou wast safe –
> And in thy minikin and embryo state,
> Attach'd to the firm leaf of some salt weed,
> Didst outlive tempests, such as wrung and rack'd
> The joints of many a stout and gallant bark,
> And whelm'd them in the unexplor'd abyss.
> Indebted to no magnet and no chart,
> Nor under guidance of the polar fire,
> Thou wast a voyager on many coasts,
> Grazing at large in meadows submarine,
> Where flat Batavia just emerging peeps
> Above the brine, – where Caledonia's rocks
> Beat back the surge, – and where Hibernia shoots
> Her wondrous causeway far into the main.
> – Wherever thou hast fed, thou little thought'st
> And I not more, that I should feed on thee.
> Peace therefore, and good health, and much good fish,
> To him who sent thee! and success, as oft
> As it descends into the billowy gulph,
> To the same drag that caught thee! – Fare thee well!
> Thy lot thy brethren of the slimy fin
> Would envy, could they know that thou wast doom'd
> To feed a bard, and to be prais'd in verse.

Apart from that pantomime grandeur, to be recited with gestures I am sure, halibut lies low again until 1826. That year, *The Cook and Housewife's Manual* was published under the aegis of Sir Walter Scott, written ostensibly by Meg Dods of the Cleikum Club, but really by a friend, Mrs Johnstone. She remarks that the halibut sometimes usurps the turbot's name in Scotland – shifty fishmongers? – but that it is excellent in its way, even if not so rich or so well flavoured as the turbot. And she suggests currying it, a brilliant suggestion. She notes that curried fish has lately become popular and is good as long you make up your own blend of spices for each dish, avoiding commercial curry powders. It is rather daunting to think that, 160 years later, cookery writers are still saying the same thing. Are lazy practices eternal?

After Mrs Johnstone, there is another silence, a conspicuous silence from Soyer, Eliza Acton and Mrs Beeton on the subject of halibut. Perhaps the explanation is to be found in *Kettner's Book of the Table* (1877). Aeneas Dallas, its author, has a lively turn of phrase: 'The most fitting appellation which has been given to the halibut is – workhouse turbot. To do the creature justice, however, he makes a good curry.' From about this time, though, halibut makes more of a showing. In *Cassell's Dictionary* of the early 1880s, there are seven recipes – 'This excellent fish is not prized as it ought to be, probably on account of its cheapness. The "tit-bits" are the flackers over the fins, and the pickings about the head.' There is also the just comment that boiling is the least satisfactory mode of cooking halibut. 'It is much better fried, baked, or put into a pie.'

It does occur to me that since halibut has a tendency to dryness and loses all its spirit if overcooked, the arrival of gas cookers and their controllable heat must have made it much easier to serve up properly done fish. I remember as a child that we had both a kitchen range and a new gas cooker, and this suddenly made finicky cooking much easier.

Our halibut in Britain comes mainly from the great sandy seabed between Norway and Scotland. There is also an immense fishery off the Pacific coast of Canada and the United States, both of the Pacific halibut and the more common California halibut. All three have a similar sweetly mild and close flesh, though the California halibut is not quite as good as the Pacific kind. Nowadays, of course, the fishing is organized in a starkly efficient manner. In the last century, though, the Red Indians would go out by the hundred in their canoes, 19 km (12 miles) offshore, and catch these immense creatures with their hooks of Douglas pine or yew, and lines of dried seaweed and deer sinew. When the fish bit on the trailing lines, they would pull them in and spear them, and drag them into the canoes. In a high sea, inflated seal skins, turned inside-out and painted, were fixed to each side of the canoes to keep them buoyant with their heavy loads.

Alan Davidson in his *North Atlantic Seafood* reproduces a small engraving from the end of the last century that shows a rather similar style. Two men in a dory that sits low on the water are 'hauling the trawl, gaffing and clubbing the halibut'. In the background is a similar dory and the halibut schooner to which they will take back their load. He also gives a recipe for an Icelandic halibut soup, thickened with a little flour and butter, sharpened with vinegar and lemon, and enlivened with prunes or rhubarb. Which reminds me to say that grilled halibut tastes splendid with butter flavoured with orange or lime juice.

HOW TO CHOOSE AND PREPARE HALIBUT

Properly fresh halibut – frozen is decidedly second best, though passable – has a look of bright juicy whiteness. Steaks vary enormously in size according to the halibut: the biggest I have seen weighed about 1 kg (2 lb) and was nearly 2½ cm (1 inch) thick, a giant slice cut right across. If one ever had the chance of buying from one of the rare enormous halibut one reads about, I cannot quite imagine how large across it would be. In any case, recipes are easy enough to adapt, as it is the thickness of any piece of fish that dictates cooking time, not its weight or surface area.

In California, they sometimes sell halibut in long fillet strips known as flitches, cut parallel to the backbone. This seems to have been a Victorian practice in England since there were special flitching knives made for cutting halibut. They are featured in the 1884 supplement to Knight's *Practical Dictionary of Mechanics*, but not in the original publication of 1874–77. This fact, plus the sudden increase in halibut recipes in books of the 1880s, date the rise of its coming into favour. Perhaps the practice still continues somewhere.

Another Californian delicacy is halibut cheeks: I have never eaten them, but they are said to be good. Something I can believe, as the little nuggets known as knobs and cheeks (often, in fact, the arrowhead-shaped muscle under the jaw) from other fish are always worth buying.

Something you may see is chicken halibut – chicken meaning young

– weighing about 1 kg (2 lb). They are well worth eating and make an attractive dish for three or four people. Just trim off the fins and neaten the tail: the fishmonger will have cleaned them. Once or twice, I had smoked chicken halibut from the Hamburg shop in Brewer Street in London – now there no longer. It was lightly smoked. All you needed to do was to strip off the skin and serve it in thin slices with horseradish cream, bread and butter.

Don't be fooled by long fillets of fish labelled Greenland halibut. They do come from a related flounder; the flesh is undistinguished, quite pleasant, but without the firm true sweetness of the real thing.

HALIBUT AND CHEESE GRATIN

This is a good way of cooking halibut with its tendency to dryness. Really you are putting a Welsh rabbit on top of the steaks to keep all the moisture inside. For me, it is very much a dish for midday, or family supper, when you might not otherwise be serving cheese. Provide new potatoes, or firm fleshed winter potatoes rather than the floury kind (p. 187), and a salad of mixed greenery that includes crisp and bitter leaves.

This is a good recipe, too, for cod and other firm white fish steaks.

Serves 6

6 halibut steaks
salt, pepper, cayenne
3 tablespoons melted butter
175 g (6 oz) grated Gruyère, Swiss or Gouda cheese
60 g (2 oz) grated Parmesan
1 tablespoon Dijon mustard
3 tablespoons single cream

Switch on the oven to gas 5–6, 190–200 °C (375–400 °F).

Season the halibut with salt, pepper and a good pinch of cayenne. Choose a gratin dish that will accommodate the steaks in a single layer, fitting them closely. Pour in the melted butter, swill it around the base and up the sides and arrange the halibut on it.

Mix the remaining items to a paste. You may need a shade more cream or mustard so that you can spread this paste more easily over the top surface of the fish, but it should not be liquid.

Bake for 15–20 minutes. If the cheese becomes brown quickly, protect it from burning by putting butter papers on top. When the halibut is cooked, serve the dish from the oven, sizzling hot.

HALIBUT AND COCONUT CURRY

The sweetness of spiced coconut milk goes particularly well with halibut, and the dish can be served cold. However, if you intend to do this, keep the sauce a little on the liquid side as it will thicken as it cools. To make coconut milk, turn to p. 478; otherwise, use creamed coconut which works well in highly spiced dishes. You can also buy tinned coconut milk.

Serves 4

1 chicken halibut or 4 halibut steaks, about 1 kg (2 lb) in all
concentrated butter, ghee or clarified butter
375 ml (12 fl oz) coconut milk
3 tablespoons cider vinegar
1 teaspoon rice flour or ground rice
1 teaspoon ground coriander seed
1 teaspoon turmeric
salt, cayenne pepper
1 medium onion, finely chopped
1 clove garlic, crushed, skinned, finely chopped
about 150 ml (5 fl oz) plain yoghurt
chopped fresh green fennel, dill or coriander leaves

Choose a heavy non-stick pan into which the halibut fits neatly. In it, cook the fish in the minimum of butter or ghee so that it is lightly coloured on both sides, but not cooked. Remove the fish to a plate. If the juices in the pan are still fresh and buttery, leave them. If not, wash the pan out.

Meanwhile, add the vinegar, rice flour, spices, salt and a little cayenne pepper to the coconut milk in a separate bowl.

Stew the onion slowly in the pan, adding extra butter or ghee if necessary. As it softens and turns yellow, stir in the garlic. Whisk up the coconut milk mixture with a fork, and pour it into the pan. When it begins to bubble, put the fish back and complete the cooking at a mild simmer. Keep spooning the sauce over the chicken halibut, or turn the halibut steaks for even cooking. If the sauce gets too thick and clotted, smooth it out with a little hot water. Transfer the cooked fish to a warm serving platter or individual plates. Check the sauce for seasoning and pour it over the halibut.

Quickly stir the yoghurt into the pan. It will acquire a pale yellow colour from the remains of the sauce. Spoon it down the centre of the fish, and scatter it with the chopped herbs and dust lightly with cayenne.

Serve with rice or potatoes, and strips of grilled, skinned sweet peppers – yellow and red ones make a happy contrast both of flavour and colour. Or serve a cucumber raita (p. 183), or plain batons of cucumber, a wonderfully refreshing garnish.

HALIBUT STEAMED IN ITS OWN JUICE

People who earn a living through food in the States, and take it seriously, are much indebted to Sheryl Julian, who – with Lora Brody – founded the Boston Women's Culinary Guild in 1978. Since then, food professionals in other cities have organized similar groups, not necessarily confined to women, for mutual assistance. As a visiting foreigner, I was bewildered by the usual problem of collecting information in a short time, and the Boston Guild came to my rescue with a speedy efficacy that amazed me. And to cap it all, Sheryl Julian gave me this excellent idea for cooking halibut: it can be used for other firm fish, too.

Serves 4

¾ –1 kg (1½–2 lb) skinned halibut fillet in 1 piece
4 tablespoons softened unsalted butter
salt, pepper
1 small handful of dill sprigs, finely chopped
1 small handful of parsley sprigs, finely chopped (flat-leaf parsley for
*   preference)*
½ shallot, very finely chopped
2 medium tomatoes, skinned, seeded, coarsely chopped
4 slices of lemon, 4 sprigs of dill for garnish

Holding the small end of the fillet towards you, skinned side down, cut eight thick 'scallops' at an angle of 45°, using a long thin sharp knife.

Grease a 35–38-cm (14–15-inch) sauté pan with half the butter. Set the scallops in the pan and sprinkle the remaining ingredients over them evenly in the order given, apart from the garnish.

Cut a round of baking parchment or greaseproof paper to fit closely inside the pan and spread it with the remaining butter. Put it into the pan, buttered side down, on to the fish. Cover with a tight-fitting lid. Set the pan over a medium-high heat for about 8 minutes, until the fish turns opaque in colour and firm to the touch. It should flake easily.

Remove the paper. Carefully transfer two pieces of fish to each of four hot plates, arranging them in a V. Twist four slices of lemon and set one in the middle of each V with a sprig of dill. Serve with boiled new potatoes, turned in a little butter, parsley and dill.

JONGHE MARC'S HALIBUT (Flétan de Jonghe Marc)

A reader living in America sent me this recipe many years ago. I think it came from the March 1972 issue of *Gourmet* magazine and I have made it many times, sometimes with cod or hake or brill. Do not be put off by the quantity of garlic, or by the use of dry vermouth rather than dry white wine. These ingredients and the style of cooking give a most appetizing liveliness that helps any fish with a tendency to be a little solid or boring. Halibut steaks or other similar steaks can be used rather than fillets. The point is to aim for a thickness of 2½ cm (1 inch). With the looser flaked fish, cod for instance, it is sensible to leave the steaks whole, or just to remove the two thick pieces from either side of the main bone; if you attempt to cut cubes, the fish will fall apart when cooked and look messy.

Serves 6

generous 1 kg (2½ lb) halibut fillet
salt, pepper
250 g (8 oz) fresh white or light wholemeal breadcrumbs
250 ml (8 fl oz) melted butter
8 tablespoons dry white vermouth
4 cloves garlic, crushed, skinned, finely chopped

Cut the fish into 2½-cm (1-inch) cubes and season them. Choose a baking dish into which they will be able to fit closely together in a single layer. Grease it with a butter paper.

Switch on the oven to gas 5, 190°C (375°F).

Put the crumbs into a bowl and pour on half the butter, and the vermouth into which you have stirred the garlic. Mix to a moist paste. Add a little more vermouth if the paste is too dry to spread.

Put half of this paste over the base of the baking dish and arrange the halibut on top. Spread the rest of the paste over it. Pour on the rest of the butter.

Bake for about 20 minutes, or until cooked. Check after 15 minutes. Complete the browning under a preheated grill.

This is a good dish for lunchtime, early in the summer when broad beans come in or some of the first slightly bitter salads, endive and rocket (or arugula) for instance.

WRAPPED HALIBUT WITH CORIANDER

A light bitterness seems to me to go well with fish, particularly when there is a butter sauce to go with it. With some of us, coriander can become a passion, others hate it. There is no point in trying to overcome this hatred: I understand that to some people it tastes like soap which must indeed be vile. This is a chemical effect, and cannot be changed. For such people, I would suggest using dill or fennel instead of coriander.

Serves 4

4 halibut steaks, each about 150 g (5 oz)
salt, pepper, cayenne, lemon juice
4 tablespoons chopped shallot or *onion*
½ clove garlic, finely chopped
2–3 tablespoons butter
400 g (14 oz) piece of flaky or *puff pastry*
12 sprigs coriander, each about 10 cm (4 inches)
beaten egg or *light cream to glaze*

GARNISH
2 bitter gourds, each about 8 cm (3 inches) long
12-cm (5-inch) piece cucumber, peeled, sliced across
3 small-to-medium tomatoes, skinned
2–3 tablespoons butter
4 sprigs coriander

Season the fish with salt, pepper, cayenne and a few drops of lemon juice. Set aside.

Stew the shallot or onion and garlic in half the butter in a non-stick pan until it becomes yellow and tender. Scoop it into a bowl with a slotted spoon, and leave to cool. Add the rest of the butter to the juices in the pan and, over a higher temperature, colour the halibut lightly on both sides. Cool to barely lukewarm.

Switch on the oven to gas 8, 230 °C (450 °F).

Divide the pastry into four and roll out each piece until it is large enough to enclose a halibut steak. In the middle of each, spread an island of cooked shallot or onion, using half the quantity. Lay two sprigs of coriander across each island, and put the halibut on top. Spread the remaining shallot or onion over the fish and top with the remaining four coriander sprigs.

Using some of the egg or cream as glue, wrap the pastry round the halibut, fastening it firmly and cutting away lumpy surplus dough.

Turn the four packages over on to a baking sheet, smooth side up. Brush over with egg or cream. Make a discreet decoration, if you like, with the dough trimmings, and brush them with egg or cream too. Make small central slits and bake for 15 minutes, or until the pastry is nicely browned and the fish inside tender.

Serve on warm, not very hot plates with the garnish.

TO PREPARE THE GARNISH Scrape the skin from the bitter gourds with a knife, to remove the majority of the bumpiness. Then slice them in quarters downwards and remove the seeds and pulp with a spoon. Boil them in salted water for 3 minutes, then drain. This reduces the bitterness to an agreeable level: taste a little bit if you are not used to bitter gourds, but also bear in mind that it is being eaten more as a flavouring than as a vegetable in this particular dish. Complete the cooking in a little butter with a scrap of garlic.

Push out the central seeds of the cucumber. Cook briefly in a little salted water, and drain.

Skin the tomatoes, quarter them into wedges and scoop out the centre part (use up in another dish). Cook the pieces in butter until they are tender and season them.

Trim the coriander sprigs.

† HERRING

Clupea harengus

I remember as a child listening to my father's tales of going out with herring boats from South Shields or Tynemouth. He talked about the cold and the fierce seas, the sudden energy required and the cups of strong sweet tea that kept them going. When the nets were hauled in – great walls, I suppose, of drift nets – the silver catch tumbled into the boat for what seemed like hours, the mesh stuck solid with fish. He understood well, as did many in the north-east, Scott's remark in *The Antiquary*, 'It's nae fish ye're buying, it's men's lives'. Something even a child could understand on certain Sundays of bad weather, when voices surged and swirled over one's head, losing their usual genteel decorum as they sang of those in peril on the sea.

Such things had gone on for ever, would go on for ever. The vast shoals would appear as usual at the expected times and places, even if their arrival was no longer predicted by the arrival of the Scottish fisher girls in their striped skirts as it once was. These women knew the seasons and would appear up and down the coast, ready to gut and barrel the herrings, a vast trade for export. A whole complete world enclosed the herring trade, with its own customs and movement and vocabulary. Do you know the meaning of klondyking, farlanes, gipping, crabs, lasts, redding? Did you know that the herring's scales are described as deciduous because they fall as easily as leaves from autumn trees? Did you know that the word herring means 'army' – because of the vast shoals they travel in? One shoal, measured in 1877, was 18 fathoms deep (118 feet): it covered an area which would have reached from Marble Arch to the London docks beyond the Tower, and from the House of Commons to Euston Station. At one time people thought the herrings moved about, like the fisher girls, but in fact it is different races of herring that appear together at certain times in certain parts of the sea on both sides of the Atlantic.

Even a tiny shoal of herring in an aquarium swimming round and round is an impressive and unnerving sight, millions of 'soldiers' moving blindly on. Perhaps this explains why the herring was rather beyond the capacity, outside the interest of early fishermen. This fish which caused battles, wars and created vast wealth from the late Middle Ages has left no traces in the prehistoric settlements of northern Europe. Salmon bones appear in excavation, but never a herring bone. Amsterdam is said to have been built on herring bones, but Amsterdam is a late town with no prehistory. Archaeologists have speculated on the matter. Boats were developed enough, since curraghs, which are survivals of early boats, have been used for fishing herring until recent times.

The conclusion seems to be that the construction of a drift net, the long wall of net which the herring swim in to and are caught by, takes too much time for a small community to bother with. Vast catches were just not needed, or not until the fast days of Christian Europe ruled that people, however far inland they might be, had to eat fish at least once a week, sometimes twice or more. And so the herring, the curable herring, became the great fish of northern life, the trade having its origin in the Dark Ages (the first recorded use of our word 'herring' occurs in the eighth century AD). Other towns were built on herrings, Great Yarmouth and Lowestoft for instance. Herrings caused skirmishes as East Anglian and Dutch fishermen raced for the first huge catch in the spring. The way of life of millions of people has been shaped by the herring. Not bad for a small fish weighing on average 150 g (5 oz).

It never occurred to most of us that herring might vanish from our shops. They were eternal, a natural plunder that would never fail. But they did fail. Nets and trawling techniques became so efficiently vacuum-cleaner-like that even the vaster shoals were sucked up. So depleted were they that for several years herring fishing was forbidden. Only in 1984 was it allowed again.

Herrings are on the slab once more, it is true, but what has happened to them? The ones I see are poor limp things compared to the crisp bright 'silver darlings' of the old days. Is this because they are lying about too long in ice? Is it because my local fishmongers do not buy the top of the catch? Is it because we fished the heart out of the herring tribe and the few years' peace we allowed them has not been enough to restore their vigour? Now they seem to have a weary grey pappiness that needs the tonic of sharp and savoury ingredients. Once all they needed was plain grilling and an accompanying wedge of lemon with some bread and butter and mustard, just as Swift wrote for the Irish women crying herrings in London streets:

> Be not sparing,
> Leave off swearing,
> Buy my Herring
> Fresh from Malahide,
> Better ne'er was try'd.
> Come eat 'em with pure fresh Butter and Mustard,
> Their Bellies are soft, and white as a Custard.
> Come Sixpence a Dozen to get me some Bread,
> Or, like my own Herrings, I soon shall be dead.

Now more than ever we need some of the more elaborate devices thought up by chefs in the past, to dress up this simple and excellent fish – maître d'hôtel butter*, orange* or mustard butter*, purées of gooseberries* and sorrel*. Flavours that are strong and clear. In these last years, too, it has been noticeable the strides made in popularizing pickled herrings of all kinds (p. 191).

HOW TO PREPARE HERRINGS

Since the scales of herring fall off so easily, all they need is rinsing under the tap with the minimum of help from the back of a knife. Gutting can be done via the gills, or by slitting the belly first with a pair of scissors. Any trace of blood remaining can be rubbed away with a finger dipped in salt.

Herring roe is much prized, especially the soft male roe or milt. It will be of better quality, coming directly from the fish, than the roe you buy from thawed blocks at the fishmonger's. Keep it for stuffing herring and other fish, for using in an omelette such as the Curé's omelette (p. 430) or tartlets. Recipes are given later in this section.

The head of herring is not generally removed unless you wish to bone the fish or remove the fillets. Boning is simple enough. Slit the herring, after cutting off the head, fins and tail, clean the cavity and continue the cut right to the tail. Put it on a board, backbone up, spreading the two flaps where it was cut to either side. Starting at the head end, press down along the backbone firmly to the tail. You will hear or rather feel the crunch as it loosens. Turn the fish over and pick off the backbone: remove any tiny bones with tweezers if you cannot easily raise them.

Another way of opening the herring is to cut along the backbone with a sharp knife, after removing the head. This is the way kippers are cut. You can then open it out, and scrape away the backbone and rinse out the innards. Keeping the roe, of course.

For fillets, cut the boned herring in half. It is also quite easy to skin large herrings, if you wish. Put them skin side down on the board, tail end towards you. Separate the fillet by scraping along the skin with a small pointed knife.

Since herring go from 150–375 g (5–12 oz), it is easy to adapt sardine and mackerel recipes to them, or bluefish recipes. They all have similar oily flesh and take contrasts of sharp acidity and sweetness very well. Spices and saltiness – bacon, anchovies, olives – and piquancy are also to be recommended.

After preparing oily fish – and this includes mackerel, sardines, bluefish and pilchards – you can best get rid of the oily smell on fingers and utensils by running them under cold water. Then they can be washed in the usual way.

BAKED HERRING IN VARIOUS GUISES

An excellent way of dealing with herrings is to bake them with a lively stuffing, but not too much or their delicate flavour will be drowned. There are three options:
(1) stuff the cavity of the fish, after cleaning it.
(2) bone the fish, spread it with a layer of stuffing and then roll it up from the tail, skin side out. A wooden cocktail stick, pushed through, is needed to secure the shape.
(3) bone the fish, stuff it more liberally, then fold it over into its original shape.

The oven temperature should be hot, gas 6–7, 200–220 °C (400–425 °F); the time will vary from 15–30 minutes, according to the size of the herring and the treatment you choose.

Serve the baked fish simply with lemon quarters, or with a yoghurt sauce of the kind given below. If you baste the fish as it cooks, with wine or citrus juice or a flavoured oil, the juices may well be sauce enough.

You can have a great deal of experimental fun with herrings. They are even now not too expensive. They are robust enough to stand up to lively flavours, and do not trail the aura of sole or turbot which demand to be treated with a certain reverence. With herrings you

have the relaxation of feeding family and close friends, you can risk a
jeu d'esprit.

All quantities below are for 6 herrings

WITH CUCUMBER

STUFFING
125 g (4 oz) soft white breadcrumbs
8-cm (3-inch) piece cucumber, peeled, diced small
2 tablespoons chopped parsley
1 teaspoon thyme
½ teaspoon chopped sage
3 shallots or 1 small onion, chopped
4 tablespoons butter
juice and grated peel of 1 lime
1 egg
salt, pepper

Mix the crumbs, cucumber and herbs. Soften the shallot or onion in
the butter, and add to the crumbs with the lime juice, peel, egg and
seasoning. Serve with:

SAUCE
250 ml (8 fl oz) Greek yoghurt
3–4 tablespoons double cream
10-cm (4-inch) piece of cucumber, peeled, diced small
2 tablespoons parsley
1 tablespoon lime juice
salt, pepper

Mix the ingredients together in the order given, flavouring finally to
taste with lime juice, salt and pepper.

NOTE   This dish can be prepared with bluefish, p. 59.

WITH APPLE AND BEETROOT

STUFFING
125 g (4 oz) soft breadcrumbs
1 sharp eating apple
¼ teaspoon cinnamon
1 teaspoon caster sugar
3 shallots or 1 small onion, chopped
4 tablespoons butter
1 egg
salt, pepper
about 2 tablespoons chopped celery or walnut (optional)

Put the crumbs in a basin. Peel, core and dice the apple, mixing it in with the crumbs as you go. Add cinnamon and caster sugar. Meanwhile, soften the shallot or onion in the butter. Add it to the crumbs with egg and seasoning. Finally, mix in the celery or walnut, if you like. Serve with:

SAUCE
250 ml (8 fl oz) Greek yoghurt
3–4 tablespoons double cream
2 small beetroot, golf-ball sized, boiled or lightly pickled, peeled, chopped
1 small eating apple, peeled, cored, diced
lemon juice
salt, pepper, sugar
horseradish

Mix all the ingredients together, seasoning with lemon, salt, pepper and sugar to taste. The beetroot will turn the sauce rather a lurid pink – use horseradish to give a counter-balancing edge of flavour.

WITH MUSHROOMS

STUFFING
125 g (4 oz) soft breadcrumbs
3 shallots or 1 small onion, chopped
4 tablespoons butter
125–175 g (4–6 oz) mushrooms, finely chopped
2 tablespoons parsley
1 clove garlic, finely chopped
good pinch of oregano or marjoram
salt, pepper
lemon juice
2 tablespoons grated Parmesan cheese (optional)

Put the crumbs in a bowl. Soften the shallot or onion in the butter, add the mushrooms, parsley and garlic, raising the heat as the mushroom juices run. Mix in the oregano or marjoram, seasoning and lemon juice to taste. If you would like an extra piquancy, add the cheese.

I prefer this dish without a sauce, though a glass of white wine poured over the herring does not come amiss. Lemon wedges and small new potatoes go with it well. Should you have the luck to pick girolles or other woodland mushrooms, or some good field mushrooms, this dish will be even more successful.

WITH GOOSEBERRIES Instead of mushrooms in the recipe above, use small green gooseberries with some sugar. Omit the garlic and use a little thyme rather than oregano or marjoram. Serve the fish on its own, or with one of the gooseberry sauces* – but keep the quantity small or the herring will be overwhelmed.

WITH SOFT ROE STUFFING See the mackerel recipe on p. 190.

DEVILLED HERRINGS

Like mackerel and sprats, herring are an ideal fish for grilling because they are so rich in oil. If you have a charcoal fire burning out of doors in the summer, cook herrings on it so that their skins catch the heat and you will not have much cause to regret the sardines of Portugal, Spain and France.

If the herrings are to be grilled whole, as in this recipe, slash them twice or three times, on either side of the backbone. This helps the heat to penetrate the thickest part and makes for even cooking. If the herrings are boned, they will need less cooking time: heat the grill rack first, brush the boned side with butter and seasoning and put them skin side to the heat. There will be no need to turn them over.

Serves 6

6 herring with soft roes
3 tablespoons Dijon mustard
2 teaspoons sunflower oil
¾ teaspoon cayenne pepper
salt
125 g (4 oz) fine breadcrumbs from stale bread
125 g (4 oz) butter, melted

Gut the herrings via the gills, extracting the roes carefully and leaving the heads in place. Slash the fish on either side of the backbone. Rinse and dry both herring and roes.

Mix together mustard, oil, cayenne and salt. Brush the cavities with this mixture and put the roes back. Tip the crumbs on to a tray, brush the herring with the mustard mixture and roll them in the crumbs to coat them. They should now go into the refrigerator for the coating to firm up, and can be left there for some time.

Preheat the grill. Line the grill pan with foil and put the rack in place. Brush it with oil and lay the herrings on top carefully. Sprinkle with melted butter and slide under the grill. Baste the fish from time to time and turn them once. Total time, including time required for basting, should be about 12 minutes, but check to see the herring are not overdone. They should be a nice golden brown.

The French would serve fried potatoes with this dish, but new potatoes turned in a little parsley butter or plain bread are good alternatives.

FRIED HERRING WITH CREAM AND ROE SAUCE

If you can persuade the fishmonger to choose you soft-roed herrings, this is an agreeable way of serving them.

Serves 6

6 herrings with their roes
3 shallots, chopped
about 6 tablespoons butter
300 ml (10 fl oz) crème fraîche or half soured, half double cream
chopped parsley, chives and chervil
salt, pepper
lemon juice
seasoned flour

Clean the herrings, removing the roes carefully. Cook the shallots in a little of the butter in a small pan until they are soft but not coloured. Process or blend the roes with the cream(s). Off the heat, stir this mixture into the shallots, add chopped herbs, seasoning and a little lemon juice to taste. Just before serving, put back on to a low heat and stir all the time until slightly thickened.

For the herrings, turn them in seasoned flour and cook them in the minimum of butter. Do not have the heat too high as this is a mild dish: you do not want the butter or the skin of the fish to burn.

Put the herrings on to a warm serving dish, with small new potatoes, and pour the sauce over the fish.

VARIATION   If your herrings do not all have soft roes, add what you can muster to a Sauce verte de Chausey*.

HERRING FRIED IN THE SCOTTISH FASHION

This is many people's favourite way of cooking herrings. I used to dip them in coarse oatmeal but now have more success with fine or medium oatmeal which clings better. This is not a recipe for small herrings. You need the larger more robust kind. Go for Ayrshire bacon if you can, or the even fattier Yorkshire bacon which gives plenty of fat for the fish. Serve oatcakes with the herring if you want to be precise in your tradition. I prefer bread, especially if it incorporates oatmeal with the flour, or potatoes that are floury.

To test for this, try the potatoes in a bucket of water before you cook them, adding 1 part salt to 11 parts water. Waxy potatoes will float, floury ones will sink. I am indebted to Harold McGee for this invaluable bit of information from his *On Food and Cooking: The Science and Lore of the Kitchen.*

Serves 6

6 fine herrings, boned
salt, pepper
fine or medium oatmeal
12 rashers of bacon, best quality
4–6 tablespoons bacon fat or lard
a little chopped parsley
6 lemon wedges

Season the herrings well and press them firmly down into a tray of oatmeal so that they are well coated on both sides.

Fry the bacon, crisp if you can and brown, in the bacon fat or lard. Keep them warm, then fry the herrings in the fat until nicely browned, turning them carefully so as to lose as little oatmeal as possible. Serve them with the bacon, scattered very lightly with a little parsley, and with the lemon wedges.

WELSH SUPPER HERRINGS (Swper Scadan)

This is a Welsh version of a gratin of a kind popular over much of northern Europe. The old way was to put the various ingredients together raw, then to cook them in a moderate oven for about an hour. This does have the effect of overcooking the fish but gives the flavours plenty of chance to blend together, so that it ends up as a comforting soft sort of mixture. Today I blanch the potato slices – the slowest cooking ingredient – so that the fish retains more of its personality after a much briefer stay in the oven.

Serves 6

1 kg (2 lb) potatoes, peeled, sliced
6 filleted herrings
mustard, salt, pepper
2 cooking apples or 2 large sharp eating apples, peeled, cored, sliced
1 large onion, sliced paper thin
¼ teaspoon dried sage
2 tablespoons butter, melted

Preheat the oven to gas 7, 220 °C (425 °F). Choose a gratin dish large enough to hold the herrings in a single layer, and rub it out with a butter paper.

Blanch the potato slices in salted boiling water until they are opaque and almost cooked. Drain and cool slightly, while preparing the rest of the dish.

Open the herrings, spread them with mustard and seasoning. Fold them back into shape, or roll them over loosely.

Put half the potatoes in the base of the dish, with half the apples and half the onion. Put the herrings on top with seasoning and sage, then apple and onion, and a top layer of the rest of the potatoes. Pour the butter, or brush it, evenly over the potato. Bake for 20 minutes, then test and see if the herrings need more time. The top should brown nicely but it can always be finished off under the grill.

SOFT HERRING ROES

The creamy texture of soft roes lends itself to some delicious recipes. Provided, that is, you can find them in good shape. Often they have been flung together and frozen into an enormous damaged heap, so that they are good for nothing but the sieve. Keep these poor creatures for the roe paste or roe stuffing, below, or to make a creamy sauce for shrimp and prawn boats. Unblemished, dignified pairs of roes may be fried in butter and served on fried bread, with lemon quarters, or cooked as follows. The recipes following may also be used for mackerel and other soft roes.

DEVILLED SOFT ROES

Turn the roes in seasoned flour liberally spiked with cayenne pepper. Fry in clarified butter. Serve on buttered toast, sprinkled with chopped parsley. Provide lemon wedges. Allow 3 pairs of roes per person.

FRITURE DE LAITANCE AVEC SAUCE MOUTARDE

Serves 6

18 pairs of large herring roes (more will be needed if they are small)
salt, pepper
oil for frying

BATTER
125 g (4 oz) plain flour
pinch of salt
2 tablespoons oil
175 ml (6 fl oz) tepid water or beer
2 small egg whites
mustard sauce*

Divide and season the herring roes. Set them aside. Make the batter by mixing together flour, salt and oil with the tepid water or beer – aim for a pouring custard consistency. Leave to stand for a while, if this is convenient. Beat the egg whites until stiff and fold into the batter just before it is required. Make the mustard sauce and keep it warm.

Coat the roes in batter and fry golden brown on both sides in oil (or use a deep-frying pan). As each batch is cooked – it is important not to overcrowd the pan – keep it warm on crumpled kitchen paper, set on a baking tray in the oven. When all are cooked, serve with the mustard sauce.

This is one of the best dishes in the book. I've adapted it slightly from a recipe in Ali Bab's *Gastronomie Pratique*.

OMELETTE WITH SOFT HERRING ROE

Soft herring roes make a good filling for an omelette. Fry them gently in butter, season with lemon and parsley and use as a filling. Or else cook them gently in butter, chop them and add them to the beaten eggs before making the omelette in the usual way. For a dozen eggs, allow 250 g (8 oz) of soft roes.

ROE PUFFS

If you cannot find roes in good shape, an enjoyable, if second-best, solution is to make soft roe puffs. Buy 250 g (8 oz) of roes. Chop them into a rough purée and season with salt, pepper and lemon juice. Make up the batter above, but with rather less liquid: 150 ml (5 fl oz) will be enough. Mix the soft roes into the batter before folding in the stiffly beaten egg whites. Drop spoonfuls of the mixture into hot, deep oil. Remove when they are crisp and golden brown. Keep warm in the oven until the batter is used up. Serve with mustard sauce, or with lemon quarters.

SOFT ROE AND CREAM SAUCE   *See* p. 186.

SOFT ROE PASTE

Like the smoked salmon pastes on p. 324, this makes a good first course. Serve with brown bread and butter, or with baked bread.

Fry 125 g (4 oz) of soft roes in a little butter. Season well and sieve or mash to a paste. Mix in 90 g (3 oz) of softened, unsalted butter, and 1 tablespoon of double cream. Taste, and add more salt and pepper if necessary, and a little lemon juice to sharpen the flavour. Cayenne pepper can also be used to spice this very smooth and delicate mixture, or a few drops of chilli sauce.

SOFT ROE STUFFING

> *soft roes*
> *60 g (2 oz) white breadcrumbs*
> *milk*
> *1 medium onion, chopped*
> *60 g (2 oz) butter*
> *heaped tablespoon chopped fresh herbs: parsley and chives* or *tarragon*
> *grated rind of ½ lemon*
> *1 teaspoon anchovy essence* or *2 anchovy fillets chopped*
> *salt, pepper, lemon juice*

Chop the soft roes. Soak the breadcrumbs in a little milk, then squeeze out any surplus liquid. Sweat the onion in butter until soft and golden. Mix in all other ingredients, seasoning to taste.

SALTED, SMOKED AND PICKLED HERRING

If wind-dried fish (p. 494) were suited to early nomadic life, salted fish indicates a settled pattern of existence; a pattern of hamlets, of fishing, and fishing communities where people were skilled enough to catch quantities of fish at a time. And had storage space, and adequate containers for salting down the catch to last the winter. It also indicates the developed working of salt mines and salt pans, which took place from the seventh century BC onwards. I suppose a tub of salted fish is as much a symbol of civilization as a gold torque.

Barrels of salt herring must have been excessively cumbersome to move about. Obviously, drying them by smoking would solve the problem of getting them inland, to people who for health – and for religious reasons – needed a particularly cheap and abundant form of protein. Gradually a most efficient technique was evolved. Salted herring were smoked, then left to drip for two days, before being smoked and smoked again. They hung over slow fires – like row upon row of washing in Venetian alleys – suspended from rods in great smoke houses. The resulting dryish red object, the 'red herring', was then able to stand up to changes of humidity and temperature without going bad: and it was tough enough to survive the rough jolting of ancient transport.

THE RED HERRING This even had its poet, Thomas Nashe, Shakespeare's contemporary. According to him: 'The poorer sort make it three parts of their sustenance; with it, for his dinner, the patchedest *Leather pilche laborattro* may dine like a Spanish Duke . . . it sets a-work thousands, who live all the rest of the year gaily well by what in some few weeks they scratch up then' – i.e. in the herring season. 'Carpenters, shipwrights, makers of lines, ropes and cables, dressers of hemp, spinners of thread, and net weavers it gives their handfuls to, set up so many salt houses to make salt, and salt upon salt; keeps in earnings the cooper, brewer, the baker, and numbers of other people to gill, wash and pack it, and carry it and recarry it.' He might as well have been writing about the herring trade of Germany and Holland.

With the development of refrigeration in the nineteenth century, the red herring disappeared in favour of less harshly cured fish.

Henry Sutton of Great Yarmouth still make them, but almost entirely for export to hot countries (although a few delicatessens in this country do stock them for their West Indian customers). They are still required where domestic refrigerators are few. There is even a 'black herring' imported by Africa and the West Indies: it will, it seems, stand up to any climate, indefinitely, without cold storage. When I heard that Zimbabwean farmers buy them to supplement the porridgey diet of their black workers, I felt that herrings were still too close reminders of slavery to be comfortable. (Southern American and West Indian plantations once provided a huge market for our hard-cured herrings.)

Cookery books of the past instruct you to soak red herrings in small beer or milk – often poured over them boiling. Hannah Glasse says that two hours should be long enough, which makes me think that our ancestors had a far greater taste for smoky saltness than we have. The herrings were then grilled, or toasted on forks in front of the fire. Butter was used to baste them, or olive oil, which 'supples, and supplies the fish with a kind of artificial Juices'. Egg sauce, scrambled or buttered eggs, or potatoes mashed and well buttered, mollified the sharp piquant flavour. Cut into strips they could be used like anchovies.

THE BLOATER By comparison, the bloater is a decadent upstart with a pedigree going back a mere three or four centuries. Its lighter cure reflects pleasure,the realization by many ordinary people that eating could be a source of delight as well as survival. The bloater being ungutted, like the red herring, keeps a certain gaminess of flavour, but it has been 'roused' in salt for one night only, before being smoked a mere twelve hours. Obviously it cannot be kept without refrigeration which means that until recently it was a speciality of East Anglia. However, as refrigeration is no improver of flavour, it is still true that you need to go to Great Yarmouth, or that part of the coast, to eat bloaters at their best (i.e. no more than thirty-six hours after the cure is finished).

This plumped creature – hence the name bloater or bloat herring, *bouffis* to the French – is really a mild yet piquant delicacy. Which is what Clara Peggotty, in *David Copperfield*, meant when she said she was 'proud to call herself a Yarmouth bloater'. This particular kind of curing has also been developed in Europe, in Holland in particular, and in France, where the *harengs saurs* from Boulogne are finer even than a Yarmouth bloater.

We usually grill bloaters in England, and serve them with butter. Or we turn them into bloater paste (p. 190). Like salted herring, kippers, etc., they can be used for the hot dishes on p. 198. Do not be dogmatic about cooking them because they taste delicious raw in salads of various kinds. I find that a filleted bloater (pour boiling water over first, leave for a minute, like a tomato, before skinning), mixed with two filleted kippers, make an excellent substitute for the far more expensive matjes herring of the delicatessen counter.

THE KIPPER The mildest of all cured herrings is the kipper. As you would expect, it is the latest comer. John Woodger of Seahouses, in Northumberland, decided in the 1840s to adapt the salmon-kippering process to herrings. He split the fish down the back and gutted it, soaked it briefly in brine – half an hour or more depending on the fatness of the fish – then hung it up on hooks fixed to long rods or 'tenters' to be smoked over slow oak fires for six to eighteen hours. His methods are still followed by the small family firm of Robson at Craster down the coast from Seahouses, by a firm or two on Loch Fyne, and by all kipperers on the Isle of Man.

Larger concerns cheat time and loss of weight, and make up for the skill of individual judgement, by dyeing the kippers to various shades of mahogany. The browner a kipper is, the more pains you should take to avoid it. This is not crankiness on my part. Try a silvery brown kipper from one of the places I've mentioned, and at the same time try one of those sunburnt objects from a deep-frozen package, and you will see what I mean. (Canned kippers I find disgusting: they do not come into it at all.)

The practice of dyeing was introduced during the First World War when it was excusable to pass off inferior kippers because people were hungry. The dye disguised the fact that the kipper hadn't been smoked for long enough: which meant that it had lost less weight, so it took fewer kippers to fill the boxes. Good kippers are sorted out after the curing is over: dyeing disguises the poor ones, and so lessens the need for skilled sorters who know what a kipper should be.

In *The Herring and its Fishery*, W. C. Hodgson remarks: '... in fairness to many respectable curing firms, it is true to say that, *provided the fish are properly smoked*, a little added colour will do no harm, but at the same time it is difficult to see why if colour was unnecessary in the "old days" it should be necessary now. However one looks at the problem, there is always the chance that the colour will be used to speed up the processing of the herring.'

Kippers may be grilled, skin side to the heat, baked in foil, fried, or jugged – i.e. put into a large pot, with a kettleful of boiling water, and left for 10 minutes. I like them best raw, arranged in strips round the edge of some well-buttered rye bread, with an egg yolk in the middle as sauce. Or I like them, raw again, in the herring salad recipes on p. 196. They make an excellent quiche (p. 314), or soufflé (p. 319), and are an obvious candidate for the fish paste recipe on p. 190.

Two hints from Mr Hodgson:

'Put a pair of kippers together, flesh to flesh, in the frying-pan with a small piece of butter between them. Fry very slowly, turning them over from time to time, but always keeping them together like a sandwich. In this way the oil runs continually from one kipper to the other and the result is excellent. Incidentally mustard is good with kippers, and mustard sauce is correct with most kinds of cooked fresh herrings.' (*See* p. 189.)

'Many people object to eating kippers because they have difficulty with the bones ... Eating a kipper is quite simple if it is laid correctly on the plate to start with, that is, with the skin uppermost ... With the head towards you, lift up the skin from half of the kipper by running the point of the knife along the edge and fold the skin back. This exposes the flesh *on top of the bones*, and it is quite easy to remove it in fillets, leaving the bones untouched. When this side has been eaten, turn the kipper round on the plate so that the tail is towards you and repeat the process on the other side.' This works.

MATJES AND BUCKLING   Since the war we have become familiar with two kinds of cured herring originally imported from abroad. The matjes or maatjes fillets on sale in many supermarkets and Continental stores come from young fat virgin herrings (which is the meaning of the word *matjes*) and have been cured in salt, sugar and a little saltpetre. They have a richer flavour than ordinary salted herrings, but after soaking can be used in exactly the same ways. The other kind, buckling, are a very different matter altogether, because they have been partially 'cooked' by hot-smoking. (The other smoked herrings are cold-smoked at temperatures not higher than 32°C/90°F, which flavours the fish without cooking it.) They are ungutted, so have the slightly gamey flavour of a bloater but in a milder form. Eat them, like smoked trout, with bread and butter and lemon, or with horseradish cream. If you must have them hot, reheat them as briefly as possible under the grill or in the oven. The appetizing gold colour comes from their final exposure to really dense smoke. This is the luxury fish of the herring trade.

HOW TO SALT HERRINGS AT HOME

When I first started housekeeping and was full of the enthusiasm of novelty, I came across a Danish book mainly concerned with pickling herrings. One recipe gave a splendid mixture for spiced salt, including sandalwood and Spanish hops. Chips of sandalwood I managed to find (and have some still in a jar in my spice cupboard – occasionally I unscrew the lid and the lovely smell brings back a pungent memory of the enormous enterprise we undertook). Spanish hops remained elusive, so we did without them. Macfisheries were surprised to receive an order for 100 fine fat herrings, but sent a patient young man out to our village with the load. He came in and out of the house with endless white trays of herrings. He talked to us gingerly and placatingly, as if he were not quite sure of our sanity.

Down those herrings went, into a stoneware crock, and they were excellent. At that time there were only two of us so they seemed to last for ever. But I would advise putting down 3 kg (6 lb) or so if you have a family, particularly if you live near a herring port and can buy them really fresh. The thing is to get them when they are at their fattest and most plentiful (and therefore cheapest).

You need a stoneware crock, a huge Pyrex casserole or an oblong plastic container, rinsed out with boiling soda water, then rinsed and drained upside down. Do not use earthenware: it is too porous. You also need a cool place for storage. This is not an enterprise for centrally-heated flat dwellers, I'm afraid, who would do better to try the quick alternative method below.

Buy 3 kg (6 lb) of the largest herrings. Clean them, leaving the heads in place. Keep the roes for another dish. Make up a solution of vinegar and water in the proportion of 1:2, enough to cover the fish, and leave overnight.

Meanwhile mix together the following cure:

> *250 g (8 oz) pure sea salt*
> *250 g (8 oz) sugar*
> *3 teaspoons lightly crushed peppercorns*
> *6 bay leaves*
> *4 almonds, chopped small*
> *12 whole allspice, coarsely crushed*
> *1 tablespoon Cretan dittany (optional)*

Drain and dry the herrings. Layer them into the crock or container, sprinkling on the cure and finishing with it. Put a very clean board or plate on top with a light weight to keep the fish submerged in the brine that gradually forms as the salt dissolves. Cover the whole thing and leave in a cool place. They will last for weeks. You can start removing them after 4 or 5 days: use tongs rather than fingers so as to maintain the highest standards of hygiene.

Soaking time will depend on how long the herrings have been in salt. Fillet the fish, cover them with a mixture of half milk and half water, and taste a little bit after, say, 2 hours.

DILL-PICKLED HERRING   Large, plump herrings can be cured most successfully with salt, sugar and dill weed in the gravadlax manner, *see* p. 310.

QUICK SALT HERRINGS   As anyone who has ever cured pork will know, brine acts far more quickly than dry salt but the flavour is less interesting.

Bone 4–6 herrings. Put the fillets, neatly trimmed, into a dish. Dissolve 60 g (2 oz) pure sea salt in 600 ml (1 pt) boiled water, then cool and pour over the herring. Leave about 6 hours, then drain well. The flavour is not as rich and spicy as in the method above – you can add aromatics to the brine, but they do not have time to make much of an impression on the herring unless you have time to leave them longer.

SALTED HERRING SALADS

Having made or bought your salted herrings, or matjes, bucklings and harengs saurs, they will provide you with a number of hot dishes (*see* p. 198), and, even better, with a variety of salads and hors d'oeuvre which can be varied to suit your own tastes.

BOULONNAISE SALAD   Soak and cut up the salt herring fillets; put them in the centre of a serving dish. Beat 125 ml (4 fl oz) olive oil into 1 large tablespoon of French mustard, as if you were making a mayonnaise. Pour this over the herrings and top with raw onion rings. Round them put a circle of diced, boiled beetroot (about 500 g/1 lb) dressed in a sauce of 125 ml (4 fl oz) double or soured cream, flavoured with chopped shallot, chives and lemon juice. Fork four hard-boiled eggs to crumbs and put in a ring between herring and beetroot. Chill well.

DANISH PICKLED HERRING   In Denmark, salted herrings are given a richer flavour by being soaked in a sweet-sour marinade. First of all, though, the herrings must be soaked in milk and water until they are mild in flavour.

Serves 6

6 salt herring
250 g (8 oz) granulated sugar
150 ml (5 fl oz) wine or cider vinegar
6–8 peppercorns
2 teaspoons pickling spice, including a chilli
2 or 3 large onions and a few bay leaves

Put the salt herring fillets to soak in milk and water. Simmer together the first four marinade ingredients for 3 minutes. Leave to cool. When the saltiness of the herrings is reduced to a palatable level, drain and arrange them in a plastic box or glass jar, with slices of onion and bay leaves in between. Pour over the marinade and leave for at least 5 days in the refrigerator.

The fillets can then be cut into pieces, to be eaten with bread and butter, as they are. Serve the pieces in a dish, garnished with a few slices of the onion, a bay leaf or two and the chilli. They are an essential part of the cold table in Denmark, and on a smaller scale can be included in a mixed hors d'oeuvre.

LIVONIAN SALAD   Dice 375 g (12 oz) potatoes, boiled in their skins and then peeled, 2–3 large Cox's orange pippins, half a head of Florentine fennel or 2–3 stalks of celery. Put into a bowl with vinaigrette dressing, chopped parsley, chervil and chives. Soak and drain 4 salt herring fillets, cut them into dice and fold them in last of all. Serve well chilled.

Beetroot can be added, so can a chopped dill-pickled gherkin or cucumber. Tomatoes and lemon quarters, too. Double or soured cream can take the place of vinaigrette sauce, appropriately seasoned.

MUSTARD SALAD   Make a strong mustard-flavoured mayonnaise*. Fold in 125 ml (4 fl oz) whipped cream. Pour over pieces of soaked, salted herring fillets. Garnish with dill weed. Serve very cold.

POLISH CHRISTMAS EVE HERRINGS   If the herrings are very salty, soak them. If you are using the packets of mild harengs saurs, or kipper fillets, there is no need to do this; the harengs saurs will have been treated and the kippers are ready to use straightaway. Put them on individual plates, and cover them with crème fraîche, or half soured and half double cream well seasoned with chopped onion and lemon juice. Serve with glasses of chilled vodka.

In summer, substitute chives for onion, or dill or horseradish. This is the best and simplest way I know of eating harengs saurs.

SALTED HERRINGS IN WINE AND CREAM   Cook sliced onion and bay leaf in 90 ml (3 fl oz) dry white wine for 15 minutes. When cold, stir in 125 ml (4 fl oz) double cream. Season with cayenne, dill weed and salt. Mix in pieces of soaked, salt herring. Leave in refrigerator for 2 days before serving.

SALTED HERRINGS IN OLIVE OIL   My favourite recipe for harengs saurs and kippers (neither should need soaking if you buy the harengs saurs in ready-prepared packets). Good, too, with soaked salt herring. Put fillets into a jar with enough fruity olive oil to cover. Add thyme, chillis, peppercorns, etc., according to taste, and close the lid. Leave in the refrigerator until required. Serve with potato salad, dressed with olive oil vinaigrette and chives.

TOMATO SALAD   To 300 ml (10 fl oz) of the marinara sauce*, add brown sugar, French mustard and vinegar, and some chopped onion. The mixture should be piquant. Spice with Tabasco, or with cinnamon. Pour over the soaked salt herring, garnish with onion rings, and chill well.

HOT DISHES MADE FROM SALTED AND SMOKED HERRING

Soak harengs saurs, if they haven't come in ready-prepared packets, and bloaters: buckling and kipper may be used straightaway. The recipes also work with soaked salt herring, but taste less interesting.

HARENGS SAURS À LA BRUXELLOISE   A dish of Carême's. Take half a dozen fish, preferably with soft roes. Remove the fillets, discarding skin and bones. Mash up a generous 125 g (4 oz) unsalted butter with plenty of chopped parsley, some chives, lemon juice and a little crushed garlic. Put 60 g (2 oz) chopped onion into boiling water and cook them for 2 or 3 minutes. Drain, rinse with cold water and add to the butter. Chop 125 g (4 oz) mushrooms. Spread the bottom of an ovenproof dish with most of the butter mixture. Place the mushrooms on top, then the herring fillets, with the soft roes between and bits of the remaining butter. Cover with breadcrumbs, dot with more butter, and put into a hot oven (gas 7, 220 °C/425 °F) for 20 minutes.

Carême remarks that this dish was always a great success in Lent. People grew very tired of eating fish and were glad to have something particularly good to tempt their bored appetites.

HARENGS SAURS À L'IRLANDAISE   A recipe from an American friend which is unusual and magnificent. Soak the fish if necessary and fillet them, or use kippers. Spread them out in a large dish and cover with Irish whiskey. Set it alight. When the alcohol has burnt away the fish are ready to eat.

HERRING WITH CREAM   Here are several Scandinavian versions using cream as a modifier, *see* below. They are best made in a small quantity and served as a first course, provided the rest of the meal isn't too heavy. Cook them in small individual ramekins or 8- to 10-cm (3- to 4-inch) soufflé dishes.

Butter the dishes well. Put in a layer of pieces of buckling or kipper fillet, or very well soaked harengs saurs, or bloaters.

Cover with a layer of chopped leek and about 60 ml (2 fl oz) cream. Dot with butter. Bake in hot oven (gas 7, 220°C/425°F) for 15–20 minutes.

Or sprinkle with a teaspoon of dill weed, and then pour in the cream. Dot with butter. Bake in the same way. This is the version I like best: it really is delicious.

Or cover with a nice layer of potato cut into small matchstick strips. Pour over the cream. Dot with butter. Bake in a hot oven (gas 7, 220°C/425°F) for about 30 minutes, until the potatoes are cooked and slightly browned.

Serve with rye bread and butter, or toast.

HERRING WITH POTATOES AND EGGS   In hot dishes as in cold, potatoes and eggs are the most popular modifiers of salted herring. So it is not surprising that variations of the same recipe are found all over northern Europe. In Scotland, soaked salt herring were laid on top of potatoes, which were then boiled in the usual way and eaten with butter. Scandinavia has a more refined version – potatoes are set to boil, the fish is put on to a buttered plate, which fits nicely on top, covered with foil and left to steam. The dish is finally garnished with chopped hard-boiled egg and dill, chives or parsley.

SMOKED HERRING AND EGG SAUCE   Follow the recipe for smoked Finnan haddock and egg sauce on p. 155. Ten minutes' cooking time should be enough for the fish.

BISMARCK AND ROLLMOP HERRINGS

Like the Ceviche on p. 348, Bismarck and rollmop herrings are not cooked by heat, but by an acid liquid – this time vinegar which is better suited than citrus juice to an oily fish like herring.

Bismarck herrings are boned fillets, soaked in spiced vinegar, seasoned with slices of onion, cayenne pepper and salt. Rollmops are the whole boned herring, curled up round pieces of onion, pickled cucumber and peppercorns: they are packed into jars and covered with spiced vinegar, bay leaves and mustard seeds, more onion and cucumber being added to improve the flavour.

Here are two recipes for home-made rollmops – one using fresh herrings, the other salt or matjes fillets.

(1) Serves 6

6 herrings
60 g (2 oz) salt
600 ml (1 pt) water

MARINADE
600 ml (1 pt) white wine or cider vinegar
1 tablespoon pickling spices, including chilli
peppercorns
3 bay leaves
1 large onion, sliced
2–3 sweet-sour pickled cucumbers or gherkins
onion slices and parsley for garnish

Cut the head and tail from the herrings, bone and clean them. Mix the salt with the water and leave the fish in this brine for 2–3 hours. Meanwhile make the marinade: bring the vinegar and pickling spices to the boil slowly, with peppercorns and bay leaves. Leave to cool. Drain and dry the soaked herrings. Wrap each one round a piece of onion and a piece of pickled cucumber or gherkin. Arrange the rolled herring side by side in a refrigerator box or glass or pottery jar. Pour the vinegar over them. Tuck any pieces of onion and cucumber left over between the herrings. Leave for at least 4 days before eating. Drain, and add fresh onion slices and parsley. A little soured cream can be poured over them as well. Serve with rye bread, or pumpernickel, and butter.

(2) Serves 6

12 salted or matjes fillets

MARINADE
300 ml (10 fl oz) water
300 ml (10 fl oz) wine or cider vinegar
½ teaspoon each slightly crushed allspice and juniper berries
3 cloves
1 teaspoon whole black peppercorns, crushed
3 bay leaves
German mustard
1 large onion, sliced
2–3 dill-pickled cucumbers

Soak the fillets for at least 12 hours, changing the water twice.

Make the marinade by bringing the water and vinegar slowly to the boil with the spices and bay leaves. Cool. Drain and dry the fillets; spread each one with a little mustard, then roll up round pieces of onion and cucumber. Finish as above.

SOUSED HERRING AND BRATHERINGE, AND SOUSED MACKEREL

The German method of prepared soused herring, or *Bratheringe*, is a form of Escabeche (p. 223), because the fish are fried before being soaked in a vinegar marinade. In Britain cooks use the second method which involves baking the fish in the marinade.

(1) Serves 6

6 herrings, preferably soft-roed
seasoned flour
olive oil

MARINADE
250 ml (8 fl oz) vinegar
125 ml (4 fl oz) water
4 tablespoons olive oil
1 teaspoon each peppercorns and mustard seed
3 bay leaves
1 medium onion, sliced

Remove the heads and tails from the herrings, and bone and clean them, setting the roes aside. Flour lightly, then brown them in olive oil. Cool, and arrange in a dish. Fry the roes in some fresh oil and put them on the herrings. Bring the marinade ingredients to the boil, cool, then pour over the fish and roes. Cover and leave in the refrigerator for at least twenty-four hours.

(2) Serves 6

6 herrings or *mackerel*
salt, pepper
175 ml (6 fl oz) each water and malt vinegar or *350 ml (12 fl oz) dry cider*
1 tablespoon pickling spice, including a chilli
3 bay leaves
1 medium onion, sliced

Behead, bone and clean the fish. Season them and roll up, skin side either all inwards or all outwards. Arrange closely together in an ovenproof dish. Add the rest of the ingredients. Cover with foil and bake in a cool oven (gas 1, 140°C/275°F) for about 1½ hours. Serve cold. Use the roes for another dish (*see* p. 188).

NOTE Soused herrings can be turned into large mixed salads, by following salt herring recipes on pp. 196–8.

HUSS *see* A FEW WORDS ABOUT . . . DOGFISH

† JOHN DORY

Zeus faber

This is one of the most desirable of the creatures of the sea, coming up to the sole and turbot for quality. As a Mediterranean fish it is outstanding, a star which Venetian cooks hide under the anonymous depressing title of Pesce bolito con maionnese – boiled fish with mayonnaise (*see* below). Lucky the visitor who manages to penetrate that particular language barrier before his fortnight is up. Couldn't the city of painters, architects, poets and Eastern merchants do better than that? It is certainly a reminder that if the Venetians built St Mark's, they also invented double-entry book-keeping.

Once you have eaten John Dory, you will not be surprised to learn that it has divine connections. It was sacred to Zeus – hence its scientific name of *Zeus faber*. When that deity lost his lustre, it came under the hand of St Peter the Apostle – literally, as you can see from the dark 'fingermarks' which have been there ever since the saint, at Christ's bidding, caught the fish in the Sea of Galilee, and pulled out a coin from its mouth to pay off some importunate tax collectors. Spaniards, Italians, French, Swedes, Norwegians, Icelanders all remember this story when they call *Zeus faber*, in their various languages, St Peter's fish.

Of course, a fish from the Sea of Galilee could not have been the salt water John Dory – or the salt water haddock, *see* p. 148 – but it is a nice tale and one does wonder about those dark round marks. The more likely fish is a kind of trout that flourishes in Galilee and is also called St Peter's fish, in Israel. I have eaten it grilled, a pleasant but not outstanding fish – though, to be just, overcooking did not help: that was in Tel Aviv. I looked in vain for fingermarks. Neither was there a coin in its mouth.

The English name is right out of line. At first it was dory by itself, from *dorée*, describing the golden sheen on the scales. John was added in the seventeenth century. An affectionate response to its frankly ugly but sad and amiable face? The same impulse which gave names like Jenny Wren, Jack-run-by-the-hedge and Robin Redbreast to things we have liked and felt at home with?

Not, I'm afraid, that you are likely to feel familiar with John Dory these days, and the American John Dory (*Zenopsis ocellata*) is also scarce – the fingermarks are paler, though still discernible. In Britain, hoteliers and restaurateurs snap it up but try ordering it specially from your fishmonger, and persist. Look out for it on holiday in Europe – or in the Canaries. A friend who was there just lately had one, or rather its fillets, fried in a crisp batter. He was told that if the catch had been bigger, he would not have been eating it, because the big fish merchants on the islands buy them all immediately they are landed, and export them rapidly. That particular day too few John Dories had turned up for them to bother.

HOW TO CHOOSE AND PREPARE JOHN DORY

The enormous head and large cavity of the John Dory gives you a misleading impression of its edible size. As so often with fish, you need to judge quantities with your eyes rather than the scales. The large spiny fins make it seem bigger, too. Unless you are using the Dory for Pesce bolito, ask the fishmonger to fillet it for you. Keep the debris for stock.

Many sole and turbot recipes can be used with success. Creamy and egg sauces are good, too. It is the obvious candidate for such Mediterranean dishes as Bourride and Bouillabaisse. I like it served with fennel, blanched and then finished in butter with a touch of garlic and parsley. Marsh samphire – this time a plant, not a fish, named for Saint Pierre – makes a good accompaniment, preferably the tips steamed, although the pickled version gives an agreeable sharp accent.

JOHN DORY WITH ORANGE SAUCE (Saint-Pierre à l'orange)

Orange with fish has become almost as popular again as it was in the eighteenth century. Bitter oranges were the thing then, as a rich but equally sharp substitute for lemon. Nowadays, unless you keep a supply of Sevilles in the deep-freeze – in which case, use three of them and omit the lemon in the recipe following – you have to use sweet oranges sharpened with lemon juice. As the strength and sweetness of oranges vary, use your taste as a guide when making the sauce rather than exact measures.

Serves 6

6 × 150–175 g (5–6 oz) fillets John Dory
salt, pepper, cayenne
2 oranges
1 small lemon
125 g (4 oz) butter
1 shallot or 1 small onion, chopped
125 ml (4 fl oz) Madeira or brown sherry
125 ml (4 fl oz) double cream
2 large egg yolks
1 generous handful of marsh samphire to garnish (optional)

Sprinkle the fish on both sides with seasoning and set aside. Peel off the zest of the citrus fruit and cut it into matchsticks; blanch them for 2 minutes in boiling water and drain them. Alternatively – this is better in every way – remove the outer coloured peel with a zester: these shreds are fine enough not to need blanching. Squeeze the fruit juices.

In a large shallow pan, melt a third of the butter and cook the shallot or onion gently, without browning it, until it begins to soften. Put in the fish, the citrus juices, the wine and enough water to come almost to the top of the fish. Cover and simmer until the fish is almost cooked, but still pinkish. With a slotted spoon, lift the fillets on to a serving plate and keep them warm in a very low oven: they will continue to cook slowly which gets rid of the pinkness without overcooking.

Boil down the cooking juices to a good concentration: you should end up with approximately 250 ml (8 fl oz). Remove about a third – this is your safety valve. Mix the cream with the egg yolks and stir them into the hot juices, off the stove. Put the pan back over a low heat for the sauce to thicken slightly without any risk of boiling. Add small cubes of the remaining butter and splashes of the concentrated cooking liquor that you removed. You may well not need the full quantity of either – go for a flavour that pleases you.

Pour the sauce round the fish – or else arrange the fillets on top of a pool of sauce, if you like the modern style, on individual plates – and scatter the shreds of peel on top.

If you have been able to get samphire, add some of the steamed tips (the unstringy part). Their saltiness goes well with the sauce and the fish.

PESCE BOLITO CON MAIONNESE

Choose one large John Dory or two smaller fish. Remember that the firm flesh is substantial, and so is the mayonnaise, so you will not need a large quantity.

> Serves 6
>
> *2 kg (4 lb) fish*
> *court bouillon, no 1**
> *mayonnaise, made with 3 egg yolks and 500 ml (15 fl oz) light olive oil or*
>   *mixed olive and groundnut oils**
> *2 teaspoons gelatine*
> *3 tablespoons hot water*

Put the fish into a cold court bouillon, and bring it to boiling point over a moderate heat. Let it shudder for a moment or two, then remove from the stove and let it cool to tepid. Now drain and skin the fish. Divide the fillets into portions and place them on a wire rack, over a baking tray. Make the mayonnaise and put half into a serving bowl. Melt the gelatine in the hot water, and as it cools to an egg-white consistency fold it into the remaining mayonnaise. Cover the fish with this mixture and put a chaste decoration or two in place – a sprig of tarragon, some capers. When the jellied mayonnaise has set, put the pieces of fish on to a serving plate, on leaves of crisp lettuce. Serve chilled, accompanied by the remaining half of the mayonnaise.

KING MACKEREL *see* MACKEREL

LING *see* COD

LOBSTERS & CRAWFISH

Homarus gammarus & Palinurus elephas

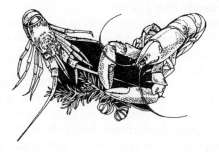

A fourteenth-century German painter, Master Bertram, who lived at Hamburg and who should therefore have known better, included a ready-boiled lobster in his painting of God creating the animals. The sturgeon and other creatures look perfectly alive and clear-eyed – but there is the lobster at the bottom of the painting flat on the ground and ready for the table.

I suppose that most of us do think of lobsters as red. (Red-coated soldiers used to be known as lobsters, although the term really started as a name for cuirassiers with shiny breastplates like the lobster's carapace.) In fact they are a dark blueish colour, which is more suitable for the rocky parts of the sea they choose to live in. It is in this state that you should buy lobster, if you want to taste it at its best. The trouble is that it usually means ordering in advance from the fishmonger. It is less trouble all round to buy one ready-boiled, and if the fishmonger has a good turnover and if you are a regular customer, you will probably not regret it. I have the feeling, though, that as lobster is one of the best things to eat in the world, and as it is one of the most expensive, too, it should only be eaten at its best and in the peak of condition. Otherwise disappointment and financial loss are too disillusioning. This means that one should, ideally, find a seaside town where lobsters are caught, and make an expedition, an occasion if you like, which will become part of one's family ritual.

Luxuries should be enjoyed with a little ceremony: deep-frozen lobster is a kind of denial, a bringing-down of excellence.

The season for fresh lobsters is from April or May to October, although many fishermen store them in tanks and caves until the prices rise in the winter. I began to understand why they are so rare and expensive after reading *Lobsters, Crabs and Crawfish* by R. C. O'Farrell. Although they are known as the Common Lobster, they are not nearly as common as one might wish. He describes from his own experience the contest between the fishermen's skill in baiting and placing lobster pots, and the animal's lack of interest in food – except when it has shed its shell and is therefore soft and unmarketable.

Thus (un)Common European lobster, and the North American lobster, are northern creatures. They like cool water and are not to be found south of the Bay of Biscay or of the coast of Maine. The crawfish or spiny or rock lobster, the lobster without the huge front claws, can live anywhere as far as temperature is concerned. This is the *langouste* and *aragosta* of Mediterranean restaurants. And it is as well to be aware of the difference, if you use Italian, Greek or Provençal cookery books, because you may be left wondering what to do with the claws of a common lobster and the fairly large supply of delicious meat in them. The answer is to remove the meat and use it to make up the tail meat, which is less copious in the lobster. I'm talking, of course, about recipes of the Thermidor type, where meat and sauce are served up in the shell.

Crawfish and lobster recipes are interchangeable, and frozen crawfish tails are now readily available. The flavour cannot be compared in quality with the lobster's, partly because it is not so good to start with, but also because of the freezing. I have eaten 'Caribbean crawfish with mayonnaise' – a standard item on one cross-Channel ferry – which was tasteless to the point of nullity; an iced chewy fibre I would not have recognized had I eaten it blindfolded. Crawfish are caught around Great Britain, too, and I imagine one would be luckier with these.

Like most expensive foods, the lobster and crawfish are simple to cook. If they are bought cooked, you need only remove the shell and serve them with mayonnaise – or split them in half, crack the claws of the lobster, and serve them as they are. The meat can also be removed and reheated in one of the delicious lobster sauces – Newburg, Américaine, Mornay and so on. The creamy part in the head of the lobster, and the coral, if there is any, should be beaten into hot or cold sauces; the tail meat is usually cut across into slices; the claw meat diced.

HOW TO BOIL A LOBSTER

The best lobsters weigh ¾–1 kg (1½–2 lb). Larger than this they become cheaper, but are not so good. I once bought a 1½–2 kg 3–4 lb) lobster, and it was very poor. It is best to buy two or three smaller lobsters, for four or six people. Mrs O'Farrell's advice is to grip the creature across the carapace, which should 'be firm and unyielding, and if there is any inward movement of the fingers it should be discarded, as this indicates a recent shell-change and resulting loss of meat. A hen lobster has a wider body and smaller claws than the cock, but there is no difference at all from the culinary point of view.'

The ideal cooking liquid is its natural element, seawater, plus enough salt to make an egg float in it. Be guided by this when using tapwater – 175 g (6 oz) salt to 1¾ litres (3 pt) water is about right. Put the lobster into the cold water, and bring it up to simmering point: weight the lid to stop the lobster jumping out. This method is recommended by the RSPCA as being painless – the lobster gets dopier as the temperature rises, and expires quietly at 26 °C (80 °F). When simmering point is reached, allow 15 minutes for the first 500 g (1 lb) and 10 minutes for each 500 g (1 lb) after that. Remove the lobster, put it on a dish and allow it to cool in the larder.

Restaurants usually stick to the old method of plunging the lobster into boiling salted water. And many people insist that the flavour of lobster cooked this way is better. Michael Field has this to say in *All Manner of Food*: 'Lobsters are at their best only if they breathe their last either in the dish in which they are cooked or moments before they are added to it. Scientists long ago demonstrated that crustaceans have nervous systems of such simplicity that they scarcely feel pain as we do.'

So you must make your choice.

HOW TO CUT UP LIVE LOBSTER

This is essential if you are using live lobster for a fine dish of Homard à l'américaine, or Lobster Newburg, as it saves you the prolonged business of boiling and cooling. It will also taste better.

The thing is to kill the lobster *instantly*. To do this, place a cleaver

across the join between carapace and tail and hammer it down with
one hard blow. Cut off the claws, and crack them. Cut the tail across
into slices, following the joints. Split the head lengthwise and discard
the sac of grit and the black intestinal canal and gills. Put coral and
lobster liquor and the creamy part, which is the liver or tomalley, into
a separate bowl for the final stages of the sauce.

LOBSTER OR CRAWFISH BUTTER

Either pound the coral and creamy parts of the lobster with an equal
amount of butter. Or dry some lobster shells in the oven, then pound
them as finely as possible. Put into a pan with an equal weight of
butter. Bring to the boil then strain through a muslin-lined sieve.

LOBSTER MAYONNAISE

This is the traditional method. Extract the soft parts, etc. from the
carapace, taking care not to damage the feelers; rub the shell over
with a little oil or a butter paper to give it a gloss, and stand it
upright at the back of the serving dish, with some small crisp lettuce
leaves. Split the tail lengthwise, *not* across in rings, and arrange the
pieces in front of the head. Crack the claws carefully so as not to spoil
their appearance and put them at either side. The rest of the garnish
can be as opulent (oysters, other shellfish) or as simple (hard-boiled
egg, tomatoes, olives, anchovies, capers) as you like. The mayonnaise
is served separately.

You can, if you like, dice up the lobster meat and fold it into the
mayonnaise along with some of the extra ingredients mentioned
above. I think this is a pity, unless you are lucky enough to eat
lobster very often. Being a luxury for most people, it should surely be
served with a little formality. This can be achieved without the realism of the carapace: just split the tail lengthwise, extract the claw
meat in one piece and arrange them, with neat rows of cucumber
and egg, or what you like, in a formal manner.

The mayonnaise* can be varied with herbs, or with cognac and
orange juice, or with a little pastis. Alexandre Dumas gives a most
delicious dressing, which many people like better than mayonnaise,
in his *Grand Dictionnaire de Cuisine*. (It can go with other shellfish, too,
such as crab or prawns.) Mix together:

Serves 6

5 tablespoons olive oil
1 tablespoon Dijon mustard
1 handful of parsley, tarragon, and chives, chopped
1 heaped tablespoon finely chopped shallot or *onion*
12 drops soy sauce
freshly ground white pepper
1 small glass of anisette, or *pastis* or *Pernod*

Fold the diced lobster into the dressing.

BISQUE DE HOMARD

I can think of no better soup than Bisque de homard, when it is made at home with the correct ingredients. It is not difficult to make, a little prolonged perhaps, and certainly expensive, but not difficult. For the best result, buy a live lobster. But a ready-boiled one is better than no Bisque de homard at all.

Serves 6

1 small lobster
2 carrots, diced
1 medium onion, diced
1 stalk celery, diced
125 g (4 oz) butter
60 ml (2 fl oz) brandy
250 ml (8 fl oz) dry white wine
1¼ litres (2 pt) fish stock
bouquet garni
3 tablespoons rice
125 ml (4 fl oz) double cream
salt, pepper, cayenne
1 bunch of parsley

Cut the lobster in pieces (*see* Lobster Introduction). Remove the coral from the meat and set aside. Cook the vegetables gently in 2 tablespoons of butter until they soften. Add the lobster. When the pieces redden, pour on the brandy and set it alight. Turn the lobster over in the flames. Pour in the white wine, and boil hard until reduced by half. Put in enough fish stock to cover the lobster and simmer for another 5 minutes until the lobster is cooked. Remove the pieces. Add the rest of the stock and the bouquet, with the rice.

Meanwhile remove lobster meat from the shells, restoring a few large bits of shell to the pan of soup. Dice the meat and set aside. When the rice is cooked, take the shell out of the pan and liquidize the rest, or sieve it, with the cream and most of the lobster meat. Season. Mix the coral with the remaining butter and add to the reheated but not boiling soup, together with the last few bits of lobster meat that were not liquidized. Sprinkle with plenty of chopped parsley and serve.

If you have a ready-boiled lobster, shell the meat and add the shell to the vegetables which have been softened in the butter. Flame with brandy, add wine and continue with the recipe above. This method is a good way of using up the shells from a lobster – it is surprising how much flavour they contain, and if you have the forethought to put aside a piece or two of lobster meat from the meal before, the bisque will be quite good. Sometimes a spoonful of tomato concentrate or chopped tomato improves this kind of economical recipe.

HOT LOBSTER DISHES

Most hot lobster dishes can be reduced to two basic methods. Once they are firmly in one's mind, a number of variations can be introduced.

The first method is to serve the lobster in a rich sauce, with rice. The second is to mix it with a small amount of sauce and some piquant flavourings, and then to grill it in the half-shell. This is a particularly appetizing way of cooking lobster; the only snag is that half a lobster is essential for each person, whereas two lobsters can be quite enough for six people when prepared by the first method.

LOBSTER WITH VARIOUS SAUCES

Serves 6

2 lobsters, live or ready boiled
125 g (4 oz) butter
1 large onion, chopped
1 clove garlic, chopped
1 glass brandy, gin or whisky
150 ml (5 fl oz) wine or fortified wine
300 ml (10 fl oz) cream, preferably double
2–3 egg yolks
salt, pepper, cayenne, herbs

Cut up live lobsters as indicated in the Lobster Introduction. Melt the butter, cook the onion and garlic until soft. Add the lobster pieces, raise the heat and turn until they are red. Flame with the brandy, gin or whisky. Remove the lobster to a dish and keep it warm. Pour the wine into the pan, and reduce to a syrupy essence. Stir in the cream; reduce slightly. Mix the egg yolks with the lobster coral, the creamy part and any liquor. Stir in a spoonful of sauce, then add to the pan and thicken without boiling in the usual way. Add seasoning to taste.

With a ready-boiled lobster, remove the meat and dice it. Add to the softened onion and garlic, reheat, and push to the side of the pan while the sauce is completed. If there is any risk of it overcooking, transfer to a covered dish, and keep warm in the oven, or over a pan of boiling water.

LOBSTER NEWBURG   No onion or garlic. Use brandy and Madeira or brown sherry as the alcohol. For the final seasoning, add salt, pepper and 60 g (2 oz) of butter cut into bits and whisked into the sauce without further cooking. Otherwise, as above.

This was a recipe invented by the French chef at Delmonico's in New York, at the end of the last century.

LOBSTER À L'ANISE   As in the basic recipe above, but add 250 g (8 oz) sliced mushrooms when cooking onion and garlic. For the alcohol, use 2 tablespoons pastis or Pernod. The herbs should include some chopped tarragon. Good, and unusual.

LOBSTER À L'AURORE   As the basic recipe above, but with white wine as the only alcohol, plus a spoonful of wine vinegar. To the cream, add 150 ml (5 fl oz) concentrated tomato purée, well seasoned. To make the purée, use fresh tomatoes, *see* Lobster à l'américaine below.

LOBSTER À LA CRÈME   Omit onions, garlic and brandy; use white wine as the alcohol. The rest unchanged.

LOBSTER À L'AMÉRICAINE

Two things are certain about the excellent dish known both as Lobster à l'américaine and Lobster à l'armoricaine – it was invented neither in America nor in Brittany, the ancient Armorica. No one disputes the first certainty. And no one who knows anything about Brittany in the last century is likely to dispute the second. Outside the main

centres, it was poor and backward. Fine cooking needs a long prosperous way of living. Glossy, tourist Brittany, with its fat strawberries
and artichokes, its up-to-date farms, is a creation of the last fifty
years. Homard à l'américaine could not be ordered in Paris
restaurants before 1873.

It was first popular at the Restaurant Bonnefoy, where Homard
bonnefoy, developed from a Mediterranean way of cooking crawfish,
probably from Langouste Niçoise, was a speciality of the chef
Constance Guillot. The name américaine was an inspiration of Pierre
Fraisse, at the Restaurant Noël Peters. He came from Sète, southern
France, but had worked in America, and soon acquired a clientele of
Americans abroad when he opened up in Paris. The delicious flavour,
the mild flattery of the name, ensured an international reputation for
the dish. In *French Provincial Cooking* Elizabeth David observes that
some Frenchmen, feeling patriotic after the First World War, cor-
rected what they chose to regard as a 'typographical error' into the
soothing 'armoricaine'.

For northern cooks, the hard point of the recipe, the point at
which it can easily fail, is the tomatoes. If you have ever eaten a
tomato in southern Europe, straight from the garden in the heat of
summer, you will understand what I mean. Our tomatoes,
particularly commercial varieties, which are so poor in flavour and in
solidity of texture, need much attention. They cannot be added to
the pan with the fish, in the French style, as they are too watery.

The original, ideal fish – no baulking at this one – is lobster,
lobster alive, not ready-boiled. The next choice, a common one in
France where lobster is even pricier than here, is monkfish, for its
texture and sweetness. Turbot works well; so do squid and scallops.

One surprising thing is the use of meat flavours; they give a rich
undertone to the sauce without being identifiable. Another is how the
recipe can be completely changed by altering a couple of secondary
ingredients. Cream instead of stock, butter instead of olive oil, turn
the southern américaine style to the northern armoricaine.

Serves 6

6 tablespoons olive oil
1 large clove garlic, crushed
500 g (1 lb) tomatoes, peeled, chopped
salt, black pepper
red wine vinegar (see *recipe*)
dark brown sugar (see *recipe*)
2 × 750 g (1½ lb) lobsters or 1½ kg (3 lb) firm fish steaks, seasoned,
*   floured or 6 squid sacs, cut in rings, floured*

1 tablespoon plain flour
1 tablespoon butter
1 small onion, chopped
2 shallots, chopped
3 tablespoons brandy, 150 ml (5 fl oz) dry white wine
  or 90 ml (3 fl oz) Madeira
3–4 tablespoons meat jelly
150 ml (5 fl oz) beef stock
cayenne pepper
chopped parsley, tarragon, chervil

Heat 3 tablespoons of oil in a 20-cm (8-inch) frying pan. Add garlic and tomatoes. Cook down to a steady boil, until you have about 250 ml (8–10 fl oz) of tomato purée – it will be fairly lumpy (sieve if you like sauces smooth). As the tomatoes cook, add salt and black pepper, with a dash of vinegar and a little sugar if they are under-privileged in flavour.

Meanwhile, if the fishmonger has not cut up the lobsters, you must deal with them, *see* Lobster Introduction. Put any coral and the creamy dark liver (the tomalley) into a basin, and mash up with the flour and butter. Set it aside. If you are not using lobster, prepare the other fish; mash the flour and butter together.

In a 25–30-cm (10–12-inch) heavy frying or sauté pan, cook onion and shallots gently in 3 tablespoons of the oil until they turn golden. Put in the lobster – or other fish – and cook until it turns red or becomes lightly browned.

Pour in the tomatoes, alcohols, jelly and stock, with a pinch of cayenne. Cover and simmer until the fish is just cooked – 10–12 minutes. Remove it to a dish (discard the lobster shell if you like), and keep warm.

Raise the heat under the sauce and boil it down hard to a good flavour. Correct seasoning. Stir in the coral/flour butter, or flour/butter mixture, in little bits: cook just under boiling point for 5 minutes until the sauce thickens. Add herbs; pour it over the fish. Serve with boiled and butter rice.

L'ARMORICAINE   Use butter instead of olive oil, and cream instead of stock – either double cream, or double and soured cream, half and half. Beat a final 30 g (1 oz) of butter into the sauce when it is ready. Add lemon juice.

LOBSTER ALLA MARINARA

This is a simpler, Italian version of Lobster à l'américaine. The seasoning of the marinara sauce can be varied – it can be made hot with cayenne, or sharpened by the addition of a tablespoon of vinegar and a teaspoon or two of French mustard. Three hundred ml (10 fl oz) of the sauce can be softened by the addition of 150 ml (5 fl oz) of boiling cream – with Marsala as a final flavouring. Warning: be sure to get the sauce right, i.e. right to your taste, before adding the lobster, and remember that mustard loses its virtue if it is cooked – always add it as a last seasoning.

Serves 4

1 large or *2 small lobsters, live*
olive oil
250–300 ml (8–10 fl oz) mussel or *clam liquor*
1 medium onion, quartered
salt, pepper
marinara sauce*
walnut-sized lump of butter

Unless you have some already prepared, prepare the ingredients for the marinara sauce, and set it to cook. Cut the lobster in pieces as for Lobster à l'américaine. Heat up a large heavy frying pan, covered with a thin layer of olive oil. Turn the lobster pieces in the hot oil until they turn red (about 10 minutes). Add the mussel or clam juice – from a previous day's cooking, or from bottle or can – and the onion. Season with salt and pepper if necessary. After another 10–15 minutes, remove the onion, and turn the lobster and juices into the pan of hot, sieved marinara sauce. Stir in the butter and serve immediately.

NOTE　If boiled lobster has to be used, simmer the mussel or clam liquor with the onion for 15 minutes. Add to the hot marinara sauce with the sliced lobster, and heat through. Add butter last of all.

GRILLED LOBSTER

3 lobsters, ready boiled or *3 crawfish*
1 onion, chopped
60 g (2 oz) butter
1 glass dry white wine or *dry sherry*
béchamel* or *Mornay** or *Normande* sauce, etc.*
mustard or *chopped anchovies* or *grated cheese (mixed Gruyère/Parmesan)*
salt, pepper, cayenne
breadcrumbs
grated Gruyère
melted butter

Remove and crack the lobster claws; take out the meat and dice it. Split the lobsters or crawfish in half lengthwise, remove the tail meat and coral and soft parts, chop them and add to the claw meat. Discard the rest, scraping the shells as cleanly as possible.

Cook the onion in butter until soft. Add the alcohol, and reduce to 1½ tablespoons. Stir in the chosen sauce and add mustard, anchovies or cheese to taste. Season. Put some of this sauce in the base of each shell, then the meat, then some more sauce. Mix the breadcrumbs and cheese and sprinkle them on top; pour a little melted butter over them. Arrange on a baking sheet, and set under the grill until hot and bubbling, and lightly browned.

To steady the half-lobsters or crawfish, put two bands of crushed kitchen foil for the ends to rest on.

CURRIED LOBSTER   Add two teaspoonfuls of curry powder, with the béchamel sauce. Do not add any other flavouring, apart from the Gruyère and breadcrumbs for the topping.

LOBSTER WITH OYSTERS (OR CLAMS OR MUSSELS)   As grilled lobster above. Use a béchamel sauce, and add anchovies only as the piquancy. Arrange a line of shelled oysters (or clams or mussels) along each half-shell before sprinkling on the breadcrumbs and cheese. Serve with lemon quarters.

LOBSTER THERMIDOR   As grilled lobster above, using a béchamel or Mornay sauce; and cheese and French mustard as the piquancy.

LOBSTER IN GIN

Under French influence, one tends to think that brandy is the only spirit worth using in cookery (or, occasionally, Calvados if the recipe is in the Normandy style). In fact whisky or gin does very well instead, gin in particular adding a delicious and subtle flavour to shellfish.

Buy and cut up 2 small live or 1 large lobster. Turn to p. 340 and follow the recipe for scallops in gin, omitting the seasoned flour. The lobster meat can be removed from the shells while the sauce is reducing.

OMELETTE DU BARON DE BARANTE

This recipe comes from a small booklet produced by François Minot, chef-patron at the famous Hôtel du Côte d'Or at Saulieu. One of his grandfathers – he is fifth in a line of chefs – spent some time in Russia, as did the famous chef Edouard de Nignon, who invented this recipe. The Baron de Barante was one of the greatest gourmets of his time.

Serves 6–8

500 g (1 lb) mushrooms, sliced
salt, pepper
butter
1 sherry glass of good port
about 600 ml (1 pt) double cream
12 thick slices cooked lobster tail
18 eggs
300 ml (10 fl oz) Mornay sauce*
grated Parmesan cheese

Season mushrooms and cook in some butter. Add port and reduce liquid by half. Pour the cream in, stir it well, and add the lobster. Cover and cook very gently, so as not to make the lobster tough and tasteless.

Make one or more omelettes with the eggs, seasoned in the usual way. Put the lobster filling inside, and roll the omelette(s) over. Pour over some Mornay sauce, sprinkle with grated cheese, and put under a hot grill until the cheese turns a fine golden glaze.

DUBLIN BAY PRAWNS OR NORWAY LOBSTERS OR LANGOUSTINES

Nephrops norvegicus

The first time I ate an unknown shellfish – unknown, that is, to me and to most English people then – called 'scampi', I thought I had discovered the secret of an earthly paradise. It was in Venice, at the very beginning of the fifties. Twenty years later, a hundred, two hundred pub lunches later, I am not so sure. How can this plateful of desiccated catering clichés, surrounded by chips, and mocked by a sprig of parsley, have anything to do with those Adriatic scampi? Or with those miniature lobsters, the langoustines of French restaurants?

And yet the *Multilingual Dictionary of Fish and Fish Products*, compiled by a galaxy of marine experts, backed by the Fisheries Division of the OECD, insists that they are all the same; whatever you call them, whatever you do to them, they are *Nephrops norvegicus* of the same family as the lobster. One cannot argue with authority of this kind.

When the first edition of this book was published, you would have been lucky to find scampi still in their shells, and if you did, they would have already been boiled to a coral pink more beautiful than the lobster's lustier tone. Thank goodness, things have improved and more enlightened fishmongers sell fresh langoustines.

If you are successful in finding some, serve them on their own or as part of a mixed array of shellfish (oysters, mussels, clams, crab) all on a bed of ice with a little seaweed to show off their beauty. This allows people the pleasure of shelling them (only the tails are eaten). A big bowl of lemon-flavoured mayonnaise should be on the table as well – never use malt vinegar for fish, least of all for shellfish. You can tartarize it or not as you please.

Alternatively the shelled tails can be reheated in a Newburg sauce, like the boiled lobster on p. 213, or in a creamy curry sauce*; or in a whisky and cream sauce – many of them do, after all, come from Scotland, or rather from Scottish waters by way of Scottish fishing boats, *see* p.220.

GRATIN DE LANGOUSTINES

From the excellent Hôtel de France at Montmorillon, in Vienne, comes this simple dish of langoustine tails, mushrooms and cream.

Serves 8

300 g (10 oz) mushrooms, sliced
60–90 g (2–3 oz) butter
1¼ kg (2½ lb) shelled langoustine tails
750 ml (25 fl oz) double cream
salt, freshly ground black pepper
grated nutmeg
pinch of cayenne
60 g (2 oz) grated Gruyère

Cook the mushrooms in the butter. When they are nearly done, add the tails. Butter a gratin dish and put the mushrooms and cooked langoustines into it. Heat the cream and season with salt, pepper and spices to taste. Pour over the fish. Sprinkle with the Gruyère and a little more nutmeg. Place under the grill to brown slightly, for 5 to 6 minutes.

LANGOUSTINES À L'ÉCOSSAISE

If you buy the langoustines in their shells, you will need about 1 ½ kg (3 lb). If they are actually alive, you should plunge them into boiling, salted water, and cook them for 10–15 minutes once the water has come back to the boil. Shell them when cool, and set the tails aside.

If the langoustines are already shelled, 750 g (1 ½ lb) should be enough. You will also need:

Serves 6

60 g (2 oz) butter
4 tablespoons whisky

SAUCE
3 large onions, chopped
1 large clove garlic, chopped
2 tablespoons oil
1 tablespoon butter
1 tablespoon plain flour
150 ml (5 fl oz) dry white wine
150 ml (5 fl oz) fish fumet or light meat stock
150 ml (5 fl oz) double cream
salt, pepper

First make the sauce by cooking the onion and garlic gently in the oil and butter, until soft but not brown. Stir in the flour, then moisten with wine, fumet or stock, and cream. Simmer for 15 to 20 minutes, longer if you like. Season.

Reheat the langoustine tails in the 60 g (2 oz) butter. Warm the whisky, set it alight and pour it over them, turning them about in the flames until they die down. Pour on the sauce. Bring to the boil. Pour into the centre of a ring of boiled rice and serve immediately.

NOTE The flour may be omitted, but flame the onions with 3 or 4 tablespoons of whisky instead, before adding the various liquid ingredients. Reduce by boiling until the sauce is of good consistency and taste.

† MACKEREL, SPANISH MACKEREL, CERO & KING MACKEREL

Scomber scombrus & *Scomberomorus* spp.

In the last sixteen years in Britain, we have seen the fall of the herring and the rise of the mackerel, which appear now in – it seems – unending shoals from Cornwall to Ullapool. One of the strangest, most eerie sights I ever saw was coming over the brow of the pass down to Loch Broom, all peaceful in the pale autumn light, and seeing far below us ships stretching to the horizon. The farther you looked, the larger they became against all the rules of perspective. It looked like a scene from some wartime newsreel of the fleet gathering before an attack. The reason for this activity, and for the many languages you hear across the Fair-Isle jerseys in Ullapool shops, is mackerel. The huge ships to sea were Russian klondykers, curing and canning non-stop we were told, and sometimes they came from Japan! If ever I revise this book again round about the year 2000 AD, I wonder if Ullapool will have sunk back into its one-storey quiet again as the herring ports of East Scotland did in the late 1970s.

Mackerel has made its way with difficulty. Older people refuse to eat it unless they can see it pretty well taken off the boat. Without freshness, it is nothing. However if the catch is properly iced from the moment it is landed or within an hour or two, according to A. J. McClane whose authority is the Fisheries Research Board of Canada, 'the eating quality of mackerel has been maintained for nineteen days'. It must be this improvement that accounts for the increasing success of mackerel at the fishmongers'.

The other thing mackerel needs is a sharp or positive flavour to balance the richness of the slightly pink flesh. This has been such a cliché of the kitchen over centuries that, in France, a gooseberry is distinguished from other currants by the name of *groseille à maquereau* (though a French cook these days is more likely to use sorrel or mustard; only in Normandy have I found a modern recipe that partners the two). Alan Davidson suggests a cranberry or rhubarb sauce, which have a similar effect of acid contrast. So, too, would red and white currants. I have also included a recipe for grilled mackerel with pears cooked in port with fresh ginger.

These svelte and beautiful fish, that winter in the cold depths of the North Sea, take no food during their long rest. I was told in Norway that people who live up on the Arctic coast refuse to eat them. For a start, they are written over in a language they cannot read – look at a mackerel next time you buy one – and the browny-reddish part is because they feed on the bodies of drowned sailors and fishermen. In fact, this 'red muscle sustains their continuous swimming, which in these pelagic fishes never ceases, and the white muscle is flexed when a burst of speed is needed'. I suppose the prejudice and the stories began because the mackerel wintering in those parts are in poor condition, and so not worth eating anyway.

I have been speaking of our northern mackerel, the Atlantic mackerel, *Scomber scombrus*, caught on both sides of the water. It has various relations in the warmer seas of the world. The finest to eat, finer than our mackerel, are the wahoo, cero and Spanish mackerel of the Mexican Gulf, where the king mackerel is also caught in abundance. Then there is the sierra of the Pacific Coast, and the Monterey Spanish mackerel, and species off the coasts of China, Japan and India. In Britain, or on holiday in southern Europe, you may well see the Spanish mackerel which has the usual pattern of dark squiggled 'writing', but on a smaller, less bold scale. All recipes for mackerel, and many recipes for bluefish, herring and sardine, are suitable for these species as well.

One aspect of mackerel that I dislike intensely is the deep-brown coloured, hot-smoked fillets and whole fish that are now so widely on sale and on the menus of many cafés and restaurants. The texture is unpleasingly soft, the taste too smoky-brown as if some essence or powder has been used.

Cold-smoked mackerel is another matter, however. Cold-smoked mackerel is a treat for the gods. Why it is so difficult to find, I do not know. A neighbour once turned up with a tray of these pale golden delicacies that he had wrested from Macfisheries in Swindon, not long before they expired. We had a share-out and I found that they kept well in the freezer. They came out for special visitors, who were often puzzled to know what fish precisely they were eating.

Another success with mackerel, large ones for preference, is the gravadlax cure of salt, sugar and dill, *see* p. 310. Really fresh mackerel, especially if you have caught them yourself, are ideal for sashimi (p. 364) or for a simple marinade of olive oil and lime juice. Lime juice is also a good treatment for mackerel fillets destined for the grill.

HOW TO PREPARE MACKEREL

Mackerel need no scaling. When you clean the cavities, guard the roes, which are a delicacy. For persistent blood marks, rub in a little salt and then rinse under the cold tap. Mackerel are best grilled, or dry-fried in an iron pan. Slash them diagonally either side of the backbone, in the plumpest part.

As with herrings, wash your hands and the utensils with plenty of cold water after dealing with mackerel. This gets rid of the smell which can be a problem with oily fish. They can then be washed in hot soapy water in the usual way.

ESCABÈCHE OLD AND NEW

The word *escabèche* has a fine sound, almost a flourish to its tail. By origin Spanish, it comes from the West Indies, where they have long used it to describe a particular method of pickling fish. In England it turns up, briskly abbreviated to caveach, in the middle of the eighteenth century. Mrs Raffald gives two recipes in *The Experienced English Housekeeper* (1769), one for sole, the other for fish in general, the only difference being in the spicing.

Hannah Glasse in *The Art of Cookery* (1747) gives the following method:

> *To pickle Mackrel, call'd, Caveach*
> 'Cut your Mackrel into round Pieces, and divide one into five or six Pieces: To six large Mackrel you may take one Ounce [30 g] of beaten Pepper, three large Nutmegs, a little Mace, and Hand-ful of Salt. Mix your Salt and beaten Spice together, then make two or three Holes in each Piece, and thrust the Seasoning into the Holes with your Finger, rub the Piece all over with the Seasoning, fry them brown in Oil, and let them stand till they

are cold; then put them into Vinegar, and cover them with Oil.
They will keep well covered a great While, and are delicious.'

I can imagine that this rich southern confection must have made a
pleasant interruption in our ancient Friday diets of salt-and-vinegar-
soused herring. The interesting thing is that the eighteenth-century
English recipes are unchanged in modern books of Central and Latin
American cooking: the fish is first fried, then submerged in oil, vinegar
and aromatics such as onion, peppers, oranges, spices – whatever the
region provides.

Modern recipes, too, vary only in the flavourings. Take this one
from Diana Kennedy's extraordinary and exciting *Cuisines of Mexico*,
for Sierra en escabèche as prepared in Yucatan. Other kinds of
mackerel can be used, p. 222, or striped bass. In Britain, you may
have to substitute other chillis for the *güeros*, which are pale yellow
and quite hot to hot with their own special flavour. Toast them by
dry-frying in a heavy iron pan, until the skin is burnt and blistered,
the flesh soft. Or grill them. Or bake them in a very hot oven. Mrs
Kennedy knows 'of a Yucatan cook who adds a few leaves of the
guava, orange and allspice trees to the escabeche, and it is wonderfully
fragrant. The best I could do was to add a few kumquat leaves that I
had found in a greengrocer's.'

Serves 6

6 × 2½-cm (1-inch) slices of sierra, kingfish or striped bass
4 tablespoons lime juice
3 teaspoons salt
½ teaspoon peppercorns
½ teaspoon coriander seeds
½ teaspoon cumin seeds
2 whole cloves
1¼-cm (½-inch) piece cinnamon stick
2 whole allspice
2 cloves garlic, skinned, crushed
300 ml (10 fl oz) wine vinegar
½ teaspoon oregano
2 small bay leaves
10 small cloves garlic, toasted in their skins and peeled
½ teaspoon caster sugar
125 ml (4 fl oz) olive oil
125 ml (4 fl oz) groundnut or safflower oil
6 güeros *chillis, toasted*
2 large purple onions, thinly sliced

Put the fish in a shallow pot. Mix the lime juice and 1 teaspoon of salt with 250 ml (8 fl oz) water and pour it over. Leave for an hour, turning the fish once.

To make the souse, crush the spices down to and including the allspice to a powder with pestle and mortar. Add the crushed garlic and reduce to a paste. Put into a pan with the remaining salt, 125 ml (4 fl oz) wine vinegar, oregano, bay leaves, toasted garlic and sugar, stir and bring to the boil. Add the olive oil, the rest of the vinegar and 300 ml (10 fl oz) water. Bring to the boil again.

Drain and dry the slices of fish. Fry them in the groundnut or safflower oil on each side, until barely cooked, 3–5 minutes a side depending on the fish. Put them into a serving dish in a single layer and pour the hot souse over them. Set aside to pickle for at least 2 hours – Mrs Kennedy remarks that although an Escabèche keeps for a long time, as Hannah Glasse pointed out, it is best just a few hours after it has been made, 'so that the fish has had time to absorb the spicy souse, but has not been left long enough to become vinegary and hard'.

Garnish finally with the chillis. Pour enough boiling water over the onion rings to cover them generously, leave them for a moment or two, then drain them and put them over the fish.

NOTE *See* p. 490 for another version of Escabèche which uses smelts.

MAQUEREAUX AUX GROSEILLES

The French may call gooseberries *groseilles à maquereau*, but this Normandy recipe is the only one I have been able to find in which the name is justified.

Serves 6

6 medium-sized mackerel, cleaned and slashed
500 g (1 lb) gooseberries, topped and tailed
60 g (2 oz) unsalted butter
6 level tablespoons stale breadcrumbs
175 ml (6 fl oz) crème fraîche or half soured, half double cream
salt, pepper, sugar

To make the stuffing and sauce, cook the gooseberries in half the butter in a covered enamel, stainless steel or non-stick pan. Mix about a third of the gooseberries with the breadcrumbs. Season and divide between the mackerel. Add the cream(s) to the gooseberries remaining, season with a little sugar and add some pepper if you like.

Grill the mackerel or bake them uncovered in a hot oven. Reheat the sauce, beating in the last of the butter. Serve with the mackerel, and plenty of wholemeal bread.

VARIATION Currants or cranberries or rhubarb could be used instead of gooseberries.

MAQUEREAU AU VIN BLANC

This is a delicious first course dish which can be prepared up to eight days in advance, and kept in the refrigerator. If you take care over cutting the vegetables, it can look most appetizing. Serve it with unsalted butter and wholemeal or rye bread, with Muscadet to drink.

Serves 6–12

6 herrings, cleaned
1 level teaspoon aniseed or pickling spice
1 fresh red hot chilli, seeded
1 bay leaf
salt
court bouillon* with white wine

Put the fish into a pan so that they fit closely, head to tail. Scatter over them the spices, chilli, bay leaf and salt. Pour on the court bouillon with its vegetables. Bring slowly to the boil, let it bubble twice vigorously, then cover and remove from the heat.

By the time the fish has cooled to tepid, it will be cooked. Remove the skin and bone, so that you have twelve nice looking fillets. Put them in a dish, with the red chilli cut into strips, 1 or 2 slices of carrot from the bouillon, and 1 bay leaf. Season if necessary.

Taste the court bouillon. It needs to be strongly flavoured, so reduce by boiling it down if necessary. When cool, strain it over the fish to cover it. Put film across the dish and refrigerate for at least 2 days.

Pour off most of the liquid before serving the mackerel, so that the dish does not look sloppy.

NOTE Herring can be treated in the same way, or pilchards and large sardines. The recipe is the French equivalent of English soused herring and mackerel, but the flavour is finer because white wine is used instead of vinegar. A good dry cider can be used instead of wine.

MACKEREL WITH PEARS, PORT AND GINGER

This is a recipe adapted from one in *The Encyclopaedia of Fish Cookery*, by A. J. McClane.

Serves 6

6 fillets of Spanish or cero mackerel or 6 whole mackerel, cleaned, slashed
salt, pepper
6 fine pears
pared rind and juice of 1 small lemon
4 tablespoons caster sugar
175 ml (6 fl oz) port
3 drained knobs of preserved ginger
375 ml (12 fl oz) soured cream
watercress salad with a light vinaigrette

Season the fish with salt and pepper. Peel, quarter and core the pears, dropping them into water with half the lemon juice.

Put 2 teaspoons of lemon juice, a wide strip of lemon rind, the sugar, port and 450 ml (15 fl oz) water into a pan. Stir until the sugar dissolves, then simmer for 5 minutes. Drain and then poach the pears in this syrup until tender, adding the ginger at the same time. Scoop out the pears and ginger to a dish. Reduce the cooking liquor to a fairly thick syrup and pour over the fruit.

Grill the mackerel in the usual way.

Put the soured cream into a bowl to serve as a sauce. Place the mackerel on warm plates, arranging the pears down one side with a very little of their syrup and the watercress salad on the other.

VARIATION   If you wish to make a nut or seed oil vinaigrette for the watercress, toast some of the appropriate nuts or seeds and scatter them over the pears and mackerel discreetly.

MAKO *see* SHARKS

MONKFISH OR ANGLER-FISH

Lophius piscatorius

The great fish apart – by which I mean sole, lobster, turbot, eel – my own favourite both to cook and eat is monkfish, or angler-fish. Its beautiful sweet flavour and succulent firmness of flesh have led some writers to compare it with lobster – not really fair, I think, to either, but it gives a hint of the monkfish's virtues.

Although a fair weight is landed in Britain each year, and although it is a common enough fish round our coasts, monkfish was not always easy to buy until recent years. Now, thankfully, it is available almost everywhere, and is found on the menus of most good restaurants.

We first came across it in Normandy, Brittany and Touraine, and now find it everywhere in France. Look out for Bourride de lotte, Gigot de mer, and dishes of monkfish with mayonnaise. We have eaten Lotte sauce Choron, the fish poached in a court bouillon and served with sauce Choron* and Lotte Normande, poached and served with a Normandy sauce* and mussels. You can prepare monkfish in the same way as Turbot au poivre (p. 436).

Monkfish is beloved of French chefs and housewives because, like sole, it can be partnered by many beautiful sauces, each enhancing the other. Cream* or hollandaise* or tomato* sauces in their variety can turn ½–1 kg (1–2 lb) of monkfish into a feast. And cold, with mayonnaise*, it is one of the best summer dishes I know.

HOW TO CHOOSE MONKFISH

In markets and fishmongers', it is always sold without its head, and can easily be passed over. The general shape is that of a slightly squashed cone, anything from 30 cm (1 foot) long upwards. The flesh looks milky and smoothly solid rather than flaked, like cod or haddock. In the centre you will observe a single cartilaginous spine. As it tends to be an expensive fish, it is usually sold in steaks cut across the body, but if you can afford it, a tailpiece of 1–1½ kg (2–3 lb) makes an excellent dish (*see* Lotte en gigot). In my experience the larger fish have the best flavour. I once bought some small tail-pieces, thinking they would be even more delicate. They weren't, they were rather tasteless. I should have taken warning from the lower price; fishmongers in France know what they are selling. The small bits and pieces sold as *joues de lotte* – what we should call monkfish 'knobs' by analogy with skate 'knobs' – are quite pleasant, but again they cannot be compared in flavour with the large steaks.

The reason for the monkfish's invariably headless state is that this appendage is thought to be too horrifying for the customer's sensibilities. In fact, it is both curious and interesting, because the first dorsal fin emerges right over the snout, and is prolonged into a supple rod with a tiny 'flag' at the end. The fish snozzles its way into the sandy or muddy bed of the sea – the French name *baudroie* is said to have the same origin as the word *boue*, meaning mud – invisible on account of its matching colour. It gently waves this plumed rod in front of its capacious jaws, waiting to lure fish into Jonah-like oblivion. It doesn't stop at fish either. This greedy and well-named angler has been known to trap quite sizeable sea birds, at low water.

LOTTE À L'AMÉRICAINE

This is one of the best way of serving monkfish which, like lobster, has a firm enough flesh to marry well with the strong flavours of the sauce.

Serves 6

1½ kg (3 lb) monkfish
seasoned flour
2 shallots, chopped
3 onions, chopped
1 large clove garlic, chopped

125 ml (4 fl oz) olive oil
90 ml (3 fl oz) brandy
generous 450 ml (15 fl oz) dry white wine
375–500 g (¾–1 lb) large ripe tomatoes, peeled, chopped
bouquet garni
1 tablespoon tomato concentrate
1 teaspoon sugar
salt, pepper, cayenne
chopped parsley and tarragon to garnish
croûtons of bread fried in olive oil to garnish

Cut the fish in pieces and turn in seasoned flour. Meanwhile fry the shallot, onion and garlic in the oil until they begin to colour. Add the fish; when it is lightly browned, warm half of the brandy, set it alight and pour it into the pan, stirring the contents about in the flames. When these die down, remove the fish to a warm plate.

Pour the wine into the pan, add tomatoes, bouquet, tomato concentrate, sugar and seasonings. Boil hard to reduce to a well-flavoured sauce – it must not be watery. Allow 20–30 minutes for this.

Return the fish to the sauce and simmer gently until cooked, about 10–15 minutes, adding the rest of the brandy at the same time. Arrange on a hot serving dish, sprinkle with parsley and tarragon, and tuck the croûtons of bread round the edge. This is one of the finest fish recipes.

LOTTE EN BROCHETTE

Monkfish cut into chunks makes an excellent fish for grilling on skewers. Here are two suggestions. Allow 10–15 minutes cooking time and turn the skewers occasionally. One and a quarter kilograms (2½ lb) of fish should be just enough for six people, but 1½ kg (3 lb) would be better.

(1) Put on the skewers 2½-cm (1-inch) cubes of monkfish with 1 large mussel, a square of unsmoked bacon, and a piece of bay leaf between them. Brush with olive oil. When grilled, serve on a bed of rice, with tomato sauce in which the juices of the grill pan have been incorporated.

(2) Soak for an hour in olive oil 2½-cm (1-inch) cubes of monkfish flavoured with rosemary and oregano, along with pieces of tomato and sweet pepper and onion which has been blanched for 5 minutes in boiling water. Cook on skewers. Serve with butter and plenty of pepper, or with the following very simplified form of beurre blanc: soften, but do not melt, 125 g (4 oz) unsalted butter

over warm water; off the heat, add the juice of a lemon, drop by drop, beating all the time as if you were making a mayonnaise. Flavour with salt and cayenne.

LOTTE EN GIGOT

A tailpiece of monkfish does have a similar shape to a leg of lamb – hence the gigot. Here, and in the next recipe, are two variations of this popular French recipe, which can also be used for other firm fish.

Serves 6

1¼–1½ kg (2½–3 lb) tailpiece of monkfish
200 ml (7 fl oz) olive oil
salt, pepper
125 ml (4 fl oz) warm water
1 kg (2 lb) tomatoes, peeled and chopped
2 cloves garlic, chopped
1 tablespoon parsley, chopped
500 g (1 lb) mushrooms, washed and quartered
125–175 ml (4–6 fl oz) double cream
lemon juice, extra parsley

Put the fish into a presentable, ovenproof dish, pour 90 ml (3 fl oz) oil over it, and season. Place in a hot oven (gas 7, 220 °C/425 °F) for 15 minutes, then turn the heat down to moderate (gas 4, 180 °C/350 °F). Add the water and leave for another 30 minutes, basting from time to time.

Meanwhile make the sauce: cook the tomatoes in 60 ml (2 fl oz) of oil until they are reduced to a thick purée; add garlic and parsley. At the same time, in another pan, cook the mushrooms in the rest of the oil. Season.

When the fish is just done, mix the tomatoes, mushrooms and cream together and pour them over the fish. Stir well, check seasoning, and add lemon juice if required, and return to a hot oven, for 5 minutes (gas 7, 220 °C/425 °F). Serve in the cooking dish.

GIGOT DE MER À LA PALAVASIENNE

This recipe is from Languedoc. *Pique* the monkfish with 4 cloves of garlic, cut into slivers, and season it. Make a Ratatouille by cooking 3 chopped onions and 3 chopped cloves of garlic in some olive oil. As they soften, add 3 sweet peppers cut in strips. As they soften in turn, add 250 g (8 oz) each of sliced aubergines and courgettes, and, after 10 minutes, 500 g (1 lb) peeled, chopped tomatoes. Simmer steadily for 45 minutes, uncovered. When you have a well-flavoured, unwatery stew, put it into an ovenproof dish, lay the fish on top and bake in a moderate to fairly hot oven (gas 4–5, 180–190 °C/350–375 °F) for 30–45 minutes. Turn the fish over from time to time.

MONKFISH FRITTERS WITH SKORDALIA

This is a favourite Greek dish and you can make it with monkfish or any white fish from fresh cod to John Dory; you can also use salt cod which has been well soaked. It is served with Skordalia, the Greek version of ailloli*, the pungent mayonnaise given solidity by the addition of breadcrumbs or potatoes. The first version of the sauce is taken from Elizabeth David's *Book of Mediterranean Food*, and the second is a recipe sent to me by a Greek reader.

> *1 kg (2 lb) monkfish*
> *salt, pepper*
> *125 g (4 oz) plain flour*
> *1 teaspoon baking powder*
> *¼ teaspoon each of powdered bay leaf and rigani*
> *1 egg*
> *1 tablespoon olive oil*
> *oil for deep frying*

Season the fish as required, after drying it. Cut it into six even-sized pieces. Mix the batter ingredients with enough warm water to give a batter consistency – about 8 tablespoons. If you are not sure about this, cook a tiny trial fritter, and add more water or flour accordingly.

Dip the fish pieces in the batter and deep-fry in the oil for about 8–10 minutes depending on the thickness of the fish. Serve at once with the Skordalia.

> (1) *6 cloves garlic*
> *2 egg yolks*
> *150 ml (5 fl oz) oil*
> *60 g (2 oz) fresh white breadcrumbs*
> *60 g (2 oz) ground almonds*
> *lemon juice, parsley*

Pound the garlic, add the yolks, then the oil, drop by drop. Stir in the breadcrumbs and almonds. Season with lemon juice and parsley.

(2) *3 or more cloves garlic*
    5-cm (2-inch) slice of stale white bread, from a small loaf
    100 g (good 3 oz) blanched, grated almonds
    125 ml (4 fl oz) olive oil
    wine vinegar, salt

Crush the garlic well in a mortar. Cut the crusts from the bread, soak it with water and squeeze out any surplus – this makes a thick paste. Add it to the garlic, pounding well, then mix in the almonds gradually, pounding all the time. When you have a homogeneous mixture, start adding the oil drop by drop at first, as for a mayonnaise. Finally sharpen and season to taste with vinegar and salt. The sauce can be made in a blender, or with an electric beater, but the garlic should be crushed by itself before you start, to make sure it is reduced enough to mix completely into the sauce.

MONKFISH IN THORNBURY CASTLE STYLE

Although a great deal of monkfish is caught around Britain, it has taken the French to show us how good it is. Kenneth Bell uses ginger, an ingredient much loved by the English, to nationalize a French method of cooking it.

Serves 4–6 (*see* recipe)

1 kg (2 lb) monkfish
60 g (2 oz) clarified butter
45 g (1½ oz) ginger preserved in syrup, thinly sliced
30 g (1 oz) carrot julienne
30 g (1 oz) celery julienne
30 g (1 oz) leek julienne
salt, pepper
150 ml (5 fl oz) Dry Martini
about 2 tablespoons Crabbies or Stone's green ginger wine
300 ml (10 fl oz) Jersey double or whipping cream
small quantity dill or parsley
puff pastry crescents (optional)

Skin and bone the fish. Cut flesh into bite-sized cubes, giving 750 g (1½ lb) weight. Heat butter in a large heavy frying pan. When very hot, stir in the fish, turning it over, then add 30 g (1 oz) of the ginger, the julienne of vegetables, seasoning, vermouth and ginger wine. Cook fast for 5 minutes, turning everything from time to time. Pour in cream. Mix and simmer 5 minutes. Check for seasoning, adding more ginger both sliced and liquid as required, or more vermouth or cream. If there is too much sauce – monkfish can give out a lot of liquid – remove the fish, which must not be overcooked, and boil down the sauce to the right syrupy consistency, then put the fish back.

Divide between four plates, with a light sprinkling of dill or parsley, and a couple of puff pastry crescents which provide the right crisp contrast.

Mr Bell's clients include many sturdy appetites: I would serve this quantity to six people as a first course.

MONKFISH STEAKS WITH BACON (Darnes de Lotte au Lard)

Steaks – *darnes* – from several kinds of white fish can be cooked in this way, with slight variations of timing according to their thickness and the texture of the fish. Ling is a favourite in Normandy, but cod, haddock and monkfish are more likely choices in this country. Buy a piece of top-quality smoked streaky bacon, rather than rashers.

The success of the dish depends on careful cooking in the early stages, never letting the butter burn. This way the flavours accumulate and blend.

> Serves 6
>
> *6 monkfish steaks*
> *salt, pepper*
> *100 g (3½ oz) unsalted butter*
> *250 g (8 oz) chopped onion*
> *200 g (7 oz) piece of smoked streaky bacon, skinned and diced*
> *seasoned flour, plus 1 tablespoon plain flour*
> *150 ml (5 fl oz) dry white wine*
> *150 ml (5 fl oz) water*
> *150 ml (5 fl oz) crème fraîche or half soured, half double cream*
> *1 tablespoon wine vinegar*
> *chopped parsley*

Season the steaks with salt and pepper and set them aside. In half the butter, soften the onion. When it is tender, raise the heat slightly and add the bacon dice. Fry them until they are lightly coloured. Push them to one side of the pan, or remove them with a slotted spoon to a bowl. Dry the fish steaks, turn them in the seasoned flour and colour them lightly on both sides in the same pan. When they are almost done but still pink at the bone, remove everything from the pan and keep warm.

Add the rest of the butter to the pan, stir in the flour and cook it for a minute. Add the wine and water gradually. Let the sauce cook down quickly, bring the crème fraîche to the boil and add it with a little of the vinegar. Check the seasoning, adding extra vinegar if you like. Put back the fish, onion and bacon and barely simmer until the fish is cooked, about 5 minutes. Transfer everything to a serving dish, sprinkle a pinch of parsley on each steak and serve.

PADANG SOUR-SHARP MONKFISH (Pangek Ikan)

The subtlety of this recipe is in the three acidities of lemon, lemon grass and star fruit. Macadamia nuts are to be found in good grocers and some health-food shops: as a last resort, use Brazil nuts, which have a similar waxiness. The dish can also be made with fresh tuna, bonito or grouper.

Serves 6

7 macadamia nuts or *Brazil nuts*
2 medium onions, sliced
2 large cloves fresh young garlic
1 level tablespoon fresh ground chilli, including seeds
2 × ½-cm (less than ¼-inch) slices ginger root, peeled
¼ level teaspoon turmeric
500 g (1 lb) sliced monkfish
1 teaspoon salt
2 tablespoons lemon juice
1 stalk lemon grass, bruised
6 small bilimbi or *3 unripe carambola* or *¼ lemon cut in thin wedges*

Chop or process the first six ingredients to a smooth paste. Set the fish to marinade for 45 minutes in the salt and lemon juice. In a heavy pan that will take the fish in a single layer, put the paste, 4 tablespoons water and the lemon grass. Bring to simmering point, slice and slip in the bilimbi or carambola, or add the lemon wedges. Cook gently for 5 minutes, stirring often to prevent sticking.

Put in the fish, turning it over so that it is coated, then cook it until just tender (about 10 minutes). Shake the pan gently and turn the fish carefully so that the slices do not collapse. Remove the pan from the heat and cool down. Cover and leave until next day.

Reheat carefully (which is why you should avoid overcooking the fish in the first place – it continues to cook as it cools down).

MOONFISH *see* A FEW WORDS ABOUT . . . OPAH

MUSKELLUNGE *see* PIKE

MUSSELS

Mytilidae spp.

Walking along the shore at Gullane a few years ago, chewing an occasional coral berry from the sea buckthorn which grows there in great banks, we were startled to see a scatter of vast mussel shells, giants of a brilliant navy blue, 10 cm (4 inches) and more long. In some of them we discovered huge mussels of a blazing orange. As we were so near the evident pollution of Edinburgh we made no attempt to gather them for a later feast, but I brought some shells home to use as little dishes for stuffed and creamed mussels of a more ordinary size.

At the other end of the scale come the small, sweet, delicate mussels grown on wooden posts in the shallow waters of western France. We visited Esnandes once, in search of its Mouclade and its spectacular fortified church. An astonishing sight, the Anse de l'Aiguillon, stuck with posts to the distant horizon, and fishermen gliding in and out in punts, harvesting the great bunches of mussels. Cultivation has been going on in the vast bay since 1253, or so legend has it. An Irishman was shipwrecked and survived by netting seabirds. Gradually he observed that increasing colonies of mussels were clinging to the posts. So he put up more of them and invented a flat-bottomed boat or *accon* to work his way from post to post. These *moules de bouchot* − *bouchot* is used both for the posts and the whole mussel-farming area − are ideal for Moules marinière as well as the local Mouclade.

This is not to say that the medium-sized mussels are to be despised, whether here or in France. Not at all. My one complaint as far as Britain is concerned is that they are not sold in the holiday season.

Why not, I wonder? It would be fun to make that strange barbecue of the Ile d'Oléron known as an *éclade* or *églade*. There it is the great family picnic on the beach. You need a really thick plank of wood, well moistened and steadied on stones so that it lies flat. In the centre you have four nails. Or else you use a large piece of thick slate and cut a potato so that it sits firmly in the centre. Against nails or potato you prop up four of your largest mussels, hinge to the sky, convex curve turned out towards you. This is your base. Around them you continue to prop up mussels in the same way, keeping the smallest for the outside, until you have a great rosette. This is covered with dry pine needles and small pine twigs to make a bed about 12½ cm (5 inches) thick. You put a light to it and by the time the flames die down, the mussels have opened and are ready to eat, with bread and plenty of Charentes butter and a dry white wine, once you have fanned away the ashes.

You may wonder why mussels do not play a larger part in our diet. It seems to me that they have, as it were, come up in the world in the last thirty years. Unlike lobsters, crabs, scallops and oysters, they have played no part – either here or in France – in grand cookery, haute cuisine. They were of interest to eighteenth-century middle-class families, judging by the recipes in cookery books of the time for scalloped mussels, mussel stews, pickled mussels. But by the mid-nineteenth century they seem to have disappeared: no recipes appear in Mrs Beeton or – and this is more surprising – in Eliza Acton. *Cassell's Dictionary* of the 1880s gives a number of mussel dishes and comments that we should eat more, but people are frightened of being poisoned. In other words mussels were an even more rapid casualty of our industrial revolution than oysters.

In France, where estuaries and shores suffered less from pollution, mussels have appeared on menus for a long time. Many of us first learned to enjoy them there. I would say they are very much part of that passionate search for regional food that began at the end of the last century and took off on Michelin tyres with Curnonsky, and with the aid of the first Michelin maps. Knowing people, the ones who read Boulestin's books in the thirties in Britain, might have served mussels from time to time, but their popularity has risen only since Elizabeth David gave a good number of recipes for them in the fifties and then in *French Provincial Cooking* in 1960. The bonus of our past neglect of mussels is their low price today. I am sure that this cannot last – remember what happened to monkfish, which in 1970 you could buy for 35p a pound. Make the most of mussels, while they are still at a price that makes experimentation possible.

TO OPEN MUSSELS

METHOD 1

Pick over the mussels and remove any that are cracked or that remain obstinately open when tapped with a sharp knife. Occasionally you will come across a mussel that is extraordinarily heavy for its size: this usually means it is full of tarry mud. Either throw it away, or open it separately if you are not quite sure.

Scrub the mussels under the cold tap, then scrape off any barnacles and accretions. Remove the fine black 'beard' with a sharp tug and rinse the mussels in a large bowl of cold water.

Have ready a colander set over a basin to take the mussels as they are opened.

Turn the heat on your hob to very high. Take a wide heavy sauté pan and put in a close single layer of mussels. Put on the lid. Set over the heat and leave for 30 seconds. Check to see if the mussels are open. Remove any that are, put back the lid and leave for another 10 seconds. The point is to give the mussels the minimum time possible over the heat (ignore cookery book instructions suggesting 2 minutes or even longer: this is unnecessary if you open mussels in single layer batches). When all are opened, remove and cook the next and subsequent batches.

Finally strain the mussel liquor through doubled muslin or other cloth to remove the sandy grit and mud.

METHOD 2

As above, but should the final preparation of the mussels involve wine, shallot, parsley and so on, put these into the sauté pan and heat to boiling before putting in the first layer of mussels. In this way you get a more thorough blend of the flavours, but no liquid is *necessary* when opening mussels.

METHOD 3

After scrubbing and scraping the mussels, open them like oysters with a thin pointed knife. This is tricky and it is easy to damage the shells, but if you intend to eat the mussels raw as part of a shellfish platter or if you intend to stuff them, this is what you need to do.

Five hundred grams (1 lb) mussels is about the same as 600 ml (1 pt). They provide you with about 90 g (3 oz) mussel meat, sometimes 125 g (4 oz).

CATALAN MUSSEL SOUP

Serves 6

1 kg (2 lb) mussels, scrubbed and scraped
150 g (5 oz) onion, chopped
3 tablespoons olive oil
375 g (12 oz) tomatoes, peeled, roughly chopped
up to 450 ml (15 fl oz) light fish stock or water
2 large cloves garlic, halved
3 good sprigs parsley
90 g (3 oz) bread, toasted
3 tablespoons brandy
½ teaspoon ground cinnamon
salt, pepper

Open the mussels by method 1. Meanwhile, stew the onions in the oil until golden. Add the tomatoes and bubble them for a few minutes before pouring in the mussel liquor and 300 ml (10 fl oz) fish stock or water.

Put the garlic, parsley, bread, brandy and cinnamon into a processor or blender and reduce to crumbs. Add to the soup which it will thicken. Dilute, according to taste, with the remaining stock or water. Correct the seasoning. Add the mussels, and serve.

CELERY AND MUSSEL SALAD (Céleri en Salade aux Moules)

If you want to serve this salad as a first course, reduce the quantities of mussels and potatoes by one-third, or more depending on the rest of the meal. I find this dish ideal for Christmas and New Year meals; the fresh flavour cuts into the heavy eating of that time of the year in a vigorous way.

Serves 6

500 g (1 lb) potatoes, preferably Desirée
3 kg (good 5 lb) mussels, opened by method 2
100 ml (3–4 fl oz) dry white wine
1 head celery
300 ml (10 fl oz) mayonnaise
Dijon mustard
4 shallots, chopped or 4 heaped tablespoons chopped onion
3 hard-boiled eggs
chopped parsley

Scrub and boil the potatoes in their skins. Peel and dice them into a bowl while still warm. Meanwhile prepare the mussels as directed, first putting in the shallots or onion and the wine, heat, and leave for 5 minutes. When mussels open, discard the shells and strain the very hot liquor over the diced potatoes. Leave the mussels and potatoes to cool.

Cut the celery into fine slices. Flavour half the mayonnaise with mustard to taste, starting with a teaspoonful. Mix in the celery. Mix the remaining mayonnaise with the cold mussels, drained potatoes and the shallot or onion. Shell and quarter the eggs.

Put the mussel salad in the centre of a large plate. Surrounded it with celery salad and arrange the eggs in a circle between the two. Scatter with parsley. Serve well chilled.

MOUCLADE AU FENOUIL

Serves 6

3 kg (6 lb) mussels, scrubbed and scraped clean
250 ml (8 fl oz) dry white wine
250 g (8 oz) onion, chopped
4 heads fennel, sliced, green leaves reserved
2 cloves garlic, skinned, sliced
150 g (5 oz) butter
salt, pepper, cayenne
125 ml (4 fl oz) single cream (optional)
small triangles of bread, fried in butter

Open the mussels as described in method 2, using the white wine. Take 12 of the mussels and break off half of their shells. Shell the remainder and keep them warm. Strain the liquor.

Meanwhile, soften the onion, fennel and garlic in two-thirds of the butter in a shallow pan. Cover it at first, then half-cover so that you end up with a juicy rather than liquid result. Chop the fennel leaves and set aside.

When the fennel is tender, tip the panful into a blender or processor and purée to a smooth sauce, adding the mussel liquor to taste. Check the seasoning. Add some of the chopped fennel leaves and reheat gently, without boiling. Beat in the remaining butter and, if you like, some cream.

Distribute the shelled mussels between six warm individual pots. Pour on the hot sauce, then add the mussels in the half shells. Dip one corner of each triangle of bread in the sauce, then in chopped fennel leaves, and serve with the stew.

MOUCLADE CHARENTAISE

If ever you are in the west of France, I can recommend a visit to
Esnandes, a village to the north of La Rochelle. Go there in the
morning to visit the extraordinary fortified church, where you can
walk on the battlements, and look out towards the marshy coast
and shallow bay where mile after mile of posts or *bouchets* diminish
towards the horizon. Lunch should be taken in the Hôtel du Port
– the flavouring there is curry powder instead of saffron, but it
works well, being used with a light hand. A Mouclade is the
Atlantic coast version of Moules marinière, the sauce being richer
and thicker.

Serves 6

3 kg (6 lb) well-scrubbed mussels, small ones if possible
bouquet garni
2 medium onions, chopped
200 ml (7 fl oz) dry white wine
large pinch of saffron
150 g (5 oz) butter, diced
6 shallots, chopped
1 tablespoon plain flour
2 large egg yolks
juice of 1 lemon
100 ml (3½ fl oz) crème fraîche or half soured, half double cream
salt, pepper
1 small bunch of parsley, chopped
2 large cloves garlic, finely chopped

Open the mussels by method 2, using the bouquet garni, onions
and wine. Strain off the liquor into a jug and add the saffron.
Remove half shells from the mussels and keep them warm in a
bowl.

Meanwhile, melt one-third of the butter and cook the shallots until
soft, without colouring. Stir in the flour and cook for 1 minute or so
to make a roux. Add the liquor and saffron and simmer for
10 minutes. Beat the yolks with half the lemon juice and the cream(s).
Stir in a little of the sauce, then stir the mixture into the rest of the
sauce. Season. Remove from the heat. Beat the rest of the butter into
the sauce with some of the parsley and the garlic. Pour over the
mussels, sprinkle with the last of the parsley and serve with bread
and a good white wine.

MOULES À LA POULETTE

This is a favourite French dish. The yellowish-white sauce looks most appetizing with the navy blue shells and orange flesh of the mussels: the flavour is wonderful, even better than the appearance of the dish.

Serves 6

3 kg (6 lb) mussels
ingredients for sauce poulette* using only 125 g (4 oz) sliced
   mushrooms

Scrub and scrape mussels, and open them by method 1. Remove them with tongs to a strainer set over a bowl. Throw away the half-shells, place the mussels in a large bowl, and keep them warm. Strain the mussel liquor carefully and use in making the sauce.

Pour the heated sauce over the bowl of mussels and serve immediately with plenty of good bread to mop up the plates.

MOULES BORDELAISE

Serves 6 as a first course

6 dozen medium to large mussels, opened by method 1
100 g (3½ oz) fresh white breadcrumbs, not too fine
4 tablespoons clarified butter*
4 tablespoons finely chopped parsley
4 large plump cloves garlic, finely chopped
extra butter (optional)

Discard all the mussel shells and keep the mussels in a covered dish. This can be done in advance.

Just before the meal, fry the breadcrumbs to a light golden brown colour in the clarified butter. Mix the parsley and garlic, and add to the crumbs. Give them a few seconds more for the garlic to soften slightly, but do not overcook, or the parsley will lose its fresh green colour and the crumbs will turn soggy.

Meanwhile, heat the mussels through gently in another pan with a little butter, if you prepared them in advance. If they have just been opened, this is unnecessary. Scoop the mussels into the pan of crumbs, leaving any liquor behind, and stir them briefly so that everything is well mixed. Divide them between six small warm pots, serve with slices of French bread and a dry white wine.

MOULES FARCIES

I do not apologize for repeating what is after all the best of all mussel dishes. If you have not tried mussels before, start with this recipe. Needless to say it can be adapted to oysters and large clams. Indeed the recipe originated with clams.

Serves 8

64 large mussels, scraped, opened by method 1
2 large cloves garlic, halved
1 shallot, quartered
leaves of 1 bunch of parsley
thinly cut zest of ½ lemon
250 g (8 oz) unsalted butter, cubed
salt, pepper
fresh breadcrumbs

Discard half the mussel shells, leaving the mussels on the half-shell. Make sure they are cut free.

In the processor, or by chopping, reduce garlic, shallot, parsley and lemon zest to a crumble and mix with the butter. Season. Put a dab of this mixture on top of each mussel.

Arrange the mussels on dimpled shellfish plates if you have them, or cut eight trenches of bread and make eight holes in each with an apple corer so that the mussels can rest steady, without wobbling. Put under a hot grill. As the butter melts, pull out the grill pan and scatter lightly with breadcrumbs. Put back to brown lightly and bubble. Serve immediately. (If your grill is small, arrange the mussels on two baking sheets and put them in a hot oven to melt the butter. Then finish them off under the grill, one at a time.)

MOULES MARINIÈRE

This is the simplest and most famous of the mussel stews, the basis from which many variations have been built up.

Serves 4

2 kg (4 lb) mussels, scrubbed and scraped
bouquet garni
4 tablespoons finely chopped shallot or onion
30 g (1 oz) unsalted butter
250 ml (8 fl oz) dry white wine
1 teaspoon lightly crushed peppercorns
3–4 tablespoons chopped parsley

Open the mussels as described in method 2 with the bouquet garni, shallot, butter, wine and peppercorns. Keep the opened mussels warm in a hot, covered soup tureen and, when all are done, strain the cooking liquor over them. Scatter with parsley and serve at once.

VARIATION   A richer version may be made by stirring a few spoon-fuls of hollandaise* into the strained mussel liquor, instead of using butter during the cooking.

MUSSEL OR OYSTER PUDDING

I suspect that one of the reasons we British think so badly of our cooking is that suet puddings, for weight reasons, are out, and suet puddings are – were? – one of the glories of our table. In fact, a good suet crust is light and pleasant to eat, crisp on the outside, a wonderful absorber of flavour. If you follow up a pudding like this one with fruit, you have an admirable lunch for a cold day that will not lie on your stomach to reproach you later on.

The secret of good suet puddings, whether savoury or sweet, is piquancy, here mussels or oysters. I daresay scallops, prawns, clams and cockles would do quite as well, but I have not tried them. Do not be tempted to use shellfish raw, as they will exude too much liquid and make the pastry doughy; cook them very lightly.

Serves 4–6

CRUST
300 g (10 oz) self-raising flour
½ level teaspoon salt
150 g (5 oz) fresh suet, chopped

FILLING
60 mussels opened by method 1 or 24 large or 36 medium oysters
100 g (3½ oz) onion, finely chopped
4–6 rashers streaky bacon (smoked or green), cut in strips, minus rind
3 tablespoons chopped parsley

SAUCE
175 g (6 oz) butter
black pepper
chopped parsley and chives

Mix the crust ingredients well together with your hands. Bind to a soft but coherent dough with cold water. Chill while you prepare the mussels or oysters.

Scrub and scrape the mussels free of barnacles, and open as directed. When open, place in a colander, then using a spoon or a loose shell half, scoop the edible part into a basin and discard the shells. Strain the liquor into a pan for later reheating.

Open the oysters with a knife as in method 3, allowing juice to fall into a small pan. Add the oysters. Set over a moderate heat and give them just long enough to firm up: remove them with a perforated spoon, leaving the liquor behind for later reheating.

All this can be done in advance. You can open the mussels with white wine rather than water, and add white wine to the oysters, but I do not think you gain anything by it. The charm of the dish is its simple contrasts.

To make up the pudding, roll out the dough into a large square or rectangle under 1 cm (¼ inch) thick. Scatter it with onion, bacon, parsley and the shellfish – you can cut the oysters in two to get a better distribution of flavour. Roll up, dampen the ends and press the ends together. Put on to a generously-buttered piece of foil, large enough to enclose the roll in a baggy parcel (the crust needs room to rise and swell). Seal it well. Enclose in a cloth if you like, for easy handling.

Bring an oblong or oval pan – I use a self-basting roaster – one-third full of water to the boil. Put a trivet in the pan, or a long shallow dish upside-down and lay the parcel on top. Cover and steam for 2 hours. Check from time to time and, if necessary, restore the original water-level with more boiling water.

Remove the pudding and take away the cloth, if used. Unwrap the foil carefully, saving any juices, and turn the pudding on to a hot serving dish. If convenient, put into a moderately hot oven to crisp the surface slightly. Melt the butter for the sauce, add plenty of pepper and heat it through, skimming off the white crust. Then add the herbs. Add any juices in the cooking foil to the shellfish juices and heat them through as well. Taste, and reduce if they seem watery. Serve butter and juices in two separate jugs. Slice the pudding and eat it on its own, although you could follow it with a salad.

MUSSEL AND SPINACH GRATIN

This is a delectable and unusual recipe from Evan Jones's *World of Cheese*. Many cheese cookery books are disappointing, but not this one – perhaps because it makes clear the special delight and relationship between vegetables and cheese, cheese of different and specified kinds. For this dish you may not be able to get Italian fontina, the creamy cheese from Piedmont. It will not be quite the same with Gruyère or Emmental, but they are the nearest thing to it on general sale.

Serves 6

3 kg (6–7 lb) mussels
1½ kg (3 lb) fresh spinach or 1 kg (2 lb) pack frozen spinach
2 tablespoons chopped shallot or spring onion
125 ml (4 fl oz) dry white wine
3 tablespoons butter
2 tablespoons plain flour
125 ml (4 fl oz) whipping or double cream
generous pinch of saffron
salt, pepper
125–150 g (4–5 oz) grated fontina cheese

Wash and scrape the mussels, discarding any that are broken, or that remain open when tapped sharply. Wash and cut the spinach into shreds with scissors, or divide the frozen block, slightly thawed, into smaller pieces. Put the shallot or onion into a large pan with the wine. Place the spinach on top, then the mussels. Cover tightly, set over a very high heat, and boil for 5 minutes. Remove the cooked mussels and discard the shells. Take the pan off the stove if the spinach is also cooked. Drain the spinach, keeping the liquor carefully.

Make a sauce with the butter, flour, liquor from the spinach and mussels, and cream. Stir in saffron and seasoning to taste. Boil for a few minutes to release the saffron yellow.

Spread out the spinach in a buttered casserole, put the mussels on top and then the sauce. Finish with grated cheese. Bake in the oven at gas 6, 200 °C (400 °F) for 10 minutes, then complete the browning under the grill. The dish should be heated through properly, without the mussels being overcooked to rubber.

MUSSELS WITH WALNUT AND TAHINA SAUCE

Serves 8

2 kg (4 lb) mussels, opened by method 1
4 tablespoons chopped parsley
4 tomatoes, skinned, seeded
salt, pepper
6 pitta bread, warmed through

SAUCE

2 slices of white bread, crusts removed
3 cloves garlic, halved
3 tablespoons tahina paste
125 g (4 oz) shelled walnuts
3 tablespoons white wine vinegar
150 ml (5 fl oz) sunflower oil
salt, freshly ground black pepper, cayenne

The sauce can be made in advance, using a blender. A processor can also be used, but you will get a finer, more coherent result in the blender. You can also pound the whole thing by hand.

Pour a little water over the bread, squeezing it with your fingers and adding more water to make a soft paste. Put the garlic and tahina into the blender and whizz at top speed. Gradually add the walnuts and the bread paste in alternate spoonfuls. The mixture will need lubricating from time to time, so add a tablespoon of the vinegar and splashes of oil occasionally – you may not need all the oil. Finally, season with the rest of the vinegar, salt, black pepper and cayenne.

Shell the mussels and toss about half of them with the parsley. Cut the tomatoes into strips, or dice them and season with salt and pepper. Cut the pitta in half across and then down, then slit the sides so that you have eight triangles from each one.

To assemble the dish, which should be served at room temperature, put a pool of sauce on to each of eight plates. Arrange the mussels overlapping the sauce slightly in a pile, plain and parsley mixed, add the tomato and two wedges of pitta – serve the rest of the pitta in a basket.

PASTA WITH MUSSELS AND ORANGE

Mussels with a cream sauce*, or a tomato sauce*, are often served with pasta. This is a lighter version that tastes as fresh as it looks. If you want a more dramatic dish – and are in the habit of making your own pasta – use squid ink to colour it black, otherwise you can use white or green fettucine or both together.

Serves 6

1½ kg (3 lb) mussels, scrubbed and opened by method 1
2 oranges
about 700 g (1½ lb) fresh pasta
125 g (4 oz) unsalted butter
3 tablespoons chopped parsley
salt, pepper

Open the mussels as directed, discard the shells and strain and reserve the liquor. Remove threads of orange peel with a zester or cut thin strips of zest and slice them into shreds. Squeeze one of the oranges.

Cook the pasta in salted water in the usual way. Melt the butter in a pan, add the orange juice, the zest and the mussel liquor. Simmer 2–3 minutes. Just before you drain the pasta, add the mussels to this sauce to heat them through briefly. Toss with the pasta, the parsley and plenty of pepper. Serve straightaway.

SALADE À LA BOULONNAISE

Channel ports of the French coast are no more to travellers these days than a minor episode of impatience on long summer journeys. As one drives away thankfully, it is startling to think that our great-grandparents might have waited nine days in such places for a wind; up to six weeks, if they could afford it, for a calm. They might even have chosen to live there for business, for economy on small pensions – and for escape. Some of them are buried under hideous tombstones in the cemetery on the steep Lille road out of Boulogne, which looks across the sea to England: 'beloved wife of . . .', 'leader of the Methodist community of this town'. If you then go, as we once did, from the cemetery to the garish duty-free booths near the Gare Maritime, it is hard to think that Boulogne has its virtues. There is the blue lung-raking air of course; but also the mild harengs saurs which are cured here, and simple fresh food à la Boulonnaise, with mussels.

The best of these Boulogne dishes, and to my mind one of the best of all salads, is this combination of sweet plump mussels and waxy potato, dressed with a fine olive oil vinaigrette and parsley.

Serves 6

1 kg (2 lb) waxy potatoes, preferably Desirée
5 tablespoons white wine
6 chopped shallots
1 good sprig of thyme
6 good sprigs of parsley
plenty of black pepper
2½–3 kg (5–6 lb) mussels, opened by method 2
about 8 tablespoons well-seasoned vinaigrette
extra chopped parsley for garnishing

Wash then boil the potatoes in their skins. When cooked, peel and slice them. Meanwhile put wine, shallots, thyme, parsley, pepper and scrubbed mussels in a large pan, and open as directed. Discard the shells, put the mussels in a dish to cool, and strain the cooking liquor over the potatoes. The potatoes are bound to cool down as you peel and slice them, so reboil the mussel liquor before pouring it over them.

Drain the potato slices when cold, mix them with the cold mussels, and pour on enough vinaigrette to moisten the salad. Arrange in a shallow dish, sprinkle chopped parsley on top, and serve well chilled. Put a covering of foil over the dish while it is in the refrigerator.

MUSSEL SALAD

This is a plain salad of mussels with curly endive and peppers. Mussels go well with salads: their small piquant richness enhances both the crispness of some vegetables such as endive or celery or the softness of potato.

Serves 4 as a first course

½–1 kg (1–2 lb) mussels, opened by method 2
250 ml (8 fl oz) white wine
1 handful of chopped parsley
2 cloves garlic, gently bruised
freshly ground black pepper
2 tablespoons tarragon vinegar
150 ml (5 fl oz) olive oil
juice of ½ lemon
1 curly endive
2 red and 2 yellow peppers, sliced
4 fronds dill
8 stalks salad burnet

Place the mussels in a pan with the white wine, parsley, garlic and pepper. Cook over a fast heat as directed above until they open.

To make the dressing, strain the cooking liquor into a bowl, add the vinegar, olive oil and lemon juice, and mix well.

To serve, arrange the salad vegetables on a plate and add the cooked, warm mussels. Dress while still warm.

NEEDLENOSE *see* A FEW WORDS ABOUT . . . GARFISH

NORWAY LOBSTERS *see* LOBSTERS

OCTOPUS *see* A FEW WORDS ABOUT . . . OCTOPUS

OPAH *see* A FEW WORDS ABOUT . . . OPAH

ORMER *see* A FEW WORDS ABOUT . . . ABALONE

OYSTERS

Ostreidae spp.

The fashion today is to praise our traditional food and cookery, out of gastronomic patriotism, without much experience of its high spots. Asparagus does not, for instance, appear on every table two or three times a week in May or June as it does in Germany. Oysters are served even less, I would say, judging by our local fishmongers. A pity this, since once they were everyone's delight from the poorest to the Prince of Wales. Today, however, we only seem to eat oysters in restaurants – foolish if you come to think of it, since their preparation is negligible and it would be far cheaper to eat them at home.

In the matter of oysters, there are two main choices. The ardent oyster-lover with a deep pocket goes for *Ostrea edulis*, native indigenous oysters which are round and flattish, their shells ridged. In Britain, the ideal might be Royal Whitstables or Pyefleets from Colchester. In France, Belons or Armoricaines or *gravettes d'Arcachon*. If you are new to oysters, go first for the very best. They are in season over the winter.

The second choice is the cheaper Portuguese or Pacific oyster *Crassostrea angulata* or *C. gigas*. Both are longer than the rounded *Ostrea edulis* and much more frilled and beautiful in their form. They are the oysters you see everywhere in French markets throughout the year, the people's oysters and, although inferior to the fine-flavoured native, by careful cultivation some specimens reach almost as distinguished a glory.

Marennes and the Ile d'Oléron provide nearly two-thirds of France's oysters. There had always been native oysters in those parts, but in 1860 a ship with a cargo of oysters from Portugal had to take refuge in the Gironde from storms in the Bay of Biscay. As time went by and the storms continued, everyone became nervous of the state of the cargo. Eventually it was thrown overboard. The oysters were not in as parlous a state as had been feared. They looked around, liked their new situation, and settled down to make a new home. All went well for a century, but latterly disease weakened the Portuguese oysters, so the Pacific oyster has been introduced with great success. As its scientific name suggests, it is a giant oyster, if left to reach full maturity. In fact it is harvested young, at Portuguese oyster size.

In Britain, where the water is too cold for them to breed, Portuguese and Pacific are started off in laboratories and sold to growers as seed oysters. This means you can have the summer pleasure of grilling scrubbed oysters over charcoal, flat side up, so that they steam open by themselves.

Beyond the simple choice that I have described, there is, as you might expect, a world of knowledge and expertise, drama and emotion (as for instance when some disease, such as bonamia, takes out famous oyster beds). My own passion for oysters began when my husband gave me a copy of *The Oysters of Loqmariaquer* by Eleanor Clark. She describes her own first acquaintance with oysters during a long stay in Brittany, and weaves in much oyster history and many anecdotes. She is poet enough to attempt a description of the oyster's special delight: 'Music or the colour of the sea are easier to describe than the taste of one of these Armoricaines, which has been lifted, turned, rebedded, taught to close its mouth while travelling, culled, sorted, kept a while in a rest home or "basin" between each change of domicile . . . It is briny first of all, and not in the sense of brine in a barrel, for the preservation of something; there is a shock of freshness to it . . . You are eating the sea, only the sensation of a gulp of sea water had been wafted out of it by some sorcery.'

OYSTERS ON THE HALF-SHELL

The best way with fine oysters is to eat them raw. But first you have to open them (don't ask the fishmonger to do this for you, or the precious liquor will be lost on the way home). You may never break the records of a professional oyster opener – one *maître écailler* reckoned he had opened 200 dozen oysters a day for forty-three years – but it is easy to acquire the skill necessary for the few dozen you are likely to buy.

The main thing is to wrap your left hand in a clean tea towel, before picking up the oyster so that it lies in the palm of your hand. The flat side should be on top. Slip a short, wide-bladed kitchen knife under the hinge and push it into the oyster. Press the middle fingers of your left hand on the shell, and with the right hand jerk the knife up slightly. The two shells will soon be forced apart, and you can finish freeing the oyster from its base. At first this is a messy, sodden business, and I find it essential to revive myself with the first two oysters (in France our fishmonger always slips in three or four extra. which I regard as the cook's perquisite). Soon, though, you will complete the operation swiftly and neatly, and be able to lay the deeper shell on the dish with oyster and liquor complete.

To serve oysters the classic way, put crushed ice on to the plates, and then if possible a layer of seaweed as it sets off the oysters so well. Arrange the oysters in a circle, pointed end inwards, and put half a lemon in the centre. About 15 minutes on ice is enough to chill the oyster without overdoing it.

All you need now is brown bread, or rye bread and butter, some lemon juice, cayenne pepper or wine vinegar with a little chopped shallot in it, and a bottle of dry white wine. 'Chablis was and remains the accepted wine to go with oysters,' said Edmund Penning-Rowsell in an article in *Country Life*, 'although to my mind these are too strong for the delicate, very dry wines of Chablis. Muscadet from near the mouth of the Loire is probably a better and less expensive choice, and if the seawater flavour gets into the wine, no great harm is done to that lesser, often rather acid, Breton favourite.' There are many people, and not just Irishmen, who say that Guinness is even better with oysters.

If a dozen oysters for each person is out of the question, you can serve eight or even six. But when you are down to this kind of quantity, a large dish of mixed seafood on ice is a more attractive way of presenting oysters. On our way to Touraine we sometimes stop the night at Mont St Michel, where this kind of hors d'oeuvre forms a regular part of the menu. The arrangement is simple but effective. Dark seaweed trails over a bed of ice, and contrasts with a large red crab, the orange of mussels in their black and pearly shells, with the shrimps and winkles and the restrained transparency of the few oysters. Sometimes there are a few raw *palourdes* (carpet-shells) as well, or *praires* which are the local clams. Lemon quarters and a generous bowl of lemon-flavoured mayonnaise are part of the dish. In France, they will usually provide you with little forks for the oyster (then you drink the juice from the shell), but I have the feeling this is frowned on in superior English circles. Not being a nimble eater myself, I think that forks are a good idea, unless you have the good luck to be eating the oysters on a quayside in the sun and it doesn't matter if you get in a mess.

If you want to cook the oysters, put them on a bed of coarse sea salt, pressing them down, or on a flat disc of bread with holes cut into it in which the shells can rest. I prefer the latter system, as any juices which spill over in preparation and cooking will be soaked up in a most edible way, and will not be wasted.

ANGELS ON HORSEBACK

I think this is a savoury which is much better eaten at the beginning of a meal. Quite apart from the work required at the wrong end of a dinner, I find that savouries spoil the sequence of wines that you may be serving.

Although this savoury came from France in the mid-nineteenth century, it was soon a top English speciality. Allow three large oysters for each person. Wrap each one, after seasoning it with a drop of anchovy essence, 2–3 drops of lemon juice and a tiny pinch of cayenne, in a thin strip of streaky bacon. Impale them on to wooden cocktail sticks, three rolls per stick. Have ready a piece of bread fried in butter for each stick. Fry the rolls in clarified butter*, or brush them with butter and grill them under a high heat, then put on the bread. The cooking should be brief and the angels eaten promptly.

Sheila Hutchins points out that mussels or pieces of scallop can be used instead of oysters.

CHICKEN AND OYSTER GUMBO

The gumbo stews of the southern states of America are often given their defining character by okra. The difference between this recipe and the Mediterranean type of stew is the inclusion of peppers and chilli or cayenne.

The stew is equally good made with mussels.

Serves 6

250 g (8 oz) gammon rasher, cubed
1 farm chicken, jointed
125 g (4 oz) chopped onion
1 clove garlic, chopped
1 red pepper, chopped, minus seeds or *1 dried chilli chopped, with seeds*
375 g (12 oz) okra, trimmed, sliced
lard and any fat from the chicken above
1 tablespoon plain flour
250 g (8 oz) chopped tomato
1 tablespoon tomato concentrate
chicken stock or *water*
bouquet garni
salt, pepper, cayenne or *Tabasco sauce*
1–2 dozen oysters
parsley

Brown the gammon and chicken, onion, garlic, red pepper or chilli and okra in the lard and chicken fat. You will have to do this in batches, transferring each item as it colours to a large pot and adding more lard as necessary; start with the meat and colour it over a sharpish heat, then lower the temperature for the vegetables, so that they soften and do not become too brown. When the last batch is ready, stir in the flour, cook for a couple of minutes, then add the tomato, concentrate and enough stock or water to make a slightly thickened sauce. Tip this over the contents in the large pot, adding extra liquid if need be, barely to cover the meat and vegetables. Put in the bouquet and seasoning (if you use chilli rather than red peppers, go lightly with the cayenne or Tabasco). Simmer, with the pot covered, until the chicken is tender – about one hour or longer. Meanwhile open the oysters, being careful to save all their juice. Ten minutes before serving the gumbo, mix in the oysters and their liquor to heat through. Taste and adjust the seasoning. Remove the bouquet, and add a good chopping of parsley. Served with boiled rice.

HUÎTRES FARCIES GRILLÉES

This is my favourite way of cooking oysters (it also happens to be my favourite way of cooking mussels – and clams). No other recipe can equal it for piquancy and delight. Garlic butter goes beautifully with oysters, the top layer of crumbs and grated cheese give the dish a crisp edge. Put plenty of good bread on the table, so that all the juices can be mopped up and enjoyed.

Serves 6

48 oysters, scrubbed and opened
6 dinner-plate circles of bread cut from a round loaf
butter
4 level tablespoons finely grated dry Cheddar cheese

GARLIC BUTTER
2 cloves garlic, finely chopped
3 level tablespoons finely chopped shallot
6–8 tablespoons finely chopped parsley
375 g (12 oz) unsalted butter
salt, freshly ground black pepper

Pour off the liquor from the oysters and keep in the freezer for another dish. Cut 8 holes in each circle of bread with a petit fours cutter and finely crumb the bread you remove. Lightly butter enough baking sheets or heatproof plates to take the circles of bread. Mix the breadcrumbs with the Cheddar.

Make the garlic butter, *see* p. 244. Spread the butter over the oysters and settle 8 oysters on each bread circle. Scatter the tops with the breadcrumb and cheese mixture and put under the grill or in a very hot oven until they are browned and bubbling.

In ordinary household circumstances, use both oven and grill, swopping the trays round so that everything is ready at the same time. The cooking time should be brief, as overdone oysters can be tough – 10 minutes maximum.

NOTE The method is the same for mussels and clams, except that they are opened in a different way, in a saucepan over a good heat (*see* pp. 239 and 78).

OMELETTE AUX HUÎTRES (OR MOULES)

Allow 6 oysters or 8 large mussels per person. Open the shellfish in the usual way and drain. Stew a tablespoon of chopped shallot per person in some butter until soft and golden, add a little chopped garlic and rather more chopped parsley. Then put in the shellfish to heat through briefly but be very careful not to overcook them.

Make the omelette(s) in the usual way, with eggs, butter and seasoning, and put the filling in the centre before flipping it over. Serve immediately.

Omelette Normande

Use fewer oysters or mussels and add some peeled shrimps or prawns together with about 250 g (8 oz) mushrooms – for 4–6 servings. Make 450 ml (15 fl oz) sauce Normande* and use half this to bind together the shellfish; heat through gently, taking care not to overcook the shellfish.

Make the omelette(s) in the usual way, and put the filling in the centre. Pour the remaining sauce, which should also be hot, round the omelette and, if possible, decorate with slices of black truffle. Serve immediately.

OYSTERS IN STEAK AND KIDNEY PUDDING

This favourite English dish does not, it seems, go back more than around 150 years. Eliza Acton, in *Modern Cookery* of 1845, calls a steak pudding John Bull's pudding which suggests a certain national fame which had spread to other countries. Mrs Beeton's recipe in *Household Management* of 1859 is the first to add the essential kidney. The recipe was sent to Mrs Beeton by a reader of Mr Beeton's magazine for women, *The Englishwoman's Domestic Magazine*; the reader came from Sussex, a county which had been famous for its puddings of all kinds for at least a century so it is fitting that such a well-liked national dish should have had its roots there.

Oysters or mushrooms were the extra flavouring ingredient. In those days, oysters were the cheaper of the two as mushroom cultivation in Europe was a spasmodic and ill-understood business, except around Paris, until the end of the century. The great boom in mushroom production in England didn't occur until after the Second World War by which time, of course, oysters had far outpriced them. Which would have surprised Mrs Beeton because for her and her readers oysters were still commonplace although becoming scarcer with the increase in the population and the pollution of estuaries.

Make the steak and kidney filling in the usual way, leaving it to cool for several hours or overnight. When you wish to make up the pudding, take a critical look at the liquid part of the filling. If it is on the copious and watery side, it is important to strain it off into a pan and boil it down to a more acceptable flavour and consistency because the oysters will contribute their own delicious liquor to the sauce. When you are satisfied with the liquid, open the oysters – 18–24 for 6 people – add them, liquor and all, to the meat and mushroom ingredients. Taste and correct the seasoning. Then finish off the pudding in the usual way.

Oysters are equally delicious in steak and kidney pie.

OYSTERS IN A WHITE WINE SAUCE

Jonathan Swift tried his hand at verses for the women who cry their wares in and around Dublin. He wrote of Malahide herrings to be eaten with pure fresh butter and mustard – 'their bellies are soft, and white as a custard' – and of the erotic pleasures stimulated by oysters:

>Charming Oysters I cry,
>My Masters come buy,
>So plump and so fresh
>So sweet is their Flesh,
>No *Colchester* Oyster,
>Is sweeter and moister,
>Your Stomach they settle,
>And rouse up your Mettle,
>They'll make you a Dad
>Of a Lass or a Lad;
>And Madam your Wife
>They'll please to the Life;
>Be she barren, be she old,
>Be she Slut, or be she Scold,
>Eat my Oysters, and lie near her,
>She'll be fruitful, never fear her.

I should not pin too much hope on this – except that oysters are said to be a most nourishing food, and excellent for your health in general. This latter proposition I find no difficulty in believing. The most exhilarating lunch in the world is a dozen large oysters, a glass or two of white wine, with bread and butter. After it, you feel light and ready for anything, well fed without fullness.

For dinner, especially dinner with friends who are not used to oysters and might not care to tackle them raw, try this way of cooking them that I came across in Ireland.

Serves 6

48 large oysters
375 ml (12–13 fl oz) dry white wine
30 g (1 oz) shallot, chopped
4 large egg yolks
250 g (8 oz) unsalted butter
300 ml (10 fl oz) double cream, whipped until almost stiff
salt, pepper

Open the oysters over a pan, dropping them in with their juice. Arrange eight deep shells on each of six oyster plates, or plates with a stabilizing layer of seaweed or pierced trencher of bread. Boil wine and shallot until there is barely a tablespoon of wine left. Cool to tepid, beat in the yolks, then beat in the very hot melted butter gradually, to make a hollandaise sauce*. Fold in the whipped cream off the heat and season.

Put oysters over the heat until just stiff – a few seconds. Drain – keeping liquor for another dish – and put into the shells. Cover each one with sauce and brown under the grill. Serve immediately.

NOTE Scallops can be used instead, allowing three in one shell to each person.

OYSTER LOAVES

Another of my favourite recipes for cooking oysters is an old one, popular here and in America in the eighteenth and nineteenth centuries when oysters were abundant, were the food of the poor.

Serves 6

6 brioches or baps
150 g (5 oz) unsalted butter, melted
24–30 oysters, opened, drained, liquor reserved and strained
300 ml (10 fl oz) whipping cream or crème fraîche
cayenne pepper or Tabasco sauce
salt, freshly ground black pepper
lemon juice (optional)

Cut the lids neatly from the brioches or baps and take out the crumb, leaving a strong wall. Put 3 tablespoons of the butter into a small non-stick frying pan about 20 cm (8 inches) across. Use the rest to brush out the inside of the brioches or baps; any left over can be brushed over the outside. Put them on a baking sheet into the oven preheated to gas 7, 220°C (425°F) until they are crisp and nicely toasted. This takes about 10 minutes but the lids can catch easily, so be prepared to remove them after 5 minutes. Switch off the oven and leave the door ajar.

Meanwhile, stiffen the oysters briefly in the 3 tablespoons of butter. Scoop them out and cut them into halves, if large. Tip the oyster juice into the pan and boil it down to a strong essence. Stir in the cream or crème fraîche and bubble steadily until you have a thick-looking sauce. Taste occasionally. If there is a lot of oyster liquor, you may need extra cream – alternatively you can stir in some extra unsalted butter at the end. The sauce should be strong but not belligerent. Add the cayenne or Tabasco, seasoning as required and add a few drops of lemon juice if you like.

Place the oysters in the sauce and heat briefly. Divide them between the crisp brioches or baps, replace the lids, garnish with samphire and julienne strips of carrot, and serve, sprinkled with cayenne.

OYSTERS ROCKEFELLER

This famous dish is said to have been invented at Antoine's, the famous New Orleans restaurant, at the end of the last century. Some inspired customer is said to have remarked that the oysters stuffed in this particular way were 'as rich as Rockefeller'.

Serves 4–6

4 dozen oysters, opened
125 g (4 oz) butter
8 slices crisply cooked bacon, crushed
2 handfuls of spinach, finely chopped
3 tablespoons chopped parsley
3 tablespoons chopped celery leaves
3 tablespoons chopped spring onion
6 tablespoons dry breadcrumbs
½ teaspoon salt
Tabasco or pepper and paprika
1 teaspoon Pernod or pastis Ricard

For this dish the oysters are usually arranged, on a bed of coarse salt, in 4 or 6 shallow ovenproof plates according to whether you are serving 4 or 6 people.

Melt the butter. Add the bacon crumbs and spinach, and the rest of the ingredients. Cook for 5 or 10 minutes over a low heat, stirring the mixture until you have a lightly cooked stuffing. Taste and adjust the seasonings. Divide among the oysters. Grill or place in a hot oven until the oysters are bubbling and lightly browned. Serve on the plates of salt. Put a few drops of Pernod on each oyster, just before serving; a tip I recommend is to do this with an eye-dropper.

OYSTER SOUP

This is the most delicate of fish soups, and is the easiest of all to make. Until oysters become cheap again, you might prefer to substitute mussels, clams or cockles. (This is not a bad joke: with modern methods of fish farming, oysters will be large, plentiful and less expensive before many years have passed.)

Serves 6

2 dozen oysters or 1 kg (2 lb) shellfish
60 g (2 oz) butter
2 tablespoons plain flour
600 ml (1 pt) hot milk or veal stock
¾ teaspoon anchovy essence
nutmeg, cayenne pepper
150 ml (5 fl oz) double cream
salt, pepper
lemon juice, parsley

Clean and open the oysters or other shellfish in the usual way. Discard the shells, but keep the liquor carefully.

Melt the butter in a large pan, stir in the flour and cook gently for 2 or 3 minutes. Add the milk or stock gradually so that the mixture remains smooth. Season with the anchovy essence and a little nutmeg and cayenne. Put in the cream. Simmer for 15–30 minutes. Just before serving, add the oysters and their liquor to the pan to heat through. (Don't overcook shellfish, they become tough; oysters are ready when they *start* to curl at the edges.) Correct the seasoning with salt, pepper, and more nutmeg and cayenne if you like. If the flavour is not quite sharp enough, lemon juice will bring it out. Pour the soup into a hot bowl, scatter a little parsley on top and don't wait for the dilatory guest to appear because the shellfish will go on cooking in the heat of the soup.

OYSTER STEW

Serves 4

700 ml (24 fl oz) single cream or half milk and half double cream
24 large oysters, opened, drained, liquor reserved and strained
Tabasco sauce
salt
4 teaspoons butter
paprika

For this simple classic of American cookery, heat the cream with the strained oyster liquor. Add a dash of Tabasco, salt if required and the oysters. Place 1 teaspoon of butter in four bowls and, when the oysters are firm, pour the stew into the bowls. Sprinkle paprika on top and serve with hot buttered toast, or oyster crackers if you can get them.

POULTRY WITH OYSTER STUFFING AND SAUCE

This is an excellent stuffing and sauce for turkey; for a large chicken, halve the quantities of both recipes. The Portuguese oysters are ideal, but if you cannot buy oysters, try this recipe with mussels. It is a good idea to try the recipe with chicken to start with, to ensure that you like the flavours together.

Oyster Stuffing

enough for a 7 kg (14 lb) turkey

2–3 dozen oysters
300 g (10 oz) white breadcrumbs made from stale bread
150 g (5 oz) chopped suet
2 tablespoons heaped parsley
grated rind of 1 lemon
2 heaped teaspoons thyme
¼ teaspoon each mace, nutmeg
pinch of cayenne pepper
salt, pepper
2 large eggs, beaten

Open the oysters. Save their liquor for the oyster sauce which is usually served at the same time. Chop the oysters in four, so that the pieces are quite large. Mix them with the remaining ingredients, adding salt and pepper to taste. Stuff the bird and cook as usual.

Oyster Sauce

2 dozen oysters
60 g (2 oz) butter
2 tablespoons plain flour
300 ml (10 fl oz) milk
150 ml (5 fl oz) double cream
grated nutmeg
pinch of cayenne pepper
lemon juice

Open the oysters, saving their liquor carefully. Put it with the liquor from the stuffing oysters. Chop the oysters themselves into fairly large pieces. With the butter, flour, milk and cream make a smooth béchamel sauce*; add the oyster liquor and simmer for 20 minutes. Season to taste, and sharpen with a little lemon juice. Just before serving the sauce, stir in the chopped oysters – they will dilute it slightly. The sauce should be about the consistency of double cream or a little thinner.

SCALLOPED OYSTERS

Serves 4

24–32 oysters
12 teaspoons butter, melted
8 tablespoons breadcrumbs
1 handful of chopped parsley
freshly ground black pepper

Open and rinse the oysters in their own juice. Drain them well, reserving the juice. Using a little of the melted butter, brush out four ramekins. Mix the breadcrumbs with the parsley; scatter a fine layer of crumbs into each dish, then put on 3 or 4 oysters, some more crumbs, a little pepper and a teaspoon of melted butter. Put 3 or 4 more oysters on top, then the last of the crumbs and butter. Strain the oyster liquid through a muslin and put a teaspoonful into each ramekin.

Stand the ramekins in a metal grill pan and place under a preheated grill until the top crumbs are lightly browned and the oysters are just firm.

† PERCH & YELLOW PERCH, WALLEYE, ZANDER & FOGAS

Perca fluviatilis & *P. flavescens, Stizostedion vitreum, S. lucioperca*

Perch of all kinds is undoubtedly worth pursuing, a most desirable fish; one fifteenth-century writer described it as 'daynteous and holsom'. The snag is that one rarely finds any of the perch family for sale, even in France where *sandre*, the zander or pike-perch, is a special treat of the spring and early summer in Loire country. Fogas in Hungary is, I would judge, more widely sold at least on the shores of Lake Balaton. Obviously perch fishermen, across Europe to China, try to keep their treasure for themselves. As it has been placed next to salmon and trout for deliciousness, and sometimes above trout, one can hardly blame them for their piscatorial greed.

Americans have a better chance than we do in Europe, though the name perch spells confusion since it can include the redfish that we know in Britain, called ocean perch, the white perch which is a kind of bass and the surfperch of California, all unrelated species. However the yellow perch is very close to our European perch, and is to be found in quantity around Lake Erie; the Great Lakes, too, are the place for the walleye or walleye pike or yellow pike, the same fish under different names. Most confusing, as it is not a pike at all. It is much fished in Canada in the winter, and is an altogether delicious prospect for the cook who can use sole, trout and pike recipes as well as the ones given below.

Perches have a certain firmness of texture, which is most attractive, though it means you must take care not to overcook them. Small perch can simply be fried, or they can be filleted and turned into fritters. Larger perch can be stuffed and braised in red or white wine, or stewed with prunes, *see* Matelote of eel, p. 136. A favourite recipe of the past was the Dutch freshwater fish stew known here as Watersouchy.

The name perch goes back to ancient Greece, where the fish was known as περχη. A word of the same origin, apparently, as the adjective meaning dusky, like grapes or olives when they begin to ripen. A good description of its body tone. The fins and tail of our European *Perca fluviatilis* are sometimes the most vivid orange and red, which may account for the Italian name, *pesce persico*, the fish of ancient Persia.

HAIRDRESSER'S PERCH AND EEL

Hairdressing in France is so expensive (and prolonged) that I've become ruthless in exacting compensation. The man who used to do my hair when I wrote the first edition of this book specialized in mushrooms; he was also a great fisherman. Alas no display of English simplicity has managed to extract a map reference for the morels and ceps he found by the kilo every year (such information is part of a family's inheritance, I gather). But with river fish, it was another matter. Between explanations of what was going on at the back of my head, he would deliver himself of heretical culinary opinions.

Take perch, of about 750 g (1½ lb), scaled, brined and cleaned. He insisted that the best method is to fry them *very slowly* in butter, half an hour on each side – I recommend the use of an asbestos mat and clarified butter. The skin turns thick and crisp, a rich golden brown. 'And inside – *no*, Madame, it does *not* get overcooked – inside the flesh is moist and full of flavour. But of course, you must drink a good white wine with it. Of course. But better still, when you have a bottle of good white wine, is to drink it as an apéritif with little bits of eel – yes, little bits, ooh not much more than a centimetre [about half an inch] long. Flour them and shake them and put them in a chip basket. Keep them in deep hot oil until they are a nice brown. You have to try one to see.' The little bits are turned on to a plate and quickly sprinkled with salt. He was right – they go much better with the wine than salted nuts or crisps or even olives.

PERCH DELMONICO

A pleasant old-fashioned gratin of perch, that can be used for other river fish, and white fish from the sea.

Serves 6–8

1–1½ kg (2–3 lb) perch
2 litres (4 pt) court bouillon, no. 1*
6 hard-boiled eggs
double quantity velouté sauce*, made with bouillon, milk and cream
  or a creamy mushroom sauce* about 725 ml (1¼ pt)
60 g (2 oz) grated Gruyère cheese
3 tablespoons fresh breadcrumbs
salt, pepper, paprika

Put the scaled and cleaned perch into the cold court bouillon. Bring to the boil and simmer until the fish is just cooked – about 20 minutes. Remove the skin and take off the fillets in smallish pieces. Put them into a gratin dish. Cut 12 neat slices from the eggs, as a garnish, and cut the rest into wedges and put them into the dish with the perch. Pour over the hot velouté sauce. Mix the cheese and crumbs and scatter over the top. Brown under the grill. Lay the 12 slices of egg down the centre, scatter with a little salt, pepper and a nice dusting of paprika and serve very hot.

PESCE PERSICO ALLA SALVIA

Since the Middle Ages, or I suppose one should say since Roman times, the perch has been appreciated in Italy; a fish 'of great esteem'. Sometimes it is served in the Milanese style (dipped in egg and breadcrumbs, then fried in butter and served with lemon wedges). But this recipe, given in Ada Boni's *Italian Regional Cooking*, is more unusual and quite delicious. The Italians are as fond of sage as we are, and they use it more adroitly, with a greater variety of food.

Serves 6

12 fillets of perch
seasoned flour
2 eggs, lightly beaten
fine, dry breadcrumbs
125 g (4 oz) butter
3 tablespoons olive oil
12 leaves of sage, roughly chopped

MARINADE
6–8 tablespoons olive oil
juice of 1 lemon
1 green spring onion, chopped
salt, pepper

Mix ingredients to make the marinade, and steep the fish fillets in it for at least an hour, turning them occasionally. Drain and dry. Dip in flour, egg and breadcrumbs. Fry in 90 g (3 oz) butter, and all the oil, until nicely browned. Remove to a warm serving dish. Add the rest of the butter and the chopped sage to the pan. Bring to the boil, stirring vigorously, pour over the fish, and serve at once.

NOTE   If you cannot get perch, try this recipe with grayling.

ZANDER WITH A PIQUANT SAUCE

Zander, also known as pike-perch, is caught by fishermen in East Anglian waterways. Sometimes, Ann Jarman, who runs the Old Fire Engine House restaurant at Ely, manages to get hold of one, and this is how she cooks it. She also treats pike in the same way. The ideal, if you have a fish kettle, is a zander weighing 1½–2 kg (3–4 lb) but the recipe can be adapted to steaks from a larger fish.

Serves 6–8

butter
carrot and shallot or *onion* (see *recipe*)
zander, scaled and cleaned
dry white wine (see *recipe*)
bouquet of 2 bay leaves, large sprig parsley

STOCK
trimmings of the zander
2 onions, chopped
1 carrot, chopped
bouquet of 2 bay leaves, parsley and, if possible, dill
salt, pepper

SAUCE
125 g (4 oz) unsalted butter
2 medium onions, chopped
2 tablespoons plain flour

4 ripe tomatoes, skinned, chopped or 2 teaspoons tomato concentrate
1 scant tablespoon tarragon vinegar
3–4 pickled gherkins, sliced
Dijon mustard to taste
3 tablespoons chopped parsley
salt, pepper

First make the stock. Put the ingredients into a pan with water to cover generously. Simmer for 40 minutes, covered; strain, taste and add extra seasoning.

To cook the fish, butter a pot or fish kettle generously. Cover the base with chopped carrot and shallot or onion and lay the fish on this bed. Pour in dry white wine to come 2 cm (¾ inch) up the pan, then enough of the stock to bring the liquid level two-thirds of the way up the fish and the bouquet. Should you be short on stock, add other fish stock or water. Dot the top of the fish with little knobs of butter.

Preheat the oven to gas 5–6, 190–200 °C (375–400 °F), unless the fish kettle is too large to go into it, in which case you will have to simmer the fish on top of the stove.

Cover the kettle or pot with foil and the lid. Give it 25–35 minutes in the oven, or a slightly shorter time if you are cooking steaks of zander, or simmering the kettle on top of the stove.

The point is to catch the fish when it comes away from the bone. Baste it after 10–15 minutes and check up on its progress. Remove it to a serving dish, cover with the foil or butter papers, and keep the dish warm while you complete the sauce.

Make a roux for the sauce while the fish cooks. Melt half the butter and cook the onion in it until soft and yellow. Stir in the flour and cook for a minute or so. The roux should be loose. Set it aside until the fish is cooked.

Strain the cooking liquor from the fish to a shallow pan. Taste and reduce it until you have about 750 ml (1¼ pt). Reheat the roux and add this liquor to make a smooth sauce. Put in the tomato and vinegar. Boil hard to concentrate the flavour. Finally add the gherkins, and mustard to taste, whisk in the rest of the butter and the parsley. Check for salt and pepper.

PICKEREL *see* PIKE

† PIKE & MUSKELLUNGE or PICKEREL

Esox lucius & E. masquinongy

The long-snouted, tyrannical pike is the hero of one of the best chapters in *The Compleat Angler*. Izaak Walton obviously enjoyed the prolonged game of wits involved in catching it. He comments on the age that some pikes live to and observes that this makes them expensive to maintain as it means 'the death of so many other fish, even those of their own kind; which has made him by some writers to be called the tyrant of the rivers, or the fresh-water wolf, by reason of his bold, greedy, devouring disposition'. He related a story that a girl in Poland had her foot bitten by a pike as she was washing the clothes: 'and I have heard the like of a woman in Killingworth pond, not far from Coventry'. Then he goes on to describe how you catch such a fish – and finally how you cook it (*see* below).

Pike fishing is again popular in Britain. I read that many pike are caught in a year, some of them over 20 kg (40 lb) in weight. Yet one never sees them for sale, as one does in France. I wonder why? Do pike fishermen treasure them for their own secret enjoyment? Or would it be more accurate to assume that hundreds of these fine fish are thrown back into the water every year?

So you must excuse me if most of the following recipes come from France where pike is one of the more highly-regarded – and expensive – of fish. Do not be chauvinistic in the matter, for all the recipes can be applied with equal felicity to the pike of this country, or to the pike and rather larger muskellunge – or pickerels as both are sometimes called – of Canada and the United States. Muskellunge, and the *masquinongy* of the specific name, is the Ojibwa for this large pike of North America. It means ugly fish, but French settlers took it to mean *masque allongé* (which it undoubtedly is) and that did not help the spelling which can be something of a muddle.

A great snag of pike is held to be the odd y-shaped bones. As long as you are forewarned they are not so much of a nuisance, and as the fish gets larger the problem gets less. Both for texture and flavour, this is one of my favourite fish. It is a good market-day in Montoire when I see its unmistakable presence on the fish stall, with the grey and yellow markings and the lengthy nose.

HOW TO CHOOSE AND PREPARE PIKE

If you want a whole fish for baking, consider the size of your oven before you buy. The northern pike is a long fish: American and Canadian cooks would perhaps do better with a middle-cut of muskellunge – being thicker, it will need a longer baking time. The other alternative is to cut the fish in steaks, but then you cannot stuff it. Sometimes cutting the head off is enough.

Because of the slimy film, scaling the fish can be messy. Put it in the bath if it is too long for any of your bowls, and pour a kettle of boiling water over it. Then turn it over and repeat the exercise. The scales should come away fairly easily.

When cleaning the fish, save the liver but not the roe, which can be indigestible. The liver can go into any stuffing, or be added, chopped, to some sauces towards the end of cooking time.

Baking, poaching and – for fillets – frying are all suitable for pike. Suitable sauces go from the richest and most complex to a jug of melted butter and a little bowl of freshly grated horseradish (*see* the turbot recipe, p. 435).

IZAAK WALTON'S PIKE

Here is the recipe as given by Izaak Walton in *The Compleat Angler* for cooking pike: 'This dish of meat is too good for any but anglers or very honest men; and I trust you will prove both, and therefore I have trusted you with the secret.'

In Walton's day, the pike was cooked on a spit. Inside the fish with the flavouring items there was 500 g (1 lb) of butter and no crumbs, not a stuffing at all but an interior sauce that fell out at the end to mingle with the claret the pike was basted with as it turned before the fire. Today we have to bake the fish, and there is no reason why you shouldn't reduce the butter to go inside the fish, and add breadcrumbs. Although sweet oranges were beginning to come in from about 1660, the orange used for cooking was the bitter or Seville orange – if you do not have any in the freezer use the juice of 2 sweet oranges and 1 lemon.

First open your Pike at the gills, and if need be, cut also a little slit towards the belly. Out of these take his guts; and keep his liver, which you are to shred very small with thyme, sweet marjoram and a little winter-savoury; to these put some pickled oysters, and some anchovies, two or three; both these last whole, for the anchovies will melt, and the oysters should not; to these you must add also a pound [500 g] of sweet butter, which you are to mix with the herbs that are shred, and let them all be well salted (if the Pike be more than a yard [10 m] long, then you may put into these herbs more than a pound, or if he be less, then less butter will suffice): these, being thus mixed, with a blade or two of mace, must be put into the Pike's belly, and then his belly so sewed up as to keep all the butter in his belly if it be possible; if not, then as much of it as you possible can. But take not off the scales.

Then you are to thrust the spit through his mouth, out at his tail. And then take four or five or six split sticks, or very thin laths, and a convenient quantity of tape or filleting; these laths are to be tied round about the Pike's body, from his head to his tail, and the tape tied somewhat thick, to prevent his breaking or falling off from the spit. Let him be roasted very leisurely, and often basted with claret wine, and anchovies and butter mixed together, and also with what moisture falls from him into the pan. When you have roasted him sufficiently, you are to hold under him, when you unwind or cut the tape that ties him, such a dish as you purpose to eat him out of; and let him fall into it with the sauce that is roasted in his belly; and by this means the Pike will be kept unbroken and complete.

Then, to the sauce which was within, and also that sauce in the pan, you are to add a fit quantity of the best butter, and to squeeze the juice of three or four oranges. Lastly, you may either put into the Pike, with the oysters, two cloves of garlick, and take it whole out, when the Pike is cut off the spit; or, to give the sauce a hogo [*haut goût* or good flavour] let the dish into which you let the Pike fall be rubbed with it: the using or not using of this garlick is left to your discretion.

The garlic is a good idea. Bake the fish at first in a hot oven, gas 6–7, 200–220 °C (400–425 °F), then after about 15 minutes, lower the heat down to gas 2, 150 °C (300 °F) until the pike is cooked. Baste every 10 minutes, using about half a bottle of claret and reduce the liquid at the end, beating in butter and the juice.

If you have an oven problem, cut off the pike's head. And if none of your dishes is long enough, make a nest of doubled foil.

DOS DE BROCHET AU MEURSAULT

The best dish of pike I have ever eaten was at Saulieu in Burgundy. It was brought to the table in neat pieces, dressed with a delicious sauce and surrounded with crescents of freshwater crayfish in puff pastry, and small quenelles of pike, containing truffles. *See* p. 275.

One cannot hope to emulate Monsieur Minot, who was chef-patron of the Côte d'Or at Saulieu at the time, but I asked him for the recipe, and assure you that even a simplified version is worth attempting.

A pike weighing 1½ kg (3 lb) is first skinned and filleted, then larded. For six hours, the long strips of fish lie in a bath of brandy and old Madeira, with a seasoning of salt and pepper. The fish is drained and turned in seasoned flour before being fried gently in butter.

When the fish is cooked – here is one secret – divide the fillets into 5-cm (2-inch) slices and remove the bones which pop up automatically from between the flakes as the knife goes through. Keep the fish warm, while you pour 2 glasses of Meursault into the cooking pan. Reduce it to almost nothing, then quickly stir in plenty of double cream. Correct the seasoning and boil down to the right consistency.

Up to this point, the recipe is not too difficult for any enthusiastic cook. It tastes very good without the final touches that are only within the resources of a first-class French restaurant. Finish the sauce with a spoonful or two of hollandaise* and sauce Nantua (p. 465) to taste; garnish with crayfish tails in puff pastry, and the quenelles already mentioned.

PIKE BAKED IN THE LOIR STYLE I

Turn to Trout and other river fish baked in the Loir style, p. 421, and add fish stock almost to cover the pike. After the pike is done, boil down the liquid for the sauce.

PIKE IN THE LOIR STYLE II

Serves 6

1 pike weighing 1½ kg (3 lb)
sorrel purée*
new potatoes
beurre blanc*

COURT BOUILLON*
½ bottle white wine, Coteaux du Loir or other dry white wine
equal quantity of water
1 carrot, sliced
1 onion, sliced
bouquet garni
5-cm (2-inch) piece of celery
salt, 8 peppercorns

Put the bouillon ingredients into a pan, and simmer them for half an hour. Wine from the coteaux du Loir is not easy to come by. I'm lucky enough to live near Jasnières, by La Chartre-sur-Loir, but if I can't get hold of a bottle (or can't afford it) I use an ordinary dry white wine.

If the pike is alive, stun and clean it without washing or scaling it (the treatment is similar to that of Trout au bleu, p. 420). If the pike is dead, it can be cleaned and scaled with the aid of boiling water – but as little as possible.

Put the fish on to the strainer of a fish kettle. Pour the tepid bouillon slowly round it, through a sieve. Bring to the boil and simmer until the pike is cooked.

Prepare the sorrel and potatoes while the court bouillon is simmering on its own. It won't hurt if they are kept warm while the pike cooks. Beurre blanc, apart from the initial reduction, must be prepared at the last minute. So, if possible, get somebody else to drain and dish up the pike and vegetables, while you concentrate on the sauce.

NOTE   Remember that spinach and lemon juice can be substituted for sorrel. Or else tart gooseberries.

QUENELLES

A quenelle is a kind of dumpling, an aristocratic dumpling I hurry to say, a light and delicate confection with little resemblance to the doughy bullet of mass catering.

In the past, quenelles have really been a garnishing element in grand cookery, part of the delicious bits and pieces surrounding a large carp or salmon, or a dish of sole. The wonderful dishes that Carême invented in his kitchens at Brighton, for the Prince Regent, often contained quenelles; with a crayfish purée, poached oysters, poached soft roes, slices of truffle and mushroom heads, they were certainly a garnish *à la régence*. Later, less majestic chefs formed the quenelles round a couple of poached oysters or a piece of soft roe, and served them on their own with a fine sauce. Thanks to electricity (instead of a collection of kitchen boys) we can now make them at home, store them in the deep freeze (after they have been rolled into shape), and produce them whenever a light but tempting dish is required in the evening.

There are two basic kinds, for which recipes follow. I advise you to attempt neither unless your kitchen has electrical machinery such as a liquidizer or processor. Pike is the classic fish to use, which is why the recipes are placed at this point in the book, but any good firm fish can be used instead – sole, salmon, turbot, sea bream, John Dory, whiting or monkfish.

Both kinds of quenelle are poached in barely simmering water or fish fumet*, and served with a fine creamy sauce. The best is sauce Nantua (p. 465), or lobster sauce (p. 212); but for most of us a sauce aurore*, a white wine sauce*, mushroom sauce* or Mornay sauce* is more practical.

Quenelles de Brochet

This recipe produces the more solid, cylindrical quenelles that are sold in cans and frozen packages in many French grocery shops. You will sometimes see them in high-class food shops in this country. They are not cheaper to make at home, but you will be sure of the ingredients and of a finer flavour.

> *500 g (1 lb) pike or other firm fish fillets*
> *250 g (8 oz) fresh white breadcrumbs*
> *125 ml (4 fl oz) milk*
> *200 g (7 oz) unsalted butter*
> *2 eggs plus 2 egg yolks*
> *salt, pepper, nutmeg*

Purée the fish in a blender or processor. Mix the breadcrumbs with the milk and squeeze them together in your hand so that the surplus milk runs away and you are left with a thick paste. Cut up and soften the butter. Using the electric beater, mix the bread paste, then the softened butter, into the fish, until the mixture is smooth and firm. Add the eggs and yolks one by one. Mix well, season and chill.

Roll into sausage shapes on a floured board, or put through a forcing bag with a wide, plain nozzle. Most quenelles of this type are about 2 cm (¾ inch) in diameter, and 10–12½ cm (4–5 inches) long.

Cook them in a shallow pan of water if you like, but preferably in a well-flavoured fish fumet* made from the bones of the fish being used. The quenelles will disintegrate in boiling liquid, so the water or fumet should barely simmer. Serve with one of the sauces mentioned already, and with boiled rice if the quenelles are to be the main course.

Quenelles de Mousseline

You will get the best result if the three main ingredients, and the utensils, are well chilled before you start work. Electrical equipment is what has made such laborious items popular again, after a long gap while we adjusted to the idea of kitchens without slaves.

500 g (1 lb) fillets of pike
4 large egg whites
600 ml (1 pt) double cream
salt, pepper, nutmeg

Cut up the fillets and reduce them to a purée, with the egg whites, in a blender or processor. Push the purée through a fine sieve (electrical, again). Whip the cream until it is very thick but not stiff. Fold it into the fish until you have a thick, homogeneous mass. The problem with quenelles is to get the fish to absorb the cream; the egg whites help, and if you are attempting the recipe by hand, the bowl should stand in a larger bowl with plenty of ice cubes.

Season the mixture, and leave it in the refrigerator to chill for several hours. As the meal approaches, make the sauce (*see* above) and keep it warm: boiled rice is sometimes served as well, so cook that too. Last of all, put a wide flat pan of salted water on to boil. Shape a quenelle with two warmed tablespoons and slip it into the water which should barely simmer; the quenelle will disintegrate in boiling liquid. Add more quenelles until the pan is comfortably full. Remove them with a perforated spoon as they are cooked – 8 to 10 minutes should be right, but taste the first quenelle to make sure;

the inside should be a little creamy. Keep hot, and serve with the sauce poured over them.

This light rich mousseline is also used for steaming in small and large moulds, either on its own, or as the basis of a fish terrine with layers of contrasting shellfish or smoked fish or strips of sole and salmon. Oil the moulds, stand them on a rack or a wad of newspapers in a roasting pan with about 2½ cm (1 inch) boiling water. Poach them on top of the stove with a sheet of foil over the top, or in the oven preheated to gas 5, 190 °C (375 °F). The centre should be just firm when lightly pressed – according to size and cooking this can take about 20–40 minutes.

PILCHARDS *see* SARDINES

PLAICE *see* SOLE

POLLACK, POLLOCK *see* COD

PORBEAGLE *see* SHARKS

PORGY *see* SEA BREAM

PRAWNS & SHRIMPS

Palaemon serratus & *Crangon crangon*

I agree with something I read once about prawns and shrimps – the prawn was described as a 'tasty morsel', but the writer – R. C. O'Farrell in *Lobsters, Crabs and Crawfish* – went on to say that it was 'less of a palate-tickler than a freshly-cooked brown shrimp', preferably eaten out of a paper bag while walking along the promenade at Morecambe. A rare food pleasure I remember from the war years was walking along Morecambe Bay with my sister, each of us with a brown paper bag of shrimps. They were small and brown, the best kind. We chewed without bothering to peel all of them. Something of their vivid sweetness came through in potted shrimps when they went on sale again as food became easier. But then they began to taste dull. Eventually, I discovered why – it was not my increasing age, as I had feared, but a complete change in production.

In the old days, the catch was cooked on board and brought in at all hours. Whatever the time of day or night the fishermen's wives, mothers, daughters, aunts, sisters and grandmothers would set to and pick (shell) the shrimps, then they would pot them in butter, catching the fresh flavour. This used to be done at home in the family kitchen but now it is a formal process carried out in a centre – still by the wives, etc. – where the shrimps are chilled and then shelled, all in ordinary working hours. What is more, they are augmented with frozen shrimp from elsewhere. You have only to think of a crab you have boiled yourself and eaten within an hour or two, and a packet of frozen crab meat to understand the difference.

The odd thing is that these delicate creatures feed on the rubbish of the sea and shore. This tends to be glossed over in modern books on the subject, by the use of genteel latinate words – 'organic remains' – and scientific phrases. For realism one has to go to the Victorians who took a very concrete look at the animal life they were describing – 'If a dead small bird or frog be placed where ants can have access to it, those insects will speedily reduce the body to a closely cleared skeleton. The shrimp family, acting in hosts, as speedily remove all traces of fish or flesh from the bones of any dead animal exposed to their ravages. They are, in short, the principal scavengers of the ocean; and, notwithstanding their office, they are highly prized as nutritious and delicious food.'

Precisely. One has only to think of the hygienic insipidity of a battery hen's food, and the manure heap picked over by a farmyard hen, to see that fine flavour is not always produced in the way we might prefer.

The word prawn does cover an enormous variety of shellfish these days. The large pink prawn we are used to, *Palaemon serratus*, the one the French call *bouquet rose*, is now jostled by deep-frozen prawns from many other parts of the world including the striped tiger prawn from Asia. The situation is further confused by our habit of calling the Norway lobster a Dublin Bay prawn. And in America many of the creatures we label prawns are called shrimps.

This need not worry the cook, apart from plain curiosity. Try all these exotic shrimps or prawns, and you will probably agree that none of them can beat the shrimps or prawns from our own seas. There is no comparison between freshly-caught, freshly-boiled shellfish and the deep-frozen kind – and the smaller the shellfish the more this seems to apply. As to cooking, tiny shrimps and prawns are suitable for eating out of a paper bag, for potting (below), for making sauces. More can be done with the larger ones without spoiling their immediacy of flavour – all large prawns can be used in the same kinds of recipe, so don't let distant origin and strange appearance put you off.

TO COOK PRAWNS AND SHRIMPS

I have assumed that the prawns and shrimps you buy have been boiled already by the fishmonger. But if you are handed a bucket of live ones, this is what you do.

(a) Bring a big pan of seawater to the boil, plus salt. Or a pan of tap-water, plus enough salt to make a strong enough brine for an egg to float in (*see* p. 112). Put in the shrimps or prawns. By the time the water comes back to the boil the shrimps will probably be done (i.e. the tiny shrimps, not American large shrimps). Prawns and larger American shrimps will take 5 to 6 minutes further boiling. Be guided by the change of colour and keep trying them. Under-boiled ones are mushy. Overboiled ones are hard.

(b) In *The Home Book of Greek Cookery*, Joyce M. Stubbs says that prawns lose far less flavour if they are put without water in a tightly covered pan and set over a high heat to cook in their own juice (the mussel system). Shake the pan occasionally, for about 10 minutes. Cool a little before shelling.

TO SHELL SHRIMPS AND PRAWNS

'Take hold of the creature by the head and tail and straighten it out. Then press head and tail towards each other in a straight line, and afterwards pull them apart. The entire coat of mail will come away in your right hand, merely leaving the edible portion to be tweaked from the head.'   (*Pottery* by A. Potter)

PRAWN OR SHRIMP BUTTER

In the old days, one had to pound shrimp or prawn meat with the butter but nowadays it is easy to crush the whole thing in a blender. Melt an equal weight of butter, then add the prawn or shrimp mixture to the pan. When the mixture boils, pour through a muslin-lined sieve into small containers.

ELIZABETH DAVID'S PRAWN PASTE

I first came across this recipe in Elizabeth David's booklet, *Dried Herbs, Aromatics and Condiments*, and have used it many times. If you are in a hurry, put all the ingredients into a liquidizer and blend at top speed; it may be necessary to add a little more olive oil. The combination of prawn and basil is delightful.

Serves 3–4

250 g (8 oz) cooked, peeled prawns
4–6 teaspoons olive oil
cayenne pepper, dried basil
juice of 1 lime or *½ lemon*
1 saltspoon crushed coriander or *cumin seed (optional)*

'Mash or pound the prawns to a paste. Very gradually add the olive oil. Season with cayenne pepper and about half a teaspoonful of dried basil warmed in the oven and finely crumbled. Add the strained juice of half a lemon or of a whole fresh lime (when available, the lime is much the better choice). When the mixture is smooth, and is seasoned to your satisfaction – salt may or may not be necessary, that depends how much has already been cooked with the prawns – pack it into a little jar or terrine. Cover and store in the refrigerator. Serve chilled, with hot thin toast. Do not attempt to store for more than a couple of days.'

If you are using freshly boiled prawns in the shell, allow approximately 1 litre (1¾ pt) gross measure. The shells and heads will make the basis of a good shellfish soup (*see* p. 288).

PRAWN SAUCE

A beautiful sauce which goes with a variety of white fish – cod, sole, turbot, brill, halibut, hake, monkfish, John Dory, bream and porgies – and enhances the pleasure of lobster, scallops and octopus.

250 g (8 oz) prawns in their shells
60 g (2 oz) butter
1 heaped tablespoon plain flour
up to 1 tablespoon tomato concentrate
1 dessertspoon wine vinegar
1 lump sugar
90 ml (3 fl oz) double cream
150 ml (5 fl oz) Marsala
salt, pepper
walnut-sized lump of butter

Shell the prawns and set the flesh on one side. Then put the shells only into a pan, and cover with 450 ml (15 fl oz) water. Simmer for about 20 minutes, then liquidize. Pour the resulting gritty mixture through a fine sieve, and keep warm.

Melt the butter in a clean pan, stir in the flour and cook for 2 or 3 minutes. Stir in the sieved shell liquid gradually, until the sauce is smooth. After 10 minutes' simmering, or a little more, flavour with tomato concentrate. Add vinegar and sugar. Cook for another 5 minutes before stirring in the cream, then the Marsala, little by little, to taste. Correct the seasoning before putting in the prawns to heat through. Remove from the heat, stir in the final nut of butter and serve immediately.

To serve, pour some of the sauce over the poached, or lightly-fried fish, and hand round the rest in a sauceboat. Any sauce left over can be mixed with a spoonful or so of mayonnaise, and used as a dressing for cold fish.

SHRIMP SAUCE

To a velouté sauce* add at the last moment a 125 g (4 oz) carton of potted shrimps. The spiced butter gives an excellent flavour to the sauce. (Potted shrimps can be added to a béchamel sauce* in the same way.)

ARTICHOKE AND SHRIMP SALAD (Fonds d'artichauts Ninette)

This is a fine way to start a special meal – the flavour of shellfish harmonizes beautifully with artichoke. Mayonnaise adds zest and richness. Do not be tempted to use canned artichokes; they have no flavour and lack consistency.

Serves 6

7 cooked artichoke bottoms
cooked purée scraped from the leaves
250 ml (8 fl oz) mayonnaise
mustard
fresh parsley, chervil, tarragon, chives, chopped
200 g (7 oz) shelled shrimps or prawns
6 prawns in their shells (optional)

Chop then mash one of the artichoke bottoms with the purée from the leaves. Mix with the mayonnaise and add a little mustard, then the chopped herbs. Fold in the shrimps or prawns. Pile this mixture up on the artichoke bottoms remaining and put a prawn in its shell on top of each. Serve chilled on a bed of lettuce.

If the artichoke bottoms are on the small side, and there is too much shrimp salad, pile the remainder in the centre of the serving dish and put the artichoke bottoms round it.

BAKED AVOCADO WITH SHRIMPS, PRAWNS, OR CRAB

Here is the most successful way of serving avocados hot. The flavour is not lost in the brief cooking and blends deliciously with the shellfish and cheese sauce.

Serves 6

3 large avocados
lemon juice
300 ml (10 fl oz) thick béchamel sauce*
2 heaped tablespoons grated Cheddar
1 heaped tablespoon grated Parmesan
3 tablespoons double cream
175 g (6 oz) peeled shrimps or prawns or crab meat
salt, pepper
breadcrumbs, melted butter

Halve the avocados and remove the stones. Enlarge the cavities, but leave a good firm shell behind. Cube the avocado you have cut away. Sprinkle it with lemon juice, and brush more lemon juice over the avocado halves, to prevent discoloration.

Heat two-thirds of the sauce, which should be very thick indeed as it is a binding sauce. Keep it well below boiling point. Leave the pan on the stove while you stir in the cheeses, gradually, to taste. The flavour should be lively, but not too strong. Mix in the cream and shellfish, with seasoning, and the avocado cubes. If the mixture is very solid, add the remaining sauce. You need to strike a balance between firmness and sloppiness; in the final baking the sauce should not run about all over the place, but keep the shellfish and avocado cubes nicely positioned.

Put the avocado halves into a baking dish. Divide the stuffing between the cavities, mounding it up. Scatter on the breadcrumbs and pour a little butter over them. Bake for 15 minutes at gas 6, 200°C (400°F) and complete the browning under the grill if necessary. Do not keep the avocados in the oven any longer than this, as they do not improve with prolonged heating.

BAKED GIANT PRAWNS (Camarão no forno)

A bonus from writing about food is that it is an easy way of making friends. Last summer I took a cab in Paris and soon discovered that the driver was Portuguese. I asked her what dishes made her feel homesick. We were still talking – or rather she was still talking – when I arrived at my destination, and she would not let me go until she made sure I understood how to make this recipe.

'I make this dish, Madame, when we have something to celebrate. Or just when I want to think about home. Sometimes I can only afford one prawn each, but the oil is so good, Madame, that nobody minds!' Back at home, I made it with the huge prawns now on sale at good fishmongers: I thought it the best thing I had eaten for months. The oil is indeed delicious, so provide plenty of bread.

> For each person
>
> *2–3 huge prawns (the Mediterranean type)*
> *1 tiny red chilli*
> *1 small clove juicy garlic, sliced*
> *olive oil*
> *salt, pepper*
> *1 ramekin about 10 × 2 ½ cm (4 × 1 inches) deep*

Set the oven at very hot, gas 8, 230 °C (450 °F). Fit the prawns – you need to push them into place – into each ramekin. Tuck in the chilli and the garlic. Pour over oil to come level with the top of the prawns. Sprinkle with plenty of salt. You can leave them to marinade for several hours in the refrigerator, if this suits you.

Stand the ramekins on a baking sheet and put them into the heated oven for 10 minutes. After this time the oil should be boiling ferociously, and the top of the prawn shells lightly browned. Let the dishes stand for a minute or two, then serve with plenty of bread to mop up the oil. A mixture of wheatmeal and strong plain white flour gives a good loaf for this kind of food. Put finger bowls on the table as well.

NOTE Do not let anyone swallow the chilli, unless they have leather throats. The garlic can be eaten, and serve sprigs of parsley afterwards if people are worried about breathing over their neighbours.

CURRIED PRAWNS

Serves 6

750 g (1½ lb) prawns
1 large onion, chopped
60 g (2 oz) butter
1 heaped teaspoon curry powder
1 rounded tablespoon plain flour
300 ml (10 fl oz) fish stock*
150 ml (5 fl oz) double cream
salt, pepper

Shell the prawns (use the shells for making the stock). Melt the onion in butter until soft. Stir in the curry powder and flour and moisten with the strained stock and the cream. Reduce to a thick sauce and season to taste. Reheat the prawns in the sauce for a few seconds, just before serving.

MANGO PRAWNS

'I was a long way from the sea when I heard about this one,' wrote Alan Davidson in the *Seafood of South-East Asia*, 'precisely, at Ban Houei Sai, the enchanting village which stands on soil studded with sapphires in the Golden Triangle area of Laos. I was on the trail of *Pangasianodon gigas*, the giant catfish of the Mekong. Peter Law, a narcotics expert from Hong Kong, was following other trails of his own; but he is also a gastronome and was moved by some turn in the conversation to impart this recipe to me ... may be used for crab instead of prawns. Whichever you use, the amount of crustacean and the amount of mango should be about equal.'

Use the large cooked Mediterranean prawns that a number of fishmongers now sell, otherwise go for crab.

Serves 4

8 prawns
4 mangos

DRESSING
300 ml (10 fl oz) mayonnaise or double cream
2 tablespoons freshly grated horseradish
a squeeze of lemon or lime juice
1 teaspoonful sugar
a little freshly ground pepper
a little single cream or creamy milk to thin dressing, if necessary

Peel the prawns, and cut up into chunks. Prepare the mangos so that you are left with the empty skins and the flesh cubed.

Mix prawns and mango. Mix the dressing ingredients, then stir it gradually into the prawn and mango. Stop when the mixture is nicely bound and not in the least liquid. Divide between the empty mango skins, and arrange on a dish. Garnish with strips of sweet red or green pepper and mint leaves. Serve chilled.

MELON AND PRAWN VINAIGRETTE

This is a very good dish to take on a picnic. Carry the salad in a plastic container and spoon it into the melon shells when you are settled in your picnic spot.

Serves 6

3 small Charentais melons
2 kiwi fruit
6 small tomatoes, peeled
300 g (10 oz) prawns, cooked
1 tablespoon chopped dill
2 tablespoons hazelnut oil
2 tablespoons lemon juice
salt, freshly ground black pepper
sprigs of dill

Cut the melons in half and discard the seeds. Scoop the flesh into balls, using a melon baller, and wrap the melon shells in plastic wrap.

Peel the kiwi fruit, cut in half and slice. Cut each tomato into eight wedges, discarding the seeds, and place in a plastic container with the melon balls, kiwi fruit, prawns and chopped dill. Mix the oil, lemon juice and seasoning together in a jar.

Just before serving, tip off any juices that have collected from the melon mixture. Shake the dressing well to mix and pour over the melon, kiwi fruit and prawns. Spoon into the melon shells and garnish with the sprigs of dill.

PRAWNS AND MUSSELS IN A CREAM SAUCE

Serves 6

1 onion, chopped
300 ml (10 fl oz) dry white wine

bouquet garni
about 2 kg (4 lb) mussels
2 shallots, chopped
45 g (1½ oz) butter
30 g (1 oz) plain flour
90–125 ml (3–4 fl oz) double cream
salt, pepper, parsley
375 g (12 oz) prawns

Put the onion, wine and bouquet into a pan, and bring to the boil. Add the mussels and leave them to open in the usual way (p. 239). Discard the shells and strain the liquor. Cook the shallots gently in butter until soft. Stir in the flour, moisten with mussel liquor and cream, and reduce to a good thick consistency. Season to taste. Meanwhile, shell the prawns. Reheat the prawns and mussels for a few seconds in the sauce just before serving.

PRAWNS IN TOMATO AND VERMOUTH

This recipe comes from *Home Book of Greek Cookery* by Joyce M. Stubbs.

Serves 4

750 g (1½ lb) prawns
1 small onion, chopped
2 cloves garlic, chopped
60 g (2 oz) butter
250 g (8 oz) peeled, chopped tomato
1 sprig rosemary or sweet basil
good pinch of cinnamon
salt, pepper
1 teaspoon sugar
60–90 ml (2–3 fl oz) vermouth
60–90 ml (2–3 fl oz) double cream

Shell the prawns. With a tiny teaspoon, scrape the soft part from the heads and set it aside. Melt the onion and garlic, until soft, in the butter. Add the scrapings from the prawns, tomato, rosemary or basil and cinnamon. Season with salt, pepper and sugar (eventually, with northern tomatoes, you may find it necessary to add more sugar and plenty more pepper). Simmer, uncovered, for half an hour. Sieve into a clean pan. Pour in the vermouth and the cream and stir the sauce together. Reheat the prawns in it at the last moment.

PRAWNS WITH RICE, AND PRAWNS IN PASTRY CASES

Prawns are so full of flavour that they are the ideal fish for serving in rich sauce with boiled and buttered rice. This is usually pressed into a ring mould, before being turned on to a serving dish; the prawns in their sauce are poured into the centre. If for rice you substitute deep-fried caissettes – 5-cm (2-inch) thick, crustless slices of bread, hollowed out in the middle – you have an even better method of making a few prawns go a long way. If you are pampered by the proximity of a first-class pastrycook, you can buy brioches and use them to hold the prawns and sauce (scrape out the soft dough inside first, having removed the little topknot). A solution which is open to everyone is to buy or make puff pastry or shortcrust pastry cases. Any of the three mixtures in the recipes for Curried prawns, Prawns and mussels in a cream sauce or Prawns in tomato and vermouth are offered as suggestions – they can easily be varied to suit your resources and tastes.

POTTED SHRIMPS

Fresh shrimps should be used at all times. The best ploy is to buy lots, eat some fresh and then pot the rest, and this should be done as soon as possible after you have bought them.

To every 600 ml (1 pt) of picked shrimps – which will serve 6–8 when potted – allow 100–125 g (3–4 oz) butter. Melt it slowly with a blade of mace, cayenne and a shade of grated nutmeg. Stir in the shrimps and heat them through without boiling. Stir all the time. Remove the mace, and then divide between little pots. Cool quickly in the refrigerator. Cover with clarified butter.

To serve, warm them slightly. Provide brown bread and butter. Prawns, crab and lobster can all be potted in the same way.

SHRIMP AND TOMATO BISQUE (Potage à la crevette)

Whatever the attractions of travel or Paris were for Dumas, he was always drawn back to the sea (he quotes Byron: 'Oh sea, the only love to whom I have been faithful'). He wrote much of his *Dictionnaire* at Roscoff in Brittany, and some in Normandy at Le Havre, where he met Courbet and Monet. He loved the shrimps and *bouquets roses* of that coast, and invented this soup for them. In the end he died near the sea.

Judging by a similar recipe in the soup section in the *Dictionnaire*, this dish was invented by Dumas himself. Ideally, it should be made with the remains of a *pot-au-feu* liquid and live shrimps. If you cannot manage this, use a good beef stock and boiled shrimps (or prawns, or mussels opened with white wine – *see* method 2 on p. 239).

Serves 4

750 g (1½ lb) tomatoes, peeled, chopped
500 g (1 lb) onions, sliced
150–200 g (5–7 oz) shrimps
white wine
salt, pepper, cayenne
bouillon from pot-au-feu or beef stock

Cook tomatoes and onions slowly in a covered pan. When the tomato juices flow, raise the heat and remove the lid. Simmer steadily for about 45 minutes, then sieve.

Meanwhile cover the shrimps generously with white wine, add salt, pepper, cayenne. Bring to the boil, and cook briefly for a moment or two. Try one to see if it is ready. Strain off the liquid.† Peel the shrimps, setting aside the edible tail part. Put the debris back into the pan with the liquid, and simmer for 15 minutes to extract all flavour from the shells, etc. Strain, pressing as much through as possible. Measure this shrimp liquid, and add an equal quantity both of the tomato purée and beef stock. Bring to the boil, taste for seasoning, and adjust the quantities if you like, adding a little more tomato or stock, or both. A pinch of sugar will help bring out the flavour if the tomatoes were not particularly good.

Put in the shrimp meats, and heat for a moment, then serve. Do not keep the soup waiting as this will toughen the shrimp tails.

NOTE If you use cooked shrimps or prawns, start their preparation at †, covering the debris very generously with white wine.

TEMPURA

In other words fritters, because the European fritter is thought to have been the origin of this popular Japanese food. When the Jesuit missionaries arrived with Saint Francis Xavier in sixteenth-century Japan, they ate the dish on Ember Days, fast days occurring at four periods of the year – the *quattuor tempora* – when ordinations could take place. The first Tokugawa ruler, Ieyasu, died about sixty years later from a surfeit of *tai tempura*, fritters of sea bream or *tai*, the most prized of Japanese fish. Some at least of the missionaries' works had made devoted converts.

If you have an electric deep frier, you will find tempura easy to organize on the *fondue bourguignonne* principle – which is to say that all the separate ingredients that go to make up a tempura are prepared beforehand, and the cooking is done last of all at table with no loss of sociability for the cook. This is the ideal, because these rather delicate fritters should be eaten immediately, straight from the pan, each person dipping his piece into a small bowl of sauce the moment it is ready.

In Japan, chopsticks are used for both cooking and eating tempura. But unless you are very skilful with them, you will find it easier, when cooking, to make use of a perforated spoon in the normal way. Fondue forks are the obvious solution, if you have them.

Prepare the three elements of the dish – sauce, seafood and vegetables, batter – in the following order:

Serves 4

SAUCE
2 tablespoons sake } or *3 tablespoons mirin or dry sherry with some sugar*
1 tablespoon mirin
2 tablespoons sugar
150 ml (5 fl oz) dashi or stock

Simmer together for two minutes. Pour into a bowl, or individual bowls, and leave to cool.

FISH AND VEGETABLES
16 mushrooms or dried shiitake
24 large prawns in their shells
24 mussels, scrubbed and scraped
2 aubergines
4 spring onions

Cut the stalks of fresh mushrooms level with the caps, or soak the shiitake until soft, drain them, and discard the stems. Shell the prawns. Open the mussels in a large pan, covered, over a very high heat (*see* p. 239); remove them from their shells (keep the cooking liquor for another dish). Cut the aubergines into 8 or 12 pieces each, according to their size. Trim roots and damaged outer skin from the spring onions. Arrange elegantly on a dish. (Other ingredients can be added – e.g. cubes of firm white fish fillets, pieces of young carrot, red and green pepper and so on.)

BATTER   The master of a tempura restaurant in Tokyo, the famous Tenichi restaurant, has written a small book on the special foods of the capital. In it he gives this recipe for the correct, very light batter. He observes that the old way of reading the characters of the word *tempura* gives you 'flour' and 'silk-gauze'. 'The whole word could mean to wear light stuff of flour, as a woman wears silk-gauze that desire may be stimulated in the beholder by glimpses of the beauty underneath.' This gives you a good idea of what the fritters should look like when they are ready to eat.

Break an egg into a measuring container, and whisk it smooth. Add four times its bulk of water, then five times its bulk of flour. In other words, if your egg occupies 30 ml (1 fl oz), you should end up with 300 ml (10 fl oz) of batter. Whisk well.

TO COOK   Heat a pan of deep oil to 177–182 °C (350–360 °F). Dip the individual pieces of food into the batter, shake off the surplus, and deep-fry for a few minutes until the coating is crisp and a rather whitish brown. With the spring onions, you will find it easier to use your fingers for dipping them into the batter rather than a perforated spoon. If you are not handing out the cooked fritters straight from the pan, arrange them on an elegantly folded napkin on a serving plate and keep them warm in the oven. Obviously the cooking has to be done in batches, so that there is no risk of the oil losing heat.

WINTER ARTICHOKE SALAD

I discovered by accident how well the earthy flavour of Jerusalem artichoke combines with the sweetness of prawns. Christmas came round one year, and there was no possibility of having the usual smoked eel or smoked salmon. I bought some prawns in their shells instead. Wondering exactly how I was going to serve them, I drove home and came in through the back kitchen past a basket of Jerusalem artichokes. The dish was a great success. It looked beautiful with the contrast of grey, pink and green: the flavour was fresh and unusual, an appetizing start for the lengthy Christmas dinner. It is also good before strong and substantial game dishes.

The quantity of prawns can be varied; you want enough to provide the contrast, but not so many that they become too dominant. I sometimes buy 750 g (1 ½ lb) prawns in their shells (for six people), set a few aside for decoration, then shell the rest; the debris goes into a pot with fish bones to make the next day's soup, or stock for a prawn sauce to serve with cauliflower, p. 281.

Serves 6

1 kg (2 lb) Jerusalem artichokes
about 125 g (4 oz) shelled prawns or shrimps
olive oil vinaigrette
plenty of chopped parsley and chives or *spring onion*
6 prawns in their shells

Cook the artichokes in their skins. Peel and slice them neatly. This means discarding the squashy parts, but do not throw them away – they can be used to flavour mashed potato, or potato soup. Put the slices in a shallow dish and dot the prawns or shrimps over the top. Pour on enough vinaigrette to moisten the salad and add a good scattering of herbs. Arrange the prawns in their shells on top. Serve well chilled.

NOTE The artichokes can be cooked and sliced well in advance. Cover them with vinaigrette. Add the shellfish an hour before serving, and chill.

RAY *see* A FEW WORDS ABOUT ... SKATE

† RED MULLET

Mullus surmuletus

Red mullet is one of the finest fish in the sea, though sadly for Americans it is confined to the Mediterranean, the Black Sea and the Atlantic coast of Europe: it can also be one of the most confusing. First of all, your eye may be deceived by the similar but paler rose-coral of the gurnard (and, in France, by the similar name of *rouget*). Secondly, your ear can be deceived so that you buy other, cheaper mullet – grey or rainbow or striped for instance – thinking they are going to taste the same, or at least similar: they do not, and belong to quite another family, the *Mugilidae* or true mullets. The red mullet is a goatfish of the *Mullidae* family, and far superior in flavour.

Sometimes it is called sea woodcock, because of its liver which must on no account be discarded with the other innards (the woodcock is always cooked with its trail). This delectable item was much prized by the Romans who had a passion for red mullet. Martial exhorted his readers not to sully their gold dishes with mullet weighing less that 1 kg (2 lb) – the Romans had a vulgar weakness for size. Personally, I am grateful for any red mullet I see, and have never noticed any difference in flavour between medium and large fish – the small mullet you sometimes see in frozen blocks are tasteless, but this is not their fault. In markets in Provence, I have seen these miniature fish in the mixtures sold for making Bouillabaisse and other fish soups; they are part of the general rock fish mixture.

It is a commonplace of cookery that the best fish need the simplest cooking. One or two flavourings, though, have become part of the red mullet tradition, fennel, for instance, and tomatoes. Olives, too.

Certainly such things are a help, not because the mullet needs them but because it is too expensive a fish to buy in lavish quantities.

I sometimes meditate ruefully on the subject, and recall that one night in August 1819, 5,000 red mullet were taken in Weymouth Bay. The sea was red with them. Now if Constable had been there then, instead of three years earlier in 1816, the pink glow of that vast catch might have been reflected in his paintings of the bay. These days, the red mullet are snapped up by restaurateurs, and eschewed by provincial fishmongers who think their clients won't pay the price. Go on asking your fishmonger, be persistent, and one day he may listen to you.

HOW TO PREPARE RED MULLET

Some cooks leave the scales of the mullet in place if they are going to grill or deep-fry it: they form an impermeable coating so that the fish cooks in its own juices, steams one might say, inside a carapace. Mostly, though, it is best to scale mullet and be able to eat the skin, or so I think. Try to do this without using a lot of water, so that you keep the reddish-pink tones as lively as possible.

When gutting the mullet, treat the liver delicately, be on the look-out for it, and return it to the cavity as it is the best part.

Recipes for grey mullet, bream, bass and bluefish can often be adapted to red mullet. Orange juice, especially bitter orange juice, used discreetly, or orange wedges, can be substituted for lemon.

GRILLED RED MULLET WITH FENNEL (Rouget grillé au fenouil)

About twenty and more years ago there was a passion for serving grilled fennel on a bed of dried fennel stalks which were then set alight with alcohol. It was indeed a delightful dish, especially on holiday in Provence where, in some small restaurant, it was done for you. People came home and tried it for themselves and for a while there was quite a market for dried fennel stalks. Clever business, that. In fact, fennel of the kind used, *Foeniculum vulgare*, grows like a weed in any garden here and the stalks are perfectly easy to dry. I suppose it was when cooks realized that once they had a plant of fennel in the backyard, they would have a fennel jungle next year, that the dish began to go out of fashion. And all the little burnt bits of fennel stopped you eating the skin of the fish, too, which with grilled mullet especially is one of the bonuses.

Serves 6

6 red mullet each weighing 250–300 g (8–10 oz), scaled
1 green leafy fennel stalk, cut from the top of Florentine fennel
    or a little pastis
a little clarified butter*
salt, pepper
6 heads of Florentine fennel, quartered
1 medium onion, chopped
1 large clove garlic, chopped fine
4 tablespoons butter
2 tablespoons Parmesan cheese

Gut the mullet from the gills, removing and saving the livers. Into the cavities, put a short stalk of green fennel, or brush them out with pastis, and replace the livers. Slash the fish two or three times on either side. Brush over with butter and season, paying particular attention to the slashes.

Meanwhile, cook the fennel quarters in boiling salted water until just tender, and cook the onion and garlic slowly in the butter. Drain the fennel and add the pieces to the onion pan, mixing everything well so that the fennel is bathed in buttery juices. Put into a heatproof dish, sprinkle with the cheese and brown nicely under a preheated grill. Keep the fennel warm while you grill the mullet on both sides, about 7 minutes in all.

Serve mullet and fennel together, with bread and dry white wine.

RED MULLET WITH MUSHROOMS

The deliberate flavour of red mullet is well set off by mushrooms. In the autumn, try the dish with ceps or girolles: use them on their own, or with cultivated mushrooms, weighing them when prepared as there can be a fair amount of waste.

Serves 6

3 large mullet or 6 medium-sized mullet, scaled, cleaned
salt, pepper
125 g (4 oz) chopped onion
4 tablespoons butter
375 g (12 oz) mushrooms, chopped

60 g (2 oz) breadcrumbs
leaves of 1 handful of parsley, chopped
lemon wedges

Preheat the oven to gas 5, 190 °C (375 °F).

Season the cavities of the mullet with salt and pepper and replace the livers. Grease an ovenproof gratin dish large enough to hold the mullet in a single layer with a butter paper.

Cook the onion until soft in the butter, without browning it. Add the mushrooms, cooking them slowly until the juices run: if you use wild mushrooms, you may need at this point to turn up the heat to evaporate excessive wateriness. Aim to end up with a moist rather than a wet result.

Stir in the breadcrumbs and plenty of parsley. Spread out in the gratin dish and put the mullet on top. Bake for 20–30 minutes, or until cooked.

If you have three mullet, it helps with the serving to fillet the fish and lay the six halves skin side up on the breadcrumb base.

Tuck the lemon wedges between the fish and serve.

ROUGETS BARBETS À LA BOURGUIGNONNE

In southern France, red mullet are sometimes wrapped in vine leaves before being grilled. In this recipe from Burgundy, they are wrapped in vine leaves and stuffed with grapes before being baked. The sauce is a variation of beurre blanc*, using a reduction of white wine and the juices, with shallots, as the base. If you don't have access to a vine, you will find packets of the leaves in brine at a delicatessen. Soak them to reduce the saltiness: only blanch them if they are not supple enough to bend round the fish without breaking.

Serves 6

6 mullet of medium size, scaled, cleaned
salt, pepper
375 g (12 oz) white grapes, skinned, halved, seeded
12 vine leaves, blanched 30 seconds
250 ml (8 fl oz) Chablis or other dry white wine
4 tablespoons finely chopped shallot
4 tablespoons crème fraîche or double cream
175 g (6 oz) unsalted butter, diced

Preheat the oven to gas 7, 220 °C (425 °F).

Season the mullet with salt and pepper, put back the livers into each cavity with some grape halves. Wrap two vine leaves round each fish. Put them closely together in an ovenproof dish, so that the leaves do not unwrap. Pour in a little of the wine, cover with foil and bake for 20 minutes or until done. Keep warm.

As the fish cook, boil down the remaining wine and the shallots in a shallow pan until you are left with 3 or 4 tablespoons of moist purée. Add the juices from cooking the fish plus the cream and boil down again by half. Let the reduction cool slightly, then whisk in the butter, keeping the pan off the heat so that there is no chance of the butter oiling. Add the remaining grapes. Reheat cautiously, check for seasoning. Put the fish on separate plates or one large dish and pour the sauce round.

SURMULETS AUX AUBERGINES

Aubergines or egg plants go well with certain fish, ones that have a pronounced flavour like red mullet, but they need a little tomato as a go-between.

Serves 6

3 large mullet or *6 medium-sized mullet*
salt, pepper
2–3 long aubergines
1 medium onion, chopped fine
olive oil
500 g (1 lb) tomatoes, skinned, seeded, chopped
1 large clove garlic, chopped fine
1 level teaspoon sugar (optional)
cayenne pepper
125 ml (4 fl oz) dry white wine or *1 tablespoon sherry vinegar*
up to 250 ml (8 fl oz) fish, veal or poultry stock
bouquet garni, basil, coriander or chervil

Preheat the oven to gas 7, 220 °C (425 °F). Season the cavities of the fish and put back the livers.

Slice the aubergines, unpeeled, so that you get 30 slices plus a couple to act as tasters (use up the rounded ends in another dish). Blanch them for 2 minutes in boiling salted water, then drain and dry them on kitchen paper.

Make a tomato purée by softening the onion in a minimum of oil in a wide pan over a low heat, then adding tomato and garlic. Cook fast and briefly so that you end up with a coherent and unwatery but fresh-tasting mass of tomato; check for seasoning and add the sugar as well as some cayenne if it needs livening up.

Spread out the aubergine slices on an oiled baking tray and put a mound of tomato on top of each. Slide into the top of the oven. Check after 10 minutes. Be prepared to give longer.

Brush out a baking dish that will accommodate the mullet closely with olive oil. Lay the fish in it, put in wine or vinegar and enough stock to bring the liquid level just a little way up the fish, about ½ cm (¼ inch). Add the bouquet and put the fish into the centre of the oven for 20–30 minutes, or until just cooked. Pour off and reduce the cooking liquor to a little syrupy sauce.

TO EAT HOT Fillet the larger fish and put them on to a hot serving platter, surrounded by the aubergine slices. Or arrange on individual plates. Pour a little of the sauce over the aubergine slices, as a seasoning, and round the fish. You can, if you like, turn it into a richer sauce by whisking in butter at the last minute, but to my thinking this spoils the simplicity of the dish. Put a light sprinkle of chopped basil or coriander over the dish.

TO EAT COLD Bring the fish out of the oven when it is barely cooked, since it will continue to cook in its own heat. Let it cool, then fillet the larger fish. Pour the reduced sauce over the hot aubergine slices, then allow them to cool. Serve the two together as above, sprinkled with basil or chervil, or coriander if you are addicted to it (I like it best with hot food, but you may not agree).

Red mullet andalouse

The sauce andalouse*, with its flavouring of sweet peppers, goes well with plainly grilled red mullet. By extension, red peppers on their own, or mixed in with tomato cooked as in the recipe above, show off its flavour, too.

RED SNAPPER *see* A FEW WORDS ABOUT . . . RED SNAPPER

RIGG *see* A FEW WORDS ABOUT . . . DOGFISH

ROCK TURBOT *see* A FEW WORDS ABOUT . . . CATFISH

† SALMON & SALMON TROUT

Salmo salar, Onchorhynchus spp & *Salmo trutta*

Salmon is, to man at least, the king of the fish. Much of its life history is unknown and mysterious. Its taste is so fastidious that it can only survive in pure waters (the appearance or disappearance of salmon is a barometer of a river's pollution).

The salmon is one of those anadromous fish, like eel and shad, which spend most of their lives in seawater, yet return to the rivers, mainly to the rivers of their birth, to spawn. And to be caught. The tiny salmon is called a fingerling, then a parr until it leaves the river at anything from one to three years old. After that the salmon are known as smolt. From this point they disappear completely until their return, either a year later as grilse, weight up to 3 kg (6 lb), or up to three years later as large and handsome salmon weighing up to 15 kg (30 lb) or more. The grilse are often of a size to be confused with salmon trout and large brown trout; not that this need bother the cook, as similar recipes are suitable for all three.

The difference in size, and development, and age of the returning fish has puzzled the scientists. Obviously some salmon go much farther away into the Atlantic to feed. But why? And where? One answer to the second question was discovered in the last part of the 1950s. A US nuclear submarine, cruising below the ice between Greenland and Baffin Island, 'spotted thousands and thousands of fish hanging like silver icicles from the underside of the pack', feeding on the rich plankton. Luckily no one has yet discovered where the grilse feed, which must obviously be much nearer the coasts of Europe. By the time they do, let us hope there is adequate legislation to preserve them from the intensive greedy fishing which has threatened the survival of salmon off the west of Greenland.

But whether grilse, or larger salmon who have made the long journey from the other side of the Atlantic, most of them return to their native rivers. Exactly how is another mystery. They gather in the waters of the estuary, fine fat fish in prime condition, and make their way upstream, sometimes with those immense leaps that have given the salmon the name of *salar*, the leaper, *Salmo salar*.

From the moment they enter the sweet water, they eat nothing until they return to the sea again. Which means, to the cook, that the sooner they are caught the better. A spent kelt which is managing to get back to the sea – many of them die – is a dish for nobody.

The universal feeling in Europe, and perhaps beyond, is that Scottish salmon is the best. Salmon from the Tweed, perhaps. Someone told me that he arrived at a small hotel near Berwick some years ago and had to stumble his way across the hall floor which was covered with salmon, thirty, forty, even a hundred. Not that he minded picking his way round, trying not to slip, not at all. Salmon for dinner he thought happily, as he checked in and went upstairs. Salmon for dinner he thought, as he washed and changed and made a slow journey downstairs to the dining-room. 'Well,' said the waitress, when she had settled him down, 'what'll it be? Lamb or chicken?'

'But what about salmon? All that salmon in the hall?'

'Oh *that*. It's going down to London by the night train.'

And that kind of salmon, pink and curdy, precious, occasional, was the standard one judged by. There were other sorts of salmon about, frozen Canadian, useful for fishcakes. Then there was canned salmon of the north country high tea and the larder standby for a soufflé or mousse. Canned salmon has strange romantic names on the label, which mystified me for years – chinook and coho, sockeye and chum. What could they mean? Now I know that chinook and coho are the best Pacific salmon, and that springtime chinook from the Copper River in Alaska may well equal Scottish salmon if you eat it fresh on the spot. Chum salmon is the least fat of these salmon, and so the least good of the canned ones. But there again, confusion – as quality also depends on the state of the salmon when it is caught and canned. General good advice is to stick to a brand that you find satisfactory. I remember a tasting of canned salmon about six years ago. Considering the price, none of them was much good. I imagine that with so much farm salmon around, at low prices, sales of canned salmon must drop.

Farming, or aquaculture, is the new thing in salmon. One can see the point and importance of it. The system is a good idea. Judging by the disastrous trout farming industry in Britain, it is the people who run the system who are not always a good idea. They are after fast growth and the quick buck, the spiv mentality, fine for a ten-year bonanza (if that, judging by the disappearance of trout farms in some areas).

Will this happen to farm salmon? I would think not.[1] For a start the whole enterprise is bigger, needs more capital, more planning. And there is the high standard already set by Norway.

A few years ago, we went to Bergen to see the salmon farming there. We had already come across a good deal of Norwegian salmon in local markets in France. It was good when fresh. The smoked sides tend to be bright pink and coarse in flavour – although there are excellent smokers supplying the best shops and restaurants, their skills do not seem to reach provincial sales – but that is not the salmon's fault or the salmon farmer's. In Bergen, we were in the capable hands of Mr Mowinkle. He had inherited a jam factory when he was still quite young, a modest affair. Jam, I gather, did not appeal to him very much. He set off round Germany, because it was the richest country in Europe, to see whether he couldn't discover something that German chefs would like to have that he could produce, something that was in short or capricious supply. Salmon was the answer, high quality salmon.

Mr Mowinkle took off in a small way, then grew bigger and bigger. Now up and down the west coast of Norway, he has tucked netted pens of salmon into grooves and inlets of the low grey rocky shore. They are fed judicious mixtures of fish pounded into a feed with krill (the tiny crustacea that it contains is what keeps the salmon an elegant pink, a colour that in Scottish farms is supplied by cathaxanthin often with horrible garish results that make a reasonably discriminating buyer wary). Mr Mowinkle's salmon are carefully handled, laid into boxes of crushed ice for their journeys to Europe and North America, even to Japan so high is the quality. And each salmon is tagged at the gills with the grey MOWI mark. I wish this system would be adopted here, then if one buys a salmon one

---

[1] Since Jane Grigson wrote this, salmon farming has increased phenomenally, to the point where it is now in crisis. Salmon is now too common to sustain the high prices, and there is growing concern about the chemicals used in intensive fish farming and their effects on the environment. There is beginning to be an interest in salmon 'ranching', i.e. rearing salmon in huge pens in the open sea, where there is no need to treat them with chemicals to prevent disease. Salmon raised this way are much closer in taste and texture to wild salmon, and many chefs, including the Roux brothers, have given their stamp of approval.

particularly likes, a pleasant experience has a good chance of being repeated.

Farm salmon of this quality is indeed difficult to distinguish from the wild kind. Often it can be better. For a start, the handling of the fish is more careful, and an autumn farm salmon can be as good as a spring farm salmon, which is not the case with wild fish. In other words, the reliable quality can make up for the less subtle flavour. Outwardly, there is little difference to the casual eye. If you look more carefully, you see that a farm salmon is stubbier, not as streamlined and slender as the salmon which has battled through the seas on long journeys: the tail too is not as vigorously developed on account of its lazier life. When it comes to tasting, if you shut your eyes you may well find it difficult to tell the difference. I should not like to stake my life on getting it right. Once you open your eyes, of course, and see that mind-blasting colour compared with the gentle milky pink of the best wild salmon, you may feel more certain of knowing which is which.

Whenever I get the chance, I buy salmon trout alias sea trout alias (in Wales) sewin, preferably when they are about 60 cm (2 feet) long. The choice of names is confusing, since there are many more in Britain and the States beyond these three – phinock, gillaroo, Galway or Orkney sea trout, orange fin, black tail or fin, bull trout and seal, brown trout – all referring to the same species. For many people, it is the finest river fish, just as sole is the supreme fish of the seas.

There is an effort being made to reduce this nomenclature to sea trout, but when I tried this out at the fishmonger's I was met with a blank stare. *Salmon* trout, ah yes! I am sure that this name will stick because it describes so well the excellence of *Salmo trutta* which combines the good qualities of salmon and trout, and is better than either. It may be no more than a sea-going variety of our native brown trout, but there is a difference in flavour. The pink flesh is firm, without the salmon's tendency to dry up, and the tidy disposition of the flakes most happily resembles the trout's. As it weighs ¾–2 kg (1½–4 lb), it is the ideal fish for a small dinner or lunch party in the spring and midsummer. Worth saving up for.

Mrs Bobby Freeman, who writes about Welsh food and ran the Compton House Hotel at Fishguard some years ago, was famous for her Welsh specialities at a time when everyone else in the principality was still engulfed in Windsor Brown Soup and prawn cocktail. She always cooked and served sewin 'in the local way, i.e. simply and gently grilled, with salty butter, and rough brown bread. The rough texture of the local brown bread contrasts marvellously with the smooth delicate texture of the fish. We advise people to put lots of the salty butter on the hot flesh as they work through the fish as this brings out the delicate flavour best of all.'

Sometimes she served a cucumber sauce (béchamel flavoured with a purée of peeled, steamed cucumber). Rich and highly-flavoured sauces will not do for sewin, she feels, and the cooking must be simple: 'I once baked a biggish sewin with one or two fresh sage leaves and a thin strip of lemon rind along its inside, and it ruined it.'

HOW TO CHOOSE AND PREPARE SALMON

Children are coloured indelibly, it seems, by their mother's expertise – or lack of it – in choosing food. Conversations with butcher, baker, nurseryman, are picked up by a pair of ears at counter level and stored in the infant lumber room. So when I came to buy salmon in my turn, I found myself echoing my mother's words: 'The tailpiece, please.' In restaurants, at weddings and parties, I have often eaten the middle cut with pleasure, but when I have to put my own money down on the fishmonger's counter, it is the moister and better-flavoured tailpiece that I buy. The lower price (bargaining advisable) compensates for the higher proportion of bone to flesh.

Instead of a piece of salmon, you might think of buying a whole fish – grilse and salmon trout come in handy sizes for a small party, grilse up to 3 kg (6 lb), salmon trout up to 2 kg (4 lb). Nowadays salmon is sold in long fillets as well as in the more familiar steaks. You will notice that farm salmon tends to be fatter, which makes it ideal for grilling.

Recipes for salmon and salmon trout are interchangeable (except of course where 1 kg/2 lb of middle-cut is required, which can only be provided by salmon, as even the biggest salmon trout are no more than 2 kg/4 lb in all). Especially in some of the new recipes, quite small escalopes are required which can come equally well from both.

The problem with *Salmo salar* and his relations is that although they are rich – and therefore filling – they also have a tendency to dryness. In the past this has been balanced mainly by unctuous sauces made with egg yolk, butter, cream, and by crisp salads of cucumber or sharp sorrel purées and sauces. In the last twenty years, chefs and cooks have concentrated on not overcooking the fish in the first place, in applying heat so that the salmon sets in the centre rather than cooks to the opaque, flaky style of the old days. The new taste for eating salmon 'cooked' by other means, citrus juices or vinegar or salt and sugar cures, means that we have come to expect a new freshness in salmon.

When you prepare the salmon, you should first scale it. Clean out the cavity, saving any roe, especially the hard roe (*see* Caviare). If you have the head removed, save it for soup and stock.

HOW TO DEAL WITH A WHOLE SALMON

One of my most persistent early memories of Three Choirs Festival at Gloucester is, I am ashamed to say, not the music but the spectacle of a whole boiled salmon, a large one, consumed at a luncheon party. It came from the Severn or Wye, and tasted glorious. The cooking of it must have been agony.

Salmon these days seem to be smaller, or at least only the smaller ones seem to be sold in one piece. Larger sizes go for steaks and fillets. And in spite of the perfection of that great salmon, fifty years ago, I would rather prepare three 2-kg (4-lb) grilse salmon for a party, than one salmon at 6 kg (12 lb). My feeling is that the smaller ones taste better, and make for easier serving as well.

Since the point of the following methods is to keep the flavours of the salmon inside the salmon, they are only suitable for wild salmon and the very best farmed salmon. Lower quality fish needs purifying, as it were, by fire: open it up, season and/or marinade it in advance and grill it as in the next recipe. That is the only way to transform the flat river-bottom taste and the soft mushy texture into something worth eating.

If the salmon is too long for the fish kettle or oven, cut off the head and cook it separately (or keep it for soup). When dishing it up, the separation can be disguised by a ruff or parsley, or bay or cucumber.

METHOD 1: With a Fish Kettle

Builders and architects make kitchens too small: equipment manufacturers collude by making pans and machines too small. They have a picture of dolls cooking in a doll's kitchen. Break out and buy a fish kettle. You will find it surprisingly useful for other things.

Keep the measurements of the fish kettle in your head when you buy a salmon, which you should have cleaned and scaled by the fishmonger.

Fill the kettle half-full of water. In it, dissolve 175 g (6 oz) coarse salt for every 2 litres (4½ pt). Salting at this strength, which is even stronger than seawater, has an excellent effect on fish without spoiling its flavour. You can make up a court bouillon* if you like – wine, vinegar, vegetables, aromatics – but I now conclude that there is no point in it. A good salmon keeps more of its good flavour when cooked in brine.

Put the fish on to the strainer tray and lower it into the kettle. Put a long dish or board on top to keep it submerged. Add extra water and salt, if need be, to cover it.

Place the kettle across two burners on the stove.

TO EAT HOT   Suspend a thermometer in the pan. Switch on the heat and bring the water to 65 °C (150 °F). Make sure it never goes above 80 °C (175 °F) while the salmon cooks: if it shows signs of doing so, and you cannot make a swift adjustment to the burners, pour in a little cold water.

Assuming the fish to be about 5 cm (2 inches) thick, give it 15 minutes at this temperature. Raise the strainer tray, rest it across the pan and pull out a bit of the back fin: it should come away with a little tug. To assure yourself of the cooking, explore the cavity with the aid of a pointed knife. If it is still transparent at the centre, give it longer in the water.

TO EAT WARM   Bring the pan to boiling point, one good bubble, then put on the lid, remove the pan from the stove, but keep it in a warm place. Leave 10 minutes, then test as above.

TO EAT COLD   Bring the pan to boiling point, one good bubble, at the most two, then put on the lid, remove the pan to the larder or somewhere cool and leave until you can comfortably put your hands in the water and pull out a back fin. In theory, you can leave the salmon until it is quite cold, but it can be overcooked.

METHOD 2: With Foil

If you have a really fine salmon and require its juices to serve as sauce, or to add to a sauce, you should wrap the fish in foil before following any of the above cooking methods.

To do this, cut a piece of heavy freezer foil that will be large enough to enclose the salmon in a baggy parcel. Lay it on the table and brush with melted butter if the salmon is to be eaten hot, or with oil if it is to be eaten cold (butter would congeal in unappetizing blobs).

Make two straps of folded foil and put them across the narrow width of the large piece. Brush them with butter or oil. Lay the salmon across them, positioning them so that when the cooked salmon is transferred to a serving dish, they will take the weight at its heftiest parts. Bring up the sides of the foil.

Season the salmon well, pour on a glass of wine, add herbs with discretion and a squeeze of lemon. Fold the straps over the fish, then fasten the large piece tightly into a loose parcel. Ease on to the strainer tray and cover with plain water (no salt). Put a dish or board on top to keep the parcel submerged.

Cook as outlined in method 1.

Unwrap the fish, lift it on to a serving dish with the help of the straps (and, if possible, a helper who will make sure the tail does not crack or break).

Pour off the juices directly into a hot jug if you want to serve them simply as they are (taste for seasoning). Or into a pan to make sauce Bercy*.

METHOD 3: Baked in Foil

The advantages of this method are obvious if you haven't got a fish kettle. In theory, it should be just as good as the fish kettle methods, and I think it is for smaller fish – the 500–750 g (1–1 ½ lb) size. Larger ones seem to work better when submerged in water, as above.

Wrap the fish in foil as above – no need for the straps when the fish are 1 kg (2 lb) or under. If it is too long for your oven, cut off the head and wrap it in foil in a separate parcel: the two pieces can be reunited with a concealing ruff of parsley or bay or cucumber.

Preheat the over to gas 7, 220 °C (425 °F). Check on a 1 ½–2 kg (3–4 lb) fish after 20 minutes.

When cooking a salmon in the oven, you may wish to stuff it for eating hot. Try a cucumber stuffing (p. 183) or the mushroom stuffing on p. 184. With farmed salmon, you could try adding sharper ingredients to a breadcrumb stuffing, chopped olives, capers or anchovies for instance. Whatever you decide to use, keep it clear in flavour rather than spicy.

SAUCES

With hot salmon, melted butter can be enough, or the buttery wine juices from a salmon cooked in foil. Any of the cream* and butter* sauces are an obvious choice, because although salmon is rich, it is also a little dry in tone: hollandaise* or one of its derivatives comes in very nicely, and with new potatoes and asparagus, it may not be a very original dish but it is hard to beat. Sorrel* or rediscovered samphire* also make a good sauce for salmon.

For cold salmon, mayonnaise* obviously. Heaven knows a proper mayonnaise is rare enough. Try Montpellier butter* as a change, especially if you are a gardener.

PRESENTATION

In high class cookery, salmon and salmon trout are invariably served without their skin if they are to be eaten cold. This is practical. It is also practical, after removing the skin, to go one further and remove the bones. This is done by raising the top part of the fish – only for the neat-fingered – and turning it over on to a long serving dish. The bone is removed from the underneath part of the fish, which is then placed boned side down on top of the first part, so that the salmon is then restored to its usual form. Put the head back.

At this point, the professional caterer will mask the salmon with a chaudfroid (jellied mayonnaise*) and decorative motifs from the higher kitsch of catering. That is his fun, but it does not have to be ours. It has its practical side, of course, in that the salmon can be dressed up like Tom Kitten hours in advance, without drying up. When you run a business, that is a perfectly proper and decent precaution to take.

A simpler way, that the neat-fingered can undertake, is to brush the skinned and filleted fish with aspic and cover it with transparent half-moons of small unpeeled cucumber, to look like scales. A friend of mine does them like this, and they are a joy to behold. They have a debonair, frilled appearance like a brushed child at the beginning of a party.

My own preference is to leave the salmon alone, removing the skin and bone for the sake of easy serving, and putting a line of sprigs of fennel or dill or tarragon, whatever is appropriate or best in the garden, down the lateral line. Or else a bed or garland of herbs.

There is much to be said for cucumber salad with cold salmon. A reader once took me to task for suggesting that one might try salting the cucumber slices first: he said that the crisp fresh slices of recently cut cucumber were just right with salmon. You must take your choice.

When it comes to cucumber with salmon, I prefer them both hot or at least warm. The cucumber cut longways into slices, or into little batons, and quickly heated through in clarified butter*, then well peppered.

Florentine fennel, blanched and finished in butter, still a little crisp, is another good vegetable with the best salmon. A hint of pastis can be added to the sauce, but very little.

CAVEACH OF SALMON

This way of treating salmon is more like a seviche (p. 348) than a true caveach which consists of frying fish and then pickling it in vinegar – but one can see the attraction of the name and why Kenneth Ball used it to, as it were, domesticate, or anglicize, this really very foreign dish for his menu at Thornbury Castle. What I like about it especially is his manner of cutting the salmon into thin steaks. Marinaded fish of this type is usually presented in transparent veils – this cut is closer to the Japanese sashimi style.

Serves 8–10

750 g (1½ lb) centre cut of salmon
175 ml (6 fl oz) dry white wine
1 tablespoon salt
¼ teaspoon ground black pepper
juice of 1 lemon
juice of 1 orange
¼ medium onion, finely chopped
¼ clove garlic, finely chopped to a mash
4 tablespoons very best olive oil
shreds of orange and lemon peel, 16–20 slices of avocado pear and a few
    leaves of chicory or endive to garnish

Half-chill the salmon, remove the fillets from each side of the backbone and skin them. Cut each fillet down into slices of just over ½ cm (¼ inch). Arrange them in a single layer in a shallow plastic box or on a large plate.

Mix together the remaining ingredients, apart from the garnish, and pour over the salmon. Cover with the lid or plastic film and leave in the refrigerator for 5 hours, turning the slices every so often. If you want to keep the salmon for longer, I find it is best to scrape off the onion and garlic after 6 or 7 hours, put the salmon on to a fresh plate and strain a little of the marinade over it.

Arrange the slices on a dish or plates with the garnish ingredients. Serve very cold but not chilled to tastelessness.

ESCALOPE OF COLD SALMON MAÎTRE ALBERT

Anjou is a country of just the right *douceur* to have produced that good king, René, Count of Anjou and Provence, King of Sicily. In warlike times, he loved painting and music and tapestries (in particular the Apocalypse tapestries now on display in his castle of Angers), and his two wives adored him. The hotel at Les Rosiers on the Loire is called after his second wife, Jeanne de Laval, and there, in the long quiet dining-room, one may eat the most delicious fish and seafood imaginable. The natural advantages of Loire and Atlantic are submitted to the skill of French cookery in the person of Monsieur Augerau, the proprietor, 'Maître Albert', who invented this summer dish.

One hears so often that it was the Troisgros brothers who brought salmon escalopes and sorrel together at Roanne: Monsieur Augerau was making such a dish a generation before them. The style is a little different – the Troisgros escalopes are beaten flat, cooked briefly in a non-stick pan and then served on a cream and butter sauce flavoured with sorrel and made on a reduction of shallot, white wine, vermouth and fish fumet*.

Serves 6

1 kg (2 lb) middle cut of salmon
butter
shallots or mild onion
250 kg (8 oz) mushrooms, chopped
½ bottle dry white wine
3 large tablespoons double cream
2 large egg yolks
125 g (4 oz) unsalted butter
1 large handful of sorrel
salt, freshly ground black pepper

Ask the fishmonger to skin and fillet the salmon. Cut it into slices about ½ cm (¼ inch) thick. Butter a large shallow pan and cover the base with a layer of chopped shallots. Put in the slices of salmon, slightly overlapping each other, and scatter the mushrooms on top. Pour on enough white wine to cover. Bring to the boil and simmer until the salmon is barely cooked. Transfer the slices to a serving dish, cover with foil and keep warm. Add the cream to the mixture in which the salmon was cooked. Boil hard, until the liquid is reduced by approximately one-third. Strain into a small pan, and whisk the egg yolks into the tepid liquid, which should be kept over a low heat – not enough to cause it to boil. When the sauce is thick, lift the pan from the heat and stir in the butter in little knobs.

Meanwhile, in another pan cook the sorrel in 2 tablespoons of butter. It will rapidly turn to a thick purée. Season well with salt and pepper. Add the purée to the sauce, pour it over the warm salmon slices and chill as quickly as possible in the refrigerator.

NOTE   Cold fish tastes better when it is eaten the day it is cooked. This is a recipe that could be used for firm white fish of good flavour. And it could be served hot – but cold is better.

GRAVADLAX, MAKRILL, FORELL, SILL

In other words, marinaded salmon, mackerel, trout or herring, and one of the great gifts of Scandinavia to the rest of Europe. When I first came across it in 1966 in Denmark, it seemed to me the most delicious thing I had ever eaten. And when the friend at whose table we had eaten it said she would give me the very simple recipe, I could hardly believe that it was going to be possible to make it at home, and with other fish than salmon.

The name means 'buried salmon'. Indeed, the fish is buried in salt, sugar and dill weed, but perhaps the name may refer to far older ways of preserving food than we know about today – to the time when food was buried to keep it fresh, or to make a cure work in a special way, though I cannot imagine how one would prevent it being devoured by wildlife: salmon is a spring and summer catch after all, so the ground would not be frozen.

The sensible minimum – especially since it can be frozen most successfully – is a 1-kg (2-lb) piece of salmon, scaled and filleted, but with the skin left in place. The cure for this quantity consists of:

1 tablespoon coarse sea salt
1–2 tablespoons sugar
1 handful of fresh dill sprigs or 1 tablespoon dried dill weed

The quantity of sugar can be varied to taste. Extra items can be added from plenty of coarsely ground pepper to a tablespoonful of brandy. Mix the salt and sugar together, plus 1 tablespoon of leaves from fresh dill or dried dill weed.

Choose a shallow-sided dish that the salmon will fit into comfortably. Scatter a quarter of the cure over the base. Put in one piece of filleted salmon, skin side down. Sprinkle most of the remaining cure over it, lay the sprigs of fresh dill across and put on the second fillet, skin side up, and with the thick side over the thin side of the fillet below. Sprinkle the rest of the cure over the top. Lay on a piece of foil, then a heavy plate and leave for at least 12 hours, turning the fillet sandwich over once at least. The gravadlax will be good for at least a week, but it will begin to get too salty. It is best eaten within 5 or 6 days, or else drained, wrapped in cling film and put into the freezer.

In any case, gravadlax should be chilled until very firm before slicing, otherwise it can be lumpy and unappetizing. Cut it down in fairly thick slices, or slice it thinly on the diagonal or even parallel to the skin, like smoked salmon.

It can be heated through – see the first recipe following. Usually, though, it is served cold or lightly chilled, with strips of the skin dry-fried to a nicely browned crispness. It can make a course on its own, with rye or wholemeal bread or potatoes, or one dish among many on a *smörgasbörd*. The sauce that accompanies it is flavoured with dill, sugar and mustard. I give the Swedish quantities, but there is no harm done in reducing the sugar:

2 level tablespoons Swedish, German or Dijon mustard
2 level teaspoons sugar
1 egg yolk (optional)
150 ml (5 fl oz) sunflower or groundnut oil
1 generous teaspoon or more chopped dill weed
salt, pepper

Mix mustard and sugar with the egg yolk if used. Gradually beat in the oil as if you were making a mayonnaise. Fold in the dill gradually to taste and season.

GRAVADLAX EN PAPILLOTE

This recipe is based on an idea of Frances Bissell's for cooking salmon with hot potato salad en papillote. With gravadlax, it is extra good.

per person:

2 teaspoons butter
½ teaspoon Swedish, German or Dijon mustard
2–3 small new potatoes, cooked, diced
1 teaspoon finely chopped shallot
¼ teaspoon chopped fresh dill or pinch of dried dill weed
125 g (4 oz) thinly sliced gravadlax
1 tablespoon fish stock*

Preheat the over to gas 5, 190 °C (375 °F). Cut a large heart from a sheet of baking parchment or foil. Melt the butter, mix with mustard and brush it over the heart. To one side of centre, make a bed of potato mixed with shallot and dill. Lay the salmon on top, sprinkle with stock and fold the heart over, twisting the edge to make a sealed package. Put on to a baking sheet and give it 10 minutes in the oven. Slide on to a hot plate to serve.

KULEBIAKA OR SALMON PIE

Fish pie is one of the great dishes of institutional catering. Even in middle age, I find it impossible to forget its gluey texture – and the smell, the revolting smell which hung, as insistently as the smell of *Phallus impudicus* in an autumn wood, over Friday morning lessons.

So at first I hesitated to try recipes for Kulebiaka (especially some of the more majestic ones containing *viziga*, which is the dried spinal cord of sturgeons). Then the possibilities of the ingredients conquered prejudice. I found that in this version of the famous Russian fish pie, they blended to a flavour which was both rich and fresh.

Serves 6

flaky pastry or brioche dough, made with 500 g (1 lb) plain flour
750 g (1½ lb) filleted salmon or turbot or eel
250 g (8 oz) butter, unsalted
250 g (8 oz) chopped shallot or mild onion
250 g (8 oz) mushrooms, coarsely chopped
juice of 1 lemon
175 g (6 oz) rice

2 teaspoons dried dill weed or *2 tablespoons fresh dill*
4 tablespoons chopped parsley
salt, pepper, nutmeg
3 hard-boiled eggs, sliced
egg yolk or *cream* or *top of the milk, for glazing*

Make the pastry or dough. While it is chilling, or rising, prepare the filling. Cut the fish into thin slices. Fry briefly until stiff in 4 tablespoons of the butter; the fish should not be cooked through. Melt half the chopped shallot or onion in another 4 tablespoons of butter, without browning them. When they are soft and golden, put in the mushrooms. Stew them for 5 minutes. Stir in the lemon juice and seasoning to taste.

Fry the rest of the onion gently in 2 tablespoons of butter, until it is soft. Add the rice, and stir about until every grain is coated with melted butter. Pour in 450 ml (15 fl oz) of water (or chicken stock, if you have any: but don't use a cube) and leave to cook gently in the usual way. Add more liquid if necessary, and when the rice is soft, remove from the heat and flavour with dill, parsley, salt, pepper and nutmeg.

Take a heavy baking sheet. Roll out half the pastry to an oblong. Put half the rice on to it, leaving a good margin free. The slices of fish go on next, then the slices of hard-boiled eggs and the mushroom mixture. Last of all the rest of the rice. Roll out the remaining pastry to a similar sized oblong. Brush the rim of the pastry, round the filling, with cream, or top of the milk, or egg, and lay the second layer on top. Press down round the rim to seal the pie. Turn over the rim to double it, and nick the edge all round to make sure of a firm seal. Decorate the pie with leaves made from pastry or dough trimmings, and pierce a central hole for the steam to escape. Brush pie and rim over with beaten egg and cream, or a mixture of both. Leave to rest for 30 minutes – in a warm place if using brioche dough. Bake in a fairly hot oven (gas 5–6, 190–200 °C/375–400 °F) for an hour. If the pastry browns quickly, protect it with buttered paper. When the pie is ready, have the rest of the unsalted butter melted in a little pan. Pour it through the central hole just before serving: a little more won't come amiss. Serve with a separate jug of melted butter, or, better still, sour cream.

NOTE Kulebiaka could be made with cooked salmon. In this case omit the quick frying in butter.

Roasted *kasha* can be used instead of rice, should you be able to get it.

QUICHE DE SAUMON

Serves 6

250 g (8 oz) flaky or *shortcrust pastry*
375 g (12 oz) cooked, flaked salmon
2 teaspoons dill weed or *chopped green fennel leaves*
2 tablespoons Parmesan
2 tablespoons Gruyère or *Cheddar*
2 large eggs, plus 2 egg yolks
300 ml (10 fl oz) single or *whipping cream*
salt, pepper, cayenne

Line a 25-cm (10-inch) tart tin, with a removable base, with the pastry. Bake blind in the oven for 15 minutes – flaky at hot (gas 7, 220°C/425°F), and shortcrust at fairly hot (gas 6, 200°C/400°F).

Spread the salmon evenly over the base. Sprinkle with the herbs and cheese. Beat the eggs and cream together, season well and pour over the salmon mixture. Bake in a fairly hot oven (gas 6, 200°C/400°F) for 30–40 minutes, or until the filling is nicely risen and brown. Serve hot, or warm.

VARIATIONS   Instead of salmon and dill weed or fennel, use the following combinations:

Tuna with capers or anchovies.

Jugged kipper with 1 tablespoon French mustard, and juice of 1 lemon, squeezed over before serving.

Good white fish with vermouth, Pernod or anisette.

Mixed shellfish. Reduce oyster and mussel liquor to concentrated essence, and add to eggs and cream.

SALMON BAKED IN PASTRY WITH GINGER

When I wrote *Fish Cookery* at the beginning of the seventies, George Perry-Smith, the inventor of this dish, was still high priest at the Hole in the Wall restaurant in Bath (these days it is run by two of his pupils, Sue and Tim Cumming). Joyce Molyneux, now at the Carved Angel in Dartmouth, sweetly remonstrated with me when I suggested that frozen salmon could be used. 'We always waited for the best Wye salmon!' And now his other pupils and assistants, with restaurants of their own in various parts of the country, all make this dish with the best local salmon they can find, as a badge almost of their training.

I asked once how the idea of putting ginger with salmon had come about, and was told that some medieval recipe was the source. In fact, a number of medieval fish recipes use ginger – powdered ginger, it seems – as a seasoning, but no early recipe comes as close as John Nott's in his *Cook's and Confectioner's Dictionary* of 1726: 'Scale the salmon, wash and dry him, chine him and season him with salt, pepper, ginger, cloves and mace; lay him on a sheet of paste, and form it in the shape of a salmon, lay in slices of ginger, large mace, and butter upon the fish, and turn up the other half of your sheet of paste on the back, closing them on the belly-side from head to tail, bringing him into proportion with head, fins, gills and tail: scale him, leave a funnel to pour in butter, and when it is baked, set it by to cool.'

A friend who was preparing the dish for visitors who do not like raisins had the brilliant idea of substituting lime. The juice and thin-shredded zest of a lime are added to the butter and ginger: juice and shreds of a second lime are added to melted, skimmed butter to make a sauce. I like this variation very much, lime gives a skip to the substantial delicacy of the dish. Here, though, is the true original version, as sent to me by George Perry-Smith who keeps it on the menu of his Riverside restaurant at Helford in Cornwall.

Serves 6

1–1¼ kg (2–2½ lb) piece of wild salmon, skinned, filleted
salt, pepper
125 g (4 oz) butter, lightly salted
4 well-drained knobs of ginger in syrup, chopped
30 g (1 oz) currants

PASTRY
500 g (1 lb) plain flour
275 g (9 oz) butter
egg yolk, beaten, to glaze

SAUCE
600 ml (1 pt) single cream
2 egg yolks
2 level teaspoons Dijon mustard
2 level teaspoons plain flour
125 g (4 oz) softened butter
juice of 1 lemon
½ small onion, finely chopped
1 small bunch each of tarragon, parsley and chervil
salt, pepper

Season the two pieces of salmon with salt and pepper on both cut and skinned sides. Mash butter with the ginger and currants. Spread half on the cut side of one fillet: put the second fillet on top, like a sandwich, cut side down, and spread the remaining butter mixture on top.

Make the pastry in the usual way, mixing it with iced water. Roll out and wrap neatly round the salmon, cutting away surplus lumps of pastry. If you are using a small salmon or a tailpiece and are feeling fanciful, you could try John Nott's idea of making it look like a pastry fish, marking scales, etc. with the tip of a sharp knife. Brush with egg yolk. Chill until just before the meal.

Preheat the oven to gas 8, 230°C (450°F). Bake for about 30 minutes – time will depend on the thickness of the salmon. Test it after 20 minutes with a skewer. By this time a tailpiece may be done.

To make the sauce, whirl the ingredients in a blender. Cook in a double saucepan, stirring, until thickened. Serve a cucumber salad as well.

SALMON BUTTERFLY GRILL

In most trades – cooking, the law, plumbing, medicine – people plod along steadily, taking the day as it comes, thankful to be paid for doing what they would be happy to do unpaid if they had the means of survival. Occasionally, though, some bit of information, some discovery changes the shape of the trivial round, giving it a new aspect. Perhaps because I never had any training as a cook, this happens to me with a particular force once or even twice a year if I am lucky. As far as fish is concerned, the discoveries often seem to be concerned with salmon – they can often then be applied to other fish, sea bass for instance.

The first was when we visited a friend in Denmark, in 1966, and she gave us gravadlax, and the recipe, which went into the *Observer* four years later, and into *Good Things*. The second came from a home economist connected with fish cookery who told me how to cook whole salmon by bringing it to the boil, then removing the whole thing from the stove, so that the fish could continue to cook in the water as it cooled. A third came from Helen Burke who many years ago pointed out that when grilling salmon steaks, there is no need to turn them over. And the fourth – this recipe from a friend in Aix-en-Provence, a brilliant cook – disclosed a foolproof method of grilling whole farmed salmon, or large pieces of salmon, which minimizes its faults of softness and leaves one in complete control. I should also say that it is now my preferred way of cooking farm salmon for eating cold later on: the svelte silver appearance of a whole poached fish is lost, and perhaps it should be kept only for the finest wild salmon, but the flavour and consistency is much improved.

The presentation can be less cucumbered, less finicky, to emphasize the difference.

Serves 6

1½–2 kg (3–4 lb) salmon or salmon trout
salt, pepper
lemon juice (optional, see recipe)
oil

SAUCE
olive oil vinaigrette*
plenty of chopped parsley and basil or chervil or tarragon
finely chopped red onion or shallot
capers
anchovies
olives

Scale the fish, cut off the head and tail. Clean out the cavity without slitting the belly, using salt to rub away stubborn traces of blood. Cut away the fins and slit down the back, keeping closely to the bone, until the salmon lies flat in a butterfly-shaped wedge. Cut away the bone. Season the fish all over on the cut side, and – if you like – sprinkle it with lemon juice or other form of marinade. Leave for 30 minutes, longer if you like.

Switch on the grill to maximum and make sure it is very hot. Cover the rack of the grill pan with foil, making a nest for the fish. Brush it over with oil. Put the salmon on to the foil, cut side down, skin up. Slide it under the grill and leave for 4 minutes. The skin should be nicely browned and blistered. Turn the salmon over on to a warmed serving dish of a kind that can stand up to heat. Remove the foil from the rack and put the dish on top. Slide it under the grill, switch off the grill and leave the salmon to complete its cooking in the declining heat. It will lose its transparent look and turn milky; investigate with the point of a knife to see how much longer is required for the salmon to become firm all through. It should lose its rawness, but never gain that dry chalky pink look of overdone salmon.

Serve on very hot plates with a vinaigrette sauce that has been embellished by herbs, onion or shallot, and chopped pickles to taste. In the season, asparagus and hollandaise* or mayonnaise* are good accompaniments to the salmon, whether it is hot, warm or cold. Samphire makes another good companion, or new potatoes and laverbread heated up with orange juice and a squeeze of lemon. Since you are dealing with a fish that becomes more and more buy-able, and less exquisite sometimes in the process, try experimenting a little: mild purées of sweet red or yellow pepper, or of Jerusalem artichokes with a light chopping of toasted hazelnuts. A redcurrant sauce, or cranberries, or even plums to give a sharp contrast.

SALMON HEAD SOUP

The heads of large fish make the cheapest of fine soups, with the bonus of extra sweet pickings from the cheeks and under the jaw for the final garnishing. This is my basic recipe, since all the other ingredients are usually to hand. If I happen to be out of white wine, I use dry white vermouth or dry sherry, or a fine vinegar with a little sugar. If there is a head of fennel, that might go into the pot instead of carrot. If the rest of the meal is on the frugal side, cream or yoghurt or fromage frais or a lump of unsalted butter will make the soup a little richer.

Serves 4

1 salmon head
500 g (1 lb) bones from filleting flounders and white fish
3 tablespoons pudding rice, tied loosely into a muslin bag
1 onion, quartered
1 medium carrot, sliced
1 large tomato, cut up
2 cloves garlic
bouquet garni
250 ml (8 fl oz) dry white wine
salt, pepper, sugar
sprigs of chervil or sorrel leaves, as garnish

Put the salmon head and bones into a large pan. Suspend the bag of rice from the pan handle so that it lies well down. Put in the vegetables, garlic and bouquet with the wine and enough water to cover all the ingredients comfortably. Bring the pan to the boil, then adjust the heat to keep the liquid simmering for 45 minutes. When the head is cooked, remove it and extract the nice pink bits of salmon. Set these on one side. Put the bony parts back into the pan as you work.

Strain off the liquid. You need a little under 1 litre (32 fl oz). If there is too much, boil it down. Blend or process most of the rice with the liquid. Aim for a smooth texture with a light agreeable graininess on the tongue: with some processors, you may feel the need to put the soup through a fine sieve afterwards.

Put the soup back into the rinsed out pan, with the last of the rice, the flakes of cooked salmon and seasoning to taste. Reheat to a bare simmer and serve with sprigs of chervil, or the sorrel leaves rolled up and cut across so that they fall into a chiffonade of ribbons which will cook instantly in the heat of the soup.

SALMON MOUSSE

Serves 6

250 g (8 oz) cooked salmon, free of skin and bone
5 tablespoons good fish or beef stock, very hot
15 g (½ oz) gelatine
2 teaspoons wine vinegar or lemon juice
1 tablespoon brandy, dry sherry or dry vermouth
2 tablespoons grated Parmesan
salt, pepper, cayenne
300 ml (10 fl oz) crème fraîche or whipping cream
2 egg whites

Flake the salmon. In a liquidizer or processor, whizz the hot stock and gelatine, then add the fish gradually, plus the various liquids, cheese and seasonings to taste. Whip the cream until stiff and fold in the salmon mixture. Put in a cool place until almost set, but just loose enough to stir. Taste again for seasoning. Beat the whites to soft peaks and fold into the salmon. Turn into a soufflé dish. Serve with a cucumber salad.

VARIATIONS   A proportion of smoked salmon can be substituted for up to half of the cooked salmon – a good way to make use of the cheap bits and pieces left over from slicing a side.

SALMON SOUFFLÉ

Since I've adopted the system of baking soufflés in a shallow dish – which I learned from Alice Waters – I make them much more often. They have an open golden bubbly look, and the inside is creamy enough to provide its own sauce. Another thing she taught me is not to be afraid of using quite a lot of cheese to make the general flavour much more savoury.

Serves 6

250 g (8 oz) cooked salmon, free of bone and skin
salt, pepper
125 g (4 oz) butter
5 tablespoons plain flour
300 ml (10 fl oz) each single cream and milk, heated together
cayenne, ground mace
1 tablespoon tomato concentrate (optional)
5 egg yolks
60 g (2 oz) Gruyère or Gouda, grated
60 g (2 oz) Parmesan, grated
6 egg whites

Flake the salmon, breaking it up as much as possible, and season it. Use a quarter of the butter to grease a shallow oval gratin dish, at least 30 cm (12 inches) long.

Melt the rest of the butter, stir in the flour to make a roux. Then moisten gradually with the cream and milk. Add salt, pepper, cayenne and mace. Simmer half-covered for at least half an hour, stirring occasionally: this can be done in a bain-marie for an hour with even better results. Remove the pan from the heat, stir in the salmon and tomato, if used, and then the egg yolks when the mixture has cooled down a little. Add the Gruyère or Gouda and about half the Parmesan. Taste and adjust the seasoning, bearing in mind the softening effect the whites will have.

Beat the whites until stiff, mix a good tablespoon into the salmon mixture to slacken it, then fold in the rest. Spread into the buttered dish lightly and evenly. Scatter with the remaining Parmesan.

Bake in the oven preheated to gas 8, 230°C (450°F), on the top shelf, for 12 to 15 minutes, or until nicely browned on top but still a little wobbly underneath the crust in the centre.

SALMON STEAKS IN CREAM

I owe this deliciously simple recipe to Mrs Charlotte Sawyer, of Woodsville, New Hampshire. It could equally well be used for cod steaks, or slices of angler-fish, or porbeagle (Blue Dod, as it is sometimes called in North America); but it is particularly good for the dryness of salmon. The ingredients may sound expensive, but they aren't really as they include the sauce for the fish. Some new potatoes are all that is needed to accompany the salmon.

Serves 6

6 thick salmon steaks
salt, pepper
butter
300 ml (10 fl oz) single cream or crème fraîche
1 bay leaf
6 lemon quarters

Season the salmon steaks well with salt and freshly ground black pepper. Choose an oven dish into which the steaks will fit closely in one layer, without being jammed tightly together. Butter the dish lavishly, then put in the steaks and enough cream to cover them well. Tuck in a small bay leaf, and bake in a fairly hot oven (gas 5, 190 °C/ 375 °F) for 20–25 minutes, until the steaks are cooked. Baste them once or twice with the cream, adding more if it reduces enough to leave the surface of the salmon much exposed. Serve with lemon quarters, in case people like to sharpen the sauce a little.

SALMON TARTARE

It seems to have been the Minchelli brothers, or rather Paul Minchelli who is the chef, who introduced the French to the pleasures of gravadlax and sashimi and seviche. Since they are natives of the Ile de Ré, where they opened their first restaurant in 1963, they grew up taking the freshness of fish for granted. And to serve fish raw, or cooked purely by salt or lemon juice, it must be of top quality. 'Our rules, our three unities, are draconian,' says Jean Minchelli, 'The fish must just be caught, its preparation must be simple and it must be eaten the same day. In our restaurants there are no left-overs and no deep-freeze ... What is not sold at the end of the day is eaten by us, or given or thrown away.' Nowadays they have restaurants in Paris, in the Boulevard Raspail, and in the Seychelles.

I suppose that Paul Minchelli turned to the idea of steak tartare for this particular dish, an idea that is well within the French tradition, and a title that would not frighten his clients. This treatment can be used for sea bass, scallops, very fine pale tuna and swordfish – almost any fish that is truly fresh is delicious served in this way. Keep the quantities small. Sometimes salmon tartare comes in teaspoonful

in tiny pastry cases with an apéritif. More usually it will be nested
in salad greenery: steamed samphire tips (p. 83) are a natural
companion.

Allow 125 g (4 oz) fresh salmon per person. Dice it as evenly as
you can, after cutting away the skin and bone, then chop it coarsely.
The pieces should end up about the size of tiny petits pois, a chopped
rather than a mashed effect. Add just enough of the sauce tartare on
p. 41 to bind the mixture lightly – you should really not be aware of
the sauce as you are, for instance, with a cooked salmon mayonnaise
or a Russian salad of vegetables. The point of it is to get the seasonings
mixed evenly through the fish and bind the mixture so that it can be
piled up a little.

SALMON WITH WATERCRESS AND CHIVE BUTTER SAUCE
(Le saumon à la tombée de cresson et au beurre de
ciboulette)

This is an example of the light cooking of Bernard Loiseau at the
Côte d'Or at Saulieu in Burgundy. No elaborate stocks are used in
his kitchen, or simple ones either, but water. This makes some col-
leagues raise their eyebrows. It also makes the sauces tricky to handle.
You need to practise. If they overheat, they separate and turn oily.

Lesser cooks than Monsieur Loiseau may perhaps be forgiven if
they beat a failed sauce into a couple of egg yolks, as if they were
making a version of an hollandaise*. The method of cooking the
salmon, though, is easily mastered and it can be used for other fish.

Serves 4

500 g (1 lb) piece of long salmon fillet
salt, pepper
1 large bunch of chives, chopped
125 g (4 oz) unsalted butter
leaves from 2 large bunches of watercress
olive oil
lemon juice

Lay the salmon skin side down on a board and slice it diagonally
into 4 escalopes of roughly equal size. Season them with salt and
pepper. Discard the skin.

Process the chives with three-quarters of the butter: it should be
very thick with the green, much more than for normal chive butter.
Chill well.

Cook the cress leaves in a little water with the remaining butter, salt and pepper. Drain when tender, dry on kitchen paper and keep hot.

Warm a non-stick frying pan until fairly hot. Quickly dip the salmon pieces in olive oil on both sides and put in the pan. Cook gently, *without turning them*, on one side only. This prevents overcooking. There will be a gradation of effect from opaque next to the pan, to a slight translucency on top. Dry on kitchen paper and arrange on four warm plates with some of the cress.

While the salmon cooks, make the sauce. Bring 125 ml (4 fl oz) water to the boil in a small wide pan. Whisk in the chive butter, bit by bit, raising the pan from the heat so that you end up with an emulsified sauce (beurre blanc technique). Season with salt, pepper and lemon. Pour round the salmon, and serve.

SMOKED SALMON

'These days there's a salmon smoker behind every hedge,' as one producer remarked the other day. I was asking him about the difference between the Scotch and London smoked salmon, in the old days, before things became so confused. He said that the curers in the north, having been used to dealing with kippers and haddock and such, were too heavy-handed with the smoke for such a delicate fish. And so Jewish fishmongers in London started producing it in their own smoke houses, but clean air acts closed them down over the last twenty-five years. Now there is no precise territorial difference, every smoker follows his own taste. And the result will also depend on whether he uses one of the enclosed stainless steel Torry smokers or has made himself a smoke hole.

My own favourite smoked salmon I have bought by post from Ritchie's on the Isle of Bute for many years now. In 1987, being up in those parts, we thought it would be an amiable detour to visit the brothers who had been so friendly at the other end of a telephone for the best part of fifteen years. We were directed to a tiny fishmonger's shop in a side street. Nobody there. I coughed discreetly and moved over to a door at the left where the most amazing sight, a fleet of wild salmon, covered the floor of a long narrow room. At the end were the mahogany-coloured walls of the brick-built smoke holes. And just about to begin work, slitting, cleaning, curing, were the tall brothers calmly surveying the labours of the week ahead. All the same, they had time to stop and talk, to show me the tenterhooks on which the sides of salmon hang, taking on flavour from the cool smoke of smouldering sawdust on the floor below.

From this plain, humble-looking place, untouched it seems since the time of the First World War when their fathers built it, comes some of the finest smoked salmon you can ever hope to eat, as delicate as any London cure. The other day I heard about the largest smoke hole in existence, Skarl's of Brooklyn, where there is room for thousands of salmon sides, with ladders and terraces and walkways. There, too, the cure is delicate. Which all goes to show, there is no rule in the matter as far as size is concerned: in the end, it is the taste of the producer that counts.

If you are ever in the happy position of catching enough salmon to spare some for smoking, I suggest you first consult a good book on the subject. You can buy smokers small enough for home curing, too, by which I do not mean the little metal boxes large enough for a few trout, but the Torry Mini Kiln which has a maximum capacity of 25 kg (56 lb) (marketed by Afos Ltd, Anlaby, Hull, North Humberside). The old home method was to convert a barrel, but you will do far better to build something more convenient. Various designs are given in *Home Smoking and Curing*, by Keith Erlandson, an excellent book with cures and recipes and such cogent advice as 'Do not let your ducks catch fire.'

When it comes to heating smoked salmon, you would do best to leave first-quality salmon alone: serve it with wheatmeal or wholemeal bread and butter and be thankful. Some people like lemon wedges so that they can squeeze a few drops over the salmon. Second-quality smoked salmon is just right for adding to scrambled eggs, or wrapping round a cold soft-cooked egg which can be steadied on a circle of bread and butter – a Wiltshire restaurateur, Christopher Snow, added a thick sauce of smoked cod's roe beaten up with some cream to smooth down the flavour.

For adding to tarts, or making small quantities of salmon rillettes, buy the odd bits and pieces and chunks left over from slicing a whole salmon side. When I first wrote *Fish Cookery*, these off-cuts were almost cheap. Now everyone is wise to this particular dodge, and prices have gone up accordingly. A pity, since they are ideal for giving a lift to cold fresh salmon when you are making a mousse (*see* above), or for pounding with butter or cream or mixing into mayonnaise, to enliven sandwiches, pancakes, baked potatoes and salads of poached white fish. You can make a mild salmon paste by pounding 175 g (6 oz) smoked salmon and adding it to 125 g (4 oz) ricotta cheese and 150 ml (5 fl oz) thick whipped cream: season with pepper and lemon juice.

One of Albert Roux's most famous dishes at the Gavroche is a mousse of smoked salmon with cream and fish aspic wrapped in an envelope of smoked salmon like a little cushion, Papillote Claudine.

There is no end to the ingenuity of it all. But when all is said and done, it is not the ingenuity of chefs that is important, but the skill of the smoker – and the fun of finding the smoked salmon that you like best.

SMOKED SALMON BUTTER

Pound 125 g (4 oz) smoked salmon trimmings with 125 g (4 oz) unsalted butter.

SALMON RILLETTES

Rillettes is the name given to potted pork in France. Chunks of meat are cooked slowly for a long time, then reduced to a thready mass and stored in stoneware pots under a covering of lard. Every household in Touraine, Anjou and Brittany has rillettes in the refrigerator for snacks and easy first courses. The name has been taken up by chefs working in the new style and applied to salmon, potted salmon in effect, although long cooking and long preservation is the last thing they have in mind. Here are two versions:

ANNE WILLAN

Serves 8

Poach a 500 g (1 lb) piece of salmon in a white wine fumet*, without added salt. Cool and shred with a fork, discarding skin and bone first.

Melt 2 tablespoons butter in a sauté pan with a tablespoon of water. Put in a piece of smoked salmon, weighing 375 g (12 oz). Cover and cook for 3 minutes, or until no longer transparent. Cool and shred.

Mix the salmons and beat in 350 g (11 oz) unsalted butter, which has been softened and creamed. Season with salt, pepper and nutmeg. Pack into eight small terrines or one large one. Serve as a first course, well chilled, with toast or bread.

This potted salmon, which is very close to the English style of potted fish, can be kept for up to a week in the refrigerator under a layer of clarified butter.

PAUL MINCHELLI

Serves 4–6

Remove the skin and bone from a 400 g (14 oz) piece of fresh salmon. Slice and chop it coarsely. Do the same thing with a similar sized piece of smoked salmon. Remove the fine skin from 175 g (6 oz) smoked cod's roe, mash the roe and add a couple of tablespoons of crème fraîche, 2 teaspoons of cognac and 2 teaspoons green peppercorns. Mix everything together, sharpening to taste with lime juice. Serve chilled with toast, with an apéritif or as a first course.

SALMON TROUT *see* SALMON

SAND-EEL *see* A FEW WORDS ABOUT . . . SAND-EEL

SAND-LANCE *see* A FEW WORDS ABOUT . . . SAND-EEL

† SARDINES & PILCHARDS

Sardina pilchardus

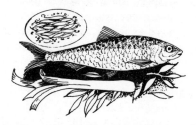

It irritates me to see fresh sardines on sale presented as an exotic fish (at an exotic price) for the travelled and knowing customer, when they are really no more than infant pilchards. It irritates me even more to see pilchards in tomato sauce, can upon can of this rather coarse confection, in the shops and never a fresh pilchard at the fishmonger's. In 1985, I think, there was a brief hooray, pilchards were on the increase off the Cornish coast, but I suppose the canners or the Cornish got in first. The little paragraph that had appeared in *The Guardian* was filed, and that was the last we saw of pilchards.

Sardines are too young and tender to swim up into our bracing waters. Although they do support the business of freezing quite well, they never taste as good in Britain as they do on summer nights further south, when the air is warm. They are part of the holiday nostalgia that recalls their appetizing smell when they are grilled out of doors and eaten with bread and butter, a squeeze of lemon, and several glasses of white wine, whilst forgetting the mosquitoes and the sunburn and (other people's) grizzling children. To cook sardine recipes in this country, you will do better to substitute small herring or large sprats – if they are fresh.

Pilchards have always been a Cornish speciality, swimming to their northern limit at one time in great shoals, leaving the younger sardines behind.

'The least fish in bigness, greatest for gain, and most in number is the pilchard,' says Richard Carew, in his *Survey of Cornwall* (he became High Sheriff of Cornwall in 1586). The picturesque fishery of Elizabethan times that he described continued unchanged until the beginning of this century. It was quite as exciting as the Mediterranean fishing of sardines and anchovies, which takes place more romantically – for the spectator at least – in darkness, with the aid of flaring lamps which attract the fish.

When the shoals were expected, 'between harvest and Allhallowtide', boats with seine nets would 'lie hovering upon the coast'. The masters turned their eyes towards a man stationed on the cliffs, sometimes in a special tower or towered house like the one at Newquay. This was the Huer. It was his job to direct the boats when he saw the dark red shadow approaching, by making a hue and cry with a loud voice, 'whistling through his fingers, and wheazing certain diversified and significant signs with a bush which he holdeth in his hand. At his appointment they cast out their net, draw it to either hands as the shoal lieth or fareth, beat with their oars to keep in the fish, and at last either close and tuck it up in the sea, or draw the same on land with more certain profit, if the ground be not rough of rocks.' There would be several waves of boats, each with their seine nets drawn round as much of the shoal as possible. On shore the country people waited with their horses and baskets; so did the merchants who would 'greedily and speedily' seize the major part of the catch.

Daniel Defoe describes the general excitement in Dartmouth in 1720 when a shoal was sighted – 'the town was all in a kind of an uproar' – and the dinner of fresh pilchards, grilled simply with pepper and salt, that cost the whole party no more than three farthings.

When my husband was a child at the beginning of the century, pilchards were brought round to the village near Looe by a man with a cartload of spanking fresh fish, but the main concern had for centuries been the export trade. Pilchards would be salted and pressed and barrelled for France, or salted and smoked for hotter countries like Italy and Spain. Local people would pickle the fish in rather different ways for their own use. They might bake them in a marinade of spiced vinegar like the soused herring on p. 201. For more immediate use, some of them were split and hung up in the open air to dry for a couple of days like the wind-dried and rizzered haddock of Scotland (p. 149). With a nice skill in judging weather and humidity, the fish would be taken down 'in the very nick of time' and put in pairs, skin sides out, on a gridiron over the fire, to roast or 'scrowl'. The insides were well peppered first, just as Defoe ate them.

I am a little suspicious of the first recipe, perhaps unfairly, but am keeping it in the book because it tastes good.

HOW TO PREPARE SARDINES AND PILCHARDS

As for herring. Some people do not clean out sardines before they grill them, and indeed it can be a fiddly job unless you are good with a hairpin or the point of a small knife at hooking the guts out through the gills. They look raggedy if you slit them with a knife to clean them: scissors do a neater job, but even so they are rarely tidy.

Pilchards, being larger, are easier, and I recommend the idea of splitting them – remove the backbone if you can – seasoning them and sandwiching them, skin side out, before they go on the grill. You can also spread the inside with butter, flavoured in some way or plain. Sardines can be treated in the same manner. Another alternative is to marinade the fish in roughly equal quantities of oil and lemon juice, with finely chopped garlic, parsley and salt.

Those with strong digestions may enjoy sardine fritters. For obvious reasons, you should bone the fish and discard the heads, then you can marinade and pair them up before dipping them in batter. This kind of food needs to be eaten straight from the pan while the batter is crisp: plenty of bread and a glass of white wine is also a good idea.

For myself, I stick with sardines grilled simply. Or else dry-fried in a heavy non-stick pan: rub the surface over with kitchen paper dipped in a little oil, heat the pan and put in the sardines. When one side is brown and crusty, turn them over. This is next best to sardines grilled over charcoal.

SARDINE WARBLERS (Sarde a beccafico)

This is most savoury and appetizing dish from Palermo in Sicily. Its sweet-sour mixture of ingredients – pine kernels, sultanas, anchovies and lemon juice – echoes ancient and modern dishes from the Arab world. This isn't surprising as Sicily belonged to the Saracens from the beginning of the ninth century until the end of the eleventh century, when the Normans arrived. Even then Muslim culture wasn't wiped out, but continued to flourish under the benign influence of Roger II, King of Sicily. I like to think of tough Normans encountering the delights of sherbet and of dishes like this one, then taking the recipes back home to their families beyond the Alps. Such mixtures as this are the background to mincemeat and plum porridges, in which dried fruits were mixed sometimes with meat, sometimes with herrings. (One must admit that the hands of northern cooks were cruder and heavier in their enthusiastic gallimaufries.)

Beccafico is the Italian word for a warbler. It refers to the shape of the stuffed sardines, tucked side by side in the baking dish like a row of little birds.

The recipe, which can be used for other oily fish, or even slices of firm white fish (pile the stuffing on top), is adapted from Ada Boni's *Italian Regional Cooking*. Other versions substitute olives and capers for the anchovies.

Serves 6

1 kg (2¼ lb) sardines, split and boned
salt, pepper
olive oil
12 tablespoons soft white breadcrumbs
60 g (2 oz) sultanas
60 g (2 oz) pine kernels
6 salted anchovies, boned, soaked or 12 fillets tinned in oil, soaked
2 tablespoons chopped parsley
2 tablespoons very finely chopped onion
1–2 lemons or oranges or 1 of each
3 bay leaves

Season the sardines with salt and pepper. Switch on the oven to gas 6, 200°C (400°F). Choose a gratin dish into which the sardines will fit in a single layer.

In a thin layer of oil, brown 9 tablespoons of breadcrumbs lightly, then mix them with sultanas and pine kernels. Pound or chop anchovies, and add them to the breadcrumb mixture with plenty of pepper, the parsley and onion. The original recipe added sugar at this point, about a teaspoon, but I don't think it is necessary, especially if you are using orange juice. An addition I sometimes make is a little finely grated zest from the lemon.

Put some stuffing on to each sardine and roll it from the wide end so that eventually the tail sticks up. Brush the baking dish lightly with oil, put in any stuffing left over and place the rolls in it, close together. Tear the bay leaves into pieces, sprinkle them over the top with the remaining breadcrumbs. Spray them with a little oil, or sprinkle it on.

Bake for 15 minutes, then check on the sardines which should be cooked and the crumbs which should be browned. Pour lemon or lemon and orange juice over the dish immediately before serving it. Or else serve the dish with the citrus fruit cut into wedges.

STARGAZY PIE

The quaint name is a puzzle. The small sail at the top of a mast was called a stargazer and so is a horse that insists on keeping its head back. The pie is a speciality of Mousehole in Cornwall where they make it on Tom Bawcock's Eve, 23 December. This heroic fisherman went out in a roaring sea to catch fish because the town had nothing to eat for Christmas. Nobody thought he would return, but he did, and with a mixed bag large enough to feed everybody. There is a certain lack of evidence on the unusual construction of the pie: I would feel happier about it if I could find some evidence for it before the 1950s.

There are other Cornish pies that sound much more authentic. One has alternate layers of soaked salted pilchards and leeks that have been scalded in milk. When everything is cooked, the crust is raised at one side, the liquor drained off and replaced with scalded cream. In another, boned and rolled herring or mackerel are packed into a dish with breadcrumbs. On top go some slices of bacon with a gill of cream and a splash of tarragon vinegar. The dish is covered with pastry, apart from the fish heads which are arranged in the centre. When you serve the pie, a sprig of parsley is put into the mouth of each fish. Those recipes were recorded in 1929.

To make a good effect with stargazy pie, you need eight pilchards or small herrings or large sardines and a shallow pie dish that will take them tail to tail in the centre, their heads leaning on the rim. You also need 750 g (1½ lb) shortcrust pastry: roll out half and line the pie dish.

Clean and bone the fish, leaving their heads in place. Season inside lavishly with salt and pepper, then either chopped herbs or French mustard. Fold them back into shape and arrange on the dish so that their heads lie evenly on the rim. Fill the gaps between the fish with a mixture of chopped streaky bacon, crumbled hard-boiled egg and breadcrumbs, in roughly equal quantities.

Cover with the remaining pastry, pressing it down firmly between the heads so that the fish lie underneath a wavy blanket. Make a central hole and brush with beaten egg. Bake in the oven preheated to gas 7, 220 °C (425 °F), for about 20 minutes, to firm and colour the pastry lightly. Then give it 25 minutes more at gas 4, 180 °C (350 °F), or until done.

CANNED SARDINES

Sardines were the first fish to be canned – in the 1820s, in Nantes, many years before the Canadians started to can salmon. The best of the Nantes sardines – the market is of the *caveat emptor* kind and likely to become more so – are still the first in flavour, too. This is because the methods of canning have produced not just a poor substitute for the real thing (like canned crab and lobster) but something worth eating in its own right.

From the north to the south of Europe, and the North Africa, one can make a choice between many brands, offering roughly three categories of sardine.

There are the brisling, tiny fish which are really sprats and not sardines at all. Smoking is what gives them their individual flavour. They are eaten in the same way as sardines, and most people think of them as Skipper's sardines, whatever the law says about nomenclature (they are conscientiously described on the label as Norwegian smoked brisling, and we are being encouraged just to call them Skippers).

Then there are the sardines that are really quite large – a little too large – from Portugal, Spain and North Africa. They are steamed in oil and packed in the same oil, which in not necessarily olive oil. The trade to Great Britain is enormous. Look for the Marie Elisabeth brand, partly on account of the excellent olive oil used but also because the sardines have been allowed to mature for a year in the can before being put out for sale. This is important. The ideal thing is to make a store of sardines, and turn them regularly every few months, using them in rotation: this gives the olive oil and fish juices a chance to intermingle, to the benefit of the flavour of the sardine.

Some of these fish may not be sardines at all, so read the small print. What is even more important, as Alan Davidson pointed out in *Petits Propos Culinaires*, No 2, 1979, is what the fish are canned in. Again read the small print. Avoid any that are canned in other oils than olive oil, and beware of those that suffer in tomato sauce.

The third category is the fine French sardine from Brittany and the Atlantic coast, down as far as Royan at the mouth of the Gironde.

This is the famous frisky sardine celebrated by Desnos in one of his nonsense poems:

> *Une sardine de Royan*
> *Nageait dans l'eau de la Gironde.*
> *Le ciel est grand, la terre est ronde,*
> *J'irai me baigner à Royan.*
> *Avec la sardine,*
> *Avec la Gironde,*
> *Vive la marine!*
> *Et salut au monde!*

Since the sardine is seasonal, arriving in incalculable quantities, the problem was, in the past, preservation of the catch. Salting in barrels was the usual answer, but – or so the story goes – a Mademoiselle Le Guillou of Lorient had the idea of frying them in olive oil, then putting them up in jars filled with fresh oil to keep out the air. A fellow citizen, Monsieur Brancart, began commercial production. In her famous *Spectator* article on sardines, reprinted in *An Omelette and a Glass of Wine*, Elizabeth David describes the clay *oules* that held them and goes far more deeply into the early and continuing history than I can here.

This happened at the start of the nineteenth century when Nicolas Appert, who as distiller and confectioner had been much occupied with preservation, set up a factory for bottling food at Massy, near Paris. The advances were made when he tackled the problem of feeding the Navy, and people making sea journeys. His products were sent to Brest to be kept at sea for several months: when the bottles were opened in April, 1807, the partridges and peas and other meats were in a good edible condition. Appert published his methods in 1810.

The next substantial progress was made by an Englishman, Bryan Donkin, who saw the weak point of Appert's method – the breakable jars – and adapted it to tin-plated cans. The British Navy was as impressed as the French had been. So were the better-off travellers who could afford to eat canned rather than salted meat on board ship. In 1824 William Parry took canned beef, veal, soup and vegetables on his expedition to discover the North-West Passage – and a confectioner of Nantes, Joseph Colin, began to can sardines. They were of course a luxury – unlike the canned Pacific salmon that was produced forty years later when such goods were becoming a godsend to the mass market of growing industrial towns, and America was getting the blame for exploiting what was after all an English invention. What is surprising is the way old attitudes survive – bottled fruit and vegetables are still reckoned superior to canned and a tin of salmon is still the treat for Sunday tea in many thousands of families in Britain.

In France you will find a much wider choice in the quality of canned sardines than in any other country. Check the small print. You can see from the label that sardines in olive oil *à l'ancienne* are something special. Category 1, 'Extra', are worth going for, too, as this means the sardines used were all fresh and matched for size. Once frozen fish enters into a product (category 2, 'Choice', includes frozen as well as fresh sardines) there is inevitably a deterioration as there has been so sadly in Lancashire potted shrimps. The best Breton sardine is slightly smaller than the Portuguese. It has been brined, beheaded and gutted, rinsed in seawater, and dried in currents of warm air. It is then lightly cooked in olive oil before being packed in fresh olive oil with aromatics. The quality of the French product depends, too, on coolness – on the coolness of the waters from which the fish are caught, on the coolness of the climate of Nantes, Douarnenez and Concarneau where they are processed. For these considerations, you must expect to pay a little more.

You can do a number of things with canned sardines, but none of the recipes that involves heating them is to be recommended. There is always another fish – herring or anchovy – which would give a better result. When you buy a good brand of sardines, serve them on their own with decent bread, fine butter and some lemon, or as part of a mixed first course. In France they sometimes come to table in their can to indicate the quality of the brand. Once upon a time the firm of Amieux had specially decorated plates made to hold the cans, but you won't find them outside a secondhand shop. Another way is to set the sardines on a round plate like the spokes of a wheel, with lemon wedges in the centre.

Left-over sardines, or not-quite-the-best sardines make an admirable fish paste if you mash them with unsalted butter (*see* p. 190).

SAURY *see* A FEW WORDS ABOUT . . . GARFISH

† SCALLOPS, SMALL & LARGE

Argopecten irradians, Chlamys opercularis, Pecten maximus,
Placopecten magellicanus

I daresay American readers will disagree with me, particularly those with their own special place on Cape Cod, but for scallops I would go to Boston. Never have I eaten scallops of such sweetness as the ones that lie about in a box in one of Turner's sheds on the quay, so that people splashing by can pop a couple into their mouths like sugar lumps. A sashimi of scallops may be more civilized in terms of dining, but those tiny bay scallops need no sauce and no surroundings.

For a start, they are so full of life in their flavour that I was not surprised to read Howard Mitcham's description of them jumping around in the tidal pools of Cape Cod, or tangled in the eel grass when the water was out, bobbing along by clapping their shells together fast. 'It's truly an amazing sight . . . it gives you a shock of bewilderment.' We have tiny scallops in Europe, too, but all at the fishmongers from deep water, not in rock pools at low tide. Queen scallops and the less familiar princess scallops are pink-marked and beautiful, not the same species as the bay scallops, *Argopecten irradians*, that enliven the beaches at Providence and elsewhere on the Cape. Alan Davidson describes eating them at the No Name restaurant in Boston, simply grilled on a baking sheet smeared with margarine. What could be better? was his conclusion. The first time we had queens, *vanneaux* on the menu card, was at the Café de Paris at Cherbourg, and they, too, had been grilled, though with butter. Still, I think, there is nothing to beat them untouched, Turner-style. It is the freshness that counts.

The Americans have a large scallop, too, the Atlantic deep-sea scallop, *Placopecten magellicanus*. Was it Magellan who first found them as he beat his way down to Tierra del Fuego? They usually come much the same size as our European scallops, but they can grow as large as dinner plates. 'These beautiful large sea scallop shells' – Howard Mitcham again – 'are very common in Provincetown ... You can buy them from kids who peddle them on the street, or from gift shops or, if you're lucky enough to know a scallop fisherman, he will give you hundreds of them free .... They should be scraped clean and boiled in a strong solution of water and bicarbonate of soda for an hour or more so you can get them completely clean and sterile. Never use soap or detergents to clean your scallop shells; they are porous and will absorb chemicals and odors from the soaps, making them useless for cooking. These shells make a perfect baking or serving dish and are almost indispensable for the classic Coquilles St Jacques recipes.' I must confess I have always scrubbed scallop shells with hot water and put them into the washing-up machine, without noticing any taste of soap next time I used them. But I pass the tip on.

On a second visit to Boston I tried these larger scallops, which seem mainly to be much the same diameter as ours in Europe. This was at the Maison Robert, where I tasted again the freshness, the sweetness of the sea that had not been smothered with culinary love and fuss. One odd thing, though, scallops in America are often deprived of their corals before sale. This is beginning to change – presumably under the weight of protest from chefs and writers? – and it should. The slightly hooked coral is the roe, the deep orange being the female roe and the cream that often, though not always underpins it the male. Apart from being delicious in itself, it can be crushed and creamed with butter or the liquids of the recipe to colour the sauce. To me, the whole appearance of a dish of scallops is lifted by this bright tone.

Appearance is an important part of the scallop's attraction. It has become so companionable a part of our European civilization. One looks up at an eighteenth-century doorway and sees the shell porch or fanlight; sees a child baptized with water from a shell scoop, takes tea from a caddy with a silver scallop shell caddy spoon; the beauty of the shape is never exhausted. It may surprise one in opening the doors of an old corner cupboard; it brings delight, it is never taken for granted. It belongs to great painting. Aphrodite floating in on a scallop shell, flecks of real gold in her hair. It belongs to the poor, who went on pilgrimages to Spain to the church of St James at Compostela wearing the *coquille St Jacques* on their broad-brimmed hats. In our cave village in France, a room in one house in the cliff has an alcove with a scallop shell carved into the rock as ceiling. Nothing grand. It is said that the room was a chapel for the pilgrims who crossed the Loir to worship at the church of St Jacques on the other side of the river, as they journeyed to Spain.

And I suppose that with the deep-freezing of scallop meat in packages, we shall eventually lose even the shell and have to look at petrol pumps to remind ourselves.

HOW TO CHOOSE AND PREPARE SCALLOPS

Most fishmongers sell scallops all prepared and shining, a few on the shell to set them off, the rest nicely grouped around. If they are a good size, you may get away with two large scallops per person for some dishes, but three or four is a more kindly number. With the tiny princesses, queens and bay scallops, a dozen is a reasonable helping: gauge the size with your eye, 4 or perhaps 5 are the equivalent to the normal size. Reflect, too, that scallops are a particularly fine shellfish: nobody expects to gulp them down in mindless quantities.

Sometimes you may have the chance of buying scallops as they leave the sea. They will look far less attractive, gritty, dirty, greyish, but buy them all the same. Ask the fishmonger to open the shells for you, if they are mainly closed. Before you clean this natural-looking creature, take a good look. Round the edge, there is this grey transparent frill edged with half a hundred pearly-looking eyes, a beautiful sight. Once you remove this and the gills, rinsing the whole thing briefly, you are down to the edible part which emerges from its veil of a mantle shining and clean, a plump white disc – the adductor muscle – and the dazzling pointed coral roe. Separate the two gently, cut off any black bit attached to the coral and peel away the little hard knobbly bit attached to one side of the disc.

Keep the deep shells at least and clean them as suggested above. They can serve as little dishes for cooked scallops, or as moulds for baking pastry shells. There is a restaurant dish in which one or two scallops are put into one deep shell with aromatics: a rim of puff pastry is pressed round the edge, then on goes the flat upper shell. The whole thing is baked in a very hot oven, so that the scallops cook in their own steam, and the hinge of puff pastry rises to accommodate the steam. At table, you crack open your scallop shells, as if you expected to see Aphrodite pushing up the shell like a Tanagra figure.

Scallops can be cooked in so many ways. Try them instead of squid in the Borshch recipe on p. 408. Rich sauces have been devised for them, and do have the benefit of extending their wonderful flavour; as an occasional treat, they should not be despised.

SCALLOPS AU NATUREL

As with all fish and shellfish, rinse scallops as briefly as possible. For eating without further cooking, use only the white part. The coral roe is too soft and creamy, and should be kept for sauces and soups when it will be lightly cooked.

Tiny scallops need no more dressing than a drop or two of lemon, lime or bitter orange juice. They look attractive heaped on to red and cream radicchio leaves, or nested into some curly endive. Serve wholemeal bread with them, and white wine. Put a pepper mill handy and some cayenne.

Larger scallops will benefit from slicing across into two or three discs or more. Taste them before you season them with any salt. Brush a plate over with a top quality olive oil, arrange the slices on it and brush them over lightly with more oil. Keep it very light, the oil.

For a simpler effect, slice the discs across as thinly as you can and put them into a bowl in which you have mixed 125 ml (4 fl oz) olive oil and the juice of a large lemon, pepper and salt. Stir the slices gently, but thoroughly, then drain and arrange them in little heaps – say in the shell, or in the centre of a pile of salad – just before you serve them. Do not leave the scallops in the oil for any length of time.

You can add steamed samphire tips (p. 83) and, if you want to make a contrast, a little salmon tartare (p. 321). Scallops prepared in this way, with oil, could be put into scallops shells with a half-wreath of samphire. Steady the shells on a little mound of coarse salt or a circle of seaweed.

If you rejoice in a supply of really fine fresh fish and shellfish, sashimi on p. 364 is a good way of making the most of it, scallops and three other fish of contrasting texture and colour do very well.

CORAL SAUCE

There are a number of ways of using corals to flavour – and colour – a sauce. You can, for instance, use them when making an hollandaise*: liquidize or process them with hot melted butter after cooking them for a few seconds in the butter just to stiffen them slightly. It is important to avoid overcooking the coral part.

This kind of sauce goes well with a scallop mousseline or a fish terrine in which the white part of scallops has been used, along with other fish, p. 512.

Serves 4

500 ml (15 fl oz) fish stock*
1 tablespoon chopped shallot
6 peppercorns, lightly crushed
4 tablespoons dry white wine
175 ml (6 fl oz) crème fraîche
corals from 12 scallops or more, any black bits removed
60 g (2 oz) unsalted butter
salt, pepper, cayenne

If the fish stock had been made with a proportion of shellfish debris, so much the better. It can also include any juices left from cooking the white part of the scallops, or the fish it is to accompany.

Cook the shallot, peppercorns and wine until you have no more liquid, just a moist purée. Add half the cream and reduce by half. Meanwhile, liquidize or process the remaining cream with the corals and set aside.

Add the stock to the shallot and cream reduction and reduce again to a lightly syrupy consistency. Lower the heat, stir in the coral/cream mixture, then the butter – keep shaking the pan, or stirring it, so that the sauce thickens slightly without the butter oiling. Lift the pan from the heat every so often, to prevent overheating. Finally, season to taste.

COQUILLES SAINT-JACQUES À LA PROVENÇALE

As this recipe is often given in cookery books, here is a quick summary of it with one important improvement – the separate cooking of the breadcrumbs.

Fry the white part of scallops with garlic and sliced mushrooms –
250 g (8 oz) to 20 scallops – adding coral at the end of the cooking
time. At the same time fry about 60 g (2 oz) white breadcrumbs in
butter in another pan, with 2 tablespoons of olive oil as well. Mix in
plenty of chopped parsley. Drain scallops and mushrooms, mix with
the breadcrumbs and serve quickly with lemon quarters.

COQUILLES SAINT-JACQUES FLAMBÉES 'GORDON'

Searching after the fish in Normandy and its purlieus one year, we
seemed rather to find Joan of Arc instead. At Le Crotoy, near its
famous seafood restaurant (Moules à ma façon, Gurnards
provençales), we saw a tablet in the ruined castle wall to sour our
sleep. Here the French had handed Joan of Arc over to the English,
and from here on 8 December she had walked across the mouth of
the Somme towards her trial and death at Rouen. We looked beyond
the exquisite iron cross on the sea wall, over the wide estuary, grey
now at low tide, and felt the cold sucking of her feet in the mud and
seaweed, as the party forded the crossing to St Valéry. The Somme is
a bitter enough river in spring and autumn; but in December?

Then in Rouen, pursuing the best source of local food, being told
again and again 'La Couronne', by a policeman, a hotel-keeper and
an anglophile bookshop-owner, we passed another tablet – 'Ah
Rouen, Rouen, I had never thought you would be my tomb' – and
we felt the prickings of historic conscience. But the head waiter, the
liveliest of his breed, came and placed before us some of the most
delicious scallops we had ever eaten. We began to feel at peace in
that wooden medieval room. 'Gin's the secret,' said the head waiter as
he glided by.

Serves 4

puff pastry (optional, see recipe)
12 scallops
seasoned flour
4 tablespoons butter
1 tablespoon oil
175 ml (6 fl oz) crème fraîche
4 tablespoons Gordon's gin
salt, pepper
lemon juice
chopped parsley

Preheat the oven to gas 8, 230 °C (450 °F).

Roll out the pastry thinly. Cut into 4 squares. Rub the *back* of 4 deep scallop shells with a butter paper (or brush with vegetable oil). Fit the pastry over the back of the shells, pressing it over the rims to keep it from shrinking. Bake for 15 minutes, pastry side up, or until nicely browned. Cut round the edges, so that the shell can be separated. If the inside of the pastry shells is steamy, put them back into the oven for a minute or two to dry out. Keep them warm.

If you have no puff pastry to hand, use the scallop shell themselves as containers, or small soufflé dishes.

Slice the scallops across into 2 discs each. Turn them in seasoned flour. Cook them in butter and oil, turning them once. Meanwhile heat the cream and reduce it slightly. When the scallops are done, warm the gin, set it alight and pour it over the scallops in their pan. Add salt, pepper and the boiling cream; cook for a few seconds and add a little lemon juice to taste.

Place the scallops in their shells or pots, pour the sauce over them, and sprinkle with chopped parsley. Serve very hot.

NOTE Lobster can be cooked in this way, too. *See* p. 217.

CURRIED SCALLOPS

The Newburg recipe (p. 344) is easily adapted to other seasonings. One of the most popular is curry powder, which is used in an entirely French way. Most delicious.

For the brandy and Madeira in the Newburg recipe, substitute the white wine cooking stock, reduced by boiling to 125 ml (4 fl oz). When the butter is added to the scallops, put in 2 teaspoons of curry powder.

When you serve the scallops, a light scatter of chopped green coriander of chervil goes harmoniously with the sauce.

HANNAH GLASSE'S STEWED SCALLOPS

A slightly adapted version of a recipe from *The Art of Cooking*, published in 1747. Over 200 years later, it is still a good way of cooking scallops. The seasoning of Seville orange juice is unusual and piquant.

Serves 6

150 ml (5 fl oz) dry white wine
150 ml (5 fl oz) water
1 scant tablespoon white wine vinegar
½ teaspoon mace
2 cloves
salt, pepper
18 scallops
1 tablespoon butter
1 tablespoon plain flour
juice of 1 Seville orange

Put wine, water, vinegar, mace and cloves into a pan. Bring them to the boil, and simmer covered for 5 or 10 minutes. Add salt and pepper to taste, and judge whether or not the spices should be increased. Meanwhile, slice the whies of the scallops in half across, then slide them into the liquid with the corals and cook gently for 4–5 minutes. They should not be overcooked.

Pour off the liquor and measure it: if there is more than 300 ml (10 fl oz), boil it down. Mash butter and flour together, then add to the simmering liquid in smallish pieces, stirring them in. This will thicken the sauce. Finally, season with Seville orange juice, and more salt and pepper if required. Pour over the scallops and serve at once.

GRILLED SCALLOPS

The simplest and many would say the best way of cooking scallops is to grill them.

First switch on the grill so that it is really hot by the time you come to cook the fish. Find a flat baking sheet or fireproof shallow dish that will stand up to the heat, and brush it over with butter or olive oil.

Prepare the scallops, cutting the thicker ones across into two discs. Set them out in a single layer on the sheet or dish, having turned them in seasoned olive oil. Alternatively, dab them with butter or brush with melted butter, and season them once they are in place. Put the corals round the edge, where the heat will not be so intense.

Slip them under the grill, at a distance of 8–10 cm (3–4 inches). Turn them once, as the tops colour lightly. Depending on the thickness of the scallops, they will take between 3 and 5 minutes in all. It is wise to include an extra scallop as a tester.

VARIATION Flavour the oil in which you turn the scallops with chopped garlic and lemon juice. Add cayenne pepper to the seasonings.

VARIATION By mixing a proportion of olive oil into a flavoured butter, you get a soft consistency that makes it easier to dab on shellfish. Here is an example, quantities for 4 people:

> *3 tablespoons olive oil*
> *3 halved cloves garlic*
> *6 anchovy fillets*
> *leaves of 1 medium bunch of parsley, chervil and chives*
> *125 g (4 oz) lightly salted Lurpak or unsalted butter*
> *salt, pepper*

Process the first four ingredients to an even crumbly mixture, then add the butter, cut in cubes. Season to taste. Serve with lemon wedges.

VARIATION Grill the white parts only of the scallops. Turn the corals into a sauce to go with them, *see* following recipe.

VARIATION Certain vegetables go well with scallops. Leeks cut into slivers and cooked down with a knob of butter, in their own juices. Red and yellow peppers roasted in a very hot oven, then skinned, seeded and cut in pieces when they are very soft: they can be reheated and dressed with a little of the flavoured butter used for basting the scallops, or just a light chopping of garlic, parsley, and lemon peel thinly removed with a zester.

Sea vegetables, laverbread reheated with orange and lemon juice perhaps, or steamed marsh samphire are good accompaniments.

SCALLOPS EN BROCHETTE

Scallops with bacon does not seem as surprising as it did twenty years ago, now that we have become used to mixtures of fish and meat (surf 'n' turf as it is unpleasantly, if snappily, described in some quarters). Monkfish, tope and the other meaty fishes, cod, mussels and oysters are all good treated the same way.

The basic treatment is simple enough, and easy to vary according to your fancy. The important thing is to acquire excellent bacon, smoked or not according to your tastes. Streaky cured in the German style is good. In Britain, Ayrshire or Yorkshire bacon sliced very thin is superb – the fat it provides bastes the scallops and drips away, while the bacon itself turns crisp (with many modern whizz cures only a whitish sort of brine emerges and the bacon goes tough).

Allow 3–4 scallops per person and enough thinly cut bacon to provide 7 or 9 squares, roughly the same size as the scallops.

You also need a nice chopping of parsley and garlic, with a pinch of thyme, and a little sunflower or safflower oil.

Slice the white part of the scallops into two discs. Put them on to 6 skewers, interspersed with the bacon pieces and the corals. Brush them over with oil and roll in the herbs and garlic so that they are nicely but not thickly speckled.

Put under a preheated grill for about 5 minutes, turning at least once. The scallops should be just cooked, the edges of the bacon slightly caught by the heat.

Serve on warm plates, with lemon wedges, bread and a bottle of dry white wine, Muscadet being the obvious choice. A jug of hot melted butter is all you need by way of sauce: many people will find they need nothing, but give them the option.

SCALLOPS NEWBURG

The famous Delmonico recipe for lobster is easily adapted to scallops, as it is to other sweet, firm fish such as monkfish. It is the kind of recipe that is out of favour these days, with its cream and egg yolks and lavish blends of wine and brandy, but if you are having a meal that is light in other courses with an emphasis on vegetables and fruit, my advice would be to relax and enjoy it.

Serves 6

18–24 scallops
125 ml (4 fl oz) dry white wine
bouquet garni
6 tablespoons butter
4 tablespoons brandy
125 ml (4 fl oz) Madeira or medium dry or brown sherry
salt, pepper
250 ml (8 fl oz) double cream
2 medium egg yolks plus 2 tablespoon single cream

Slice the scallops across into 2 discs, having separated the corals. Meanwhile, simmer the wine, an equal quantity of water and the bouquet for 5 minutes. Add the white scallop slices and stir until half cooked – they should still be a little transparent, about 2 minutes. Remove the bouquet, pour off the liquor and keep for another dish. Stir in 4 tablespoons of butter and toss the scallops in it until they are coated and just bubbling. Flame with the brandy, then pour in the Madeira or sherry and add the scallop corals. Leave to complete the cooking – do not overcook. Scoop the pieces of scallop on to a warm serving dish, season and keep warm.

Pour in the double cream and boil down the sauce to reduce it a little. Beat the yolks with the single cream, amalgamate with the sauce in the usual way, being careful not to overheat it. Stir in the remaining butter. Taste and check the seasoning. Pour the sauce over the scallops.

Serve with plainly boiled rice. You could shape the rice into a ring in a buttered mould, turn it out and fill the centre with the scallops.

SCALLOPS SANTIAGO

As I was writing this section of the book, they dug up the body of a man who had been buried in his pilgrim's garments, complete with a scallop shell. A medieval burial, somewhere in the Midlands, I think. That ancient desire to face eternity remembering the greatest journey of his life, reminded me of the evenings we sat out of doors on our shelf of a garden in France looking at the Milky Way – the great procession of pilgrims going down to Spain – and longing to go there ourselves. Not for religious reasons, but from a desire to share a little of that dominating experience of the past.

At last, in 1981, Franco gone, we found ourselves in September wandering round the cathedral and the processional spaces of Santiago de Compostela, a long journey from Trôo even in the car. How much longer on foot, with a staff and a gourd of water? How frightening very often, even with the hospitals provided by those early tour operators, the monastic orders. We ended up eating scallops in the hotel beside the cathedral, and to tell the truth they were overcooked. Why scallops anyway? They have nothing to do with St James's life as far as it is known, but legend has it that a knight was crossing a difficult inlet and in danger of drowning so called on St James to help him. He emerged safely, with his horse, both of them covered in scallop shells.

Serves 6

18 scallops
125 g (4 oz) chopped onion
olive oil
3 cloves garlic, finely chopped
leaves of 1 medium bunch of parsley, chopped
salt, pepper
powdered cloves
nutmeg
6 tablespoons fine fresh white breadcrumbs

Put 6 deep scallop shells on a baking sheet, steadying them with circles of crumpled foil. Set the oven at gas 7, 220 °C (425 °F).

Separate and reserve the corals from the scallops. Trim and dice the white part. Soften the onion in a little oil until soft and golden. Mix in the garlic and most of the parsley and remove from the heat. Season with salt and pepper, and a pinch or two of cloves and grated nutmeg to taste. Then add the scallop dice, mixing everything well together. Divide between the shells, tucking in the corals on top. Sprinkle with the breadcrumbs and drip a little olive oil over each.

Bake at the top of the oven, for 10–15 minutes, until the scallops are just done before the crumbs lightly browned. If you find the scallops are done before the crumbs are right, finish them under the grill. Scatter a pinch of parsley over each and serve.

SCALLOPS WITH WHITE WINE AND JERUSALEM ARTICHOKES

I don't know whether it was Margaret Costa who first brought Jerusalem artichokes and scallops together in one of her articles for the *Sunday Times* in the 1960s, but that was the first time I had ever come across the idea. She made a soup from the artichokes with some potato and chicken stock, onion softened in butter, then finished it with a few scallops cut into dice and poached in milk, some egg yolks and cream, and a scatter of parsley and the corals.

About twenty years later, in 1985, I chose scallops and artichokes from Joyce Molyneux's menu at the Carved Angel in Dartmouth. This is her recipe. I have tried other, more elaborate, but hers is a winner.

Serves 6

12 large scallops
about 500 g (1 lb) Jerusalem artichokes
90 g (3 oz) butter
6 tablespoons dry white wine
salt, pepper
chopped parsley
lemon juice

Remove the corals carefully, discard the tough white part and slice the scallops across into 24 discs. Peel, trim and cut up enough artichokes to give you a good 250 g (8–9 oz) matchstick strips – or use a mandolin if you have managed to get a good smooth variety of artichoke. Keep the trimmings for soup or stock.

Cook the artichokes gently in butter. When almost tender, season and add the scallop discs and white wine. Cook for a minute, then turn the scallop discs and add the corals. Leave a further minute or two, but avoid overcooking.

Scoop out all the pieces on to six hot plates, or a serving dish. Reduce the liquid if necessary by fast boiling. Check the seasoning, and add parsley and lemon to taste. Pour over scallops and serve immediately.

NOTE Joyce Molyneux also uses this recipe for lamb neck fillets. Sear them first, then add artichoke sticks and butter, then wine.

SCARISTA SCALLOPS IN OATMEAL

In Harris – this recipe comes from Alison Johnson who with her husband runs a hotel on the shore, Scarista House – scallops are always called clams. Most confusing. 'The biggest and best are got by diving, and these select shellfish cost half as much again as the dredged catch. Clam-divers are invested with high earning and an air of romance – till something goes wrong. It is a physically taxing and very risky career. We always try to buy from divers. Not only are their scallops finer, smelling of the sea rather than bilge water, but they do no harm to the sea-bed. A dredge claws the bottom like a giant harrow tearing out every scallop, large and tiny, whole and broken, and devastating the entire plant and animal community of the sea-bed. Regeneration takes years, if indeed it ever happens.'

When I walked into the kitchen of Scarista House, to meet Alison Johnson for the first time, on the draining board was a vast pile of these magnificent scallops, still in their shells, just delivered and waiting to be opened.

Serves 6

18–24 large plump scallops, cleaned
fine oatmeal
*up to 125 g (4 oz) butter, preferably clarified**
shredded heart of 1 lettuce
1 lemon, cut into 6 wedges

Set 6 deep scallop shells or small shallow pots of a similar size to warm in a baking sheet in the oven.

Slice the white part of the scallops across into two or three discs according to thickness. Separate the corals, cut off the dark end but leave them whole otherwise. Toss them all in a shallow wide bowl of oatmeal to coat them.

Heat a quarter of the butter in a heavy non-stick pan. Cook the white part of the scallops on both sides, until they are just cooked, 2–3 minutes. Go carefully, adding extra butter as required. Finally, cook the corals.

Divide the lettuce between the shells or pots. Put scallops and corals on top, with a wedge of lemon.

SEVICHE, CEVICHE OR CEBICHE

However you choose to spell the word, it should be pronounced se-veech-ee. The best place to eat it is Peru, according to fortunate travellers, but you will also find it elsewhere in Latin America. It is one of the most delicious ways of eating fish, and one of the most magical since the fillets are 'cooked' not by heat but by the acidity of lime juice which turns them just as opaque. Many fish are suitable for the treatment, but choose for freshness rather than superiority of status.

Scallops, especially the tiny bay scallops, are magnificent. Sole and the better flounders are an obvious choice, so is sea bass or striped bass or grouper or pompano. Wild trout do well, and so do small whiting. In Central America, oily fish of the mackerel tribe (p. 221) find themselves in cebiche.

The basic proportions are:

500 g (1 lb) scallops or *filleted, skinned fish* or *a mixture*
juice of 6–7 limes
salt
2 bay leaves
1 hot red chilli or *chilli flakes*
1 medium onion, sliced

Cut the fish into neat strips or pieces, or, if the scallops are large, slice them across into 2 or 3 discs. Put them in a refrigerator box, fitting closely. Remove the fine green peel from the limes with a zester and keep for a final decoration. Squeeze the limes. Sprinkle the fish with salt, tuck in the bay leaves, put the chilli or chilli flakes on top with the onion. Pour over the lime juice. Cover and leave in the refrigerator until the fish is completely opaque, turning it once. This can be as little as 2 hours or as much as 5, depending on the thickness of the pieces.

The seviche can now be arranged as simply or grandly as the occasion demands, once the fish is drained:

(1) since the dish has Polynesian origins, try the Tahiti style of covering it with about 300 ml (10 fl oz) coconut milk, mixed with a finely chopped clove of garlic and a couple of chopped spring onions.

(2) arrange it with some greenery, tomato and purple onion rings, with a few olives. Since a bitter contrast is a good idea, use curly endive, or mix rocket in with other sweeter greenery, or scatter the whole thing with chopped green coriander leaves.

Instead of olives, try sliced canned jalapeño chillis, or some strips of roasted, skinned sweet pepper.

(3) arrange more formally on a large dish with contrasting soft and crisp vegetables; avocados dressed with an olive oil and lime juice vinaigrette (those tiny avocados you sometimes see are ideal); slices of different coloured sweet peppers whether raw or roasted and skinned; different coloured sweetcorn, either the very small ones, or larger ones cooked and sliced across; celery or fennel; sweet potato, cooked and sliced; hard-boiled egg; a few slices of orange; sliced jalapeño chillis or scraps of hotter chillis.

Do not use all these things at once, or the fish will be overwhelmed.

SEA BASS, SEA PERCH & GROUPERS

Percichthyidae & *Serranidae* spp.

To walk into the fishmonger's and see a tray of sea bass is a beautiful sight. Their scales, arranged in exact gradation of colour, shine with silver and dark grey markings. Their shape is slim and elegant. I find that the white flesh can be a little on the soft side, and for this reason prefer them baked or cooked in a crisp style, rather than poached in white wine or court bouillon. The bass, or *spigola*, is a great speciality of Naples. When very fresh, it is simply stuffed with garlic and a chopping of herbs, brushed with olive oil, sprinkled with crumbs, and baked in the oven. Olive oil and lemon juice are used for basting. For a bass which is not so newly arrived from the water, an interesting stuffing should be added to the simple formula. Alice B. Toklas's recipe for Carp with chestnuts, on p. 70, can be adapted to it most successfully, but be sure to leave the chestnuts in a crumbly state; if reduced to a purée they make the mixture too heavy.

Many fish recipes – recipes for sole (Florentine or meunière for the smaller fish), recipes for salmon, bream, John Dory and so on – can be used for bass, although, as I've observed, a little vigour is preferable to a bland mildness.

The bass we normally see is only one of a huge family of fish, the *Serranidae* or sea perches. It includes the groupers, which unfortunately have a marked preference for the warm seas of the Caribbean and Mediterranean. In the *Mediterranean Seafood*, Alan Davidson comments on the superiority in firmness and flavour of the dusky sea perch or grouper over the generality of the *Serranidae*. It is apparently imported from time to time, so look out for it. The Latin name *Epinephelus gigas* gives you a clue to its appearance, as Alan Davidson observes; the first word means 'with clouds upon it', which is a good description of the dark patches blurring the yellow or reddish-brown of the skin. Groupers have chameleon-like qualities, with Nassau grouper apparently capable of eight different colourings.

These firmer fish can be treated like turbot and John Dory. Alan Davidson gives one particularly unusual and piquant recipe, a Spanish one, for grilled or fried steaks of grouper with orange sauce, really a sauce bigarade. He also recommends the following recipe.

MÉROU AU BRESSE BLEU

Serves 6

6 slices grouper (or turbot, halibut, monkfish, etc.) from 150–200 g (5–7 oz) each
seasoned flour
*clarified butter**
1 baby Bresse Bleu cheese
*1¼ litres (2 pt) fish velouté**
3 egg yolks
salt, pepper (see *recipe*)

The slices should be even and well trimmed. Flour and cook them à la meunière in the clarified butter. Grate the cheese and work it over a low heat in a small pan until it turns to a paste. In another pan heat the velouté sauce, thicken it with the egg yolks and add the cheese paste. Season if necessary. Put the fish slices into a buttered ovenproof dish, in a single layer, and cover with the sauce. Glaze in a hot oven for a moment or two.

The recipe came originally from Monsieur Max Maupuy of the Restaurant Max in Paris. He also suggests serving mérou, poached in a court bouillon* and left to cool, with a choice of two sauces. The first is Rougaille, which is simply the drained chopped flesh of 1 kg (2 lb) of tomatoes, chilled and mixed with a tablespoon of strong French mustard, and seasoned. The second consists of half a baby Bresse Bleu cheese mixed with a generous 450 ml (15 fl oz) of double cream, and passed through a fine sieve; the seasoning is a pinch of cayenne pepper. Serve the sauce cold but not chilled.

SEA BASS ANISETTE

Serves 4

1 kg (2 lb) sea bass fillets
Pernod-flavoured mayonnaise*
3 heads fennel
125 g (4 oz) butter
salt

MARINADE
¼ teaspoon coriander leaves, chopped
¼ teaspoon ground mace
8 peppercorns, slightly crushed
6 tablespoons olive oil

Leave the fish in the marinade for 3 hours before cooking it. Make the mayonnaise. Slice up the fennel, putting one-third aside. The rest can either be served as a salad with vinaigrette dressing, or it can be blanched in boiling salted water for 10 minutes, then cooked gently in 60–90 g (2–3 oz) of butter until soft – I think the second way is best if the fish is being eaten hot.

Butter a grill pan, lay the reserved fennel on it, then the fish fillets (dispense with the grill rack) which should be cooked under a medium-hot grill for 7 or 8 minutes a side. Sprinkle with salt.

Serve the fish immediately with the cooked fennel and the Pernod-flavoured mayonnaise; with new potatoes as well if you like. Or leave it to cool, and serve it with the fennel salad and the mayonnaise.

SEA BASS OR BREAM À LA VENDANGEUSE

The name of this dish – bass in grape-picker's style – isn't the fancy of some Parisian chef. It reflects the reality of a land where, in many districts, the ordinary person's food is still genuinely local. Main items such as meat and fish are cooked with what is to hand. So in September and October, after a day in the vines, pickers will go home with a basketful of grapes. Grape-picking is an affair of sweat and ribaldry. No autumn melancholy in the air, but the shrieks of women pickers trying to bring some young man to his knees as they pile more and more grapes into his huge shoulder basket. He escapes at last, leaves and fruit in his ears, and staggers to the press.

Serves 4–6

*1–1½ kg (2–3 lb) sea bass or sea bream (or John Dory or grey or red
mullet)*
125 g (4 oz) butter
1 large mild onion, chopped
2 cloves garlic, chopped
bouquet garni
salt, pepper
300 ml (10 fl oz) dry white wine
250–375 g (8–12 oz) large white grapes
30 g (1 oz) plain flour
juice of ½ lemon
chopped parsley

Ask the fishmonger to clean and scale the fish, but to leave the head
on. Using 60 g (2 oz) of butter, grease an oval dish large enough to
hold the fish. Make a layer of onion and garlic, put the bouquet in
the middle, and the fish on top. Season well. Pour over the wine.
Bake in a hot over (gas 7, 220 °C/425 °F) for 20 to 25 minutes, until
the fish is cooked. Meanwhile peel and pip the grapes, and mash the
flour into a paste with 30 g (1 oz) of butter.

Transfer the cooked fish to a serving dish, and strain the juices into
a saucepan. Bring to simmering point, and add the beurre manié in
small knobs, stirring it into the sauce to thicken it. Season with lemon
juice, and more salt and pepper if necessary. Keeping the sauce
below the boil, beat in the last 30 g (1 oz) of butter (this gives the
sauce a delicious flavour, and a beautifully glossy appearance). Add
the grapes, still keeping the sauce below boiling point, and leave for
1 minute, then pour round the fish. Scatter chopped parsley on top.
Make sure that the plates are very hot, and whatever you do, *don't
overcook the fish.*

NOTE This is a homely recipe for fish with grapes. Turn to p. 380
for the more elegant sole with grapes, Sole Véronique. I'm not implying
a preference – each dish has its place and occasion. Or to p. 296 for
Rougets Barbets à la bourguignonne with the vine leaves and grapes.

SEA BASS IN A PASTRY CASE (Bar en croûte)

One of the pleasures of Normandy in the late sixties and early seventies was staying at the Hôtel de la Marine on the edge of the Seine

under the great curve of the Pont Tancarville. As the sun set and the lights went on the scene took on the noble simplicity of a Japanese woodcut. And there was dinner, cooked by Monsieur Morisse and including dishes like this one, to look forward to.

This recipe can be used for other fish, grey mullet for instance, or a freshwater fish. Soft roes can be included in the stuffing.

2 kg (4 lb) bass, skinned and filleted
60 g (2 oz) butter
salt, pepper
750 g (1½ lb) puff pastry
beaten egg, to glaze

STUFFING
100 g (3½ oz) unsalted butter
6 tablespoons chopped shallots
60 g (2 oz) mushrooms, chopped
100 g (3½ oz) 2-day-old breadcrumbs
a little milk
2 hard-boiled eggs, chopped
2–3 tablespoons chopped parsley
1 tablespoon chopped chervil
1 egg, beaten

Cook the fillets on both sides in the butter just to stiffen them. Season them and leave them to cool.

For the stuffing, cook the butter, shallots and mushrooms together until they are soft, but not browned. Moisten the breadcrumbs with milk, using very little and squeezing out any surplus. Add them to the pan, mix well and turn everything into a basin. Add the chopped eggs and the herbs, and mix in the raw egg to bind the mixture.

Roll out just under half the pastry and put it on a baking sheet lined with baking parchment. Place a bass fillet on top, skin-side down. Put the stuffing on top and then the second fillet, skin-side up. Trim the pastry to leave a 1½-cm (¾-inch) rim and brush the rim with beaten egg.

Roll out the remaining pastry and cover the fish with it, pressing the edges down together. If your fancy takes you, shape the pastry to make a fish complete with head. Score it lightly with scales, mouth and eyes. Brush it over with beaten egg. Chill it for at least 45 minutes, or up to 3 hours.

Preheat the oven to gas 7, 220 °C (425 °F). Bake the fish for 25–35 minutes, until the pastry is well risen and brown. Serve with sauce Choron*.

SEA BASS WITH TARATOR SAUCE (Samak tarator)

From Claudia Roden's classic *Book of Middle Eastern Food* comes a tremendous dish which is particularly popular in Egypt, Syria and Lebanon. In those countries, it is usually served with lavish decorations in a variety of bright colours and traditional designs. In France, the decorations are generally more traditional.

'Choose a large fish such as sea bass, bream or John Dory. Clean and wash it. Leave the head on but remove the eyes. Rub all over with salt, pepper and olive oil, and bake in an oiled baking dish (45 minutes for a 1–1½ kg (2–3 lb) fish at gas 3, 160 °C/325 °F) or wrapped in foil (an hour at gas 4, 180 °C/350 °F).

'Serve the fish on a large dish on a bed or parsley or lettuce. Decorate it with lemon slices, sliced green pickles, black olives, radishes, fried pine nuts or almonds, and pieces of pimento. Make an oriental design, for example a criss-cross pattern. Serve cold, accompanied by bowls of *tarator* sauce', *see* p. 45.

'A delightful version of this dish is boned fish *tarator*. Prepare the fish and bake it in foil. Allow to cool. Cut off the head and tail neatly and set aside.

'Skin the body of the fish and bone the flesh. Season to taste with salt and pepper. Place the boned fish on a large serving dish, patting it back into its original shape. Place the head and tail at each end and mask the whole body of the fish with *tarator* sauce.

'Serve decorated with whole pine nuts or almonds, lightly fried, pickles, olives, and whatever else you like.

'This method of boning and reassembling the fish is particularly useful if dealing with a very large fish that does not fit into the oven. It can be cut into manageable pieces instead, and then baked in foil as usual.'

† SEA BREAM & PORGY

Sparidae spp.

The French have *daurade* or *dorade*, *pageau*, *pagre* and *denté*. The Spaniards *besugo* and *denton*. And sometimes you may see the pandora – *pageau* – imported from Greece under the name of *lithrini*, which is confusing if you try to look it up in a general cookery book. Undoubtedly, the spread of the sea breams is worldwide. In Japan it is the most prized of holiday fish in the form of the *tai* or red sea bream. Unfortunately for Pacific-coast Americans, I gather that an inferior species is sometimes sold under the honourable name of *tai* – a typical trick of the sharp food trade, akin to advertising margarine with pictures of cows knee-deep in summer meadows.

In one form and another sea bream swim up and down the American Atlantic coast under the cheerful names of porgy and, occasionally, scup. Both come from the same Narragansett Indian word, *mishcuppauog*, the plural of *mishcupp* which means thick-scaled, something you will understand if you have ever prepared a sea bream yourself. A compiler of a mid-nineteenth century dictionary of Americanisms was quite taken with the odd humour of the thing: 'It is singular that one half the original name, scup, should be retained for this fish in Rhode Island, and the other half, paug, changed into paugi or porgy, in New York.' Another member of the family is the sheepshead. It has a mild sort of look, but – for a fish – very strong teeth a bit like a sheep's incisors, and it crunches up the barnacles and crustaceans that it likes to eat. It is a good fish for poaching. In Louisiana they serve it with a creamy egg sauce. You might try it, too, with one of the hot sea-urchin sauces on p. 482, or something similar flavoured with the coral of scallops.

To the British the idea of porgy is familiar but mysterious. They know the cheerful ballad that begins:

My father was the keeper of the Eddystone Light,
Who slept with a mermaid one fine night,
And of that union there came three –
A porpoise, a porgy and the other was me.

You may recall that the porgy ended up in a chafing dish, presumably being pan-fried, which is the best fate for this kind of fish when it comes in small sizes. Try the American style of dipping the fish in egg beaten with twice its volume of milk, then roll them in a mixture of equal quantities of cornmeal, flour and cornflour. Pan-fry them in oil or bacon fat and serve them with lemon and parsley.

What I cannot recommend is the false sea bream displayed on some fish counters. A confident ticket is stuck usually into large fillets 30 cm (1 foot) long displaying a skin of pink and silver light, the tones of the skirt of Velasquez' Infanta. Do not be deluded. This is a most ordinary fish, one of the Sebastes species and not a true sea bream at all. Other names for it are Norway haddock or ocean perch. It is all right. It is dull. It is fish good for soup-making as a background flavour. No more than that.

I discovered this the hard way, in 1970. We had been to eat in London's first Japanese restaurant. The first experience of sashimi. And we had been told that the favourite Japanese fish for it was a red sea bream, the famous *tai* mentioned above. Next week I saw some fillets labelled 'bream' at the fishmonger's. Were they fresh, very fresh? I asked. The answer was yes. And I bought some. My sashimi was not a success: in fact it was repulsive because the texture was wrong – the 'bream' was really Norway haddock.

This is not to say that true sea bream, as a general rule, are one of the world's greatest gastronomic treats. They are not, but some varieties like the gilt-head bream (the true *daurade*, named for its golden colour) are very good. And even the more ordinary ones do not deserve to be confused with redfish. I once saw a sea bream in our Montoire market in France which stood out because of its colour. The consistent deep rose was astonishing, as brilliant almost as Zéphirine Drouhin in full flower. It was irresistible, but I have to confess that the flavour, though pleasant, was not outstanding.

Perhaps the most sombre, mute-looking sheepshead would have been a better choice for dinner, in spite of its sad appearance. The five dark stripes that run down the skin from top to belly reminded people of prison uniforms and they called it convict fish: the skin is tough, too, and needs to be removed as a rule, especially for fillets. Otherwise, no special preparation is required apart from the obvious cleaning and scaling.

BAKED BREAM I (Besugo al horno)

Here and in the next two recipes are versions of the Spanish way of cooking sea bream. They are all lively in flavour, especially the second and third recipes which depend on two particular techniques of Spanish cookery – a *majado* being a pounded mixture of nuts much used in Catalan and Mediterranean cooking, and a *sofrito* being a blend of onion, garlic and tomato slowly fried to a purée. Both can be used on their own, as in these recipes, or as the basis or flavouring of sauces, soups and stews.

> Serves 4
>
> *1½ kg (3 lb) sea bream, cleaned, scaled*
> *1 small lemon*
> *salt, pepper*
> *olive oil*
> *500–750 g (1–1½ lb) potatoes or 2 large onions*
> *3 large cloves garlic, sliced*
> *8 tablespoons fresh breadcrumbs*
> *leaves of 1 small bunch of parsley, chopped*

Preheat the oven to gas 7, 220°C (425°F). Choose a gratin dish that will take the bream comfortably on its bed of potatoes or onions.

Slash the plumpest part of the bream three times on each side of the backbone. Slice the lemon so that you have enough thin slices to tuck into the slashes and 4 wedges to go with the finished dish. Season the bream and put the slices in place. Brush out the gratin dish with oil.

Peel and slice the potatoes or onions. Plunge the slices into rapidly boiling salted water until they are half-cooked, then drain them and spread them out in the dish. On top lay the bream, trying not to dislodge the lemon slices on the under side.

Heat 175 ml (6 fl oz) olive oil in a small pan and fry the garlic until it is pale brown and the oil well flavoured. Mix breadcrumbs and parsley and add the lukewarm oil through a strainer. Spread this mixture over the bream. Bake for about 30 minutes, or until the fish is cooked. Serve with the lemon wedges.

BAKED BREAM II (Besugo al horno)

Serves 4

bream as in Baked bream I above or 2 smaller bream, cleaned, scaled
olive oil
1 lemon, cut into slices and wedges, as above
salt, pepper
125 ml (4 fl oz) dry white wine

MAJADO
3 ripe firm tomatoes, medium to large size
4 large cloves garlic in their skins
2–3 tablespoons blanched, slivered almonds
1–2 tablespoons pine kernels
125 ml (4 fl oz) dry white wine
leaves of about 10 sprigs parsley
salt, cayenne, paprika

Preheat the oven to gas 7, 220 °C (425 °F).

Start by preparing the majado. Brush out a small oven dish with oil and in it put the whole tomatoes and garlic. Bake in the oven until the skins darken, about 20 minutes. Peel and cut up and seed the tomatoes. Skin the garlic. Put the almonds into the oven on a baking sheet and leave briefly until they are a pale toasty colour. Put all these items, with the pine kernels, into a processor or mortar and reduce to a purée with the aid of the white wine. Add the parsley (roughly chopped if you are using a mortar) and seasoning to taste.

Choose a gratin dish that will hold the bream comfortably but rather more closely than for the recipe above. Brush it out with oil. Slash the bream and put lemon slices into the cuts; season. Put into the dish, pour over the wine and bake for 10–15 minutes, depending on size. Spoon the majado over the fish, lower the heat slightly and complete the cooking – 20–30 minutes – basting occasionally.

Serve with the lemon wedges.

BAKED AND STUFFED SEA BREAM (Besugo relleno al horno)

This is a recipe for the neat-fingered, though the characteristic structure of the bream makes the business of boning it much easier than you might have supposed. Obviously the larger the fish, the better. For this recipe buy one large bream rather than two smaller ones: 1½ kg (3 lb) will give you plenty for four. Ask the fishmonger to clean out the innards via the gills, leaving the belly intact. He should also scale the fish.

Serves 4

1 sea bream weighing 1½ kg (3 lb)
olive oil
salt, pepper
125 g (4 oz) chopped onion
2 large cloves garlic, skinned, crushed, finely chopped
500 g (1 lb) ripe firm tomatoes, skinned, seeded
leaves of 1 small handful of parsley, chopped
1 small hot chilli

STUFFING: see *squid stuffing, p. 406*

Put the bream on a board. With a small sharp knife, cut along the dark central line that runs from head to tail down the centre of the body. Ease away from this cut up towards the top of the fish, then towards the bottom, scraping and cutting the flesh from the bones. Snip the backbone at head and tail ends, and draw it out – the tricky part. The bream is now a floppy pocket, ready to be stuffed. Brush a baking dish with olive oil and put the fish into it. Season and set aside.

Next make the sofrito which acts as sauce. It is best to use an earthenware dish so that everything cooks slowly; with gas and electric, it is wise to slip a heat-diffuser beneath it. In the dish, cook the onion and garlic gently in enough oil to cover the base. As they become tender, add the tomato, parsley and chilli. Cook to an unwatery purée, tasting from time to time and removing the chilli when the sofrito is piquant enough. Add seasoning, too.

Meanwhile, make the stuffing and fill the bream pocket. Skewer the cut edges with wooden cocktail sticks, leaving them slightly apart to show the stuffing.

Spoon the sofrito round the fish and bake as in the recipes above. If need be, protect the top of the bream with butter papers, and baste the fish occasionally.

FILETS DE DORADE À L'ANTILLAISE

I was surprised to read this recipe in a local French newspaper, as rum in the kitchen is usually kept for sweet things, chocolate desserts in particular. I tried it and everyone like it. The secret is not to overdo the rum. (I'm not sure how genuinely West Indian the recipe is, or whether the title is just a genuflection by some French cook to the source of the most powerful ingredient.) Croakers and drums, and other lively tasting white fish, adapt well to this treatment.

Serves 6

6 fillets of sea bream, porgy, etc.
4 tablespoons rum
salt, pepper, cayenne
4 tablespoons butter
250 ml (8 fl oz) crème fraîche or *mixed soured and double or whipping cream*
2 large egg yolks

Preheat the oven to gas 6–7, 200–220 °C (400–425 °F). Choose a dish into which the fillets fit closely in a single layer; rub it out with a butter paper.

Trim the fish, skin it if you like, or if you are cooking sheepshead fillets. Pour the rum over, season and leave for at least an hour.

Dot the fish with the butter and bake for about 20 minutes, or until just done.

Meanwhile, make the sauce by beating together the cream(s) and egg yolks in a basin over barely simmering water – or directly over a low heat if you are confident with egg sauces. Season, especially with cayenne. Spoon any juices from the cooked fish into the sauce and then pour the whole thing over the fish.

The original recipe had a garnish of puff pastry crescents, but that seems to me fussy and out of place. Pasta with a light finish of chopped green coriander seems a better idea.

PEBBLE-ROASTED FISH (Horoku-yaki)

This is a most attractive and healthy way of cooking fish. I would suggest however that you try it out first with some cheaper fish than sea bream, to see how well you manage it.

Attend first of all to your equipment. You need a large shallow pottery or metal dish of agreeable design, filled with a tight layer of well-washed pebbles the size of large cherries. On some beaches you will find banks of even-sized round grey stones, and they are ideal. The next item, though not essential, is a handy pine tree. Pick and rinse enough small branches of pine needles to cover the stones, with some left over. Lastly cut a piece of foil that will be large enough to cover and balloon up over the dish.

Serves 6

3 sea bream, each weighing about 375 g (12 oz), scaled
sea salt
6 huge prawns or langoustines
12 large mussels, scrubbed, scraped
12 fresh shiitake, stems removed or other mushrooms

SAUCE
3 tablespoons lemon juice
3 tablespoons soy sauce
3 tablespoons dashi or chicken broth
8-cm (3-inch) piece white radish, peeled, shredded hair-fine
10-cm (4-inch) length Welsh or spring onion, sliced

If they have not been cleaned by the fishmonger, remove the innards of the sea bream through a cut made to one side. On the same side, slash the fish three times in the thickest part. Sprinkle 2 teaspoons of salt over them and leave at least 30 minutes.

De-vein the prawns or langoustines, removing the heads if they are very large, but leaving the shells in place; put with the mussels. Slice the mushrooms thickly.

Put the dish of pebbles into a cold oven, then switch it on to gas 8, 230°C (450°F). Leave at least 15 minutes, or until the temperature is well set. Take out the dish, scatter on the pine branches and put the bream on top, slashed sides down. Put the remaining items round them quickly and decoratively. Encase your hands in oven gloves and fix the foil in place, pressing it tightly round the edge of the dish, and ballooning it up so that it clears the contents.

Put the whole thing back into the oven. Leave for 6 minutes, then check and remove the mussels which should be open, and the prawns or langoustines if they are cooked: keep them warm. Re-cover the dish and put back for about another 8 minutes, until you judge the fish is ready.

Meanwhile mix the sauce ingredients together, and divide between six little bowls.

Remove the dish from the oven, discard the foil and, using kitchen tongs, replace any unsightly pine needles with fresh ones. Put back the mussels and prawns or langoustines and serve immediately.

In Japan, Horoku-yaki would be accompanied by soup and a salad dish. Usually it is served in winter-time, but the method fits in well with our own style of summer eating – with or without pine needles.

SALT-GRILLED SEA BREAM (Tai Shioyaki)

When I wrote *Fish Cookery* in 1971 and 1972, it seemed necessary to apologize for the eccentricity of including a few Japanese recipes such as this one. Then came the new cookery, and Japanese and Chinese ideas were effortlessly incorporated into the French repertoire: now they are taken for granted. Sashimi (*see* the following recipe) has perhaps been the most noticeable newcomer. Another has been the cooking of chicken and fish in mounds of coarse sea salt. Recently I was offered a leaflet of such recipes in Britanny, when buying a bag of sea salt near Guérandes, at the back of La Baule. Nothing was said to indicate that the recipes were anything other than local, yet I have never found such a thing in earlier Breton cookery books, only in Chinese ones. It is easy to understand that the owners of the last saltings, coming by chance upon such a recipe in a smart cookery magazine, seized on it with rapture since it makes use of such a quantity of his declining product.

For that particular system of cooking with salt, turn to p. 367. This recipe uses rather less. A number of fish are suitable for salt-grilling, but the Japanese use it especially for the particular sea bream known to them as *tai*. They regard *tai* as a special and superior fish, the lucky fish to be eaten on ceremonial occasions, since it sounds like *medetai*, meaning happy. 'This kind of symbolic pun ... helps the Japanese in their quest for harmony with nature. To the Japanese, nothing on earth, even a common fish, can exist in isolation; everything must be accorded its rightful place in the universal scheme of things. All aspects of a creature, its soul, its colour and character, even its name, are duly honoured.'[1] I like that idea.

Serves 6

3 sea bream each weighing approx. 500 g (1 lb) scaled
unadulterated sea salt

Make a cut below the pectoral fin and take out the innards: wash the cavity of each fish. Weigh them, then calculate two per cent of their weight in salt – this will be something around 30 g (1 oz). Put the fish on a plate and pour the salt over them. Leave for 30 minutes at room

[1] Rafael Steinberg, *Cooking of Japan*, Time/Life, 1970.

temperature rather than in the refrigerator. Wipe the fish dry and free of salt just before grilling.

You can cook the fish at this point, protecting the fins and tail with bits of foil. Charcoal gives the best result – about 4 minutes a side.

The alternative, if you have long wooden skewers, looks more attractive, and is what a Japanese cook would do. Put the fish on a board, heads to the left. Push in a skewer just below the eye, pass it through the fish and through the tail, curving it up slightly. The second skewer goes in below the first and should emerge underneath the tail. These skewers hold the upward curve of the tail. Rub the fish over again with salt, particularly around the tail. Grill over charcoal if possible, or under a preheated grill, cooking the 'front', i.e. head-to-the-left side, first.

To serve, put on a serving plate, remove the foil and skewers and decorate with lemon slices or white radish grated into threads as fine as angel's hair scattered with a few pinches of chopped parsley.

For a dipping sauce for fish, which is by no means essential, mix together:

> 6 tablespoons shoyu (*Japanese soy sauce*)
> 2 tablespoons rice vinegar or *white wine vinegar*
> 1 tablespoon fresh peeled ginger, grated

Divide between six little pots.

SASHIMI I

Of all the ways of eating fish, this is the best. But – and there is a but especially as far as Britain is concerned – the fish must be fresh, sparkling almost. On the fishmonger's slab, it should look irresistible, scales gleaming, skin pearly and full of light.

Always try to buy two contrasting tones and textures of fish. Three is even better. Favourites are sea bream, the better flounders and flatfish, tuna, mackerel, cuttlefish, and in Japan and the Pacific two *Sillago* species, the Indian or Silver whiting and the Trumpeter whiting, as well as half-beak (*Hemirhamphus marginatus*) which is similar to flying fish in flavour and texture.

As the fish for sashimi are not cured in the sense that gravadlax is cured with salt, sugar and dill, the accompanying sauce is important to show off the fish. A number of French chefs have taken the whole idea over and transformed the look of the dish: they tend to slice the fish paper-thin, arrange it on plates like smoked salmon, and brush it over with flavoured oils and lemon juice just before serving. Another popular style, especially with salmon, is to chop the fish into tiny dice and mix it with a very little mayonnaise and herbs: delicate quantities are heaped into minute tartlet cases or on to circles of buttered bread or piled more generously on to bitter salad leaves. Such dishes will be called marinaded sea bass or salmon tartare, and I imagine that their particular arrangement is to disguise from western sensibilities the raw nature of the fish. Everybody, or so I imagine, knows that it is raw, but their eyes are not assailed. And that makes all the difference. There is no barrier between them and the delicious tasting reality.

With sashimi, the raw nature of the fish is directly apparent. What makes it acceptable is the seductive brilliance of really fresh fish and the beauty of the slicing and general arrangement, including the choice of the bowl or plate. I shall never forget reading an observation of D. H. Enright's in his book on Japan, that even the most untutored housemaid knows how to present food with elegant grace. By contrast most of us are cack-handed in such matters. But it is fun to try.

If you are filleting whole fish, say a sea bream, cut off the two sides from the bone, skin them and then, if they are from a good-sized fish, divide the fillets down their length. Use the plumpest part for preference. With enormous fish, buy a nicely shaped piece of fillet. Scallops are excellent for sashimi: choose well-formed discs and trim them neatly, and slice them across once or twice according to their thickness.

Here are some of the cuts – beginners will find it easiest to chill the softer fish until it is firm in the freezer, but do not freeze it completely or attempt to use frozen fish.

(1) cut down straight into ½-cm (¼-inch) slices
(2) cut these straight slices across into strips and pile them in a small mound
(3) cut the strips across again into dice – a good cut for firm fish like tuna
(4) slice diagonally downwards in paper-thin slices
(5) cut down at a slight angle into ½-cm (¼-inch) slices
(6) with squid or cuttlefish, cut a flat piece from the bag, make parallel cuts almost but not quite through, then slice completely through at right angles; you can then curve each strip round slightly in a cock's-comb effect.

Straight cut slices may be served as they were cut, in a close piece.

Diagonal slanting slices are arranged like overlapping tiles. Dice, like the strips, can be heaped into little mounds. Scallop discs could be fanned, and a piece or two of squid used as a decoration.

Serves 6

750 g (1½ lb) sea bream or 500 g (1 lb) sole
250 g (8 oz) slice of pink tuna or 375 g (12 oz) mackerel
6 fine scallops, white part only
10-cm (4-inch) length white radish, peeled
1 tablespoon wasabi (green horseradish powder) or 2 tablespoons peeled
  and finely grated green ginger
6 spring onions, cut into curly brushes

SAUCE
6 tablespoons shoyu (Japanese soy sauce)
6 tablespoons lime juice

Scale, fillet and skin the whole fish. Skin the tuna. Wrap in cling film and chill until very firm – up to 2 hours – in the freezer. Peel and finely shred the white radish.

No more than an hour before the meal, mix the wasabi to a thick paste with a little water, then let it stand for 20 minutes. If you choose ginger, form it into six little cone-shaped mounds.

Remove the fish from the freezer and cut it into appropriate slices with a very very sharp knife. Use trimmings for fish stock.

TO SERVE Either arrange the fish on six cold plates with a blob of wasabi or a mound of ginger and a loose heap of shredded radish. Decorate with a spring onion brush, and serve bowls of the shoyu and lime juice mixed together. Or else arrange the fish elegantly on one central serving plate, and give each person a tiny bowl of sauce. You could make a sunflower of thin slices of sea bream or bass, with an inner circle of pink tuna or mackerel slices, and a central blob of wasabi. The idea is to help yourself from the plate to a piece of fish, with chopsticks or a fork, dip it into the sauce and then eat it.

TO MAKE SPRING ONION BRUSHES Cut the lower part of spring onions into 3–4-cm (1½-inch) lengths, keeping the green tops for another occasion. Slice one end of each piece down about halfway, then slice across it. Put the pieces into a covered plastic box of ice water. Store in the refrigerator, and in a little while the cut ends will curl. Drain and serve.

SASHIMI II

Here is another way of preparing fish for sashimi, in which the skin sides of the fillets are partially cooked.

Use fillets of fish that are not too thick. Sea bream for instance, but not tuna which is too solid and meaty. Sea bass would be a good alternative.

Cut the fillets, leaving the skin in place, and cut each fillet lengthways in two pieces. Put them on a heavy chopping board, skin side up. Tilt the board in a sink. Bring a kettle of water to the boil and pour it slowly over the fish and the skin will contract. Rinse in cold water, dry thoroughly and then remove the skin before slicing the fish.

Serve with shredded white radish and shoyu, or soy sauce mixed with an equal amount of lemon or lime juice.

SEA BREAM BAKED IN SALT

Choose a pot into which the sea bream, or other fish, fits with about 3 cm (1½ inches) to spare all round. Line with heavy or doubled foil. Put 3 cm (1½ inches) of salt in the bottom. Place the fish in the pot and pour in enough salt to bury it completely, with a 2-cm (1-inch) layer on top. Put in a preheated oven, gas 8–9, 230–240°C (450–475°F), and leave for 30 minutes for a larger mackerel, or other fish weighing 500 g (1 lb).

Turn out on to a large baking sheet. Tap it carefully with a hammer. Brush off the salt and serve.

SEA EAR *see* A FEW WORDS ABOUT . . . ABALONE

SEA PERCH *see* SEA BASS

SEA-URCHINS *see* A FEW WORDS ABOUT . . . SEA-URCHINS

SHAD *see* A FEW WORDS ABOUT . . . SHAD

† SHARKS – PORBEAGLE, MAKO & TOPE

Lamna nasus, Isurus oxyrinchus & Galeorhinus galeus

To see a shark brought low on a marble slab is disturbing; as if the wildness of the sea can no longer be relied on, when such creatures are harvested, or caught like cattle. Scientists, too, have taken away our fantasies. They assure us that sharks, requiem sharks in particular, do not all deserve their tolling name of doom. They do not hover behind ships waiting for a careless lurch overboard. We shall never see a shark swimming off with a dinner-jacketed arm protruding from its awful jaws, like the mousetail from a cat's. One writer ominously remarks that they are 'not averse to dead meat'. Another says that it is the ship's garbage they are after. They are no more than a scavenging nuisance. Think of it – the man-eating shark a nuisance and no more. They spoil fishing nets and gnaw pointlessly at the profitable shoals of herring; they gobble the bait from the lines. Not much Melville or *Moby Dick* here.

As far as the cook is concerned, there are no horrors either; shark is delicious and easy to prepare. The two kinds I first came across are undoubtedly only a couple amongst a number that are worth trying. Admittedly neither was in the first rank of fish – sole, lobster, turbot, salmon, eel and so on – but both were above the ordinary humdrum level. As well as good flavour and texture, they have the advantages of no bones, beyond a central spine and its few attachments, and of cheapness. This latter must be a reflection of conservative taste and poor cooking ability, because sharks are a rare fish by comparison with the daily fare of saithe, ling, etc.

We first saw the immense porbeagle, or a part of it, at the Wednesday market in Montoire. Its matt velour-like skin stood out among the scaly fish and white fillets around it. The fishmonger's wife explained that it is called *taupe* in France on account of this mole-coloured skin (which makes an excellent shagreen). Then she turned the piece towards us so that we could see the pale pink, lightly fibred flesh. 'It's just like veal,' she said. 'We sometimes call it *veau de mer*.' She took her great knife across the piece, then cut a section the right size for our small family of three. 'Treat it like veal,' she called after us. We found that she was right; the flavour is so delicate, and the texture so substantial, that I think few people would realize they weren't eating meat.

Americans will find the pink, veal-like quality of porbeagle in the mako shark which is sometimes, I believe, sold as 'swordfish' though it is deeper in tone. Sharks of several species become more and more popular on both coasts: 'the public has accepted shark on its own terms. It is no longer the bargain it was a few years ago,' say the authors of *The California Seafood Cookbook*, 'but it is still reasonably priced.'

Confusion in the matter of sharks comes, at least for shoppers in Europe, with tope. It is tempting to believe it is the fish that one sees in French markets labelled *taupe*, which – *see* above – is the name for porbeagle. Once you have seen both, you understand instantly that they cannot be the same (and indeed the tope is *milandre* or *ha* in French). What amuses me is that the great national dictionaries on either side of the Channel are defeated by the names – but then neither is very good at food words, as if eating were a shameful need of nature that a person of intellect should despise. The *Grand Robert* ignores it, concentrating on *taupe* as mole, with all the mining derivatives you could imagine. At least the vaster *Oxford English Dictionary* gives a little space to 'tope', confessing weakly that its origin is obscure, Cornish dialect, since tope is much caught off the Cornish coast: then it goes on cheerily to columns on 'tope' (verb) and 'topers' (noun), cheerful drinking words of known ancestry.

Oddly enough, the first tope we ever saw was in Oxford market. There were a couple of them, about 1½ m (5 feet) long, slender compared to the tight swelling girth of the porbeagle. Tope are much whippier, more like a dogfish in shape. These two creatures laid low were dark on the back, but with a brownish tinge, fading to a strange old-rose colour on their bellies which reminded me of curtains my grandmother had in the thirties when old-rose was a favourite colour in furnishing. The flesh, though, was translucent and white. It clustered in tight sections around the central bone, a brilliant rosette. My only regret was that we never thought to ask for the fins, we were so taken aback at seeing shark on a fishmonger's slab at all.

In Ceylon and the Philippines they are treated with hot wood ash and fine salt, then dried to a brittle blue-grey crispness in smoke or sun. At last they go to Chinese cooks to be made into soup, a valued ingredient on account of their fine-tasting gelatine (flavour comes from other items, including pork).

The tope is called Sweet William in some places, sarcastically on account of its ammoniac smell. Something to look out for, but don't let it put you off. It is not the poor tope's fault, but part of its physical make-up which cannot be helped. It does not impugn its freshness, or the eventual pleasure of its flavour. Just take care to marinade the fish before cooking in lime or lemon juice, or cider or wine vinegar. Soaking in brine – see tuna, p. 429 – also gets rid of it.

Next point, there is no mileage in eating shark's skin – endless tough chew, so always remove it.

Having arrived at this point, the rest is easy. You can adapt it without fuss to swordfish, tuna and halibut recipes, just be careful not to overcook it.

A Californian idea is to dry-fry it in a sauté pan that has been warmed up with a tablespoon of oil, adding a couple of skinned chopped tomatoes: serve scattered with basil and a bowl of pesto.

Steaks can be briefly fried in clarified butter and served finished like Sole meunière (p. 388). Or they can be first be dipped in egg and breadcrumbs, then fried, and served with lemon quarters, or a purée of sorrel*. Tomato sauce* and créole sauce* are obvious partners, so are white wine sauces* and butter sauces*.

These shark can be given a delicate treatment, or something more jovial. Because they are not yet too expensive, you can have fun experimenting with them. Some of the curried fish recipes in this book – pp. 174 and 404 – might first be tried with porbeagle or tope or mako. Or the strange and sweet Sicilian swordfish pie, p. 412.

BARBECUED SHARK

This is a dish that makes a lively family meal.

Serves 4

750 g (1½ lb) shark
salt, pepper

> *juice of 2 lemons* (see *recipe*)
> *8 tablespoons olive oil* (see *recipe*)
> *6 rashers bacon, smoked or green, or both*
> *250 g (8 oz) mushrooms, halved*
> *4 large bay leaves, each cut into 4 pieces*
> *olive oil or melted butter for basting*

Skin and cut the shark into a number of similar sized chunks, divisible by four. Season lightly with salt and pepper. Marinade them, if there is time, with the juice of 2 lemons and about 8 tablespoons olive oil.

Preheat the grill to maximum.

Cut the rind from the bacon and cut it into the same number of pieces as there are chunks of shark, plus four.

Lay out the shark and bacon, alternating in four rows on a board, fitting pieces of mushroom and bay leaf in between in an equitable manner. Now it is an easy matter to thread the skewers. Brush with oil or butter and grill, turning at least once, until the edges are nicely caught and the fish turns just opaque at the centre. Serve with rice, and melted butter, plenty of pepper and lemon quarters.

SPICED PORBEAGLE

All the sharks take very well to spices. Try this recipe, too, with monkfish and halibut.

> Serves 6
>
> *6 steaks*
> *4 dry red chillis*
> *2 tablespoons finely chopped garlic*
> *3 teaspoons cumin seeds*
> *¾ teaspoon ground tumeric*
> *2 teaspoons tamarind paste or pulp*
> *2 teaspoons brown sugar*
> *1½ teaspoons salt*
> *clarified butter or sunflower oil*

Put the steaks on a dish in a single layer. Reduce the spices, garlic, tamarind, sugar and salt to a paste in a mortar and spread over the fish on both sides. Leave for at least 4 hours.

Brush a non-stick frying pan over with butter or oil and cook the steaks in it, adding extra butter or oil if necessary when turning them. Serve with a cucumber raita (p. 183) and rice.

TOPE EN BROCHETTE

The diameter of the steaks we bought was about 15 cm (6 inches). I found that five of them gave enough for six people. Marinading them for several hours, even overnight, improves their flavour: remove the skin and cut each piece into six chunks. Put them into a dish and pour over equal quantities of olive oil and lemon juice, with seasoning and, if you like, chopped garlic. You will also need:

Serves 6

6 long thin rashers green streaky bacon, each cut into 5 pieces
6 long thin rashers smoked streaky bacon, each cut into 5 pieces
12 or 18 small mushrooms
6 large bay leaves, each cut into 4 pieces
salt, pepper

Drain and arrange the chunks of fish into 6 lines, and fit the rest of the ingredients equitably between them, including the bay leaves. It is an easy matter to thread and season the skewers. Grill until the fish is opaque to the centre, turning regularly and brushing with the remaining marinade. Serve with rice.

SHRIMPS *see* PRAWNS

SILVER HAKE *see* HAKE

SILVERSIDE *see* A FEW WORDS ABOUT . . . SMELT

SKATE *see* A FEW WORDS ABOUT . . . SKATE

SMELT *see* A FEW WORDS ABOUT . . . SMELT

SOLE, DAB & PLAICE

It must be confessed that the life history of the sole is not entertaining, delicious though it may taste. Mostly it lies supine on the bed of the sea, dark side up, attracting as little attention as possible. Its name means 'flat', like the sole of the foot. The most dramatic episode of its life – to the outside observer – is when the left eye of the perfectly normal, fish-shaped larva moves up and over the head to the right side, as the sole flattens into its characteristic shape. But then, this happens to the humblest of the flatfish, one way or the other (sometimes the right eye moves to the left side, as with the turbot). The sole also shares the chameleon quality of other flatfish, though not with such enthusiasm as the plaice, whose rust-coloured spots change to white when it lies on a pebbly patch of the sea-bed.

But why should we expect the sole to astonish or entertain us, to provide us with the pleasures of intellectual excitement? Such expectations seem tawdry by comparison with its gift of exquisite flavour and firm but dissolving texture. The sole is the darling of the sea, of all the things we eat the greatest stimulus to chefly lyricism. It is cherished in cream and good wine, set off by muscat grapes, truffles, mushrooms and shellfish, yet is arguably as its most beautiful when unadorned by amorous attentions, when served à la meunière or plainly grilled, with no more fuss than a few pieces of lemon.

The secret of the sole's flavour is, it appears, no more than an accident of chemistry. 'The palatability of a fish,' explains J. R. Norman in *A History of Fishes*, 'is due to the presence of some peculiar chemical substance in the muscles which gives it its characteristic flavour … In the Plaice, as in most other fishes, the chemical substance is present in the flesh when the fish is alive, but unless it is eaten soon after capture this soon fades away and the flesh becomes comparatively tasteless. In the Sole, on the other hand, the characteristic flavour is only developed two or three days after death in consequence of the formation of a chemical substance by the process of decomposition; thus it forms a tasty dish even when brought long distances.'

What a shame that this accident should not have happened to the superabundant plaice (*Pleuronectes platessa*). In Europe every year between 100 and 120 thousand tons of plaice are landed, over four times the weight of sole, and more than all the other flatfish put together.

For the practical cook, flatfish fall into two different groups, small (sole, plaice, dabs) and enormous (halibut and turbot). Recipes therefore designated for sole in this chapter can also be used for dabs and plaice. I have to say, however, that for the lover of good things, the groups given above are immaterial. There are only two flatfish – the sole and the turbot. They shine out among all the fish of the sea. Whilst plaice can be cooked in the manner of sole (and brill in the manner of turbot), they won't taste the same. Some restaurateurs substitute weever for sole, so it is worth enquiring about sole dishes, *see* p. 491. Which is not to say that they won't be enjoyable and worth eating, especially if the sauces are good.

Here are some of those other flatfish which may be cooked in the style of the true sole (*Solea solea*) – but need more culinary attentions:

THE DAB   This is called a *limande* in French, and has more right to the name, seeing that it is *Limanda limanda* in scientific terminology (from the Latin *lima*, a file, on account of its rough skin).

THE FLOUNDER OR FLUKE   This fish has a poor reputation, and is not particularly good to eat, though it hardly deserves one description which compares it to wet flannel. I suppose one must here specify European flounder because in America 'flounder' includes a number of flatfish that can be good eating when they are freshly caught. The names vary in different parts of the US, but the most common varieties are black back (winter) flounder, summer flounder (fluke), dab (yellowtail), gray sole and lemon sole.

LEMON SOLE   This has the delightful Latin name of *Microstomus kitt*, and a decidedly yellowish-brown appearance. Again, it is not a true sole. Other names are merry or Mary Sole, and sweet fluke. The

French name is *sole-limande*, which is thoroughly confusing because the French name for the dab is so similar.

MEGRIM, WHIFF, SAIL-FLUKE, OR WEST COAST SOLE This has a thinner, translucent appearance, and the name of *Lepidorhombus whiff-iagonis* – there's invention for you – and *cardine* in French.

TORBAY SOLE OR WITCH A beautiful pinkish-purple marble-skinned creature, not unlike the sole in its blunted shape. You can be caught out both by the name and appearance of this fish, if you are not too familiar with the true sole. The French name is *plie grise*.

The average weight of a sole is about 375 g (12 oz). Some are larger, some can be tiny. In France we buy very cheaply minute creatures, 7–10 cm (3–4 inches) long, called *séteaux*. They are a true sole and quite good eating for this reason, in spite of their small size. They are not, as we at first thought, infant Dover soles, but a species on their own, first recognized I believe by Jonathan Couch, the great naturalist of Polperro in Cornwall, in the last century.

At present prices, a 500 g (1 lb) sole has to do for two people. For a meal which may have several courses, this is not unreasonable. Better to eat a small amount of something delicious (and fill the corners up with some good bread) than a lot of something mediocre. Ask the fishmonger to skin it for you, and grab the skin before he throws it into the waste bucket; this will give you the opportunity of asking him for the bones and skin of other flatfish which he has filletted already, so that you have the all-important basic material for fish stock for the sauce.

If you have to skin the fish yourself, or produce fillets, see the instructions on p. 4.

FILETS DE SOLE À LA NORMANDE

If a dish requires extra time and attention, a cookery writer is supposed to be apologetic. I fail to see why. People spend hours developing photographs in a dark room, or watching birds. Why shouldn't a cook be allowed to enjoy an hour or two with an interesting occupation? Sole normande is certainly that. Purists may complain that it can only taste as it should in Normandy (on account of the butter and cream there, which differ from ours in texture and flavour). In fact the dish was probably invented in Paris by Carême – not by a fisherman stirring his iron pot over a driftwood fire in a smoky cabin. Of course nowadays the dish in one form or another is on the menu of most self-respecting Normandy restaurants – a tribute to modern communications and cross-fertilization rather than to authenticity.

Serves 6

fillets of 3 large sole or 1 ½ kg (3 lb) brill or turbot fillets
salt, pepper
125 g (4 oz) unsalted butter
150 ml (5 fl oz) dry white wine or cider
36 mussels or oysters
24 button mushrooms
1 tablespoon lemon juice
*450 ml (15 fl oz) velouté sauce**
125 ml (4 fl oz) crème fraîche or double cream
4 egg yolks

Grease a heatproof dish with butter paper, put in the fish fillets in a single layer and season them. Dot them with 15 g (½ oz) butter and pour on the wine or cider. Open the mussels, if used, over a high heat, as briefly as possible (*see* p. 239). Discard the shells and strain the liquor through a cloth over the fillets. With oysters, open them and simmer them briefly in their liquor; strain the liquor over the fillets. Keep the mussels or oysters warm. Either simmer the fish on top of the stove for 3–4 minutes or in a hot oven at gas 6, 200 °C (400 °F) until it is half-cooked.

Meanwhile, cook the mushrooms in 45 g (1 ½ oz) butter with the lemon juice and seasoning. Strain the liquor into the velouté sauce. Keep the mushrooms warm. Pour off the liquor from the fish into the sauce and reduce this sauce back to its original volume.

Arrange the fish on a warm, heatproof serving dish and surround it with a border of the mussels or oysters and mushrooms. Put butter papers or greaseproof paper over the top and leave it to keep warm in a low oven. It will continue to cook gently. Preheat the grill to its maximum temperature. Bring the crème fraîche just to the boil, if using it.

To complete the sauce, beat the egg yolks with half the crème fraîche or cream, add some of the sauce and then stir the cream mixture into the pan. Keep stirring while the sauce thickens over a low heat, without letting the sauce boil. Stir in the rest of the crème fraîche or cream to taste and then – off the heat – the last of the butter, cut into cubes. Check seasoning.

Spoon some of the sauce carefully over the fish, inside the border of shellfish and mushrooms. Put the serving dish under the grill for a few moments to glaze (don't brown it). Serve the rest of the sauce in a separate jug.

VARIATION   Soles à la Dieppoise: Substitute 250 g (8 oz) shelled, cooked prawns or langoustines for the mushrooms. Heat through in butter. Make stock from the shells and add to the sauce. Scatter with chopped parsley before glazing.

FILET DE SOLE MARGUERY

Marguery's, on the Boulevard de Bonne-Nouvelle in Paris, was a famous restaurant of the Belle Époque. It was celebrated for its picturesque rooms, 'some oriental, others medieval, yet others recalling Potsdam', for its lively and loquacious and mixed clientele – and for the great dish of Filets de sole Marguery.

Everyone was after the 'secret'. Chefs all over Europe and America tried to imitate it. Every cookery book of the time had some stab at the recipe. One enthusiast who persuaded the recipe out of Monsieur Marguery was Claude Monet. He gave wonderful dinners in his yellow dining-room at Giverny, and undoubtedly saw how good the dish would look – as well as taste – on the yellow- and blue-rimmed dinner service he had designed for himself.

A much odder, greedier enthusiast was Diamond Jim Brady of New York, a man whose diamond rings matched his appetite. His favourite restaurant was Rector's in New York. One night someone in his party there rhapsodized about the wonderful dish he had recently eaten at Marguery's. This caught Brady's imagination. Indeed, it became an obsession, and he delivered an ultimatum to Rector: 'If you cannot put this dish on your menu, I shall go elsewhere.'

A serious business. Rector removed his son from Cornell University and sent him off to Paris as a gastronomical spy. The boy started at Marguery's as a dishwasher, *plongeur*, lowest of the low, and worked his way up. After two years he reached the magic circle and the recipe, and set off home. As the boat sailed towards the dock, he could make out Diamond Jim on the quay, bellowing 'Have you got the recipe?'

That night Diamond Jim ate nine helpings of Filet de sole Marguery. He went to the kitchen to congratulate the chef: 'If you poured some of the sauce over a Turkish towel, I believe I could eat all of it.'

But what was the recipe? An American, James M. Andrews, pursued the story in the 1970s and happened to tell a friend, Nina Lobanov, about it. She in turn told her landlady, to amuse her one day when she was ill.

By extraordinary coincidence, this lady, Mrs Burmister, had visited the restaurant fifty years earlier in 1926, and charmed the recipe out of the maître-chef, Monsieur Manguin, who had ruled the kitchen for over thirty years. And she had kept it.

Serves 4

2 large fillets of sole, trimmed bones, heads, etc.
2–3 shallots, chopped
1 sprig of thyme
¼ bay leaf
2 sprigs of parsley
salt, white pepper
375 ml (12 fl oz) dry white wine
generous 1 kg (2½ lb) mussels
400 g (14 oz) unsalted French butter
6 egg yolks

GARNISH
500 g (1 lb) prawns, shelled
125 g (4 oz) winkles (optional)

Put bones, trimmings, etc., into a pan with shallots and herbs, seasoning and two-thirds of the wine. Add water barely to cover. Boil steadily for 20 minutes, skimming. Strain into a measuring jug.

Clean and open mussels in the usual way (*see* p. 239) with the remaining white wine. Discard shells. Keep mussels covered in a cool oven. Strain liquor into a measuring jug.

With 60 g (2 oz) butter, grease a flameproof non-stick or enamel pan and butter a piece of greaseproof paper, cut to fit on top. Flatten the fillets slightly, season and put into the pan in a single layer. Pour on enough of the sole and mussel stock almost to cover. Put on the paper, butter side down, and half-cook over a steady heat. Take the pan off the heat and pour off the liquor into a measuring jug. Keep the sole under its paper. It will continue to cook in its own warmth.

Boil the stock down hard to a syrupy concentration, about 300 ml (10 fl oz), but go by flavour. This takes the place of lemon and wine vinegar in what is virtually a hollandaise sauce. Strain about 150 ml (5 fl oz), through muslin this time, into a pan, off the heat. The stock should still be hot. Beat in the yolks.

Dice the remainder of the butter and beat to a cream in another pan over a low heat. Gradually beat the butter into the egg and stock mixture, to make a thick sauce. Keep raising the pan from a low to a moderate heat, or use a bain-marie. Overheating will curdle the egg. Add extra stock and seasoning to taste.

With a fish slice, lift the sole on to a large hot serving dish. Arrange mussels, prawns and winkles, if used (provide pins and little bowls of water for washing fingers if you do), in three close but separate rows round the sole. Pour over enough sauce to cover generously, without swamping the garnish: serve the rest separately. Put the serving dish into a hot oven or under a preheated grill to glaze (not brown). Serve immediately, with bread and white wine.

The 'secret' of the dish – as of most of the great chefs' recipes, I suspect – is using the best ingredients with the special taste of one particular person. In this instance this means knowing exactly how much to reduce the fish stock, and exactly how much to add to the sauce for the finest result.

FILLETS OF SOLE SAINT-GERMAIN

This is a delicious recipe for the summer when fresh tarragon is available for the sauce béarnaise.

Serves 6

175 g (6 oz) butter
12 fillets of sole
seasoned flour
breadcrumbs
500 g (1 lb) new potatoes, scraped and diced
salt, pepper
sauce béarnaise*

First clarify the butter (*see* p. 14), and strain it into a frying pan which is off the heat. Dip the sole fillets in flour and shake off all surplus. Pour off a little of the clarified butter into a bowl, and with a brush spread it over the sole fillets, then press them gently but firmly in breadcrumbs. Put the frying pan on to the heat and cook the potato dice, stirring them about so that they brown evenly. Keep the heat moderate. Season the potatoes when done.

Meanwhile, grill the sole under a low to moderate heat to avoid burning the breadcrumbs. Allow about 10 minutes, turning them over at half time.

Arrange the grilled sole on a serving dish, surround with the potatoes, and serve with sauce béarnaise (which the prudent cook will have made in advance of cooking the fish and potatoes, leaving it to keep warm over a pan of hot water. Hot, not boiling or even simmering water).

NOTE   Grilled sole and potatoes fried in clarified butter can also be served with sauce Choron* which is a béarnaise flavoured with tomato purée. Sprinkle the potatoes with a little chopped parsley before arranging them on the serving dish.

FILETS DE SOLE VÉRONIQUE

'Monsieur Malley, *saucier* at the Paris Ritz and later *chef des cuisines* at the London Ritz, was my professional ideal . . .' writes Louis Diat, the inventor of Crème Vichyssoise glacée. 'Malley had a fertile mind, and many of the fish sauces served in good restaurants today were originated by him. Filets de sole Véronique, for instance, was a Malley invention. A special party was planned, and Malley decided to add tiny white grapes to the white-wine sauce for the fish course. He gave instructions to a trusted under-chef, and went out, as usual, for the afternoon. When he returned, he found the young man so excited that he could hardly work. Monsieur Malley discovered that the young man's wife had just presented him with a baby girl, their first child. Monsieur Malley asked what they would name the child. "Véronique," was the reply. "*Alors*," said the *chef des cuisines*, "we'll call the new dish *filets de sole Véronique*." And so it is called to this day.'

Serves 4

60 g (2 oz) butter
2 shallots or ½ small onion, finely chopped
8 fine fillets of sole
salt, pepper
150 ml (5 fl oz) dry white wine
150 ml (5 fl oz) béchamel sauce*
4 tablespoons double cream
1 egg yolk
250–375 g (½–¾ lb) seedless white grapes or muscatels

Grease a shallow pan with 1 tablespoon of butter, and put in the chopped shallot or onion. Roll up the fillets of sole, salting and peppering them first, and secure with a cocktail stick. Arrange them on top of the onion. Pour in wine and the same amount of water, cover with foil, and either simmer on top of the stove for about 10 minutes, or else bake in a hot oven (gas 7, 220 °C/425 °F) for 15 minutes: the first way is best. When the fillets are just cooked, transfer them to a heatproof serving dish and keep them warm.

Strain the cooking liquid into a clean pan and boil it down to 300 ml (10 fl oz). Stir in the béchamel sauce, which should be on the firm side, and 2 tablespoons of cream, beaten up with the egg yolk. Cook without boiling until the sauce thickens nicely, stirring all the time. Place the pan over another pan of simmering water, so that it keeps warm but doesn't cook any further while you finish the recipe.

Whisk the remaining 2 tablespoons of cream until they are light and stiff. Heat the grapes through in just-boiling water, then arrange them round the fish. Stir the last 2 tablespoons of butter into the sauce to give it a good gloss and flavour. Lastly fold in the whipped cream and pour the sauce over fish and grapes. Brown lightly under a hot grill and serve immediately.

NOTE   Small seedless grapes do not have a long season, neither do the muscatel grapes recommended by Elizabeth David as the right ones for this fine and delicate dish.

If the only white grapes on sale are the coarser Almerian, which will need skinning and de-pipping, buy a cheaper fish and follow the recipe on p. 352 for Sea bass or bream à la vendangeuse. (I wonder if this country dish was the original inspiration for M. Malley's Sole Véronique?)

FILETS DE SOLE WALEWSKA

This dish – invented, I believe, by Escoffier – is named after Napoleon's Polish mistress, Marie Walewska. It is simple to prepare, but expensive on account of the lobster and truffles. Dublin Bay prawns could be used instead, or crawfish tails.

Serves 4

8 fillets of sole
*450 ml (15 fl oz) fish stock**
*600 ml (1 pt) béchamel sauce**
1 ½ tablespoons grated Parmesan cheese
30 g (1 oz) butter
8 slices truffle
8–12 slices cooked lobster or cooked prawns or shrimps

Poach the sole in the fish stock. When just cooked, transfer it to a serving dish and keep warm. Boil the stock down vigorously until it has a strong concentrated flavour. Heat the béchamel sauce, add the stock to it, and boil them both together for a few moments. Off the heat, stir the cheese and butter into the sauce. Arrange the truffle slices and lobster or prawns on top of the sole, pour the sauce over them, and place under a very hot grill for a few moments to glaze.

FILLETS OF SOLE WITH BANANAS

A friend once told me that she had eaten a delightful dish of fresh haddock with banana cubes, lightly fried in butter. With that on my mind, I tried to find similar recipes for banana with fish, and came at last to a French version. In it, new potatoes and sticks of fresh coconut were deep-fried with the fish fillets. This you can do, but I prefer the method given below.

Serves 6

12 fillets of sole (whiting can be used)
salt, pepper
3 large bananas
seasoned flour
coconut cream, p. 478
18 small new potatoes
3 medium carrots
grated zest and juice of 1 large orange
1 good teaspoon butter

Season the fish. Peel and cut each banana into three across, then into nice little sticks. Sprinkle a tray with seasoned flour, and put the fish on it, skin or skinned side up. At the wider end of each piece, lay a bundle of banana sticks. Roll up and secure with cocktail sticks or tie with thread. Set aside in a cool place.

Prepare the coconut cream, and set it to heat through over the pan in which you boil the potatoes. Grate the carrots coarsely into a pan which already holds the orange zest and juice and the butter. Cover closely and cook briefly, so that the shreds are tender but still a little crisp. Strain off the small amount of carrot juice into the coconut sauce, and add a tablespoon of carrot, swirling it round.

Finally deep-fry the fish until it is nicely browned: beware of over-cooking. Arrange on a warm dish with potatoes and carrots. Pour on a little of the sauce, and serve the rest separately.

FILLETS OF SOLE WITH CREAM AND MUSHROOM SAUCE

This recipe is suitable for almost all fillets of white fish – although obviously with sole, turbot and John Dory or monkfish it will be better than with sea bream or cod. I make it often with fillets of chicken halibut, really fresh inshore fish, which is firm and not as dry as the huge halibut one sees occupying 1½ m (5 feet) of the counter. The recipe is variable – if you have no time to make some fish stock, use light chicken or veal stock. Instead of using parsley, you could flavour the sauce with nutmeg or mace.

Serves 6

1–1½ kg (2–3 lb) fish fillets or steaks
salt, pepper
4 heaped tablespoons finely chopped shallots or onions
250 g (8 oz) mushrooms, thinly sliced
parsley, finely chopped
225 ml (7½ fl oz) dry white wine
225 ml (7½ fl oz) fish stock*
butter
100 ml (3½ fl oz) double cream
lemon quarters

Season the fish with salt and pepper. Put the shallots or onion, mushrooms and some parsley into a buttered ovenproof dish, season, and place the fish fillets on top. Pour on the wine and stock, and dab small amounts of butter over the fish. Bake at gas 5, 190°C (375°F), for about 20 minutes, but check after 15 minutes – the length of time required will depend on the fish's texture and the thickness of the pieces. Transfer the cooked fish to a warm serving plate. Pour everything else into a pan, and reduce by hard boiling to a strongly flavoured concentrated sauce. Stir in the cream, and cook again for a few moments. Correct the seasoning, beat in a few tablespoons of butter, and pour over the fish. Sprinkle with parsley, tuck lemon quarters round the edges, and serve.

GRILLED SOLE

Choose fish of about 250–300 g (8–10 oz), and allow one for each person (reflect that you will be saving money on sauce and garnishing). They need to be skinned both sides, the heads left on.

Brush with butter – clarified butter* gives the best results in colour and flavour – and grill for about 5 minutes a side. Time depends, obviously, on the thickness rather than the weight of the fish. Do not salt before grilling, but serve with two or three pats of savoury butter* arranged down the centre of each sole. The usual one is maître d'hôtel* (parsley and lemon), but you might like to try something different for a change. The butter, melting in the heat of the fish, forms a small amount of concentrated sauce which gives all the seasoning required.

Sometimes grilled sole is served with a sauce, a proper sauce with a pronounced flavour.

LEMON OR TORBAY SOLE WITH PARMESAN

This recipe is intended for proper sole, Dover sole, but to me so good a fish is not improved by the strength of Parmesan cheese. I find the method more suitable for the second and third ranks of flatfish, where extra interest is needed to compensate for the fact that they are not Dover sole. The idea is a simple one, and can be adapted to several fish or one or two large ones.

Switch on the grill and leave it to warm up while you cook the fish. Skin and clean them if the fishmonger has not done so already. Flour them lightly and fry in butter on both sides until they are pale golden brown. Pour into the pan enough fish, shellfish or chicken stock to come 5 mm (scant ¼ inch) up the sides of the pan. Complete the cooking at a steady boil, so that the stock reduces a little: do not overcook the fish which should remain slightly pink at the bone.

Scatter the fish with a layer of grated Parmesan cheese, not too thickly. Baste with stock, being careful not to dislodge the cheese. Put under the grill until the cheese melts. Baste again. Put back for the cheese to colour lightly, and baste again. Put back for the cheese to turn an appetizing but pale brown. The basting will have given the cheese a juicy, shiny appearance. There will be little stock left.

PAUPIETTES DE SOLES SOPHIE

The simple method of baking sole in the oven (or poaching it), can be elaborated into the favourite restaurant dish of Paupiettes de soles. Fillets, spread with some delicious mixture, are rolled into a neat shape and cooked in white wine, or wine and stock: the cooking liquor is finally used in the making of a creamy sauce. Although such dishes look pretty and often taste agreeable, I do confess to a preference for sole on the bone; it keeps more of its natural flavour when cooked that way. But I make an exception for this recipe from *Les Recettes Secrètes des Meilleurs Restaurants de France*. At first the title and ingredients were irresistible; then I found that the smoked salmon adds a most delicious flavour to the sauce, an unexpected piquancy.

Here you have the basic recipe for all paupiettes of fish; it can be adapted to humble herring fillets or varied to make many dishes of sole, lemon sole and turbot. The fish bones can be used to make a little stock to go with the white wine when a larger amount of sauce is required.

Serves 4

8 fillets of sole
salt, pepper
30 g (1 oz) butter
125 ml (4 fl oz) dry white wine – Chablis or Sancerre
1 large egg yolk
1½ generous tablespoons single cream

SALMON BUTTER
60–90 g (2–3 oz) smoked salmon
30 g (1 oz) butter, softened
salt, pepper, lemon juice

MUSHROOM DUXELLES
250 g (8 oz) mushrooms, chopped
30 g (1 oz) butter
salt, pepper, lemon juice
1 generous tablespoons double cream

First make the salmon butter. Reduce the smoked salmon to a purée in a liquidizer with the butter. Season to taste with salt, pepper and lemon juice.

Season the cut side of each sole fillet; spread with salmon butter and roll up – use cocktail sticks to keep the fillets in shape. Butter an oval ovenproof dish and place the rolled fillets in it, packed closely together, side by side. Pour the white wine over them. Bring the liquid to the boil, cover with aluminium foil, and either place in a moderate oven for up to 10 minutes (gas 4, 180 °C/350 °F) or leave to simmer gently on top of the stove for 5–7 minutes, turning the paupiettes once. Whichever method you use, do not overcook the fish.

Meanwhile cook the mushrooms quickly in the butter. Season with salt, pepper and lemon juice. Remove from the heat, stir in the cream and put onto a warm serving dish.

Pour cooking liquid off the sole into a saucepan, and reduce it by half. Beat the egg yolks and cream together, stir a tablespoon or two of the reduced liquid into this mixture; return to the saucepan and cook slowly without boiling until thick. Place paupiettes on the mushrooms, coat them with the sauce and serve. At the Domaine de la Tortinière at Montbazon, where this dish is on the menu, small fish shapes are cut out of a piece of smoked salmon and used to garnish the paupiettes.

SEVICHE OF SOLE WITH SCALLOPS

Serves 6

6 fillets of sole, skinned
4 scallops, white part only
175 ml (6 fl oz) fresh lime or lemon juice
2 hot red chillis, sliced
salt, freshly ground black pepper
1 medium red onion or *sweet Spanish onion, thinly sliced*
1 red and 1 yellow pepper, seeded, thinly sliced
1 small clove of garlic, crushed
5 tablespoons sunflower oil
1 large ripe avocado pear
1 good handful of lettuce leaves
3 limes, thinly sliced

Cut the sole into diagonal strips and put into a bowl. Slice each scallop disc into three or more rounds and place evenly over the sole. Pour over the lime or lemon juice. Scatter the chillis over the fish and season. Cover and leave for an hour in the refrigerator. Turn the pieces gently, cover again and leave for a further hour, or until both sole and scallops are opaque.

Meanwhile, season the onion and peppers. Mix the garlic with the oil. Peel, stone and slice the avocado and pour the oil over it, with seasoning and a little of the citrus juice from the fish.

Wash, dry and place the salad leaves at one end of a serving platter. Drain the fish and avocado and arrange them attractively with the pieces of vegetable and slices of lime on the platter.

SOLE À LA BONNE FEMME

Although this and the following are two of the classic recipes for sole as given by Escoffier, they can equally well be used for other firm fish of quality. By this I mean turbot, or chicken halibut, or John Dory, which all have something of the firm, well-divided flesh which makes the sole such a desirable fish. It can also be used for lesser lights, lemon sole, flounders, brill and so on, but there is always something disappointing in the unresistant softness of their flesh.

Serves 2

1 chopped shallot
½ teaspoon finely chopped parsley
60 g (2 oz) mushrooms, chopped
1 large sole about 375–400 g (12–14 oz), cleaned and skinned
60 ml (2 fl oz) dry white wine
salt, pepper
juice of ½ lemon
3 tablespoons butter
1 tablespoon plain flour

Rub an ovenproof oval dish with buttered paper. Put shallot, parsley and mushrooms over the base in an even layer and lay the sole on top. Pour the wine and the same amount of hot water over it, and season with salt, pepper and lemon juice. Cover with foil, and bake in a moderate oven, gas 4, 180 °C (350 °F) for 5 minutes. Meanwhile mash up one-third of the butter with the flour, to make beurre manié, and add it in little pieces to the sole liquor. Return to the oven until the sole is cooked – about 10 minutes, or a little longer.

Transfer the sole to a warm serving dish. Whisk the remaining butter into the cooking juices and pour over the sole. Put under a hot grill for a few minutes to brown lightly.

SOLE À LA FERMIÈRE

Fish cooked in red wine (in the style of the farmer's wife) – another myth tumbles to the ground. Drink the rest of the bottle with the sole.

Serves 2

1 shallot, chopped
½ teaspoon chopped parsley
1 sprig of thyme
½ bay leaf
175 g (6 oz) mushrooms
1 large sole about 375–400 g (12–14 oz)
175 ml (6 fl oz) red wine
salt, pepper
75 g (2½ oz) butter
1 teaspoon plain flour

Grease an oval flameproof dish, and put in the shallot, parsley, thyme and bay leaf. Chop 60 g (2 oz) of the mushrooms, and add them. Lay the sole on top, pour in the wine, and add seasoning. Cover and cook gently on top of the stove until the sole is cooked. Meanwhile, slice the remaining mushrooms neatly and cook them in 30 g (1 oz) of the butter, tossing them about so that they are golden but still firm and in no danger of being overcooked. Arrange them round the edge of an oval serving dish, and place the cooked sole in the middle. Keep it warm while you finish the sauce. Boil it down to half quantity. Mash together the flour with an equal amount of butter to make a beurre manié and add it to the sauce in pieces. When the sauce is ready, whisk in the remaining butter off the heat, and strain it over the fish. Place under a hot grill for a moment or two to glaze.

SOLE À LA MEUNIÈRE

The miller has rarely enjoyed the respectful admiration of his fellow citizens. (Old remarks such as : 'Hair grows in the palm of an honest miller', were brought up to date not so long ago by an actress who described her ex-boss, owner of many flour mills and cinemas, as having 'the sack in one hand and corn in the other'.) But the miller's wife, *la meunière*, is another matter. In cooking at least her reputation is high. What could be more delicious than a fresh trout or sole, dipped in flour and fried golden brown in butter?

It is the ideal method to show off a fine, fresh fish and was invented, so the story goes, at Royat, near Clermont Ferrand, at the mill which is now an hotel, La Belle Meunière.

Sole meunière is not the dish for a large party, as it needs last minute attention: keep it as a special treat for 2 or 4 people. Although it is basically a simple dish, there is a snag. Butter burns at a low temperature. If you don't want your beautiful fish to come to table with a covering of black flecks, you must clarify the butter first, *see* p. 14.

Serves 4

125 g (4 oz), slightly salted butter
4 whole sole, skinned or 8 large fillets
seasoned flour
sprigs of parsley
lemon quarters
125 g (4 oz) unsalted butter

Clarify 125 g (4 oz) of the butter. Turn the fillets or skinned sole in seasoned flour and shake off the surplus. Fry until golden brown in the clarified butter, turning once. Remove to a hot serving dish and garnish with the parsley sprigs and lemon quarters. Wipe the pan out with kitchen paper. Put the unsalted butter into the pan and rapidly bring it to a golden brown foam; it should now smell deliciously of hazelnuts. Pour this over the fish and rush it to the table. Not a dish to be kept hanging around.

SOLE À LA ROUENNAISE

This sole in the Rouen style is another exception to the rule of white wine with fish. You will not find that the robust flavour of red wine spoils the delicate sole and shellfish.

Serves 2

1 large sole, skinned
125 ml (4 fl oz) red wine
2 shallots, finely chopped
125 g (4 oz) butter
12 large mussels
12 oysters (if possible)
12 cooked prawns or shrimps in their shells
125 g (4 oz) button mushrooms
1 egg yolk
salt, pepper

Put the sole into a shallow pan. Add wine, shallots and 30 g (1 oz) of butter. Simmer until cooked.

Meanwhile open the mussels in the usual way (p. 239). Discard their shells and strain their cooking liquor into a bowl. Open the oysters (p. 254); simmer them in their own liquor for a few moments until their edges just start to curl. Strain the cooking juice into the mussel liquor. Peel eight of the prawns or shrimps. Cook the mushrooms in 30 g (1 oz) of the butter. These mussels, oysters, prawns or shrimps and mushrooms are the garnishes for the sole. Keep them warm. The mussel and oyster juice will be required for the sauce.

Remove the cooked sole to a hot serving dish. (Pour its cooking juices into the mussel and oyster juices.) Arrange the garnishes around the sole and keep everything warm.

Pour the fish juices into a pan and reduce to a fairly strong-flavoured liquid. Beat the egg yolk with a little of this liquid, then tip it back into the pan and stir over a low heat until the sauce thickens (*do not boil, or it will curdle*). Off the heat, whisk in the remaining butter, season and strain the sauce over the sole. Place the four unshelled prawns in the centre, and serve.

SOLE MEUNIÈRE AUX POIREAUX

Proust was inordinately fond of fried sole; indeed, it was the only dish he ever finished during the last years of his life.

Proust: My dear Céleste, I think I could manage a fried sole. How quickly do you think I could have one, if it's not too much trouble?
Céleste: Straightaway, Monsieur.
Proust: How kind you are, Céleste.

And good, kind, patient Céleste would rush out to a fishmonger's nearby in the place Saint-Augustin, run back with the sole, cook it and present it to Proust on a clean, doubled napkin – to soak up any fat that might remain – with four lemon halves, one at each napkin corner.

Had Proust been alive today, and a young man, he would I think have appreciated a new French version of Sole meunière, a version with lightly cooked, shredded leeks, not too many, just enough to make the fish even more appetizing than usual. The two secrets are clarified butter and finely cut leek. Other fish can be substituted, obviously other flatfish, from turbot down to plaice, or small filleted whiting.

Serves 4

250 g (8 oz) butter, clarified*
1½ kg (3 lb) skinned sole, preferably two large ones
seasoned flour
cayenne pepper
4 medium leeks, trimmed to their white stalks
salt
lemon quarters (optional)

Strain the clarified butter into two fish pans, large enough to accommodate one sole each, with room to spare. It is helpful to be able to cook all the fish at the same time: see the note at the end if not.

Turn the fish in seasoned flour, to which you have added cayenne according to taste: I add enough just to make the flour slightly pink. Heat the pans, shake any surplus flour from the fish, and put in to cook – not too fast. After 3–4 minutes, according to the thickness of the fish, see if it is nicely browned underneath. Turn it over, if so, otherwise leave a little longer.

As it cooks, slice the leeks thinly so that they tumble into green and white shreds.

Add the leeks to the turned fish, and stir them about carefully so that they cook lightly in the butter. They should not entirely lose their crispness, neither should they brown – a few patches of light gold are all right, but no more. Salt the leeks, and leave them in the pan for a minute as you remove the sole to its warmed serving dish. Remove the leeks with a slotted spoon and put them round the sole in little piles or in a circle. Arrange the lemon quarters at intervals among the leeks. Serve immediately with bread, and a dry white wine.

NOTE Unfortunately the new French cookery depends for its light effect on brief cooking and prompt service. Easy to manage if you have help in the kitchen that you can trust, or if you always eat in the kitchen and do not mind leaving the table to cook between courses. If your problem is the lack of a second fish pan, remember that the sole will survive waiting around better than the leek shreds. Brown the sole in turn, using half the butter, over a slightly higher heat (golden-brown, not black-brown), and put them on their dish in the oven set at gas 2, 150 °C (300 °F) to complete their cooking while you cook the leeks in their juices, refreshed with the remaining butter. If something is served before the sole, this really must be done between courses.

SOLE MOUSSELINE WITH BUTTER AND CREAM SAUCE

I think it was Drew Smith, editor of the *Good Food Guide*, who remarked that Dover sole brought out the worst in chefs: he was thinking of the enormous list of sole recipes in Escoffier's *Guide Culinaire* I suspect. Reading it, you do feel that the fish has been submerged in champagne, cheese sauce, grapes, potato balls, cucumber balls, turned mushrooms, oysters, truffles, aubergines, sliced oranges, crayfish, smoked salmon, asparagus, spaghetti and lobster sauce, until it seems to have no existence of its own except in the floury hands of the miller's wife. But then she had nothing to cook it with but butter. Temptation was not her problem, temptation of that kind at least.

Today, chefs have calmed down and produce restrained dishes of sole that depend on good fresh fish and a few simple ingredients of quality to set it off. In this, Colin Wood of the Old House Hotel in the Square at Wickham in Hampshire learned well from his training at the Box Tree at Ilkley (*see* their sole recipe on p. 394).

Serves 4

100 g (3–4 oz) filleted sole
2 medium eggs
150 ml (5 fl oz) double cream
salt, pepper
milk
parsley

SAUCE
125 ml (4 fl oz) dry white wine
125 ml (4 fl oz) white wine vinegar
½ medium onion, chopped
1 bay leaf
250 ml (8 fl oz) double cream
30 g (1 oz) butter
salt, pepper
shreds of carrot and leek

Chill the processor bowl or liquidizer. Chop sole roughly and reduce to a paste in the chilled processor or liquidizer. Add the eggs, and when everything is smooth, pour in the cream. Taste the mixture for seasoning. Turn into a bowl, cover and chill for 2 hours.

To make the sauce, reduce by two-thirds the wine and vinegar with the onion and bay leaf. Add the cream and boil 1 minute – keep tasting and remove the bay leaf before it becomes too strong. Beat in the butter and season to taste.

Boil the matchstick shreds of carrot for 1 minute, add the leek and return to the boil. Tip into a sieve and cool under the running tap. Keep on one side.

For the final cooking of the mousseline, prepare a shallow pan half full of milk and bring it to simmering point. Adjust the heat to keep it this way. Using two tablespoons, shape an 'egg' of mousseline and slip it into the milk to poach for 5 minutes turning it once. Do the same thing with the remaining mousseline, as quickly and neatly as you can, to give you 4 'eggs'.

Meanwhile, reheat the sauce gently and stir in the vegetable strips. Put each mousseline on a plate. Coat it with the sauce, which should run down on to the plate. Sprinkle the top with a pinch of parsley and serve immediately.

SOLE SUR LE PLAT

This is one of the simplest ways of cooking sole, baked in the oven, preferably with wine. There are many variations possible with this excellent method.

The recipes which follow are all for 2 people; they require a sole weighing about 500 g (1 lb).

> *1 large sole, skinned and trimmed*
> *salt, freshly ground black pepper*
> *nut of butter*
> *4 tablespoons dry white wine*
> *4 tablespoons fish stock**
> *juice of ½ lemon*
> *sprigs of cress*
> *1 handful of curly endive*
> *lemon wedges and strips of zest*

Rinse and dry the sole, then season it. Butter an ovenproof oval plate or dish and add the sole. Pour the wine and stock over it, with a few drops of the lemon juice. Bake in the oven preheated to gas 6, 200 °C (400 °F) for about 8 minutes, basting with the juices twice. (The sole should be almost done.) Taste the juices and add more lemon if necessary.

Put the sole under a very hot grill just to glaze the fish and complete the cooking. Transfer to a warmed plate and garnish with sprigs of cress, curly endive, lemon wedges and strips of zest.

VARIATIONS   The variations on this simple theme are endless: you can work up the juices with butter, or cream and butter. You can put the fish on to a bed of lightly cooked tomato with a little onion. Instead of the white wine and stock, you can use a splendid red Burgundy – omit the lemon, add a slice or two of onion and thicken the sauce lightly with beurre manié.

SOLE FLORENTINE   Bake the sole in fish fumet*, in a buttered dish. Spread a layer of cooked, well drained, and buttered spinach on a serving dish. Lay the sole on top. Cover with Mornay sauce*, then sprinkle on some grated cheese – Gruyère and Parmesan are best – and glaze under a hot grill.

SOLE SUR LE PLAT AUX MOULES   Open 600 ml (1 pt) of mussels in
the usual way (p. 239); remove from their shells. Use the strained
mussel liquor to replace the water in the Sole sur le plat recipe, and
add a shallot chopped almost to pulp. When the sole is cooked, place
the mussels round it and sprinkle the sole with a mixture of parsley
and white breadcrumbs. Cook a moment or two longer under the
grill and serve.

SOLE WITH CIDER

Our best meal of the tour of Great Britain whilst researching for
British Cookery, was at the Box Tree in Ilkley and was as good as any
I have had in France in recent years. We arrived on a pouring night,
feeling damp and sceptical. Kindly girls removed dripping umbrellas.
Warm Yorkshire voices sounded piquant and welcoming among the
treasures that Malcolm Reid and Colin Long had collected over
the years.

They started off nearly forty years ago with a snack bar in Leeds;
then came a tea-room in Ilkley which stretched and grew into the
sequence of rooms we see today like some fairy-tale cottage, small
outside, endless within. (Helen Avis now owns the restaurant.)

Here is one of their deceptively simple recipes to test your skill –
not just as a cook, but as a buyer of fish since you need sole from the
top of the catch.

Serves 2

750 g (1½ lb) sole, filleted
30 g (1 oz) butter
275 ml (9 fl oz) dry cider
90 ml (3 fl oz) water
2 rounded teaspoons plain flour
lemon juice, salt, pepper
2 rounded teaspoons chopped parsley
2 tablespoons single cream

Fold fillets over, skinned side under. Lay in an ovenproof dish rubbed
with a little of the butter. Pour on liquids, lay butter papers on top,
and poach in the oven preheated to gas 4, 180°C (350°F) for 12–
15 minutes. Keep an eye on it to avoid overcooking.

Meanwhile melt the rest of the butter in a small pan, stir in the
flour off the heat, then return to the heat and cook gently for
2 minutes, stirring. Set aside until the sole is ready, then strain the

liquor from the fish on to the butter and flour and cook the resulting sauce, stirring, until it loses any taste of flour. Season with a squeeze of lemon, salt and pepper. Add parsley and cream. Pour enough of the sauce over the sole fillets, arranged on a clean warm serving dish, to coat them nicely and serve at once.

SOLE WITH ORANGE SAUCE

Serves 6

2 large sweet oranges
juice of 1 lemon
3 large sole
salt, freshly ground black pepper, cayenne
300 ml (10 fl oz) fish stock*
150 ml (5 fl oz) dry white wine
6 tablespoons whipping cream
3 large egg yolks
175 g (6 oz) unsalted French butter
seasoned flour
parsley or chervil, chopped

With a zester remove the thin outer peel of one of the oranges. Reserve the fine shreds for the garnish. Squeeze both oranges and add the lemon juice.

Season the sole fillets, place them on a shallow dish and pour over half the citrus juice. Set aside for at least an hour.

To make the sauce: boil down the stock and wine to 150 ml (5 fl oz). Add the remaining citrus juice and boil again briefly. Stir in the cream, boil for 1 minute and then, off the heat, whisk in the egg yolks. Return to a very low heat and beat in two-thirds of the butter, bit by bit. Season to taste, pour into a sauceboat and keep warm.

Drain the fish, pat dry with kitchen paper and flour lightly. Cook gently in the remaining butter, then transfer it to a hot serving dish. Scatter with the herbs and orange zest and serve with the sauce.

VOL-AU-VENT À LA NORMANDE

This is a fine dish which can be adjusted to suit the resources of your fishmonger. Turbot, brill or John Dory could be used instead of sole. Prawns instead of oysters (include their shells when making stock for the sauce Normande).

Serves 6

500–750 g (1–1½ lb) sole or other white fish
dry cider or dry white wine
12 oysters or 18 cooked prawns or shrimps
1 kg (2 lb) mussels
sauce Normande*, made very thick
250 g (8 oz) mushrooms
60 g (2 oz) butter
parsley, chopped
1 large or 12 small baked vol-au-vent cases

Poach the sole or other fish in just enough cider or wine to cover.

Open the oysters and mussels in the usual way (*see* pp. 254 and 239); add juice with the sole juices to the sauce Normande. Cook the mushrooms gently in the butter: strain off the juice and add it to the sauce.

Divide the cooked sole or white fish into suitably small pieces. Reheat in the completed sauce with the oysters or prawns, and the mussels and mushrooms. Lastly mix in some parsley. Pour into the reheated vol-au-vent case(s) and serve immediately.

This is a recipe which can be prepared entirely in advance, apart from the final reheating.

SPANISH MACKEREL *see* MACKEREL

SPRAT *see* A FEW WORDS ABOUT . . . SPRAT

† SQUID & CUTTLEFISH

Loligo spp. & *Sepia officinalis*

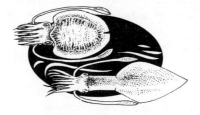

Although octopus and cuttlefish and squid are much eaten in southern Europe, the cephalopod most usually encountered at the fishmonger's shop, whether in Britain or the States, is the squid. It is tender and delicious and easy to cook. Some squid are tiny, the body part about 7 cm (3 inches) long: they are the ones for quick frying. Others are most substantial, the body part over 12½ cm (5 inches) long: they are the ones for stuffing and stewing and gentle frying. Whatever the size, they will have two triangular finny flaps, attached to the body. Unless the fishmonger has removed it, there will also be a fine purplish red veil of delicate transparency: this, alas, has to be removed as its appearance is spoiled by cooking, though it is not inedible. Tentacles and 'arms' tassel out from the head, ten of them, if you care to count. All in all a strange and beautiful creature.

Or don't you agree? Perhaps the appearance is a little daunting to the cook the first time he or she encounters squid. Even more daunting is the sight of a frozen block of 14 kg (28 lb) or even 30 kg (60 lb) of squid, looking like a compressed Last Judgement. Some fishmongers have to buy them this way. They are tender and good, but not so good as fresh ones, which may look inky and muddled by comparison.

The first encounter with a squid can be memorable and messy. Mine happened years ago, in 1959, when squid was still an exotic, something one ate in Greek-Cypriot restaurants in London. Yet we saw this creature on top of a pile of crabs on the quay at Seahouses in Northumberland. It looked improbable. Surely it should have come out of the Mediterranean, not the bitter North Sea.

We took it back to the cottage in Craster where we were staying. We looked at it. Tentacles, bag of a body – where did one start? How could so rubbery an object be transformed into our favourite Kalamarakia stew? We rang the restaurant where we had often eaten it. Through the crackling of a bad line, we heard the manager Epaminondas, a patient man, give the simple instructions of this recipe. We followed them and the flavour was fine, just right, but that squid must have been the old man of the Farne Islands. It could have done with a high proportion of the ninety-nine bashings that, it is said, are necessary before it is tender enough to eat.

That was an unfair representative of the squid which do, in fact, flourish sweetly and tenderly quite far north in Atlantic and Pacific waters. I don't understand why they aren't a regular part of our diet, but until recently they seem to have been regarded only as bait for other fish. The fact that squid are now seen more and more is mainly thanks to foreigners, at least in Britain, and to such popularizers as Isaac Cronin in the States who has fished squid in the Monterey Bay and written a book about it, *The International Squid Book*. He notes that the first American squid festival took place the year before in Santa Cruz. The species that he mainly writes about is *Loligo opalescens*, which is similar to *Loligo pealei* eaten on the East Coast, and to the two species favoured in the Mediterranean and northern Europe. What we do not have in Europe, it seems, is the Grande Calamari of Mexican waters, that is tenderized before sale and sold in flat fillets or steaks.

Mr Cronin wisely points out that 'squid protein becomes firm rapidly and then turns chewy until long cooking breaks down the muscle. Much of the squid's reputation as a tough food comes from lack of knowledge of this simple fact. Sautés should be cooked no longer than three minutes and stews no less than twenty minutes.'

This is an opinion I respect, but I am not totally convinced. Those squid rings that form part of the Greek *meze*, for instance: they are best regarded as a form of marine chewing gum, to be nibbled at steadily while the flavour lasts, then to be politely discarded rather than swallowed. For this reason I never fry squid rings at home, only the youngest, tenderest squid.

At their best, nothing in the vast trawl of fish from the sea can compare with the cephalopods – squid, cuttlefish and octopus – for the combination of sweetness and delicate bite. Nothing else has their power to colour a dish all the deepening shades of brown to sepia – from the Greek name for cuttlefish, that once was the sole source of that colour from its abundant ink. A sepia that seems at times black in its velvety depths. I much enjoy dishes that exploit this romantic quality. It reminds me of licking the paintbrush when I was a child, though mostly its light flat taste is obscured by other items in the dish. In the case of squid, this scholarly note is taken further by the transparent piece of plastic, a rudimentary shell, in the mantle or body sack that is just the shape of an old-fashioned pen nib.

Squid seems to be a variant of the word squirt, from the cephalopod habit of blasting out a cloud of ink to discourage its predators. People used to think this was purely a smokescreen behind which the poor creature might make a retreat. Now they say that the idea is to foil the attacker into thinking that the ink itself is the prey. Presumably it then wears itself out stupidly gnashing and lungeing at an incorporeal darkness that is only a semblance of the creature. This is a psychological nicety which, although it has led to an admiration of cephalopods as the intellectuals of the sea, Mensa level, Oxbridge and Ivy League, need not, I think, detain the cook.

What is more interesting from the culinary standpoint is the bodily form of the squid, which provides a convenient bag for a stuffing. The cuttlefish derives its name from this – like cod, and, more understandably codpiece, it comes from the Norse *kaute*, meaning a bag. This, however, is no good to the cook since the bag must be slit to free it from the chalky oval that takes the place of the transparent pen of the squid; sometimes you see these light dry shapes in the tideline on a beach in Europe, or in a bird cage for the canary or budgerigar to peck at. This means that cuttlefish are confined to soups and stews – when full use can be made of its copious inky resources – and stir-fried dishes.

Should you be housekeeping in the Mediterranean, look out for tiny *supions* or *soupions*, squat and minuscule cuttlefish that need little preparation beyond removing the small cuttle and rinsing – but check with the fishmonger in case he has already done this. They taste particularly good when cooked with rice (*see* Arroz nero), or deep fried, in which case, half-cover and stand back to avoid the splutters.

The great areas for squid cookery are southern Europe and the Far East. In both its sweetness is underlined, inevitably by tomato in Spain, Portugal and the Mediterranean. The Japanese use mirin and sugar with soy sauce, depending on whether they marinade and grill little pieces on wooden skewers, or slice it into translucent water-lilies to decorate a dish of sashimi with its sweet and fiery sauce. Chinese cooks slice the squid bag into two triangles, score them in a diaper pattern and stir-fry these pieces with chilli, garlic and coriander – the bitterness enhances the sweetness, too – with extra embellishments such as peanuts and sweet pepper. Tiny squid may be stuffed simply with pork seasoned with coriander and soy, and then poached tenderly in clear chicken soup. In South-East Asia, coconut milk underlines the sweetness, so too does hot chilli (*see* Sri Owen's red hot sambal on p. 403).

HOW TO PREPARE SQUID AND CUTTLEFISH

Work close to the sink and have paper towels and a couple of bowls handy, for the different pieces.

After rinsing the squid, lay them on a board parallel to each other, tentacles all one way. Squeeze gently behind the hard part of each head, so that the round 'beaks' pop out between the tentacles. Throw these away. Now cut off the cluster of tentacles and arms so that they are still just held together by a ring. Remove any fine purplish skin and put the clusters in one of the bowls.

The next stage is to pull the heads gently away from the body sacks. Much of the soft innards will come away with them. You will be able to see a shadowed silver streak: this is the ink sac. Gently slip a small knife beneath it and ease it free. Put it into the other bowl. The rest of the head and innards can be kept for stock.

From the body sacks, hook out with your finger the transparent plastic-looking pen nib, if it has not come away already with the innards.

Now rinse the body sacks, pulling away the fine purple veil of a skin (deep-frozen squid may already have been skinned), and check that the inside is completely empty. Pat the sacks dry. At this stage, or earlier, you can cut away the two finny flaps. They are often chopped with the tentacles.

The body sacks can be left as they are for stuffing, cut across into rings or slit into two triangles and then scored in a diaper pattern, depending on the recipe you intend to follow.

If you intend to use the ink sacs, you can just leave them as they are and add them to the sauce if it will be sieved eventually: crushing them with a little water first helps to release all the ink quickly, but is not strictly necessary. If the sauce will not be sieved, put a sieve across the pan, crush the sacs with a little water or stock and tip them into the sieve, pressing down to make sure the ink goes through either with a pestle or a wooden spoon.

Cuttlefish are prepared in the same way, except that you will find it more difficult to remove the chalky oval part. If it has to be cut away, you may well slit the body sack: it can be sewn up with button thread if you want to stuff the cuttlefish, but this spoils the appearance. Cuttlefish produce more ink than squid, so be prepared.

BLACK RICE (Arroz negro)

This is a dramatic-looking dish of Spanish cookery that I received from Merce Navarro, chef-proprietor of the Roig Robi restaurant in Barcelona. There you may sample Catalan and Spanish food at its finest, cooked with great skill and attention to the modern style.

Serves 4–6

600 g (1¼ lb) small to medium-sized squid
1 medium onion, chopped
olive oil
150 g (5 oz) skinned, seeded, chopped tomato
1 large clove garlic, crushed, skinned, chopped
400 g (14 oz) Spanish or Italian rice, suitable for risotto
600 ml (1 pt) good fish stock*
salt, pepper

Prepare the squid as described earlier in this section, setting the ink sacs carefully aside in a basin with a little water. Chop the tentacles, cut the main part into four or more convenient size pieces.

Cook the onion in a little olive oil, slowly. When it is soft, add the tomato and cook to a thick purée. Add the squid pieces, the garlic and the rice, stirring them about in the oil for a minute or two.

Remove the pan from the heat, put a sieve over the top. Crush the ink sacs into their water, tip the whole thing into the sieve and, adding stock as you go, push through as much inkiness as you can manage. Put the pan back on the heat and simmer for 15 minutes, uncovered, or half-covered, until the liquid is absorbed. At this point, the top of the rice will be pocked with small craters. If the rice is still too firm, you will need to add extra stock or water. When it is just tender, jam the lid on the pan with a cloth, and leave for 5 minutes, over the lowest possible heat. The rice then steams to a melting tenderness. Season, if necessary.

Serve hot on its own, or with a bowl of garlic mayonnaise*.

CACCIUCCO ALLA LIVORNESE

Cacciucco is the fish stew of Leghorn and the coast thereabouts – the north of Italy's west coast. It is black, black as Chinese ink, and the first time I encountered it only a well-drilled upbringing prevented me from asking for something else – and from missing one of the best experiences in European food. Family friends, the Gisalbertis, descended on Florence where I was a student. They took me to Viareggio for the day. At a small restaurant in a back street at lunchtime this strange dish appeared. Being poor I was excessively hungry, which no doubt helped my manners, but I dipped my spoon in carefully. Cacciucco turned out to be the best thing I had ever eaten. Afterwards we sat on a fallen pine tree on the beach to digest our food. We looked towards the thunderous Carrara mountains, white against purple grey, as Mario talked about the Etruscans and their strange, hidden gaiety. And about this soup.

Even if you are not in Italy, you can make this soup with a fair degree of success since its dominant notes are provided by cuttlefish and squid; small octopus if you can find one is also a good idea. Shellfish provide more sweetness and a pink contrast to the dark soup, with some firm white fish – monkfish, whiting, John Dory, red mullet or gurnard – for the cheaper bulk of the stew. As with so many fish stews and soups, aim to get the liquid part right first, properly flavoured, strained and the right consistency. In it you poach the fish. This is quite the opposite technique to a meat stew or soup.

And as with so many Mediterranean dishes, be prepared to reinforce our pallid northern tomatoes. Dried tomatoes do this very well as their flavour has a deeper subtlety than tomato purée or concentrate. In an emergency have recourse to a splash of vinegar and a couple of lumps of sugar, or even to Heinz tomato ketchup.

750 g (1½ lb) squid and cuttlefish
½–1 kg (1–2 lb) mixed lobster, langoustines, prawns, shrimps, mussels, as available
1½ kg (3 lb) mixed white fish – hake, John Dory, weever, whiting, monkfish, rascasse, gurnard, red mullet, as available
salt, pepper
olive oil
1 large onion, finely chopped
1 medium carrot, finely chopped
2 stalks celery, finely chopped
300 ml (10 fl oz) red wine
bouquet of 2 bay leaves, 4 sprigs thyme, 6 sprigs parsley
1 fresh hot chilli
3 cloves garlic, quartered
1 kg (2 lb) tomatoes, skinned, chopped
sugar, tomato concentrate or dried tomatoes
12–16 slices toasted or fried bread

NOTE   Oily fish are not suitable, e.g. herring and mackerel.

Prepare and slice the squid and cuttlefish as described at the beginning of this section, keeping the ink sacs carefully in a bowl, slicing tentacles and body sacks, and retaining the soft inner debris.

As you are unlikely to buy most shellfish uncooked, remove the shells and put them with the squid debris. Open the mussels in the usual way (p. 239) discard the shells and strain the liquid over the debris, etc. Keep all cooked shellfish together on a plate: only lobster needs slicing.

Clean the mixed fish. Cut off any heads and put with the debris. Discard the innards, apart from the red mullet livers which can be put with the shellfish. Slice the fish into pieces that can conveniently be eaten with a spoon, putting the firmer fish on one plate, the rest on another. Season them. This can be done an hour or so in advance.

Prepare the soup in a large saucepan. Heat enough oil to cover the base and brown the vegetables lightly. Pour in the wine and boil down by half. Add the bouquet, chilli, garlic and tomatoes; then the debris of the shellfish, squid and other fish with the mussel liquid, plus a good litre (1¾ pt) of water. Boil slowly for 30 minutes, removing the chilli when the liquid is as piquant as you like it. Meanwhile pound the ink sacs with a little water to release the ink. Add to the soup, give it 10 more minutes and then sieve into a bowl, pushing through enough vegetable to give some consistency. Taste and season, boil down a little if the flavour needs concentrating. Reinforce it with a little sugar, or with tomato concentrate or one or two pieces of dried tomato, chopped up, if your tomatoes were on the poor side. Get the soup right at this stage, then pour it into a serving pot and leave it to brew gently over a low heat. Keep it very hot without further boiling or even simmering.

About 20 minutes before the meal, attend finally to the fish. Fry the cuttlefish and squid in olive oil, then add them into the soup when they are nicely coloured and almost tender. In the same pan, cook the firm fish for 5 minutes, keeping it on the go, then add the tender fish. When they are all just cooked, transfer to the soup. Finally add the shellfish to the soup, give it 5 minutes to heat through, and then serve.

Put the toast or fried bread into people's bowls and ladle the Cacciucco on top, aiming for an equitable distribution of the fish.

SAMBAL GORENG CUMI-CUMI

This recipe for squid in a red hot sauce comes from Sri Owen's *Indonesian Food and Cookery*. She says that if you are nervous of the heat of 6 large red chillis, substitute some sweet red pepper; the sauce must be a fine robust colour. The ingredients are available from oriental stores, and Macadamia nuts can be used instead of kemiri.

Serves 4 as a main dish, or 6 as a side dish

1 kg (2 lb) squid
1 tablespoon white vinegar
5 kemiri (candlenuts)
6 large red fresh chillis, seeded
6 shallots or 1 onion
1 slice trassi or blachan (optional)
2 teaspoons powdered ginger
¼ teaspoon ground cumin
¼ teaspoon turmeric
¼ teaspoon powdered lemon grass
2 teaspoons peanut oil
3 tablespoons tamarind water
1 teaspoon brown sugar
salt

Clean the squid, keeping only the body sack which should be cut into small squares and the tentacles and arms which should be cut into 1-cm (½-inch) lengths. Mix the vinegar with 600 ml (1 pt) water, stir in the squid and straightaway tip the whole thing into a sieve over the sink. Leave the squid to drain.

Pound the next ingredients down to and including the lemon grass into a paste. Fry it in the oil in a sauté pan for 1 minute, put in the squid and tamarind water and cook for 3 minutes more. Add sugar, some salt and 150 ml (5 fl oz) water, and cook for about 5 more minutes, stirring often. Serve hot, with rice.

SQUID AND COCONUT CURRY

A somewhat westernized form of cooking squid, this makes a most delightful dish – so long as you like coconut. The recipe works well for firm white fish such as halibut, weever and monkfish, and for tuna or swordfish or tope.

Serves 4–6

1 kg (2 lb) medium-sized squid
peanut oil

175 g (6 oz) chopped shallot or red onion
4 cloves garlic, finely chopped
2 tablespoons chopped Macadamia nuts
3 teaspoons lightly crushed coriander seeds
1 fresh chilli pepper, seeded, chopped, plus 1 whole chilli, seeded
1 teaspoon ground turmeric
1 teaspoon grated ginger
1 stalk lemon grass or a little lemon juice
4–6 tablespoons tamarind water
scant ½ litre (16 fl oz) coconut milk
salt

Clean the squid, saving the body sack (cut into squares) and the tentacles and arms (cut into short lengths). Fry them briefly in a little oil to colour them lightly.

If you like the sauce very smooth, process or blend in a liquidizer the shallot or onion, garlic, nuts and coriander; fry the resulting paste. Or fry just the shallots or onions on their own, adding garlic, nuts, and coriander when they are soft. Add the remaining spices and tamarind water. Simmer it all together for a minute or two, then put in the squid. When it is almost tender, add the coconut milk. As the dish cooks, taste it and remove the whole chilli when it is as hot as you like it and add salt, if necessary. The sauce should end up thick and spicy: if it seems to be thickening too fast before the squid is done, add a little water and cover it.

Serve with rice and sticks of cucumber.

STUFFED SQUID IN ITS OWN INK (Calamares en su tinta)

To me, this is the perfect way of cooking squid. It reminds me of endless summer lunches in the sun, under the lime tree, usually on Thursdays, the day after Montoire market, because squid keeps reasonably well in the refrigerator and this is essentially a lunchtime dish; delicacies such as weever or miniature sole belonged to Wednesday night. I should qualify this picture by remarking that if you are nimble with your fingers and unlikely to be interrupted, you could make the dish on a small scale, with small squid, as the first course for a dinner: the secret of success is to allow room for the stuffing to swell and to make sure the cooking temperature is below boiling point, barely shouldering a simmer.

The particular blend of ingredients brings out the sweetness of squid, shows it off with sharp and savoury contrasts. The resistant texture of squid is reduced to an agreeable bite. Variations on the theme are numerous. I give some of them below.

Serves 6

6 medium squid, with bags measuring 15 cm (6 inches)
8 tablespoons white or red wine
olive oil
3 medium onions, chopped small
3–4 cloves garlic, crushed, skinned, chopped small
60 g (2 oz) serrano or Bayonne or other smoked ham, chopped
90 g (3 oz) fresh breadcrumbs
1 small bunch of parsley chopped
salt, pepper, cayenne
250 g (8 oz) firm, ripe tomato, skinned, chopped
small fried triangles of bread or fried, round slices of French bread to garnish

Prepare the squid as described above, putting the ink sacs into a basin with just under half the wine. Crush together so that the ink runs, and then set aside.

Chop the squid tentacles and side flaps. Discard the rest of the head, and peel off the fine purple membrane from the cleaned bags.

To make the stuffing, heat up enough oil to cover the base of a wide shallow pan. In it, soften the onion with the garlic. When soft and yellow, remove half the onion to keep for the sauce. To the pan add the chopped tentacles, etc. As they begin to brown lightly, put in the ham. Mix the breadcrumbs with the rest of the wine and stir the resulting, rather lumpy paste into the pan as well. Cook briefly, add parsley and seasonings, then cool slightly. With a teaspoon, put the stuffing into the squid bags, leaving them one-third empty. Take a stitch in the top of each bag, with a wooden cocktail stick, to close them.

For the sauce, put the onion you set aside into a heavy shallow pan or earthenware serving dish. Add the tomato, any left-over stuffing and seasoning. Lay in the squid, top to tail. Put in a little water to bring the liquid level to the top of the squid, and check seasoning. Simmer on top of the stove, or in the oven if it happens to be on at a moderate temperature. Turn the squid occasionally, with great care, and keep the heat down. Allow 30 to 45 minutes on top of the stove, longer in the oven, uncovered in either case, so that the sauce reduces.

Five minutes before serving the squid, sieve the ink into the sauce. You could also then sieve the sauce if you prefer to have it smooth.

Tuck the bread into the dish, round the side, and scatter the little white cushions of squid with a discreet amount of chopped parsley.

Chipirones a la bilbaina

Prepare the squid as above, retaining none of the ink. Make the stuffing as above, with the same ingredients. Stuff the squid, colour them lightly in a little olive oil and put into a pan or pot. For the sauce, you will need:

> cooked onion from the stuffing
> 500 g (1 lb) mussels, opened, their liquor strained
> lemon juice
> 2 medium tomatoes, skinned, seeded, chopped
> salt, pepper, cayenne
> a little fine chopped parsley

Put the onion, the mussel liquor, 2 teaspoons lemon juice and the tomatoes in with the squid. Cook gently as above. Sieve the sauce or process it, if you like. Check the seasoning and pour round the squid. Stir in the mussels, minus their shells, and heat through as briefly as possible. Sprinkle with parsley. Serve immediately, with bread.

Kalamarakia yemista

Prepare the squid in the usual way. Keep the ink for another dish. You will also need:

> 175 g (6 oz) chopped onion
> chopped tentacles and flaps from the squid
> olive oil
> 125 g (4 oz) brown or long grain rice
> 75 g (2½ oz) pine kernels
> 100 g (3½ oz) currants or raisins
> 1 small bunch of parsley, chopped
> salt, pepper
> 125 ml (4 fl oz) dry white or red wine
> 375 ml (12 fl oz) tomato juice
> 3 pieces dried tomato, chopped or tomato paste

Cook the onion and tentacles in the minimum of oil until soft. Stir in the rice, and 125 ml (4 fl oz) water. When the water is absorbed, add the pine kernels, currants or raisins and enough chopped parsley to make a good speckled effect. Season and stuff the squid, as above.

Brown the squid lightly in a little oil. Add wine, tomato juice, dried tomato or tomato paste. Keep the pan at a simmer, until the squid are tender. If the sauce reduces too fast, half-cover the pan and lower the heat. Add seasoning towards the end.

SUMMER BORSHCH WITH SQUID

Serves 6

500 g (1 lb) squid of medium size
fish stock or water, about 1½ litres (3 pt)
500 g (1 lb) beetroot, plus 1 extra
about 3 tablespoons red wine vinegar
2 medium carrots
1 small head of fennel or the heart of a small head of celery
2 ripe tomatoes, peeled, seeded, chopped
bundle of 6–8 spring onions, chopped
12 tiny new potatoes, scraped
125 g (4 oz) small courgettes, sliced diagonally
salt, pepper
3 cloves
bouquet garni including a sprig of dill
smetana or soured cream and finely chopped dill to garnish

Clean the squid, retaining the body sacks and tentacles and leaving them unsliced. If you have no fish stock, boil up the innards and heads with the water to give it a little flavour.

Keep any lively looking stalks and leaves from the beetroot. Peel and grate the extra beetroot into a small pan. Pour enough boiling water over it to cover completely and add 3 tablespoons of vinegar. Bring slowly to the boil, then cover and set aside to infuse for 20 minutes while you make the borshch: this is the brilliant coloured beetroot stock that you use at the end to revive the colour.

Peel the rest of the beetroot and grate it coarsely into matchstick shreds directly into a large pan. A mandolin is the ideal implement. Do the same with the carrots. Add the squid and cover with fish stock or water. Simmer for 20 minutes, removing the squid pieces when tender: slice them into strips and keep to one side. Add the rest of the vegetables to the pan with extra stock or water to keep them well covered as they cook. Slice the beetroot stalks and leaves and put them in as well, with all the seasonings. Simmer until the vegetable are just done, then put back the squid to heat through. Keeping the heat low, strain in the beetroot stock and adjust seasoning.

Ladle the soup into bowls and add a spoonful of smetana or soured cream with a sprinkling of dill.

SUNFISH *see* A FEW WORDS ABOUT . . . OPAH

† SWORDFISH

Xiphias gladius

Swordfish are found all over the world, but usually in warmer waters than ours. Americans are not short of swordfish, neither are Spaniards, Italians, Greeks and other dwellers to the east. Occasionally they swim to our shores, but normally prefer the Mediterranean which is where you should look out for them on menus and market stalls.

In October of 1970, there was excitement on the Atlantic coast of France because the fishermen of La Rochelle had encountered a huge shoal of swordfish. The trawlers concerned, the *Vieux marin* and the *Claude Jean Robert* from the Île d'Yeu, usually brought in no more than two or three tons of fish. This catch weighed twenty tons, and was uncommon enough to justify two or three paragraphs in the French papers. I asked our weekly fishmonger at Montoire market about it. She explained that the firm-fleshed *espadon* was a great treat – the shoal would bring much profitable joy to the fishmongers and merchants of La Rochelle. She obviously envied them. So did I, as swordfish was something I had never cooked.

There was no mention in the paper of any damage caused by this tonnage of swift and powerful fish. I had hoped for some modern record echoing the old reports that a swordfish strikes with the 'accumulated force of fifteen double-headed hammers', and can pierce through 50 cm (20 inches) of timber, even oak.

If you go down to the foot of Italy, to the Tyrrhenian Sea and the Straits of Messina, you soon discover that things do not always go the swordfishes' way. When they go down to the African coast every year to spawn, the sharp-eyed fishermen are on the look-out and are prepared for the hunt. The strange boats they use can be seen at Bagnara, say, or Scilla. They have tall thin metal look-out towers, ladderlike in their silhouette, and long metal platforms that jetty out over the sea like a murderous arm. That and the ferocious tuna fishing are sights of antique barbarity and blood that one is hypocritically happy not to see. The August and September traveller sees swordfish for ever on the menu, and groans as it is so often overcooked.

Like tuna, or porbeagle and other sharks, swordfish is sold in steaks and intended, mostly, for the grill. First it will be marinaded in olive oil with garlic and parsley and lemon, then turned over charcoal and served with lemon. In *Honey from a Weed* Patience Gray describes a Catalan roasting technique, by which the marinaded fish is slapped down directly on the hot plate of a kitchen range. After a while it is turned and 'roasted' on the other side, then it comes to table with a pounded romesco sauce*. Often swordfish will be sealed in hot oil, then stewed gently in tomato with piquant additions such as capers, olives and anchovies. Alan Davidson describes a most oddsounding sandwich of a pie in his *Mediterranean Seafood*. For years I jibbed at the sweet pastry – it is a recipe that takes one back in mind to the Arab occupation of Sicily, like the beccafico sardines on p. 329 – then took courage when swordfish began to appear regularly at Waitrose and tried it. It is most delicious and not odd at all, well worth trying.

HOW TO PREPARE SWORDFISH

Swordfish is sold in convenient steaks. Nothing much to do, unless you need to remove the bone and leathery skin for the recipe you are following. If the steaks are to be grilled or 'roasted', no need to bother.

Serve it simply with lemon quarters, or the Sicilian Salmoriglio which Ada Boni recommends: this is made by beating together, in the top of a double boiler, 250 ml (8 fl oz) of olive oil, the juice of 2 lemons and a couple of tablespoons of water. Flavour it with a generous tablespoon of chopped parsley, 2 teaspoons fresh oregano or rather less dried oregano and some salt.

IMPANATA DI PESCE SPADA

This is Sicilian swordfish pie from Alan Davidson's *Mediterranean Seafood*. Other firm fish can be used: he suggests halibut, I would add white tuna, porbeagle and monkfish.

Serves 8

PASTRY
400 g (14 oz) plain flour
200 g (7 oz) butter
175 g (6 oz) caster sugar
4–5 egg yolks
finely grated peel of 1 lemon
pinch of salt

FILLING
500 g (1 lb) swordfish
salt, pepper
2 medium onions, chopped
olive oil
2 tablespoons tomato paste, diluted with a little water
2 celery stalks, finely chopped
100 g (3½ oz) green olives, stoned, chopped
2 tablespoons capers
4–5 courgettes
1 beaten egg
seasoned flour

Make a short pastry dough with the listed ingredients, using a little iced water only if absolutely necessary. Chill for an hour.

Meanwhile, cut the swordfish into tiny pieces and season them. Brown the onion in a little oil in a sauté pan. Add tomato paste, celery, olives, capers and fish. Cook gently to get rid of wateriness.

Cut the courgettes into 5-cm (2-inch) strips, coat the pieces with egg and flour and fry in hot oil, then drain on kitchen paper.

Rub a pie dish with a butter paper and flour it – choose one that is about 20 cm (8 inches) across and 7 cm (3 inches) deep. If it has hinged sides, so much the better. Divide the pastry into three. Roll out the first bit, making it large enough to lay in the dish and come a little way up the side. Put on half the swordfish mixture and half the courgettes. Put on the second layer of pastry. Repeat with layers of swordfish and courgettes, then top with a third layer of pastry, tucking it down the side of the dish to meet the bottom layer. Brush with the last of the beaten egg and bake in the oven preheated to gas 5, 190 °C (375 °F), for 50–55 minutes. Check occasionally and turn the heat down slightly, or protect the pastry with paper, if it becomes too brown.

GEORGE LANG'S SWORDFISH STEAK WITH SOFT-SHELLED CRAB

The crispness of soft-shell crab when it is cooked, the biscuity quality and spiced flavour make a good contrast with swordfish. The combination was George Lang's idea. It appears in his *Café des Artistes Cook Book* and on the menu of the Café in New York. There you eat warm and lively food, food of an energetic delight that is not pale or mechanical or pretentiously fashionable. Every time I go there, I come out with ideas and a feeling of general satisfaction. Once it was a glorious dessert of fruit, cut into elegant, convenient pieces and arranged like a painting on a big Victorian serving dish: the waiter put it down in the centre of the table, we were each given a fork and we were able to spear the bits we fancied and keep on talking. An ideal dessert, I should say in parenthesis, after a main course of fish. Another time I left the Café happy was after the first experience of eating fresh sturgeon.

Now that swordfish is not difficult to find in Britain, and soft-shell crabs are making an appearance, try this recipe for a special occasion.

Serves 4

4 medium soft-shell crabs
plain flour
6 tablespoons unsalted butter
salt, pepper
4 thick swordfish steaks, about 175 g (6 oz) each
2 tablespoons melted unsalted butter
2 lemons, halved with a zigzag cut, like crowns

Switch on the grill. Rinse the crabs and dry them. Flour them lightly, shake off the excess and fry them gently in the butter over a medium heat. Give them 5 minutes a side – they should end up golden brown and crisp-looking. Season them with salt and pepper.

Meanwhile, brush the swordfish lightly with the melted unsalted butter and season them. Grill them for 3 minutes, turn and complete the cooking – another 3 minutes. Serve each steak with a crab on top and half a lemon on the side.

SWORDFISH GRATIN ON TOAST

This will make a supper dish for two people, and can be adapted to your taste and what happens to be in the larder. By adding extra liquid to the egg mixture and building up the main ingredients in a baked pastry case rather than on toast, you can make an appetizing tart: it will need to be cooked in the oven.

Serves 2

1 slice swordfish, about 200 g (7 oz), sliced thinly on the diagonal
375 g (12 oz) firm tomato, skinned, sliced
salt, pepper, cayenne
2 medium onions, sliced
3 tablespoons single or whipping cream
2 egg yolks
2 anchovy fillets, drained, chopped
1 tablespoon each chopped parsley and basil
2 teaspoons small capers
2 large slivers of a melting cheese – mozzarella, fontina, single Gloucester,
    Gouda, Lancashire, etc. or 2 tablespoons each grated Gruyère and
    Parmesan
2 large slices bread
olive oil

Season the fingers of swordfish and the tomato with salt, pepper and cayenne. Simmer the onion in the least possible salted water until just tender, and drain. Beat together the cream, egg yolks, anchovy fillets, herbs, capers and – if used – the *grated* cheeses.

Preheat the grill and toast the bread. Put it on to a serving dish and keep warm.

Heat a large sauté pan over a medium heat and brush thinly with olive oil. Cook the swordfish briefly, seconds a side, until it turns opaque. Remove and quickly put in the tomato in a single layer. Cook fast on both sides until the slices blur and are just about tender, but still in shape. Remove and, if need be, reheat the onion slices quickly. Put them on the toast evenly, then make a layer of the fish, then the tomatoes. Put on the large slivers of melting cheese, if used, and pour over the egg mixture. Put under the grill, lower the heat a little and leave until lightly browned. Serve immediately

VARIATION   You could substitute fresh – or canned – tuna for the swordfish. Heat the caned tuna through very briefly or it will become stringy and dry.

SWORDFISH STEAKS WITH FENNEL

This combination of swordfish, fennel and basil is based on a recipe of Paul Minchelli's. He was one of the first in France to serve marinaded fish and very lightly cooked fish in his restaurants. He has revolutionized the cooking of the firm meaty fish, such as tuna, swordfish, porbeagle and tope. In the old days, you were told to cook them 'as if they were veal', i.e. for at least 35 minutes, even longer: nowadays, the cooking is brief and to the point, the fish in consequence is no longer dry and stringy.

Serves 6

6 slices of swordfish, 1½ cm (½ inch) thick
salt, pepper
olive oil
4 cloves garlic, crushed, skinned, finely chopped
6 small bulbs of fennel, sliced, some of the leaves saved
6 slices mozzarella cheese
2 tablespoons pine kernels
leaves of 1 small bunch of basil
3 tablespoons grated Sardinian pecorino or Parmesan or the two mixed

Season the fish with salt and pepper and set aside. Pour a thin layer of oil into a sauté pan and cook the chopped garlic in it slowly to perfume the oil. Do not let it colour. After about 5 minutes, add the sliced fennel and let it cook for 10 minutes. Taste it from time to time – you may like it harder than I do.

Heat up a heavy non-stick pan and put in the swordfish to cook like a steak. Turn it after 30 seconds, and give it another 30 seconds. Put it on top of the gently bubbling fennel, cover the pan and give it another minute. The fish should be supple and soft, if you press it.

Remove the fish, mix the reserved fennel leaves, chopped, into the cooked fennel and then put it all on a serving plate. Place the fish on top, then the slices of the mozzarella on the fish. Keep this warm while you chop the pine kernels and basil, and mix with the cheese. Spread over the fish, put under the grill until the mixture softens on top of the swordfish and the nuts turn a light brown. Serve immediately.

TOPE *see* SHARKS

† TROUT, CHAR, GRAYLING & WHITEFISH

Salmo spp., *Salvelinus* spp., *Thymallus* spp.

& *Coregonus* spp.

The best trout, whatever the size, variety or place may be, is the one you catch yourself and eat within an hour or two. Given these happy circumstances, the style of cooking hardly matters at all – baking in newspaper, frying, grilling, simmering in salted water; whatever you do, it will taste perfect. If anyone can suggest a finer food, apart from salmon trout, I should be grateful to know about it.

This is one reason why people pay apparently ridiculous sums for a stretch of trout fishing, and why people since the Middle Ages have been studying the trout's habits with that passionate, contradictory love that hunters seem to devote to their prey.

In their book on trout, in Collins's New Naturalist series, W. E. Frost and M. E. Brown point out that long before Izaak Walton was born, Dame Juliana Berners was discoursing on the joys of trout fishing and the correct comportment of trout fisherman (to be summed up as 'Don't be greedy'). The two modern authors delight in the variety of size and colouring in our native brown trout. In Lough Derg and Lake Windermere the trout are large and silvery with black spots. In the small brown tarns near Windermere, the little fish have 'yellow bellies and red spots on their dark sides'. Some trout have pink flesh like salmon – they are the best of all to eat – some have white flesh. 'As trout swim and turn gracefully in their native waters – in rushing becks, placid lakes or yellow bog-pool – they are, simply, beautiful.'

That great American fisherman and expert, A. J. McClane takes a mildly reproachful view of trout. The shades of Izaak Walton and Charles Cotton do not daunt someone who has caught at least half a million – though he didn't eat them all, I hasten to say. With such experience, he has found that the quality of wild trout can be most variable according to the waters they come from, with, as you would expect in this polluted world, the best ones being found in high clear mountain streams.

One of the things that intrigued me most in his descriptions of trout was the history he gives of trout farming. As long ago as the fourteenth century, a French monk, Dom Pichon, discovered that trout eggs could be artificially impregnated. It took another five centuries before the idea was developed and the French government had a hatchery built in 1852. The first American farm was begun in 1864 by Seth Green, at Mumford, New York, and as one clerical angler made clear, some years later, doom was nigh: 'Trout will be hatched by machinery and raised in ponds, and fattened on chopped liver, and grow flabby and lose their spots. The trout of the restaurant will not cease to be but he is no more like a trout of the wild river than the fat and songless reed-bird is like the bobolink. Gross feeding and easy pond life enervate and deprave him.'

Precisely. I shall silently honour the Reverend Myron Reed on the rare occasions when I cannot avoid eating farm trout. Of course, just as trout from different waters vary, so do trout from different farms and farm trout handled in different ways. Mr McClane's great experience bears out my own empiric conclusions that a flash-frozen Danish trout, packaged and bought from the supermarket, can taste much better than the more romantically acquired trout from a local farm where the fish may be overcrowded and overfed with what looks like pellets of cat food. And when these local trout have been lying around on ice at the fishmonger's, they can be poor eating indeed, with a strange muddy taste that reminds me of London tapwater.

Chars are rare now in our country. They include the Arctic char, once so prolific in Windermere that locally potted char became a famous delicacy that was sent down to London. Occasionally one finds the shallow dishes they were packed in: white pottery with gaily coloured fish swimming round the outside, and a high price ticket underneath. Celia Fiennes in her way round England in the late seventeenth century commented on the Lake District char, 'part of the whole skin and the fin and tail is red like the fins of a perch, and the inside flesh looks as red as any salmon . . . their taste is very rich and fat tho' not so strong or clogging as the lampreys are, but it's as fat and rich a food.' Char are still caught, though in smaller numbers, and if you go to the Rothay Manor Hotel at the head of the lake at Ambleside you may be able to see the silver spinners used in catching the char collected by Mrs Bronwen Nixon, whose recipe I give later on, and who until her tragic death ran the hotel. Char elsewhere may be white-fleshed – it all depends on what and where they eat and the time of year. Char are very much cold water fish, as their Latin name *Salvelinus alpinus*, also implies. They have their treasured localities and in the French Alps, *omble chevalier* on the menu is something to look out for. Not all the localities are land-locked. If you get the chance of an Alpine char from the sea, take it. Char to look out for in North America – don't let the word trout confuse you – are the Dolly Varden, and Lake and Brooktrout.

Grayling seems to be almost entirely an angler's fish. Only from a friend, or at some small inn near the right rivers, will you get the opportunity of sampling it. The white flesh falls beautifully from the bone, it is firm like the trout's but lighter in flavour. When newly caught, they are thought to smell of thyme – hence *Thymallus*. A few hours later this is not perceptible, any more than the cucumber fragrance of smelts survives their journey to the kitchen. *Ombre* is the French for grayling: don't confuse it with *omble* meaning char. *Ombre* being a shadow in non-piscatorial French, I imagine that it refers – like grayling – to the beautiful grey colour that we associate with it in western Europe. Elsewhere it can be almost purple depending on the species and where it lives. Grayling in England – *Thymallus thymallus* – as Charles Cotton wrote in *The Compleat Angler* caught in the winter is 'little inferior to the best trout.' Incidentally you need to scale grayling.

Whitefish are not as interesting in Britain, at least as char or grayling, although elsewhere they can be abundant and worthwhile. The name is confusing to the ear, if not on paper, and more memorable names have been thought up. At Lake Annecy in France they appear as lavarets (*Coregonus lavaretus*) which are known in Britain as the powan. There are six species which go under the name of cisco – shortnose cisco, longjaw cisco and so on – which are sold widely in North America as smoked chub: a seventh cisco – to us it is known as vendace – provides the lovely golden caviare of Scandinavia which I have managed to buy from the Swedish Table, now located at Unit 21, Parkroyal Metro Centre, Britannia Way in London. In America the best known whitefish is the lake whitefish (*C. clupeaformis*).

These fish vary in size, colour and texture, but any of the salmon and trout recipes are suitable for them. As a general rule, I would say the fresher they are, the simpler the cooking should be – but that applies to almost every fish one can think of, whether from salt or sweet water. Some you may want to poach, but there are trout fishermen who declare that the skin of the fish when fried in butter is the best part of all, crisp and succulent. It profits from a fine but unmistakable sanding of freshly ground black pepper. This adds a marvellous piquancy to the rich skin, without being in the least too much for the lovely flavour of the fish inside it.

BAKED TROUT IN A SOUFFLÉ CHEESE SAUCE

This is a lovely dish from the Sharrow Bay Hotel on Ullswater, one of the most beautifully placed and best-fed hotels in Britain. The recipe is intended for the best wild Lakeland trout, but it can be worth doing with top quality farm trout. Or, better, with large fillets of sole or other reputable flounder.

Serves 4

4 trout, cleaned
milk
seasoned flour
clarified butter*

SAUCE
2 tablespoons butter
1 tablespoon plain flour
300 ml (10 fl oz) single cream or milk, heated
2 egg yolks
75 g (2½ oz) grated Double Gloucester or good hard cheese
¼ teaspoon grated nutmeg
salt, pepper
6 egg whites

Remove fins from the trout, but leave heads and tails in place. Cut them along the belly from head to tail, then turn them backbone up on to a board and press down firmly along the backbone to loosen it. Turn the trout over and remove the bones.

Next make the sauce by melting the butter, stirring in the flour and cooking for a minute or more. Keep this roux pale. Pour in the cream or milk, stirring, and then beat to make a smooth consistency. Cool slightly, then mix in the yolks, the cheese and seasoning. Pour a little clarified butter over the top to prevent a skin forming.

Rinse the trout, dip them in milk, then in flour and brown them in butter on both sides without cooking them through. Do this one or two at a time. Put them side by side in an oval gratin dish which has been brushed out with butter.

Whisk the egg whites until stiff. Fold a little into the cheese sauce to slacken it, then fold the rest into the mixture lightly. Pile on to the trout and bake in the oven preheated to gas 6, 200 °C (400 °F) until the soufflé is puffed and golden brown – 10–15 minutes. Serve immediately.

A.J. McCLANE'S BLUE TROUT

By this method of cooking, the natural film of slime on the trout's skin is turned to a slatey-blue of great softness. The important thing is that the trout should be killed and cleaned just before going into the pot (although I find that one gets quite a good colour from frozen Danish trout). I have always slipped the trout into a couple of litres (about 3½ pt) of boiling water, acidulated with 6 tablespoons of wine vinegar, and simmered them until just cooked.

Mr McClane, who is after all a great fisherman, has much stronger views on what is right: and with his experience I cannot argue. This is what he does.

He makes a court bouillon of 4 parts of water to 1 of white wine and flavours it with the usual pot herbs and aromatics. Then he strains it into a clean pan and keeps it bubbling on one burner. On another burner he has a large pan containing 2 parts of water to 1 of tarragon vinegar. When this boils, he grabs his newly caught, newly killed and newly cleaned trout with a pair of tongs and lowers them into the vinegar-water. When the colour is appropriately blue, he transfers the trout to the court bouillon. This knocks it off the boil, but when it bubbles again, he puts on the lid, removes the pan from the heat and leaves the trout to complete their cooking.

'Classically, blue trout are served with marble-size new potatoes bathed in butter and garnished with parsley. There should also be a side dish of fresh asparagus smothered in mousseline sauce . . . A dry white wine would be the proper mate to such rich fare. A watercress salad is a must.'

I would put in a plea for a walnut and horseradish sauce*.

TROUT IN WHITE WINE JELLY

A cool dish for a warm day, either as a first course or a main course at midday.

Serves 6

6 trout, about 250 g (8 oz) each
450 ml (15 fl oz) water
150 ml (5 fl oz) dry white wine
1 tablespoon white wine vinegar
1 onion, sliced
1 small carrot, sliced
½ bay leaf
2 sprigs of parsley
2 sprigs of thyme
¼ teaspoon salt
1 level teaspoon peppercorns

Clean the trout and set aside. Simmer the remaining ingredients together in a covered pan for 30 minutes or a little longer. Leave to cool.

Put the trout in a pan, side by side. Strain over them the cold bouillon and bring gently to the boil. Barely simmer for 8 minutes, or until the trout are cooked. Remove them, take off the skin and then carefully fillet the fish. Lay the fillets side by side in a shallow dish. Put the skin, bone and debris into the bouillon and simmer down to half the original quantity. Taste for seasoning – the flavour should be fairly strong. Strain over the trout, and put into the refrigerator to chill. The liquid sets to a light jelly.

TROUT OR OTHER RIVER FISH BAKED IN THE LOIR STYLE

Every cook in the val du Loir – and in north and western France, I suspect – uses this recipe for river fish because the ingredients are always in house or garden. The sudden return of a fishing party causes no flurry. By the time a couple of bottles are emptied, the fish is on the table, its freshness in no way masked, but honoured without pretension.

This kind of recipe has felicity and seemliness – like our church at Trôo, whose Norman walls, tower, capitals and keystones, arches and arcades have been cut and dragged out of the cliff which it crowns, and which shelters still a number of its parishioners.

Serves 3–8

butter
shallots and onion
parsley
salt, pepper
¾–2 kg (1½–4 lb) whole fish, scaled and cleaned
175 ml (6 fl oz) dry white wine
175 ml (6 fl oz) crème fraîche or double cream
lemon juice

Butter generously an ovenproof dish which is large enough to hold the fish, without too much room to spare. Put in enough chopped shallots and onions to cover the base thinly. Scatter the parsley, salt and pepper. Lay in the fish, and brush it with melted butter. Bake in a fairly hot oven (gas 6, 200°C/400°F) for 10–15 minutes according to size, then pour in the wine. Baste occasionally with the juices, until the flesh turns opaque. Pour over the cream, and return to the oven for 5 minutes. A squeeze of lemon juice before serving compensates for the blandness of English cream. Serve scattered lightly with parsley and with plenty of bread or plainly boiled potatoes.

You can, if you like, stuff the fish – particularly the larger fish.

Egg and mushroom stuffing

The simplest stuffing for any fish, whether it comes from sea or river, is made from breadcrumbs mixed with butter, parsley and seasoning. Chopped shallot, bacon or prosciutto and grated cheese may be added for extra flavour. If you are presented with a fine trout or other river fish, a bream, tench, barbel or perch, I suggest you follow another excellent French recipe, and combine hard-boiled egg and mushroom in a more elaborate recipe.

For 6 fish

4 tablespoons butter
2 tablespoons chopped shallot or onion
60–90 g (2–3 oz) roughly chopped mushrooms
3–4 tablespoons breadcrumbs
salt, pepper, nutmeg
grated rind of ½ lemon
about 1 tablespoon each, chopped chives and parsley
1 large hard-boiled egg, chopped
double cream

Melt the butter and fry the shallot or onion gently in it for 5 minutes. Add the mushrooms, raise the heat slightly and cook for 10 minutes. Stir in the breadcrumbs – a little more or less according to the size of the fish – and remove from the heat. Season to taste with salt, freshly ground pepper and freshly grated nutmeg. Stir in lemon rind and herbs, then the hard-boiled egg. Mix in a little cream, so that you have a lightly bound, not pasty, consistency. Correct the seasoning.

Any stuffing left over can be augmented with some extra onion, plus mushroom if you like, and laid on the well-buttered base of the baking dish. Follow the recipe above, but omit the final addition of cream. A little more white wine may be needed.

TROUT WITH MUSHROOM AND WINE SAUCE

The ideal mushroom for this recipe is the cep, *Boletus edulis*, but as it does not, alas, flourish in every wood, most of us have to fall back on cultivated mushrooms. Even so this is a good dish.

Serves 6

6 trout
150 ml (5 fl oz) dry white wine
150 ml (5 fl oz) light meat stock
1 medium onion, chopped
3 tablespoons butter
2 teaspoons plain flour
1 ½ tablespoons tomato concentrate
175 g (6 oz) cultivated mushrooms, sliced or 375 g (12 oz) prepared
   sliced ceps
2 tablespoons chopped parsley
salt, pepper

Put the trout into a shallow pan. Pour over wine and stock, and simmer gently until just cooked, turning the fish after 5 minutes. Drain off the liquid, retaining it, and keep the trout warm.

Meanwhile soften the onion in the butter, stir in the flour and moisten with the liquid in which the trout have cooked. Add the tomato concentrate gradually, stopping when the flavour is spicy and rich, but not conspicuously of tomato, then put in the mushrooms. Simmer for about 10 minutes. Add parsley and seasoning, and pour the sauce over the fish. Glaze under the grill for a few seconds.

NOTE You may need to add more stock or wine or both to the sauce – this will depend on how much moisture is given out by the mushrooms.

TRUITE DU GAVE

This is one of the best trout recipes; it comes from the Pyrenees where the fish are taken from the *gaves* or mountain torrents. Measure out the pastis carefully – a lavish hand can sometimes be the cook's undoing.

For each trout allow:

> *seasoned flour*
> *2 tablespoons clarified butter**
> *90 g (3 oz) ceps or sliced mushrooms*
> *½ clove garlic, crushed*
> *salt, pepper*
> *1 teaspoon pastis Ricard*
> *2 tablespoons crème fraîche or double cream*

Turn the trout in seasoned flour, shaking off the surplus. Fry in butter over a moderate heat, allowing 5 minutes a side. Remove to a serving dish and keep warm. Cook the mushrooms in the pan juices, together with the garlic. Season well. Stir in the pastis; let it bubble hard for a moment or two, then add the cream and stir everything well together until the sauce is amalgamated. Correct seasoning, adding extra pastis if you like. Pour round the trout and serve at once.

MRS NIXON'S POTTED CHAR

The recipe can be used for all the fish in this section, and for salmon trout.

Serves 6–8

> *6 char, each weighing 175 g (6 oz)*
> *about 300 ml (10 fl oz) dry white wine*
> *1 bay leaf, 2 sprigs of parsley, 1 curl of lemon peel*
> *¼ teaspoon powdered ginger*

¼ teaspoon powdered mace
250 g (8 oz) unsalted butter
150 ml (5 fl oz) double cream
lemon juice, salt, pepper
clarified butter* to cover

Put the fish into an ovenproof dish that fits them closely. Pour enough wine over them to cover – the quantity you need will depend on the tightness of the fit. Put in a bay leaf, parsley and lemon, with the spices, and some of the butter dotted over the top.

Bake in the oven preheated to gas 2, 150 °C (300 °F) until just cooked – 30 minutes or so.

Remove the fish, raise the fillets, discarding skin, bone and head, and flake them into a processor or blender. Strain the cooking juice into a shallow pan and boil it down to a syrupy essence, then beat in the butter, bit by bit, off the heat, until it melts. Pour on to the fish, add the cream and whizz to a paste. Check for seasoning and add lemon, salt and pepper as required.

Put into one shallow pot, or six to eight small pots and chill. When firm, pour on a layer of melted clarified butter. Chill again and cover with cling film. Store in the refrigerator for 24–36 hours. Serve with brown bread and butter.

GRILLED GRAYLING WITH FENNEL

Brush scaled grayling with clarified butter*, and sand them generously with freshly ground black pepper. Grill them in the usual way.

Serve them on a bed of Florentine fennel and onion – *see* recipe on p. 294 for Grilled red mullet with fennel – cooked in butter. Serve with pats of tarragon butter and lemon quarters, with a sprinkling of chopped green fennel leaves.

WHITEFISH (OR GRAYLING) WITH MORELS

The flavour of morels is so exceptional that it is worth buying a small packet of dried ones to make this dish, if you aren't lucky enough to find your own. This recipe is also suitable for perch and pike, and sole.

Serves 6

1–1½ kg (2–3 lb) whitefish fillets
salt, pepper, pinch of paprika
500 g (1 lb) fresh morels or 45–60 g (1½–2 oz) packet dried morels
1 shallot, chopped
175 g (6 oz) butter
125 ml (4 fl oz) dry white wine
1 tablespoon beurre manié*
juice of 1 lemon
125 ml (4 fl oz) crème fraîche or double cream
seasoned flour
2 eggs, beaten
slices of lemon
chopped parsley and chives

Season the fish, and leave in a cool place while you prepare the sauce.

Wash the morels carefully and slice them up (or soak the dried ones according to instructions on the packet). Put into a pan with the shallot, 2 tablespoons of butter, and the wine. Simmer for 20 minutes. Thicken with the beurre manié, and add lemon juice, seasoning and cream. Keep just under the boil for a few moments. Pour on to a serving dish and keep warm.

Dip the fish into flour, then egg, and fry in 4 tablespoons of the butter until golden brown. Place on top of the morel sauce. Cook the remaining butter in a small pan until golden brown and pour over the fish. Arrange the lemon slices on top, sprinkle with herbs, and serve.

† TUNA OR TUNNY & BONITO

Thunnus thynnus & related spp.

My earliest sight of tuna was at Scarborough before the war, when tuna-fishing first became a fashionable sport there. I remember dark perfect shapes hanging against the usual grey summer sky. Their tails brushed the ground almost, but tall men had to put their heads back to look up at them. In 1933 a record-breaking tuna was landed there, weighing 425 kg (851 lb). These fish were *Thunnus thynnus* I suppose, the bluefin tuna or *thon rouge*, caught on the way north to recuperate in the rich seas after spawning, and all of 2 m (7 feet) long.

The second time I saw tuna, many years later, was in Spain on the Basque coast. This time it was a smaller species, *T. alalunga*, which the French call *germon* and the Americans albacore, the prized white tuna, the only one allowed to be sold as *white* meat tuna in the USA. Fat fisherwomen were pulling these tight-skinned shapes over the quays of the small port of Llanes. Natural slime and blood greased the way so that they survived the brutal handling unblemished. We did not eat tuna for dinner that evening.

Next day we were glad to blot out that over-truthful image with a visit to the cave of Pindal where a palaeolithic tuna swims gracefully on the wall. One has to step up on to a stone to make out the engraved lines. And all the time the smell of sea and wild flowers hangs about the cave. I suppose that women have been lugging these meaty, full-skinned fish over the ground hereabouts for 25,000 years and longer. Palaeolithic tuna must have been rather an indigestible chew, without the peppers and potatoes and tomatoes that now seem such an essential part of tuna cooked in the Basque style.

There are a number of other species which come under the general heading of tuna – the yellowfin (*T. albacares*) of the Pacific is what people in California think of as tuna. A. J. McClane, the great fish expert, is happiest when his Florida waters bring him a blackfin (*T. atlanticus*). The small skipjack (*Euthynnus pelamis*) provide the Japanese with a favourite sashimi as well as the flakes of dried fish used in making the basic stocks of their cookery: when you read the word *katsuo* in a list of ingredients, this is the fish that is meant. Add to that the various small fish somewhere between a mackerel and tuna proper that pass under the name of bonito – the true bonito of the Atlantic and Mediterranean (*Sarda sarda*) had relations in the Pacific, but the name is used for the skipjack in France and elsewhere, too, although with a qualifying adjective.

This sounds more daunting than it really is, unless you are a marine biologist. If you are a cook with a bit of experience, your eye tells you that whatever the name may be, these are solid, meaty fish and these qualities are what count in the kitchen. When I first wrote *Fish Cookery*, fresh tuna was a rarity in Britain. Now it is quite easy to find thanks to the immigrant communities that have so enlarged our choice of good things to eat in the last twenty years. Holidays abroad have helped, too; tuna is now more than just a handy store cupboard fish in a can. It does help to know that the best part of tuna comes from the belly. This is what you should buy at the market, and what you should look for on the can should it come from Italy – *ventresca* is the word.

There are various standards of canned tuna. The best consists mainly of large pieces of fish, packed in with flaky bits. The lowest quality is all flakes. For a Salade Niçoise (p. 57), you should choose the chunkiest. For sandwiches, the bitty kind is more practical. In France they often can the fish in brine – *au naturel* – which many people prefer to tuna in oil, especially for dishes which already contain a good deal of oil already, a salad with mayonnaise for instance. It is better, too, for the Curé's omelette, p. 430.

Whether we shall ever see the range of pickled tunas that one sees in a Spanish market, I do not know. Knowledge of Spain, imports from Spain must surely increase. It seems we have taken tea and chips to Spain and not yet brought anything back. The big market in Barcelona was an extraordinary sight when at last a friend from Madrid took me round, explaining the unfamiliar sights on the fish stalls. Rationally I should have expected it, but no amount of reading and visiting fish markets elsewhere and eating fish on every occasion had prepared me for the strangeness, the abundant vigour, and those great slabs of tuna pickled in various ways, strange tawny colours of pink, looking reserved and a little dry and disapproving as the prawns escaped their boxes and crawled out of sight.

HOW TO PREPARE TUNA

Don't be put off tuna because it has a disconcerting look of beef with extra dark patches. This can vary, but even in quite pale steaks there can be deep red streaks along the bone. Just cut them away, and discard them with the skin and bone. Another problem, although this does not apply to all species, is a general bloody look, something one does not have to deal with often in fish. American cooks are used to soaking tuna in brine, which clears it – dissolve about 125 g (4 oz) sea salt in 1 litre (1¾ pt) of water, put in the tuna and stand in the refrigerator for an hour or so.

Now you can poach, fry or grill it, depending on its quality. If you have not cooked tuna before, start off with a good sauce – try the recipe from the Château-Renault market (p. 431), or give it the treatment à l'américaine (p. 213). The Basque stew is the kind of dish most people enjoy. Or else cook it au poivre (p. 436). The thing is not to overcook tuna, but not to undercook it too much either. When it is done, it should still be very slightly pink at the centre. Be quite ruthless about piercing it with the point of a knife to see how it is getting on. You can always remove it, and let the sauce cook on by itself should it be necessary.

BASQUE TUNA AND POTATO STEW

This is a recipe with many variations; sometimes there are no tomatoes, sometimes there are not so many onions, and so on. The basic ingredients are tuna, garlic, olive oil and potatoes. If possible, cook this stew in a large shallow glazed earthenware dish, using a heat-diffuser with gas.

Serves 6

750 g (1½ lb) tuna
2 large onions, sliced
4 cloves garlic, chopped
125 ml (4 fl oz) olive oil
6 or more potatoes, peeled
500 g (1 lb) tomatoes, peeled, chopped
4 sweet red peppers, seeded, sliced
salt, pepper
6 slices bread

Cut the tuna into chunks 2½–3½ cm (1–1½ inches) – discarding skin and bones. Cook the onion and garlic in the oil until lightly coloured. Add the potatoes, tomatoes and peppers, and cook them for about 15–20 minutes. Put in the tuna, making sure it is well embedded in the tomato stew. Simmer on top of the stove; keep a watch to see that the tuna does not overcook. Check the seasoning. The bread can be crumbled or cut into squares and added at the end of the cooking time or the slices can be toasted in the oven and put on top of the stew before serving.

CROSTINI DI TONNO FRESCO

A recipe for fresh, good quality tuna fish. Be sure to place the sage leaves next to it on the skewers for the full benefit of the flavour.

Serves 6

625 g (1¼ lb) tuna
bread
small sage leaves
olive oil
salt, pepper
lemon juice

Cut the tuna into regular slices about the thickness of a finger, and divide the slices into squares. Cut an equal number of squares of bread, without crusts, of a similar size. Wash plenty of sage leaves.

Thread the tuna and bread on to six skewers, with sage leaves on either side of each piece of tuna. Half-leaves of bay can be substituted for some of the sage leaves.

Brush the skewers with olive oil, and season them. Grill at a very moderate temperature for about half an hour, brushing tuna and bread with oil whenever they begin to look in the least dry.

Squeeze lemon juice over them and serve.

THE CURÉ'S OMELETTE

In the *Physiologie du Goût*, Brillat-Savarin tells the story of how Madame B, a society beauty who occupied herself with good works, called on a curé one evening in the poor part of Paris. He was dining

at an unfashionably early hour, and welcomed her to join him. Poor
and unfashionable he may have been, but he ate well (and copiously).
After he had finished a salmon trout, the housekeeper brought in a
tuna and carp roe omelette which smelled and tasted so good that
Madame B could talk of nothing else at the dinner she went on to.

I thought the story much exaggerated – until I tried the omelette.
Admittedly herring roes had to stand in for carp, and canned tuna
for fresh, but the result was still superb.

Serves 4

250 g (8 oz) soft roes
6 tablespoons butter
1 small shallot, finely chopped
125 g (4 oz) fresh or canned tuna, chopped
salt, pepper
8 eggs, beaten
*maître d'hôtel butter**

Pour boiling water over the roes and leave for a few seconds to
become slightly firm. Drain and chop roughly. Melt 4 tablespoons
butter in a pan, and cook the shallot gently until soft. Add the tuna
and stir for a few seconds, then add the soft roes. After a moment or
two, remove the pan from the heat: the roes must stay creamy.
Season and cool. Stir into the seasoned eggs. Using the 2 remaining
tablespoons of butter, make the omelette in the usual way – or make
four smaller omelettes. Don't overcook; omelettes should be just liquid
in the centre. Spread the maître d'hôtel butter on a warm dish and
place the omelette(s) on top. Serve immediately. The heat of the
omelette should melt the butter into a sauce.

THE FISHMONGER'S TUNA

Around Trôo, there is a market almost every day of the week, in one
or another small town, which means that we know exactly which day
we may be invited out for a meal in any particular area. Or which
day to choose, if we are given a choice. Tuesday means Château-
Renault where there is a good convivial fishmonger, and one
September lunchtime we were given this dish by a triumphant friend
who had acquired the recipe that morning as her purchases were
being wrapped. Most of the vegetables came from her huge kitchen
garden. It was very much an autumn country lunch, a small harvest
festival.

Serves 6

¾–1 kg (1½–2 lb) tuna slices
salt, pepper, cayenne
olive oil
2 cloves garlic, sliced
500 g (1 lb) chopped onion
250 g (8 oz) sliced carrots
about 500 g (1 lb) aubergines, sliced, salted
about 500 g (1 lb) small courgettes, sliced, salted
about 500 g (1 lb) tomatoes, skinned, seeded, chopped
1–2 red peppers, toasted, skinned and cut in strips
wine vinegar
sugar
about 60 g (2 oz) black olives
chopped parsley and basil or *green coriander*

Season the fish with salt, pepper and cayenne and leave for 30 minutes. Heat a large sauté pan with a thin layer of olive oil in it. Add the garlic and onion, with the carrot. Cook slowly until the onion is tender. Push to one side and gently cook the tuna 3 minutes on each side. Put it onto a warm serving dish and keep it in a low oven, where it will continue to cook through very very slowly – gas ½, 130 °C (250 °F).

To the pan, add the remaining vegetables. Cook down to a thick sauce. Season, add a splash of vinegar if you like and a little sugar if the vegetables are watery in flavour. Pour over and round the tuna. Scatter with olives, parsley and basil or coriander. Serve with rounds or triangles of bread rubbed with garlic and fried in olive oil.

VARIATION   You could substitute parboiled small new potatoes for the aubergines, and increase the quantity of peppers and tomatoes in the vegetable stew, which is a kind of Ratatouille and variable.

† TURBOT

Rombus maximus

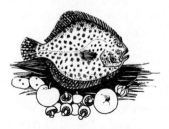

One thing I do resent – having to be in France, 240 km (150 miles) from the sea, before I can count on buying turbot. No doubt if I lived in London, things would be different, but like most of the population of these islands, I don't. And yet turbot has been vaunted – until recently at any rate – as a national delicacy. Dover sole class, right at the top of life's gastronomic experiences.

Nowadays, looking round grand houses and coming at last to the kitchens, we stand and stare at the diamond-shaped copper turbot kettles artistically nailed to the wall. Many people in the party (sometimes including the guide) have no idea of the use to which some enormous pans were put. How could they, rarely having seen a lusty, knobble-skinned turbot on the fishmonger's counter?

It is this lumpy dark skin – the white skinned side is smooth – that gives the turbot its name: *-bot*, as also in hali*but*, means flounder and *tur-* thorny. That is something of an exaggeration, but if you run your fingers over the humps and lumps you will find the sensation quite unlike any other you have experienced; it is even a little disquieting. This dark side is turned uppermost on the bed of the sea, so that the turbot melts into the background. Cooks usually cut through it to the backbone so that the white side remains smooth and uncracked, but some nineteenth-century epicures considered that the flesh under the dark side tasted better and ordered it that side up with no cuts made. Another point of turbot gastronomy is the fins which are considered a delicacy. Maria Edgeworth, the novelist, 'relates an anecdote of a Bishop – and we doubt not that he came to be an

Archbishop – who, descending to his kitchen to superintend the dressing of a turbot, and finding that his cook had stupidly cut away the fins, set about sewing them on again with his own Episcopal fingers. This dignitary knew the value of turbot.'

Another man who knew the value of turbot was Brillat-Savarin. The problem he was faced with was more fundamental. He arrived at a cousin's country house in Villecresnes, to the south-east of Paris, round about seven one evening, to find the family in an uproar over the turbot. It was grand and beautiful and plump, and they had nothing to cook it in. The husband had an axe in his hand determined to cut it in two. The wife was distraught.

'That turbot will remain in one piece!' said Brillat-Savarin. Everybody calmed down, and followed him from room to room as he searched for the answer. And this is what he did. He cut the wicker base from a basket that held fifty bottles of wine and covered it with a layer of *bulbes*, which I take to be onions and leeks, and *herbes de haut goût*. On went the turbot, with more *bulbes* and *herbes* on top. This was set over the household copper, half full of boiling water. A tub was turned upside-down over the fish, and sand was heaped round to prevent steam escaping. The turbot was, of course, perfection. The party was delighted, especially the curé who rolled his eyes to the ceiling as a sign of ecstasy. Everyone agreed that turbot steamed in such fragrance was far better than turbot which had been cooked in boiling water in a *turbotière*.

HOW TO CHOOSE AND PREPARE TURBOT

Look out for the small chicken turbot which weigh about 1 kg (2 lb). They make a handsome dish for a dinner party and are not difficult to cook. Use a large glazed earthenware dish of the kind imported from France to cook them in (unless, of course, you are the lucky possessor of a turbot kettle). Another way is to wrap the fish in foil and cook it on a baking sheet in the oven in its own steam, at gas 7–8, 220–230 °C (425–450 °F): butter the foil, include appropriate aromatics and make a tightly closed but baggy parcel. Check the condition of the fish at 15 minutes: assuming the chicken turbot to have been 2½ cm (1 inch) thick, it should be ready.

Since whiteness is supposed to be one of the virtues of turbot, it is usually poached in milk and water with slices of lemon, or in water with lemon alone. To keep the white-skinned side unblemished, the dark side is cut through, down to and along the central bone. The fins are left in place, and the head. Cooks had problems with vast turbot, even with a turbot kettle of the right size, and all kinds of stratagems were required to prevent the skin cracking and the flesh breaking which would spoil the presentation. Sometimes the fish were wound in muslin cloths to this end: I am sure this worked as far as the cooking went, but how did you remove the cloth and slide the turbot on to its serving dish without damaging it? My feeling is, thank heaven for chicken turbot and smaller parties.

Larger turbot these days are usually filleted, and sold in steaks. You buy what you require and cook it in any way suitable for white fish. Most of the finer recipes for cod, monkfish and sole are suitable for turbot. If you enjoy making sauces, turbot gives you a chance to show off your skill. Wild mushrooms cooked with a little shallot, parsley and butter are a worthy partner for turbot. Hollandaise and its derivatives*, cream sauces* and shellfish sauces* are the classic accompaniments.

Don't neglect any left-overs. Cold turbot is fine for a salad, or for making a filling for puff pastry. The poaching liquid, and carcase, can be turned into the most excellent jellied stock for a chowder or soup if seasonings and lemon were not too strong.

POACHED TURBOT WITH HORSERADISH

At Krogs Restaurant in Copenhagen, they serve the freshest and finest turbot you are ever likely to eat. Ours had come out of the water that morning. It had been seasoned and left for a while to absorb the flavour. Then it had been poached in a well-flavoured court bouillon* while we waited.

It came to our table with a fine scatter of grated horseradish root, a sauceboat of melted butter and a sauceboat of hollandaise*. There were also some small new potatoes, and extra horseradish in a bowl.

When the fish was served, everyone helped themselves to the horseradish, sprinkling it over the fish. Then melted butter was poured over the whole thing. It was really excellent. The surprising thing was the horseradish, which was sweetly piquant. The butter provided the emollient richness that poached fish require. We hardly needed the hollandaise.

To do this yourself at home, say with a chicken turbot, cover the fish with cold court bouillon (Krogs did not seem to be concerned with whiteness as Victorian cooks used to be, so no lemon or milk).

Bring it to the boil, then immediately lower to a simmer and give it 8–9 minutes, assuming it is 2½ cm (1 inch) at the thickest part.

Meanwhile, grate fresh horseradish from the outside of the root (the inner core is the hot part), and melt a packet of lightly salted Danish Lurpak butter, straining off the crusty white bits. Serve potatoes and hollandaise sauce, too, if you like.

TURBOT À LA CRÈME

Left-over turbot can be turned into an honourable dish. Mrs Beeton has an excellent way with it, very simple. She made a cream and butter sauce* – you melt 125 g (4 oz) of unsalted butter in a shallow pan, then stir in 175 ml (6 fl oz) of the thickest cream you can find, preferably Jersey. This makes a thick unctuous sauce to which seasoning can be added, and in which the flaked turbot – about 375 g (12 oz) – is briefly reheated.

The mixture is then used to fill split oblongs of puff pastry, or vol-au-vent cases, or shortcrust tartlets. Another way is to divide it between little pots, one per person, and tuck in triangles of toast. Sprinkle on top a little cayenne, or some chopped green herbs.

TURBOT AU POIVRE

Since I first wrote *Fish Cookery*, *steak au poivre* has had its moment of glory and mostly disappeared, but I find that visitors much enjoy fish cooked in the same way. It seemed original and attractive in 1971 and it still seems original now, although one or two writers have copied it from me. But then I had the idea from an obscure French source, so perhaps I should not complain that they make no acknowledgement!

The recipe is easily adapted to halibut, monkfish, even cod and its relations. The thing is that you must have a steak, i.e. a slice cut across a fish, and not a piece of fillet, so that the pepperiness can penetrate the fish.

> Serves 6
>
> *6 turbot steaks, about 2 cm (just under 1 inch) thick*
> *salt*
> *6 tablespoons black peppercorns*
> *2 tablespoons plain flour*
> *1 tablespoon sunflower oil*

125 g (4 oz) unsalted butter
4 tablespoons brandy
4 tablespoons port
175 ml (6 fl oz) light beef or veal or chicken stock
125 ml (4 fl oz) crème fraîche or double cream

Salt the fish steaks. Crush the peppercorns coarsely, using an electric mill, and mix them with the flour. Dry the fish and press the pepper mixture into both sides of each steak. Brown them lightly in the oil plus half the butter, on both sides. Flame them with brandy and deglaze with port, then the stock. Remove the fish when it is just cooked, and keep warm in a low oven.

Boil down the pan juices slightly, stir in the cream and continue to reduce until the sauce is rich and thick. Check the saltiness, put in the remaining butter in bits and strain round the fish. Serve very hot, on hot plates, with small boiled potatoes.

Some people like to eat the peppery coating, but others will prefer to remove most of it to one side.

This is one of the best fish recipes.

TURBOT SALAD

Cut or flake cooked turbot neatly and put it into a dish. Make an olive oil and lemon vinaigrette*, flavoured with chopped parsley, tarragon or chervil, and chives, a few capers, and 2–3 chopped anchovy fillets. Pour over the fish and leave it for at least 4 hours. Scatter with chopped hard-boiled egg, or put half-slices of hard-boiled egg round the edge.

Shellfish can be added to extend the salad, mussels, or shrimps, or crab. Mayonnaise* and similar oil-based sauces or sauces of the rouille* or romesco* type are also a good idea with cold turbot.

TURBOT VALLÉE D'AUGE

It may seem odd to cook fish with fruit, but it does enchance the natural sweetness of the fish. And apple also makes a good marriage with onion flavourings such as leek. In Normandy they might well use Calville or reinette apples: here you might choose a Charles Ross or a Newton Wonder, varieties which lie between the dessert and cooker categories, or an aromatic Cox. This recipe is particularly worth trying with brill as well as turbot.

Serves 4

white part of 1 large leek, trimmed, sliced
2 apples, peeled, cored, sliced
salt, pepper
1¼–1½ kg (2½–3 lb) turbot
300 ml (10 fl oz) dry cider or white wine
300 ml (10 fl oz) fish stock*
175 ml (6 fl oz) crème fraîche or double cream
butter, about 125 g (4 oz)
250 g (8 oz) small mushrooms
lemon juice

Heat the oven to gas 7, 220 °C (425 °F).

Choose a dish into which the turbot will fit closely and butter it. Scatter over it the leek and apple. Season lightly. Score the dark side of the turbot along the lateral line, through to the bone and put it into the dish, dark side down. Pour on the cider or wine and enough stock barely to cover the fish: lay a butter paper on top.

Bring to simmering point on top of the stove, using a heat-diffuser mat if need be. Then transfer to the oven and leave until the turbot is just cooked – start checking after 20 minutes. Remove the fish to a hot serving plate and keep warm.

Strain the cooking liquor into a shallow pan, pressing the juices through. Add any stock you did not use. Reduce by half. Whisk in the cream, reduce again, and finish with 4–6 tablespoons of butter. Season to taste. Meanwhile cook the mushrooms in a little butter, squeezing a little lemon juice over them to keep them white. Season them.

Put the mushrooms round the turbot, and serve the sauce in a separate sauceboat.

TURBOT WITH LOBSTER OR SHRIMP SAUCE

Here is one of the great dishes of English cookery, one that nobody ever sneered at. It is an example of the dictum that the finer the fish, the less you should do to it. To keep their end up, chefs devised a way of decorating it with an outline scallop of lobster eggs – which is fun to do, but unnecessary unless you have to prove genius in lieu of hard work.

If lobster is too difficult to find, and shrimp seems too ordinary, try an oyster sauce instead, p. 263. If shellfish is your allergy, remember that Thackeray who knew a great deal about food liked turbot best with plain melted butter.

Serves 4

1 chicken turbot, weighing about 1½ kg (3 lb)
½ lemon, sliced
milk (optional)
white wine vinegar (optional)
salt

SAUCE

1 small hen lobster, boiled, complete with eggs or 250 ml (8 fl oz) shelled
   shrimps or prawns, a hard-boiled egg and some chopped parsley
½ leek or medium-sized onion, sliced
1 stalk celery, sliced
fish stock* (see recipe)
125 g (4 oz) unsalted butter
2 teaspoons plain flour
salt, pepper, cayenne

The fishmonger will have cleaned the turbot, but you will find it a help with evenness of cooking if you score deeply through the dark skin, through to the bone.

Next take a piece of paper, roughly the size of the turbot and well within it, draw the shape of a scallop shell – try and make this reasonably graceful not like a petrol station sign. Carefully cut out this outline and a few ribs to make a stencil: this you need for the final garnishing.

The next job is the stock for the sauce. Put the lobster or shrimp shells and debris into a pan. Cover completely with water, add leek or onion and celery and simmer for 40 minutes: if you happen to have plain fish stock handy in the freezer, use this instead of the water, but it is not essential.

Strain off the liquid and reduce it to 175 ml (6 fl oz). Put the softer shells hot into the processor with the butter and whizz them to a sludge-like state. Push what you can of this sludge through a fine sieve: you should end up with a quantity of lobster or shrimp butter roughly equal to the amount you put into the processor.

Mix the flour with a little cold water in a small heavy pan. Heat gently while you stir, so that the liquid thickens without coming to the boil or even close to it. Take the pan from the heat and stir in the shellfish butter. When the turbot is dished up and ready to serve, put the pan back on the heat and continue to stir until you feel the weight of the sauce against the spoon. Taste it, correct the seasoning, add cayenne, then the lobster cut up or shrimps or prawns.

Returning to the turbot, put it into a pan that will hold it in reasonable comfort. If you anticipate problems removing it to a serving dish later on, slip a wide band of double foil underneath. Put in the lemon slices, the milk or a good splash of white wine vinegar, then enough cold water to cover the fish. Add plenty of salt: if you do not intend to keep the cooking liquor, make it very salty indeed.

Bring – or as one authority said, lead – the liquid to the boil and then stop the boiling at once, maintaining the temperature at just below boiling point until the fish is done. Look after 8 minutes where you made the underneath cut, to see how things are going. You will then be able to judge how much longer will be needed.

Slide the turbot on to its warm dish. Put the stencil on top and scatter it with the sieved lobster eggs, or hard-boiled egg and parsley. Decorate with little bunches of parsley, tucked underneath. Carefully raise the stencil so as not to disturb the elegant scallop. Serve with the sauce in a separate bowl or sauceboat.

TURBOT WITH MUSHROOM RAGOÛT

We were standing dejectedly, one Wednesday afternoon, by the fish stall at Montoire market, comparing the size of the turbot in front of us with the size of my largest frying pan. Madame Soarès clumped up to us briskly in her Wellington boots. 'Don't worry. I'll cut you a beautiful fillet. And I'll give you a recipe. *Extrà*!' In Madame Soarès' hands, we are as spineless as squid; she treats us like gentle barbarians who need to be shown the light, and to be pushed a little for their own good. We watched her remove a large section from the majestic creature, then shape two pieces from it of exactly the right size. 'Now,' she said, leaning forward earnestly, 'this is what you do . . .'

That scene took place, alas, over twenty years ago. Madame Soarès retired a few years later and comes no more to market in Montoire. The fish stall now is poor by comparison with those days. You have excellent service, but no good advice, although the friendliness is unabated. The French are feeling the pinch so choice and freshness are not quite what they were, although still remarkable by British standards. To be sure of something special we have to go to Vendôme, where Jacky Soarès, the son, sells good fish, or to Tours where in the covered market at the first stall on the right you can choose from between eighty-five and a hundred kinds of fish, shellfish and cured fish.

Serves 6

6 pieces of turbot fillet
salt, pepper
turbot bones
175 g (6 oz) unsalted butter
375 g (12 oz) trimmed mushrooms, sliced, woodland mushrooms or
    cultivated or the two mixed
1 clove garlic, finely chopped
6 tablespoons crème fraîche (see *recipe*)
chopped parsley
seasoned flour

Season the turbot with salt and pepper. Use the bones to make a little fish stock*, with the usual aromatics: you will need about 250 ml (8 fl oz). Clarify half the butter.

Melt the rest of the butter in a sauté pan and cook the mushrooms with the garlic. If they are the cultivated kind, cover the pan to conserve the juice at the start. Moisten the mushrooms with a little of the stock as they cook, adding more as the liquid reduces. Add seasoning and keep tasting. Add cream gradually to taste – you may not need it all. The point is that different kinds of mushroom produce different quantities of liquid as they cook. This means adding more or less stock as you go. Be guided by taste rather than by precise measures. Use the cream to soften the effect. Aim to end up with a moist ragoût rather than a lot of liquid. Pour it on to the warm serving dish. Scatter lightly with parsley.

Start cooking the turbot when the mushrooms are nearly ready. Dry and flour the pieces and cook them to a nice golden colour in the clarified butter. Allow about 2 minutes a side, but be guided by their thickness. Arrange them on top of the mushrooms, and serve. If it is the season, new potatoes go well with this dish.

TWAITE SHAD *see* A FEW WORDS ABOUT . . . SHAD

WALLEYE *see* PERCH

WEEVER *see* A FEW WORDS ABOUT . . . WEEVER

† WHITEBAIT

One of the treats I best remember as a child was being taken by my mother – rather stealthily – to Lyons Corner House, at Piccadilly Circus, for the purpose of eating whitebait, with lemon and brown bread and butter. It was a dish of her nostalgic youth in London, when she was an art student. Now she lived in the north, and felt that my education was lacking in this essential experience, and must be remedied. At first I was alarmed at the crisp mound of minuscule bodies, complete with eyes, which were placed in front of me. Then I saw my mother tucking in with an impressive wave of her fork, and had to follow suit. I soon found out how right she had been. By the way she talked, I understood that whitebait was an inalienable right for Londoners, and at the time accepted her enthusiasm without enquiry. Only thirty years later, when whitebait began to appear quite frequently on pub menus outside London, did the story of this tiny fish and its enormous fame begin to reveal itself.

Whitebait is not, in fact, a separate species, but the small fry mainly of herrings and sprats. They used to be caught in shoals in the Thames off Blackwall and Greenwich, from the early spring to the end of August. As far as I can make out, the idea of whitebait dinners as a goal for excursions began with some enterprising restaurateur in Blackwall towards the end of the eighteenth century, but what gave these tiny fish their particular cachet was their appearance at the annual ministerial whitebait dinner held during most of the nineteenth century at Greenwich (I think the last one was held in 1894).

These dinners had their origin in a close political friendship. The MP for Dover, Robert Preston, a rich merchant of Scotland and Nova Scotia, had a cottage on the banks of Dagenham Reach, an idyllic sort of place. He was in the habit of inviting a friend of his, George Rose, commonly known as Old George Rose, down for the day near the end of the parliamentary session, some time towards the end of May. One year, Old George, then Secretary to the Treasury, asked if he could bring another close friend of his, Pitt, the Prime Minister. The day went well, the three men got on happily over the bottles and the occasion was repeated. The only snag was the long journey in those pre-railway days. To make things easier, Robert Preston invited the two men to dine at Greenwich; a fourth and then a fifth friend, both in the government, were invited along and eventually the annual whitebait dinner became a semi-official way of celebrating the end of the parliamentary session. The original three were all members of Trinity House, the date was fixed each year soon after Trinity Monday just before the House rose, and the dinners went on long after the deaths of Pitt and Old George and Robert Preston.

Other Londoners, rich and poor, Whig as well as Tory, delighted in what was then a jaunt to the countryside, to eat whitebait. Everyone set out to have a good time. Like the Trinity House trio, they drank too much, which led occasionally to rioting and fights among the lower orders; the nobs, I take it, got drunk more quietly. 'The peculiar attraction . . . consists in the trip, the locality, the fresh air, and perhaps the whitebait − for it loses its delicacy by transportation, and is seldom so well dressed as in the immediate proximity of its haunts.'

Whitebait dinners could be ordered that were far more than a picnic or a pub lunch. In 1835, according to Thomas Walker, in his short-lived weekly, *The Original*, the smart place to go was Lovegrove's in Blackwall. There he had ordered the following dinner for a party of eight: 'Turtle, followed by no other fish but whitebait; which is to be followed by no other meat but grouse; which are to be succeeded by apple fritters and jelly.' They finished off with ices and a good dessert. They drank punch with the turtle, claret with the grouse − and champagne with the whitebait. The post-mortem concluded that a Water-souchy of flounders should have come after the turtle.

That was a simple little meal compared with the feast described by that splendid gastronome, Thomas Love Peacock who, a few years on, made his way there with friends, in the heat of the summer:

All day we sat, until the sun went down –
'Twas summer, and the Dog-star scorched the town –
At fam'd Blackwall, O Thames! upon thy shore,
Where Lovegrove's tables groan beneath their store;
We feasted full on every famous dish,
Dress'd many ways, of sea and river fish –
Perch, mullet, eels, and salmon, all were there,
And whitebait, daintiest of our fishy fare;
Then meat of many kinds, and venison last,
Quails, fruits, and ices crowned the rich repast.
Thy fields, Champagne, supplied us with our wine,
Madeira's Island, and the rocks of Rhine.
The sun was set, and twilight veiled the land:
Then all stood up – all who had strength to stand,
And pouring down, of Maraschino, fit
Libations to the gods of wine and wit,
In steam-wing'd chariots, and on iron roads,
Sought the great city, and our own abodes.

In other words, they went home by train.

As a comment on occasions such as this, I quote a distich by Tennyson's eccentric elder brother, Frederick:

I had a vision very late
After a dinner of whitebait.

It might seem from all this that whitebait is an exclusively English delicacy and, perhaps in the scale of its celebrations over more than a century, it is indeed unique. Many other countries, though, eat similar dishes. The riverside Friture de poisson in France has the same air of country festivity, although the fish tend to be larger. There are also *blanchailles* to be found (*bianchetti* in Italy) and a melange of pellucid sole and other minute items of the *Gobiidae* family found in the Mediterranean area under the name of *nonnats*. They eat such things, too, in New Zealand and South America, and I dare say in Africa, Australia and China. And 'virtually any saltwater bay along the East or West coasts of America will provide a whitebait dinner', consisting mainly of tiny sand-eels and silversides. The Japanese eat whitebait – *shirasu* – and have regarded them with an admiring delight as they shimmer in their close thousands beneath the surface.

As though the colour of the water
were moving.

Bashô, the great haiku poet, saw in them the situation of powerless masses restrained by the power of the few:

> The whitebait
> Opens its black eyes
> In the net of the Law.

Quite a thought next time you buy a package of frozen whitebait!

HOW TO BUY AND PREPARE WHITEBAIT

Of course, whitebait should be eaten fresh whatever species it may consist of and wherever you may find them. In some places you might be able to catch them yourself – 'a simple haul seine (a 10-foot [3-m] length of net with a fine mesh) is all that's required.'

In Britain, we are unlikely to see whitebait fresh at all except, I would suppose, at Southend when they have the annual whitebait festival. What we do have is frozen whitebait of reasonable quality, which can be bought at the better groceries and freezer centres. Pubs serve them sometimes, quite properly with brown bread and butter and a wedge of lemon. They make a much better choice than ginger-crumbed plaice or extruded scampi in armoured batter.

There is only one way to cook whitebait, fresh or thawed. Do not attempt to gut the tiny creatures, just rinse and drain them and divide them into batches, according to the capacity of your deep-fryer.

Dip the first batch into milk, then shake them in a paper bag containing some seasoned flour. Put them into the fryer basket, shaking off excess flour, and plunge them into the hot oil until they are brown and crisp. Serve immediately.

For devilled whitebait, which is even more of a pleasure, add cayenne to the seasoned flour, and sprinkle the cooked fish with more cayenne.

WHITEFISH *see* TROUT

† WHITING

Merlangius merlangus

Some people do not care for whiting. They remember small grey fish coming to table curled round so that the tail was stuck through the eye sockets – a perverted fancy sometimes known as *merlans en colère*. They may also remember how wholesome this object was supposed to be (wholesome was once the English excuse for serving tasteless and watery food to children). They shudder at such recollections.

It is not worth arguing against prejudice of this kind. Just buy filleted whiting, and present them under their old name of marling or merling. Make sure, of course, that they taste delicious, which they will do if you cook them in the Dieppe style or serve them with Alan Davidson's samphire sauce* or an orange sauce* which suits them particularly well. When filleted, whiting lack their blunted heads and have an attractive kipper shape because they are boned out from the back and not from the belly. These small whiting are the best to eat directly. Fillets of some length from larger whiting are the thing to buy for fish terrines and quenelles.

What are the advantages of whiting? For a start, it is one of the more rewarding members of the cod family. Not, you may think, a relationship to raise the cook's blood pressure, but it does mean that the flesh is firm, with sweet flakes, and a kind of pearly quality, and that it is abundant – in other words, cheap. Much whiting is landed in Scotland (*see* wind-dried fish, p. 494), where it has a much stronger identity in people's minds than it does in England. A pity since, in my experience, whiting comes to the fishmonger's counter in the south in far better shape than most cod, and of such quality that it can be used in sole dishes without inviting sour comments, rather as mussels can be used in oyster recipes without disgrace.

The French who know a good fish when they see one, recognize this. They serve whiting with beautiful sauces like those which follow. They turn them into *jeux d'esprit* such as quenelles (p. 275) and dish them up with white wine*, mushroom* or shrimp* sauces. They may simply dip them in egg and breadcrumbs, and fry them in butter, or turn them into delicate stuffings for other fish and for terrines, or use them in soups and stews.

HOW TO CHOOSE AND PREPARE WHITING

Never be fobbed off with tired whiting. After all the fresh is easy enough to spot; it has a bright look. Faded whiting blurs to a flop as truthfully as any rose. Buy whiting whole if you can. Their plump bellies give an indication of their freshness, as well as the brightness of their eye. If you do this, you can clean them yourself and retain the livers which you incorporate into the sauce sometimes (*see* the Le Duc recipe, below) or cook briefly when you cook the fish. Scrape off the few scales and rinse, then dry before cooking them.

To fillet the fish, chop off the heads and remove the guts. With a small sharp knife, slit down the back, scrape one side from the bone and lay it flat, skin side down. Then, holding the bone, scrape the other side free, until you have a neat triangular shape lying in front of you, skin side down. Season and set aside for 20 or 30 minutes.

BASIC FISH TERRINE

One of the pleasures of Paris is analysing the fish terrines in the windows of Fauchon's, in the Place Madeleine. One in particular appeals to me, with its bands of pink and white, touches of yellow and streaks of grey. I did once buy a slice and was, inevitably, disappointed even though the central fish was eel. The trouble is that for slicing neatly, the texture has to be too solid for good eating – like those party jellies of one's youth that failed to melt in the mouth. I suppose you might describe a fish terrine as a type of blancmange: for success, they need delicate handling and the best ingredients.

The basis of a fish terrine is a mousseline, for which whiting is an ideal choice. *As long as you have a processor*, it is simple to make. If you have no machinery, turn to another recipe altogether. Unless, of course, you want to give yourself a history lesson, Squeers style, and discover why such things disappeared from our menus when skivvies abandoned our kitchens.

If you decide to cook the mousseline mixture in small moulds to be served individually, the contrasting interest will lie in the sauce (or sauces, since the plate might be partly covered with a red pepper purée, and partly with a yellow pepper purée, before the moulds are turned out). If you decide to make the loaf-shaped terrine that is cut across into slices, contrast comes from bits and pieces of special virtue that are layered with the mousseline, as well as from the sauce. These could range from fillets of a contrasting fish to oysters, mussels and shrimps, which should all be lightly cooked and free of their shells; herbs and lightly cooked, bright vegetables and mushrooms should also be considered.

Since wateriness is a danger, never use a raw item that loses liquid as it cooks, oysters and mussels for instance, tomato, mushrooms especially girolles. Cook them lightly first, and cool them. Also reflect that since the oven heat will be kept low, any central treasures that you put in to vary the terrine must be agreeably edible both in themselves and in contrast with the smooth mousseline. A sliver of raw pepper or a teaspoon of raw peas spells disaster.

Terrines are luxuries, and by definition expensive. However cheap the fish you use – say whiting and Finnan haddock – you will have quite a bill when you add on the cream required, and the sauce. You can tackle the cost of reducing the ingredients and cooking the mixture in small individual pots. Or you can do something quite different in method but similar in effect, by making a cream instead, or what is sometimes called – trust the English – a fish custard.

Mousseline

Classic fish are whiting, pike and sole, *see* pp. 276 and 391. Scallops are the current choice. Salmon, eel, halibut all do well, so do turbot and sea bream and John Dory.

> *500 g (1 lb) trimmed, skinned, fillets of the chosen fish* or *trimmed scallops, white part only*
> *2 egg whites*
> *250 ml (8 fl oz) crème fraîche, double* or *whipping cream*
> *salt, pepper, cayenne*
> *lemon juice, herbs, etc. to taste*

Chill the first three ingredients, plus the processor bowl and blade, for an hour. Turn out a couple of trays of ice cubes into a handy bowl and keep them in the fridge or freezer until needed.

Set the processor whirling, quickly cut up the fish and drop it on to the blades, alternating with egg white. Using the pulse switch for close control, pour in the cream. You should end up with a smooth light bulky mass. Season to taste. Put into the refrigerator while you prepare the contrasting bits and pieces. Work fast so that everything remains as cold as possible.

SPECIAL INTEREST
375 g (12 oz) trimmed fish fillet of a contrasting colour or *shelled cooked*
    shrimps, oysters, mussels or *a mixture that includes Finnan haddock*
chopped parsley, chervil, tarragon or chives or *cooked spinach, sorrel or*
    laverbread or *the cooked tender tips of samphire*
salt, pepper, cayenne, and nutmeg if appropriate

Cut the fish into long thin strips and season them. Range the other items beside them, ready to hand.

TO ASSEMBLE   Brush a terrine or non-stick loaf tin or 1½ litres (2½ pt) capacity lightly with sunflower oil. Make two strips of doubled foil, one long enough to go down the sides and length of the tin with a little over, the second long enough to go across the tin. Press them into place and brush them with oil, too. When you come to turning out the terrine, you will be able to ease it by moving the ends of these strips.

Into the terrine put three layers of mousseline divided by two layers of the special items you have chosen. Should you be using shrimp, remember not to put them flat but upright, stuck slightly into the mousseline so that they appear in the slices as tight round pink coils. Knock the base of the terrine on the table so that the layers shake down together.

Cover with a buttered paper and either the lid of the terrine or a double layer of foil, tied in place.

TO COOK   Switch on the oven to gas 4, 180 °C, 350 °F. Put together a bain-marie on top of the stove: place a low rack in a deep roasting tin and stand the terrine on the rack. Pour almost boiling water into the tin, enough to come up to the base of the terrine. Turn on the heat and bring the water to boiling point. Transfer the whole thing to the pre-heated oven. Leave for about 30 minutes. Stick a skewer into the centre. If it comes out hot and the terrine seems firm, it is ready to come out.

TO SERVE HOT OR WARM   Let the terrine cool slightly, then turn it out on to a hot serving dish. Pour round it a white wine* or Normandy* sauce, or serve an hollandaise* or sauce Choron* separately.

If you want to leave the terrine to keep warm for 10 minutes, do not remove the cooking terrine or tin but leave it in place over the inverted terrine on its serving dish; this prevents collapse.

TO SERVE COLD   Leave to cool, then ease the straps of foil and turn the whole thing over on to a dish. Leave until next day in the refrigerator; the terrine will have parted company from the mould, which can then be lifted off.

LES FILETS DE MERLAN VALLÉE D'AUGE

The Pays d'Auge, the region surrounding the river and its valley, is the heartland of Normandy cooking. All the good things are to be found there – cider and Calvados, excellent cream, Camembert and Livarot cheeses (though Gruyere is used in this recipe, which is the norm in French cookery). In spite of agribusiness and the demands of the EEC, it is still a pretty place, timbered farms and manors with dovecots, farm buildings put down like toys into orchards, with irises growing along the roof ridges. They could be wrapped up and sold at Hamley's or Harrods' toy department.

Add to all these advantages, a coastline of ports able to supply the freshest of fish, and you may find a steely envy tightening your jaw. Especially if you live just across the Channel in Kent, where things could be, but are not the same.

This recipe is simple, which means that the ingredients must be good. The fish should be sparkling fresh, the cider good enough to drink with the meal.

Serves 6

6 filleted whiting
salt, pepper, cayenne
*5 tablespoons clarified butter**
300 g (10 oz) chopped onion
300 ml (10 fl oz) dry cider
6 tablespoons grated Gruyère cheese

Choose a shallow earthenware or gratin dish large enough to take the open whiting in a single layer. You will also need a heat-diffusing mat.

Season the whiting with salt, pepper and a little cayenne. Heat the butter in the dish and, when it melts, stir in the onion, spreading it out to cover the base of the dish. Cook over a low heat until it is tender. Lay the whiting on top, skin side down. Raise the heat to moderate, pour in the cider and sprinkle the tops of the fish with cheese.

When the cider comes just to boiling point, complete the cooking briefly either under a preheated grill or on the top shelf of the oven, preheated to gas 7, 220 °C (425 °F). Check after 3 minutes, and do not overcook.

MERLANS À LA DIEPPOISE

Whiting with mussels and mushrooms, in a white wine sauce.

Serves 6

6 filleted whiting
salt, pepper
1 kg (2 lb) mussels, cleaned
375 g (12 oz) button mushrooms, left whole
lemon juice
6 tablespoons unsalted butter
300 ml (10 fl oz) dry white wine or half wine, half fish stock
2 teaspoons plain flour (optional)

Season the fillets and place them in a single layer, head to tail, in a flameproof pan, skin side down.

Open the mussels in the usual way (p. 239), discard the shells and strain the liquor into a basin. Cook the mushrooms, with a little lemon juice to keep them white, in 4 tablespoons of butter: if they are on the large side – small buttons are not always easy to buy – quarter them. Strain off their juice into the mussel liquor, and add the wine. Keep mussels and mushrooms warm.

Pour the liquor over the fish. Bring to simmering point on top of the stove and cook until just done. Remove the whiting to a warm serving dish and surround them with the mussels and mushrooms. Keep warm while you finish the sauce.

Strain the cooking juices into a clean pan. Taste and reduce them to improve the strength of flavour. Mash the flour with the remaining tablespoons of butter, if you like – this was the original style – and use to thicken the sauce, adding it in little bits gradually (beurre manié technique). If you are one of today's farinophobes, you may prefer to reduce the liquid to a more robust strength and beat in the last of the butter (monter au beurre technique).

MERLANS À LA VERDURETTE

The title of this recipe, adapted from one given by Madame Prunier, might be translated as 'Whiting with a little greenery'. It is for wise and knowing people who collect woodland mushrooms, or for the lucky ones who can buy them. The quantity of mushrooms required is inevitably vague since, with ceps in particular, the damaged parts are difficult to gauge until you are back at home cleaning them. Girolles lose a lot of moisture in the cooking, although again this will vary with the season. Aim to end up with 500 g (1 lb) of cookable mushrooms, if you can, although you can get away fairly successfully with 375 g (12 oz) – a consideration, if you are buying them.

Serves 6

6 filleted whiting
salt, pepper
beaten egg and breadcrumbs or *seasoned flour*
clarified butter*
375–500 g (¾–1 lb) chopped chanterelles (girolles) or *ceps (boletus)*
   or *other woodland mushrooms*
sunflower oil
6 tablespoons butter, unsalted
4 tablespoons chopped shallot
2 teaspoons each chopped parsley, chervil and chives
4 tarragon leaves, chopped
salt, pepper
lemon juice

Season the whiting with salt and pepper, in advance if possible. Then dry it, and coat it with egg and breadcrumbs, or seasoned flour. Fry in clarified butter until golden, then keep warm.

    Meanwhile, deal with the sauce. Cook the mushrooms in a little sunflower oil until the juices flow and they are almost done. Pour off the juice (use on another occasion), and add the butter and shallot. Continue to cook for a minute or two to soften the shallot slightly (be careful not to colour it). Stir in the herbs and season, adding a little lemon juice if you like. Pour over the fish and serve.

MERLANS AU VIN ROUGE

In this recipe from the Minchelli brothers' restaurant, Le Duc, in Paris, a glass of reasonable claret is used to cook the whiting. Since the dish is for two, they obviously see the rest of the bottle being drunk with the dish and the cheese that will follow. A Premières Côtes de Bordeaux is recommended.

Serves 2

2 nice plump whiting, heads removed
4 shallots
1 long chive stalk
3 tablespoons lightly salted butter
1 clove garlic still in its skin, but crushed
6 tablespoons fish stock*
125 ml (4 fl oz) red wine
2 tablespoons crème fraîche
salt, pepper, sugar

Switch on the oven to gas 7, 220 °C (425 °F). Choose a gratin dish that will hold the whiting when they are filleted, spread out in a single layer, and set a heat-diffuser mat on the stove, if necessary.

Clean the whiting through the gills, saving the livers. Split and bone them from the back and lay them flat.

Chop the shallots with the chive stalk and cook it gently in the butter in the gratin dish, with the garlic. After a minute, pour in the stock and reduce by half, then add the wine. When it bubbles, put in the whiting, skin side down, and head to tail to save space. When the wine begins to bubble again, transfer to the oven. Check after 3 minutes, removing the dish when the whiting are just cooked. Transfer the whiting to a serving dish and keep warm.

Strain the juices into a small pan with a heavy base. Add the livers and the cream. Reduce over a moderate heat, stirring quietly with a wooden spoon. Taste and check the seasoning, adding a pinch or so of sugar to counteract the acidity of the wine. Pour over fish and serve immediately.

WHITING WITH AUBERGINE IN TWO FASHIONS

By cooking aubergine in two very different ways, you can make a lively accompaniment to whiting that sets off its pearly texture well.

If you feel that the coating of egg and breadcrumbs is too much, content yourself with flouring the fish before you cook it.

Serves 6

6 small filleted whiting
salt
6 aubergines, medium size, peeled
plain flour
sunflower oil
about 6 tablespoons olive oil
4 cloves garlic, crushed, finely chopped
2–3 tablespoons chopped parsley
beaten egg
plenty of fine breadcrumbs or *fine cornmeal*
clarified butter
lemon wedges or *fresh tomato sauce**

Season the whiting with salt and set aside. Pick out the two longest aubergines, cut them in halves across, then downwards into very thin slices. Dice the rest of the aubergines (including any lumpy bits left from the slicing) and put them into a colander, salting lightly as you go. Lay the slices on top and salt them, too, then weight them down with a dish. Leave for an hour. This preparation means the aubergines will absorb less oil.

Dry the thin slices carefully, flour them, shaking off any excess and deep-fry them in sunflower oil until crisp. This happens fast. Drain these crisps on kitchen paper in a low oven.

Next dry and cook the diced aubergines slowly in the olive oil, turning them about. When they are juicy and almost tender, turn up the heat and scatter on the garlic. Cook 3 minutes more. Season, stir in the parsley and keep warm.

Finally dry the whiting; flour, egg and breadcrumb them, or turn them in fine cornmeal. Fry in clarified butter until cooked and nicely coloured. Serve with the two lots of aubergines, with either lemon wedges or very fresh tomato sauce.

WOLF-FISH *see* A FEW WORDS ABOUT . . . CATFISH

YELLOW PERCH *see* PERCH

ZANDER *see* PERCH

A FEW WORDS ABOUT OTHER FISH & CRUSTACEANS

ABALONE, ORMER & SEA EAR
Haliotis tuberculata

It is easy to collect shells, whether from the beach or the junk shop, without ever realizing that each once had an occupant; in the case of the beautiful ormer or ear shell, with its nacreous lining of green, purple and silver lights, it was an occupant of a most desirable kind. In California they come in enormous sizes, and the edible white muscle is sold in large slices, already beaten (if they aren't beaten they are quite exceedingly tough). In Brittany, they are smaller but may still need beating. As far as the British Isles are concerned, you are unlikely to find them north of the Channel Islands.

There are two main ways of cooking them. The American system is to marinade the slices in oil and white wine, flavoured with chopped herbs and shallot. After a while they are removed and dried, and then cooked in butter very briefly like a steak. They are also chopped up and used in chowders and soups. The Breton and Channel Island system is to turn them into a stew.

ORMEAUX AU MUSCADET

Serves 6

1 kg (2 lb) shelled ormers
250 g (8 oz) unsalted butter
salt, pepper
1 clove garlic, chopped
1 large onion, chopped
plenty of parsley
3 cloves
bouquet garni
generous 450 ml (14 fl oz) Muscadet
beurre manié*

Having beaten the ormers energetically with a mallet, arrange them in layers in a flameproof casserole, dotting each layer with butter, seasoning, chopped garlic, onion and parsley. Add the cloves, bouquet garni and wine. Bring to the boil and simmer steadily for 30–45 minutes until the ormers are tender. Strain off the liquid; stir in the beurre manié in little pieces until the sauce thickens – keep it over a low heat so that it does not boil. Pour the sauce over the ormers, sprinkle on a little more parsley, and serve.

CARPET-SHELLS *Venerupis decussata*

Although two kinds of carpet-shell, the Cross-cut (*Tapes decussata*) and Pullet (*Tapes pullastra*), are common in Great Britain, I have never seen them on sale in a fishmonger's or on the menu of a restaurant. To eat them you will have to go to Brittany, where *palourdes farcies grillées* has made the name of several restaurants, or to Paris – or you will have to go and dig them up yourself. Equip the family with rakes and spoons – the advice of one French writer – and find a large extent of muddy, gravelly shore. Consult *Collins' Guide to the Sea Shore* for a description and illustration.

Open them like oysters or clams. The best recipe, in Breton style, is on p. 256, under Huîtres farcies grillées.

CATFISH, WOLF-FISH OR ROCK TURBOT *Anarhichas lupus*

This fierce creature, with its blunted head like a fold-eared cat, makes good eating. The long single-boned body provides firm flesh which, like tuna and angler-fish, can be treated like veal. The first time we bought it – in France – we were advised to pierce it with slivers of garlic, and either bake it in tomato sauce (*see* Lotte à l'américaine, p. 229), or fry it in clarified butter*. It benefits from a little sharpness, such as vinegar or lemon, in the final seasoning. You could also try it *au poivre* as in the turbot recipe, p. 436.

Owing to its fierce aspect, catfish is sold without the head and skin. In Britain the pinkish white fillets appear under the name of rock turbot – or rock salmon, which is more usually applied to dogfish. I dislike such names: they make comparisons which lead inevitably to the lesser fish's disadvantage. The French call it sea wolf. Are we too squeamish for this – or for the straightforward catfish or wolf-fish?

CATFISH WITH FENNEL AND BEURRE NOISETTE

Serves 6

3 large heads Florentine fennel, sliced
125 g (4 oz) butter
2 large onions, chopped
salt, pepper
3 cloves garlic
1–1½ kg (2–3 lb) tailpiece or fillet catfish
seasoned flour
*60 g (2 oz) clarified butter**
wine vinegar
parsley

Cook the fennel in boiling, salted water for 5 minutes, drain. Melt 60 g (2 oz) butter; stew the onion and fennel in it for about 20 minutes, until cooked but not brown. Season. Cut the garlic into slivers and push into incisions made in the fish with a sharp pointed knife. Turn the fish in seasoned flour, and fry gently in the clarified butter. Put the vegetables on a dish, with the catfish on top. Clean the fish pan and melt the last 60 g (2 oz) butter in it. When golden brown, pour it over the fish. Swill out the pan with a good dash of vinegar and pour on top of the butter. Sprinkle with chopped parsley and serve.

CONGER EEL *Conger conger*

When it is my turn for the ferry boat across the Styx, one of the people I hope to encounter in Hades is Nereus of Chios, a Greek chef who worked in Sybaris. He was famous for his preparation of conger eel, and I should like to know how he did it. I suspect he followed the cookery tradition of classical times and drowned the fish in seasonings and strong sauces. Now conger eel, being firm and insistent in flavour, might survive this treatment well – better, at any rate, than delicate fish like sole or turbot. The sauce for roast conger eel given some two thousand years ago by Apicius (who got his recipes mainly from Greek cooks working in Italy) included pepper, lovage, grilled cumin, oregano, dried onion, yolks of hard-boiled eggs, wine, honeyed wine, vinegar and *garum* – which was a fermented fish sauce (*see* p. 48) with a good deal more kick than anchovy essence.

I do not suggest that you follow Apicius to the letter, but remember that a little conger eel goes a long way and can stand up to a collection of other flavours. For this reason it is an excellent fish for soup, as you will see if you try the Breton recipe, below, or the Matelote Normande on p. 499. The conger makes a good basis of fish flavour.

Do not be fooled by writers who instruct you to cook conger eel like the silver eel from the Sargasso sea, *Anguilla anguilla*, one of the finest fish you can eat. General shape apart, they have nothing in common and your expectations will be disappointed. I suspect that this instruction is merely handed down from cookery book to cookery book, without anyone trying it out. I have, several times, and it was a disastrous waste. The only possible eel recipe would be the red wine and prunes matelote (p. 134) where, Apicius-style, the almost unpleasant flavour of conger in the piece is well subdued by stronger presences.

As a subsistence fish, it has its own little history. In Cornwall, until the end of the last century, 'conger-doust' was exported in quantity to Catholic countries, largely, I gather, for soup-making on fast days. This was conger, split, and dried without salting; a kind of stockfish. In Normandy, fishermen do the same thing, but season the boned conger with salt and pepper before drying it in the sun. It is eaten for breakfast with bread and butter, and milky coffee, just as the Scots used to eat wind-dried whiting and haddock (p. 495). Conger eel is also cooked, with onions and herbs, in vinegar, and stored as a preserve, like soused herring (p. 201). Pieces are removed from time to time and served at the beginning of a meal with oil and herbs, and bread and butter.

Always buy a thick piece of conger eel from the head end. The bones seem to multiply alarmingly towards the tail.

BRETON CONGER EEL SOUP

This is a good homely soup, to which extra vegetables can be added to taste; for instance, soaked haricot beans, a small amount of turnip, or onion.

Serves 6

750 g (1½ lb) conger eel
2 large leeks
oil
400 g (14 oz) can tomatoes
750 g (1½ lb) potatoes, peeled
bouquet garni
salt, pepper

Cut the conger eel into thick slices; then cook gently with the leeks in a large saucepan, with just enough oil to cover the base of the pan in a thin layer. Don't let them brown, but turn them about for 5 minutes. Add 1¾ litres (3 pt) of water. When it boils, add the tomatoes, the potatoes cut into dice, and the bouquet garni. Simmer for 45 minutes, skimming off the murky looking foam which rises. Remove the conger eel, discard the skin and bones and return the pieces to the soup. Discard, too, the bouquet. Correct the seasoning and serve.

CROAKERS & DRUMS *Sciaenidae* spp.

There are many kinds of croakers and drums spread all over the world. Like the gurnard, they owe their names to the pronounced noises they make by vibrating a muscle attached to the air-bladder, which then acts as a resonator (*see* p. 468). The drums include the corvina of Peru, the fish traditionally used to make Ceviche (p. 348); the weakfish and kingfish of North America; the kabeljou of South Africa; and the mulloway of Australia. Also in the family is the meagre, which I first came across in France: it lay on the fish stall, plump and silvery-grey, looking like a sea bass. This was not surprising as these fish are related to the sea perches, or groupers, of which the bass is one: the recipes for bass and bream are all suitable for the meagre.

Large drums and croakers can be cooked according to recipes for cod steaks and fillets; really small fish can be grilled, or else dipped in beaten egg and breadcrumbs and deep-fried (in America cornmeal would be used instead of breadcrumbs).

Our fish was 375 g (12 oz) in weight. Madame Soarès, who sold it to us, suggested we should bake it in the oven. Then remembering we had no oven, she suggested we fry it meunière, in clarified butter. This was most successful because the skin turned to a golden crispness which made an excellent contrast to the sweet flavour and soft texture of the bass-like flesh. Some lemon juice and a few potatoes were all the addition it needed.

† DOGFISH alias FLAKE, HUSS or RIGG

Scyliorhinus canicula

I cannot be the only person to associate dogfish with the appalling smell of formalin. On dissecting days at school, too often Fridays, the smell became unforgettably united, about halfway up the stairs, with the smell of fish pie. A cacophony of smell. No wonder the fish authorities have preferred the names of flake, huss and rigg.

There is good warrant for these names. Frank Buckland visited Folkestone harbour in the last century and saw that most of the fishermen's houses were adorned 'with festoons of fish hung out to dry. There was no head, tail or fins to them ... the rough skin on their reverse side told me at once that they were a species of dogfish. I asked what they were? "Folkestone beef," was the reply. What sort of fish is that? "That's a Rig", and this? "That's a Huss", and this other? "That! A 'bull huss'."' He went on to say that as soon as the boats arrived, the fish-dealers could be seen cutting off the heads, tails and fins and halving the fish, which were then salted and hung out to dry. When grilled, they tasted like veal chops, and were eaten 'by the poorer class, as a relish for breakfast'.

The word dogfish covers a variety of small sharks, as fierce as a pack of wild dogs. They have a keen sense of smell, and hunt mackerel, herring and whiting like a pack of hounds.

All this being said, the name will not do. We are too closely attached to family dogs to eat anything that bears their name. The same with cats. I think that flake, huss and rigg are therefore reasonable. Rock salmon or rock turbot for catfish is a less happy choice of alias. It verges on a con trick, because catfish is not remotely like salmon or turbot at any point; rockfish is a better choice.

Good quality huss is certainly a wiser buy than a piece of tired white fillet of nothing-in-particular. It repays attention. Cut it into 8-cm (3-inch) pieces – the body is long and roughly eel-shaped – and coat them in seasoned flour. Fry gently until a true golden-brown, in butter, or preferably clarified butter*. Serve them with natural brown rice, boiled and tender, and with a creamy sauce. The curry sauce* is an excellent choice. So is sauce aurore*, or a white wine sauce; seasoning and richness.

Another way is to brown the floured pieces lightly in olive oil flavoured with garlic, and to transfer them to a tomato*, créole* or américaine* sauce to finish cooking.

Very fresh huss can be deep-fried in batter* and served hot or cold, with an olive oil and lemon vinaigrette*, or one of the highly flavoured mayonnaises*.

DOLPHINFISH OR DORADO

One of the fish now being imported from the Caribbean is the dolphinfish or dorado. It is also fairly common in the Mediterranean where it usually appears under the name of lampuga.

This strange grey and gilded creature, with a blunt, cat-like head and unbroken fins down its long body, has a delicious flavour. It should be better known. Do not be put off by the name – this fish has nothing to do with true dolphins which are mammals.

Dolphinfish is a suitable candidate for the américaine treatment, (p. 213). In general it should be treated in a southern style – for instance, steaks baked in the oven with some kind of chopped and moistened mixture on top. The pine-kernel stuffing on p. 359 is good, or a chop-up of onions, butter, herbs and a few breadcrumbs, with grated lemon peel (what the Italians call a *battuto*).

If steaks are to be grilled, it is wise to marinade them first (oil, lemon, garlic); or if there is not time for this, wrap them in foil before grilling (buttered foil, plus lemon, finely chopped onion and so on). The parcels can always be opened for the last part of the cooking in order to brown the tops.

FLYING FISH *Atheriniformes* spp.

Several varieties are caught in the tropical and sub-tropical seas of the world. Their flight is more apparent than the garfish's or saury's, lasting for quite a few seconds with the help of the huge pectoral fins which sustain the leaping movements of the tail. Their head is a conventional fish-shape, with no protracted beak. When you spread out the spiny fins, they give an almost bird-like impression of flight.

Flying fish used to come to this country only as frozen, grey-black creatures, about 20–25 cm (8–10 inches) long, fins plastered to their body by ice. However, I have occasionally been able to buy flying fish from enterprising fishmongers. In my experience, it is not the flavour or the texture of flying fish that is so remarkable but their beautiful shape with the wing-like fins that enable them to leap from the sea.

When grilled, the flesh is firm, almost white, pinkish-brownish, in nice flakes. It has a slightly cured taste, with a hint of buckling about it. It is not as oily as mackerel, but richer than garfish. As we ate it the first time, I reflected that fish from warm seas do not have the flavour of northern fish. Many people have said this so I don't think that the observation is a matter of cold-climate chauvinism.

The recipes for gurnard would also be suitable for flying fish; so would some of the baked herring and mackerel recipes on pp. 182–5 and 223–7.

FLYING FISH PIE

Serves 4–6

3 kg (1½ lb) fillets of flying fish
salt, pepper
butter
1 kg (2 lb) yams
1 large onion
1 large tomato
2 hard-boiled eggs
2 egg yolks
2 tablespoons groundnut or *sunflower oil*
2 tablespoons unsalted butter
1 tablespoon Worcestershire sauce
6 tablespoons dry sherry

Season the fillets and fry them lightly on both sides in butter. Then cut the pieces in two. Peel and cook the yams, cool and slice thinly. Slice the onion thinly, also the tomato and the hard-boiled eggs. Beat together the egg yolks, oil, melted unsalted butter, Worcestershire sauce and sherry.

Butter a deep dish lavishly. Put in half the fish; scatter on top half the onion-tomato-egg mixture. Then cover neatly with half the yams. Repeat with another layer, and brush the top with melted butter. Pour over the egg-yolk mixture.

Bake in an oven preheated to gas 4, 180 °C (350 °F) for about half an hour until the top is brown and everything heated through. Be prepared to give it a little longer, but avoid overcooking at all costs.

FRESHWATER CRAYFISH
Astacus pallipes & *A. fluviatilis*

Pollution has not helped the freshwater crayfish, which likes very clear, oxygenated streams. These miniature lobsters have been favourite eating for a long time. Hannah Glasse gives recipes for crayfish soup, one demanding fifty, and the other two hundred: 'save out about 20, then pick the rest from the shells'. But there are less extravagant and more delectable ways of cooking them, for those who are lucky enough to live in chalk and limestone parts of the country where they can indulge in crayfishing parties at night. (The best bait is not-too-fresh meat; a sheep's head is the thing, or some bits of meat concealed in the centre of a faggot of sticks: the crayfish cling to the head, or crawl right into the sticks, and can then be drawn out of the water in quantity – this is the theory.)

The most famous of all crayfish recipes is, I suppose, Sauce Nantua, but a simpler crayfish sauce is also excellent with chicken, as you will see if you try the following recipe.

CHICKEN WITH CRAYFISH

This is a beautiful recipe from Le Lièvre Amoureux at Saint Lattier in the Isère.

Serves 6

1 chicken, cut into joints
8 tablespoons butter
salt, pepper
375 ml (12 fl oz) dry white wine
2 large tomatoes, peeled, chopped
1 kg (2 lb) crayfish
1 tablespoon chopped shallot
1 clove garlic, crushed
1 glass cognac
2 tablespoons plain flour
125 ml (4 fl oz) chicken stock
pinch of saffron
90 ml (3 fl oz) Madeira
3 tablespoons double cream
1 tablespoon fresh chervil, chopped

Fry the chicken in half the butter until lightly browned. Season, and add a third of the wine. Cover and leave to simmer, adding the rest of the wine at intervals. About 10 minutes before the chicken is cooked, put the tomatoes into the pan and finish cooking.

To cook the crayfish, fry them in the rest of the butter until they turn red. Add the shallot and garlic, stirring them into the pan. Pour on the cognac and set it alight. Sprinkle on the flour, let it brown a little and moisten with the chicken stock and dry white wine. Add the saffron and seasoning, and leave to simmer for 3 minutes. Pour in the chicken and its cooking liquor. Cover and leave for another 3 minutes. Finally stir in the Madeira and cream.

Put the chicken pieces on a warm serving dish with the crayfish, keeping a few of these to garnish the top. Pour the sauce over, without sieving it, and sprinkle with chervil.

ÉCREVISSES À LA NAGE

This is a favourite French way of serving these rare and delicious creatures so long as you have plenty. Allow a minimum of 6 per person: 9 or 12 will be more gratefully received.

Serves 6

white wine court bouillon, no. 5*
a few grains of aniseed

cayenne pepper
½ stick celery
36 or more crayfish

Boil the court bouillon, with the extra aromatics, until reduced by half.

Meanwhile, wash the live crayfish in plenty of water, drain them well. Remove the intestine if you can, by pulling out the middle tail fin. Tip them into the fast-boiling liquid and simmer for 12 minutes, with the lid on the pan.

Put the unshelled crayfish into a bowl (they are often piled up in an elegant arrangement) and strain the bouillon over them.

SAUCE NANTUA

This is a fine sauce made with freshwater crayfish – *not with lobster*. Any dish with the word Nantua attached to it means 'garnished with freshwater crayfish and serve with Sauce Nantua'.

Once after a brief holiday at Lake Annecy, we stopped at this small town in the mountains with its own calm blue lake. I went to buy picnic food, and remembered being disappointed that the streets were not paved with écrevisses. There weren't any in the shops either. Perhaps I was just unlucky. Perhaps it was the wrong day. Perhaps the entire haul of those miniature lobsters from the many streams around the town is taken by the two best hotels. Certainly their menus proclaimed Quenelles de brochet Nantua, Gratin d'écrevisses Nantua, Croustade de queues d'écrevisses.

In our part of western France the lack of crayfish is lamented. Detergents are blamed, so are chemical fertilizers and weed-killers washed by rain from the soil into small streams. If you are lucky and live in the Cotswolds, or some other part of England where crayfish are to be found, plan to make this delicious sauce. Then go out and find pike for the quenelles on p. 275 or else invest in a boiling fowl, as this is good with Sauce Nantua: or serve the sauce with poached sole or salmon.

Once you have achieved the crayfish, your troubles are over. To a béchamel sauce*, add 300 ml (10 fl oz) single cream and reduce to about 450 ml (15 fl oz) – a nice creamy consistency. Finish with 3 tablespoons double cream, 3–5 tablespoons of crayfish butter (p. 210), and a generous tablespoon of shelled crayfish tails. Truffles and truffle juice may be added, but for most people this is even further beyond expectation than crayfish, or a few mushrooms stewed in butter can be used as a garnish, and their cooking juice added to the sauce.

† GARFISH & NEEDLENOSE OR SAURY
Belone belone & Scomberesox saurus

Garfish may not be an epicure's delight, but they have some enchanting characteristics, more than enough to enhance the good but unexciting flavour. Although they are plentiful enough in our waters, we saw them first in France at our weekly market. The blueish-green glow of their long narrow bodies stood out amongst the herring and mussels; so did the protracted beaks armoured with a row of tiny vicious teeth (garfish – the name goes back to the Middle Ages – means spearfish or javelinfish, from the shape of this beaky snout). The label said orphies. Name and appearance were worthy of a fairy tale, or one of the lighter stories of mythology. In her quick way, Madame Soarès the fishmonger saw we were hooked, and came over to explain that the glowing sheen of the skin was repeated in the bones. 'I'll cut one up to show you . . . See?' Sure enough they were an exquisite greenish-blue, like Persian plates in a museum. The colour doesn't disappear in the heat of cooking either, so you have an elegant articulation of peacock glory against the white flesh on your plate. (It is caused by a harmless phosphate of iron, discovered in 1823 by J. G. Vivian and named vivianite.)

Another amiable characteristic is the way garfish leap out of the water to escape prowling tuna fish, or to snap at the tiny herrings and sprats they live on. It is not the real flight of a bird, a flight which changes direction and soars and dips, but more of a 'skittering' over the sea propelled by strong tail movements.

Garfish arrive on the west coast of England in early summer, swimming into shallow water just ahead of the mackerel – in some parts they are called mackerel guide or mackerel scout – to spawn in the seaweed. Apparently housewives in the East End of London like to buy them. The rest of England doesn't get much of a chance. No demand. (I always wonder how we are expected to 'demand' fish we have never had the opportunity of seeing or hearing about.)

Madame Soarès doesn't suffer from that kind of fishmonger's laziness and stupidity. She delights in the unusual. The moment your eye flickers towards something new, she is there. Like a Colette of the marketplace, she pours out information with feeling and drama, from a treasure of hoarded experience. Usually there is a recitative on the history, capture and character traits of the fish, rising to an aria of recipes and sauces. In this case the recitative was the thing, because the garfish doesn't offer much scope for culinary enterprise.

The saury (*Scomberesox saurus*) is related to the garfish, and looks very like it. The beak is similarly protracted – for which reason Americans call it needlenose and needlefish. It leaps from the water, too, though rather more vigorously, and is sometimes called skipper. One thing distinguishes it instantly from its cousin – two rows of small tuftlike fins between the dorsal fins and the tail. When you cook and eat it, you could not guess the difference since the bones have a greeny peacock glory too. It is caught down the east coast of America and in the Caribbean, as well as in Europe and North Africa. Other related species are found in the Atlantic and Pacific: occasionally they can be bought in cans.

How to prepare garfish and needlenose

Cut off the head, tail and fins. Clean out well. Cut across into 5–7-cm (2–3-inch) pieces. Dip them in seasoned flour and fry them in clarified butter. A few lemon quarters, some bread or potatoes in butter, a glass of white wine, and there you are – simple gustatory pleasure with plenty of conversation.

The Danes who eat a good deal of hornfisk (garfish) sometimes poach it in very salty water or a court bouillon*. French friends have recommended a green sauce sharpened with sorrel* which is fine if you feel the occasion requires embellishment, or if garfish often comes your way and you want a change. I prefer the simplest style of all.

GURNARD *Triglidae* spp.

Three species of gurnard are commonly caught in the Atlantic and Mediterranean: the grey gurnard (*grondin gris*), the yellow (*grondin perlon*) and the red (*grondin rouge*). They are easily distiguished from all other fish by their strange, mail-cheeked heads, with bony plates which give them a prehistoric, almost fossil-like appearance. The body attenuates from the large head in a cone, which lacks the elegant curves of more conventionally-shaped fish such as sea bream or herring. The flesh is firm and white, good for baking, stews and soups. It is not a fish of the first water, but it is useful and cheap, well worth buying.

One snag. The lovely colour of the red gurnard, in my experience the most commonly seen of the three in this country, means that it can be confused with the red mullet. Take a good, long look at the head and general body shape, or you may be disappointed in your expectations. Not even the gurnard's most devoted admirer could say the flavours were comparable. On hotel menus in northern France, we have also been confused by the word *rouget* on the menu. Expecting *rouget-barbet* or red mullet, we learned the hard, unforgettable way that gurnard are sometimes called *rougets-grondins*.

The names of this fish reveal an interesting thing: the gurnard's ability to make short, sharp noises. Both *grondin* and gurnard come from French words for growling (*gronder*) and for grunting (*grogner*). These strange sounds are made by a special muscle in the air-bladder wall, which can vibrate many times a second: the air-bladder acts as a resonating chamber. There are other fish with the same ability, which has led to all kinds of speculation about the origin of the Sirens' song. A shoal, say of meagre or drums (p. 459), many feet below the surface of the sea, can be heard quite clearly on board a fishing boat. Like the noises made by whales and dolphins, they have not been interpreted so far.

A practical point – the size of gurnard can vary enormously. Judge the amount you require by eye, allowing for the size of the head, rather than by weight. The recipes following are based on gurnard weighing about 250 g (8 oz) each.

GURNARD WITH A CHEESE AND WINE SAUCE

The firm texture of gurnard makes it a successful fish for a gratin. The main preparation can be done several hours before the meal, with a last-minute reheating in the oven or under the grill.

Serves 6

1½ kg (3 lb) gurnards, filleted
court bouillon* or light chicken or veal stock plus a dash of
*   wine vinegar*
125 g (4 oz) butter
3 tablespoons plain flour
150 ml (5 fl oz) scant white wine
300 ml (10 fl oz) hot milk
3 or 4 tablespoons double cream (optional)
60 g (2 oz) Parmesan cheese, grated
60 g (2 oz) Gruyère cheese, grated
salt, pepper, nutmeg
60 g (2 oz) breadcrumbs

Put the cleaned and filleted gurnard into the court bouillon or stock and vinegar; there should be enough to cover it comfortably. Bring slowly to simmering point, and remove the fish the moment it is cooked. Put head, skin and bone back into the cooking stock, and continue to boil gently. Leave the fillets to drain while the sauce is made.

Melt half the butter in a small pan; stir in the flour. Cook for 2 minutes, then pour in the wine and cook for a further 2 or 3 minutes. Now pour in a good ladleful of the boiling fish liquor (through a strainer) – about 150 ml (5 fl oz) or a little more – then the hot milk. Simmer to a thick but not gluey consistency. Stir in the cream if used, then half the grated cheese. Season well with salt, pepper and nutmeg. Put a layer of the sauce into a gratin dish, then the gurnard fillets. Cover with the rest of the sauce. Mix the remaining cheese with the breadcrumbs and scatter evenly on top. Dot with the last 60 g (2 oz) of butter, and reheat in a very hot oven or under the grill until brown and bubbling.

MOULINES FARCIES À LA FÉCAMPOISE

I found this very pleasant appetizing recipe in Simone Morand's *Gastronomie Normande*. It makes the best of a most obligingly cheap fish (*mouline* is the local name for gurnard).

Serves 6

6 gurnards
2 onions or 2 large shallots, sliced
bouquet garni
2 glasses dry cider
1 tomato, sliced
2 tablespoons double cream
chopped parsley

STUFFING
90 g (3 oz) butter
300 g (10 oz) mushrooms, chopped
1 chopped shallot
2 large tablespoons good sausage meat
1-cm (½ -inch) slice bread
milk
chopped parsley
1 sprig of thyme
lemon juice
salt, pepper

Make the stuffing first. Melt the butter and fry the mushrooms and shallot and sausage meat gently. Squeeze the bread in a little milk, just to moisten it, and add to the pan. Season with parsley and thyme, lemon juice, salt and pepper. Divide this mixture between the six gurnard.

Butter an ovenproof dish which will hold the stuffed gurnard cosily. Tuck the onion slices and the bouquet into the gaps. Pour in the cider and dispose the tomato slices in a decorative manner on top. Bake in a moderate to fairly hot oven (gas 4–5, 180–190 °C/350–375 °F) until the fish are cooked – about half an hour. If the dish seems dry, add a couple of spoonfuls of water during the cooking. About 5 minutes before the end, pour the cream over the whole thing. Sprinkle with chopped parsley and serve.

† OCTOPUS *Octopus vulgaris* & *O. dofleini*

One of the most familiar sights of a trip to Greece is a fisherman on the rocky edge of a harbour or beach, beating an octopus. There is something heroic about it, a scene from an ancient Attic vase. Watching it, you feel the link with a past of two thousand years and more. Now I learn that all this muscular activity is unnecessary, no need for all this swing and bash, swing and bash nine and ninety times. The octopus has been maligned. It is as tender as a chicken.

All you need to do, once it has been cleaned, is to dip it for 4 or 5 seconds in a pan of fast-boiling water, then let it cool for a minute and dip again. Out for another minute and then back it goes for the third time, but lower the heat to maintain a bare simmer and leave for an hour. Now all you have to do is to drain it, cut it up and finish it in one of the stews or sauces from the squid or lobster chapters. You do not even need to skin it.

Enlightenment – or disillusion, according to your temperament – comes from A. J. McClane and his splendid *Encyclopaedia of Fish Cookery*. 'This process' – which is followed in Spain – 'of dipping, as opposed to submerging the octopus in boiling water, denatures the protein gradually and when left to simmer it will not toughen.'

Since we have begun at the end, I propose to return to the alpha of the matter – the cleaning. Mostly you will not need to bother about this, as all the preliminaries will have been concluded by the time the fishmonger sells you an octopus (bear in mind that it can shrink enormously in the simmering when you decide how much to buy and check that there is a double row of suckers on the tentacles since there is an inferior species which has only one row). But should you be given an octopus by an amiable fisherman, it would be a shame not to know what to do. The most obvious thing about an octopus, and the reason for its name, is its eight tentacles (*okto* and *pous* being Greek for eight and foot) encrusted with suckers. They come together and end in a collapsed looking bag, which is the head. This is easily turned inside out so that the bits and pieces inside can be removed: save the ink sac if it is needed for the recipe.

Before I learned the Spanish method above, I used to put the whole octopus into a covered Pyrex dish and leave it in a low oven – say gas 2, 150 °C (300 °F) or even lower – for an hour at least. A glance from time to time would reveal the interesting stages as the octopus turned from its original blueish-grey colour to a rusty sort of pink, and became submerged in its own liquid.

A standard way of cooking octopus is to fry an onion in olive oil with a little garlic, add tomatoes, wine, a little water and herbs, and then put in the pieces of octopus that have had their preliminary simmering. Diced potato can be added in Cypriot style, or you can flavour the sauce with ink in the Basque manner of Calamares en su tinta (p. 405). Instead of wine and ink, you might try pastis – but go carefully – or some ground cumin and harissa in North African style.

Octopus is included in fish soups, such as Cacciucco (p. 401), and in stews. Pieces are grilled over charcoal. Sometimes it is used to eke out lobster, rather as monkfish is, but nobody is fooled, I would say. You can eat it cold, making a little salad with avocados, some bitter greenery and an olive oil vinaigrette, or you can chew it with a glass of ouzo as an apéritif.

The strangest octopus recipe I have been able to find is the Maltese one which follows, from a book by two sisters, Anne and Helen Caruana Galizia, *Recipes from Malta*.

OCTOPUS STEW (Stuffat tal-qarnit)

You can cut the long cooking time of this recipe by adopting the dip-and-simmer method of preparing octopus outlined at the beginning of this section.

Serves 6

4 large onions, chopped
2 tablespoons olive oil
1 octopus weighing about 750 g (1½ lb), cleaned and cut into pieces
*   convenient for eating*
2 tablespoons tomato purée
1 tablespoon small capers
1 tablespoon chopped mint leaves
8 black olives
1 handful of walnuts
1 handful of raisins
300 ml (10 fl oz) red wine
1 teaspoon mixed spice
1 teaspoon curry powder

Cook the onion in the oil, fairly slowly, until golden. Stir in the octopus pieces and continue to cook gently for a few minutes. Add the remaining ingredients and simmer for 2 hours, stirring quite often, and adding a little hot water so that the octopus does not dry out – it should bathe in enough liquid barely to cover.

Serve as a sauce over spaghetti. Alternatively, turn the dish into a main course by adding 750 g (1½ lb) peeled and quartered potatoes (and extra water) for the last 30–40 minutes.

'The addition of the curry and spice may sound outrageous,' say the authors, 'but it is a typical Maltese addition and we think it should be tried.'

Another Maltese cookery book gives a simpler variation of this stew – minus capers, mint leaves and spices – adding peas rather than potatoes at the end.

† OPAH, MOONFISH OR SUNFISH

Lampris regius

A large fish, of curves and perfect beauty of colour. The aspect of its round eyes and rounded head is mild, almost dolphin-like. The huge, plump body, a taut oval up to 2 m (6 feet) long, is softly spotted with white. The main blue-grey and green of its skin reflects an iridescence of rose, purple and gold. The fins are a brilliant red. The sickly tail has reminded people of the moon's shape; the ribs of its fins have seemed like the scarlet rays of the sun. Earlier, scientists gave it the magnificent rank of *Zeus luna*. Now it is more correctly classified as *Lampris regius*, which could be translated as 'creature of kingly radiance'.

The opah likes the warm waters of the world (*opah* from W. African *uba*), but in summer it is sometimes caught in the North Atlantic. I saw one at Swindon, in the warm autumn season of 1971. It had been taken on 29 October, off the North Cape of Iceland, by the trawler *Lucida* – appropriate name – and was in perfect condition over a week later. I was given two steaks cut from the centre of this 63 kg (9 stone) majesty; each one weighed 2½ kg (5 lb). Round the central bone, the flesh fell into closely curved sections the colour of salmon. The flavour and richness, too, were salmon-like (the practical Norwegians eschew poetic names and call it, simply, the 'large salmon', *laksestørje*). The taste was less fishy than salmon; the texture more meaty yet not so dry as similarly meaty fish like tuna or porbeagle.

Ask your fishmonger about opah (or Jerusalem haddock, or sunfish, or moonfish; or mariposa, or kingfish if he happens to be American). He might have the chance of some one day. Then you will be able to try one of the best fish it is possible to eat.

Alan Davidson, friend and learned author of many books on fish, was able to track down this magnificent fish through another friend, Jack Shiells, the liveliest and most erudite fish purveyor in Billingsgate. They tackled the fish in their own kitchens. Jack Shiells liked the darker part sliced thin in Japanese sashimi style (p. 365). He also approved my sunfish in cream recipe. The Davidson family concluded that the best thing of all was steaks from the upper rear end, grilled, and the shoulder baked in the oven. On no account should the skin be neglected. Alan Davidson also gives a Danish recipe from the writer Mogens Brandt who lives at Skagen where opah is landed occasionally. Slices 1 cm (½ inch) thick are floured and fried with curry powder in butter. Then they go on to a bed of chopped shallots, cooked gently until soft and transparent, surrounded with small peeled tomatoes. Double cream is stirred into the pan juices to make a sauce. Pour it over the fish. Put the whole thing into a low oven for 10 minutes. This is good, and it works well with salmon.

Opah is also very successful when pickled in the Danish – or rather Scandinavian – gravadlax style (p. 310). If you are given to Beef Stroganoff, try making it with opah instead.

POACHED SUNFISH

Although sunfish can be poached in court bouillon of the usual kind, I think it is better to use a veal or chicken stock, sharpened with a spoonful or two of lemon juice or wine vinegar. Plenty of flavour without heaviness is the secret.

Put the piece of fish flat into a pan and cover it generously with the stock. Bring slowly to the boil. After three or four strong, convulsive bubblings, put the lid on and remove the pan from the stove to the larder to cool down. By this time the fish will be perfectly cooked.

Serve it with the kinds of salad appropriate to salmon – cucumber in cream (p. 183), hard-boiled egg, slices of tomato and so on. Plus a large bowl of mayonnaise. Or you could flavour the cooking stock with tarragon, and serve with tarragon-flavoured whipped cream sharpened with lemon juice. A small amount of orange and tomato salad, with black olives, is also very good with sunfish.

Should you want to eat the sunfish hot, leave it to simmer gently until the centre loses all transparency. This takes about 10 minutes, but the time will vary according to the thickness of the fish, and how slowly it came to the boil. Serve with new potatoes turned in parsley butter. Sauces to choose are hollandaise* or Maltese*, sauce aurore* or a cream* or butter* sauce. Again tarragon is a good flavouring.

SCALLOPED SUNFISH

Firm fish can be reheated successfully, provided this is done not too long after the original cooking. One way is to make a creamy sauce and add the fish to it at the last moment like the turbot recipe on p. 436. Another is to construct a piquant gratin with a béchamel-based sauce. The second method is best if you have only a small amount of fish to go round. By using scallop shells or individual pots, you can produce an excellent first course for a dinner party without the idea of left-overs crossing anyone's mind.

The thing is to flavour the sauce in an appetizingly positive way. Choose an anchovy (p. 49) or Mornay* sauce, for instance, rather than a plain béchamel*, and spice it with French mustard. Sauce aurore* and white wine sauces* can be enriched with grated Parmesan and Gruyère cheese.

Put a layer of whichever sauce you choose into the base of individual ramekins or scallop shells. Then a layer of the flaked fish, then sauce to cover. Cook fine fresh breadcrumbs briefly in melted butter. Cool them and scatter them over the sauce and reheat the whole thing under the grill until bubbling and golden brown.

SUNFISH À LA CRÉOLE

Fish stews need quite a different technique from meat stews. Meat, shin of beef say, or neck of lamb, goes into the oven with the sauce ingredients; they all cook together for several hours. Now with fish, the method must be quite different because even the most solid, meaty-looking piece of tuna needs a comparatively short cooking time. It is one of the advantages of buying fish. So get the sauce right first, see that it is properly reduced and correctly seasoned. Then add the fish, which may or may not need to be lightly browned first. This is the method of matelotes, chowders, Cacciucco, and of Sunfish à la créole:

> Serves 4–6
>
> *créole sauce**
> *salt, pepper*
> *750 g (1½ lb) piece of sunfish*
> *butter*

Make the sauce and adjust the seasoning (this can be done well in advance – the day before if you like). A good half an hour before the meal, brown the sunfish steak lightly in butter and then lower it into the pan of simmering sauce. Allow half an hour's cooking time, but test after 20 minutes to see if the fish is ready.

It may be imagination on my part, but I think that this kind of dish is best cooked in a large round shallow earthenware pot of the Spanish or Portuguese kind. Use a heat-diffuser if you cook by gas. Put the sauce in to reheat, add the browned sunfish and complete the cooking as above.

SUNFISH IN CREAM

A beautiful recipe of great simplicity. Baked in cream, the sunfish becomes soft and unctuous, delicately flavoured with the aromatic seasonings.

> Serves 6
>
> *1 kg (2 lb) piece of sunfish*
> *small onions*
> *pieces of carrot*
> *bay leaf, parsley, thyme*
> *salt, pepper, nutmeg*
> *up to 500 ml (18 oz) single or whipping cream*
> *60 g (2 oz) butter*
> *2 large egg yolks*

Choose a pot into which the sunfish fits closely. Pack the gaps with onions and pieces of carrot. Lay a large bay leaf on top of the fish, tuck a couple of sprigs each of parsley and thyme down the side. Season well with salt, freshly ground black pepper and nutmeg. Pour in enough cream to cover the fish by ½ cm (¼ inch) – the better your packing, the less cream will be required. Dab the butter on top. Cover with kitchen foil or the lid of the pot and bake in a fairly hot oven (gas 5–6, 190–200 °C/375–400 °F). Test after 25 minutes. The centre should have lost its transparent look entirely – on the other hand, you don't want to overcook fish, particularly solid-fleshed creatures like sunfish, tuna, sturgeon and so on.

When it is just cooked, transfer the fish with its bay leaf to a serving plate, and keep warm while you finish the sauce. Strain the cooking liquid into a small pan. Beat the egg yolks in a basin, add a little of the cooking liquid, then pour the lot into the pan again. Set over a low heat, and stir until the consistency is that of smooth, thick cream. *Don't let it boil* or the eggs will curdle. Check the seasoning and pour over the fish.

Serve with a few small boiled potatoes, or brown bread of not too strong a flavour.

RED SNAPPER *Lutjanidae* spp.

Red snappers are easily recognized. They look as if a designer has improved the conventional fish shape by emphasizing the curve of the head and back, flattening the belly and pointing the nose; an elegant adjustment. The scales blush from silver-pink to a deep rose-red; although much of this colour has to be removed before the fish is cooked, something remains of its beauty. The flesh is firm and pleasant.

Freshly caught red snapper on the Atlantic sea coast of America is good eating. In Britain, we used to have to buy from small frozen shoals which needed chiselling apart. Although they are more readily available now, bream or any firm-fleshed fish could be used instead.

BLAFF OF BOURGEOIS

A lively cheerful dish, with an elegant turn, which is not surprising since it comes from Anne Rosenzweig, chef and co-proprietor of New York's Arcadia restaurant. She is one of the bright stars of American cookery. The red pepper marmalade can be made at the same time as the rest of the dish, or in advance; I've found that any left over goes well with other fish, with poultry and also with cheese and vegetable dishes.

Serves 6

800 g (1¾ lb) fillet of snapper
salt, freshly ground black pepper
500 g (1 lb) red onions
1 tablespoon chopped shallot
1 tablespoon chopped garlic
2 tablespoons olive oil
2 litres (3½ pt) shellfish stock*
2 large heads of fennel, cut in julienne strips
2 large potatoes, peeled and cut in julienne strips
300 ml (10 fl oz) red pepper marmalade (below)
4 spring onions, sliced diagonally

Set the oven at gas 8, 230°C, (450°F). Cut the fish diagonally into 6 pieces and season them. Set aside in the refrigerator. Put the red onions into a dish and bake in the oven for 25 minutes. Cool, skin and slice them.

In a large pan, stew the shallot and garlic in the oil for 1 minute without browning them. Add the stock, onions, fennel and potatoes. Bring to the boil and simmer for 1 minute. Put in the fish pieces, cover and poach at barely a simmer until almost done but still a little pink. Remove the fish and keep it warm, but be careful not to complete the cooking.

Stir 175 ml (6 fl oz) of the red pepper marmalade into the pan and boil down until the sauce looks smooth and creamy. Taste for seasoning. Put the fish back to complete the cooking and heat through. Divide between six hot soup plates, arranging the pieces of fish and the julienne of vegetables in the centre. Garnish with the spring onions and remaining pepper marmalade, and serve toasted bread rubbed with fresh garlic separately. You could also serve the fish in one large hot serving dish, if this is easier.

Red Pepper Marmalade

Makes 300 ml (10 fl oz)

6 large red peppers, seeded, ribs removed
2 large beefsteak or Marmande tomatoes, halved and seeded
1 large onion, peeled
3 large cloves garlic, peeled
4 tablespoons red wine vinegar
1 tablespoon sugar
salt, freshly ground black pepper

Preheat the oven to gas 8, 230 °C (450 °F). Put the vegetables and garlic into a dish. Cover with foil and bake for 45 minutes, or until the vegetables are completely soft. Process them and then sieve. Season to taste with the vinegar, sugar, salt and pepper.

FILIPINO FISH AND GUAVA SALAD

This recipe, with slight alterations, comes from *Maria Y Orosa, Her Life and Work* (with 700 recipes) which was published in the Philippines in 1970. It was given in Alan Davidson's *Seafood of South-East Asia*, a book I would recommend for a number of reasons, but particularly for its range of fish and fruit dishes. We do not always take into account the sweetness of fish, and how well this is emphasized by fruit other than lemon. The intention of the recipe, in a guava-growing country, was frugality, extending expensive fish. For us, economy might mean cutting down on the guavas: there is no reason why the salad should not be served in small ramekins, which means a saving of fifteen guavas.

Serves 6

500 g (1 lb) snapper
125 ml (4 fl oz) coconut cream, see recipe
25 ripe guavas
1 orange, peeled
3 bananas, peeled

Poach the fish in well-seasoned water. Cool and flake the flesh. Make the coconut cream by breaking up some solid coconut cream which can be bought in blocks and diluting it with water or cream; mixed in the blender you can achieve a smooth, very white consistency. If all you can get is desiccated coconut, do not despair. Heat a cupful with a cupful of single cream, to just below boiling. Whizz in a blender and then leave to cool. Sieve into a basin, adding a cupful of boiling water towards the end. Add salt to taste.

Peel 10 guavas thinly, halve them and discard the seeds. Chop the rest into small pieces. Divide the orange into segments and remove the thin white skins and pips. Cut the banana into smallish pieces and mix all this fruit together, with the fish. Stir in the coconut cream gently. Cover the bowl with plastic film and chill thoroughly.

Cut lids from the remaining guavas. Scoop out the seeds to make 'shells'. Put into a plastic bag and fasten, then leave in the refrigerator to chill until needed. Just before serving, divide the salad between the shells and replace the lids.

RED SNAPPER CRÉOLE

This is a good sauce which can be used for herrings as well. My feeling is that the Worcestershire sauce makes all the difference to the flavour.

Serves 6

6 red snappers (about 1¾ kg/3½ lb), cleaned
seasoned flour
1 lemon

SAUCE
375 g (12 oz) chopped onion
3 stalks celery, chopped
175 g (6 oz) chopped green pepper
60 g (2 oz) butter
2 cloves
grated rind of the lemon
60 g (2 oz) chopped parsley
½ teaspoon each rosemary and thyme
1 bay leaf
2 cloves garlic, finely chopped
2 × 400 g (14-oz) cans tomatoes
1 tablespoon Worcestershire sauce
Tabasco
salt, freshly ground black pepper, sugar

Make the sauce first, taking trouble to get the reduction and seasonings to your taste before baking the fish. It is an elaborated version of the créole sauce*.

Put onion, celery and pepper into a frying pan with the butter.

Cook gently until soft. Add cloves, lemon rind and herbs, including the garlic. Quickly drain the tomatoes and add them (keep the juice for another recipe). Leave this mixture to boil down busily for about 20 minutes, or until it has lost its wateriness and has become a liquid purée. Stir in the Worcestershire sauce, then add the rest of the seasonings to taste.

Sprinkle the fish with seasoned flour and place them in an ovenproof baking dish. Arrange slices of lemon on top, two to each fish, and pour the sauce round and between them.

Bake in a moderate oven (gas 4, 180°C/350°F) for about 20 minutes until the fish is done. Baste occasionally.

NOTE One large red snapper can be used instead of six little ones; it will take longer to cook: 35–45 minutes.

VARIATION Some recipes suggest making the sauce above in half-quantity, and adding enough breadcrumbs and egg to bind it to a stuffing. Chopped shrimps and prawns are sometimes mixed in as well. Filled with this mixture, the fish are then baked in the juice from the tomatoes, plus a little water and lemon juice, or simply in a well-buttered dish.

† SAND-EEL, SAND-LANCE *Ammodytes* spp.

Sand-eels and sand-lances look like miniature eels, long and silvery and darting – but this is where the resemblance stops. The flavour is pleasant rather than distinguished. The flesh is firm and sweet, but without the rich delicacy of eel.

Équilles and *lançons* are more popular in France than sand-eels and sand-lances are here or in America. We often see them at our weekly markets in the Bas-Vendômois, especially at the equinox when tides are full – *'à la Saint-Denis, on pêche l'équille d'assis'*, around 9 October, which is the fête of France's patron Saint Denis, you can catch sand-eels without budging, according to fishermen in Normandy. In nineteenth-century Britain they provided a lively holiday occupation, as they still do in France today: 'When it is discovered that a shoal of sand-eels have hidden themselves in the sand' – this is at low tide – 'sea-side visitors should sally out, armed with spades, shovels, rakes and forks, and dig them out. When extricated from the sand-beds, the fish leap about with singular agility, and afford much sport.' So said Frank Buckland in his *History of British Fishes* (1880). The professionals, whether or not they have to budge, use nets, and catch the fish at sea.

The great pleasure of these fish is to eat them crisply fried. Some French cooks soak them in milk for half an hour after cutting off the heads and cleaning them. They are then dried, floured and deep-fried for 4 minutes, and served immediately with parsley, lemon wedges, bread and white wine. You can also fry them in clarified butter or olive oil, but the temperature has to be lower which means the fish will be less crisp.

They are also an excellent addition to a mixed bag of small fish for a Fritto misto di mare, Italian style.

SEA-URCHINS *Strongylocentrus droebachiensis*

'Sea-urchins (there are several edible varieties) are a menace to bathers on the shore of the Mediterranean, for they cluster by the hundred in shallow waters, hidden in the rocks, and anyone who has ever trodden on a sea-urchin with a bare foot knows how painful and tedious a business it is to remove their sharp little spines from the skin. They are, however, delicious to eat for those who like food redolent of the sea, iodine, and salt. They are served cut in half, and the coral flesh so exposed is scooped out with a piece of bread; they are at their best eaten within sight and sound of the sea, preferably after a long swim, and washed down with plenty of some cold local white wine ... Sea-urchins are wrested from their lairs in the rocks with wooden pincers, or can be picked up by hand provided you wear gloves.'

So speaks the voice of experience – Elizabeth David on sea-urchins in her *Italian Food*.

If, the first time, you eat sea-urchins which are not perfectly fresh, you may well wonder why anyone bothers with them. But fresh from the sea, as Mrs David urges, they are an experience.

A special delight of Irish eating is the sea-urchins. They are dived for in England and Scotland too, so bully your fishmonger in the summer. In fact, they are at Billingsgate very nearly all the year round since native stocks are supplemented by imports from the Mediterranean. You can boil them for a few minutes like an egg, then cut off the cap, remove the bright orange creamy inside and mix it with a little cream (for eating hot) or with mayonnaise (for eating cold). Or you can make a sauce, as Colin O'Daly used to do at the Park Hotel in Kenmare. From the hotel dining-room, you could look down to the sea creek and across very nearly to where the O'Connors live and tend their stocks of shellfish and sea-urchins off the rhododendron-fringed Beara Peninsula. They bring in other fish too from the neighbourhood and supply all the good hotels.

FILLETS OF SOLE WITH SALMON SOUFFLÉ STUFFING AND SEA-URCHIN SAUCE

Serves 2

750 g (1½ lb) sole, skinned (in Ireland, black sole)
a few extra white fish bones for stock
½ onion, diced
½ carrot, diced
1 small bay leaf
175 ml (6 fl oz) dry white wine

STUFFING
2 scallops
350 g (11–12 oz) salmon fillet
1 egg white
150 ml (5 fl oz) double cream
salt, pepper

SAUCE
300 ml (10 fl oz) fish stock (see recipe)
150 ml (5 fl oz) double cream
5 sea-urchins
60 g (2 oz) butter, diced
salt, pepper

Skin and fillet the sole, which will give you 4 fillets. Put bones and skin with extra bones into a pan with the diced vegetables, add the bay leaf and white wine and enough water to cover. Simmer gently for 30–40 minutes, then strain and reduce to the 300 ml (10 fl oz) required by the sauce.

Next make the stuffing. Blend or process scallops and salmon together. Transfer to a bowl set over ice and work in the egg white gradually, then the cream, using a wooden spoon. Taste for seasoning.

Spread it over the skinned side of two of the fillets, placed on two pieces of cling film. Roll them up with the aid of the cling film and put them to chill for at least an hour so that you can get two wooden cocktail sticks through without squeezing out all the stuffing.

Take the two fillets left, cut each one into three lengthwise without cutting through at the top, so that the three pieces are held together. Then plait them.

Strain the fish stock into a pan, add the cream and bring back to the boil. Simmer down a little. Slice the tops from the sea-urchins, add their contents to the sauce and simmer down again.

Unwrap the rolled fillets, and steam them and the plaited fillets for 3–4 minutes. Whisk the butter into the sauce just before serving, then strain it and correct the seasoning.

Pour the sauce on to a hot serving dish. Arrange the sole on top. Decorate with empty urchin shells and lemon quarters.

SHAD – ALLIS SHAD, TWAITE SHAD AND AMERICAN SHAD
Alosa alosa, A. fallax and A. sapidissima

The shad, of whatever kind, is a fine fat member of the herring family – it is sometimes known as the king of the herrings – which has the unherring-like habit of coming into rivers to spawn. And it is in rivers that it is caught. The allis and twaite shads used to honour the Wye and Severn, but now you have to go to the Loire or Garonne, or even further south, if you want to enjoy one. Going there to eat shad with sorrel sauce, or sorrel stuffing, and beurre blanc is one of the springtime rituals of the French who are lucky enough to live near the Loire. And I notice a similar air of celebration about American recipes.

All three kinds of shad have the richness of herring, and a good flavour. Alas, they also have its bones. I pass on two American ways of causing the bones to disintegrate, but feel the price paid – 5 and 6 hours in the oven – is probably too high for any fish.

The great delight of shad is the roe. The soft milt is good, but the hard roe has a moist crunch, a most delightful texture that begins to approach the foothills of caviare. This is because the individual eggs are almost the size of those coloured beads which adorn some dressmaking pins.

How to get rid of Shad Bones

1.THE OLD WAY   Grease the bottom of an oval, lidded, ovenproof pot. Put in the cleaned fish, without its roe, and with slices of unsmoked bacon in the central cavity and on top. Pour in enough water to leave the top part bare. Season. Bring to the simmer, then transfer to a very cool oven (gas ½, 130°C/250°F) and leave for 5 hours.

2.THE MODERN WAY   Clean shad, brush inside and out with seasoned melted butter. Take a large sheet of foil, brush it with cooking oil and put the fish on it. Seal the edges tightly. Place in an oval covered pot and bake in a very cool oven (gas ½, 130°C/250°F) for 6 hours.

ALOSE À L'OSEILLE

Shad, as I have said, is a favourite fish of the Loire springtime. Usually it is baked, and served with sorrel purée or sorrel stuffing. At other times, it is poached, and served with beurre blanc*. The second recipe I give combines both these accompanying delights in a dish of ceremony. The two recipes come from *La Vraie Cuisine de l'Anjou et de la Touraine* by Roger Lallemand:

> Serves 4
>
> *500–875 g (1–1¾ lb) shad, cleaned and scaled*
> *125 g (4 oz) softened butter*
> *salt, pepper*
> *500 g (1 lb) sorrel*
> *90 ml (3 fl oz) double cream*
> *nutmeg*

Butter an ovenproof dish generously. Place the shad in it and dab the rest of the butter on top. Season well, and bake in a fairly hot oven (gas 5, 190 °C/375 °F) until cooked – about 30 minutes. Baste often. Meanwhile wash the sorrel and cut it into strips with a pair of scissors.

When the shad is ready, pour off the butter and juices into a saucepan. Cover the fish with foil; put it back into the oven – reducing the temperature – to keep warm. Stir the sorrel into the butter and juices, and cook rapidly to a thick purée. (Spinach with lemon, or tart gooseberries, can be substituted: the point is to provide the fish with a sharp but rich sauce.) Stir in the cream. Season with salt, freshly ground black pepper, and nutmeg. Pour on to a long serving dish, and place the shad on top.

ALOSE FARCIE À L'ANGEVINE

Serves 4

3 shallots, chopped or *90 g (3 oz) mild onions*
60 g (2 oz) butter
250 g (8 oz) sorrel
250 g (8 oz) spinach
salt, pepper
2 full tablespoons double cream
2 hard-boiled eggs
500–875 g (1–1¾ lb) shad, cleaned and scaled

Melt the shallots or onion in the butter. They should cook until soft, without browning. Cut the sorrel and spinach into strips, and stir in. Cook until the purée is thick and all wateriness has disappeared. Season and bind with the cream. Shell the hard-boiled eggs and fork them to crumbliness. Stir into the stuffing. Place this mixture in the cavity of the fish, and sew it up well so that none – or very little – can escape. Bake in butter, as in the recipe above.

Serve with beurre blanc*. Beurre blanc is also served with shad poached in a white wine court bouillon*, but I think that this recipe is better, as shad, to me at any rate, needs sharpness.

NOTE If you are lucky enough to buy a female shad, stir the eggs into the stuffing.

BAKED STUFFED SHAD

This is a French recipe with a delicious whiting stuffing.

Serves 6

1½ (3 lb) shad

STUFFING
300 g (10 oz) whiting fillet, without bones or skin
1 egg, separated
150 ml (5 fl oz) double cream
3 tablespoons chopped almonds
1 tablespoon each parsley and chives
salt, pepper

SAUCE
60 g (2 oz) butter
3 tablespoons chopped shallot
200 g (7 oz) mushrooms, chopped
salt, pepper, lemon juice
scant 300 ml (10 fl oz) dry white wine
scant 300 ml (10 fl oz) court bouillon* or light stock
1 tablespoon plain flour
300 ml (10 fl oz) cream
2 tablespoons chopped chives

Clean, scale and rinse the shad. Prepare the stuffing – liquidize the whiting with the egg white, then add the cream little by little. Transfer to a bowl and incorporate the egg yolk and chopped almonds. Add herbs and seasoning. Now stuff the shad.

Butter an ovenproof dish with half the butter. Put in the shallot and mushrooms, season with salt, pepper and lemon, then place the stuffed fish on top. Pour in wine and bouillon or stock. Cover with kitchen foil and bake in a fairly hot oven (gas 6, 200 °C/400 °F) for 30 minutes.

Meanwhile fork the flour into the remaining butter to produce beurre manié. When the fish is cooked, transfer it to a serving dish. Pour the cooking liquor, etc., into a pan, reduce it by boiling to half quantity, and pour in the cream. Thicken with the beurre manié in the usual way. Add chives and seasoning, and serve.

SKATE OR RAY *Rajidae* spp.

The ribbed wings of skate are sometimes described as 'coarse', which I resent. Those rosy wedges, leaved one over the other on a white tray at the fishmonger's, do not deserve such an adjective. The French have more discrimination and describe the flesh as very fine; delicate.

It can be cooked in several different ways, and is always a success particularly with children. The ribs of flesh part sweetly and easily from the layer of soft, unvicious bone, a relief after the troublesome and spiky nature of herrings. Skate, like dogfish and shark, belongs to the cartilaginous *Selachians*: this makes all the difference to a child dealing with fish. I remember admiring the neat way it was all put together, but had no idea of the kite-shaped beauty of the total creature, with its long tail, until I saw the shimmering skate of James Ensor's painting many years later. As children, our only contact with its reality was the black, four-handled egg sacs that washed up on the beach with the seaweed; we called them 'witch's purses'.

The pieces of skate one eats are taken from the wings only, though sometimes small nuggets are cut from the tail and sold as 'skate nobs' (in French, *joues de raie*, skate's cheeks). Floured and fried in butter, and served with lemon, they are delicious. Apparently they are popular in the north-west, at Lytham in Lancashire, but I have never seen them in the south of England. They are worth looking out for. Incidentally do not be put off by a slight smell of ammonia, it disappears in cooking.

FRIED AND BATTERED SKATE

If the pieces are small, each whole wing weighing about 250 g (8 oz), they will be tender enough to be fried in clarified butter, or half butter and half oil. Turn them in seasoned flour first, and give them 4 minutes a side, until the flesh begins to part from the bone easily and loses its transparent look. Serve with a creamy caper sauce, or a shrimp sauce to which capers have been added: *see* pp. 49 and 281.

Pieces of skate make good fritters. Cut the wings into manageable strips or wedges. Dip them in batter* and deep-fry. Serve with lemon quarters or a piquant mayonnaise.

Large pieces of skate may also be fried, but they should first be cooked briefly in a court bouillon* as in the next recipe.

RAIE AU BEURRE NOIR

The classic recipe for skate, particularly suitable for larger wings. These are usually sold cut into pieces; choose the thick middle strips, rather than the side wedge pieces. Put them into cold court bouillon no. 2* and bring to the boil. After one strong bubble, lower the heat to keep the liquid below simmering point. In 15 minutes the skate should be cooked (10 minutes will be enough if you wish to fry it as in the recipe above).

For six people, you will need 1½ kg (3 lb) skate, prepared as above. Drain the pieces and put them on a warm serving dish, while you make the beurre noisette*.

Having poured the beurre noisette over the fish, swill out the pan with a couple of tablespoons of wine vinegar, bubble it for a few seconds and pour that over the fish, too. Scatter with capers and chopped parsley and serve immediately.

Boiled potatoes, preferably new, go well with this dish. Turn them in parsley butter.

RAIE À LA CRÈME

This is a particularly rich and good recipe.

> Serves 6
>
> *1½ kg (3 lb) skate*
> *125 g (4 oz) unsalted or lightly salted butter*
> *150 ml (5 fl oz) double cream*
> *2 egg yolks, beaten*
> *2–3 tablespoons parsley*

Cook the skate in court bouillon no. 2* as in recipe above. Drain, arrange the pieces on a serving dish, and keep warm. Melt the butter in a frying pan, pour in the cream and stir until it is well amalgamated and bubbling; a few moments, that is all. Pour on to the beaten yolks, whisking with a fork, then return to the pan and heat without boiling until very thick. Add the parsley. Pour some of the sauce over the fish and serve the rest in a sauceboat.

SKATE MAYONNAISE

> Serves 6
>
> *1½ (3 lb) skate*
> *vinaigrette dressing**
> *mayonnaise**
> *crisp lettuce, such as Webb's Wonder*

Cook the skate in court bouillon in the way described above. When just done, remove and drain well. Put on a plate and pour over it, while it is still warm, a little vinaigrette dressing, made with lemon juice and olive oil.

Choose a lemon mayonnaise, or any other with a sharp seasoning. Put some lettuce leaves on a dish, arrange the skate on top and pour the mayonnaise over. Decorate with capers, olives or anchovies (depending on what kind of mayonnaise you have chosen to make) and chopped parsley. Serve chilled.

NOTE   It is a refinement to remove the skate from the bones before arranging it on the lettuce, though not strictly necessary.

† SMELT, CAPELIN, ARGENTINE & SILVERSIDE *Osmerus eperlanus, Mallotus villosus, Argentina silus & A.sphyraena, Menidia menidia*

These slim silver fish, all much of a length when you see them in the market, about 15 cm (6 inches), are delicacies that should not be passed over. They are usually fried, traditionally deep-fried in the manner described by the Reverend George Musgrave in *A Ramble Through Normandy* that he made in 1854. One night he ended up at the Hôtel du Louvre at Pont Audemer, a simple place, where the landlady was 'a capital cook ... with an extraordinarily expeditious way of frying smelts. I had bespoken a score and a half (after having seen some in the market), and they were dished as they were fried, with two skewers, fifteen on each skewer, the slender pin passing through the heads, and the ring at its extremity serving to turn them in the pan all at once, for the more even frying.' And beside the description there is a neat little drawing of his plate, with the two rows of fish. Chefs of the past have loved the smelt, and used it as part of their elaborate garnishing. Now, like the other small fish it resembles, it is more likely to provide a quick supper or the first course of the meal.

The great quality of the smelt – and I understand this applies to the capelin as well – is its smell of cucumber when freshly caught. By the time they appear at the fishmongers', there is no trace of this elegant fragrance. My experience of the capelin is limited to Norway, where it is used as part of the feed thrown to salmon in their farm pens. The female roe is often removed and treated as caviare; we were given some with perfectly ripe avocados and it was good (it looked beautiful, too, being a pale orange-gold).

The Argentine or silver smelt provides the colouring for artificial pearls, but is well worth eating, especially the larger *Argentina silus*. So, too, is the silverside which in its tiniest form does duty as whitebait for Americans of the east coast.

For something a little more unusual, try the following recipe which has the effect of lightly pickling the fish.

ESCABÈCHE

This is an old recipe, particularly useful in pre-refrigeration days when supplies of fresh fish were erratic. You will find versions of it in English cookery books under the name of caveach, but the dish was by origin Spanish. The recipe is also a good one for fillets of larger fish such as herring and mackerel. By arranging the vegetables and herbs neatly, you can make the whole thing most attractive.

Serves 4

500–750 g (1–1½ lb) smelts or other small fish
milk
seasoned flour
about 300 ml (10 fl oz) olive oil
1 medium carrot, sliced
1 medium onion, sliced
2 large cloves garlic, halved
125 ml (4 fl oz) wine vinegar
bouquet garni
salt, pepper, cayenne
an extra bay leaf

Dip the fish in milk, drain and coat them in flour, shaking off the surplus. Fry not too fast in half the oil, then transfer them to a serving dish when they are nicely browned. Refresh the oil with what remains and cook the vegetables and garlic until lightly coloured – do not allow the oil to overheat or blacken. Add the vinegar and the bouquet with 4 tablespoons of water. Simmer until the vegetables are cooked, then distribute them over the fish with salt, pepper and cayenne, and the extra bay leaf. Bring the liquid left in the pan to the boil and strain it carefully over the fish so as not to dislodge the decorative bits and pieces.

Leave to cool, then cover and chill. This keeps well for two days.

† SPRAT *Sprattus sprattus*

Although sprats may look – hopefully – like smelts, it is wise to distinguish between the two for culinary reasons. The sprat, being a member of the herring family, is rich in oil and therefore tastes best when grilled. The smelt, being related to the salmon family, is less rich and usually fried.

Confusing them is not, however, a matter of anxiety. For one thing, the sprat has a tubbier, more homely appearance. For another, it is by many times the more common of the two. According to official lists, over a million hundredweight of them are landed annually. Smelts do not even rate an individual mention.

As with sardines, there seems to be little point in attempting to gut sprats. If you do feel the need, extract what you can via the gills with a hairpin. If you slit their bellies they become raggedy as they cook. Make the grill very hot and give them 2–3 minutes a side. Serve with lemon quarters, or a piquant French mustard, bread and butter. They can be turned into an Escabèche like smelts (p. 490) but are better baked in a hot oven, then skinned and left to marinade in oil and lemon with plenty of chopped green herbs, including chives or spring onion.

Smoked sprats are also a bargain, most delicious. As they can be indigestible, I think they are best served as part of a mixed hors d'oeuvre. Skin and fillet them. Range them neatly in an oblong dish, or on a round one like spokes of a wheel, and pour a little dry white wine over them, then sprinkle with a very little salt and plenty of black pepper. They can also be heated quickly under the grill (skin them or not as you please – if skinned, they need brushing with clarified butter*). Serve with bread, butter and lemon wedges.

Note that the tiny Skippers sardines are not sardines at all, but brisling, i.e. tiny sprats. They are not as easy to find as they once were, but persist. They, too, are fine for an hors d'oeuvre, or for crushing with butter for sandwiches.

† WEEVER *Trachinus draco*

First acquaintance with weevers can, quite literally, be agonizing. Walking barefoot on a sandy beach in Cornwall (or in many other places of the kind in Europe, although not I think in America), you may suddenly feel the most excruciating, stabbing pain. One friend insists that it vanished suddenly and completely after 15 minutes: other accounts are not so cheerful, and add inflammation and itching as well. These spiky fish like to bury themselves in sand, right up to the eyes (which are positioned at the top of the head), with just the spines of the first dorsal fin sticking up, almost invisibly, through the sand. They are really waiting for shrimps, although you may not appreciate this at the time, and are more of a nuisance to the shrimpers of Lancashire than they are to holiday-makers. Even the strongest and most knowledgeable of these fishermen are sometimes caught as they walk through the shallow waters of that coast, and can be laid up for a fortnight.

Along these spines, and along another strong spine attached to the gill-covers, are grooves that conduct the poison from the fish's poison glands to the victim. Not surprisingly, both French and English names – *vive* and weever – seem to derive from the Old French *wivre*, meaning viper. But don't be put off because the flesh has an excellent firm texture and good flavour. Ask the fishmonger to remove the poisonous spines: if he is unwilling, it is quite easy to do this yourself at home with a pair of kitchen scissors. Weevers are easy to recognize from the slanting streaks of yellow and greyish brown which look oddly straight for fish markings; they are separated by long lines running parallel to the backbone which gives the impression of a geological slip as pictured in a diagram. The fillets come away cleanly and neatly, like a sole's – and I believe that unscrupulous restaurateurs have been known to substitute them, a far more convincing ploy than lemon sole where the likeness is verbal only, in sole dishes (always enquire when a menu declares 'sole' to make sure you are getting the real right thing).

A likely place to come across weevers is a market in France, especially Brittany or Provence where they are a useful part of the mixed bag of fish sold for soup. Interestingly William Verral, master of the White Hart Inn at Lewes in Sussex, observed that weevers did very well in a fricassée, especially when combined with whiting livers – 'In the whiting season you may have plenty of livers at any fishmonger's shop', but this was in the middle of the eighteenth century. Another person who was cooking weevers at about the same time was Hannah Glasse. Both recipes are included since they are easy to adapt to our times, and I hope you will be lucky enough to see a weever or two at the fish counter. You will see that the method favoured in both cases is broiling, a word that the Americans have retained for the practice that we now refer to as grilling.

TO BROIL WEEVERS

'Gut them and wash them clean, dry them in a clean cloth, flour them, then broil them, and have melted butter in a cup. They are fine fish, and cut as firm as a sole; but you must take care not to hurt yourself with the two sharp bones in the head.' (Hannah Glasse, *The Art of Cookery*, 1747).

BROILED WEEVERS WITH BAY LEAVES, WITH SAUCE POIVRADE (Des puavivres grillés, aux feuilles de lauriers, sauce poivrade)

'Notch your fish' – slash them in the thickest part – 'and lay them in a marinade of white wine and vinegar, &c, and a few bay leaves, let 'em remain an hour, and dry them in a cloth, broil them of a nice brown colour, with a bay leaf or two upon each, and prepare your sauce with a spoonful or two of gravy' – light beef stock – 'a little white wine and vinegar, some shallot, pepper, salt and parsley, boil it but a minute or two, and send it up in a fish-boat or cup, for most choose these fish with orange or lemon only.' (William Verral, *The Cook's Paradise*, 1759).

In the marinade, which should mainly consist of white wine with a little vinegar, the '&c' could be some aromatic vegetables. Use some of this strained marinade for the sauce. The oranges should be bitter ones of the Seville type that we use for making marmalade: out of season, use lemon.

† WIND-DRIED or WIND-BLOWN FISH

(BLAWNS, SPELDINGS, SILLOCKS, BOMBAY DUCK, BOKKEMS, ETC)

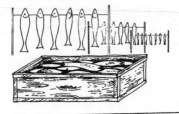

A favourite book of mine is *The Herring and Its Fishery* by W. C. Hodgson. It is written with a vivid eye, with an immediacy that makes me feel that his experiences have been mine as well. The nuggets of information, recipes, strange facts, become part of the reader's existence. Try his way of making wind-dried herrings, still apparently a favourite in East Anglia. 'It is most successful in the winter months, and a frosty night in November is admirably suitable. Take half a dozen fresh herrings and sprinkle them with salt, then leave them in a dish overnight. Then thread them on to a stick passed through the gills and mouths of the herrings, and hang them out in the open air where the wind can get at them. In cold weather time does not matter very much, and they can be eaten any time after they have hung for a day or two. They should be opened and cleaned, and the backbone should be removed before frying.'

We can choose the night, the month, the fish. We can avoid humidity, that enemy of drying food. We can eat wind-drieds as a delicious variation to our everyday diet. This and other curing methods, though, belong to early communities of the prehistoric Atlantic coast. They depended on them to survive the winter. They had to dry fish precisely as and where it was caught; mainly I suppose in the early summer, when salmon and sturgeon leapt up the rivers in a profusion we now find unimaginable. Even allowing for the different climate, I imagine that this was as much a period of changing humidity as it is today, so it became necessary to help the drying along artificially by fire. Wind-blown salmon, smoked salmon – what a feast.

Fish was dried on a large scale until recently in Scotland, and it still is in communities which are cut off from regular supplies in the winter; in Shetland today, washing-lines of split and salted piltock (saithe) are pegged out in the summer winds, until they are stiff and hard enough to be put by in boxes. A good description of the traditional method was given by Marian McNeill in *The Scots Kitchen*. Whiting were the favourite fish, and they were not always cured for long keeping. They might just be dipped in salt, and hung up in a draughty passage (as a native of the north-east coast of England, I begin at last to see the point of that hard north-eastern wind forever blowing – from Siberia, according to my mother, who rubbed cold cream gently on her peeling skin every night. Obviously she should instead have been hanging fish up to dry).

Next day these blawns – i.e. blown whiting – would be eaten for breakfast, grilled or boiled, with butter; barley bannocks, wheat scones and tea were put on the table as well. Alexis Soyer, the famous chef of the Reform Club in the mid-nineteenth century, considered that they made a fine and delicate breakfast dish. This was not the opinion of Dr Johnson. Boswell once insisted on '*scottifying* his palate' with just a taste of one of these dried whiting which were habitually on sale in London. Johnson let 'a bit of one of them lie in his mouth. He did not like it.'

It surprises me that Dr Johnson should have found blawns so strange, because Hannah Glasse gives instructions for curing mackerel in the sun in the 1758 appendix to *The Art of Cookery*. There is nothing to indicate that her instructions would seem odd to her middle-class readers. The mackerel were opened down the back and cleaned – like kippers or Finnan haddock – then salted and laid out to dry 'on inclining stones facing the sun; never leaving them out when the sun is off, nor lay them out before the sun has dispersed the dews, and the stones you lay them on be dry and warm. A week's time of fine weather perfectly cures them.'

Hannah Glasse came from the north of England, near Hexham. Perhaps she learned to cure fish up there. Her technique puts me in mind of the way speldings were cured in Aberdeenshire, according to Catherine Brown in *Scottish Regional Recipes*. They began life as haddock, surplus haddock to the requirements of fresh eating or transformation into lightly cured and short-lived Finnan haddies. They were split and gutted – heads left on – and then soaked in a strong brine. They were laid out on 'smooth pebbles on the beach during the day. If it rained they had to be brought in. After a few days, as they hardened, they were pressed with more flat stones. The drying process took about a week, depending on the size of the fish, and at the end of it they were a greenish-red colour and quite hard.'

Sillocks in Shetland were immature coalfish or saithe that were cleaned and washed in salt water and hung up in bunches outside, until quite hard. 'They were eaten uncooked and are very popular with the school-bairns of Ultima Thule as a relish with their midday "piece" of oatcake or bere bannock.'

That, I reckon, makes sillock a version of Bombay duck which, as anyone who had ever listened to a radio quiz will know, is not a feathered friend but a fish, *Harpodon nehereus*. They catch it in such quantities on the west coast of India that over three-quarters of the haul is split, boned and sunburned dry on racks on the beach. The smell, as Tom Stobart recalls in *The Cook's Encyclopaedia*, is 'like a fish-glue factory in full spate. It blows through the fishing villages of the Bombay coast: you can smell it on the breeze amongst the coconut palms or across the black mud of mangrove-bordered creeks. And this picturesque smell invades the kitchens of curry addicts the world over because Bombay duck is not only eaten around Bombay but is exported.'

The addict of Indian food knows that cooking transforms the oddity of smell into the most delightful piquancy. There is no reason not to use it in Western cooking – one suggestion is to break it up and cook it briefly in butter before you pour the whole thing, foaming, over fish cooked in the meunière style. Here, though, is a recipe from Harvey Day's *Complete Book of Curries*, which gives you the Indian style:

BOMBAY DUCK AND BRINJAL CURRY (Boomla begga ka salna)

Brinjal is the Indian name for aubergine. *Boomla*, meaning Bombay duck, is sometimes anglicized as bummelow.

Serves 2

1 large aubergine
1 large onion, sliced thin
mustard or *sunflower oil*
4 cloves garlic, sliced thin
1 teaspoon ground coriander seed
½ teaspoon ground cumin
½ teaspoon ground turmeric
½ teaspoon salt
¼ teaspoon cayenne or *chilli pepper*
12 pieces Bombay duck
2 tablespoons dessicated coconut
juice of 1 lemon

Cut the aubergine in half lengthways, then across into 2-cm (¾-inch) slices. Fry the onion in 3 tablespoons of the oil until it is well browned. Keep stirring. Add the garlic, spices, salt and pepper and cook gently for 5 minutes. Put in the aubergine with 300 ml (10 fl oz) water. Simmer until cooked. Cut the pieces of Bombay duck into four each and add them to the pan, with the coconut. Pour on the lemon juice and give everything another 5 minutes before serving, with rice.

This idea of dried fish as a relish to the stolid realities of every day eating links those school-bairns of the Shetlands more closely with fishermen of the Bombay coast than with us today. Today our food is almost all relish. The habit of using small, sharp flavours to get down bowlfuls of rice or manioc or pasta is quite alien to us – how odd an Italian peasant would find Alice Waters' instructions, in her book of pasta, to provide roughly as much sauce or embellishment as pasta itself.

We have lost, or are losing, the dried fish of Scotland and Shetland. What a pity they cannot be kept in our sights as bokkem are in South Africa. They are made from mullet (*haarder*), horse mackerel (*maasbanker*), bass (*steenbrass*) and shad (*elf*) in the same sort of way as blawns. First the salting, then a day in the sun and up to a week in the cool of shadowy verandahs. The idea came from the Netherlands. They can be chewed as a relish and are said to taste like biltong. Or they can be lightly grilled and eaten with butter – and a glass of white wine.

I regret that refrigeration has driven out many old curing methods, unreliable as they must often have been. After all a frozen herring is similar, if inferior, to a fresh herring, whereas a kipper or a buckling or a wind-dried is something quite different to eat. The old methods increased variety: freezing does not – the only certainty is that it diminished flavour. One has to apologize for a frozen herring, for a kipper never.

The advantages of refrigeration are all in distribution. I do not belittle this. In the old days, many people starved to death as they do today in Africa. Now in Europe and North America, they don't. Food can be kept over the winter, or bought from elsewhere, and sent where it is needed. I just hope that we shall have the sense to hang on to the old cures as well and improve them. Even if curing is destined to become a luxurious choice, I hope people will cling on to it because they like the tastes it can produce. Tastes which can be finer than they ever have been, because people are no longer dependent on curing for survival.

FISH SOUPS AND STEWS

There are many recipes which contain a mixture of fish and this section caters for them. Other soups, stews and chowders which contain one main fish will be found under the relevant section, i.e. Breton crab soup, Sedgmoor eel stew or Clam chowder.

FISH SOUPS

FISHERMAN'S SOUP (Kakavia)

This is the old soup of romantic association, and still a reality for some fishermen – a soup cooked over the fire on shore or in a boat, in the three-legged pot known as a *kakavi*. The fish used will depend on what have been caught. Greeks claim that Kakavia is the origin of Bouillabaisse, taken by Ionian Greeks in ancient time when they set off to colonize the place now known as Marseilles.

Enough of the same types of Greek fish can be bought in England to make a reasonable showing – red and grey mullet, snapper, bream, whiting, and John Dory. The problem comes when you try to get hold of small live lobsters and live Mediterranean prawns. You may have to be content with buying frozen ones or substituting mussels and cooked prawns, whose shells at least can be added to the basic stock.

When you choose the fish, allow extra weight to compensate for any mussels used as their shells are so heavy. Ask the fishmonger to give you bones and heads left over from filleting. When you get home, divide up the fish according to the time they take to cook, putting them on separate plates as you prepare them. Add their trimmings to the trimmings you already have.

Serves 6–8

fish trimmings, well washed
250 g (8 oz) sliced onion
125 ml (4 fl oz) olive oil

2 bay leaves
2 good sprigs parsley
½ teaspoon rigani or dried thyme
250–500 g (½–1 lb) tomatoes, peeled (optional)
1 level teaspoon peppercorns
salt
2 litres (3½ pt) water
2 kg (4 lb) mixed fish and shellfish, cleaned
lemon juice

Put the fish trimmings, onion, oil, herbs, tomatoes, peppercorns and a good pinch of salt into a large pan. Add the water, bring to the boil and cook steadily, uncovered, for 45 minutes. Sieve into a clean pan so that you now have a thick soup base.

Bring to simmering point and add the fish in batches – the thickest, firmest pieces first, together with the lobster if using, and ending up with mussels and cooked prawns, which only require a minute or two. Correct the seasoning with salt and lemon juice. Serve with bread or croûtons.

MATELOTE NORMANDE

As you would expect in a Matelote from Normandy, dry cider is substituted for red wine, and Calvados (their famous apple brandy) for eau de vie. Whisky is a possible alternative to Calvados. The fish, too, are typical of the area; the same fish that we can buy in Britain.

Serves 6

1 kg (2 lb) fish (including 250 g/8 oz conger eel, and a mixture of plaice,
    dabs, whiting and gurnard)
90 g (3 oz) butter
3–4 tablespoons Calvados
300 ml (10 fl oz) dry cider
liquor from mussels
300 ml (10 fl oz) fish or light meat stock
salt, pepper, chervil
beurre manié* –1 tablespoon each butter and flour
125 ml (4 fl oz) double cream
250 g (8 oz) mushrooms, lightly fried
1¼ litres (2 pt) mussels, opened
croûtons of bread fried in butter

Clean and cut up the fish. Cook in butter until the pieces are very lightly coloured. Pour over the warmed Calvados, set it alight, and stir the fish about in the flames. Add cider, mussel liquor and stock. Season with salt and pepper, and add some chopped chervil. Simmer until the fish is just cooked. Add the beurre manié in small knobs to thicken the cooking liquor. Pour in the cream. The sauce should not boil, but should thicken gradually over a moderate heat. (Two egg yolks can be used instead of the beurre manié, if you prefer: they should be beaten up with the cream.)

Transfer to a serving dish, and arrange mushrooms, mussels and croûtons round the fish. In Normandy, you might get oysters and crawfish as well as mussels, if you were lucky.

MEDITERRANEAN FISH SOUP

As there is no point in attempting a Bouillabaisse since we do not have the right fish, here is another Mediterranean fish soup from France which we can make successfully. The vital ingredient is saffron, followed by fennel and a dried strip of orange peel – things we can get hold of here. Be sure to buy fish with heads on, and ask the fishmonger if he can give you a collection of sole or turbot bones, skin and heads from filleting white fish (they increase the flavour, improve the texture and cost nothing).

Serves 6

generous 1 kg (2–2½ lb) fish – monkfish, conger, mullet red or grey,
    gurnard or rascasse
bones and skin
1 large leek, trimmed, sliced
1 large onion, quartered
1 medium carrot, sliced
3 large cloves garlic, sliced
outer layer trimmed from a fennel bulb, or *2 fennel stalks* or *2 level*
    teaspoons fennel seed
olive oil
bouquet garni
strip of dried orange peel
salt, pepper, cayenne, sugar
large pinch of saffron
dash white wine vinegar (optional)
125 ml (4 fl oz) white wine, reduced by half (optional)
90 g (3 oz) vermicelli or other soup pasta

Clean and cut up fish: chop bones into convenient pieces. Put vegetables, garlic and fennel into a huge pan with enough oil to cover the base. Stew with an occasional stir for about 15 minutes, until the onion is soft and yellowing. Put in fish bones, skin, fish, bouquet garni and orange peel. Bring 2 litres (3½ pt) water to the boil and pour it into the pan. Bring rapidly to the boil and boil hard for 15 minutes. Tip into a sieve laid across a large pan. Ignore the more recalcitrant objects, bones, peel, bouquet, hard bits of fennel. Push through as much of the debris as you feel inclined, to give texture to the soup. Season to taste, adding a pinch of sugar if the flavour needs enhancing. A dash of vinegar or wine can be added with the same idea.

Bring soup to the boil, tip in the pasta and simmer until it is just cooked. Serve the soup with toasted or baked bread and rouille*, either to spread on the bread or stir into the soup.

VELOUTÉ DE POISSON

This fish soup is made on the principle of a velouté sauce*, but with finer, richer ingredients.

Serves 6

1½ kg (3 lb) fish – redfish, conger, gurnard
2 carrots, chopped
2 leeks or onions, chopped
3 large tomatoes, peeled and chopped
bouquet garni
3 cloves garlic, chopped
2 cloves
cayenne, nutmeg
1 tablespoon white wine vinegar
600 ml (1 pt) dry white wine or dry cider
1¼–1¾ litres (2–3 pt) water
500 g (1 lb) shellfish – lobster, mussels, prawns
salt, pepper
2 shallots, chopped
60 g (2 oz) butter
2 heaped tablespoons plain flour
1 glass brandy (optional)
125–175 ml (4–6 fl oz) single cream
2 large egg yolks
lemon juice
chopped parsley, tarragon, chives
croûtons of bread fried in butter

Put 1½ kg (3 lb) of fish into a pan, with vegetables, bouquet, garlic, spices, vinegar, wine and water. Bring to the boil. Add live lobster if used – otherwise add *shells only* of cooked prawns and lobster; with mussels, open them and add their liquor. Set aside the meat of these shellfish. When the lobster is cooked remove it, take out the meat, set it aside, and return shell to the pan. After 10 more minutes, sieve the contents of the pan and season well.

Melt the shallots gently, without browning, in butter. Stir in the flour, then the sieved fish stock. When smooth, add brandy and seasoning, and simmer for 20 minutes. Mix the cream and egg yolks and use to thicken the soup. Sharpen with lemon juice and taste for seasoning. Stir in shellfish and chopped herbs, and serve with croûtons.

FISH STEWS AND MISCELLANEOUS FISH DISHES

This is another section where there is no main fish ingredient; more an amalgamation of three, four or more different fish and shellfish.

CATALAN FISH STEW (Zarzuela)

A *zarzuela* is an operetta, a musical entertainment, very gay and brightly coloured, frivolous – a good name for this splendid Catalan fish stew with its different tones of red and white, touched with saffron yellow. As with Paella, you may find it difficult to make because of the lack of fine fresh shellfish. Of course cooked and even frozen shellfish can be used, but the dish loses something of its pell-mell sweet intensity of flavour. As far as the plainer fish are concerned, squid and monkfish are essential as they have a hint of shellfish texture and flavour, after them come hake, sole or John Dory. In Spain, grouper (*mero*) is important to Zarzuela, but this is not a common fish. Substitutions can be made of course, so long as you have a variety of textures and tastes. Use the ingredient list as a guide only. Even if the result is not authentically Spanish, it may be just as delicious in its own way.

Serves 10–14

2 kg (4 lb) mixed fish – monkfish, hake, sole, John Dory, halibut, weever
500 g (1 lb) prawns in their shells or shrimp, mixed kinds and sizes, uncooked
  if possible
1 kg (2 lb) lobster, cut into 10 pieces
125 g (4 oz) onion, chopped
6 cloves garlic, peeled, sliced thin
olive oil
750 g (1½ lb) tomatoes, peeled, seeded, chopped
leaves of 1 handful of parsley
large pinch of saffron dissolved in 125 ml (4 fl oz) hot water
150 ml (5 fl oz) dry white wine
salt, pepper

Prepare, sort and slice the fish. Put all trimmings, tentacles, heads, bones and shells of cooked shellfish (apart from a few left whole to garnish) into a large pan. Cover with water, and boil for 30 minutes to make some stock. Aim to end up with 250 ml (8–9 fl oz).

From the next five ingredients, make a sofrito. This means something lightly fried and is the basis of many Spanish dishes and sauces. Sweat the onion and garlic slowly in the olive oil. As it turns golden, add the tomato and parsley. Cook to a thick, unwatery paste. When it is mellow add saffron and its water, wine and stock, with seasoning. When boiling hard, add the firmest fish and uncooked large shellfish. Simmer 5 minutes, then add softer fish and smaller shellfish and lobster pieces. Bring back to simmering point and simmer for 5 more minutes. Add cooked shellfish and give it 2 more minutes. Pour into a hot tureen and serve.

CORNISH BOUILLABAISSE

This magnificent stew of fish comes from Gidleigh Park Hotel on the edge of Dartmoor. It is made with the best ingredients that the western coast can supply and the quantities vary according to what is available.

Serves 8–10

¾–1 kg (1½–2 lb) lobster, uncooked
1–1½ kg (2–3 lb) mussels
1 large gurnard
750 g (1½ lb) monkfish or turbot
500 g (1 lb) red mullet
1 good kg (at least 2 lb) fish bones, heads, trimmings

1 large onion, chopped
2 medium carrots, diced small
white part of 2 leeks, diced small
2 medium stalks celery, diced small
olive oil
175 ml (6 fl oz) dry white wine
large pinch of saffron
lemon juice
2 tablespoons Pernod
1 head fennel, outer layer removed, then diced
250 g (8 oz) tomatoes, skinned, seeded and chopped
salt, pepper, cayenne

Ask the fishmonger to cut the lobster across into slices, and crack the claws if you feel unable to tackle this yourself. Loosely tie the bits into a piece of butter muslin. Scrub and scrape the mussels, discarding any that are cracked or that obstinately stay open when tapped: tie them into another piece of butter muslin, leaving plenty of room for them to open. Scale, clean and fillet the remaining fish, as necessary, putting skin, bones, heads, etc. into a large pan with the fish trimmings and 2 litres (3½ pt) of water. Make a stock while you cut the fillets into convenient pieces for eating with a spoon, and prepare the vegetables.

Sweat the onion and diced vegetables in a little olive oil in a huge pot: they should soften and turn golden without browning. Strain on the fish stock. Add wine, saffron and a tablespoon of lemon juice. When everything is boiling vigorously, put in the bag of mussels and leave boiling for 2 minutes. Remove and cool. Do the same with the bag of lobster, leaving it to boil for 3 minutes before removing it. Reduce the stock until it has an agreeably concentrated flavour. Strain the liquor off into a clean pot, pushing through a certain amount of the debris to give it a little body.

Open the bag of mussels, discard all but 8–10 of the shells. Put in a bowl. Open the lobster bag, clean away any debris and useless shell, but leave most of the lobster in its shell. Add to the mussels.

Up to this point, the recipe can be prepared in advance, but only by an hour or two.

Twenty minutes before serving, have everything ready on the table and a bowl of garlic croûtons keeping warm. Bring the liquor up to boiling point. Add Pernod, fennel and tomatoes and boil vigorously for 10 minutes. Check the seasoning at this point, adding extra lemon juice or Pernod if it seems a good idea, but be careful not to overdo either. Add salt and pepper, a pinch or two of cayenne. Keep at a vigorous boil and put in the monkfish or turbot pieces; leave 1 minute. Put in the red mullet, leave 1 minute, then the gurnard, and leave 30 seconds. Switch off the heat, stir in mussels and lobster meat. Taste again, and serve.

Be careful about the timings, and keep them on the short side: the fish should just be cooked through, no more, and remember it will continue to cook as you bring it to table. Serve into hot bowls, giving an equal distribution of fish and shellfish, with the garlic croûtons.

MEURETTE À LA BOURGUIGNONNE

Meurette is the famous Burgundian stew of river fish cooked in red wine. Pochouse or pauchouse is a similar concoction made with white wine, Meursault preferably, and garnished with small caramelized onions as well as triangles of bread. They are both a form of Matelote, *see* p. 499. Incidentally, Meurette shows that red wine goes as well with fish as white; one more 'rule' tumbling to the ground. (You can think of sole with Chambertin as well as the rich-fleshed salmon.)

This is a fisherman's recipe; when a bag of mixed fish is presented to you, it is an excellent way of dealing with them. Divide them into thick, medium and thin piles, so that none gets overcooked.

Serves 6

1½–2 kg (3–4 lb) river fish – pike, tench, eel, bream, etc.
3 large carrots, sliced
2 large onions, sliced
4 cloves garlic
thyme, bay leaf, bunch of parsley
salt, freshly ground black pepper
1 bottle red wine (from Burgundy for preference)
3 or 4 slices of bread
125 g (4 oz) butter
1 tablespoon plain flour
liqueur glass of marc or brandy

Clean the fish. Cut off the heads and tails (and put them into a piece of muslin if they are numerous and muddled). Chop the fish into roughly equal pieces and season them.

Butter a sauté pan with a butter paper. Line it with rings of carrot and onion, 3 of the 4 cloves of garlic crushed, the thyme, bay leaf, parsley stalks and seasoning. Put in the bottle of wine and bring to the boil. Tie the muslin bag of fish heads to the pan handle, and let it sink well into the bubbling liquid. Simmer for 20 minutes.

Meanwhile cut the bread into triangles and rub them with the fourth clove of garlic. Fry them in 30 g (1 oz) of the butter, on both sides, and keep warm. Mash up another 30 g (1 oz) of butter with the flour and divide the resulting paste into little pieces (beurre manié); leave to one side until later on.

Put the thickest pieces of fish into the sauté pan. After 5 minutes' cooking, add the medium ones. After 5 minutes again, the thinnest ones. In another 5 minutes or less everything should be cooked. Discard the fishes' heads, in or out of the muslin. Pour off the liquor into a saucepan. Warm the marc, set it alight and tip it over the fish and vegetables, stirring them about in the flames. Keep warm, while you finish the sauce.

Add the little pieces of flour and butter to the liquor in the saucepan, keeping it just below boiling point. Stir until the sauce thickens nicely, adjust the seasoning. Beat in the remaining 60 g (2 oz) of butter, and the chopped parsley leaves. Pour over the fish and vegetables. Tuck in the triangles of bread and serve straightaway (with some more red wine to drink).

PAELLA

Paella is one of those magnificent dishes that need a party to share them. A picnic by the sea in this case, I think, with the shallow pan bubbling gently over a driftwood fire. There is no one 'right' recipe: the only essential ingredients are rice and saffron (do not be tempted to substitute turmeric – make your economies elsewhere if necessary). Flavourings can be meat and poultry alone, or fish and shellfish alone, or vegetables alone. Or – as in this recipe – a mixture of all three. I have come to regard squid as essential for its piquant sweetness; mussels help to flavour the broth, and huge *gambas* (Mediterranean prawns) give an air of luxury, though the usual pink prawns do well enough.

Serves 8–10

1¾ kg (3½ lb) roasting chicken, with giblets
2 litres (3½ pt) light stock or water
1 small lobster, uncooked or ready-boiled, cut up by the fishmonger

1 medium-sized squid, approx. 250 g (8 oz) in weight
500 g (1 lb) prawns, preferably of varying sizes
500 g (1 lb) mussels
250 g (8 oz) monkfish
olive oil
1 large onion, chopped finely
250 g (8 oz) tomatoes, peeled and chopped
1 heaped teaspoon paprika
3 large cloves garlic, chopped finely
salt, pepper
tomato paste or *sugar, if needed* (see *recipe*)
500 ml (15 fl oz) Spanish or *Italian rice (approx. 400 g/14 oz)*
generous pinch of saffron
175 g (6 oz) shelled young peas
1 large red pepper, grilled, skinned, seeded and sliced
4 large artichoke hearts, cooked (optional)
3 lemons, quartered

Use a wide, shallow pan or *paellera* of at least 35 cm (14 inches) diameter. Alternatively, use two pans once the rice is half-cooked, transferring some of the rice to a second pan before putting in the chicken. Paella is not a dish for the small family. Remember that if you alter the quantity of rice, you need to alter that of the liquid.

First, prepare the chicken and fish. If you intend to make the paella out of doors, on a picnic, this should all be done in advance, leaving the final cooking of the rice and so on to be done on the spot.

Set aside the chicken wings and drumsticks. Cut away the chicken breast and keep for another meal, if you are only feeding 8 people. Cut the thigh meat off the bone, dividing each piece into three, and remove the oysters. If you are using the chicken breasts, bone them and cut into two pieces each. Leave the carcase to simmer in the stock or water. Cut up the lobster so that there will be a chunk for each person.

Clean the squid (*see* p. 400) and cut the bag into rings and the tentacles into short lengths: keep the trimmings and left-overs. Peel most of the prawns, leaving a few whole for garnishing: put the debris with the squid's. Open the scrubbed mussels in a heavy covered pan over a high heat (p. 239); shell most of the mussels, keeping some for the garnishings, and strain the juice into the chicken stock pan. Add the fish trimmings after the stock has been simmering for at least half an hour. Cut the monkfish into chunks: add the bone and skin, and the small claws of the lobster, to the stock pot. Give it another half hour and then strain off the stock – you will need just over 1 litre (approx. 2 pt) or a little more, so add water if you are short, or boil it down if there is much too much. Season the chicken and fish.

Now you are ready for the cooking. Bring the stock to simmering point and keep it there. In a large pan or *paellera* heat enough olive oil to cover the base. Put in the onion and cook it slowly until soft and yellow. Add the tomatoes, paprika, garlic, seasoning and a little tomato paste or sugar unless your tomatoes are very well ripened. When the mixture is a thick purée, push it to the side of the pan and brown the chicken pieces. Remove them to a plate. Stir in the rice and move it about until it looks transparent. Pour about half the hot stock on to the rice. Pour a little more stock into a cup and dissolve the saffron in it. Leave the rice to bubble gently.

When the rice is half-cooked, put in the chicken, pushing it down so that only the drumstick and wing bones stick up. Pour in the saffron stock and most of the remaining stock.

After 10 minutes put in the squid. In another 5 minutes, add the vegetables and uncooked lobster pieces. Check the chicken breast pieces and remove them if they are done: they should not get too dry and can be put back at the end to heat through with the prawns and mussels. Another 8–10 minutes and everything should be cooked. Add any remaining stock or water, if necessary to prevent sticking. Shake the pan from time to time, but avoid stirring it up.

Just before serving, put in the shelled mussels and cut-up, cooked lobster meat, if you had to buy a ready-boiled lobster. Then add the shelled prawns. Last of all, arrange the reserved whole prawns and mussels in their shells on top, after checking the seasoning. Tuck in the lemon wedges and serve.

NOTE   In Spanish restaurants, the *paellera* is sometimes placed in a slightly larger basket tray, with a ring of flowers and fruit in the gap – red and white carnations, yellow lemons, echoing the colours of the food. Festive but confusing.

PLATEAU DE FRUITS DE MER

Our first meal in France, at Avranches or Mont St Michel, or our last before the boat at Cherbourg, is a vast platter of shellfish with a bowl of mayonnaise and a little pot of mignonette sauce. To go with this feast there is a basket of bread, butter and a bottle of white wine from Alsace.

The oval metal dish is placed ceremonially in the centre of the table on a stand. Arranged like a still-life on top of a bed of crushed ice and seaweed there will be winkles, whelks, opened clams and oysters, rising to a central height of prawns, langoustines, spider crabs and, if you are lucky, lobster. The whole thing has a glorious freshness. One picks and eats slowly. Always I am amazed that the whelks, which in Britain are impossibly rubbery, are in France agreeably chewy.

To make such a show here is not easy – for a start our best shellfish seem to go to France. But if you happen to live near the west coast of Scotland, or in some blessed spot near Weymouth or Wells and Cley in Norfolk, you may be lucky.

Quantities need to be judged by eye, and will depend of course on what you can get. Half a decent-sized crab or lobster per person, four oysters, six large mussels, three large langoustines (Dublin Bay prawns), with a scattering of prawns, shrimps and winkles would be reasonable. Always buy shellfish the day you intend to eat it, and if possible cook it yourself. Otherwise you can buy crab and lobsters ready-cooked. At large fishmongers in France you can buy bottled seawater by the litre: be careful about seawater in Britain, it may well be polluted, judging by how few beaches we have that are safe for swimming. Safer to dissolve sea salt in water until an egg will float in it.

Serve everybody with a needle stuck into a cork for winkles, with a long slender lobster pick or snail fork for lobster and crab, and lobster shears or nutcrackers for the lobster and crab claws. And large cloth napkins!

CRABS   If you are cooking it yourself, take it home as soon as possible. Plunge it into boiling salt water, give it 10 minutes boiling and then simmer it for a further 15 minutes, for a crab weighing just under 1 kg (2 lb). When cold, cut it in half with a cleaver, or a large knife knocked smartly down with a mallet.

LANGOUSTINES, PRAWNS AND SHRIMPS   Bring a large pan half-full of very salty water to the boil. Plunge in the shellfish. By the time the water returns to the boil, the shrimps are likely to be done (try one to see). Prawns will take a couple of minutes or more according to size. The moment they change colour, try one. Once you are used to cooking shellfish, you can tie the different kinds into pieces of muslin and cook them at the same time, removing each bag at the appropriate moment.

LOBSTER　Can be cooked like crab, but is better steamed if you are cooking it yourself. At home choose a large pan, put in 2 cm (¾ inch) of water, 4 teaspoons sea salt and 4 of vinegar. When boiling, put in the lobster, cover it and cook it for 15 minutes. Remove it with tongs and uncurl the tail with a wooden spoon; if it springs back efficiently, it is cooked.

MUSSELS　Scrub and scrape mussels under the cold tap. Tug away the beard and discard any that are cracked. Arrange them in batches in a single layer in a heavy pan. Set the pan over a very high heat, covered, and leave it for 1 minute. Inspect to see if the mussels are open. Give them a few seconds longer, if not. For the best flavour, never leave them longer than necessary. Tip them into a colander set over a bowl. Remove a half-shell from each or leave them as they are. Discard any that remain shut when the rest have opened. Strain the liquor and keep it for soup or stock and sauces.

OYSTERS, CLAMS AND COCKLES　Scrub them and then, holding each one in a cloth-wrapped hand, insert an oyster knife, or any thin, short, stubby knife, between the shells as close to the hinge as seems practical. Lever off the top, i.e. flatter shell, freeing the attached oysters. Clams and cockles have twin shells, so it doesn't much matter which one you discard. Ease the fish from the shell to make it easier for the eater.

SCALLOPS　I have never seen scallops on a French platter of shellfish, but there is no reason not to include them, especially if your choice is limited. Tiny queen scallops, if very fresh, could be served as they are, once washed well. So of course could the larger kind: slice them thinly across the disc.

To cook them, rinse them well and remove the frill and tough muscle, leaving only the tender white disc and the coral. Halve the discs across and poach all the pieces in a little fish stock until they are just opaque. Serve the pieces from 3 or 4 scallops in one deeper shell, allowing 3 or 4 scallops per person.

Scallops at the fish counter have usually been opened, and the edible part cleaned, the rest thrown away. If, however, you get the chance of buying closed, uncleaned scallops, they are likely to be fresher. Open them like mussels, or put them into a preheated very hot oven. Inside you will finds an unaccustomed murkiness, the gritty frill and so on. Under the cold tap remove and rinse until you are down to the edible part.

FISH CAKES

I was never fond of northern ways with fish – fish pies and muddles of that kind, and overcooking generally – but fish cakes are another matter. Especially when made with smoked haddock or salmon or crab, or the fresh inshore cod which was taken for granted until lately, but seems such a treat now. I read somewhere a few years ago that Newcastle eats more fish fingers than anywhere else in the country – which seems scandalous for a place that has the makings of excellent fish cakes to hand.

Sometimes fish cakes are smartened up, but I think that food of such basic purity and goodness should be left alone. Anchovy essence is the one permitted flavouring, Lazenby's according to my husband but unfortunately you cannot get it now: I have the feeling that modern brands are not as good.

Makes 6–8

250–375 g (8–12 oz) cooked fish, flaked
250 g (8 oz) cooked potato, the fresher the better
yolk of 1 large egg
about 2 tablespoons chopped parsley
1 teaspoon anchovy essence
60 g (2 oz) butter
salt, pepper
large egg white, beaten slightly
fresh white breadcrumbs
clarified butter* or bacon fat (see recipe)

Mix the first five ingredients. Melt the butter in a pan over a very low heat and put in the mixture, beating them together – the warming through makes this easier, but the mixture should not cook properly. Season to taste, then spread out on a plate in a thick layer and cool.

When cold, form into cakes of whatever size is convenient – tiny fish cakes served with a little crisp bacon make a good first course. Dip in the egg white, then the crumbs and fry in clarified butter or bacon fat according to the fish used: the more delicate the fish, the more delicate the cooking medium. Have the fat 1 cm (¼ inch) deep in the pan, so that the cakes brown at the sides.

Drain on kitchen paper, and serve very hot with a béchamel* or velouté* sauce flavoured with anchovy and parsley. Or just serve them on their own with bread and butter.

FISH TERRINE (Terrine de poisson)

Making fish terrines – or pâtés, as they are often called – is one of the most entertaining exercises of French cookery. It gives you a chance to make something beautiful and delicious that is completely your own. Seeing the works of art in Fauchon's in Paris first gave me the hint of what could be done: some terrines are simple layers of two or three mixtures, interspersed with an occasional layer of finely chopped herbs or mushrooms: others look like pink marble, studded with strips of sole or eel. At home it is wise to eschew the fussier effects of a professional caterer's kitchen, but that is no reason not to enjoy the fun.

Loaf tins can be used if you intend to turn the terrine out before slicing it. I prefer an oblong earthenware dish and serve the terrine from it: the slices hang together far better this way. When making your choice of decorative centre ingredients, reflect on whether they are likely to shrink in cooking, and give up much liquid: if they are, it is wise to cook them lightly and cool them down before layering them into place.

A mousseline should be what its name implies: very fine and smooth. This used to be achieved by pounding and sieving, and more sieving. Today, we have blenders and processors, which account for the return of this kind of dish to our tables.

Serves 8–10

500 g (1 lb) whiting, sole, salmon, eel, or red mullet, etc.
    weighed after boning
2 large egg whites
300 ml (10 fl oz) whipping or double cream
salt, pepper, cayenne
lemon juice
250–375 g (8–12 oz) fillets of fish (sole or salmon) or scallops with
    shellfish (shrimps, prawns, crab) or mussels, weighed without shells
    or mixed smoked fish, cut in strips
chopped parsley, chives and tarragon
fish stock* or white wine if scallops are used

Cut the fish into pieces and drop them on to the whirling blades of a blender or processor and reduce them to a purée. This purée will now go easily through a sieve into a bowl set over ice. With an electric beater, mix in the egg whites then the cream, bit by bit, and salt, pepper and cayenne, until it becomes a bulky lightness. Taste and add extra seasoning and lemon juice.

For the filling, first season the fish fillets then cut them neatly, bearing in mind that they will be set longways through the terrine, so that each cut slice will contain a piece. Roll the fish pieces in the herbs. If you use scallops, which do shrink, slice the cleaned white discs across, horizontally, into two: cut off any black bits from the corals. Steam or poach them in a little fish stock or white wine. Cool and season them.

If the terrine is to be served cold, brush the dish or tin out with a tasteless oil. If it is to be turned out, cut a long strip of non-stick baking paper the narrow width of the base of the dish or tin, and run it down one end, along the base and up the other end. Brush it with oil. Put in another oiled strip, cut to fit widthways.

If the terrine is to be served hot or warm, line it in the same way and brush with butter instead of oil.

Beginning and ending with mousseline, layer in the mixtures. Cut a butter paper to fit on top, then cover with double foil. The preparation so far can be completed earlier in the day, and chilled until required, if you wish to serve the terrine hot or warm for dinner.

Set oven at moderate, gas 4, 180 °C (350 °F). Stand the terrine on a rack in a roasting tin, pour hot water round to come about halfway up the sides, bring to the boil on top of the stove. Transfer to the heated oven and cook for 30 minutes.

Inspect the terrine: if it seems firm and if a skewer or larding needle pushed into the centre feels hot on the back of your hand, it is done. Remember that it will continue to cook a little as it cools.

Serve hot with beurre blanc* or vin blanc* sauces or cold with mayonnaise* flavoured with an appropriate herb, or coloured and flavoured pink with tomato, or green with spinach juice or the juice of a bouquet of green herbs and watercress, blanched and squeezed in muslin.

FRUITS DE MER FILLING

A recipe for seafood bound with a rich velouté sauce is a most useful one to know. It can be rolled into crêpes or piled into a large, pre-cooked, flaky pastry case, or spooned into vol-au-vent cases. Most simply of all, it can be served inside a ring of rice or egg noodles.

The quantities given here are enough for six helpings. If you have problems getting one or other of the fish or shellfish suggested, substitute what you can get that is good and fresh: in all you need a minimum of 750 g (1 ½ lb) total edible weight.

Serves 6

750 ml (1¼ pt) fumet de poisson*
250–300 g (8–10 oz) boned monkfish, cut in little cubes or strips
    or John Dory, weever or Dover sole fillets, cut in strips
6 large scallops
175 g (6 oz) prawns, large shrimps or langoustines
12 mussels or oysters, shelled, liquid added to fumet
meat of a boiled crab or lobster weighing about 500 g (1 lb) or about
    175 g (6 oz) shelled crab or lobster meat
salt, pepper

SAUCE
60 g (2 oz) unsalted butter
4 tablespoons plain flour
100 g (3½ oz) mushrooms, chopped
150 ml (5 fl oz) crème fraîche or double cream
salt, pepper, lemon juice

Bring the fumet to simmering point and poach the white fish until it just becomes opaque. Remove the fish with a slotted spoon, season it and set it aside. Slice the white part of the scallops across, reserving the corals. Cook the discs of white scallop meat in the fumet. Remove them, season them and set them aside. Strain the fumet and reserve it. Shell the prawns, shrimps or langoustines, reserving any eggs. When the fish has cooled, mix it with all the shellfish and season to taste.

Meanwhile, make the sauce by melting the butter, stirring in the flour and cooking it for 2 minutes. Add the strained fumet and mushrooms. Cook the sauce down steadily until it is thick but not gluey. Mix enough sauce into the shellfish mixture to bind it nicely, and check the seasoning, adding lemon juice if it seems a good idea. Sieve the crème fraîche or cream, scallop corals and shellfish eggs together, and mix in the remaining sauce with salt, pepper and lemon juice as required.

You now have your filling and sauce ready for use and subsequent reheating. Remember that shellfish is best eaten the day you buy it.

CHOWDER, CHAUDRÉE AND COTRAIDE

These are the fish and potato stews of the Atlantic coasts of France and America, seamen's food that can be prepared in a boat; a rough food that can be softened on land with the resources of gardens and store cupboards. I had thought that chowder sounded a thoroughly American word, even a Red Indian word; in fact it is an anglicization of *chaudière*, the large iron cauldron in which Breton fishermen off Newfoundland and Iceland made their soup. (It was also used on whaling ships for boiling down the blubber . . .) *Chaudrée* means 'cooked in a *chaudière*'. The meaning of cotriade is more difficult to track down: a *cotriade* should be cooked over a wood fire, and *cotret* means a faggot – perhaps that is the origin of the word. The odd thing is that it always contains potato, and the recipes are closer to the American chowder recipes than the *chaudrées* of the French Charentes, which only contain potato in some districts.

They are the sort of recipes I like because the result tastes different every time. They are an invitation to experiment, to try adding something from the garden or larder that wasn't available last week. Such recipes are a stated principle, not a detailed plan of construction. Each person will have an individual view of the most important ingredients. For me it is the bay leaf, which, with the milk of a chowder, produces the most deliciously fresh-tasting background for cod or shellfish.

COD AND SHELLFISH CHOWDER

A most satisfying dish when everyone is tired at the end of the day. Don't despise the frozen packs of cod or haddock on sale in the grocery, they do nicely for chowders; so do frozen scallops or prawns if clams and fresh mussels aren't available.

Serves 6

125 g (4 oz) salt belly of pork or *streaky bacon, diced*
175–250 g (6–8 oz) chopped onion
1 tablespoon lard or *butter*
1 heaped tablespoon plain flour
450 ml (15 fl oz) water or *fish stock*
450 ml (15 fl oz) milk
bouquet garni, including a bay leaf
6 medium potatoes, diced
salt, mace, freshly ground pepper, cayenne
750 g (1½ lb) cod or *other firm white fish*
150 ml (5 fl oz) cream
at least 125 g (4 oz) shelled mussels, clams, scallops, etc.
parsley and chives for garnish

Brown pork (or bacon) and onion lightly in the fat. Stir in the flour and cook for a couple of minutes. Add the water or fish stock gradually, then the milk, bouquet, and potatoes. Season well with salt, mace and peppers.

When the potatoes are almost cooked, put in the cod, cut into rough 2½-cm (1-inch) pieces. After 5 minutes, stir in the cream and shellfish (and any liquor from opening mussels, etc). When the soup returns to the boil remove from the heat. Remember that the cod continues to cook in the heat of the chowder as it comes to table, and should not be overcooked – neither should the shellfish. Correct the seasoning and sprinkle with parsley and chives. Hot buttered toast or hot crackers usually accompany a chowder: ship's biscuits if you can get them.

NOTE Curry powder can be added with the flour. Final garnishes can include sweet red pepper or sweetcorn. Every town on the East Coast has its own small variations.

LA CHAUDRÉE

Here is another 'chowder', this time from La Rochelle, but without the seaman's flavouring of salt pork. The liquid should be white wine (ideally from the Île d'Oléron or the Île de Ré, islands off the south-west coast of France); and the *chaudron*, or cauldron in which the soup is made, should be buried in a fire of prunings from the island vines, which are fertilized with seaweed. Even if you haven't the possibility of such an aromatic smoke as flavouring, or the right wind Chaudrée is an excellent dish. This recipe comes from *Recettes des Provinces de France*, chosen by Curnonsky.

Serves 6

12 onions, quartered
1 clove garlic
large bouquet garni
salt, peppercorns
3 cloves
125 g (4 oz) butter
whole potatoes (optional)
2 kg (4 lb) assorted fish, small sole, plaice, eel
1 litre (1¾ pt) white wine or half wine half water

In a large pot arrange the onions, garlic and bouquet. Season, with not too much salt; add about 8 peppercorns and the cloves; dot with butter. Next, if you like, put in the potatoes, well-scrubbed but not peeled – one per person, or more if they are small; they turn the soup into a meal, a filling one, on American chowder lines. Arrange the cleaned fish on top – eel should be cut into chunks. Cover with wine, or wine and water; bring to the boil and simmer for half an hour or more. Remove the fish to a warm plate as it is cooked, do the same with the potatoes. Reduce the liquid to half by boiling down, and correct the seasoning. Restore fish and potatoes to the pot and serve immediately.

THREE COTRIADES

The fish soup of Brittany; or, if you like, the fish supper, because the liquid is drunk first, as soup, with the fish and potatoes as a main course to follow. The cooking method for the first two recipes is close to that of American chowder. All three come from Simone Morand's *Gastronomie Bretonne*. The point of variation between the three, and between so many other fish soups, lies in the different resources of the places where they are made. For this reason, mackerel is included – an unusual creature in most fish soups.

Cotriades are excellent food for large parties or people. One cooking pot to watch (and wash up), the simplest of preparations which means that everyone can help, and a lavish result after a short cooking time. The only possible mistake is to overcook the fish. Provide a great deal of butter to eat with the fish and potatoes. (Breton butter is often salted, unlike Normandy butter which is too softly creamy for this kind of food.) Failing butter, a vinaigrette will do instead. Provide plenty of bread, too, and toast some of it lightly for the soup. Another essential item is a bottle of full-bodied red wine.

Simone Morand so feelingly implores her readers not to cut off the heads of the fish, that I'm reminded of a Chinese cookery writer who declared that Westerners missed something through feeling unable to look at a fish with its head on, 'they miss experiencing the delicate taste of fish head'. True.

COTRAIDE DES BORDS DE LA RANCE

Serves 6

2 onions, chopped
1 spoonful of lard
3 cloves garlic, chopped
1 kg (2 lb) potatoes, quartered
chervil, parsley, chives in quantity
salt, pepper
2 medium mackerel, 3 gurnard, piece of conger eel sliced, 2 whiting, 1 bream

COTRIADE FROM CORNOUAILLE

Serves 6

1 onion, chopped
lump of lard or butter
good handful of sorrel
1 kg (2 lb) potatoes, sliced
bouquet garni
salt, pepper
1 gurnard, 1 red mullet, 1 garfish, cod etc.

Cook the onion in the fat until it is lightly browned. Add vegetables, herbs and seasoning, and scant 2 litres (3 pt) of water. Cover the pan, and simmer until the potatoes are almost cooked, then add the fish, cut into chunks. Add more water if necessary to cover all the ingredients. Bring back to the boil, and simmer for a further 10 minutes until the fish is cooked, but not overcooked.

COTRIADE FROM BELLE-ÎLE

Serves 6

firm fish – conger, mackerel, pollack, saithe
soft fish – sardines, skate, cod, ballan wrasse, etc.
shellfish – crawfish, lobster, crabs of various kinds, mussels, shrimps
1 kg (2 lb) potatoes, sliced
4 onions, sliced
6 large tomatoes, peeled, seeded and chopped
1 stalk of celery, chopped
white part of 2 or 3 leeks, chopped
salt, pepper
parsley, chervil, thyme, bay leaf
pinch of saffron
tumbler of olive oil or melted butter

The method is slightly different for this feast. First season and cut up the various fish. Put the firm-fleshed ones on a plate with crawfish, lobster and crab. Put the soft-fleshed ones on another plate with mussels and shrimps or prawns. Pour the oil or butter over both piles. Leave while the vegetables cook in plenty of water, with seasoning, herbs and saffron. When the potatoes are nearly done, add the firm-fleshed fish etc. Boil hard for 5 minutes exactly. Add the soft-fleshed fish, etc., and boil hard for another 5 minutes. Not a moment longer. Serve separately in the usual way, after correcting the seasoning of the soup.

BOUILLABAISSE, BOURRIDE AND CACCIUCCO

These Mediterranean stews have an air of romantic gastronomy about them. Their reality is in fact as simple as Atlantic chaudrées and chowders. The cook assembles whatever freshly caught fish he can, stews them in water with vegetables, embellishes them with such grace notes as the district can offer, and serves the whole thing up with bread. Of course if the local fish include lobster, John Dory and squid, the local vegetables huge sweet tomatoes and onions, and the grace notes olive oil, saffron and garlic, the stew is likely to be a winner.

At the opposite end of existence, it can be perfectly disgusting. A friend told me recently that his grandmother once went into a dark cottage in the Highlands of Scotland. There she saw a woman, apparently alone except for a cow, stirring a pot over the fire. In a few moments she poured the contents of the pot on to a pile of heather in front of the hearth. And from a shadowy hole in the wall darted two filthy children, who grabbed as many potatoes and raggy herrings as they could, and darted back again to eat them in obscurity. The liquor drained away through the heather stalks to be soaked up by the mud floor. That woman's resources were poor, her skills undeveloped, in such circumstances of life; but the method of cooking the stew was the same as the one used by any Marseillais fisherman to make his Bouillabaisse. The result could have been perfectly edible, if the fish hadn't been overcooked, and if there had been plenty of butter to eat with it.

In other words, it is the clemency of nature plus the skill of the cook which makes everyone seek out Bouillabaisse, Bourride or Cacciucco rather than tatties an' herrin'. Another sad truth about such dishes is that they cannot be reproduced elsewhere, not satisfactorily. Even if by some magic, you could acquire a spiny and beautiful rascasse (scorpionfish), always claimed to be the key fish of Bouillabaisse, along with the other proper ingredients, the results in Manchester or Milwaukee can never come up to the real thing in Marseilles. Cooking – thank heavens – still knows this particular disillusionment, in spite of the universal sameness of frozen food. In the autumn I always bring back tomatoes from France, olive oil, sea salt, fresh basil, yet the tomato salad I make in Wiltshire never tastes the same as it did when I used the same ingredients in France two days earlier. If you do not believe me, reflect on the unsuccessful efforts made to produce Scotch whisky outside Scotland.

Of course there is no reason why you shouldn't use the recipes for your own entertainment and this book would be incomplete without it. But to avoid disillusion, remember the uniqueness of local food when you visit an inland restaurant far from France, which has Bouillabaisse on the menu, at a reverential price.

Bourride and Cacciucco are less sacrosanct. They, after all, were not 'discovered' by Prosper Merimée, the French writer who was a friend of Napoleon III. Bouillabaisse comes into his *Colomba* (1840). Cookery writers have since tried to give it a pedigree, and have traced it, with a considerable number of gaps, back to a recipe given by the Roman gastronome Apicius for scorpionfish. For a longer discussion of Bouillabaisse, turn to *The French at Table* by Raymond Oliver, or to Elizabeth David's *French Provincial Cooking*. She gives two excellent recipes; here is a third, from a Marseilles restaurant, the Brasserie des Catalans:

BOUILLABAISSE

The interesting thing about Bouillabaisse and Bourride is that the fish is removed from the soup, but served with it; and the enrichment is provided by large bowls of ailloli and rouille. The bread is toasted, then fried in olive oil, and finally rubbed with garlic before being put into a basket for the table. As the soup itself doesn't take long to cook, prepare all the accompanying dishes first.

Use the following kinds of fish: monkfish, conger eel, John Dory, weaver, gurnard, crawfish or spiny lobster, Dublin Bay prawns, mussels (if prawns are not available).

Serves 6–8

3¼ kg (6½ lb) fresh fish
125 g (4 oz) olive oil
2 large onions, chopped
white part of 2 leeks, chopped
4–6 cloves garlic
2 huge tomatoes, peeled and chopped
parsley, fennel
1 small chilli
good pinch of saffron filaments
cayenne pepper, salt
4 potatoes, sliced
3 litres (5 pt) water, warm
12 slices French bread, toasted lightly in the oven, fried in olive oil and
    rubbed with garlic
bowl of rouille*
bowl of ailloli*

Sort out the fish and clean them. Put oil, vegetables (except potatoes), herbs, and seasonings into a large pot. Add the thickest fish (conger, monkfish) on top of the vegetables, and top with slices of potato. Pour on the water, bring to the boil and boil hard (this enables the water and oil to thicken together). After 5 minutes add the crawfish. After another 5 minutes add the Dublin Bay prawns, and John Dory. After another 5 minutes add the rest of the fish, and the mussels if you are not using Dublin Bay prawns. Boil 4–5 minutes.

Remove fish and potatoes to a hot serving dish, split the crawfish head in two and slice the tail. Prawns and mussels are left in their shells. Taste the soup and correct the seasoning. Boil hard for a few moments, then pour through a strainer into a soup tureen. Serve immediately with the fish and potatoes, the bread and sauces.

The correct wine is a rosé de Provence, well chilled. Other rosé wines can be substituted.

NOTE   A friend told me that the water by Marseilles is becoming so polluted that the fisherman's Bouillabaisse, caught and cooked on the spot, is becoming impossible to contemplate with serenity . . .

BOURRIDE

Any firm white fish can be used; one alone, or a mixture. The ideal fish is monkfish, turbot or John Dory, but squid make an excellent Bourride as well. Saffron is occasionally used to scent and colour the soup, but the most usual flavouring is orange peel, one or two good strips of it, preferably from a Seville orange. The ailloli is used to thicken the soup. Croûtons rubbed with garlic are served with it, as with Bouillabaisse. Potatoes can be cooked and presented separately, or included in the soup.

Serves 6

1½–2 kg (3–4 lb) firm white fish or squid
2 large onions, chopped
1 leek, chopped
4 cloves garlic
2 tomatoes (optional)
500 g (1 lb) potatoes, sliced (see above)
bouquet of herbs: thyme, fennel parsley, bay
strips of orange peel
salt, pepper
ailloli*
*12 slices French bread toasted lightly in the oven, fried in olive oil, and
    rubbed with garlic*

Clean the fish and cut into good-sized slices. Put onions, leek, garlic, tomatoes, and potatoes (if included), into a large pot. Lay the fish on top, with the herbs, orange peel, and seasoning. Add 1 ¼ litres (2 pt) of water, or enough to cover the fish; stock made from head and bones of fish can be used instead for a finer result; in some places seawater is used. Cook *gently* for 10 minutes at simmering point. Remove fish, and potatoes, to a warm serving plate.

Boil the liquor hard to less than 600 ml (1 pt). Correct the seasoning. Then strain slowly on to the ailloli, in a large bowl, mixing the two together carefully. Return to a clean pan and stir over a low heat until the mixture thickens slightly. Pour over the fish, sprinkle with extra parsley, and serve with bread as above, and with potatoes if not included in the soup-making.

CACCIUCCO ALLA LIVORNESE, *see* p. 401.

CAVIARE & OTHER HARD ROES

Caviare is a grand and painful subject. It is one of the most delicious, most simple things to eat in the world (and one of the most nutritious, too, but that is an academic point). It is also one of the most expensive. It has an air of mythical luxury – mythical to our modern experience at any rate. The food of Czars, of those incredible tyrants who cherished fine fat fleas and Fabergé knick-knacks, while most of their subjects lived in a poverty of indescribable squalor. The mainstay, along with champagne and oysters, of *La Belle Époque*. Odd that the caviare trade should never have been so efficiently organized as now, under the Russians and their pupils in the business the Iranians.

Another odd thing: caviare isn't a Russian word at all (it is called *ikra* in the former Soviet Union). It seems to be a word of Turkish-Italian origin, derived perhaps from the port of Kaffa, on the south-east coast of the Crimea, which had been important even in classical times. Under the Genoese, from the mid-thirteenth century, to the mid-fifteenth century when it fell to the Turks, Kaffa was a vast international port, a depot on the trade route to China.

The origins of caviare must be as difficult to trace as the word itself. Aristotle remarked that the sturgeon was prized for caviare. The Chinese had developed methods of treating and trading in caviare as early as the tenth century AD. Probably earlier, as they had long used refrigeration to protect delicate foods on journeys across China to the Emperor's court. Edward H. Schafer, Professor of Chinese[1] at Berkeley University, California, sent me this reference from the *T'ai ping huan yü chi*, a tenth-century official gazetteer, which says: '. . . at Pa-ling, where the Yangtze river flows out from Lake Tung-t'ing, an area also noted for its tea, the natives catch sturgeon, simmer the roe in an infusion of Gleditschia sinensis seeds (an acacia-like plant, normally used as a black dye), then pickle it in brine . . . extremely delicious!' It sounds like an early form of pasteurization.

[1] Author of *The Golden Peaches of Samarkand*, a study of exotics imported into China in the T'ang dynasty; recommended to anyone who is interested in food, wine, spices.

I think, though, that one has to look much further back for the origins of caviare. Consider the reality, the basic nature of the product – really no more than the salted hard roe of a sturgeon. Once man came to the skill of being able to trap and catch fish, and to organize a supply of salt, he could not avoid the experience of caviare. Imagine him, squatting over a sturgeon by the mouth of some great grey river on the Baltic or North Sea, slitting up the belly and diving into the incredible mass of eggs – up to twenty per cent of the total weight – with a handful of salt. I'm sure he reflected gratefully that this part at least he could not smoke or dry for winter stores: it must have been a bonus in the hard realities of mesolithic survival. A crude affair by comparison with the finest *malossol* Beluga perhaps but still caviare.

Caviare today is a pampered product compared with those mesolithic feasts. It has to be, because of the problem of conveying a food, which should be eaten immediately, to the far-off societies that can afford it. We have killed our own sturgeon population, and have to look to the Caspian Sea, the only place where these vast creatures survive in any quantity. Even there they are in danger from Russian oil drilling, from hydro-electric stations and from the sinking level of the sea itself. There is also the problem of human greed, politely described as 'over-fishing'. Now, the Caspian sturgeon seek the southern rivers of the sea, the ones flowing down to the Iranian coast, for their spawning. The Persians produce 210 tons of caviare a year, in consequence, which is not so far behind the Russians with 320 tons. They have learned everything they can, from Soviet technicians, about processing caviare, and about farming the fish, and with state control produce caviare of the highest standard. (The Rumanians produce tiny amounts – comparatively speaking – from Black Sea sturgeon; so do the Turks.)

The three main kinds of caviare are called after the species of sturgeon which provide them. The largest-grained and therefore most expensive (the price is based on appearance and not flavour) is taken from the Beluga, *Huso huso*, a giant 3½ m (12 feet), which can live to a hundred years, and which reaches maturity at the same age as a human being. It may – with luck – contain 65 kg (130 lb) of eggs, from deep grey to a soft moon-white. Next largest are the eggs of the Osetr, *Acipenser gueldenstaedtii*; they are sometimes golden-brown, sometimes greenish, or grey, and are first in flavour with people who know about caviare. The smallest-grained, and therefore the cheapest, come from the Sevruga, *Acipenser stellatus*: it is the one most widely on sale, and the most reliably steady in flavour.

With these three divisions, caviare is graded. The finest is *malossol*, which means slightly salted. Any of the caviares are best eaten fresh, which is only possible in the largest towns: for the provinces, where trade is not brisk and conditions of storage less ideal, it must be pasteurized. The difference in quality is comparable with the difference between fresh and potted *foie gras* – or between fresh and pasteurized milk and cheese. To me pasteurization spoils the pleasure of eating these foods, because the elusive, vital flavour has been killed.

Caviare is exported fresh in 2-kg (4-lb) tins, which have been piled up with salted eggs. Sliding lids are placed on top, then gently pressed down at intervals so that all surplus brine is excluded. A rubber band is stretched round to make an air-tight seal. The tins travel in ice in refrigerated containers, to keep the caviare at the correct temperature of − 1 °C (30 °F); one pamphlet observes that it is fatal to put caviare in the deep-freeze: 'it is reduced straightaway to a somewhat expensive soup!' An importer will re-pack it, sending fresh caviare twice a week to London's best hotels and grocers, and putting smaller amounts of pasteurized caviare into little pots, for distribution to delicatessen stores all over the country.

At the offices of W. G. White Ltd I was shown the most beautiful of gastronomic spectacles: a tray with three of these tins on it, opened, with a little bowl of Osetr caviare and a pot of salmon caviare, often known by its Russian name of *keta*. The Beluga in one tin was silky in texture, and lightly delicious. The Sevruga in another tin had a more pronounced and sea-like flavour. The Osetr in the bowl had been pasteurized, so it was difficult to judge if it really was the finest of all: again, the taste was different. The salmon eggs were enormous, and a translucent vermilion. They were certainly the visual stars of the tray by comparison with the Quaker-greys and sombre greens of the caviare, but after the others they tasted bitter. The third tin contained a tacky seaweed-coloured substance, in which the form of the eggs could hardly be seen. This was pressed caviare, made from the damaged eggs of the various species of sturgeon, salted and impacted together. I liked the taste very much, and the slightly toffee-ish substance. Considering that the price is less than half the Sevruga, I recommend it as an ideal candidate for a first sampling of caviare. Everyone needs a celebration occasionally and I think it is worth saving up for caviare: the pressed kind is a possible extravagance for people whose incomes do not quite come up to their appreciation of food. Which, I think, means most of us.

Red caviare is so different. It is delicious enough, like a superior smoked cod's roe, but it is not in the same class as caviare proper. Neither is lumpfish caviare from Iceland or Denmark, which is dyed black like those tenth-century roes from the sturgeon of Lake

Tung-t'ing (though not with *Gleditschia sinensis* seeds). They are not to be despised, but keep them for lesser occasions.

TO SERVE CAVIARE

First of all, the amount – allow 30 g (1 oz) per person as a decent minimum, 45 g (1 ½ oz) is luxurious. Keep the pot in the refrigerator until required, then place it on a dish and surround with ice. As nothing should impair the delicate flavour of this greatest of all luxuries, avoid wine and vodka. And do not be tempted to mix in some cream cheese to make it go further. All that is required is toast, or water biscuits, or rye bread, or – best of all – the buckwheat Blini below.

So much for the finest quality. With lesser grades or pressed caviare, you could add unsalted butter for the toast or rye bread, or melted butter for Blini. Perhaps some sour cream as well, or lemon juice. Pressed caviare is delicious spread on small split potatoes, baked in their jackets and not larger than duck's eggs (unless you can afford a great deal of caviare).

When it comes to the 'caviare' of other fish, chopped spring onions, hard-boiled eggs, or cream cheese which has not been too processed, can all be added to make a large hors d'oeuvre. And when it is a question of the following recipe for homemade 'caviare', you can experiment as much as you like. Personally I like it quite on its own, too. It is very good, but I won't pretend that it compares with the finest Russian and Iranian product, which has transformed the slightly porridgey quality of hard roe into a most poetic texture.

HOMEMADE 'CAVIARE'

My first and best experience of homemade 'caviare' I owe to a fishmonger in Oxford market, who presented me with the unfamiliar grey-crested body of a lump-sucker (otherwise known, being female in this instance, as a hen-paddle). We found that it was stuffed with a vast quantity of eggs, which I didn't count after reading that there might be anything between 80 and 136 thousand of them. It was easy to see how Iceland manages to can and export 32 tons of 'lumpfish caviare' every year. (The rest of the fish was not so good:

there is a grey fatty layer between flesh and skin which is difficult to remove, and unpleasant to eat. Apparently the flesh must be smoked; then it tastes all right.)

The strange thing about the eggs is that the male or cock-paddle takes such great care of them, once they have been deposited in rocky crevices above low water-mark, in the spring. As J. R. Norman remarks in *A History of Fishes*, there can be few better cases of parental devotion ... 'For weeks and even months he devotes himself to the care of the eggs, fasting rather than leave his post, from time to time pressing his head into the clump of spawn to allow the water to penetrate to the centre, and thus ensuring the proper aeration of the eggs, a process which he further helps by blowing upon them with his mouth and fanning them with his pectoral fins ... While on guard the males have been described as being attacked by rooks and carrion crows, which thrust their sharp beaks through the abdominal walls and feast on the liver of the unfortunate fishes. If removed from the eggs and then released, they will at once rush back to their posts, and after a heavy storm that has swept masses of eggs from their normal positions high up on the beach, as soon as the sea becomes calm again the parents may be seen anxiously searching for their charges.'

Lump-suckers owe this particular name to the powerful suction disc, between the pelvic fins, which enables them to cling tightly to rocks: cock- and hen-paddle refer to the very pronounced crest along its back. Unfortunately you won't find this most interesting creature very often at the fishmonger's. Instead you can use the eggs of the cod, catfish, mullet, salmon, shad, pile, turbot, or whiting – quite a choice.

Remove the membrane from the eggs, and turn them into a basin. Season with salt and freshly ground white pepper, then with a little onion chopped almost to a pulp, some lemon juice, and brandy if you have it to spare. These seasonings should be added to taste.

Serve the eggs with toast and butter, or rye bread. You can give them the full caviare treatment, and make some Blini from the recipe following. As I have remarked above, hard-boiled eggs, spring onions – both chopped – and some good cream cheese which hasn't been over-processed can all be added if you want to make an hors d'oeuvre.

BLINI OR RUSSIAN BUCKWHEAT PANCAKES

In the west, we think of Blini as the proper accompaniment to caviare, but in Russia they are served with other kinds of preserved fish (and

with quite different foods as well – jam, cheese, mushrooms, etc).
Although the preparation is lengthy, it is not laborious or painful.
The flavour is quite different from our Shrove Tuesday pancakes on
account of the yeast – and the buckwheat flour, which can be
obtained from good health food stores.

Serves 6

30 g (1 oz) fresh or 15 g (½ oz) dried yeast
6 tablespoons lukewarm water
250 g (8 oz) plain flour ⎱ *or 375 g (12 oz) plain flour*
125 g (4 oz) buckwheat flour ⎰
450 ml (15 fl oz) lukewarm milk
3 large egg yolks
1 teaspoon sugar
good pinch of salt
3 scant tablespoons sour cream
125 g (4 oz) melted butter
3 egg whites

Fork yeast and lukewarm water together; leave for 10 minutes, until
it froths up. Put the plain flour and half the buckwheat flour into a
large warm mixing bowl. Make a well in the middle and pour in the
yeast mixture, then 300 ml (10 fl oz) of the milk. Beat to a smooth
batter. Leave for 3 hours, covered, in a warm place – the rack of a
solid fuel stove is ideal, but anywhere out of a draught will do. Next
stir in the rest of the buckwheat flour, and leave again for two hours.
Beat together lightly the egg yolks, sugar, salt, sour cream and
3 scant tablespoons of the melted butter. Add to the dough, mixing
well. Whisk the egg whites stiff, then fold them in carefully. Leave for
half an hour.

Have a baking tray, lined with a clean cloth, in a warm oven.
Take a large, preferably non-stick, frying pan or griddle, and brush it
over with melted butter. Cook the batter in the usual way, allowing a
couple of tablespoons or so per pancake, which should be about 7 cm
(3 inches) across when done: several can be done at once if the pan is
large. When bubbles begin to show through on the upper side, after a
couple of minutes or so, brush with butter and turn over. Keep the
cooked pancakes warm on the baking tray in the oven, while you
cook the rest.

Serve with a big bowl of sour cream, another bowl of melted
butter, and dishes of black caviare, or red caviare, or homemade
'caviare'. Smoked salmon, smoked sturgeon, and smoked cod's roe
provide excellent alternatives: so do the Danish pickled herrings on

p. 195. Sliced kipper, served raw with lemon juice, makes another good filling.

BOTARGO

Another hard roe luxury. This time provided by the grey mullet, like the true Taramasalata, below. The roes are salted, dried, pressed into black-skinned, orange-brown firmness, a salami firmness; perfectly adapted, unlike caviare, to the hot climate of the Mediterranean, and the exigencies of transport in all weathers. In Italy *bottarga* or *buttariga* is served in thin slices with bread, and either olive oil or butter; sometimes with fresh figs, like Parma ham. In southern France *poutargue* is a speciality of Martigues: it is eaten in thin strips with a seasoning of pepper, olive oil and lemon juice. Sometimes it is added, anchovy style, to salads of haricot beans or chick peas to give them piquancy. It was once a popular import here, in England. On 5 June, 1661, Pepys remarks in his *Diary* that he and Sir William Penn, father of Pennsylvania Penn, made their way home after a sociable evening with friends. It was so hot that they went out upon the leads in the garden, Sir William in his shirt sleeves. Pepys played his 'flagilette' and the two men stayed there 'talking and singing and drinking of great draughts of Clarret and eating botargo and bread and butter till 12 at night, it being moonshine'. Next day Pepys had a dreadful headache – but not, I think, from Botargo.

It is difficult to find Botargo in England nowadays. The best thing is to look out for it if you are visiting Paris, or the Mediterranean countries, and bring it home as a souvenir. Or you can make it. Claudia Roden, who writes about *batarekh* from her Egyptian experience, in *Middle Eastern Food*, gives a couple of recipes. One came from Canada, where in Montreal at least one may buy frozen grey mullet roes. In Britain, fresh cod roes have to do instead.

Make sure, before you buy them, that the skins of the roes are perfectly undamaged. Roll them in kitchen or sea salt, and lay them on a wad of absorbent paper. As the paper becomes damp, put a fresh wad down and turn over and salt the roes again. When the paper is at last dry, after several days, hang the roes up in a good draught (steamy kitchens are to be avoided, as always, for drying food). Leave them for 8 days or so, until they are hard and dry. They can now be eaten, or stored in a refrigerator in tightly-sealed polythene bags. Miss Roden remarks that the drying process can be hurried up by putting the roes into a turned-off warm oven from time to time; leave the door open. The danger is that the botargo may over-dry to crumbliness.

A quicker recipe makes use of smoked cod's roe. Put it into the oven, when it has been turned off, from time to time, and hang it up in a dry airy place between whiles. This takes only a few days and little effort.

TARAMASALATA

The pride of the Abbazia di Loreto, an eighteenth-century monastery of curves and colour at the back of Vesuvius, is the pharmacy. The original 300 majolica jars stand elegantly on the shelves. Even more elegant is the mortar, placed in the centre of one wall. I suppose that mortars were the main piece of equipment in a pharmacy in those days. This one takes the form of a hollowed out Corinthian capital decorated with gold, and mounted on a waist-high column of pink marble. How much time people had then, how many people were needed about the place, how hard and steadily they worked.

Taramasalata belongs to that pestle and mortar life, which survives, in part at least, in Greece and Turkey still. It is a cream salad, like the *tahina* salads on p. 43. And I'm sure it wouldn't be as popular with us as it is, if electric beaters and liquidizers hadn't come to save work in so many kitchens. And yet, when we first ate Taramasalata twenty years ago, the head waiter declared that it had been made by hand: 'Downstairs in the kitchen. Here.' I believe him now – I was sceptical at the time – because however I vary proportions and method, I never quite achieve the cool, granular texture of his hand-made Taramasalata. But it is still delicious and worth making:

Serves 6

> 125 g (4 oz) tarama (*salted grey mullet roe*) or *smoked cod roe*
> 1¼-cm (½-inch) thick slice of bread
> 1 clove garlic, crushed or 1 tablespoon chopped onion
> 300–450 ml (10–15 fl oz) olive or corn oil
> juice of 1–2 lemons
> black olives or capers

If you are using a piece of cod's roe, remove the skin first. Soak *tarama* or cod's roe in water for an hour or two to abate the saltiness. Moisten the bread with a little water so that it turns to a thickish paste (cut the crusts off first), then put it into the blender with garlic or onion, and enough oil to keep the mixture moving. Gradually add the *tarama* or roe, and the oil, alternately to the blender. Should the mixture become unworkably stiff, put in a spoonful or two of water.

The amount of oil required depends on your taste and the consistency of the Taramasalata. Finally, season with lemon juice.

If you intend to use an electric beater it is a good idea to start off with an egg yolk. Beat it with a little lemon juice, then add the bread, garlic or onion, and roe, gradually in small amounts, lubricating the mixture with olive oil or corn oil. This mayonnaise technique ensures that the oil doesn't separate at all from the mixture.

Serve on a dish, well-chilled, and garnished with black olives. Thin toast or bread go with it. Taramasalata is also good when served in small pre-cooked pastry boats or tartlets and decorated with capers. Make sure the pastry is thin and crisp, and don't put the Taramasalata into it more than an hour or two before the meal.

BIBLIOGRAPHY

American Heritage Cook Book, London, Penguin, 1967.

The International Squid Book, Berkeley, Calif., Aris Books, 1981.

Les Recettes Secrètes des Meilleurs Restaurants de France, Paris, Albin Michel, 1972.

Acton, Eliza. *Modern Cookery*, 1845, reprinted London, Elek Books, 1966.

Ali-Bab. *Gastronomie Pratique*, Maidenhead, McGraw-Hill, 1976.

Beeton, Mrs Isabella. *The Book of Household Management*, 1859, facsimile of 1861 ed, London, Cape, 1968.

Boni, Ada. *Italian Regional Cooking*, London, Thomas Nelson.

Brennan, Jennifer. *Thai Cooking*, London, Futura, 1984.

de Brillat-Savarin, Jean-Anthelme. *La Physiologie du Goût*, Paris, A. Sauteret et Cie, 1826.

Brissenden, Rosemary. *South East Asian Food*, London, Penguin, 1970.

Brown, Catherine. *Scottish Regional Recipes*, London, Penguin, 1983.

Buckland, Frank. *The Natural History of British Fishes*, London, SPCK, 1883.

Carew, Richard. *The Survey of Cornwall*, New York, Augustus M. Kelly, 1969.

Caruana Galizia, Anne and Helen. *Recipes from Malta*, 2nd ed, Valletta, 1974.

Clark, Eleanor. *The Oysters of Loqmariaquer*, Chicago, University of Chicago Press, 1978.

de Croze, Count Austin. *Les Plats Régionaux de France*, Paris, 1928.

Dallas, E. S. *Kettner's Book of the Table*, 1877, reprinted London, Centaur Press, 1968.

David, Elizabeth. *Book of Mediterranean Food*, London, Penguin, 1987.

—— *Dried Herbs, Aromatics and Condiments*

—— *English Potted Meats and Fish Pastes*, London, Elizabeth David, 1968.

—— *French Provincial Cooking*, London, Penguin, 1986.

—— *Italian Food*, London, Barrie & Jenkins, 1987.

—— *An Omelette and a Glass of Wine*, London, Penguin, 1990.

—— *Spices, Salt and Aromatics in the English Kitchen*, London, Penguin, 1987.

Davidson, Alan. *Mediterranean Seafood*, London, Penguin, 1987.

—— *North Atlantic Seafood*, London, Penguin, 1980.

—— *Seafood of South-East Asia*, London, Macmillan, 1978.

Day, Harvey. *The Complete Book of Curries*, Tadworth, Kaye & Ward, 1970.

Dods, Meg. *The Cook and Housewife's Manual*, London, Rosters, 1988.

Dumas, Alexandre. *Dumas on Food: Selections from 'Le Grand Dictionnaire de Cuisine'*, trans. A. & J. Davidson, London, Michael Joseph, 1979.

Echevarria, Juan Dº de. *Gastronomia Vasconum*, Bilbao, Eduardo Izquierdo.

Erlandson, Keith. *Home Smoking and Curing*, London, Century, 1989.

Escoffier, Auguste. *Guide Culinaire*, trans as *The Complete Guide to the Art of Modern Cookery*, trans. H. L. Cracknell & R. J. Kaufmann, London, Heinemann, 1979.

FAO (Food and Agriculture Organization of the United Nations), *Atlas of the Living Resources of the Seas*, London, HMSO, 1981.

Farmer, Fanny. *The Fanny Farmer Cook Book*, London, Robert Hale, 1988.

Field, Michael. *All Manner of Food*, ECCO Press, US, 1984.

Frederick, J. George and Joyce, J. *Long Island Sea Food Cook Book*, New York, Dover Publications, 1971.

Freeman, Bobby. *Welsh Fish*, Dyfed, Lolfa, 1988.

Frost, W. E. and Brown, M. E. *Trout*, London, Collins, 1967.

Glasse, Hannah. *The Art of Cookery Made Plain and Easy*, 1747, reprinted London, Prospect Books, 1983.

Gray, Patience. *Honey from a Weed*, London, Prospect Books, 1986.

de Gouy, Louis P. *The Gold Cook Book*, Greenberg, 1948.

Hodgson, W. C. *The Herring and Its Fishery*, London, Routledge, 1957.

Jones, Evan. *The World of Cheese*, New York, Alfred A. Knopf, 1976.

Kennedy, Diana. *Cuisines of Mexico*, New York, Harper & Row, 1990.

Kitchiner, Dr William. *Apicius Redivivus, or The Cook's Oracle*, 1817–43.

Lang, George. *The Cuisine of Hungary*, London, Penguin, 1985.

Leyel, Mrs C. F. and Hartley, Miss Olga. *The Gentle Art of Cookery*, 1925, reprinted London, Chatto & Windus, 1970.

Manjón, Maite and O'Brien, Catherine. *Spanish Cooking*, London, Book Club Associates, 1976.

McClane, A. J. *The Encyclopaedia of Fish Cookery*, London, Holt, Rinehart, Winston, 1977.

McGee, Harold. *On Food and Cooking: The Science and Lore of the Kitchen*, London, Unwin Hyman, 1988.

McNeill, F. Marian. *The Scots Kitchen*, London, Mayflower Books, 1974.

Mitcham, Howard. *The Provincetown Seafood Cookbook*, Reading, Mass., Addison-Wesley, 1975.

Morand, Simone. *Gastronomie normande d'hier et d'aujourd'hui*, Paris, Flammarion, 1970.

Musgrave, Rev. George M. *A Ramble Through Normandy, or Scenes, Characters and Incidents in a Sketching Excursion Through Calvados*, London, David Bogue, 1855.

Nott, John. *Cook's and Confectioner's Dictionary*, 1726, facsimile reprint, Rivington, 1980.

OECD. *Multilingual Dictionary of Fish and Fish Products*, Paris, 1968.

Oliver, Raymond. *The French at Table*, London, Michael Joseph/Wine and Food Society, 1967.

Owen, Sri. *Indonesian Food and Cookery*, 2nd r.e., London, Prospect Books, 1986.

Petersen, Bengt. *Delicious Fish Dishes*, Göteborg, 1975.

'A Potter'. *Pottery, Home-made Potted Foods, Meats and Fish Pastes, Savoury Butters and Others, by a Potter*, London, Wine and Food Society, 1946.

Raffald, Elizabeth. *The Experienced English Housekeeper*, 1769, facsimile of 1782 ed, London, E & W Books.

Roden, Claudia. *A Book of Middle Eastern Food*, 2nd r.e., London, Viking, 1985.

Rombauer, I. S. and Beck, Simone. *The Joy of Cooking*, London, Dent, 1975.

Stobart, Tom. *The Cook's Encyclopaedia*, London, Macmillan, 1982.

Stubbs, Joyce M. *Home Book of Greek Cookery*, London, Faber & Faber, 1967.

Toklas, Alice. *The Alice B. Toklas Cookbook*, London, Brilliance Books, 1983.

Verral, William. *The Cook's Paradise, being William Verral's 'Complete System of Cookery'*, 1759, reprinted London, The Sylvan Press, 1948.

Walton, Izaak. *The Compleat Angler*, London, Penguin, 1985.

Watt, Alexander. *The Art of Simple French Cookery*, 1960.

Wright, Carol. *Portuguese Food*, London, Dent, 1969.

Yonge, C. M. *The Sea Shore*, London, Collins, 1949.

INDEX